M000304003

Janie's Journal

Volume 2

1988-1991

Also by Janie Tippett

Four Lines a Day

Janie's Journal
Vol 1: 1984-1987
Vol 2: 1988-1991
Vol 3: 1992-1996
Vol 4: 1997-2004
Vol 5: 2005-2009
Vol 6: 2010-2015

Janie's work appears in
the following anthologies:

*Talking On Paper: An Anthology
of Oregon Letters and Diaries*

*Crazy Woman Creek:
Women Rewrite the American West*

Janie's Journal

VOLUME 2

1988-1991

Janie Tippett

Lucky Marmot Press

www.luckymarmotpress.com

Wallowa, Oregon

JANIE'S JOURNAL, VOLUME TWO: 1988-1991
was originally published in the weekly Agri-Times NW.
These columns are collected here with permission of the publisher.

Copyright 2021 by Janie Tippett. All rights reserved.
First Edition. Printed in the United States of America.

No part of this book may be used or reproduced in any manner whatsoever
without written permission, except in the case of brief quotations.

All photos were taken by Janie Tippett as part of her photojournalism
for Agri-Times NW, except where noted in the captions.
All photos are used with permission.

The cover photo of Doug and Janie was taken by Max Gorsline at the
Imnaha River headwaters, in front of Cusick Mountain under Hawkins Pass.

ISBN 978-1-7334833-2-2 (paperback)
ISBN 978-1-7334833-5-3 (ebook)

This volume was collected, digitized, edited, and published by
Lucky Marmot Press in Wallowa, Oregon.
https://www.luckymarmotpress.com

For my large and extended family,
who provided constant fodder
for my writing.

Tippett cattle move across the east moraine of Wallowa Lake.

1988

January 1—We slept in until 7 on New Year's morning. The thermometer registered five below zero. Bundled to the teeth to chore and feed the animals.

Later, sipping a steaming cup of Postum, I watched the Rose Bowl Parade taking place in sunny, warm Pasadena on our TV. I always marvel at the lovely flower-bedecked floats, and at how many hours it must take in the planning and creating of them.

Sunlight spilled into our living room and seemed especially bright as it was reflected off the snowy yard. That afternoon I began to undecorate our home of its Christmas trappings.

Doug and Ben spent most of the day feeding the nearly 1,000 head of cattle, a monumental job that goes on every day of the long, cold winter. I left strings of popcorn on the Christmas tree and stood it out in the snow for the little birds to eat. Roasted a chicken in the wood stove oven. Had filled the cavity with onion, sage and celery, which made the house smell wonderful.

Five degrees at 5 o'clock, zero at 6 o'clock, and still falling! I baked buttermilk biscuits, made gravy and used my new food processor to turn out a carrot salad. We enjoyed the hot meal on a cold, moonlit night, and thus began 1988.

January 2—Dave Nelson, our local radio announcer, says it is 12 below zero in Enterprise this morning, and it is eight below here! A cold fog hovers over us, and the wire fence around the chicken pen is a work of frozen art. Frozen fog crystals float in the air.

After chores, I gathered up my cross-country skis and met Grace and Bill before driving to the Ferguson Ridge ski area, where we tried out our ski legs for the first time this winter.

Driving to upper Prairie Creek, we left the fog behind and came into beautiful, warm sunshine. It was refreshing to be out in the clean air. From Ferguson Ridge, we could look down on the valley with its layer of fog still hanging below us. The exercise was invigorating and at noon we ate our lunches on the sunny, wooden deck of the warming shack.

Soon the cold settled in and by 4 o'clock it was five degrees, zero at 5, and at 6, five below! Doug and I finished off the leftover chicken dinner tonight, built a fire in the fireplace, read and watched TV. Outside the white light of a January moon brightens our world, which lies in a frozen trance.

January 3—Repeat of yesterday morning, hoarfrost on everything. After chores Scotty, Bill and I headed for Salt Creek Summit to do some ski touring. Above the fog, we drove over packed snow to the summit and parked the four-wheel-drive pickup. Shouldering our day packs, we skied up a groomed trail that climbed a gradual hill before leveling off.

After skiing about three quarters of a mile, we arrived at a wide open meadow where snowmobilers and cross-country ski enthusiasts had made tracks everywhere. At the edge of the opening stood a newly constructed warming shack. The rustic log building was built in a woodsy area, and contained a barrel stove and a stack of firewood. We were to learn later that the log structure had been built by a local snowmobiler club.

Trails took off in many directions, following the ridges. We skied down one that wound through the frozen woods and resembled a Christmas card. Snow covered the evergreens and the packed ski trails made for good stride-and-glide skiing. We moved along at a brisk pace and were soon warmed by the exertion.

A few more skiers appeared and an occasional snowmobile whizzed by; otherwise the forest was silent. We saw many tracks of deer, elk and snowshoe rabbits. As we turned around to head back we noticed that clouds were forming and a brisk wind began blowing the snow off the laden branches of the trees. We hurried back to the pickup and ate our lunches before slowly making our way down the slick road to the Sheep Creek highway and home.

There is the smell of snow in the air. Our constantly changing weather will be different tomorrow.

January 4—Temperatures continue below zero in the mornings, warming to around 10 by chore time. Son Steve is off to Blue Mountain Community College again. He will attend winter term to pick up the required credits to graduate. Doug and Ben sorted some cows we will cull and sell.

January 5—Cloudy and much warmer. Twenty degrees when I chored. Took some of my elk in to be ground for elk burger at Jerry's Market in Joseph.

Paid Aunt Opal a visit in her Enterprise apartment this morning. I gave her an amaryllis bulb to grow. She will enjoy watching the bud form and then open into beautiful blossoms. Later, I took Opal to lunch at the "Common Good Market Place," where we ordered chicken soup and visited.

This great little lady spent 50 years of her life out on Pine Creek, married to Charley Tippett and rearing her children. She remembers with clarity the beavers playing in Pine Creek, and the Indians who camped on their ranch while passing through.

"Not very many people still living that remember how things were in those early days," says Opal. True.

Baked yams in the wood stove oven and fried lamb chops for supper.

January 6—Deciding to give up desserts for a while. I will continue baking for my husband and family, who are spoiled when it comes to "somethin' from the oven."

Had a meeting of the "Wallowa Story" committee here this morning, and we tied up the loose ends on meeting the requirements of the humanities grant. It is such a good feeling to be through with this project.

Baked a loaf of french bread and made chili using chunks of my elk meat, garlic, onions, tomatoes, peppers, sauce and spices. Simmered slowly in the dutch oven, it turned out pretty tasty, without beans yet! Wallowa County Seed Potato Growers held a meeting in our home tonight.

January 7—Thirteen degrees and much warmer. While choring, I tried to sort in my mind what to take and pack for a three-week absence. The plan is to drive to Portland for the Oregon potato conference, stay over for the Northwest Chili Cookoff, and then head south for our annual visit with the California relatives.

It was foggy this evening, when Max and Dorothy Gorsline arrived to take us to dinner at "The Country Place on Pete's Pond." We so enjoyed the delicious steaks, the conversation, and the pleasant company of two dear friends.

January 8—Startch is now officially in the condition known as "dry," thus my chores are reduced to tending the chickens. In our absence, Ben will gather the eggs, and feed and water the laying hens and Chester.

This morning the bankers will count our cattle, and most likely stay for lunch. Jim Stubblefield will also be here to help corral the cattle. Leaving a big dutch oven full of elk hamburger and vegetable soup simmering on the wood stove, I left for Enterprise to show "The Wallowa Story" for the noon luncheon meeting of the Rotary Club.

Being a guest of Rotary brought back memories of when I was a young girl in 4-H. We had organized an all-girl team that put on a program which consisted of us leading a purebred Guernsey heifer right into the meeting room of the Lincoln Rotary Club.

We laid down a tarp, plugged in a pair of clippers and went to work on that heifer, preparing her for show. I remember wielding the clippers while sister Mary Ann worked on polishing the horns. Sally and Beverly brushed her smooth coat and fluffed out her switch.

The heifer's name was Oakcrest Jennifer and she was one of my 4-H dairy projects. She behaved beautifully, and we later took her to other organizations and put on the same demonstration. The Rotarians were sitting on the edge of their seats when we led the spit and polished heifer out the door.

I hurried home to help at the chutes, but found they had plenty of hands and Fred Bornstedt was already preg-testing the cows we will sell. The fellas had obviously enjoyed the soup and bread; there wasn't much of anything left.

Darkness comes a little later now as winter progresses. Daylight, however, is slow to arrive in January. Most mornings, the sun is just coming over the hill when I return from the barn or chicken pen.

January 9—Snowed during the night and it is 26 degrees this morning. Doug is on the phone lining up extra help to feed on weekends while we are gone. If it weren't for faithful Ben, we wouldn't be able to leave the ranch at all. We certainly do appreciate the efforts of such a trustworthy employee.

January 10—A wind blows at 6 a.m., and it is snowing. Startch's heifer, now weaned with the other yearlings, still comes to the end of the corral and looks longingly at her old home. She misses the T.L.C., but she will survive.

Sloshed through deep snow to tend my chickens, thinking it would be three weeks until I see them again.

We gathered up props for the cattlemen's booth at the chili cookoff, and loaded the mountain of gear for our extended absence, which included Doug's gold-panning paraphernalia. It was around 1:30 before we got away. The roads were bare and rain clouds threatened overhead as we pulled into Pendleton to visit briefly with daughter Linda before heading down the freeway toward Portland.

Leaving Wallowa County far behind us in distance, but not in memory, we headed west in the foggy darkness bordering the Columbia River. It soon began to rain, and we could see that snow lay alongside the highway.

We ate supper at a truck stop at Bigg's Junction and made it safely to Troutdale where we spent the night at a Shiloh Inn.

January 11—As we pulled into the Red Lion, a sea gull swooped down to welcome us! Dappled sun fell through clouds over Portland and the city was rain-washed. From our room on the ninth floor, bright sunlight glinted off the windows on nearby tall buildings. Pretty clouds continued to float overhead. Below, "The Max," a trolley-like city train, rumbled by in front of the Red Lion on its way downtown.

While Doug attended a meeting, I set up my portable typewriter in our high room that overlooked the city and caught up on some writing. Met Doug for lunch and, while dining at Maxi's, we were gladdened to see a blue jay through the large glass windows that separated us from a garden-pool area outside. Many birds were singing in a nearby park when I later took a walk across the street to Lloyd Center.

Entering Meier and Frank, I noticed a sign that read, *With your Meier and Frank credit card YOU are in control here.* So, trying to feel in control, I wandered around looking for a pair of jeans. Plain blue jeans. Not faded, Calvin Klein versions, but new, blue denim.

No luck. I searched high and low to no avail, and was told these jeans had been washed many times and then treated with acid to make them have that "lived in" look. I have plenty at home with "that look," I replied, and they are in the rag bag to wipe off Startch's udder or to be used for shop rags.

The sales lady looked at me blankly and continued: "These jeans are washed so many times to get them soft that they have to dye them again to put the color back." Prices on them went up proportionately with how badly they were damaged, some as high as $50 a pair.

I began to notice women around me shopping in these worn, faded jeans, and even jackets. The sales lady began to think I was some sort of freak, wanting new unwashed jeans!

Needless to say, I didn't make a purchase, but when I get home I'll look in the rag bag. Who knows, I might possibly have a "high fashion" pair and not even know it.

As I left the store, I patted my credit card. Thank goodness, I was still "in control."

January 13—This is the final day of the potato conference and, while our husbands attend more meetings, we wives—Donna, Gail and I—decide to take in the Sellwood antique area. Although I didn't purchase anything, it was fun to browse around and look at the shops filled with old-time relics.

We ate lunch at Thadius' Pantry and ordered hot cream cheese and oyster sandwiches, which were delicious and different from ordinary fare. The "Pantry" was an old house turned eating place that could accommodate only a few people.

Tonight our Wallowa County delegation secured a table close to the area where a slide show would later be presented at the banquet. And what a banquet the Red Lion puts on! Steve James and Luther and Joyce Fitch joined us as we enjoyed a meal featuring boned chicken breasts simmered in mushroom sauce. The food was served in elegant style by a trained professional staff.

Entertainment for the evening, extremely interesting, was a slide show given by Ken and Jan Warren of Portland. Ken is the famed, white-water guide-outfitter of the Warren Expeditions. As Jan projected more than two hours of spectacular color slides, husband Ken narrated their experiences while rafting down the Yangtze River.

We were transported to this rarely seen no-man's land, traveling the high Tibetan plateau at elevations up to 14,000 feet as the expedition made its way to the source of the Yangtze. We watched as the mountain of gear was transferred from trucks to the backs of patient yaks. This stocky, long-haired, wild ox has been domesticated as a pack animal in Tibet, and what a sight this unusual pack train made in that haunting setting.

The journey began at the glacier-fed source of the river, continuing down through treacherous wild white water. Mile after mile, the expedition navigated the ever-widening Yangtze. What amazed me was that they could carry all this sophisticated photographic equipment in that wild water, and have photographers survive to film it!

Often from the bank, the film crew recorded the daredevil plunges of the roped-together rafts as they literally spilled over waterfalls. This perilous trip was not without mishap. One man became ill and died along the way. We watched and felt like we were there when the mourners erected a crude cross to mark the grave.

Because of damage to the rafts and the wild water, the expedition was forced to halt 800 miles short of its destination. Rather amazing what some people will do for the sake of adventure, and if I were younger...

Somehow, the name Warren rang a bell. When the program ended, I visited briefly with Ken and learned he was, in fact, the same man who had been coming into the Wallowa country to hunt for 25 years.

I still dream about that high Tibetan plateau and remember one special slide: an incredible timed exposure of the moon shining above the birth place of the Yangtze River. Raining over Portland tonight.

January 14—We had time to kill, waiting for the Northwest chili cookoff in the Expo Center at the P.I. What does one do to pass the time in the city, when one is a country person? It was pouring rain as I sat at the window of our ninth floor room and pondered the problem.

I watched the "Max" speed by as I gazed out across the wet city, and wondered what it would be like to ride on it. After lunch, and finally convincing Doug it would be fun, as well as looking like country bumpkins, we walked in the rain to wait for the train.

The small trolley soon arrived, whereupon we simply climbed aboard, took our seats and waited for someone to sell us a ticket. No one did. We had no idea where we were headed, and didn't really care. Fun. As we zoomed along, Doug became a bit concerned about the entire procedure, of which we knew nothing.

Picking up a brochure, he read where this route would take us downtown. We watched with fascination the passengers who boarded at every stop. Up front, hidden from view, the ghost-like voice of the conductor whispered "22nd, 23rd," and those around us familiar with the territory pulled an overhead rope to signal they wanted off, which triggered a bell... *ding, ding.* To open the door, they pressed a button.

The little trolley ran swiftly and quietly over tracks that laced the rain-soaked streets, and soon we were crossing a bridge that spanned the Willamette River. People on board represented a cross section of Portland: the wealthy, the poor, young and old. Downtown, the train stopped and everyone got off, except us.

Finally we got to meet the "ghost" conductor when he walked back to tell us this was the end of the line. We replied that we were just along for the ride. He smiled and explained we had to get off here regardless, and then perhaps we could catch a return trolley one block west. So off in the rain we went to find the little shelter station and hop the next train.

While waiting I peered through the large windows of what appeared to be some sort of art shop. It contained things my country eyes had never seen: rabbits sculpted in clay sat in chairs having a tea party in the window, and a stuffed zebra standing upright, wearing tennis shoes.

Inside I glimpsed beautiful basketry and raku pottery.

Suddenly the train appeared, and still no one asked for tickets. We couldn't believe you could ride this jolly little trolley for free. Nothing in the city, so far, had been free. Far from it.

Most of the people who boarded wore dull, sullen expressions on their faces, clutched shopping bags and stared blankly out the windows. Not us. Sitting opposite each other, we smiled, turned around, visited, and were constantly entertained by it all.

The train stopped and a grimy, pitiful little man got on and sat down beside me. He mumbled something about loading luggage and kept repeating it over and over every time the trolley stopped. His clothes looked like they were pilfered from someone's garbage can. Bell bottom pants, soaked and dripping water, hung from his small frame. Looking down at his feet, I was shocked to see he was wearing women's patent leather shoes and no socks. His feet looked wet and cold.

Unlike the other passengers, he smiled and shot me a toothless grin as he disembarked carrying a white plastic bucket, which probably contained his earthly possessions. This lost little soul was one of Portland's street people, but he could still smile. I smiled back. As the train rolled on I could still see him trudging along in the rain, carrying his pail.

We returned to Lloyd Center, then decided to continue riding and see where else the trolley could take us. After all, it was free! And a way to spend the time. A strong wind had come up and sheets of rain blew across the city. The wind whistled outside the windows and we fairly flew along, heading for Gresham.

I glimpsed a sign, The Dalles 84 East, and thought of home. We raced along concrete abutments and, after what seemed like hours, entered a neighborhood of little ticky-tacky houses, cluttered yards and scattered trees. We had struck up a conversation with a college girl who commuted daily from her Gresham home to school. She was very kind and seemed to understand we were definitely not city dwellers, as she informed us we were supposed to purchase tickets prior to boarding.

When we got off in Gresham, we looked around the small depot and found the info she spoke of. Doug slid a dollar bill into a slot, which immediately "ate" it, only to spit it out moments later. Soon the conductor appeared.

"Put the bill in like it says, George Washington side up," he said. Doug did as told and the machine digested it, and soon a ticket appeared from another slot. Still pouring rain and blowing up a hurricane as Doug procured two tickets.

To get under shelter, I jumped aboard a waiting train, which chose that moment to take off. The door closed and through the rain-streaked window I could see Doug's grinning face. I yelled "stop the train" and a kindly woman, noting the panic in my voice, told me to press the button.

The door flew open and Doug, running alongside, leaped on. Whew! The train picked up speed and we were off. Doug thought it was most hilarious, and I could have killed him. We were now legal passengers. I wondered if our city cousins have as much trouble adapting to "country" as we to "city."

January 16—We spent all day at the Great Northwest Chili Cookoff at the P.I. Expo Center. We had a blast! Quite an experience. The activities lasted all day and it was 6 p.m. before we left Portland and headed south on I-5 in the rain.

Four hours later, we arrived in Roseburg and tried vainly in thick, pea soup fog to locate the Matthews' place. We eventually gave up, found our way back to Roseburg, and called Bill and Carolee, who arrived to lead us to their country place.

January 18—We stayed until this morning with our good friends, my son-in-law Bill's parents. Enjoyed their hospitality, good food, and comfortable country home. Their baby lambs were being born and the rolling, oak tree-studded hills were refreshing after our week-long stay in the city.

Awoke to see a new snowfall covered the landscape. The bare-limbed oak trees were transformed into works of art. Driving south again on I-5, heading for California, we stopped briefly in Rogue River to rest. We encountered icy road conditions going through the Siskiyous, but made it over the summit safety and pulled into Weed for lunch.

Mt. Shasta was hidden by snow clouds, which quickly dispersed and blue skies greeted us as we drove on down through Northern California. The warm sunshine streamed in through our windshield as we whizzed by Redding, Red Bluff, Marysville and looked at the miles of walnut, almond, prune and pear orchards that line the road on both sides.

We arrived at my sister Mary Ann's in Auburn around 6 p.m. After a delicious ham dinner we walked the couple of blocks to where my mother and new husband, Bill, live in a new apartment complex. Felt wonderful to be out stretching our legs after all that driving.

January 19—While Doug was off panning for gold in Doty's Ravine, I sat myself down in front of Mary Ann's word processor and typed out some journalism assignments. Couldn't believe how that thing worked!

Of course, my sister's assistance helped; she teaches a class in word processing.

I found a photo shop in Auburn that developed my film shot at the chili cookoff. After meeting these deadlines, Mary Ann and I hiked down an old stagecoach road to the American River. It was a lovely afternoon and we enjoyed the walk down the steep road that ended at the river.

Red Toyon berries, huge digger pines and oak trees lined the trail and the smell of the Sierra foothills reminded me of long-ago youthful excursions.

January 20—Mary Ann, Doug and I drove to Forest Hill. I hadn't been back up there since I was a young girl, and remembered the narrow, winding 17-mile drive as being a bit hairy. Today it is a good paved road that is traveled by many who commute to Auburn and even Sacramento to live out of the fog and smog. It is snow country, however, and snow lay all around, reminding us of home.

I had fun photographing the old hotel, stage-stop, general store and we ate lunch in a cafe across the street. We drove out on Mosquito Ridge and gazed across the airy canyons to snow-covered Sierra Nevadas that included the Crystal Mountain range, beyond which lay Desolation Valley.

I had packed into this area for many years during the '50s and '60s with my family. We toured around Todd Valley Estates, following a maze of roads that led to secluded homes hidden in the pines. People wanting to escape the city are now living in this heretofore uninhabited area that used to be a large ranch.

That night mom and Bill took us to dinner at the Sizzler in Auburn. The place was so popular that we had to wait in line.

January 21—After being delayed in a terrific traffic jam, caused by an overturned propane truck on Interstate 80, we drove to Grass Valley to meet Lee and Gary Roberts for lunch at Miner's Camp. I can still see that line of backed-up cars that stretched for seven miles. Helicopters hovered overhead and a school had to be evacuated.

Such occurrences are common in California, where everywhere is felt this crush of people. People, who have been coming to the Golden State until it is no longer golden...but the color of smog, and yet the construction goes on and on.

In my youth I remembered an old slaughter house; it stood on a lonely hill near the small town of Auburn, commanding a view of oak tree-dotted hills. Today a new subdivision is going up on the site. How long will the lovely oak trees last, surrounded by concrete and over-watered by people who do not understand the trees?

January 22—On the morning, I mixed up a batch of sourdough hotcakes, having brought my trusty starter with me from Oregon. Mary Ann invited her neighbor Paul to breakfast, as he said he had dreamed of eating sourdough pancakes since reading my column.

The weather continued warm, sunny, nearly 70 degrees. We drove down to the Mt. Pleasant Ranch, where I was raised, and visited my brother Jim's family before Doug went back to his gold-panning. While he worked the creek I went for a walk.

Two hawks wheeled overhead, filling the air with their mating cries. A carpet of green grass pushed its way through winter-killed debris. The tall, leafless water oaks stood silent in the woods and mossy rocks were covered with blackberry bramble. A covey of quail called from their sanctuary in a wild grape thicket.

Now people inhabit new, fancy homes that sit atop every knoll or hill in this area, but there are still little bits of wild habitat left, like this one on Doty's Ravine. Mary Ann arrived with our lunch and we picnicked by a large granite rock near the creek. As the bright sunshine filtered through oak trees, it was hard to believe the temperature had been zero at home when Doug called Ben this morning.

Later I wandered through my father's garden. Runaway ivy trailed in profusion from oak trees and a variety of succulents spilled out of their containers. Daddy's handmade cement-form creations and planters remained permanent and creeping Myrtle covered the ground underfoot.

The garden remains, a monument built by a man who loved all things in nature. My niece Jeanette and her husband, Don, live there now. The house has been redone. Things change, people change and time goes on; but somehow I felt my father's presence in his garden.

I walked back to the creek where Doug showed me the tiny flakes of gold that represented his day's labor, which is a labor of love, Driving back to Auburn we noticed blooming daffodil, Camellias and citrus trees laden with grapefruit, oranges and lemons.

That night 16 members of my large, extended family met at an Auburn restaurant for our annual get-together. Fun visiting while we stuff ourselves with an eight-dish Oriental meal.

January 23—My three sisters—Mary Ann, Caroline and Kathryn—and I drove to Grass Valley and looked up the old Barnegat Ranch. Mary Ann had researched beforehand and we easily found the place. In the 1930s my father had been herdsman at Barnegat when I was a baby.

Sister Mary Ann and brother Jim had been born while my parents lived there.

Barnegat was quite a ranch in its heyday, where my father was in charge of the registered Guernseys. Aside from being a bit rundown, the old place had not lost its charm. The milk house still stood, as did the enormous old barns. The house where we lived was still there and had been restored over the years to its original rambling style.

A Mr. and Mrs. Savage had purchased the property, which remained intact all these years; he having worked on the place as a young boy, had realized a dream of one day returning. We photographed the old milk house where milk had been cooled with piped-in spring water that flowed from a cistern on a nearby hill.

Here, butterfat tests and production records were kept on each cow. My father had started the first milk delivery in Grass Valley and Mr. Savage gave us sisters some cardboard milk bottle caps that read: Golden Guernsey milk, Barnegat Ranch, Grass Valley, California.

We found the cement base of an old silo and several concrete watering troughs. High on a hill, in a pasture, we looked down on the ranch and across at Wolf Mountain and picnicked in the sunshine. The four Bachman sisters sharing a special day in a special way.

January 24—We drove through Beckwourth Pass and down into Chilcoot, where we will spend five days visiting daughter Ramona's young family.

January 25—Packed up and left, with Ramona and the children, to join son-in-law Charley at Fish Springs Ranch in Nevada where he works. The temperature was five degrees—shades of Wallowa County!

On the way we stopped at the Chilcoot Post Office to mail my column, and then at Wiggin's Trading Post, where we purchased pork chops and fix'ins for grandson Shawn's traditional birthday dinner. Leaving the pavement at Doyle, we continued on a dirt road that wound through miles of frosted sagebrush.

This remote Nevada ranch is located on the ancient Lahontan Lake bed that covers much of the area near Pyramid Lake. As we rounded the final bend to the ranch, we saw hundreds of Canadian honkers feeding on alfalfa stubble. Fish Springs has no electricity, except for a generator, which at the moment was out of order. It was good to get in out of the cold desert air and into the cozy modern house where a wood stove kept the place warm.

All hands were, at the time, working on the generator, which is necessary to keep the freezer, refrigerator and water pump operating.

We heated some soup on the wood stove for lunch, and by afternoon the generator once again roared to life, and all the appliances began humming.

I took a photo of "Henry," the legendary 10-year-old Hereford steer. Wearing an impressive set of horns, he resembled a Charles Russell painting.

I walked out to a nearby field this afternoon, where I had spotted an old beaver slide hay stacker. Here I found other ancient pieces of horse-drawn equipment that had been discarded over the years. A long time ago this place was a well-known stage stop where weary desert travelers stopped to water their horses at the large natural spring, rest in the shade of the giant cottonwoods, or perhaps spend the night in the boarding house.

As I wandered around the partly frozen meadow, investigating sturdy old corrals made of railroad ties, I thought of how the ranch must have been in its heyday. Suddenly I came upon the honkers, which took to the air at my approach.

Before me stretched the desert, the alkali slick, shimmering waves of distance, and the silence. New fences were being built, and slowly but surely the old place is being brought to life again. A huge semi-truck-trailer rumbled out onto the dirt road, having loaded up with alfalfa hay destined for a California dairy.

Circling around the large sheds of baled hay, I climbed a hill over-looking the ranch buildings. Bending every once in a while to look for arrowheads that sometimes surface after a rain, I returned to the house.

That evening we had a great birthday supper for grandson Shawn, who turned 14. At twilight I listened to the honking of the geese, return-ing to feed on the meadow. Far out on the slick a coyote yipped and the ranch dogs set up a howl.

January 27—Awoke to a much warmer day. The distant, snow-covered mountains that bordered the ranch gleamed brightly across the expanse of desert. Leaving Fish Springs, we returned to Chilcoot.

After delivering the children to school, we stopped to visit the Alvin Lombardis, fans of this column, who live in the Sierra Valley town of Loyalton. Such friendly folks, it was good to see them both in good health.

This afternoon I made a pie from some apples given to us by the Lombardis. A chinook wind warmed the valley and soon dripping and thawing began to take place. The school bus brought the children home from Loyalton and I spoiled them with apple pie.

January 28—Left this morning after seeing the children off to school. I was becoming increasingly anxious about the arrival of a new grandchild in Wallowa County. We'd been keeping close tabs on Liza, who was due in early February, and all was well, but I'd feel better being home.

Heading for Reno, then turning north to Lovelock, Winnemucca and the miles of sagebrush desert in between, we finally pulled into McDermitt. I looked up Bob and Mary Kay Pace, a young couple from Wallowa County who teach school there.

They were very surprised to see someone from home and from what I observed, Wallowa County's loss was McDermitt's gain. Bob told me that 90 percent of the children were Indians from the Fort McDermitt Indian Reservation nearby. "A great bunch of kids" and fun to work with, Bob said.

We stopped in Jordan Valley long enough to have a bowl of soup at the old Basque Inn. A watercolor painting sunset created a startling background for the darkened sheep corrals made of sticks, and the long lines of cattle eating their hay along the willow-bordered bottoms. We wound through the Owyhees in darkness and descended into the big basin and on to Ontario, where we spent the night.

January 29—We awoke to a freezing rain, which, thankfully, melted by the time we entered the northbound freeway. The farther north we traveled, the drier it became, and when we drove down Ladd Canyon into the valley of the Grande Ronde, we were greeted by Mount Emily, shining under a blanket of snow.

We were soon back in Wallowa County. Hurrah! The Minam Canyon was a welcome sight after all our travels, and sunlight glanced off the clear waters of the beautiful Minam River. Sunny and mild for January, with much thawing and melting as we drove into the ranch.

The barn cats and Stubby, the dog, ran to greet us. Great to be home. Just entered the house when the phone rang. It was Scotty. She had our tickets for the Robert Burns dinner that night in Joseph.

So, we went, and what a great time we had at this Scottish celebration of tradition. We ate haggis, listened to Robert Burns' poems, many of which were recited by Scotty, and watched a slide show of Scotland. The lads wore kilts and the lassies were clad in colorful plaid skirts and saucy little caps. There was a toast to the haggis.

Ron Peterson, who owns the Blue Willow Sausage Kitchen, had made the concoction, which he marched in carrying on a platter. He was followed by another fellow wearing kilts, who played the bagpipes. Rich Wandschneider brought up the rear, brandishing a large carving knife.

In addition to several of these steaming haggises, which are cooked in the lining of a sheep's stomach and contain many things which I would just as soon not know of, except for the oats, we had mashed rutabagas, mashed potatoes and hot biscuits.

For dessert there was a tableful of shortbread, scones, oat cakes and trifle, that sinful combination of custard, sponge cake, strawberries and whipped cream. We were entertained by three lovely young women who sang a medley of haunting Scottish folk songs. Bob Perry, accompanied by wife, Liz, on the piano, sang a Scottish love song.

When we stepped from Scotland back into the Wallowa County night, it was snowing!

January 30—Checked out my livestock, which had survived my absence quite well. Max's sackful of black cats looked healthy, and the laying hens produced their usual large brown eggs. I checked in with our large family and found everyone well and looking forward eagerly to the new baby.

January 31—It snowed again today, as the month ended with a low of 10 degrees.

February 1—Lightly snowing. Two inches of new snow here, five inches on Alder Slope, and nine inches down in the lower valley, around Wallowa. Shipped our calves today. C&B Livestock in Hermiston has purchased them.

It cleared off this afternoon. Brilliant sunshine transformed snow crystals into glittering diamonds. The snow is so light and airy that our footfalls stir snow dust.

One of the largest calves, weighing 800 pounds, was out of one of my milk cows and sired by a Simmental bull. Little Guernsey May earned her keep this year by producing this steer, and raising a grafted orphan as well.

This evening, as a cold moon glows early in a pink sky, our thermometer reads zero.

February 2—Winter seemed far from over this morning. It was 13 below zero at 6:30 and the dawn's light revealed mountain peaks surfacing above ghostly layers of fog. A cold, pale moon hung around to watch a pink glow steal across the faces of Chief Joseph Mountain, Mt. Howard and Ruby Peak. Cold vapors trail above stretches of open water in the creeks as the warmer temperature of the water mingles with the colder air.

Today was Groundhog Day. The fabled rodent emerged from his den and didn't see his shadow, which means, of course, that spring is just around this frigid corner somewhere.

This evening a magnificent full moon pushed itself up from behind an eastern hill and flooded the valley with cold, white light. The livestock endures this bitter cold, but requires large amounts of feed, and day by day the long hay stacks diminish.

February 3—A wind came up in the night, sifting the snow into drifts. It warmed to four below zero this morning!

After tending to my livestock, I baked a pie using a new recipe sent to me by Wanda Doud of Elgin, a mincemeat custard crunch pie that turned out to be a delicious new way to use my homemade mincemeat.

Scotty and I went cross-country skiing today on Alder Slope. The snow was perfect: dry, powdery and soft as down. After trudging up a long hill on our long fiberglass skis, good exercise, we gleefully skied down the slop, practicing our turns. After many such assaults on the hill, the sun sank over Ruby Peak and the temperature did likewise. We called it a day.

At home I split a wheelbarrow full of wood to feed the hungry woodstove and cooked supper.

February 4—Four above zero, foggy and cold, with a coating of hoarfrost on everything. Carried a boiling teakettle of water to thaw the ice in my chickens' drinking water.

Met with Kathy Siebe today at noon at the "Country Place on Pete's Pond" to plan the publicity for our Wallowa Valley Festival of Arts, which will, in addition to an art show, feature the Montana Repertory Theater production of "Cowboy." This is a musical based on the life of cowboy artist Charley Russell.

This year's event promises to be better than ever, with a juried art show, cowboy poet gathering and a catered dinner, two live performances of "Cowboy" and a dance. The annual Arts Festival will be April 22-24 in Joseph and Enterprise.

As Kathy and I discussed our plans over lunch, a flock of wild geese flew over frozen Pete's Pond and gracefully landed in a path of blue open water.

February 5—I took grandson Chad skiing with me today, as Enterprise students are let out at noon on Fridays. We drove to the nearby Ferguson Ridge ski area, where I rented boots and skis for Chad. The snow was still great and we skied all afternoon. Although this was only

Chad's second experience at downhill skiing, he learned quickly and was soon skiing circles around grandma.

When I drove Chad home, the entire family was glued to the living room window, watching Rowdy's cow give birth to a calf. Rowdy, who is quite the animal lover, led me to the barn and proudly showed me his twin Dorset lambs.

Back at the house everyone soon let out a cheer when the calf made its appearance. Then everyone shook the beaming Rowdy's hand.

February 6—Daughter Jackie arrived this morning with her two children. I had promised them their annual ski outing at Ferguson Ridge today. The children were so excited they could hardly wait. We put together a picnic lunch and headed for the slopes.

It was partly cloudy and around 20 degrees, with areas of blue sky and intermittent sunshine creating magic on the mountains. After fitting the children with their rented skis and boots, we were finally ready to ski.

Seven-year-old tow-headed Buck was persistent and very determined to master the tow rope, and finally got the job done. From then on, he scarcely took a break all day, except to eat. He took plenty of spills, but got up to try again, undaunted.

His sister Mona was just gaining some degree of confidence when she had an unfortunate mishap on the tow rope and that ended her skiing for the day. There was no injury and she will no doubt try again.

By nightfall there were two weary children and one very weary grandma.

February 7—Doug left this morning to attend a Simmental sale in Reno, while I stayed close to home and waited for the phone call about the expected arrival of the newest grandchild. During his absence, I tackled the income tax, caught up on my letter writing, read two books, and rested my ski legs. No phone call.

February 8—We had a low last night of 23, and by 8 it had warmed to 30! I opened the door to the chicken house this morning and my laying hens cautiously ventured forth onto the snow. Chester, the banty rooster, spread his wings, flapped them back and forth and gave a hearty crow.

The warm breath of a chinook wind outside this evening is melting the snow. Doug called to say he had purchased two animals at the sale. Still waiting for our baby.

February 9—The snow is nearly gone now except for a few scattered patches. Stubby's dog bones have surfaced under the clothesline as the white coat of winter vanishes, leaving its refuse laid bare for all to see. On my way to town I noticed that Prairie Creek was running high and muddy with melted snow and ice.

Watched grandson James today while mom got some rest. We had such a good time, this little 19-month-old and I, gathering the eggs, reading books and talking about his small world. Doug arrived home safely around midnight.

February 10—A new snowfall during the night covered up the dog bones. Doug attempted to drive out to the hills to check on things there, but wasn't able to make it; the road to Salmon Creek isn't maintained during the winter.

A chicken roasts in the oven with parsnips, carrots and potatoes, as I type at the kitchen table.

February 11—Doug and I met with our accountant today to go over the income tax.

In the office, people went out muttering to themselves over this annual headache, which is becoming more and more complicated each year. What is worse, one can't vent one's frustrations on any given person. This complex system, referred to simply as "they," an unmoving, uncaring IRS machine, most apt to be operated by someone, heaven forbid, like you and me. Somehow that fact worries me the most.

Taxes are just one of many obstacles to overcome in the running of a ranch these days. One needs a good sense of humor—either laugh or go mad.

Our CowBelles served free beefy chili at the annual Les Schwab tire promotion at noon today in Enterprise. We in the beef industry appreciate the support given yearly by Mr. Schwab.

The thermometer got up to nearly 60 degrees today. We are into mud now, a yearly condition that is simply endured. This year we are glad for anything that has moisture in it, mud included.

Attended the monthly CowBelle meeting today at Pat Murrill's. The calendar is filling with busy spring projects and calving time is close at hand.

This evening I made valentines for my grandchildren by cutting out the seed catalog's colorful pictures of vegetables and fruits and pasting them on construction paper: "Peas" be mine, I "carrot" for you a lot. "Corny?" Maybe so, but the children love them, and with 12 grandchildren one must be creative and work with what's on hand.

February 12—Late morning sunshine burned off a cold fog that earlier lay over Prairie Creek.

I have hit upon a plan to bring about the birth of the baby. I am planning a dinner for the "Wallowa Story" committee Monday evening... we'll see if it works!

February 13—Under 30 degrees this morning, with an icy wind blowing off the snowy mountains, which lay hidden behind a curtain of storm clouds. As the yellow silage truck comes lumbering up the road, the cows begin to bawl and gather at the hill gate, anticipating their daily ration of fragrant silage.

Baked a peach pie for grandson Chad's pie-a-month birthday present. One more month and his year will be up.

Gathered some favorite recipes and put them in a recipe file that my mother had given me for Christmas. Hopefully, now I will be able to put my hands on a special recipe without having to tear the kitchen apart.

A rather nasty flu bug has been making the rounds in the county and several members of our family have been laid up recently.

February 14—Valentine's Day dawned cloudy and cold, with the freezing breeze lingering on. The ground is frozen again, and ice puddles dot our lane. On Upper Prairie Creek a weak sun makes the patches of snow glare on a glazed surface, resulting from recent thawing and refreezing.

Doug and I did all the feeding today, as it was Ben's day off. I am keeping a daily growth record on an amaryllis bulb that I have potted near my kitchen sink. Its rate of growth is phenomenal. The bloom stalk has grown from 4-1/2 inches to 10 inches in four days. Responding to sunlight and water, the stem reaches upward until soon the large buds will burst into enormous blooms. When there is snow outside, it is a great joy to watch this grow inside my warm kitchen.

I made a heart-shaped cherry cheesecake for Doug's valentine. Wind and light rain outside, which probably will turn to snow before long.

February 15—A phone call at 5 a.m. Liza's time had come! My plan to have the dinner party tonight had worked. I grabbed my toothbrush and, like a good grandma, left Prairie Creek for the mountain.

A wild, gusty wind was blowing snow down off Ruby Peak in great white, misty sheets as I pulled up to the Slope house. Little James, who had the flu, immediately came to me, a little bewildered at all the goings-on this early in the morning.

Son Todd disappeared with his wife into the storm to drive the few miles to Wallowa Memorial Hospital. All morning I held James until his fever broke, whereupon he felt better and we both ate some lunch. All day we read books, looked up at the storm on the mountain, and waited.

It was after 6 p.m when we received the news: Adele Marie, weighing in at a healthy 9 pounds, 4-1/2 ounces, had finally made her appearance on this stormy February night. James had a little sister, and I had my 13th grandchild.

That night James and I lay in bed and by the porch light watched swirls of loose snow blow off the roof through the bedroom window.

February 16—Hearing that her daughter was in the hospital, Liza's mom had driven all night and arrived safely in the early hours of the morning. Pretty important baby! It wasn't until later in the day that I finally got to see my newest granddaughter.

Can there be anything more precious than the sight of a newborn babe snuggled in her mother's arms? Through pink-curtained windows of Liza's hospital room, the gleaming white mountains, shot with sunlight, looked down on this newest member of our family. Wallowa County's population had swelled by one.

February 17—Baked an extra loaf of sourdough bread this morning and took it to the Alder Slope family. Mother and baby came home while I was there. It was a special time for both of us grandmas as we watched little James welcome his baby sister.

I got home just in time to help Ben and Doug drive our heifers to a dry feedlot. While moving them down the road, a mini-snow squall materialized, naturally.

Baked a chocolate "Wacky" cake for a potato growers' meeting here tonight. Snowing heavily in the mountains.

We received our annual "Mexican letter" from Duane Wiggins, who, with wife, Jane, spends his winters in Mexico. Duane does his best each year to coax us down there with stories of all the good fishing and plenty of warm sunshine. It seems the fishing wasn't as good compared to previous years, so instead Duane talked about eating armadillos and iguanas. Somehow, I think we'll stick to our winter fare of elk and beef.

February 18—Doug left this afternoon to attend a potato meeting in Corvallis while I stayed close to home where I was needed. Because it was such a bright, sunshiny day, Scotty and I took the time to do some cross-country skiing on Alder Slope. Fresh snow lay in the fields and the skiing was great.

Tonight a new moon hangs suspended over the snowy mountains. Next to it two brilliant stars glitter in the cold sky.

February 19—I had rescheduled my dinner and planned it for tonight, so began by making a shrimp tomato aspic and mixing up the sourdough. I thawed a nice steelhead and began to clean house. Another gorgeous day. Sunlight streamed through the large living room window and the bird song had a spring-like quality.

Scotty called to say, "We've got to go skiing while the conditions are so good."

"I can't," I said, then looked outside at this perfect day and changed my mind. The housework would have to wait.

We drove to Ferguson Ridge. A whole new blanket of fresh snow and not a soul around to enjoy it. We put on our skis and followed ski trails into the woods. Branches, laden with snow, let loose occasionally with a loud "swoosh" as their burden slid off. We climbed a rather steep hill and skied out on a ridge top. The pristine snow glistened in sunlight, broken only by scattered snowshoe rabbit tracks.

After eating a light lunch, I returned to the house cleaning and cooking. From my kitchen window I spied the first returning robin.

"When will the strawberries be ripe?" he chirped.

When my guests arrived, I was ready. I had also invited the other grandma for an evening out and she brought a bright bouquet of daffodils for the table. Grace arrived with her specialty, squash pie, and what a wonderful meal we had: hot sourdough bread sticks, fresh from the oven; delicious baked Snake River steelhead, the colorful aspic, creamed new potatoes and peas and pie.

It was a fitting climax to our project.

February 20—Another of those perfect Blue Bird mornings. After chores I began taking the cover off my sheepherder wagon; there are several areas that need repairing. It has been parked all winter in the calving shed and we will soon be needing the space. In a week or so we will begin calving. The spring rush is just around the corner!

The Blue Bird morning became a Blue Bird day. Clear skies, brilliant sunlit snowfields, and not the slightest breeze. Simply had to get outside on such a day, so met some friends at Ferguson Ridge and got in some downhill skiing this morning.

There were only about eight people there because the T-bar was shut down for repairs. Gardener Locke, who was operating the tow rope, offered to take three of us to the top of the hill on the snow cat. Cressie Green and I, never missing a chance for adventure, said sure, we'd go.

We climbed on the back and the snow cat began its ascent of the steep hill. The big caterpillar-like tracks grabbed and crawled straight up and the engine roared and puffed. At times the machine would give a lurch sideways, then grab a fresh hold on the snowy, steep slope. Cressie and I hung on for dear life.

The higher we went, the more beautiful the sight. We could see the Findley Buttes, Idaho's Seven Devil Mountains, the backbone of the Wallowa range and, below, the valley lay spread out like a giant colored tapestry. It was such a clear day, we could see forever.

Negotiating a rather steep face, we crawled and clung and slowly inched our way up and over a lip. We were on top! Now we could see the cut between the canyons, which marks Little Sheep Creek's course to the Imnaha. A limitless horizon of blues stretched to Washington and Idaho as we viewed our country from this northeastern tip of Oregon. A fellow who had ridden up to ski down jumped off, donned his skis, and disappeared in a cloud of powdery snow.

We returned by way of "Haze Maze" where the going wasn't as steep. The snow pack was deep with a powdery surface. Soon we arrived safely back at the warming shack, where we ate our lunches on the deck and enjoyed the warm sunshine. After a few more runs on the tow rope slope, we called it a day.

Built by volunteers, members of the Eagle Cap Ski Club, this remote ski area can hold its own when it comes to great skiing and unique wintertime scenery.

February 21—Another beautiful day. The frost goes out by mid-morning, making the ground ooze. Opened all the windows and let the fresh air blow away winter's cooped-up staleness in the house. The snow is nearly gone on Prairie Creek here, but ice remains in the irrigation ditches and on the shaded "norths."

Went for a walk around the ranch, picking up bits of plastic and baler twine. It seems we live in an age of plastic. Wood and wood products go back into the ground, but we live with these synthetics forever.

Cleaned out the flower beds alongside the house. A few primroses are bravely blooming.

Doug and I attended a sweetheart banquet this evening at the Imnaha School. As we traveled down along Little Sheep Creek, we noticed many deer feeding in the gathering dusk, and it was nearly dark when we arrived at 6.

This small two-room Bridge School is the social hub of Imnaha, and people from upriver and down were already converging for the evening festivities. From the kitchen drifted the aroma of roast beef and all the trimmings, cooked up by the ladies of Imnaha.

Many old-timers were there, including 93-year-old A.L. Duckett, looking fit as a fiddle. Also Wilson and Kate Wilde, Clyde and Rose Simmons, Bill and Cecil Mae Bailey, Bud and Thelma Maxwell. Just folks, but perhaps some of the best in the world when it comes to creating a caring, sharing community.

The younger, newer generation was represented, and a few of us from "On Top," like Max and Dorothy Gorsline. Tables had been set up and decorated in patriotic red, white and blue.

After a delicious dinner, the dessert table laden with homemade pies beckoned, and everyone had just a bit of room left to partake of a choice of pies that ranged from blackberry-custard to luscious lemon meringue.

While the pie settled, we were entertained by Don Norton on the fiddle, accompanied by wife, Vadna, on piano. Holding an old, faded copy of Gene Autry sheet music, Warren Glaus sang "My Cross-eyed Gal" as wife Rose played the piano accompaniment.

Honored guest Bob Erickson from Coeur d'Alene yodeled. And yodeled, and yodeled. Never had we heard such a performance. Hindered somewhat by a large slice of chocolate cream pie, he belted out "Cattle Call," "The Auctioneer's Song" and "I've Been Everywhere, Man" with scarcely a break. The little school house fairly rang with country songs.

Bob ended with a room full of people joining in the singing of "America the Beautiful" and the evening ended.

Driving the 30 miles home to Prairie Creek, we noticed a new moon growing and a warm wind blowing.

February 22—Another warm, clear, flawless day, in a succession of them. Although the low is 25 degrees, the morning frost melts rapidly. Hung my wash on the clothesline for the first time since fall. Mailed a birthday present to granddaughter Lacey in Wyoming. She soon will be five.

Lots of interest in our home-raised bulls. We have sold more than half of them already.

February 23—Clear, crisp morning, not a cloud in the sky, with a low of 15. The robins have returned in full force and the fields are alive with them. My amaryllis bulb has grown a 20-inch stalk and is about to burst into full bloom.

The warm afternoons have caused the lilac buds to swell, but they are too early. They are in for a shock.

February 24—Son Ken here to help drive in our spring calvers, sorting out the cows closest to calving and putting them in the lower field so we can observe them more closely. Also sorted were two of my milk cow "herd" who have been wintering with the main bunch.

Daisy and May, looking pleasingly pregnant, came ambling down Tenderfoot Valley Road toward the house. I had been baking pies and opened the door to let some fresh air in, when I saw them. I called the two cows by name, whereupon they stopped and looked at me before slowly making their heavy way down the driveway.

They seemed to know it was time for them to return to the barn lot before their calves were born. These two Guernseys, with a smidgen of Jersey thrown in, proceeded to walk into their familiar enclosure, where I closed the gate behind them. Immediately they renewed old friendships with the two Holsteins, Star and her half-Simmental offspring Startch. All too soon, my leisurely days of skiing will be over, and it will be back to the barn to graft calves, milk and care for these spoiled bovines who moo at the sight of me.

In the house to finish with the gooseberry-custard pie, another one of Wanda Doud's delicious pie recipes, and a sour cream raisin pie. The raisin pie went to son Ken for his pie-a-month.

Lawrence and Ilene Potter drove up from Little Sheep Creek to ride with Grace Bartlett and me as we drove to the Wallowa Grange Hall to show the Wallowa Story. Quite a contrast to the wild, windy night when we had attempted to show the program before and the electricity had gone out.

Orie and Rae Mahanna were there to greet us and a good crowd turned out. The audience was sprinkled with many descendants of the early pioneers: Schaeffers, Johnsons, Bechtals, to name a few. All very proud of their heritage and their lovely lower valley, a valley that was first glimpsed by the earliest settlers entering the Wallowa country when it was inhabited by the Joseph band of Nez Perce.

February 25—February continues unseasonably mild, and a typical 25-degree morning quickly warmed to around 55. Twice a day I feed hay to my pregnant milk cows as their swollen udders and bellies grow and grow.

The amaryllis buds opened into three delicate pink blossoms.

Gave a private showing of the Wallowa Story to Norma Hope in her upper Prairie Creek home. Norma, who doesn't get out often, appreciated seeing and listening to the history. It was such a gorgeous morning and the mountains, which literally rise from her pastures, gleamed brightly in snowlight.

Years ago Norma was a school teacher and taught at both the Pleasant Center and Prairie Creek one-room schools. Today she lives alone, tending her small cow herd, and in the summer grows a beautiful garden.

Finally located a pair of new, blue, unfaded jeans at Wagner's in Enterprise. Just goes to show, a person should shop in her own home town.

February 26—An especially bright, clear morning. The birds were singing, the sourdough bread was rising (in the sunlight) and Chester the rooster was crowing. Was this a false spring? The first tiny green of the tulip leaves emerged and the primroses alongside the house began to bloom. Doug spotted a bald eagle in the lower field.

The days lengthen slowly, with sunup over the hill at 6:50 a.m. Lovely days, but dry ones, and how we wish for rain. On these nice, warm days I sometimes drive to Alder Slope and watch James while his mom gets a little rest. Baby Adele grows and blossoms, all sweet and pink, like the amaryllis.

Our first baby calves have begun to arrive, and in no time the pasture will be full of them, running and playing in the sunshine.

February 27—Attended a baby shower for Liza. The guest of honor was little Adele, who slept through most of it.

Leigh Juve, who lives on Alder Slope, gave the shower, which was nice of her. It was especially fun for several of us grandmas there, as we all got to brag, in turn, about our grandchildren. There has been a rash of new babies being born lately.

Doug and I attended a potluck supper party in honor of Judy and Rich Wandschneider, who recently sold the Bookloft in Enterprise. To get into the spirit of the thing, we were told to go dressed as our favorite literary character.

I decided to go as Patrick McManus' "Rancid Crabtree," a character I adore. Just reading his name makes me laugh. This old woodsman, who is supposed to be an authority on outdoor life, who takes life with a grain of salt, enjoys each day, doesn't know the meaning of the word stress and simply reduces life to the basic functions. He goes off fishing and hunting, with nary a care in the world.

So I dug out Doug's oldest hat, decorated with a buck tail and a hawk's feather, and added a gaudy fishing lure and a piece of line to the crown I put on a fringed buckskin jacket, a pair of torn and faded jeans, some holey long johns, my old hiking boots, and smeared smudges of stove soot on my face.

A large group of the couple's friends attended, and most all of us were bookworms. It was fun to guess who the other literary characters were. They ranged from Jo, in "Little Women," to Ernest Hemingway.

Rich and Judy will be missed for their "tea and sympathy" that went with the purchase of each book, but the new owner will, I'm sure, manage just fine. All in all it was a great evening with the "roasting of Rich and Judy," songs and square dancing.

February 28—Another sunny day, our yearling bulls stretched out on the ground to soak up the warmth. In the chicken yard Chester strutted around trying to attract attention, but the hens were more concerned with digging up worms and ignored his charms altogether.

I went for daily walks to check on the calving cows. It is so amazing that these wet, newborn babies can stand and nurse within minutes after birth. The warm, sunny days are ideal for calving, even though many calves will arrive during a snow squall.

Roasted a pot roast of elk and baked a pecan pie for the Stockgrowers-CowBelles potluck. Another potluck! Due to it being calving time, many were late arriving. After eating, we listened to reports given by Oregon Cattlemen's Association President Bill Wolfe and Beef Council Chairman Reid Johnson, both from the lower valley. Wallowa County is honored to have these beef industry leaders in our midst.

February 29—Leap year day leapt away and a sprinkle of rain fell during the night as cooler air moved in. Doug hauled some yearling bulls to the vet to be semen tested today.

March 1—Came in like a lamb, a blushing pink one that tinted the early morning clouds. Some of us CowBelles organized the Cow-Belle inventory of supplies that have been stored in Jean Stubblefield's bunkhouse, a job that consumed the morning.

Doug attended a weed meeting during lunch. I received a phone call from Gay at the Grain Growers feed store. The baby chicks I ordered would be here tomorrow. Holy cow! So, I shook out the straw in the big wooden box in the calving shed, scrubbed and disinfected feeders and waterers, hooked up the extension cord for the heat lamp, and now it surely will storm.

Doug saddled a horse to drive in a heifer having trouble calving and I put supper on hold. By the time I walked to the calving shed, he had the heifer there. We ran her in and pulled the calf. Just as it was born, a sudden shower pelted the tin roof. I knew it. One way to make it rain: order baby chicks or have a heifer calve.

March 2—Thirty degrees and a slow-moving fog bank crawled in from the lower valley. It quickly dissolved and another sunny, blue day ensued. I had many errands to run before picking up the chicks. The car was packed with my week's groceries, chicken feed and the 50 peeping chicks when I finally returned to Prairie Creek.

Doug and Ben horseback sorting more cows that are closest to calving. Then Doug left for Portland to attend the quarterly Oregon Cattlemen's Association meetings. Meanwhile, back at the ranch, I held down the fort with 50 peeping chicks, and the calving cows.

Tonight I attended the annual Alder Slope Pipeline Association meeting at the home of Wilmer and Mary Cook on Alder Slope. A good turnout of members discussed assessments, leaky pipes and elected officers, before socializing over ice cream and cookies. If we don't receive more moisture, we won't have water to use in the pipeline.

I checked on the chicks when I returned and they were cozy and warm in their quarters. They won't be cute for long. Soon their feathers will appear and they will have a case of the uglies.

Two yearling sorrel colts and two older horses nibble grass between patches of snow on Wallowa County's Upper Prairie Creek on a sunny March morning.

Prior to the 1870s, this beautiful land was occupied by the Wallowa or Joseph band of Nez Perce Indians. It was their homeland, used for hunting and fishing and as a pasture for their thousands of horses and cattle. The Nez Perce wintered in the canyons, unlike the white men of today, who must feed their livestock hay through the long, cold, winter months.

Shown here are horses that inhabit upper Prairie Creek today. Tired of their winter diet of hay, they eagerly await springtime's approach. Sufficient grass won't be available here until mid-May. In the plateau or "hill country" north of here, horses are able to paw through the snow for old grass and winter quite well.

March 3—An icy tingle to the wind this morning as I walked down to the calving shed to hay and water a cow and calf, and tend to my baby chicks. Dramatic, meringue-like clouds cling to the base of the mountains, which appear brighter under a new layer of snow. It is 36 degrees, no frost!

When I took my daily walk down the road to check the calving cows, I waved a greeting to our neighbor, Hubert Rosser, who was out doing his evening chores. Tonight the full March moon rose in a cloudless sky.

Two yearling sorrel colts and two older horses nibble grass between patches of snow on Wallowa County's Upper Prairie Creek on a sunny March morning.

March 4—Seventeen degrees. The thermometer goes up and down like a yo-yo in our high mountain valley. While starting the fire in the woodstove, I enjoyed watching the pink-tinted peaks give way to cloudy skies. Six calves born today.

March 5—Snow fell during the night, and there is snow mixed with rain this morning. Doug drove from Portland and the cattlemen's meetings to Hermiston last night, so I rode with Wayne and Meleese Cook to meet him at the C&B sale. We arrived just in time to partake of the last of the steak, eggs, biscuits and honey brunch served up by Jane Baker and her crew.

The sale began and, one by one, C&B bulls entered the ring and were sold to the highest bidder. One particular bull came charging into the sale ring, decided he wanted out, and proceeded to paw his way up into the auctioneer's stand. Bill Lefty, who maintains a running dialogue, was suddenly speechless.

After a fashion, the bull exited via the opposite gate, and Bill, remaining relatively cool, said, "That bull that just left has good eyes and fine ears. I just got a really close look at them." Without more ado, Lefty straightened up the mike, shook the spilled coffee of his catalog, brushed his coat, re-set his Stetson and resumed his sing-song chant—and sold the bull.

Ran into an old Wallowa Countian, Cy Kooch, who invited me to his place down the road to see a most unusual collection. What a sight it was. Every conceivable type of horse, made from many materials: ceramic, wood, glass, plastic, cloth, metal, you name it. The collection took up an entire room and numbered around 1,000!

I enjoyed visiting Cy and his wife of nearly 50 years, Willetta. The Kooch family roots are in Wallowa County and many descendants continue to live here. Cy is a well-known draft horse judge, breeder and enthusiast.

Returning to the sale, I found that Doug had purchased a bull. Later he purchased another bull and two heifers. By late afternoon 221 lots of bulls and 26 lots of females had gone through the sale ring. Spectators and buyers were treated to crisp red apples provided by the Bakers.

As we left, steady rain began to fall. Driving up Cabbage Hill it was foggy and drippy. Traveling through the Blues we encountered sleet, rain, snow and more fog. Arriving home on Prairie Creek, we checked the cows and my chicks, which had survived my absence.

March 6—Up early to see a howling, blowing blizzard. Yep, it is March. Hayed my pregnant milk cows, hoping they wouldn't choose today to calve. Warmed some colostrum milk for a chilled calf born in the storm. Naturally, the calves come right and left with every new storm.

A flock of robins lit in the snowy yard, escaping the wind and blowing snow. Baked bread today and tried to catch up on inside chores. The sky cleared by evening, and the temperature plummeted.

March 7—Clear skies, 15 degrees.

Bundled up in insulated overalls to chore. Later I drove with a sick calf to the vet, but it expired soon thereafter due to a severe intestinal blockage complicated by pneumonia. A new calf, born in the field, was bawling, his mother not letting him nurse. I walked out with a bottle to feed him and he ate hungrily.

A bitter chill to the air this evening; the snowy mountains seem to close in on us. Attended a 4-H leaders meeting tonight at Cloverleaf Hall. I left an elk roast in the wood stove oven for Doug, who would arrive late from trucking our sale animals home from Hermiston.

March 8—Much warmer this morning when I fed the milk cows and horses, and took another bottle to the calf in the field. After drinking his bottle. he did go over and manage to get a little milk from mom, who tolerated him better this morning.

Grace, Cressie, Opal Tippett and I showed the "Wallowa Story" to the nursing home residents this evening. It was a very rewarding experience. Many residents were Wallowa County natives.

March 9—Awoke to another March blizzard, the wind blowing loose snow across the fields and plastering it against the fence posts and trees. Still struggling with two calves in the calving shed. Wish I had a milk cow fresh and wouldn't have to mess with bottles.

Early this morning Ben drove up with a chilled calf which we laid on a tarp in front of the old Monarch wood range. Why is it whenever there is a cold snap or a blizzard, something triggers these problem calvers? As if on cue from some unseen force of nature, cows decide to have complicated births. If it is sunny, dry and warm, there are no such problems. Strange indeed.

Most of the time we tube feed these new babies to get them on their feet. It is during these times that the romantic life portrayed by the Hollywood movie world simply isn't authentic. Cow-calf ranching is hard, exhausting. dirty, cold work. But however unpleasant the moment, we know spring is eternal and soon the calves will run around bucking and playing in green fields, and these times will be forgotten—until next March.

March 10—Fresh snow on the ground and the wind has a bite to it. Down to the calving shed to face the music. Liza called, said James missed his grandma, who has been so busy with baby calves that she hasn't had time for him. One storm after another sweeps across Prairie Creek and the poor little calves must be tough to survive.

Doug is attending a potato meeting in Redmond. One of our bulls got out today and wandered up Tenderfoot Valley road. I jumped in the pickup and drove him home. Doug arrived home safely around midnight.

March 11—Out to feed the calves, cows and horses, and tend the baby chicks, which have sprouted wing feathers already. It is still very cold, with areas of snow on the frozen ground. Patches of blue sky show between snow clouds. Between the calving chores, I somehow sandwiched in the grocery shopping and various errands in Enterprise today.

March 12—Icy breeze blows over frozen ground. Brief periods of sunshine between scattered clouds. Began working on publicity for the April Art Festival. Measured the old tarp on my sheepherder wagon and ordered a new one made.

March 13—Twenty-eight degrees; a flawlessly beautiful blue sky. The birds are singing and the mountains gleam in the sunlight. The frozen manure and mud around the cow's hay feeder makes walking difficult. Our newly purchased Simmental heifers look like petunias in an onion patch, next to our rough winter-coated Wallowa County cattle.

On this Sunday, Doug and I drove to Imnaha and had lunch at the Riverside Cafe, visited Jim Dorrance, and enjoyed seeing apricots, forsythia and sarvis berry in bloom. The first gauzy green tinge was appearing on the weeping willows. Spring is near!

March 14—No frost, mostly sunny, but black clouds forming out north. Fixed breakfast on the wood stove before going out to chore. Busy working on publicity for our annual Festival of the Arts. Sent news releases to several newspapers.

By mid-morning a full scale blizzard erupted from those black clouds. Cyclonic winds swirled snowflakes into the air, and they blew about like goose down. Son Ken here helping Ben sort cows during the blizzard.

Always looking for innovative ways to cook chicken, I came across a Farm Journal recipe, "Chicken with 40 cloves of garlic." The accompanying color photo looked tempting, so I gave it a go. Because I had an abundance of garlic from my fall garden, that wasn't any problem. The unpeeled garlic, stated the recipe, would impart a subtle flavor to the dish. Atop a layer of celery, carrots and surrounded with the garlic, the chicken cooked slowly in my dutch oven.

At suppertime we peeled the cooked garlic and smeared it on buttered, freshly baked sourdough bread. The chicken was wonderful, even though the house smelled of garlic for days.

When I left that evening to drive to Alder Slope, the pavement was bare. By the time I got halfway there, it began to snow. Big, fat flakes hit the windshield so thickly I could scarcely see. The storm increased and by the time I pulled up to Liza and Todd's, I stepped out into a good five inches of freshly fallen snow.

I stayed with James while mom and baby sister went out for the evening. It was still snowing lightly when I returned home. All of Prairie Creek looked like the dead of winter. Poor baby calves.

March 15—Twenty degrees. Baby calves being born right and left. Sloshed through deep, wet snow to feed. We really need this moisture, so can't complain. Baked a pie using my frozen gooseberries.

Grandchildren Buck and Mona with us this evening while their parents attended a meeting in town. They enjoyed feeding the baby chicks and eating gooseberry pie.

March 16—Bright, blue skies, brilliant sunshine and...11 degrees! Nearly 50 robins decorated the willow trees in the yard this morning, making splotches of orange on the bare limbs.

Brought James home with me this morning. This 20-month-old grandson is so much fun. We talked the entire time, through lunch, gathering eggs, going for a walk, playing the piano. His favorite thing was watching the chickens. He would gladly stay there all day, face pressed against the chicken wire, listening to the hens cluck and Chester crow.

So he would rest, I read him stories about the fox and Moses the kitten. When it came time to return my little pal, his head nodded once on the car seat and he fell fast asleep. James had such a good time at grandma's, he'd worn himself plum out.

March 17—My purebred Simmental cow gave birth to a nice, big bull calf on this sunny St. Patrick's Day morning. The sunshine felt warm in spite of a 15-degree reading on the thermometer. Made a peach pie for Chad's pie-a-month birthday present. His 12 months finally are up!

Worked on the Simmental registration records. Baked a loaf of sourdough bread. This evening we attended a "Cow Chip Lottery" at Imnaha. The school yard had been roped off and marked into squares, which people previously had purchased for $2.50 each. This wasn't your ordinary lottery. A cow was hauled to the school and turned loose inside the roped-off area. This is where the chips would fall, hopefully.

However, it got darker and darker and by the time bossy decided to cooperate, it was pretty hard to see the chip. The cow's owner, Barbara Warnock, spotted it and with much ceremony it was determined that Sally Stein had won the $100 Cow Chip Lottery. The remainder of the profit went toward the Jack and Harriet Finch Memorial Scholarship Fund. The Finches were beloved teachers at the small school.

Meanwhile the Imnaha students had been releasing helium-filled balloons that floated above rimrocks to join stars that appeared one by one in the canyon night. Written on the balloons were the number of books each child had read.

Inside the school house there was a buzz of activity as the students staged a carnival to raise money for their yearly field trip. Susie Borgerding was making green cotton candy and the machine was really spinning; most of the spidery stuff was floating toward the ceiling.

A real carnival atmosphere prevailed, with booths of ring-toss, a fish pond and rope the steer. If you weren't wearing green, a student escorted you to jail. If you couldn't pay your way out for a quarter, you were put in solitary confinement for five minutes.

The pie throwing booth was the most popular. Cream pies were thrown by the students into the faces of their teacher, Char Williams, and several of the mothers. The committee of mothers sold hot dogs, chili and Imnaha's famous homemade pies. Most of the community turned out to support the event.

Barnum and Bailey couldn't have created more enthusiasm than did these students, parents and teacher. When we left, Paul Kriley was still in solitary confinement! We checked the cows on this clear, beautiful night. Nothing calving. They are waiting for the next storm!

March 18—The birds are singing their hearts out. So warm I let the fire go out. After chores I drove to upper Prairie Creek, where I photographed for the horse issue of Agri-Times.

Gradually the snow line retreats toward the mountains, whose snow-fields are blinding white in the morning sun. A small bunch of horses was eagerly nibbling old grass between patches of melting snow. It has been a long winter for them, and they are tired of hay.

Ate lunch today at the Common Good Market Place in Enterprise, where I met with two other committee members to discuss plans for the Art Council's Festival of Arts. So much to do before April 22.

The baby calves arriving 10 at a time in the lower field today. Developed my roll of film, then later went to the Art Angle to print. Son Steve home from college, working on the ranch again, having fulfilled his graduation requirements.

March 19—Doug off to Hermiston to purchase Angus "heifer bulls." What is a "heifer bull"? Ask any rancher, and he will tell you.

Delivered eggs to customers and then attended a country auction on Hurricane Creek Road. It was a warm, beautiful day and everyone, it seemed, wanted to be out in it. An auction is a time for socializing and visiting neighbors you haven't seen all winter.

The house and property having previously been sold, the 100-year accumulation of this widow's family was disappearing rapidly. The

Although Wallowa County recorded only small amounts of moisture in February, the mountain snow pack appears to hold sufficient water to feed irrigation ditches like the one shown here on upper Prairie Creek.

auctioneer, Roger Nedrow, was standing on a trailer, and the crowd pressed forward to see each item he held up to sell.

It must have been hard for the owner to watch the possessions gathered over a lifetime be sold and scattered to the wind. Perhaps many, like me, were thinking that someday this might happen to us. Mostly everyone smiled though, because it was such a pretty spring day and the long winter was over.

March 20—Daisy calved yesterday. She chose a warm, sunny day to have her nice heifer calf. Karl and Karen Patton hauled the three Angus bulls home for us that Doug purchased in Hermiston yesterday. There isn't even any frost on this morning of the first day of spring!

After choring, I met some friends for a hike on Alder Slope. On such a day one needs to be out and about to celebrate spring. Climbing up a sunny hillside, we spied some of the season's first buttercups nestled between large rocks. As we entered the timberline area, it also became the snowline.

We crunched through hardened drifts, following an old road that led eventually to an elk trap that we had come to investigate. Don't know if any animals were captured here, but we had read where elk were being trapped and shipped to Texas in return for wild turkeys. Evidence of many elk having been in the area.

We came upon two "bearing trees" that were used years ago to mark the forest boundary. Walking along a heavily-used elk trail, we came out into an opening that lay hidden beneath the deep snows of winter. Our legs sank up to our knees with each step.

Presently we came to the old Murray homestead. The Murrays, who were Guy McCormack's mother's family, immigrated from Quebec, Canada, and settled on this secluded spot under the base of the mountains.

While trudging through deep snow we heard the howling of several wolves. People who live higher on the mountain raise them. It was like being in the far north to hear those eerie voices in that wild setting.

All that remained of the homestead was an old fruit orchard; apple, pear and plum trees, a crab apple tree, and two huge poplar trees that grew where the cabin must have stood. Several rambling lilac bushes had survived, although not even one board of the house or outbuildings could be found. We followed a dim road to a sunny clearing and ate our lunch sitting on a log.

What a perfect way to celebrate the first day of spring and the end of winter. That evening I milked out Daisy's colostrum milk and froze it for the remainder of the calving season. Felt funny milking. It will take a while to build up my wrists again. I put Daisy's calf in the barn because I will be grafting an extra calf on her soon.

March 21—Daisy bawled all night. She was happy when I let her in to nurse her calf and to milk her some. The busy days have begun! Typed my column and it seems like every minute of the day is completely filled.

Calves being born all over the field today. A light rain quickly turned to a blizzard with blowing snow. No wonder those calves decided to be born. Seed potato buyers beginning to call and come look at our seed. Soon it will be time to ship.

Attempted to put an orphan on Daisy this evening, but the calf wasn't hungry enough yet. Come morning, he will be.

March 22—Weaned Star's big bull calf yesterday, so am having to milk her out a little each day to gradually dry her up. The orphan went right to nursing this morning after I stuck his nose in a kitty dish of warm milk. Startch and May are very close to calving.

Packed water to my laying hens, changed bedding under the chicks, and made sure the feeders were full and waterers clean, a daily chore. Doug and extension agent Arleigh Isley left to attend a weed control meeting in Island City.

I met with the Art Festival committee at noon. Threatening rain or snow; very windy. Returning from town, I walked out to check my cows. Apparently May and Startch had lain down side-by-side and calved. Startch had a big heifer and May's bull was just breathing his first air. It appeared they had been born within minutes or seconds of each other. Do you suppose these two cows will compare notes on their pregnancy and talk over their calving experiences like women do? The wet newborn calves shivered in the wind until their mammas' vigorous licking warmed them up enough to stand and suck.

The high winds continued and March marched onward. Purple crocuses bloomed beside the house and the robins continued to arrive in droves. That night, sleet rattled against the window and I had nightmares about those humongous udders full of milk.

March 23—New, wet spring snow on the ground this morning. Mixed sunshine and rain as spring jumps ahead one day and falls back two. Busy at the barn.

Made a sour cream raisin pie, then Doug and I worked in the shop putting the new cover on my sheepherder wagon. We installed new stove pipe and repaired the little herder's stove.

I gave the old wagon a thorough spring cleaning and it looks pretty spiffy. It is now parked under the willow tree in the yard and ready for a spare summer bedroom. The grandchildren especially love sleeping there.

March 24—Raw, cold and freezing this morning. Whatever happened to our first day of spring weather? Chores take an hour and a half now. Mothers and babies doing well. The chicks are growing at a fantastic rate. A light snow fell on the cow barnlot mud.

Met with two representatives of the Montana Repertory Theater this morning at the Cloud 9 Bakery in Enterprise. This nice young couple have the job of going from town to town before the production of "Cowboy" arrives. They must be sure all details are "go" before this live theater troupe arrives.

After our brief meeting, we escorted them to our local KWVR radio station for a taped interview. So much of the success of our Art Festival will hinge on media coverage, getting the word out to the local citizenry. We are very excited about this great musical, based on the life of famed Western artist Charley Russell.

March 25—Snowed all night, but melted by morning. A muddy mess at the barn. Worked for several hours in the darkroom at the Art Angle in Joseph, trying to catch up on my printing.

After chores this evening, Doug and I attended the annual Grain Growers dinner meeting at Cloverleaf Hall. We enjoyed visiting neighbors as well as the delicious roast beef dinner served by members of the local Grange.

March 26—Necked Daisy's two calves together this morning. They struggled around for hours pulling opposite each other, until they broke themselves to lead. Generally after a week I can turn them loose and the cow allows the grafted calf to nurse, and accepts the fact that she is responsible for raising two instead of one.

More high wind today as large, black clouds roll across Prairie Creek. Hung five loads of wash to dry in Mother Nature's "clothes dryer." Neighbor Willie Locke harrows his fields in the wind and intermittent rain. Storms bumped into one another all day. Stinging sleet greeted Doug and me as we went out to chore this evening. Milked Startch out. What a job. One of the necked-together calves had slipped out.of his collar, so had to run them into the barn and buckle them tighter. A real night out for all the baby calves.

March 27—Icicles hang from the barn roof and a leftover cold breeze lingers. Must face the day. Two more calves to graft. The busy season is upon us.

March 27—It snowed today. Driven by a north wind, the snow plastered the sides of fence posts, tree trunks and buildings. It muted the spring colors of the landscape. In the wind and flying snow, Canadian honkers flew overhead to land on Allison's pond.

This evening I set a pan of sourdough biscuits to rise and then, on a whim, I decided to bake them out in the sheepherder wagon. I fired up the little stove and soon had things warm and cozy in the old wagon. After placing a pot of cooked beans to heat on top of the stove, I put the biscuits into bake. And just for the fun of it I informed Doug that supper would be served in the sheepherder's wagon.

Not surprised by anything I do, he accepted. For sourdough biscuits he would follow me anywhere. So while a new blizzard swept out of the north and snowflakes blew around outside, we enjoyed the lightest, goldenest sourdough biscuits you ever saw, along with ham hocks, beans, apple pie and boiled coffee, whilst sitting at the small pull-down table covered with oilcloth. Which goes to prove sourdough was made for camp stoves. Somehow it always performs better under these conditions.

The smell of freshly brewed coffee, aroma of biscuits, and soft lamplight created what is known as "atmosphere." One that could never be

Sam Loftus of Imnaha recites ones of his poems at the Wallowa Valley Festival of the Arts in Enterprise. Loftus has cowboyed all his life in Wallowa County. He was born on Elk Mountain. Poets performed to the largest crowd ever at the Cloverleaf Hall.

duplicated in the finest restaurant. In other words, it was real!

I threw Stubby, our border collie, a ham bone, and while Doug went out to check our calving cows, I lingered inside the warm, old wagon trying to conjure up the life of a sheepherder: day after day of quietness, the tinkle of a sheep's bell, morning birdsong, a gurgling stream, a coyote's wail, watching the lightning and the rain storms come and go, sunrise, moon-glow and starry nights...and coping with loneliness.

Back in my kitchen the phone began to ring and the TV blared out gloom and doom between endless commercials that marched across the screen. Perhaps the sheepherder's life isn't so bad after all.

March 28—It is eight degrees! Even though the sun shone all day, the air had a bite to it. Very busy working with my calves, necking them together to share Daisy and May's abundance of milk. Ben brought in another calf for Startch. That makes six calves on three cows.

March 29—A light snowfall and a 15-degree morning greeted us. Much of my time spent at the barn twice a day. It is paying off; cows and calves healthy and doing great. The baby chicks aren't; they are growing out of their quarters.

March 30—We awoke to see another snowfall with everything frozen. Whatever happened to spring?

March 31—The month ended on a cold note with yet another snowfall covering everything. A brilliant sun rose over the hills to bring to life a blue and white 10-degree morning. The mountains appeared very close in blinding snowlight. Almost immediately the sun's warmth began to take effect; the cattle stood still to soak it up as steam rose from their bodies. By 10 a.m. the green, new grass was exposed as the hot sun continued to burn off the snow.

Dripping everywhere; from the eaves of the house and barns. Snow slid off in great blobs from the tin roofs. As the air warmed, the birdsong intensified. "Spring again," they sang. The laying hens and Chester gossiped and scratched in the thawing earth; robins pulled huge worms from the ground; the barn cats, full of fresh cow's milk, lay sunning themselves on a bale of hay.

Action began at our potato cellars. The crew will ship the first seed out tomorrow. Our phone rang off the hook with buyers and crew communication, and March marched right off the calendar into infinity.

April 1—April Fool's Day, but we were too busy to notice. It was also Good Friday and an absolutely gorgeous day. No foolin'. Resembling a watercolor painting, the pale green began spreading like magic over the valley.

Picked up granddaughter Chelsie at noon from school, and took her to lunch at "The Country Place" on Pete's Pond. Her annual birthday present from grandma. We dined next to a window that looked out on ducks, geese and swans cavorting happily on the surface of the pond.

While eating, Chelsie remarked that her teacher had informed the class that if any child could catch a duck here, Ford Peterson would let them keep it. So seeing Ford nearby, Chelsie asked about the matter, to which he replied, "Sure, only you must use that big net over there."

The ducks, which earlier had been eating out of Chelsie's hand or had been staying close to shore stealing fish chow she fed to the trout, took one look at Chelsie approaching with that net and flew, as one body, to the center of the pond! Undaunted, my granddaughter tried sneaking up on a few wary ducks across the pond and in the process nearly stepped on a nesting swan. The gander, hissing and with outstretched wings, took after her. That ended the duck snatching spree. Just as well, as I was more worried about what to do with the duck after it was captured.

The afternoon warmed to nearly 70 degrees! The first shipment of our seed potatoes went out of the county today.

April 2—Spent the day cleaning house and cooking for Easter Sunday dinner here tomorrow. Made a strawberry cheese cake, a raspberry pie, a large potato salad, sourdough bread and am thawing out a big, cured ham. Hung three loads of wash on the line.

Listened to the 4-H radio auction on our local KWVR station. I had donated a loaf of sourdough bread, and Doug 100 pounds of potatoes for the event. By day's end the auction netted over $4,000. This money will be used for 4-H Summer Week at OSU, the State Fair, and other out-of-county trips. The local support was tremendous. Extension secretary Marsha Svendsen's donation of a pie-a-month for year sold for $105!

At 5 p.m., daughter Ramona called from Prairie City. She and her family were on their way here to spend Easter with us and haul back bulls that Fish Springs Ranch in Nevada was purchasing from us.

Our weather changed and rain showers materialized; plans for an Easter Sunday picnic on Salmon Creek faded as time went on. The family arrived safely around 11 p.m. It was so good to see them. The full moon shrouded in rain clouds when at last we went to bed.

April 3—Time springs ahead one hour on this Easter Sunday morning, ushered in by a snow storm. By mid-morning it seemed as though we plunged into the dead of winter again. A raging blizzard passed over Prairie Creek, and the big, fat flakes of snow stuck to everything.

While a 20-pound ham baked in the wood stove oven, I did my chores. There were 20 members of our family around the table today for dinner. During a brief lull in the storm, a shaft of sunlight broke through the clouds and I decided to take my "herd" of grandchildren for a walk up the road. The little "country cousins," happy to get out of the confines of the house, took off, leaving me holding onto James' hand.

We had a good walk until the next blizzard swept down on us, where-upon we ran for cover in the sheepherder's wagon. What fun the young-sters had. We built a fire in the stove, and Mona and Buck carried cups from the house; we made hot chocolate and told stories. We lit the kerosene lamp and for an hour or so I entertained them so their parents could visit.

The children ranged in age from 17 years to weeks. The oldest, Tammy, and the youngest, Adele, were too old and too young respectively to join our troop. After a hectic Easter egg hunt downstairs and a pie-eating session, the families left and various cousins spent the night with each other. It been a great day, but grandma was wiped out.

April 5—Mostly clear, frosty and cold with scattered snow showers in the forecasts. Ben helped Charley load the 10 bulls bound for Nevada. Doug left for our cellars to ship seed potatoes and I did my chores before the family hit the road. The family had gotten together again last night for dinner at "The Country Place."

It was so nice having everyone around, especially because none of us had to cook or do dishes. Didn't have much time to miss my daughter's young family as the phone began to ring the minute they left, with potato truck drivers calling.

In between relaying messages to the cellar, writing up this column, and housework, I managed to move my growing chicks to roomier quar-ters near the hen house. It took three trips in the pickup with chicks, feed, waterers and a bale of straw, but they are much happier and have considerably more room to grow. Ben shod horses today, as we will be trailing the fall calving cows to the hills this week.

To bed wondering how far my family had traveled so far on the long trip to Fish Springs Ranch, pulling the trailer full of bulls.

April 6—Cloudy, windy and warm when I milked the cow, hayed the other cows and horses, and tended my chickens, which survived their night without a heat lamp. Weaned the fall calves today. The bawling at the corrals is intense!

Feels like it could rain. Attended a meeting with my Sourdough Shutterbug 4-H Club tonight. Coming home it began to rain and rained most of the night, and later turned to snow.

April 7—Out of bed in the gray light of dawn to begin frying bacon on the wood stove. Leaving the rest of breakfast preparations to Doug, I went out to chore. The early light revealed a new snowfall. The warmer air of yesterday had been replaced by a raw, cold breeze.

After putting on layers of clothing, I made a lunch to put in my saddlebag, buckled up my chaps and put on a slicker. Could hardly mount my horse! I joined Ben and Mike McFetridge, who at nearly 80 years of age is still a mighty fine hand. He would be helping us trail the cattle to the hills today. When the cows were turned out onto the road, we kept them at a run until they got out of sight of their calves. We didn't give them an opportunity to turn back.

It was snowing lightly and a cold breeze began to blow, which made the cattle drive well. At the four corners, one black cow turned back with Mike and Ben in hot pursuit. Meanwhile, I had my hands full convincing the herd they had to go forward and not back to the calves. The cow was returned to the main bunch and we headed them out to the hills.

When we got them started up the Crow Creek road, off the pavement, Ben rode back to the ranch to finish feeding. He would join us later at the Dorrance Place, where we planned to leave the herd for the night. Doug had gone to the cellars to ship more seed potatoes, so that left just Mike and me with the cattle. The cows seemed to travel well and kept going at a pretty good clip, having forgotten about their calves and anticipating the open range and grass.

Riding up Crow Creek Pass, the storm intensified. A freezing wind bore stinging flakes of snow that plastered our bodies. It was so cold and the snow flew with such force against us that our eyelashes began to freeze shut, our cheeks becoming reddened and numb with cold. Mike commented that the weather forecasters were forever saying West Yellowstone was the coldest place in the U.S.

"Wrong," Mike said. "Crow Creek Pass is!"

I agreed.

We finally reached the top and it was all downhill from then on. The snow balled up on our horses' hooves and on Mike's dog's feet. It covered our saddles and slickers. A pretty cold deal. Mike and I grinned a frozen smile and told each other how tough we were. There wasn't much else we could do.

When we reached Circle M, the air warmed, the snow slackened and the wind laid down somewhat. What a relief. It still wasn't warm, but it was bearable. As the spring snow began to melt and expose the fields, we could see they were covered with yellow, waxy buttercups! A few shallow snowbanks remained way up high in the aspen draws, but Crow Creek gurgled with life and the moisture was causing spring to "happen" in the hills.

Soon squirrels ran across the melting snow and disappeared into their burrows. Mallard ducks flew about the marshy areas near the creek. Hawks wheeled overhead and the bright patches of buttercups shone like spilled sunlight upon the hills.

We made good time. It was nearly 12:30 when the old log cabins near the Dorrance place came into view. It had begun to turn cold again with the return of the freezing wind. I rode on ahead to open the corral gate and we drove the cows into a holding pasture where they would spend the night.

Mike and I unsaddled our horses and tied them to the corral fence. Then, stiff-legged from all those miles in the saddle, we walked into the old "pink" barn built by Church Dorrance in 1918. We tried to find relief from the bite of the wind, but drafts came through broken windows and creaky doors. We finally sat down near a manger in the old horse stall and ate our lunches.

The only other inhabitant of the large barn was a huge horned owl who resided high in the granary loft. Our hands were so numb with cold that we could scarcely hold our sandwiches. Mercifully, Ben showed up soon after with the pickup full of hay, which we spread out for the cattle. By the time we watered our saddle horses and fed them oats, it had begun to snow again. We piled into the pickup and headed back to Prairie Creek.

I was cold clear to my bones when I arrived home, so built a fire, brewed a cup of tea, and felt like I'd make it after all. Mike and I had ridden non-stop from 7 to 1. I couldn't help but admire Mike, who, in spite of his years, remains one of the last true cowboys.

Gathered eggs, read the mail; then Doug called saying he was bringing home a truck driver for supper and to spend the night. It was already 20 degrees when I hurriedly did my chores before starting supper. I added chunks of leftover Easter ham to onions, potatoes, corn and some of my milk cow's cream. Voila! Delicious corn chowder.

Heated up sourdough bread and had supper ready when Doug returned with the driver, who was quite taken with the warmth of our wood stove, not to mention the meal. He ate three heaping bowls of chowder and some leftover raspberry pie. After a hot bath I hit the hay at 8, after mixing up the sourdough for breakfast. Another long day tomorrow.

April 8—A half slice of moon appeared between clouds in center sky as dawn broke over pink-washed mountains. Out to chore, crunching through ice puddles. Seventeen degrees and mostly clear. Strained Startch's milk, mixed up the sourdough hotcakes and the three of us ate.

The truck driver is impressed with our country and wants to return for elk season. Put together my lunch and was ready to put on that mountain of clothes again before heading out to the hills in the pickup with Ben. The frost was thick on the windshield, Ben peering through a tiny hole to see as we rumbled out the Cow Creek road in the old cattle truck.

A light dusting of new snow on the ground as we arrived at the Dorrance corrals. Mike was already there waiting for us and had the horses caught. Mike, who has ridden many trails in his lifetime, can relate numerous experiences about his long career as a cowboy. When we led our horses to water, they had to break the ice with their hoofs to drink. An icy wind blew up Crow Creek and rattled the hanging boards that clung to the old barn. With each passing season, the barn deteriorates a bit more. A pity, as it is such a wonderful structure.

We saddled our horses, fed them some oats and headed the cows up Dorrance Gulch. The lead took off—they knew where they were going.

April 10—In sharp contrast to Easter a week ago, a beautiful day dawned on this Sunday. Spent the morning cleaning up the yard and flower beds, pruning the raspberries, planting purple onion sets and cleaning the corn stalks, withered squash vines and sunflowers out of the garden. Because we'd been working long hours, we decided to take a break and drive to Troy.

Doug threw in his fishing pole, I grabbed a good book, and we were off. Driving out the north highway, we saw Stangel's herd of buffalo grazing the greening hillsides. Out near the timber, large patches of snow lay in the shaded areas, melting into pools of water that formed on the low-lying meadows. We drove up Snow Hollow Hill and noted that the patches of snow were disappearing rapidly from the woods. Twenty head of mule deer crossed the road in front of us. Joseph Creek Canyon, devoid of snow, looked dry.

Turning left at the Flora junction, we enjoyed seeing green fields of winter wheat. As we drove through the small settlement of Flora, beautiful views unfolded in all directions: green fields of rolling, fertile

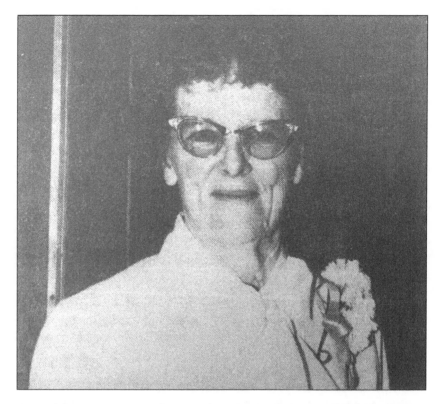

Several former court members were present at the recent Chief Joseph Days coronation dinner, including Dolores (Perren) Beach, who served on the 1948 court. Today she is a rancher's wife, Mrs. Norman Beach, and lives on Paradise Ridge in Wallowa County.

farmland edged with timber. We soon passed the Lost Prairie turnoff and began the long switchback descent to Troy.

The winding gravel road wound ever lower toward the Grande Ronde River. We could look up to see the picturesque farms scattered between the benches of Bartlett and Eden. We felt the milder climate of the Grande Ronde and opened the car windows. A carpet of grass in all shades of spring green covered the canyons. Cattle and horses grazed along the banks of the river, and the white water riffles of the Grande Ronde glinted in sunlight. Large, shiny new green leaves on the cottonwoods were a novelty to us, and gnarled old apple trees were white and pink with blossoms. The sweet fennel splashed the hillsides with golden color.

We crossed the bridge at Troy, where the Wenaha conflues with the Grande Ronde. Whereas ancient Troy stood on a hilltop above a plain and was surrounded by walls 20 feet high and resisted Greek attacks,

Troy, Oregon, is situated at the bottom of a spectacular canyon and welcomes visitors. Homer's Troy fell in 1183 B.C. Wallowa County's Troy recently underwent a facelift.

This small, remote settlement boasts a restaurant, country store and picnic areas. We ate lunch at the newly remodeled cafe and found the food delicious, the service excellent and the help friendly. We were most impressed by the cleanliness of the area.

Driving down the river, we found a place to pull over; Doug tried his luck at steelhead fishing while I stretched out in the welcome sunshine and read my book. It was quiet, save for the river sound and a pair of Canadian honkers across the river. It must have been at least 75 degrees at that elevation. Doug hooked a big one "that got away" and I reveled in the peace and quiet of the canyon.

Returning home by way of Buford grade, we stopped briefly at the Rimrock Inn, overlooking Joseph Canyon, for a cold soda.

April 11—Another clear morning, with warm, welcome sunshine. The days are lengthening and there is very little frost now. We let the fire die out during the daytime.

April 12—Awoke to another warm, balmy spring day. My chores at the barn increase daily and our cellar crew puts in many long hours sorting and shipping seed potatoes. Steve began harrowing the fields today. The recent warmth has caused the daffodils to burst into golden blooms.

The cattle, still wearing winter coats, stand around panting in 80-degree heat today. The grass is really starting to grow, but more moisture will be needed soon to keep it coming. The weaned fall calves have finally settled down and ceased their incessant bawling.

April 13—My daffodils and primroses are a riot of color. The rhubarb sends out its first reddish stalks. The large old willows by the creek sport a green tinge that deepens each day.

After chores this morning, I printed photos in the Art Angle dark-room before attending a CowBelle luncheon meeting at Pam's Pastries in Joseph. Home to chore, fix supper, then attend an Art Council meeting in Joseph where we completed plans for our big Art Festival, which is just around the corner.

Lightning lit up the sky as I drove home. Three semis of seed potatoes were shipped from our cellars today.

April 15—Cloudy and mild. Milked my cow, let calves nurse, then tended my chicks, which soon will be ready to butcher, except when will

I ever have the time?

Met other CowBelles at the Civic Center, where we served the senior citizens dinner today. Home to bake a loaf of sourdough bread for a potluck tonight. At the Legion Hall in Joseph, W.R. (Bill) Freudenberg's neighbors gathered to honor him as outgoing president of the Farmer's Water Ditch Company—after 44 years! As 85-year-old Bill accepted the plaque, he said he enjoyed every minute of those years, simply doing what he loved, living as a rancher and farmer on Prairie Creek.

April 16—Thunderheads build over the mountains this morning. Son Todd here to borrow a horse to help son Ken move his cattle to another pasture. Milked Startch. I swear that cow gives a gallon in each quarter.

After milking a gallon for house milk, I fill the kitty's dish, feed some to the dog, and still the calves can't handle it all. So I must milk the excess and feed it to the chickens. Almost hot today and, after a day of work, feel a bit wilted by evening.

As a member of the press, I attended the Chief Joseph Days coronation dinner tonight at the Civic Center. It began to rain as I drove into Joseph. After a catered prime rib dinner, we listened to a program arranged by the Joseph Chamber of Commerce, which centered around the staging of the annual Chief Joseph Days celebration.

Just as Don Green was giving a report on the Indian dances scheduled again this year, a bolt of lightning followed by a deafening roar of thunder shook the building with such impact that Don stepped back from the mike. It seemed most coincidental that this should happen, with such force, at this precise moment. Outside, we could hear the drum of rain failing steadily. Somehow this didn't seem like your ordinary April shower.

During a very impressive ceremony, Chantay Jett was crowned queen of the 1988 Chief Joseph Days court. Any one of the three lovely girls would have made a good queen, and Amy Bales and Tammi Zollman will reign as princesses.

Driving home, I could see the effects of the water spout. Debris and muddy water lay over the Imnaha highway and when I turned onto Tenderfoot Valley road, my tires crunched through several inches of hail. The black cloud had followed a narrow path across Prairie Creek and left destruction in its wake. Tiny new leaves of willow trees were beaten off the limbs and covered the road.

Later, we were to find out more rain had fallen in that short time than had been recorded during the entire month of March.

April 17—Cloudy and warm, the grass leaping at a furious rate as a result of the moisture. Guess spring must be here to stay.

April 18—Cloudy, cool, rained nearly all night. Blue sky appeared by mid-morning, and the spring transformation continued on Prairie Creek. It took more than the usual discipline to sit at my typewriter today. By nightfall four semi loads of seed potatoes were shipped from our storage cellars.

April 19—Cloudy, cool and windy. Breakfast these mornings are still cooked on the wood stove. Biscuits and blackberry jam with bacon and eggs started off our day.

I attended Orie Mahanna's funeral today. The coolish morning gave way to one of those spring days that Wallowa County bestows upon those who love the country. I will always think it was especially beautiful for Orie.

Grace Bartlett and I walked up the steps into the lovely, old Wallowa United Methodist Church, and took our seats in the polished wooden pews. Shafts of sunlight filtered through yellow, red and green colored window panes. Garlands of flowers surrounded the altar, and fragrant fir boughs were arranged with yellow mums over Orie's casket.

Looking around at the crowd, we could see that Orie had been well-loved in this small community. Although I barely knew Orie, somehow he had impressed me. His outlook on life, the kindness in his eyes; it was really hard to put into words. Guess Orie liked the same things I do: children, the great outdoors, riding horseback, milking cows. Orie had moved west when he was quite young and he was 20 years old when he came to Wallowa.

While working for the Bowman-Hicks Lumber Company, he met Rae Schaeffer. He was hauling logs on eight-wheeled wagons pulled by horses, when he drove by her home one day. Orie and Rae were married June 25, 1931, and raised their family of two girls and two boys on the Schaeffer family farm on Bear Creek.

Bear Creek might possibly be one of the prettiest places on Earth. Guess the Schaeffers thought so too, because they were some of the very first settlers to come into the Wallowa country, put down roots and stay. As we followed the funeral procession to Bramlet Memorial Cemetery, lovely shadows were cast upon the landscape by spectacular floating clouds.

Sunlight and shadow, like life is, mixed with some of both. This lovely, green lower valley was the first part of the county to be settled by the pioneers who came over Smith Mountain by way of the Grande

Ronde Valley in the 1870s. More than 100 years later, the scene is pastoral with winding creeks and waterways. Horses and cattle still graze the lush spring grasses. Willows, beginning to leaf out, line the creeks and scattered among the new buildings, old barns, weathered and gray, remain to remind us of the past.

While the valley was bursting with new life, Orie was laid to rest in the peaceful old cemetery where, nearby, the first white child born in Wallowa County is buried. Orie is gone, but the memory of him will linger. He is now as much a part of the valley as the grass, the trees and spring wildflowers that will soon cover the slopes of Smith Mountain.

Orie, and others like him, rarely written of, are representative of the solid older citizens who have over the years helped shape the destiny of Wallowa County. Quietly, without fanfare, working, living the best they know how. Such a man was Orie Mahanna, a man I met only a few times, but somehow seemed to know well.

Returned home to find the grandchildren waiting for me. They helped do chores and cook supper around a roast I'd put in the oven earlier. It began to rain again this evening, ensuring the continuation of a green, verdant spring.

April 20—Cloudy, cool. The grass is fairly leaping up! Sourdough waffles for breakfast. Cellar crew still busy shipping spuds. A light rain fell while I chored and the cows were dampened with moisture.

Doug had me drive the pickup into the Grain Growers in Enterprise to haul home a ton of rolled barley for the bulls. A fine, warm, misty rain continued all day, coaxing the earth to awaken to spring.

Baked bread. The moisture in the air helped the sourdough do its "thing." We attended a house-warming tonight on Alder Slope, and I took along a loaf of freshly-baked bread. Fast-moving, low clouds swirled around the base of Ruby Peak, leaving misty trails. Fascinating to watch. Lovely views of mountain and valley from this newer home recently purchased by some California people. Seems as though many of these places are being sold to "outsiders" these days. Lots of new faces in the county. It is nice when they are neighborly and make an attempt to know the people who live around them.

April 21—Rained all night. More than an inch of precipitation in the past 24 hours! Wonderful soaking rain penetrated the thirsty hills and canyons so desperately in need of moisture this year. Doug fixed a tarp over the heads of the potato crew as they loaded trucks today. Noticed a new snowfall on Ferguson Ridge this morning. In spite of dire predictions for a drought, it looks like we are in for a good feed year.

Baked a blueberry pie for son Ken's pie-a-month birthday present. Decided to get in and do some serious house-cleaning. I first tackled the back porch mud room. Then cleaned out the spare bedroom, as the visiting cowboy poet, Sunny Hancock, and his wife will be staying with us during the Art Festival. I raised lots of dust anyway, and burned a winter's accumulation of junk.

Still having to milk Startch twice a day, in spite of two calves nursing her. Hopefully I'll find another calf for her soon.

Attended the Enterprise FFA banquet tonight. An impressive affair. Roast beef, provided by our CowBelles, was well prepared and attractively served. The meeting was conducted orderly and on schedule. I was especially proud of several outstanding FFA members, former and present members of the Sourdough Shutterbugs 4-H Club.

April 22—The days are so full! Cloudy and cool. Red tulips opening into full bloom beside the house. I ignore the fact that my fryers are nearly ready to butcher. Still shipping potato seed at the cellar and Doug and his crew putting in many long hours there.

The Art Festival is here. It begins tonight with an artists' reception. Grandson Chad is in a track meet at Joseph, so I leave to watch him perform and spend three hours sitting in the cold with other family members. My print is framed and ready to hang at the art show. It is a photograph I took of the Lost Prairie school house. After chores, Doug and I attended the reception for the gala opening of our three-day Art Festival.

It was raining as we drove to the Joseph Civic Center, but we ranchers and farmers didn't complain one bit. The center was transformed into a wonderful art show. Hung on the walls and displayed on pedestals were creative works of sculpture, pottery, basketry, oils, pastels, watercolors, weaving, wood, metal and photography.

Doug and I had a nice visit with Dan Warnock, former Wallowa Countian who ranches near Sumpter. His wife, Alice, had a painting entered in the show. Dan was raised on Crow Creek and knows a lot of Wallowa County history.

April 23—Sunny Hancock and his wife, Alice, from Lakeview, showed up at the ranch late this afternoon. We had been looking forward to having them stay with us. Sunny was to emcee as a visiting cowboy poet during this evening's program, as part of the Art Festival. The remainder of the performing "poets" were all local cowboys, with the exception of the one cowgirl, Jennifer Isley, who now lives in Burns.

Jennifer Isley, of Burns, recites her poetry at the Art Festival in Enterprise.

After my usual busy morning with chores, I attended a critique of the art show given by Cliff Cason, a Montana gallery owner. I prepared an early supper of elk steak, sourdough biscuits, and salad, topped off with gooseberry pie, before Sunny and Alice departed for Cloverleaf Hall to meet with other cowboy poets. Later, after evening chores, Doug and I drove into Enterprise to attend the "Gathering." We arrived early enough for front row seats, so I could do some photographing.

Wallowa County poured into the hall from all directions. All seats were quickly taken and soon many people were standing six deep in the back of the room. Sunny, stepping up to the microphone, commented that this was the friendliest crowd he'd ever performed for. After Sunny's great reciting, he introduced a former Montana cowboy, Warren Glaus, now of Imnaha, who sang "Tumblin' Tumbleweeds."

He was followed by another Imnaha cowboy, Scott McClaran. Imnaha is famous for its cowboys, many of whom learn very young how to work cattle and ride in the canyons of the Snake and the Imnaha. Scott's original poems brought down the house, even though he couldn't remember a few lines.

Fred Bornstedt, popular local veterinarian, sang songs he composed himself, including "The Master of Them All." Fred, seen earlier this year sporting a new hat, opted to go bareheaded on stage, but still looked the part with his well-groomed mustache.

Jennifer Isley gave her rendition of "Swamp Creek Saturday Night," followed by her humorous poem about "Them Durn Wire Gates," which drew chuckles from us cowgals in the audience. She ended by reciting a poem that poked fun at the guides and packers. Sam Loftus, another Imnaha cowboy, was back again this year, more polished and popular than ever with the crowd.

At the conclusion of the cowboy poetry, Joni Harms, a rising western country star, backed up by her band, "Country Class," began to play their foot-stompin' music. Soon most everyone was out on the floor, kickin' up their heels. Cloverleaf Hall fairly shook with that good western music. Joni, who is a former FFA talent winner, just recently signed a contract with MCA records of Nashville and is definitely on her way up. Cowboys whirled their gals around the floor at such a furious pace it was hard to keep track of them.

Meanwhile, outside, Mike Kurtz was kept busy most of the night barbecuing 50 pounds of tri-tip steak that had been marinated in his special sauce, then skewered on sticks. This tasty tidbit was served with fresh pineapple chunks. That delicious, nutritious beef seemed to give the crowd renewed energy and they continued dancing until the early hours of the morning.

The dance had turned into a real old-fashioned Wallowa County hoedown. Doug and I, Sunny and Alice gave up the ship around 12:30. After Doug and Sunny checked the "girls" (our calving cows), we sat around the kitchen table, eating more gooseberry pie and listening to Sunny recite more poetry.

Doug got in the mood and contributed some little ditties he'd learned from the bunk-house boys when he was growing up in the canyons. Cowboy poetry has been around for a long time; it's always been a source of entertainment to the ranch hands during their long hours in the saddle. Recently, this wonderful form of folk art has been enjoying a revival and has become a popular source of western entertainment.

April 24—We were up early to greet another one of those long days and short nights. I fried bacon and eggs, heated up the sourdough biscuits, and set out the blackberry jam for our guests before they began their long drive home to Lakeview. Sunny, an old-time Arizona cowboy, sure had some interesting tales to tell.

After they left, I milked my cow and let the calves nurse. Had so much excess milk, I gave Ellie Hanks a call, and she drove up from Little Sheep Creek to pick up some for her bummer lambs.

Cold and cloudy, feels like it could snow. After giving Doug a tow to get one of the old potato trucks started, I drove to Liza and Todd's and stayed with James and baby Adele while mom and dad attended the matinee performance of "Cowboy." Just barely made it home in time to make the catered dinner at the Joseph Civic Center. Didn't have time to do my chores. Knowing Startch would be most unhappy, I opted to do them later.

Doug and I walked in just as they were serving the salad. We enjoyed good old beef and taters (prime rib and baked) and, appropriately, all of us beef and potato producers sat together. Seems as though most of us Prairie Creek ranchers are artists of some sort, whatever an artist is supposed to be anyway. Farmers and ranchers are certainly artists in their own right. They raise "state of the art" seed potatoes and Wallowa County beef is certainly some of the world's finest.

One of the reasons our living here in our high mountain valley is unique is that we can go from cow barn to live theater in a matter of minutes. I tried not to think of Startch bawling at my own cow barn, however.

Doug and I drove to the Enterprise High School gym to watch the final performance of the Montana Repertory Theater production of "Cowboy." Everyone thoroughly enjoyed this wonderful, rollicking musical based on the life of cowboy artist Charley Russell. Forming a backdrop for the large stage set was a copy of his famous painting "Waiting for a Chinook," or "The Last of Five Thousand." This small watercolor, painted by Russell in the winter of 1886-87 and depicting a starving steer humped over in a snowy setting, turned out to be one of his most famous works.

Montana Repertory Theater brought to life the drama of this "for real" young cowboy. It was all there under the wide, blue Montana skies. The play is a tribute to a great state that will be celebrating its first 100 years in 1989. Montana is pretty proud of its own C.R. Russell, whose paintings, sculptures, pen and ink drawings and letters will endure forever. Russell recorded the West as it will never be again.

The stage settings, which included sunsets, chuckwagons, campfires and saloons, transported us to another time and place. Russell watched the old West disappear and, knowing it was the end of an era, painted prolifically. With sensitive brush strokes, this self-taught artist captured the very essence of the old-time cowboy. Russell lived as he painted, and in earlier years gave many of his works to friends.

All in all it was three hours of great, young talent; most of us will probably never get to New York, or even want to, but were able to see live theater here in our own valley thanks to the efforts of our Wallowa Valley Arts Council.

It was 10:30 when I sheepishly walked out to face my cow and the live production of "Barn Chores." On a stage not so glamorous, I let the very unhappy Startch in to let the bawling calves nurse. This independent bovine informed me that she didn't much care about art festivals and would rather I returned to her schedule. The calves echoed her sentiments and gorged themselves on the full udder.

Having changed from dress and silk stockings to rubber boots and overalls, I had trudged out in the frosty night to the barn. After gathering eggs by flashlight, we Prairie Creek inhabitants finally settled down for some much-needed sleep. Before I closed my eyes, I reflected on all the hours spent on our sixth annual Art Festival and had to admit it was worth it all. It was a smash!

Columnist's Note—Time to catch up again on this column. Guess I enjoy writing so much that I sometimes get carried away and pretty soon I'm behind. Then I get a letter like the one received from Eleanor Randall of Centerville, Washington, who writes that she wishes the column could be more timely.

They like to compare their weather and ranch activities with ours, and she says when the Journal is six to eight weeks behind, this is impossible. First of all the blame rests on me, not Agri-Times. Also, copy deadline is a week prior to publication, so that puts it even more behind.

Here goes with trying to be more timely. However, I must sacrifice many interesting events on the ranch, as time and space will not permit.

April 28—I arose in the dawn's gray light to chore, make a lunch, saddle my mare, and help move our cows and calves to the hills. Mike McFetridge, Ben and I spent the better part of two days in the saddle, trailing the herd to summer range near Wet Salmon Creek. The tired, little doggies were glad when it was over. Along the way, we experienced every kind of weather Wallowa County could throw at us. The day began with sunshine, then changed to strong wind, rain, snow and sleet. After two 16-hour days in a row, sure didn't have any trouble sleeping.

A light snow frosted the spring greens as April left us. Mostly though, the days were lovely and sunlight and cloud shadows swept across the brilliant, green, grassy fields of Prairie Creek. Ben brought in another orphan calf to help me with all of Startch's milk.

May 1—Twenty-two degrees. Little chunks of ice spit out the hose when I watered the chickens. The tulips drooped, the robins didn't sing, and an icy wind blew off the snowfields.

May 2—Dropped to 18 degrees.

May 3—The sky darkened and snow began falling. At first the soft, spring snow melted on contact with the green grass, but by mid-morning, the big, fat flakes began to stick and it seemed as though the entire sky was full of goose down...and it quickly covered up SPRING!

The willows hung low under their burden, and afterwards there was an inch of moisture in the rain gauge.

May 5—Rained most of the day. Received a surprise in the mail: a beautiful, handmade cloth doll sent by a fan, Verda McClain, of Dayton, Washington. Invited Mike and Joyce McFetridge, and Opal Tippett to supper. We feasted on fried chicken, sourdough biscuits, mashed potatoes, milk-gravy, and topped the meal off with wild blackberry pie.

The real treat of the evening was listening to these Wallowa County old-timers reminisce about the times when ice was cut and stored for summer use in sawdust-walled buildings, when Opal and Joyce packed water to their kitchens, scrubbed clothes on a scrub board, prepared endless meals on the wood range for huge families, gardened, canned, and followed their husbands to sheep and cow camps, cooking for the crews, cleaning up the camps...and we think we're busy.

May 7—No frost, no rain, and the air has a much warmer feel. We watched the 114th running of the Kentucky Derby on TV. By 4:30 we were seated at the Joseph Junior Rodeo, watching five grandchildren compete in the many events. It turned cold again, which didn't seem to alter the enthusiasm of the many young contestants. Because the arena was a sea of mud, the dummy roping was held out near the parking lot. We were so proud of Buck and Chelsie, as they had been practicing for days and it showed.

Next, an unwilling goat was staked out and the youngsters were supposed to tie a ribbon on its tail! That goat proceeded to tromp, first one, then the other of the pee wees. Some got astraddle of the animal and went for an unscheduled ride. Miniature cowboys and cowgirls, wearing chaps, hats, and carrying ropes ran everywhere. The pee wee events were especially popular with the crowd.

Later, I held my breath as grandson Chad rode a steer and cousins Buck and Rowdy got bucked off in the mud in steer and mutton riding. It took many volunteers, like "The Running in Red" Cattle Company, Lyle and Mark Dawson, Char Williams, and Peggy Brennan, who tromped through the mud to stake out goats, barrels and poles; many parents pitched in to make the junior rodeo a success. These youngsters will one day be Wallowa County's new crop of cowboys, and the way some of them handle a rope and ride, the art is far from dead.

It was after 10 p.m. when we finally got home, having sat through most of the events. Wearily I walked out into the cold night to greet Startch and the three hungry calves.

May 8—Mother's Day dawned warm and mostly clear. Just like last year, I enjoyed my day watching the second go-round of the junior rodeo. I tromped around the chutes in my boots, taking photos of the contestants coming out on their steers and sheep.

When it was all said and done, Chad won the buckle for steer riding and Chelsie for dummy roping. I had watched Rowdy, Mona and Buck escape unscathed from underneath steers, goats and sheep. They were covered with mud, but it would wash off. I was a pretty proud grandma. Just watching those healthy youngsters perform was the best Mother's Day present I could ever want.

May 9—Rained, but cleared up later. The potato seed shipping went on and on.

May 10—I "cowgirled" all day. In the beautiful, springtime hills we gathered in the cows and calves and held them while Doug and Ben cut out and sorted. Different colored eartags were put in separate bunches to breed to different bulls, drys were cut out, and it lasted a long time because each calf had to be mothered up to its dam.

I enjoyed riding out there on the lush bunch grass range, the undulating green hills sprinkled with wildflowers. Birdbills, bluebells, yellow bells, phlox, wild geranium and the sweet fennel. Zephyrs gently brought the fragrance of rich, dark earth; the smell of spring. The sky was cobalt blue and rain-washed.

I wished for my camera when we were driving in the herd. What a sight it made, with the far-off snow-clad Wallowas gleaming in contrast to the green hills. That country is truly a cattleman's paradise. We ate our lunches in the cool shade of the old log barn before resuming the sorting.

May 11—Branding day began early. We drove the long miles to the hills to bring in the cows and calves once more. At first I worked the chute gates, then got the job of pushing the calves up the long wooden chute to be worked. A job I am good at, having worked with calves all my life. At day's end, we all smelled of scorched hair, mud and manure. Corral No. 5!

Red-faced from sun and wind, I attended a meeting of our Art Council that night at the Country Place. It felt so good to relax in that pleasing atmosphere. Arriving home I walked into a seed potato meeting in our living room, kept on walking and fell into bed.

May 12—Our CowBelles met at Imnaha. I took daughter-in-law Liza and the children with me, stopping along the way to pick up Ilene Potter along Little Sheep Creek. Golden balsamroot bloomed profusely on the canyon sides, and puffy white clouds floated in a blue sky. It was extremely warm in the canyons.

We enjoyed a delicious potluck meal and a good meeting at the home of Bonnie Marks. Ben and Doug brought me two more calves to raise on Startch. Five calves that makes. This cow deserves a medal of honor. Dandelions are riotous and the apple tree is in full bloom.

May 13—Baked farmhouse cookies and served them with fresh fruit at a rural health symposium held at the Joseph Civic Center. In the evening I baked pie shells for strawberry pies that I would serve the next day at the symposium for lunch.

May 14—I roasted a 25-pound prime rib roast and finished the pies; Hope McLaughlin and Scotty helped me serve the 55 people at the health meeting. Nothing like beef to focus on the health issue. If more people ate nutritious beef, we probably wouldn't need as much health care.

We all worked like troopers and had everything cleaned up by 3 p.m. Home to catch up on the ranch...and Doug and I enjoyed prime rib sandwiches for supper.

May 15—An absolutely beautiful morning! Baked (from scratch) a lemon meringue pie for son Ken's last pie-a-month; his 12 months are up! Because I must literally steal milk for the house, I began feeding one of Startch's five calves a bottle. After all, the poor cow has only four faucets.

The time I'd been dreading arrived. Leaving a kettle of water to heat on the stove, I hacked the heads off of six fryers. After I had several of them picked, Doug showed up, and together we tackled the job until we were finished. Those Cornish-cross fryers dressed out like young turkeys, with some weighing nine pounds. It was a pretty good feeling when they were all in the freezer. My Rhode Island Red pullets will do better with the competition of those voracious appetites removed.

While the chicken plucking was going on, son Ken and family stopped by with a flat of bedding plants for my belated Mother's Day gift. Scotty showed up later in the day to go mushrooming with me and two of my visiting grandchildren. Although the morels were as scarce as hen's teeth, we were treated to the sight of a white tail doe and a yearling fawn, flags flying in that peculiar way, waving back and forth in the brilliant afternoon. Hawks were out hunting red diggers, blue jays scolded us and we thoroughly enjoyed our two-mile jaunt through meadows to cool woods.

May 16—So mild we slept with the windows open all night. Steve and Ben to the hills repairing miles of fence that seems to require constant maintenance. Biggest problem is elk damage. Kelly, another hired hand, began plowing a field in readiness for planting seed potatoes. Out my kitchen window, I can see "Tucker's Mare" taking shape on the mountain. As the snow melts each spring, it forms the shape of a horse (with a little imagination).

Clouded up and the wind began to blow. Rain in the forecast. By suppertime it began and thereby put a halt to the plowing. But now the mushrooms will pop up.

May 17—Up early as usual on this cloudy, cold morning. The snow level has returned to timberline again. The forested slopes of the mountains are frosted and cold-looking. The scars that are the Ferguson Ridge Ski runs have been covered with snow. Fire in the wood stove feels good.

Voting day. Our county must decide the fate of several levies. It seems as though our rural areas jump from one financial crisis to another and, like everything else these days, it always takes more money. Personally, I think more of us need to live within our incomes.

The nine calves that Startch and I are responsible for are all growing like weeds. Printed photos in the Art Angle darkroom for three hours this morning, after which Doris treated me to lunch at "Pam's Country

Inn" in Joseph. The mountains really put on a show today as sunlight and shadow spilled alternately across their frosted slopes.

Ben and Steve trucked several loads of bulls and heifers to the hills. Most all the cattle are out on grass now. It is still too wet to get in the fields to plow. We have finally finished shipping seed potatoes from our cellars. Soon it will be time to plant. No sooner is one job finished than another begins. That's ranch life.

May 18—Cold; more new snow has fallen on the Ferguson Ridge Ski area. After milking my cow and letting her large "family" nurse, I helped Doug run a young bull into the pasture with my milk cow herd. The young Simmental-cross bull was so taken with the taste of green grass that he ignored the curious cows completely. Must have a talk with that bull.

I shed muddy overalls and began typing my column, along with several other deadlines. After a "leftover" lunch, I put on my riding gear, caught and saddled my mare, and Ben and I rode over the hill to the other side of the ranch to gather 46 bred heifers. We drove them along Liberty Grange Road and across the Imnaha highway.

A fine, misty rain began and all around us a kaleidoscope of color. The incredibly beautiful Prairie Creek landscape: snow melt running in the ditches, green leaves shining with spring newness and glistening with raindrops. Hawks were nesting in tall old cottonwoods that lined the road, dandelions, birdsong, and patches of the bluest sky, white and purple-bellied clouds, some of which periodically opened up and rained on our parade.

The grain fields were sprouting and the freshly tilled fields steamed with trailing vapors as warm earth mingled with cool air. The Wallowas swam in and out of clouds, their dark blue sides contrasted with freshly fallen snow. The air was wonderful, full of spring. Willow growth, earth, snowmelt and rain. It was a glorious ride, not work. The heifers moved right along as we approached the green moraine. Ben opened a gate and we headed the herd straight up the eastern slopes toward the lush grasses that grew there.

We were soon very close to the mountains that loomed above and across Wallowa Lake. It was like riding into the opening scenes from "The Sound of Music." Below us lay the checkerboard fields of Prairie Creek and an artist's hand had splashed the greens, browns and wildflower yellows across the land. The Seven Devils range in Idaho glistened on the eastern horizon, and we could see the rolling plateau stretch for miles out in the Zumwalt and Salmon and Pine Creek country.

While I held the herd, Ben opened another gate and we turned the heifers into their high pasture. As we rode down the moraine and loaded the horses into a truck that Doug had parked there for us, I marveled again at how very lucky we are to live among such beauty. Back in my kitchen, I put one of those nine-pound fryers in the oven to roast, cooked the giblets for gravy, baked a rice pudding using fresh eggs and milk, started a batch of sourdough biscuits to rise, and then put my feet up for a short rest before tackling the chores.

As I gathered eggs in the hen house, I walked under our apple tree, which is covered with a cloud of pink and white blooms. Cooked a kettle of mashed potatoes, made gravy, baked the biscuits and then loaded the entire meal into our car. Doug and I took dinner to our upper Prairie Creek friends and neighbors, Max and Dorothy Gorsline.

Because Dorothy has been under the weather lately and unable to cook, we thought it would be fun to share our meal with them. It was a lovely evening and the supper tasted better in the company of good friends.

May 19—Up at 5 a.m. to get ready to go to the hills. With our saddle horses loaded in the truck, we drove out to the Butte Creek place to gather 40 head of fall calvers. While I trailed them down the road, Ben rounded up the 40 head in the Johnson pasture.

It was a perfect day as I rode alone behind the cows. Not a breath of wind stirred, and huge floating clouds forever changed the colors of the landscape. The miles of bunch grass range stretched as far as the eye could see, and the silence was broken by the song of the meadow lark and the heavy breathing of the cows. The hill country glowed with balsamroot, blue bells, camas, vase flowers, shooting stars, and sweet fennel.

Soon I could see Ben bringing in the other bunch, which we joined together and drove toward Dorrance Gulch. New aspen leaves quivered on white-barked trees; patches of pink, tufted phlox covered the hills. We let the cows rest and drink the cool waters of Crow Creek, and ate our lunches near the old Dorrance log cabin homestead. It was only 1:30 when the last of the cows trailed into the holding pasture on East Crow.

We turned the horses loose with the cattle and drove home in a pickup left there for us. After chores and supper I went into Enterprise High School and played a clarinet (after 37 years) during a rehearsal of the Wallowa County Band. The thrill of a great Sousa march was still there, after not having experienced it since my high school years!

May 20—Scraped ice off the windshield before I left to drive to the hills on this beautiful clear morning. I met Ben out near Circle M. He'd gone out earlier to start the cattle to the valley. He'd left my mare impatiently waiting for me in the back of another truck, which was parked near East Crow. When I arrived she was trying to paw her way out of the truck. We joined Ben behind the herd, my mare having settled down to work.

This 17-year-old mare loves to move cattle and often lays her ears back and nips at the lagging cows. When we reached the top of Crow Creek Pass, we let the cows rest a while. After that we just tucked in the edges and let them mosey until we arrived in the valley. The cows were corraled, sprayed, then turned out into a small pasture. Tomorrow we would complete the drive.

Numerous small, yellow canaries now inhabit our yard, and they are forever flitting around and feeding on some sort of seed pods in the nearby hayfield. It was so warm we left the bedroom window open all night.

May 21—Up at 5 a.m. While Doug fixed breakfast, I did the chores, ate, and then saddled my mare before heading over the hill to the other side of the ranch where Ben and I let the cows out to begin trailing them to their summer pasture. The morning quickly warmed and the cows, which were pretty fleshy, slackened their pace.

By the time we reached the elk fence gate and started them up the east moraine, they didn't want to be driven at all. They simply wanted to shade up somewhere under the trees. The heat became intense and as we climbed higher, we had quite a time keeping them going. At this point, I would have given a thousand dollars for a dog, any dog! Our dog Stubby is still too young to work much.

After what seemed like hours of hard riding and yelling, we finally got them to the top of the ridge. After we drove them through a gate to the lake side, the real work began. If we hadn't been so intent on getting those cows to follow a steep wagon road down to the only water in the pasture, perhaps we could have enjoyed the splendid view of Wallowa Lake below. But those 80 ornery cows simply would not stay on the road and instead tried to take off on every deer trail that ran parallel to the road and always wound uphill. A few cows hadn't been in this pasture before, so we had to show them the water. Anyway, those were the "boss's" orders, and by gum, we'd better do it.

I've worked for this outfit 10 years now and hubby says I hired on to be tough. The incredibly steep hillside that forms the east moraine of

Wallowa Lake is hard for horses to negotiate, and definitely isn't for the timid rider. Several times my mare lost her footing and went down. All I could do was stay put until she got up. Trying to turn cattle on those steep inclines is a bit hairy. to put it mildly.

Our horses had worked up a sweat and we yelled until we were hoarse, and finally got them to a creek that splashed down from the side of Mt. Howard. We left the cows, then slipped and slid down through thick timber to the road below, following the fence line until we spotted Doug waiting for us with the cattle truck. Next time Ben and I plan to take a pack of dogs and at least three more cowboys!

I was too tired and hot to eat much lunch. Refreshed after a nap, I gathered up camping gear in preparation for a camp out with my 4-H group.

By 5 p.m., kids and gear were loaded into the pickup and we headed up the same road we had just driven the cows over only hours ago. The trip had been planned; no backing out now. The 4-H'ers were in high spirits; this was one of their most looked forward to excursions.

When we reached the ridge top in that "Sound of Music" setting, I parked the truck and the kids spilled out in all directions to pitch tents and make camp. There was a delightful breeze and the evening coolness was wonderful after my strenuous day. The mountains loomed across the lake and the evening light bathed the snowy ramparts in many changing colors. There were wildflowers and bluebirds in abundance.

The children loved it and, tired as I was, the sight revived my lagging spirits. The 4-H'ers did all the work of preparing supper over an open fire while I sat on a rock and rested after a long day far from over. While we were eating, close to 20 head of mule deer grazed along that high ridge, peering curiously at us before, one by one, they leaped gracefully over the fence. Far below, we could see the fishermen in their little boats, fishing for kokanee, the land-locked salmon that live in the waters of Wallowa Lake. And those cows we'd worked so hard to drive all that way down to water... were back on top!

A bluebird perched but a few feet away woke me at dawn. I had bedded down night under the Big Dipper, listening to the 4-H'ers tell stories way into the night. A warm wind whispered all night and was still blowing. There was no dew or any moisture on the grasses and the weather had been so mild most of us slept with our arms out of the sleeping bags.

Thanks to the bluebird, I was able to watch a spectacular sunrise and witness the early pink light as it spilled across the face of Chief Joseph Mountain. All this I watched from my sleeping bag.

Members of the 4-H Sourdough Shutterbugs camp at Wallowa Lake.

The children roused one by one and began frying bacon, eggs and hotcakes over a large griddle. Then we did some photographing in the early morning light, and simply sat and enjoyed. Later we went into a natural bowl, which was the site of a rodeo held in 1946 to celebrate the building of the Joseph Airport.

It seems children's lives these days are so structured, they are rushed from one stage of development to another, under constant pressure from parents and peers to succeed in all they do. Personally, I feel they need quiet times like this, where they can sit and dream, or talk to one another.

Finding an adult who will take the time to supervise these types of outings is another story. A real pity! Watching my own children profit from these experiences has made me want to help others as well. Having three of my own grandchildren in the club gives me an added incentive.

We left reluctantly, but the ranch work beckoned. Our crew is fertilizing our potato fields prior to planting. Doug roto-tilled my garden patch. Baked a sweet cream cake to go with some strawberries, and planted six Early Girl tomato plants along the warm side of the house.

The growing season is upon us and heralds the busy summer months, when we Wallowa Countians all try to get all our work done in such a brief time.

May 23—As it was cool and cloudy, I began waging the never-ending war against weeds in the strawberry patch. Later, I watched grandchildren James and Mona, while Jackie and Liza sewed on a Log Cabin quilt they are making for granddaughter Tammy's graduation gift. One of the season's many thunderstorms builds over the mountains this evening.

May 24—We could hear rumblings of thunder and see flashes of lightning through our open bedroom window before hail stones hit the roof. The storm was short-lived and rumbled off across the valley, leaving Prairie Creek refreshed with a delicious coolness that settled over the land. While choring this morning, I noticed small piles of hail stones remained alongside the barn.

We shipped seed potatoes to some local growers today, and began planting our nuclear seed. The lilac bush is just beginning to bloom.

May 25—Potato planting goes on. Three women ride the planter as it slowly makes its way up and down the rows, pulled by a tractor. Thunderheads began to build over the mountains as I planted petunias next to the house.

This evening Grace Bartlett accompanied Doug and me to Imnaha to attend the "end of school" program. Earlier a terrific thunderstorm had erupted before sweeping over Sheep Creek Hill toward Imnaha. The Sheep Creek road was rain-soaked and steam rose from the pavement. Apparently we were just behind the storm all the way down.

The canyons were lush and green with new growth, and freshened by the recent rain. Approaching Big Sheep Canyon, a most beautiful rainbow suddenly appeared. What a sight it was: dark clouds, shot through with sunlight; golden rim rocks, scattered with sarvis berry in full bloom, and Sheep Creek all frothy with snowmelt.

The storm had left its mark and, by the time we arrived at the little two-room school, chairs that had been set up outside were being carried inside. Icy patches of hail lay everywhere. The school yard was littered with white locust blossoms and the air was steamy, warm, wet and fragrant with the scent of locust. Everyone pitched in, helping move the chairs and portable stage sets inside.

The program soon began. We watched as the K-8 grades performed their clever skits and puppet shows, and sang songs. The small schoolhouse was filled with parents, grandparents and local residents from up and down the river. Naturally, I was especially impressed with my own two grandchildren, who participated in it all. It was quite a production, complete with a backdrop stage, which consisted of a large cardboard box simply turned over for each new scene change.

Am always impressed with how happy these canyon children are, and how very lucky they are to have such a fine teacher as Char Williams, whose boundless energy and love of children shines through in her work. These rural canyon children are truly unique and Imnaha residents are justly proud of them. The students were awarded certificates for the number of books they had read, and some children had read more than 200 books during the school year! The one graduating eighth grader received her diploma and will this fall enter a school on the "outside."

After enjoying cookies, cake and punch, we socialized a bit before driving the 30 miles back up "on top."

May 26—Clear and sunny. Finished weeding the strawberry patch. Planted snapdragons and worked in the flower beds. More thunderheads appeared, bringing with them the nightly storm to freshen the valley anew.

May 27—Rained lightly on and off all night. The warm rain has made everything so green and lush. What a spring we are having. The crew finished planting our nuclear seed today. This evening Doug and I attended grandson Chad's eighth grade graduation dinner and program at the Enterprise multipurpose room.

Eighth graders' mothers had decorated the room with balloons, streamers of brightly colored crepe paper, and candles, which sat in handmade wooden candle holders. It was hard for me to believe this grandson is ready for high school. The years continue to fly by with increasing speed.

May 28—Cool, cloudy and windy, so built a fire in the wood cookstove to take away the chill. Memorial Day looms and it appears as if it will be a cold one for the many campers and tourists who have come into Wallowa County for the long weekend.

It began to rain when I was in Enterprise shopping, and it continued to rain without letup the rest of the day and into the night. Wonderful, soaking rain; so good for the country.

May 29—Rain, mixed with snow. A typical Memorial Day weekend in our county. Can imagine the campers at Wallowa Lake will be pulling up stakes and heading out.

Fixed sourdough hotcakes on the woodstove. Nephew Mike Tippett from the Tri-Cities is here for the holiday and he can sure put away these hotcakes. Out to chore, bundled up in the unaccustomed cold. The snowline is on upper Prairie Creek...again!

Around 7:30 p.m. there was a clearing in the west and a brilliant burst of sunlight spread across Prairie Creek, the "Ross Light." Green fields were flooded with golden light, and Lockes' red buildings looked like part of an oil-on-canvas painting.

May 30—Memorial Day dawned cloudy and coolish. The flowers scattered on all the graves around the country will stay fresh and fragrant for a while. Fire in our old Monarch range all day felt good. Our potato crew is cutting seed so we'll be ready to plant when the ground dries out enough to do so. Mike rode out to the hills with Ben, who took some cattle out.

Printed photos in the darkroom this afternoon, trying to catch up on a backlog of assignments. The mountains are covered with a layer of clouds.

May 31—May is leaving. We were able to resume the potato planting today, as the ground is now workable. Today is a typically busy one where I must juggle housework, ranch work and writing. For me to have time to write, I must really organize every moment of my day.

It was 30 degrees this morning and ice formed under Hough's sprinklers in the hay field. Ben started our sprinkler irrigation this afternoon. It was too cloudy to see the full moon rise this evening. A pity, as it was a "once in a blue moon" moon, the "lovers" moon for those into lunar lore. I read where there was a full moon on May 1 and now again on the 31st. Only happens once in a blue moon, or so they say.

June 1—Cold, cloudy and raining. The ground is receiving a good soaking and the grass is very high and still growing. A good feed year seems assured. Ben is here each morning very early to change sprinkler pipes.

We received a terrific downpour of rain, which was accompanied by a strong wind. This was followed by a lovely pink sunset that reflected itself onto large gray clouds. Our horses frolicked in pink light and Hough's Angus cattle grazed in an ethereal glow. Such are the rare spring evenings on Prairie Creek when the last rays of sunlight reach across the valley.

June 2—Warmer, but clouds and mists linger over the mountains until a sudden breeze comes up and blows it all away. Writing occupies much of my days; am working on several articles at the moment. Also answered fan mail. The skies are a cobalt blue after the rain and the lush, maturing grasses undulate in the wind, like waves on a vast green sea. June is bustin' out all over.

June 3—I raked the soil in my garden, and found it soft, friable and warm to the touch. Time to plant. I set out the dozen cabbage plants, planted two varieties of red potatoes and a bag of yellow keeping onion sets, and sprinkled packages of lettuce, carrot and beet seeds in the rich soil.

June 4—I put in corn, peas, green beans, swiss chard, spinach, crookneck squash and zucchini. When I was through with the vegetables, I planted a row of sunflowers along the western edge of the garden and transplanted a row of giant marigolds next to the garlic. Such a satisfaction to have the garden all in. From now on it will be up to Mother Nature's whims and my hoeing and irrigation to ensure a productive, attractive garden.

Not only will this garden provide fresh, nutritious vegetables for our bodies, but it will nurture my soul as well. Hoeing and weeding is good for the mind. Thoreau planted beans, and I was reminded of Peter Meinke's poem,

A monk can do his work on bended knees
inside or out; the bishop looked askance
when Mendel labored in a row of peas
and led the combinations in their dance.
The spark of genius dominates the heavens
and sparkles in the furrow and the loam;
both earth and sky are broken down in sevens
and Christ is captured in a chromosome.

Meinke's poem from *Trying to Surprise God* was found scotch-taped to my father's bedroom wall after he died of cancer in 1984.

Liza and Jackie spent hours sewing on that beautiful patchwork quilt so it would be ready to take to California for granddaughter Tammy's high school graduation gift.

June 5—The fine growing weather continues, and everything is lush and green. Even though it is Sunday, our crew works all day planting seed potatoes.

My friend and neighbor, Wilmer Cook, called and said he had some raspberry plants if I wanted to come and dig them. So I drove up on Alder Slope, where I found Wilmer and wife, Mary, out in their garden transplanting strawberries. Together the three of us dug several pails and boxes full of new raspberry shoots with roots intact. It was fun digging the canes while visiting my friends. How I admire this couple.

I would venture to say that Wilmer and Mary are among the select few of us who have, perhaps, achieved that elusive something called success in life, a fulfillment, and ask for no more, no less and remain content with their lot. This present state has been achieved through hard work, strong family ties, honesty, and a good sense of humor, the stuff America was founded on, but which many have lost along the way somewhere. Their "wealth" is measured in happiness, zest for living, and contentment; also in raspberries, a lovely garden, children, grandchildren and a strong faith. The children have been cultivated and tended to as lovingly as the gardens and it shows.

Wilmer and Mary live in the land of milk and honey. Wilmer keeps bees and extracts the honey, and he and Mary milk cows every night and morning. They live the "simple life," which hasn't ever been or ever will be simple. In their later years they remain strong and healthy. The Cooks' place is known by a name Wilmer gave it years ago: "Cook's dairy, berry, and apiary."

Well-read, Wilmer has shelves lined with books, almost more books than I've ever seen. He also pans for gold with his wife and family. He is a retired rural mail-carrier, plumber, ditch tender, and philosopher. There isn't a whole lot Wilmer can't do.

While we dug those raspberry plants I got another dose of Wilmer's philosophy of life, which was a bonus. One more thing before I change the subject—Wilmer is the champion Chinese checkers player on Alder Slope, and perhaps the world. He'll challenge anyone.

At home Doug and I transplanted the raspberry canes on the cool Sunday afternoon and they immediately took root. Now, out of my kitchen window I keep a daily vigil over them, and the weeds grow.

The irrigating goes on. This year Ben's two young sons, Zack and Seth, change the hand lines.

Forty acres of seed potatoes have been planted, with 40 more to go. A fire in the cookstove feels good this evening. It has turned cold, with rain in the forecast.

June 6—It hails during a thunderstorm before settling into a deluge that lasts all night and into the next day, bringing the potato planting to a halt. The pipe changers go about their work in pouring rain. "That's when irrigation does the most good," says husband.

Also in pouring rain, Steve and Doug saddled up horses and chased some heifers that knocked down a panel and wandered around upper Prairie Creek all morning. By evening it clears off and the valley is incredibly lovely. So refreshing to see sky all clean and bluebird blue.

June 8—June passing by swiftly, as the busy season is upon us.

The weather turns cloudy and cool, and it begins to rain again. The ground and the pipe changers are saturated. Our electricity is off for an hour or so, and thank goodness I don't have one of those word processors or I wouldn't make my deadlines. As always, I use my portable Smith-Corona, which takes up permanent residence on my kitchen table, and doesn't rely on PP&L.

After the electricity came on, I baked a batch of sourdough cinnamon rolls and gave a pan, warm from the oven, to son Ken, who turned 35 yesterday. Daughter Jackie and the children came out from the canyons this evening to spend the night, as they would be accompanying me to Chilcoot, California, tomorrow.

June 9—We left shortly after 5 on this partially cloudy morning and therefore witnessed the most gorgeous sunrise I've ever seen. As we drove away from the ranch, a patch of sky over the Wallowas was free of cloud for the first time in days, and the sun broke over the eastern hill country and shot between dark clouds. This created a spotlight effect. The light hit the mountains first in a brilliant pink wash, and moments later turned to burnished gold.

It was a good omen. Our trip would be a safe one. After all that dramatic opener, clouds covered the sun and except for periods of sunlight here and there, a layer of fog covered the Wallowas. Driving through that misty, green lower valley was like being on the coast. Morning mists lay in pockets above the Minam River, which ran green, cold and clear. The trees dripped with moisture. Everything was pristine, fresh, and lupine and balsamroot lifted their heads, refreshed after the rain.

At the top of Minam hill, the fog lifted as I looked back on the Wallowa country and entered Union County. Through Elgin, La Grande, onto Highway 80-N, then to Ukiah via 244, following the Grande Ronde River. Through the morning mists mule deer lifted their heads from drinking, a porcupine ambled across in front of us, and we passed not one vehicle. In Ukiah we realized we were hungry, so pulled up in front of a small cafe where a handmade cardboard sign standing outside drew our attention: "World's Best Breakfast." Pretty big statement.

Inside the establishment, which also had an adjoining bar, a large fellow with a dish towel tied around his waist greeted us, and we ordered the "world's best breakfast." Aside from three men, we were the only customers. A bulletin board above the counter read, "Wanted: waitress, bartender, cook." And yet another sign, "This place for sale."

Meanwhile, the man-cook-waitress, proprietor, bartender disappeared into his kitchen and proceeded to mix us up breakfast, all from scratch. The pancakes were so large they literally draped over the sides of our plates. We did justice to what we could, but alas, they were so huge, we couldn't eat them all.

We listened to the proprietor's account of a local controversy that had divided the small town, and thought it sad that such a lovely area could have such problems. As we drove away from that little community nestled in the springtime Blues of Northeastern Oregon, the outlying meadows were covered with blue lupine and golden balsamroot.

Abandoned, weathered buildings and split rail fences left by the early settlers were everywhere as we turned left, then south, on 395, which ultimately would take us to Chilcoot.

We headed down through the heart of Eastern Oregon, a land of little human habitation, through towns with names like Fox. We passed crystal clear creeks with fascinating names and came to the North Fork of the John Day River. We entered canyon country, a vast land of rims, clouds, sagebrush, green bottom land, cowboys, coyotes and silence. Winding roads brought us to Abert Lake, alkali flats, brilliant colored rock formations and Oregon's high desert.

We pulled into Valley Falls and thank goodness they had diesel. We had been on empty for 20 miles and the children were ready to stretch their legs.

Around Lakeview the country was green and looked good, as did all of southeastern Oregon as a result of the rains. Quite suddenly we were in California, heading for Alturas, where we stopped to eat before continuing through the high desert of Northern California where the cattleman continues to reign.

Then we drove into a land of black oaks, poplars and cottonwoods, their new, green leaves blowing in the wind. The air was noticeably warmer as we passed Doyle, still following route 395. We looked out over the vast Nevada desert in the direction of Fish Springs where son-in-law Charley worked.

The children were so glad when we finally turned off onto 70 and began the climb to Beckwourth Pass and, at last, drove down into the small community of Chilcoot. It was 7:30. We had been on the road since 5:30 a.m.

The weather at 5,000 ft., near the entrance to the huge Sierra Valley, was cool and the wind was blowing. Chilcoot is an Indian word meaning something about "land where the cold wind blows." Things appeared drier there on the eastern slope of the Sierra, and the lack of moisture was quite evident.

Charley and Ramona Phillips pose with their graduating daughter, Tammy.

Granddaughter Tammy ran out to greet us, looking so grownup! My sweet 17-year-old granddaughter, whom we had all come so far to see graduate from high school. She had just received the good news that she was the recipient of a local CowBelle scholarship.

Grandson Shawn, Ramona informed us, was on a two-day campout in the mountains with his 8th grade class. Granddaughter Carrie ran out announcing that the macaroni for salad was boiling over!

Bed early for me, while my two talkative daughters burned the midnight oil, catching up. A train sped by during the night, shaking the house before its sound was replaced by the lonely Chilcoot wind.

June 10—Tammy's relatives continued to arrive throughout the day, from points west…Sacramento, Auburn, Roseville, Newcastle, Dixon, Loomis. It was turning into a family reunion! Daughter Ramona's Chilcoot home was bulging at the seams. It was fun. Tammy was to have the largest family support section at tonight's graduation at Loyalton High School—two sets of grandparents, aunts, uncles and assorted cousins, not to mention a dozen or so shirt-tails.

It was a beautiful day and the Chilcoot wind had gone off into the Sierras to play. My two younger sisters, Mary Ann and Kathryn, drove up from Auburn and Roseville. I accompanied Ramona to a "last day of school" picnic, put on by Carrie's grade school in Loyalton. What a picnic—watermelon, hamburgers and water fights, while all around the immense Sierra Valley, shimmered in that high altitude heat.

By late afternoon, Charley had driven the long desert miles from Fish Springs Ranch in Nevada, where he works, to join the gathering of the clan and be there for his daughter's graduation. Ramona, who had been cooking all day, laid out some delicious food to eat and everyone contributed something to the fare.

That night, as Tammy graduated from Loyalton High, son Steve was receiving a diploma from Blue Mountain Community College in Pendleton. Doug had gone one direction and we the other. Tammy's eyes filled with tears, as did ours, when she was presented four more scholarships. This meant the way was paved for her to attend the University of California at Davis, where she has already been accepted.

All 26 of us present shared in her big moment. I'll not soon forget the sight of this first grandchild marching down the aisle in her white gown with the gold California Scholarship Federation banner draped over her shoulder. Tammy will go to college, an opportunity denied her grandmother and her mother.

During the wee hours of the next morning, son Todd, with wife, Liza, and the babies arrived, having also driven non-stop from Wallowa County. Room was made for more bodies to sleep and I joined second cousin Libby on the living room rug.

Later on that beautiful morning, Mary Ann, Kathryn and I, armed with a picnic lunch, drove toward Loyalton, then took a narrow, dirt road that led into the mountains. We were making a planned pilgrimage back to where our great-grandmother, Electa (DeWolf) Butler, lived in the years 1873-74. The drive was incredibly lovely and followed a splashing creek bordered with newly leafed-out aspen and numerous wild flowers. We emerged from the forest into a secluded valley, heart-shaped and backgrounded by snow-streaked peaks rising in the distance.

Sardine Valley! As we walked out to photograph the meadows, a huge semi-truck-trailer rig rumbled in from the opposite direction, and soon hundreds of sheep ran down a metal ramp and began grazing the spring grasses. We wandered over and talked to the owner, a Mr. Fiddyment, whose family had been coming to Sardine Valley since the 1860s. The Spanish sheepherder immediately set out several scarecrows "to frighten away the coyotes", he said.

Three bummer lambs followed him everywhere, and we heard him telling his pets in Spanish they had to eat grass now, "no more leche." Fiddyment told us the sheep would gradually graze their way up toward

Weber Lake, which would take most of the summer, before being trucked back to the Sacramento valley for the winter.

Thunderheads had been building, and it began to rain lightly as we drove to the site where Electa had lived. Here Mary Ann read from one of Electa's letters, dated February, 1874—

High up among the Sierra Nevadas; over six thousand feet above sea level nestles the diminutive, little valley of Sardine. As I look across it, even now, covered five feet deep in its winter dress of pure white snow, I feel I can forgive the early settlers almost everything else but the name.

They must have been men who had 'no magic in their souls,' else they would have given this spot some soft musical name. Why Sardine? Tradition says that long ago two men, 'prospecting,' came to this place with their larder reduced to a box of sardines.

If they had only eaten their supper just around the hill, in what is known as Dry Valley, I should have found no fault in them; but then this might have been called Starvation Camp, or something worse. Is there nothing in a name?

Thirty-year-old Electa, fresh from the East, alone, unmarried, had secured a job with the Nathan Parsons family to teach their children. She lived at Sardine House, which lay on the old stage road from Marysville to Virginia City, known then as the "Hermit's Pass Road". Before the railroad crossed the state, it was an important thoroughfare.

The road was no longer in use by the time Electa lived there, and all travel was between Loyalton and Truckee. In addition to the station house, Parsons owned the first lumber mill in the valley. A water wheel, set in Davey's Creek, provided power for the mill. Our great grandma Butler graduated from Western Reserve Seminary at West Farmington, Ohio, in 1864, with the degree "Mistress of English Literature," which included two or three years of Latin, a good deal of German and some French.

To teach she had to pass an examination by a county board for a certificate. Electa received the only No. 1 certificate she ever saw, and it was renewed for her as long as she taught country schools. Before the way opened for her to come to California, she taught at many schools in the East, even becoming principal of one of them.

One hundred fourteen years later, Electa's great-great-great-grand-daughter graduated with honors from Loyalton High School, just 15 miles from where Electa lived. The circle is complete.

As we sat on a log under some ancient cottonwood trees and listened to the thunder roll around among the high peaks, we could feet Electa's presence. We had traveled back in time to our roots...and now Electa's great granddaughter writes about her experiences in Sardine Valley and you read about it in Agri-Times.

June 11—My two sisters, Mary Ann and Kathryn, and I returned from our pilgrimage to Sardine Valley to Ramona's Chilcoot house, only to find that our relatives had moved lock, stock and barrel out to the Nevada desert ranch of Fish Springs. So...we followed suit.

Desert primroses bloomed along the road and the desert air was fresh and wonderful due to thunderstorms that swept across the vastness of that sagebrush-covered range. We arrived at ranch headquarters to find our clan, and what a wonderful time we had. Cousins went for horseback rides or played under the huge old cottonwood trees in the yard, while their parents caught up on years of family news.

Huge alfalfa fields, watered by artesian wells that pumped water from center-pivot sprinklers, were nearly ready for their first cutting. Cattle grazed the miles of sagebrush range that comprise the huge Fish Springs Ranch.

The sunset that night was incredible. It resembled a Charles Russell painting. The clouds were touched with brush strokes of pinks, purples, crimsons and oranges, and because of the infiniteness of the horizon, it filled the desert sky with breath-taking color for an hour. Mary Ann and K. went bonkers taking pictures. I was out of film!

We kept the windows open to the desert night, listening to the "coyote chorus," and slept like rocks.

June 12—We bid our usual tearful goodbyes to daughter Ramona and her family. 14-year-old grandson Shawn and Jackie and the children loaded into the car all their baggage and we left Fish Springs. Shawn was looking forward to spending several weeks visiting us in Wallowa County.

We ate lunch at a McDonald's in Susanville before traveling the long Northern California miles through cattle country rangeland that commanded far-reaching views of high mountain valleys, meadows, lakes and steep winding roads. We arrived at cousin Terry's place in Tulelake late in the evening and, after a chicken dinner downtown, we stayed up until nearly 11 playing Pictionary and visiting. The next morning we hit the road again, early, and drove to Klamath Falls and then on up to the Diamond Lake cutoff where we rendezvoused with

Jackie's in-laws, the Matthews, who had driven over from Roseburg to meet us.

After a delicious breakfast at Malfunction Junction Cafe, Jackie and the children left us to return to Roseburg with the children's other grand-parents. Shawn and I continued northward to Redmond, where we turned northeast and headed toward Prineville. It was a beautiful drive to John Day and Prairie City. We saw the sign that led to Monument and I wanted to visit, but we didn't have the time.

We traveled through syringa-scented canyons and passed fields of hay already swathed and laying in the fields. We stopped in Mitchell and ate the best hamburger on the trip at the Blueberry Muffin Cafe. I photographed in the ghost town of Whitney, then drove through the colorful area of Sumpter Valley and on down into Baker.

It was 5 p.m. when we pulled up to the Sumpter Junction Restaurant. As we sipped our root beer floats, we marveled at the working, scale model of the Sumpter Valley Railway train as it traveled over 1,000 feet of track around the restaurant.

The train traveled through an intricate tunnel system, then blew its whistle came down alongside our booth. Shawn and I were fascinated. Truly, this had been a labor of love for the people who conceived and carried out the project. It must have taken them hundreds of hours.

We glimpsed two antelope alongside the freeway out of Baker and before we knew it we had come down out of Ladd Canyon into La Grande. On the spur of the moment, I decided to hunt up my mother and her husband, who were attending an Elderhostel week at Eastern Oregon State College. They were very surprised to see us.

Sixty more miles to Wallowa County and Prairie Creek, and the valley never looked lovelier than it did on that June evening, the Minam River running clear and unpolluted, the deer feeding in the evening light, and the mountains welcoming us home.

It was 10 p.m. when we pulled into the ranch. Doug was at the sink, cleaning kokanee he had caught that evening on Wallowa Lake.

June 17—Doug and I celebrated our 10th wedding anniversary with a delicious dinner at Vali's Alpine Delicatessen at the Lake. Hot weather arrived, but we weren't used to it and wilted. The garden loved it and grew rapidly. I had forgotten how much a 14-year-old could eat and spent a lot of time trying to satisfy Shawn's insatiable appetite. Fourteen-year-old Chad (grandson) spent one night here and the boys slept in the sheepherder wagon.

In the morning, Doug hollered out that their sheep had already left the bed ground with daylight, and they had better get up! I filled them with sourdough hotcakes and sausage, which they washed down with huge glasses of Startch's milk. Good food builds strong bodies and healthy minds.

I picked the first red shoots of rhubarb and made two juicy pies. A thunderstorm cooled the valley somewhat, so the next morning this 54-year-old grandma and three of her grandsons—11-year-old Rowdy, 14-year-old Chad, and 14-year-old Shawn—climbed Ruby Peak, the 8,874-foot mountain that towers over the small town of Enterprise.

We encountered some difficulty in locating the old trail to Murray Gap, but finally managed to intercept it, whereupon the boys took off and waited for me at the gap. Along the way up that steep trail I made my way, slowly, and came upon a small snowman fashioned by my grandsons, and then later, *HI!* written in a snowbank.

I joined the boys at the gap. As we gazed down into the snow-filled Silver Creek basin and up to the awesome crags and ridges that form Traverse Ridge, I again marveled at this magnificent backcountry. It is worth the effort of every step to get here.

We trudged through snowbanks and finally came out onto Scotch Creek saddle, whereupon I pointed to the way to the top and let the boys forge ahead. They made it by noon; I arrived, out of breath, around 1 p.m. We had made it!

Misty clouds formed around us and the valley below was obscured; then, patches of that aerial view appeared like in a dream! The air was cool, and butterflies, just hatched, flew everywhere. We were on top of the world. The boys produced a stick-and-handkerchief they had carried up, and then stuck it into a pile of rocks at the very top of the peak.

We read notes that were in a jar there and added ours to it, describing the climb and the weather, and putting the date next to our names. It was a special moment for all of us, one we would remember all our lives.

June 20—Ranch work continues; gardens to weed and irrigate, the cow to milk. My pullets began laying their first little brown eggs and Chester, the rooster, was happy, as always, about life in general. Doug took Shawn fishing at Wallowa Lake and we so enjoyed eating the delicious pink meat of the landlocked salmon that locals refer to as "Yanks."

Shawn helped me with some serious house cleaning, during which time the electricity went off for about three hours, so we packed water from the ditch to scrub and clean with. Just as we finished, the power was restored.

On top of Ruby Peak, 8,874 feet up in the Wallowas, stand grandsons Rowdy, Chad and Shawn.

June 21—Summer has officially made its appearance. How wonderful it is to have these long, hot and dry days to accomplish all that has to be done. Our men will swathe and chop hay to fill the big plastic Ag Bags. Some of the hay will also be baled, and the long stacks of hay will begin to form all over the Wallowa country; a necessity for the long, cold winter. This year, Doug is mixing some leftover potatoes with the green chop to make silage. The fall-calving cows will have a slightly different menu after the snow flies.

June 26—The seed potatoes came up beautifully and grew very quickly. James celebrated his second birthday.

Grace Bartlett and I took the "Wallowa Story" down to Imnaha so old-timers A.L. Duckett, Jim Dorrance, Inez Meyers and Ferm Warnock could view it at the Riverside Cafe. They seemed to really enjoy it, which makes such an effort worthwhile. These wonderful people and others like them are the history of Wallowa County.

The June colors of the canyons were shades of purple and blue, and the penstemon incredible. The cloying sweetness of the wild syringa (mock orange) scented the entire Imnaha.

Chuck and Sue Mehrten, cattle rancher relatives from White Rock, near Folsom, California, paid us a visit. I had a roast chicken dinner prepared for them, topped off with blackberry cobbler. That night, we took them to the top of the east moraine of Wallowa Lake to check our cows. A fine, misty rain was falling. Just what we needed for grass.

June 28—Doug caught some trout in the irrigation ditch and I cooked them for breakfast. Then we all piled into the pickup and headed for the hills, which were carpeted with wildflowers. What a sight it was. Never have I seen the hills so lovely as they were this early summer. The skies were rain-washed and cool. Periods of sunshine made the grasses glisten with freshness and brilliant green colors. Wildflower scent floated over that undulating, high plateau we know simply as "the hills." Sue went wild snapping pictures.

We drove across from Salmon Creek to Pine Creek and into the Zumwalt country, where miles of bunch grass range stretched in all directions, as far as we could see. Our rancher relatives were impressed with the grass.

"Real cattle country," we told them, "and managed by cattle people who are, above all, the best stewards of the land." They have to be. It is their livelihood, and besides, they care. Driving past the Steen Ranch on Chesnimnus Creek, we continued on to Buckhorn.

What a disappointment. We stepped up to the drop-off into the canyon by the fire lookout, but could see nothing past a solid wall of fog and mist. We stood there on the rim, smelling the syringa-scented air drifting up from the bottom of that deep canyon country, and told our guests of the wondrous sight that lay hidden.

Later, as I stood there alone (Doug, Sue and Chuck having wandered off in the opposite direction), a faint breeze began to stir, and below me the panorama began to unfold. The mist lifted like a curtain on a play, bringing canyon after canyon to brilliant life; suddenly, there they were, the drainages of the mighty Imnaha and Snake. Mile after mile of green silence with fingers of mist trailing in the draws; a glimpse of paradise, then magically, the breeze ceased and the lovely view faded from sight.

We had been privileged to witness the brief, breath-taking world below our feet.

June 30—June ended with a week's visit from my mother and her husband, Bill, who drove over after their Elderhostel week at Eastern Oregon State College in La Grande.

One morning, I treated them to a fly-in breakfast at the Wallowa Horse Ranch (formerly known as Red's Horse Ranch). Grandson Shawn, who was visiting at the time, also went, as did my friend and historian Grace Bartlett.

It was a first for all four of them. This famous dude ranch lies in the heart of the Minam Wilderness and is accessible only by horseback, hiking or airplane. They reported back to me a most enjoyable trip. Shawn, having been permitted to sit next to the pilot and mama, survived the flight.

Grace was interested in the history of "Red's," of which there is still much unrecorded and much that will never be known, but much being presently written. A very interesting place.

July 1—The moon still shone brightly in the morning sky when I jumped out of bed and hurried to the barn. I'd forgotten to let Startch in the night before to nurse her calves! My days have been so busy.

What a feeling on this fresh, new mountain morning, of a new day and a new month, and summer stretching before us. The smell of freshly raked hay and the calves gorging themselves on Startch's swollen udder. I finished mowing the lawn before the sun came up over the eastern hills.

The roses by the bunkhouse are blooming so profusely this year, for days they were a solid mass of yellow blooms. Picture-pretty clouds floated in blue skies during the annual Lostine Flea Market, and crowds were bigger than ever when Doug and I took it all in on opening day. I purchased two antique muffin tins for $1 and some old books for 25 cents each. Doug found some old tools and we bought a sack of Walla Walla Sweet onions from a vendor.

After returning to the ranch, Doug baled 600 bales of hay before Sunny and Alice Hancock drove in from Lakeview. Sunny was to perform during the Cowboy Poetry Gathering at the South Fork Grange Hall in Lostine that night. We attended with our friends, and visited other cowboy poets Jennifer Isley, Blackie Black and Leon Davis, who had traveled to Lostine from out of the county.

It was a very hot evening as local cowboy poet-rancher-longhorn breeder Fred Bornstedt emceed the program and introduced "the Possum Trotters," who played some foot stompin' music before Sunny recited a poem entitled "That Gol' Darned Wheel." Scott McClaran entertained us with poems he had written about the Imnaha and the Cow Creek Bridge. Blackie Black from Adel and Leon from Union kept us in stitches with their performances, and Sam Loftus sang "Red River Valley" as the perspiration dripped off his brow.

It was 11 before I let Startch in to nurse her calves. Thunder and lightning played around us all night, and the next morning I arose early to fry elk steaks and make sourdough waffles, bacon and eggs for our company. How we enjoy Sunny and Alice's company.

While Doug drove them out to Buckhorn for a look-see at our canyon country, I prepared food for a picnic here that day. It was a beautiful day for showing off the county to our visitors. To keep Startch on her "weird" schedule, I didn't let her calves nurse or milk her until 11 a.m.

I had chicken fried and was baking sourdough bread when Doug, Sunny and Alice returned. As Alice helped me with the meal preparations, she raved about the scenery and about seeing a cow elk. Daughter Jackie arrived with more chicken to fry, and later we had a great family picnic outside until it started to rain, whereupon we carried everything inside and continued on with our meal.

That night we had a small display of fireworks for the benefit of the young (and old) children while Sunny and Alice drove to Lostine for the second performance of the Cowboy Poetry Gathering.

July 4—What a beautiful morning, cool, with thunderheads building over the mountains. I did my cow early. Poor cow. She is now on a 6 to 6 schedule. The calves are growing and Startch takes it all in stride.

Leaving daughter Jackie fixing breakfast with Alice, I left for Haines and their big 4th of July celebration. Mainly I wanted to cover the "Old Hands" contest. It was my first trip to Haines, population 395, and the small, friendly cowtown was all decked out in red, white and blue. I looked up Harley Caudle, Mike McFetridge and Dan Warnock, who were standing around taking in the sights. Phyllis Brownlee was there and getting everyone lined up for the parade.

It had been nip and tuck just getting Harley to come down for the parade, but his family and some friends persuaded him to enter a cow penning contest that followed, and that got him there. What a surprise to Harley when he was informed he was the winner of the "Old Hand" contest and Phyllis Brownlee pinned a big, blue rosette ribbon on his shirt.

My friend Mike McFetridge was there also, and Wallowa County is equally proud of him, as we are of Dan Warnock, who was raised out on Crow Creek. Another old hand was Russell Temple of Wallowa, who wasn't able to attend.

What a feed Haines put on that day: pit barbecued beef, a huge hog-scalding kettle simmering with beans and pork, salads, rolls, and tables laden with homemade pies. I partook of the feast and headed home because it had begun to rain. As I drove the eight miles back to North

Powder and turned up toward La Grande, I was glad to have made the effort to attend Haines' Fourth of July.

All the folks were so friendly; it is a place I will always think fondly of.

July 5—It poured down rain and much of the first cuttings of hay got wet, but moisture is always welcome and we agriculturists take all we can get, whenever.

July 6—Grace Bartlett and I left "The Wallowa Story" slide tape program with the Wallow Lake State Park's program director. At summer's end, we would learn that more than 2,000 people viewed the presentation, held every Tuesday night at the outdoor amphitheater. Due to popular demand, it will again be shown in the summer of 1989.

Again, three times a week, all summer, on Joseph's main street local actors staged the re-enactment of the "Great Joseph Bank Robbery." The success of this event was due to people like Bud Zollman, who left his horse tied to a hitching rack while he tended his hardware store, then jumped astride his mount at the appointed hour, and became a bank robber! This real-life drama (hammed up, just a wee bit) was popular with the tourists.

Our rain-damaged hay dried out and Ben kept busy with the loader-stacker while his son Zack raked. Son Steve spent most of the summer tending to the 80 acres of seed potatoes.

July 7—Today was our Wallowa County Band's first summer concert. It was held in the newly constructed gazebo bandstand on the courthouse lawn during early evening. I dug out my old, blue and gold high school sweater and wore it while I played the clarinet. Felt like a high school girl of the '50s (almost) as we presented our concert. It was such a thrill, especially for our band leader, Bob Clegg, whose wonderful enthusiasm inspired all of us.

There were baskets of colorful flowers hanging from the bandstand's roof, and a good-sized crowd wandered onto the lawn to listen to and enjoy the great, old Sousa marches and other selections that we had practiced. The band, truly "Wallowa County," included housewives, children, farmers, the editor of our local newspaper, businessmen, and former students of our own "Music Man."

In years past, Bob was the band instructor at Enterprise High School. This man's entire life has been music, and he is one of those rare individuals who not only teaches but inspires as well. The difference between a student's success or failure.

July 8—I helped our CowBelles pre-cook 600 pounds of beef ribs for a barbecue they would put on the next day for Enterprise's Crazy Daze celebration. We worked like beavers and at 12:30 I left to attend the "Fishtrap Gathering" Writers Conference at Wallowa Lake. I had been looking forward to this all year. Imagine actually being able to attend a writers conference in our own area.

It was a warm, wonderful afternoon as writers drifted in from all over the West, and even some from the East. Delegates from "outside" were enthralled by the beauty of the country. The greenness, the mountains rising above the lake, the sweet fragrance of blooming wild syringa, and mule deer wandering around the lodge where the conference was held.

The theme was "Writing West of the Rockies." The name "Fishtrap" was appropriate because Wallowa is, in fact, a word the Nez Perce used to describe the tripods, made of poles, that held their fishtraps. "Fishtrap" was, for me, a long-awaited opportunity to mingle with writers, a group of people whom I admire, but from whom I feel, somehow, far-removed. After all a rancher's wife who loves to write is not considered a real writer.

As a result of "Fishtrap" I was to learn that writers come in all sizes, shape and different walks of life, and one cannot judge the contents by the wrappings. I was also to learn that we all speak a common language, a language often not understood by those who do not write. In other words, I could communicate with these people, I could identify with them and, for all of us Eastern Oregon writers, it was wonderful to be with our kind.

Grace Bartlett, my local historian-writer and friend, and I attended every session of the three-day conference, listening to and visiting with such famous Northwest writers as William Kittredge, James Welch, Craig Lesley, George Venn and Kim Stafford. And what a pleasure to meet Ursula Le Guin and find out her mother wrote *Ishi*, a story about the last Stone Age Indian. I had recently finished reading Ursula's book of poems entitled *Wild Oats and Fireweed*, a collection of her published and unpublished poetry from 1981 to 1987.

Bill Gulick, well-known author of such books as *Snake River Country* and *Nez Perce Country* was there also. The first night's program lasted until after 10 and included readings by writers and poets. How wonderful to listen to those beautiful words.

It was nearly 11 when I returned to the ranch and walked out under a star-studded sky to call in my cow Startch. Out of the night she came, into the lighted barn to let her four calves relieve her swollen udder. While the calves nursed, I savored the smell of newly mown hay on that warm July night.

Returning slowly to the house, in my old overalls that covered my new "Fishtrap" T-shirt, I wondered if one day, maybe, this writer could produce written words as beautiful as we had heard that night. In the house I re-read a manuscript I was working on, didn't like it, and went to bed... and laid awake thinking about what to write.

July 9—I did my chores and headed to the lake to have breakfast outside in the morning sunshine at the "Fishtrap" writers conference. That day's sessions centered around the subject of "Cowboys and Indians." During a stimulating audience-participation discussion, I added my two-cents worth by stating that cowboys were not being portrayed accurately by most modern-day writers.

I feel that we, as writers, have a responsibility to describe them, as well as their lifestyles, the way they really are. Personally, I believe that they are much more colorful, in truth, than the Zane Grey version of the shoot 'em up variety. As a result of the popular western stories, the East still thinks of our western cowboy as coming out of the pages of a western novel.

Many opinions were expressed. It was a great communication between East and West, between city and country, and all through it you could feel the spell of the "Wallowa." The writers sensed it. It was there in the sunlight sifting through the trees and the deer wandering around.

That evening we were treated to a wonderful experience at the Buhler Ranch. On the wooden deck of an old log building, long tables groaned with a variety of delectable dishes that included smoked turkey, barbecued pork, homemade bread, beans and salads.

The last rays of evening sunlight streamed through tall pines; visiting Indian dancers danced to the beat of their drums while dressed in their finest regalia: beautiful fringed buckskin, beadwork and feather headdresses. You could almost sense, somehow, the spirit of their ancestors in the drum beats coming through the years, filling in the time gap of memories from then to now.

A grandmother sat and watched her grandchildren dance. Her face reflected the love and pride she felt for them. A pretty young mother held a baby in her lap while her older children danced. People were seated on wooden benches in the circular outdoor amphitheater and enjoyed their meal.

Writers like Kim Stafford leaned against the tall pines and soaked it all in. The stuff writers live for. A large, middle-aged woman recited a morning prayer to the light. It was very touching.

Grandmother Blanche Hung.

Indian dancers from the Confederated Tribes of the Umatilla Indian Reservation included, among others, Irma Sams, left; Francis McFarland, wearing headdress, and Sams' son, daughter and grandson.

Startch was waiting patiently at the barn door when I got home on that warm July night. She hadn't given up on me entirely. Lying in bed that night, I remembered the hour's visit I'd had with the Indian grandmother. What a wonderful person she was. I very much respected her wisdom and her down to earth observations about life. She was not unlike my own grandmother, when spoken to in the universal language of love.

July 11—My Rhode Island Red pullets laid their first small brown eggs. Bill Gulick and his wife, Jean, visited the ranch that day, and we ate lunch out on the lawn. I fixed egg salad sandwiches with lots of fresh, garden lettuce. It was a real treat for Doug and me to visit with this interesting couple, whom I had met at the writers' conference. Bill, with Jean's help, has authored such books as *Snake River Country,* and more recently *Chief Joseph Country.*

The valley ranchers are frantically haying, scarcely taking time for little else.

July 14—A fine, misty rain falling. It would be the last moisture we would see for days.

Our "Swiss Miss," Susanne from Switzerland, paid us a visit. For two years, she had dreamed of returning to our ranch and riding Hummer, our Appaloosa cowhorse. So we saddled the horses and went for a ride on Tenderfoot Valley Road. After our ride, we walked out to visit the milk cows, Star and Startch, and the calves. For lunch we fixed BLT's and Susanne savored a glass of cold, fresh milk.

Due to the moisture and subsequent warmth, the garden grew like it was in a steamy hot house. And all over the valley, hay lay in the fields in all shapes—round bales, huge big bales, conventional bales and bread loaf haystacks. The ones I like best are Hank Bird's huge loose stacks. They remind me of the hay stacks in Montana's Big Hole Valley.

July 16—My 4-H'ers and I went on a two-day backpack trip to Minam Lake. When we left the trailhead at Two Pan at the end of the Lostine River Road, I was carrying a 35-pound pack. As we hiked up the lovely West Fork of the Lostine, the air was fragrant with huckleberry, and the trail lined with wildflowers.

The trail followed the rushing waters of the creek, which would suddenly form into clear, blue-green pools whose bottoms glittered with golden sand. Snow-covered Elkhorn Peak appeared to the west and it was here we ate our lunches. At exactly 6.2 miles, and considerably higher, we came to the headwaters of the West Fork. Through a thick stand of spruce I glimpsed the shimmery blue waters of Minam Lake, which was the source of the West Fork.

It was 4 p.m. when we selected a campsite in view of the lake. Later we cooked our supper over an open fire and ate, listening to the little wavelets lap against the shore of Minam Lake. It appeared that we were the only inhabitants on that wilderness lake, although there were two other camps hidden from view.

That night we were awakened by "crunch, munch" and the rustling noises of paper. One of the 4-H'ers said, "Willie, are you eating again?" To which a sleepy Willie answered, "No."

It was a mule deer doe we had seen feeding at dusk near our camp. She had returned to "munch out" on Willie's graham crackers. We went back to sleep, because the next morning we would head up the mountain and come out under the spectacular Eagle Cap, look down on Mirror Lake and return to Two Pan via the beautiful East Fork trail.

July 17—Dawn broke around 4 a.m., then graylight time. Later still, western peaks turned softly golden as morning sunlight stole slowly down talus slopes above timber line. Frost covered the ground, and our sleeping bags. It created pretty patterns on the wild strawberry plants. Wisps of steam-like mists hung over the lake's surface and burned off, magically, as the sun streamed down the ridges.

When the doe appeared for her morning drink at the lakeside, I was able to photograph her while the 4-H'ers slept. After finishing breakfast, we shouldered our packs and headed up a steep switchback trail that would lead to the High Lakes Basin. Because I would meet them at the top, the younger ones eagerly took off, leaving me to follow slowly.

The morning was fresh and clear, and Minam Lake appeared as I climbed higher, and Blue Lake, nestled higher up and to the southwest. High, pinnacle-like ridges rose above me, and a snow-streaked range appeared. The awesome trail was covered with red outcroppings of rock with intrusions of grey talus and granite. In the trail were several large snowbanks. The views were tremendous.

I walked through huge rock slides and gazed above to massive, jumbled boulders. This is home to the pika, the shy, little rook rabbit, who inhabits these high, rocky places. I could hear its high-pitched call, and paused to observe this tiny animal chattering at me.

Windswept trees at timberline, bent and twisted, showed the effects of winter's icy blast. It appeared we were among some of the season's first travelers on that high path. In places, larger snowbanks nearly covered up the trail. On one such patch of snow, the children had written

"HI" for me. Suddenly I looked up to see the tip of the mountain named Eagle Cap, and a few more laborious steps brought me to the top.

Nearby, the 4-H'ers were sliding down a snow bank, bug-eyed by all the beauty around them. Far below lay Mirror Lake, shimmering in the noon-day sun, and next to it lay a small blue-green pothole which the kids immediately named Sourdough Lake. Below, also, lay the entrance to the High Lakes Basin, over which reigned the beautiful, snow-covered Eagle Cap.

Descending the trail to Mirror Lake, we were accompanied by the song of water. The melting snow ran everywhere in riverlets through the low-growing pink and white mountain heather bells, splashing and cascading happily to form a larger stream that would ultimately become the East Fork of the Lostine.

Looking up, it appeared as though one of these musical little water-ways fell from the sky. Born in beauty, this river would begin its journey through a long valley, carved by an ancient Pleistocene glacier. Near Mirror Lake the trail was bordered by bright, purple penstemon and green willow scrub.

The Shutterbugs went crazy taking pictures. As we approached the lake, a great hoard of mosquitoes erupted from the grasses and bushes to attack us. Little alpine whirlwinds dissipated them for awhile, but they returned before long to plague us. It appeared we were the only souls there, until we spied some horses, swishing their tails madly at deer and horse flies, tied to some trees up in the timber. We ate our lunches near the shore of the lake, and since the air was so warm, we waded in the lake's cold water to refresh our tired feet.

Covering my face with a jacket, I was able to ward off those pesky mosquitoes and take a nap. On the opposite shore, huge snow banks hung over the edge. Once in awhile, one of these chunks would break away and splash into the lake. It was very peaceful there, and in spite of the mosquitoes, we all hated to leave.

As we left that high, alpine setting to hike out the seven miles back to Two Pan a little breeze sprang up and the insects left us pretty much alone. The trail was alternately damp and dusty, small waterfalls falling from ferny springs above the trail, and once in awhile I could glimpse sky through the fir trees along the meadows that carpeted the length of the U-shaped valley.

The valley was rimmed by steep talus slopes. The trail wandered out into the meadow and onto a rustic, wooden bridge that crossed the East Fork which, at this point, was only a small meandering stream. Patches of brilliant, blue Penstemon bordered the stream. Looking back, near the bridge, I saw a most incredible sight! In the background, rising majestically above all, the snow-capped Eagle Cap at the head of this magnificent valley, with its clear, winding stream, the wooden bridge I had just crossed...and I was out of film.

The children were far ahead as usual. Many varieties of early wild-flowers nodded in the breeze as I contemplated where I would photo-graph, if only I could! Later in the summer, I was to recognize this very scene, that haunts me still, on the cover of a promotional pamphlet on Northeastern Oregon. The cover, when opened out to include the back, reveals that incredible sight. Apparently another photographer recog-nized the uniqueness of that special place and did a most commendable job of capturing the feeling I also felt.

Nearing the trailhead the East Fork picked up speed and fell from cascading waterfalls to merge with the West Fork. It was nearing evening when I wearily reached the pickup. The last two miles had been simply putting one foot in front of the other. I was tired, and my pack seemed to get heavier. It had been a long day. The trip was, however, worth any discomfort, because these young people, no matter what path they may choose to follow in life, will always remember these experiences. And such memories will help give them the strength to cope with today's complex world.

July 23—Eight of my 4-H'ers and I back-packed into Brownie Basin. We drove up the South Fork of the Lostine and hiked from the Bowman trailhead. Several of the members had to change irrigation pipes that morning, so we got a rather late start. As usual, the 4-H'ers left me far behind, and I met some interesting hikers on the trail.

About two miles or so up the trail I stepped aside for a young mother leading a burro on whose back rode a three-year-old boy wearing a hard hat. The child waved happily to me as they passed by. Next in this procession came the daddy, carrying a baby on his back in one of those child carriers and leading a burro loaded with camping gear. Bringing up the rear was a loose burro packed with more supplies. The baby, secure in his pack and obviously enjoying it all, grinned broadly at me as they disappeared around a steep bend in the trail. What lucky children.

Farther up the trail, I caught up with Jeff. This being his first back pack trip, he was learning that there were several items in his pack he should have left at home. His pack was extremely heavy and it took us quite a long while getting to camp.

At 1:15 we finally made it and Brownie Basin looked like Shangri-La. We collapsed in the shade of a spruce tree and ate our lunches. The other

4-H'ers were already fishing the nearby lake.

Brownie Basin, a narrow mountain meadow, is rimmed in by high snow-streaked peaks and ridges, and Bowman Creek winds its way through the middle. Wildflowers, like pink elephant head, grew out of the boggy places near the stream. The basin belonged to a young two-point mule deer buck, several ground squirrels, and numerous alpine birds. In earlier years sheep grazed these high mountain meadows and the herders' summer camps were scattered throughout the area.

With happy shouts, the returning 4-H'ers came racing down from the trail to our camp, and we soon had a good cooking fire going. When the fire burned down to coals, we all turned into creative outdoor cooks and concocted everything from hobo stew to steak and corn on the cob roasted over the small grate we had packed in.

Later, as we roasted marshmallows, the moon appeared in a flawless mountain night, and the two-point buck came out to browse the willows that bordered the creek. The children named the stars and talked and talked, and the moon drifted over the mountain out of sight. Grandson Chad kept our fire burning all night, which was comforting, and the smoke discouraged the mosquitoes, and as well, we hoped, all the things that go bump in the night.

It was 10 when we packed up and left the basin the next morning. Just leaving, we met Betsy Henry leading a pack string out from North Minam Meadows. Betsy and husband, Cal, operate High Country Outfitters, which includes the Wallowa Horse Ranch on the Minam.

My group waited for me at the trailhead where they had been fishing. It being so hot and all, and we being so dusty, we decided to drive down the Lostine a few miles and find a good swimmin' hole. We found a perfect place where the river made a bend and pooled into a hole near a sandy beach. In we jumped, clothes and all, into the cold snowmelt waters of the Lostine. The boys jumped off a bank and splashed into the hole, sending up a spray of water. It was wonderfully refreshing and I felt like a kid again!

Returning home, I found my sister Mary Ann reading a book in the shade of our willow tree in the yard. She was looking forward to a long visit with us. And what a help she was: picking raspberries, doing dishes, gathering eggs. She even survived, somehow, the preparations for and the celebration of Chief Joseph Days, which, to put it mildly, is no small feat.

She went right along with the flow of ranch life, where no two days are alike and one incredible day follows another. Every day the heat became more intense, the berries ripening and the flowers wilting in the

Five members of the Sourdough Shutterbugs 4-H Club pose at the top of the pass that separates the High Lakes Basin country and the Minam drainage, in the Eagle Cap Wilderness Area. From left are Willie Zollman, Erick Johnson, Leah Svendsen, Amy Zollman and Becky Jones.

midday sun. Mary Ann and I prepared delicious meals using the garden vegetables, homegrown fryers and beef, and ate outside on the picnic table as more company arrived.

One evening we drove to the Wallowa Lake State Park amphitheater and viewed "The Wallowa Story" with more than 300 other people who had come to watch the program. Somehow we made it through Chief Joseph Days week. There was the kiddie parade on Friday, and on Saturday morning we ate outside at the Shriners' cowboy breakfast, then returned to the ranch to saddle horses for the CowBelle entry.

The small town of Joseph was crowded with throngs of people, possibly the largest crowd ever, and it was so hot. My Sourdough Shutterbugs marched in back of our CowBelle entry, which consisted of Saralynn Johnson and myself, clad in our working clothes, riding the horses and carrying the CowBelle banner. Our horses behaved well and it was fun, except our hands were full and we couldn't wave to our friends and relatives.

Mary Ann and two of the grandchildren rode with Doug on "Cyclops," which is Doug's giant three-wheeler rouging machine. After the parade we attended the Indian friendship dinner, which was followed by the Indian dance contest. On the way home that evening we stopped by to attend a get-together at Dave and Darlene Turner's lovely home, and had just enough strength left to drive to Alder Slope and watch the grandchildren while mom and dad attended the rodeo.

On Sunday, we attended the Professional Rodeo Cowboys Association (PRCA) rodeo finals. Always such a thrill to witness the opening ceremonies of each performance. This year an Indian woman sang a national anthem, which was followed by Tillie Johnson's high, clear voice singing the Star Spangled Banner. Tillie's lovely notes carried out over Joseph and the Wallowas looked down on it all, and we were proud to be Americans.

July 28—"My life is a poem I might have writ, if I had the time to live and utter it." Don't know who originally wrote that splendid little tidbit, but it describes how I feel during this last week in July 1988. As I write in the yard, pounding the portable typewriter at an old redwood picnic table in the shade of our willow tree, I can look out across Prairie Creek and see the heat burning in the hills.

I can also see Hough's sprinklers shooting jets of precious water onto the recently hayed fields. I hear Chester, the banty rooster, crow as he flies over the chicken yard fence away from his harem and picks about, eating bugs and worms before flying back to join the young Rhode Island Red pullets.

The mountains, from which the water flows, are already devoid of snow and have that soft, purple look about them that comes with the heat of summer. I find it hard to write about June on this busy July day. It is the season for company and my sister Mary Ann is here and I want to visit and go see the county with her and be a tourist and eat at the fun eating places and show her our towns and have her meet the Wallowa country's wonderful and interesting inhabitants.

While I write, the raspberries ripen in the heat, as do the strawberries, goose berries and the first tender green zucchini is appearing. There is jam to be made, berries to freeze, and the irrigating takes up so much time. And always, when it is the busiest, we have Chief Joseph Days! Our fall calving heifers are being brought in from the hills and down from the high moraine pasture so they can be watched closely in the lower field below the house.

The seed potatoes are growing well, but need constant irrigation on these blistering hot days when dry winds sap the moisture from the soil as soon as the sprinklers are moved. Doug drives "Cyclops," the three-wheeler roguing machine he built in his shop, up and down the long rows of potatoes to detect any diseased plants. Knock on wood; this year we haven't had much to rogue out, and passed our first field inspection with flying colors. Son Steve is doing a great job of managing the seed potato end of our operation.

The days run together. I spend much of that time cooking big meals for company. It was fun to eat outside on the picnic table on these warm, golden evenings. At one memorable meal there were 17 of us. Young fathers played football with a herd of young grandsons, while granddaughter Chelsie ran interference. One way to work off a meal!

These July days are full of baking rhubarb pies, watering the lawn, garden and flowers, preserving berries, butchering more fryers, attending the Wallowa County band practices...on my feet from dawn 'til dark and loving it.

The old sheepherder wagon got lots of use this summer. It was the favorite place for visiting grandchildren, who came to spend the night.

August 1—Because of our numerous visitors this past summer and fall, the sheepherder wagon, parked close to the house, is often used as a spare bedroom. The zucchini have began to produce...and produce; I will have to cook it a thousand ways. The Rhode Island Red pullets have begun to lay double yolked eggs, and the first pink blossoms appear on the cosmos. We are all down to muscle and bone, putting in long hours of summer work. The weather has grown extremely hot and dry, and irrigating has become a daily chore.

August 2—Our thermometer registered 32 degrees, which was, according to our local radio station, the coldest spot in the nation. A distinction we usually share with West Yellowstone! My sister Mary Ann, who was still with us, elected to do the barn chores and succeeded very well. This freed me to write and catch up on the myriad of other matters that seem to pile up around and over me.

August 4—In the weeks that followed, the calendar held us to something every day. The county fair, more company coming was all sandwiched between constant irrigating, ripening berries, silage making and family reunions. The Wallowa County Fair began Aug. 4 and I spent that day receiving and displaying the 4-H photography exhibit.

August 5—Horticulture division entries are being accepted this morning in Cloverleaf Hall. On my way out the door to the fair, I picked some zucchini, dug a few of my red potatoes, and cut some pink cosmos to enter.

August 10—Because my husband gives me such a bad time about my prolific zucchini, I was thrilled to receive a blue ribbon on them. Then it was the Sourdough Shutterbugs' turn to work in the food booth. I was thankful that daughter-in-law Liza and daughter Jackie showed up to help supervise while I took a break and shepherded the grandchildren around the fair. Two-year-old James was fascinated with the pigs, so we spent a good deal of time in the hog barn.

Parents, 4-H leaders, FFA advisors, townspeople and others volunteered for everything needed, and as usual the fair was a great success.

This weekend was also the Tippett family reunion in Clarkston, Washington. It began as a picnic at Chief Timothy Park, where we met daughter Lori, her husband, Tom, and children Lacey Jo and Ryan, who had driven from Thermopolis, Wyoming, and would be spending the next three weeks visiting us.

At Asotin's Gateway Inn on Saturday night, some of the Tippett boys branded the walls with electric branding irons. The next morning, we all met for breakfast at Jack and Blanche's lovely home that overlooks the Snake River. Very relaxing and delicious breakfast was served by members of the Jack Tippett family. Then it was back to the park again for a barbecue and swimming. Each year the direct descendants of Jidge Tippett meet and socialize, which is a good tradition and worth the effort.

On Sunday, I visited the Alpowai Interpretive Center at Chief Timothy Park, where I watched a slide show on the history of the area. I learned that the Snake River area had been inhabited for some 10,000 years by Indians, and after the first whites to visit the area (Lewis and Clark), trappers, missionaries, miners, farmers and ranchers began moving onto these lands and the natives began to see the end of their way of life.

Also, I was to learn that by the late 1880s a small town named Silcott had been built there at the junction of Alpowai Creek and the Snake River, on the exact spot as the former Nez Perce village. The town had a short history, however, and by the 1920s gradually disappeared.

And now, on that August Sunday, hundreds of people were swimming, boating and picnicking at Chief Timothy Park, but I was the only visitor, save two others, to the Interpretive Center, to learn of the rich history of the country's past. To me this is sad, because it is only from history that we will be able to successfully go forward.

Meanwhile, back in Wallowa County, the fair was far from over, and my 4-H'ers were again responsible for photographing the market animals for the buyers' cards to be given out at the fat stock auction. Mary Ann was enlisted in this project, which she entered into with the usual good sportsmanship. She worked well with the kids and, between all of us, we got the job done.

We had quite a time, as usual, with the hogs, until Mary Ann came up with the idea to put grain in their enclosure. So while they "pigged out" and their owners held a ribbon over the hogs' backs, we snapped the shutter. It worked like a charm.

Grandson Chad had the grand champion market steer and Rowdy the champion Dorset ewe. Even Chelsie competed in the peewee show-manship class...I am a proud grandma! The theme of this year's fair was "Bounty on parade." The bounty not only included produce, livestock and baked goods, but the youthful exhibitors, who continue to be our country's most valuable resource.

The fair ended with a fat stock auction, cow chip lottery and a beef pit barbecue put on by the FFA.

August 13—I began my day early with a stockgrowers' breakfast at the VFW Hall in Enterprise, where I took notes and photos for news articles. It was nearly noon when I drove to Wallowa to attend the CowBelles' annual luncheon meeting, which was held at the IOOF Hall. The Rebekahs, dressed in denim skirts and red blouses, served a great lunch. Outside they had barbecued beef kabobs, which were delicious.

In a way, the meeting was an end of one era, and the beginning of another, because that day it was voted to change the name from CowBelles to Wallowa County CattleWomen. It seemed especially fitting that the first CowBelle president, Berniece Arnhart, was present for the meeting.

On the way home, I noticed a sign in front of the Salt Shaker restaurant: "Immaculate housekeepers are dull women." The last glimpse I'd had of my house assured me that there was no danger of me ever becoming dull.

Doug, being the latest victim of the "Wyoming flu" that had been making the rounds of our family since relatives had arrived with it, was unable to attend the Stockgrowers' barbecue and dance that night at Cloverleaf Hall. I stayed until the presentation of the Grassman and Cattleman Of The Year awards, took my photos, and went home shortly thereafter. It had been a long day.

August 18—40 degrees. There is a feeling of fall in the air already, which is such a relief from the oppressive heat. Our Wyoming bunch has headed home; the last night they were here, I slept in the sheepherder wagon with granddaughter Lacey. I read her stories by candlelight until she went to sleep.

August 19—Friday evening get-together tonight at Reid and Marilyn Johnson's in Wallowa, in the midst of a terrific summer storm; the wind blew, lightning zig-zagged across the hot sky, thunder rolled off the mountains, and we all worried about fires in our dry forests.

August 20—After our company left around noon, Doug and I decided to take the motor home and get away for a day. We had often talked about visiting the early-day mining town of Cornucopia in Baker County.

By 1:30 we had quickly loaded the motor home and were on the road. As we headed up Salt Creek summit, the tensions of our busy summer slowly drained away. Driving down Gumboot, we surprised a yearling black bear standing at the edge of the road, feeding on thimble berries that were abundant in the area. As we drove off, the little fellow jumped into the creek, stood up on his hind legs and waved his paws at us!

We crossed the upper Imnaha near Ollokot campground, and halfway to Halfway we stopped to pick ripe huckleberries for tomorrow morning's sourdough pancakes. We entered peaceful Pine Valley with its green meadows, weathered barns, and no traffic. Leaving the small town of Halfway, we drove the final 12 miles on a gravel road that followed Pine Creek to Cornucopia. As we climbed up that steep, narrow road, we could look down and see the present-day mining activity going on below us in the creek.

Despite a rather irritating sound that had developed somewhere under our motor home, we made it safely to a camping spot. Cornucopia, steeped in history as the site of the largest gold strike in Oregon, is still a colorful place. It was after 6 p.m. and the sun had gone down behind the steep mountain ridge to the west before I was able to start cooking dumplings to go with the leftover chicken. Later, we sat around the campfire and let the silence seep into our bones, before sleeping the sleep of the exhausted.

August 21—We awoke to a beautiful morning near the old ghost, gold town of Cornucopia. There was a "fallish" chill in the air as we cooked sourdough huckleberry pancakes outside, which made them taste even better. We spent the day relaxing and hiking around with friends who had joined us.

On the way home we stopped to pick more huckleberries that grew along side the road. Refreshed, I dove into the house-cleaning, getting ready for the next company. Must have frosted while we were gone; the green beans got nipped. Spent quite a bit of time organizing our 4-H club's annual trek to Red's Horse Ranch next week. The heat became intense as day after day of hot dry conditions prevailed.

We invited friends for supper and were eating outside on the picnic table when sister Caroline and husband, Duane, drove in. Plenty of food and we enjoyed a great meal and good conversation. On the eastern horizon we watched the billowing smoke of a forest fire on the Idaho side of Hell's Canyon.

August 25—Ate breakfast on the picnic table. I fixed blueberry muffins, using freshly picked blueberries given to us by Duane, who had brought them from the Oregon coast. Also cooked zucchini omelets and fried pork chops! Summer company is fun; normally, we wouldn't have fixed such a breakfast, much less eaten outside.

August 26—Our annual trek with the 4-H'ers has arrived. We arose at 4:30 a.m., gathered our backpacks and readied ourselves to hike into the Wallowa Horse Ranch (formerly Red's Horse Ranch) in the Minam Wilderness. Sister Caroline and her husband, Duane, accompanied our 4-H excursion this year.

After driving to Cove, then up a narrow gravel road to Moss Springs, our jumping off place, it was around 9 a.m. when we hit the trail. The trail drops 1,000 feet in elevation in eight miles. A few withered Indian paintbrush plants remained along the dusty trail, and we could look into the hazy distance and see the far reaches of the headwaters of the Little Minam country.

My younger sister, Caroline, unused to the altitude, not to mention my vigorous lifestyle, was making the hike just fine. Marsha Svendsen, OSU Extension secretary and mother to one of my 4-H'ers, was also along. The trip was a first for all of them, including a new crop of 4-H'ers. Duane acted like a seasoned hiker and seemed to enjoy the walk, which was a far cry from his office work job.

Approaching the shady coolness of the Little Minam River, we noticed the first huckleberry bushes, and hidden among the leaves were plump, purple berries! Walking along in filtered shade and sunlight, we came upon more bushes and simply loaded with fruit, more than any of us had ever seen. The children ate as they hiked, but Marsha, Caroline and I really slowed down. We couldn't walk 10 feet without stopping to pick. Soon we were filling every empty container we could find in our packs.

After crossing a wooden bridge that spans the Little Minam, the trail forks one way to Jim White Ridge, the other to the Horse Ranch along the Minam River. Here we rested and competed with a swarm of yellow jackets for the contents of our lunches. Several bow hunters, packing in on horseback, rode by.

It was a relief to see the ranch sprawled out below us when we at last reached the hog's back and rested before the steep, switch-back descent. It had been a long, hot eight miles. We were greeted on the porch by Feryl Laney, the cook, who welcomed us with a glass of cold tea. We relaxed and then, because it was so hot, we all changed into our bathing suits and cooled off in the fresh, clear waters of the Minam River, which flows in front of the rustic log cabins. Felt good to wash off that trail dust and let our tired feet revitalize themselves.

Later we rolled our sleeping bags out on tarps provided by wrangler Mike Nooy. Because the weather was so warm, we decided to sleep outside on the grassy river bank. We were joined in the dining room by a group of people flown in by Russell Elmer of Cove. And what a supper: Oriental chicken, rice, coleslaw, homemade hot rolls, green beans, freshly baked cake, and cold fresh cow's milk. "Laney" says she loves to cook and it surely shows.

Colorful petunias bloomed in outside window boxes and a cool evening breeze fluttered the gingham curtains. The serenity of the place was savored by all. We slept out under the stars and fell asleep listening to the murmur of the Minam as it rolled along beside us. Because of moonlight, starlight was dimmed, and around 3 a.m. I awoke to see not one star! Then I smelled the smoke. The sky was filled with a dense haze that had drifted up the canyon from a fire threatening the small settlement of Troy on the Grande Ronde River.

By 5:30 I was up, joining "Laney" in the big kitchen where she was stirring up a batch of hotcakes with our huckleberries. More people flew in for breakfast with the latest fire reports. Mike milked the Guernsey cow, which supplied fresh cream for our sliced breakfast peaches. An eerie calm settled in the canyon and we all felt a bit uneasy, because the forests around were tinder dry. We helped Laney make our lunches before taking a walk down to the Minam Lodge and then dropped down over a bank to a remembered swimmin' hole.

The day had warmed and we were soon splashing and swimming in the cool, refreshing waters of the Minam. At first, it seemed breathlessly cold, but after the initial plunge it was pure heaven. Once we heard a splashing noise and looked to see a large spawning salmon fighting its way through some riffles. On the opposite bank, in a depression, we saw the remains of a deer and bear sign. Mike had mentioned that there were several bear in the vicinity.

We ate our lunches on a sandy beach before walking back to the ranch. The children and Marsha had ridden horses, so they went back to where they were tied to a hitching rack. When the dinner gong sounded that evening, we were treated to another of Laney's delicious meals: roast beef, mashed potatoes, gravy, zucchini casserole, topped off with a banana split dessert, sprinkled with more of our huckleberries.

Marsha and I obtained permission to sleep in an abandoned log cabin, which had been inhabited many years ago by Red Higgins' Chinese cook. Legend has it that Sing Lee haunts the cabin and nearby pond, and I wanted to meet the ghost. So Marsha and I settled down in our sleeping bags, which we laid out on two old dusty bunk beds. We left the door ajar to let fresh air come into the cabin. The ghost? Well, guess you'll just have to wait until next issue of Agri-Times to find out.

August 26, continued—Now, about that ghost that supposedly haunts the old log cabin at the Horse Ranch...

Upon entering the dusty, cobweb-strewn cabin for the night, a large toad hopped upon the doorstep. "Hop Sing" reincarnated? Well, we could handle a toad better than a ghost.

I held a small pinch flashlight in my hand as I crawled into my sleeping bag. The night was hot and the voices of the children faded away. The blood-red moon pulsed in an eerie, smoke-filled sky. All was still until, around midnight, the open door creaked, groaned and slowly closed! I squeezed my little flashlight and listened. No wind, not even the slightest breeze! The ghost? I listened again, asking my ears to please hear a wind, any wind, that would explain the slow closing of the heavy, old wooden door.

The cabin, built of chinked logs, had a roof made of hand-hewn shakes that extended over the doorway. The other cabins sported new tin roofs, but this abandoned one had been left in its original rustic state. Marsha awoke, whereupon we both began to laugh, but somehow I felt like a presence had entered the cabin. After an hour or so, we drifted back to sleep. The cabin felt close and warm and musty-smelling; creepy spiders hid in dusty corners.

All of a sudden, Marsha awoke with a start, as "something" scritched and scratched in the rafters above her head. Again I directed the small beam of light to the spot, but whatever it was had disappeared into the night via the small, partially opened window. We laughed again and wondered if something was "drooling under the bed."

We survived the night and I awoke at graylight, dressed quietly, and made my way across the meadow-cow pasture through dew-laden grass to climb the rail fence and walk into the dimly lit dining room to write notes on my nightly experience. The cook, "Laney," was beginning her day with breakfast preparations in the kitchen.

Later, the rest of the crew arose and we listened to a two-way radio in the kitchen. Conversations with bow hunters and guides. Such talk. The wilderness communication was more entertaining than a real radio. A fiery red sun rose over the canyon wall through a pink layer of smoke, and a heron lit in a tree next to a young sharp-shinned hawk.

After another terrific breakfast of freshly-baked cherry-filled sweet rolls, potato pancakes, eggs, fried apples and sausage, milk and orange juice, we shouldered our packs and headed up the winding trail to the hog's back, carrying with us wonderful memories that will gladden our hearts in years to come. As we hiked out that long, hot trail, the eight miles to Moss Springs, we wondered about the forest fires. We arrived safely by 2 p.m.

August 30—This has certainly been a berry, beary, busy summer! In fact, I've been calling it the summer of the B's: bees, wasps, yellow jackets, hornets, what have you. Then there have been berries, such berries: our high country loaded with huckleberries, elderberries, thimble berries, grouse whortle berries and on and on. And I suppose because of those luscious berries there have been bears, one of whom got too friendly with a woman who was scouting around on Ferguson Ridge with her dog.

B also stands for burn. The Tepee Butte Fire continues to rage to the north of us here on Prairie Creek. I must apologize for not getting my column out in recent weeks, but between back-to-back company, continual irrigation chores, county fairs, CattleWomen meets, berries, back-packing, 4-H'ers and more company, and now the fires, this writer has been somewhat overwhelmed and has had to, of necessity, establish new priorities and finally, whew, end this sentence—sorry.

Day after day of hot, dry conditions prevail. Smoke fills the valley and all we pray for is rain. Again, Mother Nature started the fires and she alone can extinguish them. Right now fire dominates our lives. Already several local ranchers have lost their ranges, cow camps, fences and corrals to the fires. Most of the fire area lies within the vast National Recreation Area, and therefore the main concern to ranchers is losing valuable fall and winter range.

August 31—Although our mornings begin to cool, the days continue frightfully hot and the sun bears down with a renewed vengeance. The Tepee Butte fire still burns, smoke from its massive backfires lingering all over the county. On the plus side, alfalfa hay crops are the best we've seen in years and local gardens have outdone themselves. I even raised enough cucumbers for a batch of dill pickles.

September 1—The big, yellow school bus just rumbled by here on Tenderfoot Valley Road this morning and a fall chill is in the air. However, there is the promise of a dry, scorching hot day ahead and already the thermometer under the clothesline is escalating. We ranchers who have grassy summer ranges in the Pine Creek, Zumwalt, Salmon Creek, Butte Creek and Chesnimnus country to the north are all anxious about predicted thunder and lightning storms. Conditions are such that another lightning storm could set these lands afire.

Farther north, near Cold Springs Ridge, vast areas are already blackened and the Cold Springs cow camp is no more. Doug and son Steve left a few days ago to help protect the Jim Creek Ranch, private land owned by Doug's brother, Biden, which lies along the Snake River. The house and buildings are situated about two miles from the Oregon side of the Snake. Of concern also to them is the Lime Kiln Fire, which originated in Washington but crossed State Line Creek and roared its way into Oregon. It has since been 90 percent contained and held at bay at Cache Creek. Conditions continually change, but at the moment, they seem to be holding their own.

As the sun climbs higher on this first day of September, it burns with an intense heat. From where I write, on the picnic table outside on our lawn, I can see the murky, smoke-filled horizon and smell the smoke wafting into the valley on a slight breeze. By the time I finish the final typing of this column, the mountains are obscured by a filmy, smoky haze. It is a sad time for Wallowa County, but it will change, just as it always has, and like the seasons, roll on into eternity. Meanwhile, life must go on, as it always has.

On the positive side, the second and third cuttings of hay are going up beautifully. The harvest is in full gear and most of our valley is blessed with water, that most valuable resource, lacking in other parts of the drought-stricken Northwest. Our pastures are green and the seed potatoes look great, all because of irrigation water.

Wallowa Lake's water level lowers each day and the major rivers and creeks continue to run and supply water for our valuable agricultural lands, fertile lands that are the very lifeblood of Wallowa County's economy. If it were not for agriculture (timber, livestock raising and farming), the area would indeed be depressed.

The tourist season is nearly over and they will soon "fold their tents like the Arabs" and "As silently steal away" after Labor Day. Already it is quiet at Wallowa Lake State Park. School has begun and the voices of children are gone. The family vacationer has returned to wherever. Our tourist season is short and frantic, and due to geographic isolation and cold winter climate, the remaining nine months will be relatively calm.

Now is the time to make apple sauce, bake transparent apple pies, freeze and can green beans, make pickles, put food by for the long winter, and fill the woodshed with seasoned tamarack. The last of our company has left, having taken rolls of film and stored away memories that will last a lifetime. It was fun hearing them rave about the fresh garden vegetables, about gathering eggs from under the pullets, watching them enjoy the silence on Prairie Creek and become attuned to ranch life.

That way it is good for us, too, so we won't lose our sense of "place" and take our good life for granted. For with all its trials and tribulations, our rural lives are the best there is. I suppose that is the reason we of this diminishing agricultural community are struggling so very hard to preserve that quality of life that is so dear to us.

Perhaps the example we set for the "outside" world as far as family values, traditions, and wholesome living are concerned, can in some positive way affect a better living for the future of America.

September 2—The sun rose like a fiery red ball, looking more like the moon. Extremely hot, dry day, with the sun bearing down without mercy. No rain in sight. We decided on the spur of the moment to go camping at Ollokot campground on the upper Imnaha over the Labor Day weekend. Smoke continues to fill the sky over the entire county. Never have we seen the forests so dry. We camped in the motor home that night and were joined the next day by son Todd and his family plus two more grandchildren.

September 3—Doug and I up early to drive up on McGraw to do some grouse hunting. We watched the eerie red sunrise over the Seven Devils Mountains in Idaho, and with it returned the intense heat. After Doug bagged a brush pheasant (ruffed grouse) and a blue grouse, we returned to camp and fixed breakfast. The yellow jackets were so bad Doug made a trap, using the fresh grouse entrails for bait. It worked and we soon had a bucket full of drowned bees. The children fished while we rested and tried to escape the heat, but the worry of fire never left us. We cooked a big dinner that evening and enjoyed eating outside after sundown, so the bees would leave us alone. As we left the next day to return to the valley, six ruffed grouse crossed the road in front of us and I was able to follow them into the woods and shoot a few.

Back at the ranch we discovered hornets' nests under the pump house eaves, on the sheepherder wagon, and two by the chicken house. The sunflowers remain confused; unable to find the sun in the smoke-filled sky, they don't know which way to turn.

September 4—The fire "On Top" continues to burn and will for days. A back burn has been relatively successful, but due to extreme dry conditions, can become complicated by the daily winds that materialize each afternoon.

The situation remains critical on the Tepee Butte Fire, which was reportedly the result of a lightning strike somewhere in the vicinity of Rock Creek. It quickly spread to the surrounding wilderness and consumed the Cold Springs cow camp. This place held many fond memories for the Tippett family because it was one of their summer cow camps, and Doug can remember in his youth staying in the old house that used to stand beneath the road near a spring. Once he showed me where his name was carved in the porch railing.

It is all memories now for Biden and Betty Tippett, who spent many falls in this log cow camp. For during these times of the fall gather, it was home. Now it becomes history and they will be among those who will always remember how it was.

On Monday, Doug and Steve rode horseback and led the pack mule Maud down Downey Saddle to the Jim Creek Ranch, after spending some time putting out a spot fire on a high ridge above the ranch. In fact they slept that night in bedrolls on Downey Saddle to keep watch on the spot fires. Doug reports seeing the blood-red moon rise, while high above them, on the ridge top, the burning trees glowed and crackled in that fiery wilderness.

Meanwhile, here at the ranch on Prairie Creek, my sister Caroline, her husband, Duane, and I watched that same fiery, red, waning moon appear over the dry eastern hill. We tried to envision the firefighters, some 80 miles north, watching this red moon—the fire moon.

Biden Tippett and son, Casey, along with Biden's son-in-law, Wayne Bronson, are spending days down on the Jim Creek Ranch to protect their holdings, which are the last bit of deeded land left on the Oregon side of the Snake, having been surrounded by "instant wilderness"—the National Recreation Area (NRA).

The men were able to doze a fire break around the buildings with a cat they hauled down that winding, steep canyon road. They watched and stood guard, wondering about the billowing smoke from above, as the back-burning and firefighting continued. They also wondered, having no communication, about the status of the so-called Lime Kiln fire, which raced its way toward them along the Snake. Surrounded by acres of dry grass, the situation was explosive.

As of this writing, much of Biden Tippett's winter range has been lost to the fire, and a very valuable resource of winter and fall range has been lost by other ranchers in that vast forested area in the Hells Canyon NRA. Elk have heavily grazed the grass around the Jim Creek Ranch; therefore, the grass isn't as high as it would be normally.

The elk seem to prefer grazed-over forage to rank grasses that are not allowed to be grazed by livestock. Ranching on the Snake is tough enough without having to contend with elk and the fire too.

September 5—Labor Day. The sun rose, wearing the same blood red color it wore last evening at sunset. Smoke from the Tepee Butte fire, now under control, lingers. Made several calls to neighbors Ardis Klages and Alice Rosser to PLEASE come and pick up vegetables from my prolific garden. They gladly obliged. After picking up windfalls from under our apple tree, I made a batch of apple sauce before driving to the Enterprise Livestock Auction where we CattleWomen served a steak dinner with all the trimmings to more than 300 people.

Cattle prices were up and everyone was in a good mood at our traditional Labor Day Feeder Sale.

September 6—The air is clear again. No smoke! It is wonderful to see our mountains and breathe fresh air.

September 7—Seated at my kitchen table, the typewriter opposite me, which patiently holds a blank sheet of paper, which, in turn, waits for some words of wisdom, I suddenly realize summer is all but gone! Since I last wrote, Oregon's largest forest fire has been contained.

This fire, known as the Tepee Butte blaze, has ravaged nearly 60,000 acres of our Wallowa-Whitman National Forest and Hells Canyon National Recreation Area lands. Beneath those cold, impersonal statistics lies the "rest of the story," much of which will never be completely told, or assessed, in losses to local ranchers.

That giant fire, which swept in an easterly course, finally halted on the rocky shores of the Snake River, somewhere near Eureka Bar. Owing to heroic efforts by Biden Tippett's family, the Jim Creek ranch buildings were spared. Unfortunately, the log cabin, two sheep sheds, several outbuildings and the fences at Cherry Creek were destroyed when 40 mile an hour winds gusted during nine percent humidity.

To many of us, although the property is now owned by the U.S. Forest Service, Cherry Creek was a special "place in the heart." I remember going down there with a load of corn in the fall, riding along in the Grain Growers delivery truck, when each year the Cherry Creek Sheep Company would feed its ewes the corn to "flush" them prior to breeding.

I remember seeing that old log cabin, which had been home to Joe and Marge Onaindia, and Gus and Juana Malaxa, those wonderful Basque friends who owned and managed one of the best sheep outfits in Wallowa County. As we climbed back up that steep, winding road coming out of Cherry Creek, on that perfect Indian summer day so long ago, I stopped to take a snapshot of the scene below. In those days I didn't own a 35 mm camera, just a simple Kodak Instamatic.

I can still see the scene, even though I've given the photo away to several people, one of whom later purchased the Cherry Creek Sheep Company. (Somewhere I have that negative, but where?)

Anyway, back to the scene, one I'll never forget: the log cabin, out-buildings in that peaceful setting miles from civilization, no power lines leading to it, lying amid canyon country whose hillsides were covered with the golden brown grasses of autumn, while in the draws shouted the brilliant red sumac.

The scene was one of infinite beauty, the colors of Indian summer all blended together like a watercolor painting. The photo, although not professional, looked like a painting. It was alive with color. I hope I can find the negative. It is estimated the cost of suppressing the fire will be $3.5 million. The Cherry Creek "place in the heart" has no dollar figure. The loss is not calculated in dollars! And those of us who remember how it was are sad.

Mother Nature has a way of healing fire scars, and perhaps come next spring, the area will, I hope, look somewhat better. Spring is eternal, and so is fall. And speaking of fall, that "feeling" is in the air this morning. A few real clouds appeared in a blue sky. The smoke is gone and again the sun lights up pink peaks instead of endless miles of thick, smoky haze. Suddenly, our world appears brighter, and Indian summer is just around the corner.

For me, Indian summer is a time when the ancestral urge to gather and store food for the winter conflicts with my wanderlust soul. Should I stay home and can green beans, make sauerkraut? Or strike out over the nearest hill and follow the wild goose? I am always torn which way to go. What to do? So I do both, and everything else that happens on our busy ranch and in our busy community. Consequently my days are so very full that at day's end I fade at 9 p.m., and the book I plan to write never gets started. Anyway, I am "living" and that, after all, is what life is for! To write, they say, one must first live.

Late June seems only yesterday when Doug and I took cattle rancher relatives Chuck and Sue Mehrten out to the Buckhorn Overlook. That day was such a disappointment, nothing to see from the lookout but a

Hells Canyon Mule Days chairman Max Walker, of Enterprise, has worked hard through the years to make the event what it has become today.

wall of smoke and mist. And now, two months later, country north of the old road to Eureka Bar is charred by the monster Tepee Butte fire.

Thinking back to that June day, driving out the Zumwalt Road towards Buckhorn, we glimpsed 83-year-old Mike McFetridge wearing his yellow slicker, riding for cattle on Hinkley's range, as he disappeared into the misty woods near Thomason Meadows. We drove past the lonely, deserted remains of the Zumwalt schoolhouse and later passed the old building known as Midway, an early-day stage stop between Enterprise and Imnaha.

Huge black clouds formed over the Wallowas and a freak storm swept off Ruby Peak. Later we learned that cyclonic winds and golf ball-size hailstones did severe damage to Alder Slope homes and crops. The next day, we drove up on the Slope and viewed the damage. Grasses lay over fences, hay was beaten into the ground, gardens plastered.

Everything was steamy, like being in a hot-house. That had been the start of an unreal summer. July and August went by so quickly it now seems only a dream. So much couldn't have happened in two months, but daily entries in my journal say it did.

September 9—My children and grandchildren treated me to a birthday luncheon at the "Country Place on Pete's Pond."

September 10—Mule Days began with the traditional parade. I enjoyed making the acquaintance of old hand Emory Crawford while watching the arena events on Sunday. The largest crowd ever came to watch all types of mules and their owners perform. Mule skinners and fanciers from many states converged on the small town of Enterprise to participate in this event, which started with modest beginnings. Two very deserving Wallowa County natives served as grand marshals at this year's of Hell's Canyon Mule Days. They were old-timers Mary Marks and Joe McClaran.

September 13—On the surface, the scene here on this lovely September day would seem to be one of tranquility. A gentle breeze stirs pretty pink cosmos near the front door, while other flowers growing away from the house show the effects of a recent frost. The button weed is attacking the vegetable garden, but the cabbage has won. Huge heads nestle inside gigantic pale green leaves, oblivious to the first frosts. Tops of squash vines are blackened, but yellow crookneck and bright green zucchini bravely mature.

The mornings have lately been devoid of frost and the days have warmed to summer-time temperatures. The golden sunflowers tower over all. Doug measured the tallest ones and found them to be 11 feet. Their heads turned toward the sun until they became too heavy to do so.

The green beans look sad and the cucumbers even sadder. Onions, carrots, beets and chard continue to thrive, despite the weeds. The red potatoes have grown so large I can stack them like cordwood! In the chicken pen Chester looks pretty rough. Guess the long, hot, dry summer plus those Rhode Island Red pullets nearly wore him out. But there is hope for his recovery. Luther Fitch, Umatilla County extension agent, called this morning and happened to mention that he has just the perfect little black banty hen (with a brood of chicks) and wouldn't Chester like a wife his size and breed?

I walked out in the cow pasture yesterday and visited Star. This grand old Holstein matron didn't breed back last year and is receiving a much-earned rest. She is fat and sleek and, except for some bothersome flies, has everything a contented cow could want: Shade, grass, fresh water, salt and the company of her daughter Startch and her brood of four calves.

Because my summer schedule has been so hectic, I turned Startch out with her calves back in July. It frees me to do more work, but we sure miss that fresh milk. The two Guernsey milk cows, Daisy and May, are down in the lower field, each raising two calves.

Doug, Ben and Steve are readying the potato cellar in preparation for the seed potato harvest, which is due to start on the 26th. The frost has killed the vines and so far conditions have been favorable for a good crop this fall.

Meanwhile, the kitchen table reflects my busy lifestyle. In the middle of all sits the typewriter; to the left, cooling on a rack, reposes a fragrant loaf of sourdough bread. Near the bread stands a large gallon jar of freshly made garlic dill pickles. Stacked on either side of the typewriter are proof sheets and black and white negatives, waiting for cutlines and/or articles to accompany them. This stack grows daily.

Occupying more space, waiting patiently, are minutes of a recent 4-H leaders' meeting, ready to be typed. A small vase filled with tiny, blue wildflowers cheers me, and next to that a large basket full of stick'em notes stick to each other and multiply, reminding me to "Bake enough sourdough bread (for 150 people) on Saturday." I am catering a wedding for Pam Bolen and Tom Wolf at the Edelweiss Inn at Wallowa Lake.

Other scribbled notes: attend grandson Buck's first soccer game, 5:30, Joseph Park; deliver garden vegetables to friends (so they won't go to waste); start sweet pickles; can pickled beets; mix sourdough; call people to help with Saturday. Other notes remind me to pick up beef on Friday; pick up smoked turkeys; "REST"!!!; write my column; call 4-H'ers.

And, so you see, the scene of tranquility is deceiving.

This afternoon the bride and groom-to-be arrived to pick up decorations for the log building where the wedding reception dinner will be held. They had helpers, nice young people who loaded a pickup with some of our bleached cattle skulls, wagon wheels, milk cans, lanterns, and geraniums and lobelia growing in granite-ware pots. They also picked four of those 11-foot sunflowers to decorate the hall.

So this is the scene here on Prairie Creek today: "Mule Days" have come and gone and last Saturday saw the first dusting of snow in our high country. Jack Frost arrived next morning and nipped the garden as fall made its first appearance. Now the days have warmed and it feels like Indian summer is already here.

The 75th annual Oregon Cattlemen's convention will be under way in Baker when you read this. I had so wanted to get together a group of ranchers and ride horseback through the mountains to Baker, but none, including myself, has the time to spare. It was just a dream, but I thought it would be a fitting way to commemorate this anniversary of the cattlemen's convention, especially because the very first one was held in Baker 75 years ago.

The Pendleton Round-Up begins this week and I have yet to attend one. Always too many conflicting events. However, my appaloosa mare Cal will pull a hack, driven by old hand Herb Owens, in the big parade. Then the next day she will pull a surrey that will transport the newlyweds, Pam and Tom Wolfe, to the dinner reception at the Edelweiss Inn. This mare is versatile: a cow horse, a pack horse and, when called upon, a buggy horse. She is also a good friend.

September 14—We managed to save the garden during the first killing frost by running a sprinkler all night. Although the vegetables were sheathed in ice the next morning, they were safe and once more the temperatures returned to the 70s. For some time I had been in on the planning of a big wedding for Pam and Tom, a delightful young couple who I have promised to help with their big day. This morning they showed up with friends to load two pickups full of props for the wedding reception, which will be at the Edelweiss Inn at Wallowa Lake. This rustic old log structure, earlier known as the white elephant chalet, has seen much history and was about to see a unique wedding reception. I was letting the couple borrow some of our wagon wheels, cattle skulls, single trees, milk cans, four of my 11-foot sunflowers, the blue lobelia that spills out of granite ware pots, and deer horns.

In the kitchen I was busy baking sourdough bread to freeze ahead for the reception. Those young people got a whiff of that freshly-baked bread and there went most of a loaf!

September 15—Around 2:30 this morning, I heard a coyote on the neighboring hill singing a love song to our cow dog Stubby, or at least I took it to be a love song, because "Stub" answered with such a heart felt howl! A link from the wild to our civilized world, which seems closely related in Wallowa County. Presently, however, Doug jumped out of bed and the reverie was broken with "Shut up, Stub," whereupon all was quiet once more. The phone rang off the hook with potato workers wanting to know when they could start work in the cellar or on the digger. My wedding helpers received last minute instructions and in between all of this I somehow managed to write my column.

September 16—Scotty appeared to help make a huge potato and pasta salad. I completed last minute planning and grocery shopping, and felt confident that all was in readiness for tomorrow's big day.

September 17—Cold, but two large fires blazed in the old Edelweiss Inn's stone fireplaces. On one table reposed the two cakes, one a chocolate-lover's delight groom's cake, the other the beautiful wedding cake, covered with small lily of the valley frosting flowers. On another table were no less than 15 huckleberry pies baked by the bride's aunt. Meanwhile, down the road came the surrey (with the fringe on the top) and pastel-colored balloons bobbing alongside. My mare Cal and one of Herb Owen's horses proudly pulled this handsome rig and Herb held the reins.

The bride, dressed in an old-fashioned, off-white, cutwork gown, on the arm of the handsome groom, stepped out of the surrey and walked up the wooden steps into the log building. My sunflowers and lobelia decorated the porch entrance. Inside the warm fires crackled and the wagon wheels and other Western decor filled the hall. A huge basketful of green and purple grapes added just the right touch as a centerpiece to all the food being laid out. Meanwhile, in the kitchen my crew and I dealt with smoked turkey, salads and bread, while outside, Doug got ready to unearth the buried dutch ovens full of marinated beef.

Rain mixed with snow began to fall on Tom Swanson, who faithfully tended the corn on the cob, each ear roasted in its husk and served up in a huge basket with butter. Earlier I had enlisted another guest to churn butter, which was molded into the shape of a cow. Never have wedding guests had so much fun. Pat Combes mixed my recipe for ice cream and soon the wedding guests were turning six ice-cream freezers. There was music by Sara Miller and Mike Hale. Earlier Sara had played the mountain dulcimer during the ceremony, which was held at the outdoor chapel at the lake. Later, a Western band arrived and guests ate and then danced.

I shall never forget the sight of the lovely bride, looking radiant, at seeing her dreams come true. Pam had planned this affair down to the minutest detail and others, along with myself, had carried the thing off. The bridesmaids looked like something out of an oil painting, lined up along the wall in their colorful dresses, watching the bride and groom dance. The old log walls reverberated with merriment and the fireplaces gave forth a cheery heat. That evening represented months of planning, but that one moment was worth it all!

Small tropical fish swam in bowls that were placed on the tables to honor the groom, who is an avid fisherman. Tom also works as a white water guide on such rivers as the Salmon River in Idaho. Pam is a manager of an REI store in Denver. Her grandparents, the Rameys, have a cabin at Wallowa Lake and because Pam has always loved it there, she decided this was where they would get married. The Wolfs spent their honeymoon in our county and one night we had them out to the ranch for supper.

Grand marshals of the Hells Canyon Mule Days at Enterprise were cattle-man Joe McClaran and cattlewoman and mule fancier Mary Marks, both from the Wallowa County community of Imnaha. Driving the hack is Max Walker, who was chairman of the event.

Riders mounted on mules compete in the team-roping event at Mule Days. Entries from all over the Northwest and from as far away as Colorado converged on Wallowa County for Mule Days. A mule and horse auction was included.

October 19—Here it is the middle of October already and, even as I write, precious time marches on toward winter. And the days dwindle down...But what an Indian summer we are having!

Day after day of mild, beautiful weather; golden days that enable farmers to harvest their crops and put up second and third cuttings of hay. Our seed potato harvest seemed like a piece of cake, compared to other years.

Monday evening, at precisely 5:30, our big, red potato digger made its final trip down the last row. For those of us riding that monster machine it was a relief, to say the least. We all agreed that we could stand that job for a while, but full time would be the pits.

As the sun disappeared behind Ruby Peak on that Monday evening, a sharper chill settled over Prairie Creek. The next morning our thermometer registered 26 degrees and there was a heavy frost. Our entire crop was safely stored in the cellar before the cold hit. Between the potato harvest, moving cattle, putting food by for the winter, attending 4-H, CattleWomen and other community meetings, and being a full-time grandma and ma, my fall has been full. Most ranch wives would agree that it's a great life, if you can keep up.

Despite the weeds, my garden continued to produce, and two crocks of sauerkraut are fermenting in the basement. The tangy, sour kraut smell mingles with the odor of yellow "keeping" onions stored there also. Boxes of cooking and eating apples are there along with freshly-dug red potatoes.

Last week, I pulled all the carrots and beets. Pickled beets add their deep, ruby color to the canning cupboard shelves and will zest up winter meals. One lone sunflower stands tall in the vacant garden along with a large head of cabbage (for future coleslaw). Our mule Maud got into the garden one night and feasted on corn stalks and carrot tops. Come morning, she had a very full tummy.

It rained last night, nearly a quarter of an inch of welcome moisture that freshened the dry earth. No frost this morning. Long trails of mist follow the Wallowas and lovely, purple-gray clouds move slowly across the autumn sky. Slanted rays of October sunlight brighten golden tamarack that lace the evergreen slopes on the mountains.

Down in the canyons it is a blaze of red sumac, which rivals the golden cottonwood and trembling aspen for color. It is truly a beautiful time. Our summer was most eventful and looking back on that time, I wonder how so much could have possibly happened in this remote, quiet, peaceful valley.

A young writer, attending the Fishtrap Writers Conference at Wallowa Lake, makes friends with a mule deer buck still in velvet.

October 26—The full harvest moon lit up the valley last night. It sailed on waves of Halloween-like clouds and shed its bright light on the many elk camps scattered over the Wallowa country.

This morning, the loud reports of rifle shots will pierce the stillness of our otherwise quiet outback. Our vast forests and the Zumwalt hills will be alive with hunters. It is opening of general Rocky Mountain bull elk season, as well as the first Zumwalt cow hunt. My husband is among the permit holders who left in the pre-dawn hours to head for the hills. Hopefully, by nightfall he'll return with some winter meat.

I had put in for an Alder Slope antlerless permit, and that first hunt opened last week. Many elk stories later, after trudging many miles carrying a rifle up and down the forested slopes of Ruby Peak in search of the wily Wapiti, my final story does not include what you'd call a successful hunt in bagging my elk.

These stories do, however, describe being out in those perfect October days, smelling the pine and resin-scented trees, seeing a huge six-point mule deer buck, neck swollen in the rut, and numerous does and healthy fawns—and one two-point BULL elk! They tell about arising from the womb of sleep at 5 a.m. morning after morning, waiting under a pine tree for enough daylight to see by.

They do include meeting my Alder Slope neighbors and swapping elk stories, about the ones that got away and how one fellow filled his tag in his own field. This grandma was either at the wrong place at the right time or vice versa. What I did have was loads of free advice from my sons and grandson.

Probably the best idea offered was the one son Todd came up with. Perhaps if I'd followed through with his plan, I'd have meat in the freezer by now. Somehow, the idea of jumping out of a moving vehicle into a ditch, to stay curled up in the cold, dawn hours for daylight, didn't appeal to me. Call me chicken Jane...or maybe if I'd been a few years younger.

Our gorgeous blue and gold Indian summer goes on and on. I drove into our hometown of Joseph (population 1,125) yesterday and noted some of the familiar seasonal changes taking place. Everywhere a feeling of positiveness and friendliness. The huge old maple trees that line the south end of Main Street are turning to burnished gold, the sidewalk beneath carpeted with beautiful leaves.

The Baptist church (formerly Walter Brennan's Movie Theater) is undergoing a facelift, as have the Chief Joseph Hotel and Gold Room. A pile of bright, clean bales of straw were stacked in the parking lot of Jerry's Mainstreet Market for sale to elk hunters. Across the street in the front window of Kohlhepp's Kitchen, a large orange and black sign reads: "Happy Halloween."

Colorful hanging baskets of blooming flowers still grace the entrance to Donna Butterfield's Art Angle framing shop. And up the street at Bud's True Value Hardware, sales of hunting gear are brisk. Along with the purchase of ammunition, coffee pots or gloves, goes advice to the elk hunter. "Go up high, weather has been mild, they'll be up on the mountain."

Next customer might hear: "They're all in the canyons, have to go down low for 'em."

A local chimes in, "Saw 150 head, bulls, cows and calves, in the hills day before yesterday."

Then someone from Alder Slope comes in and reports as how someone shot an elk in the neighbor's field last week. Elk are where you find them. And you are apt to find them most anywhere this year. Especially because the fire has changed much of their habitat, and they've been bow and arrowed, and cow hunted since August.

One thing for sure, there are lots of them. More elk than the total human population of the entire county. Down Main Street Joseph the hunters drive by, a steady stream of them, in all manner of rigs. Some driving elaborate motor homes, towing jeeps, many with horses and mules riding in gooseneck trailers, pickups piled high with gear.

They all share a common bond. They come to hunt, but also they come for the chance to escape the rigors of modern living. If they bag an elk they consider it a bonus. They are all in a good mood and it is obvious they have waited all year for this special time. Lately, our phone has rung off its hook; hunters asking permission to hunt our hill lands. If only half of them show up, there will be an army of them out there today.

On Monday, Mike McFetridge, Ben and I moved the fall calvers and their calves off the moraine and trailed them to Hockett's hayed-over alfalfa field on Tenderfoot Valley Road. We began riding at 8 a.m. and remained in the saddle until nearly 4 p.m. Those cows were scattered all over the lakeside hill. We got ourselves into some pretty hairy spots chasing cows out of the steep, brushy hillside where they had gone to water. It was already noon by the time we got the herd going down the east side of the moraine and out onto the road.

It was another of those flawless Indian summer days and the sight of those cows and calves trailing past the old rodeo bucking chutes near several golden aspen trees and Chief Joseph Mountain rising up to meet a cobalt sky was really something. Eighty-three-year-old Mike McFetridge riding his red roan gelding completed the scene. It more than compensated for the hard riding we had just experienced.

The cows were reluctant to leave. It wasn't winter yet, and there was still feed. However, it was time. A big snow can come any day now, and then we would have our hands full. So this is Prairie Creek on this 26th day of October, and now let's return to my hurriedly scratched notes of this summer and attempt to catch up where I left off last time.

November 2—Scattered raindrops, borne on a blustery wind, spatter the windowpanes as I write. Early this morning, before a layer of mist obscured the mountains, we noticed a new snowfall on the highest peaks. It is, after all, November. Last week we finished branding all the fall calves; some of them were pretty husky little fellows. The fall color has peaked, and after the storm, most of the pretty leaves will have been wafted away in the wind.

Last weekend Scotty and I decided to hike up the Chief Joseph Trail and bid goodbye, so to speak, to October. It was a gorgeous day and as we climbed higher, we gazed down upon the autumnal color that bordered Wallowa Lake. Our destination was a high alpine meadow that lay under the rugged, bare summits of Chief Joseph Mountain.

Soon, we could look across at Mt. Howard and eastward to far-reaching horizons that stretched forever beyond the Seven Devils Mountains in Idaho. Paths of ancient glaciers carved enormous canyons writing their story on the terrain. One such glacier, moving slowly over the ages, had scooped out what is now Wallowa Lake and left two nearly perfect moraines on the western and eastern shores.

Presently we crossed the West Fork of the Wallowa River on a wooden bridge erected high above the water. Soon the sound of thundering waterfalls reached our ears and we crossed, just under the falls on another wooden bridge, the cascading waters of B.C. Creek. It appeared that we were the only souls using this beautiful trail that morning.

Far below, splashing and cavorting on the surface of the lake, swam thousands of migrating mallard ducks. What fun they were having. The waters of the placid lake were so still, yellow aspen trees cast perfect, golden reflections, as did the east moraine, where, just last week, while riding for cattle, I had made up my mind to hike to this high meadow.

We reached that very spot around 11 and selected an old, weathered log on which to eat our lunches. I had looked up to this spot in summer to see a brilliant green carpet, then again, in winter, to see it covered with a deep layer of snow. As I write, the grasses are frosted with the season's first dusting of snow. This opening, high on the timbered slopes of the mountain, has always held a fascination for me. It was rewarding to have made the effort to climb there.

Approaching winter makes itself felt in many ways. One morning last week, on my way to town, I looked up to see a great flock of wild geese flying against the sunlit clouds. The different elk seasons roll on, in stages. This weekend the Chesnimnus bull hunters have at it. Many wild hunting tales are circulating and some of them are true.

One pretty afternoon I took two-year-old grandson James up to the lake for a promised outing. Two mule deer does stuck their heads through the car windows and James fed them an apple. Later we walked along the shores of deserted Wallowa Lake, and James was delighted at all the wild waterfowl. Personally I think fall is the most beautiful time of all at this lake, when the summer tourists have gone.

In Joseph, on the way home, we stopped at Kohlhepp's Kitchen and enjoyed strawberry ice cream cones. Halloween has come and gone. A lighted pumpkin in the front widow guided the young ghosts and goblins who came for "trick or treat." The only ones making it out this far in the country were the grandchildren, and I had made orange-frosted cupcakes for them.

One bright morning, Grace Bartlett and I drove to Imnaha to purchase winter squash and walnuts. While there we visited several friends along the river. The day was warm and the cottonwoods along Little Sheep Creek were very colorful. Clouds floated above rimrocks and brilliant red sumac marched up the draws.

A recent frost had blackened A.L. Duckett's marigolds, and as we talked with this grand old gentleman, we marveled at the food he was putting away for the winter. His canning cupboard shelves were filled with sauerkraut, pickles, peaches, apricots, apple butter and ground cherry preserves. A.L., at 90-plus, is an artist when it comes to most anything.

On the way down we had stopped to give some leftover Halloween cupcakes to two of Bill Bailey's cowboys, Bill Matthews and Skip Royes, who really appreciated the unexpected treat. They were trailing a bunch of cows down the road along Little Sheep Creek. Daughter Ramona, son-in-law Charley, and their family recently moved back to Wallowa County. It is just great having more grandchildren and children closer to home.

I have acquired a new puppy, a border collie cross named "Freckles." And now we are going through the throes of puppyhood. The whole bit. This little bundle of black and white fur terrorizes cats, drags dried horse manure to the front door, pulls jeans off the line and nips at my heels when I go outside. I'd forgotten how much boundless energy a puppy has. But they are such positive little creatures and they look at the world in a fresh, inquisitive way, like children do. Puppies and children make you happy.

November 9—The snowline has been creeping closer, and this morning it is here. I forgot to bring the potted geranium in while we were in Portland attending the quarterly Cattlemen's and annual CattleWomen's meetings; it looks pretty sad!

Last Wednesday Doug and I took the midnight to 4 a.m. shift at the elk hunters hay station, located in the Minam canyon. This station is manned by Wallowa County Stock-growers, U.S. Forest Service and State Fish and Wildlife. The purpose is to stop the hauling in of outside hay, in an effort to control noxious weeds—such as ragwort.

In the past, hunters entered our county with their horses and pack mules, bringing hay with them from other areas. Weed seed from this hay was scattered all over the hunting camp areas and contributed to the spread of noxious weeds. A terrific rain and wind storm preceded us, as we relieved Prairie Creek rancher-neighbors Rex Ziegler and Willie Locke shortly after midnight. All night long hunters pulled in to purchase local hay and straw. If they brought their own, it was taken and later burned, and replaced with local hay.

As a whole, the hunters were congenial and cooperative. We served them coffee, kept hot on an old wood-burning stove. I worked throughout the night, correcting my column, and by 4 a.m. my eyes could barely function. Finally, Van and Betty Van Blaricom arrived to take our places. Doug and I drove home and tried to sleep, but the phone and demands of the ranch kept that from happening.

It was pouring rain when we drove through the Minam Canyon on our way to Portland on Sunday. The countryside around Elgin was accentuated by numerous, red nine-bark bushes that contrasted with the pastoral colors of green winter wheat, brown plowed fields and golden stubblefields.

The Columbia Gorge's fall colors were brightened by the recent rain. And as we drove on into a brilliant "Westering" sunset, hundreds of waterfowl bobbed on the wavelets of the Columbia River. Although our visit to Portland was brief, we did feel it was worthwhile.

This morning, as I sit at the typewriter pounding out articles about those meetings, our just-weaned spring calves are bawling up their own storm down in the corrals. Their mammas, still pastured out on fall range, are out of hearing distance.

And...the election is finally over, thank goodness!

November 15—The spicy aroma of apple butter fills my kitchen. Making apple butter is fun, and a delicious way to use up all those apples left in the fall. I use an old-fashioned recipe that requires long, slow cooking, and my crockpot works well for this. After 12 hours or so, the butter is ready to can. I seem to be giving as much of it away as gets canned, but that is fun too.

The weaned calves have ceased their bawling and settled down to eat. The four calves on the two Guernsey milk cows have been weaned, and the cows turned in with "Startch," whose calves have also been taken from her, with the exception of her own heifer calf. So, after a summer of rest? I am once again milking Startch when I need house milk. The rest of the time her own calf does the milking, which is a convenient arrangement.

But when I go out to the barn now, a familiar bovine face is missing! Star, the grand old matriarch of numerous offspring, not to mention a "herd" of adopted calves, is gone. She was sent to market some time ago. No longer will she have to suffer rheumatism during the long, cold winter, but I shall miss her; and if there be a cow heaven, perhaps she has already taken her place among the stars.

Although winter hasn't, as yet, made its official appearance, according to our calendar, it would seem to be here in Wallowa County. It was a chilly 12 degrees this morning.

Last Thursday, neighbor Ardis Klages and my daughter Ramona rode with me to attend our monthly CattleWomen's meeting at Becky Wolfe's cozy little country home near Wallowa. It was cold and windy, but as we drove down to Becky's the sun came out, lighting, up the fall colors, which were still very bright in the lower valley. Cattle grazed the open, grass meadows and well-kept ranches lay scattered about. Wolfe's large ranching operation is tidy and is situated in a lovely rural setting. Becky, her husband, Gordon, and their two children live on the ranch, as do Gordon's parents, Edna June and Wayne Wolfe.

November 22—There is a temporary lull in the howling winds that hurl themselves down across Prairie Creek. The fury of the storms is really felt here, as there is an open expanse for the moving air to escape and nothing to break the relentless force we know as the Prairie Creek wind. I have just returned from the canyons of the Imnaha and it's like coming from another world down there.

Brilliant golden-yellow leaves still cling to cottonwoods and drift downstream on the waters of Little Sheep Creek. New green grass is beginning to appear due to recent rain, and way high on the rims, there is a dusting of snow. I had lunch with daughter Jackie and then we went for a walk.

Later, we drove to the school and picked up the children. Because the lower grades were studying Native American culture, they were busy painting beads. Tepees and stretched paper hides on willow sticks decorated the classroom. Teacher's aide Pat Stein and parent helper Anne Borgerding were supervising the younger grades in this project, while school marm Char Williams taught the older grades in the next room. Rancher-wife-school bus driver Barbara Warnock waited in the school van to take the children home.

The snow has mostly melted here on the ranch, but more snow is in the forecast for Thanksgiving. The snowline at the moment begins near Max Gorsline's place.

The new puppy is my constant shadow when I go to the barn. Then she pushes her chubby self through a crack in the barn door and waits for me to squirt milk in the kitty dish, whereupon she competes with the cats, lapping up the warm milk with loud slurps.

Ben and Steve feed the cows and fall calves silage on the hill. The weaned spring calves are eating grain and hay and have settled down to a routine, as have the young bulls in their pen. Although we still have cows in the hills, where there is still feed, the long winter of feeding has begun.

Last Thursday night Doug and I attended a donkey basketball game at the high school gym in Enterprise. Put on by the school support group to raise money for a playground, it was a riot! My oldest daughter and son, plus son-in-law Charley played on the school support team, which competed with town, Forest Service and faculty teams.

When the children were growing up we always had burros around and most of them were ridden frequently. Now, years later I watched my grownup offspring play, or attempt to play, basketball on them. Because these animals have no withers, once in a while a donkey would put down his head and a surprised player would ungracefully slide off over two large ears.

The donkeys wouldn't lead and baskets had to be made from their backs. If a player retrieved the ball, his donkey must accompany him. After much hilarity and confusion, a few baskets were actually made. The donkeys wore rubber shoes as as not to mar the polished gym floor. Youngsters who had the job of "pooper scoopers" luckily didn't have to perform their duty, as the donkeys were extremely well-mannered. All team members were required to wear hard hats for obvious reasons.

The weather of late has been stormy, which is good. The moisture we so desperately needed is welcome and a good snow pack is already forming in the mountains.

Yesterday I purchased a new cookbook, *Cookies and Conversation*, written by Judy Wandschneider and published by her husband, Rich, who owns Pika Press in Enterprise. It is a delightful book in that it is like a personal visit with the author. Judy tells a little story at the beginning of every recipe, and when you finish the book, you know Judy as well as all of her many friends who also have contributed to the book in the way of illustrations.

Most of the recipes, which have been developed over the years by Judy, contain tasty, nutritious baked treats, like honey, raisin bread pudding. This homey, old-fashioned dessert sounded so yummy I came directly home and made it. As it came fragrant from the oven an hour later, I thought it was a delicious way to combine all those country ingredients we always have on hand: fresh eggs, milk, whole wheat bread and honey. I baked the pudding on one of Ted Juve's handmade pottery deep-dish pie plates, which added the touch that Judy herself suggested in the recipe.

November 23—*When the m-m-m-moon shines over the cow shed, I'll be waiting at the k-k-k-kitchen door. Oh K,K,K, Katy, beautiful Katy.*
Words from that old familiar song went through my head this morning when such a moon shone over my cow shed. Glowing softly, only a few hours away from the full moon, the "Beaver Moon" hung suspended over the snow-covered mountains. Washed and hung our flannel sheets on the line, whereupon they immediately froze solid.
Walked out our lane to get the paper tonight and the full moon brightened the landscape clear as day. Even the sky around the moon was a cold blue, with white clouds hovering nearby. Moonbeams glanced off the snow under foot, and the air was fresh and cold, and it was the night before Thanksgiving.

November 24—It is 13 degrees as Thanksgiving day dawns in a pink sky. The sunlight soon spilled down on Prairie Creek and temporarily melted the clouds hanging around the mountains.
Spent all morning baking pies: mincemeat, apple, pumpkin and raspberry. Around noon Doug and I loaded the warm pies into the car and left for daughter Ramona's, where we would have our Thanksgiving meal this year. Children were everywhere…grandchildren, ranging in age from 10 months to 18 years, from diapers to college. The little cousins were buzzin' like bees. One of life's greatest satisfactions is watching one's children's children grow up, without having the full responsibility of raising them. Lucky are those children who receive that steadfast, constant love which is meted out unconditionally by grandparents.
The house smelled of Thanksgiving as a huge, golden brown turkey, overflowing with dressing, roasted in the oven. Daughter Jackie was baking whole wheat rolls. As usual everyone ate until they were miserable. Aunt Molly and I did the dishes to justify eating so much, then had room for pie! I am sure we were all thinking about how much we have to be thankful for, especially thankful, it would seem, for our large, happy family. That is, after all, what life is all about.

November 25—Yesterday morning reversed. Instead of 13 degrees, it is 31. Typical of Wallowa County. Spent the morning making inroads on the accumulated dust of country living. By noon the house was beginning to look somewhat better.

As cold weather settles in, and the pace slows down, I find time to curl up with a book. What a joy it is to read. And what wonderful books are available to us, if we only take the time to search and dig them out. I have just finished Theodora Stanwell Fletcher's *Driftwood Valley,* a book I read years ago. Now I'm into Ivan Doig's *This House of Sky,* which is a fine example of contemporary western writing.

November 26—We are fixing breakfast on the wood cookstove again, listening to sausage sizzle in a cast iron frypan, breaking fresh eggs to cook sunnyside up, popping the shells into the fire. Yes, winter has its advantages.

It was snowing heavily when I went out to chore this morning. I couldn't escape it even in the barn, as the fine snow sifted through cracks in the door. Snow blew onto the barn cats, while they waited patiently for their bowl of warm milk. Little mini-blizzards swept across Prairie Creek all day.

Aunt Molly, Ramona and the children came over this morning and I baked a batch of Highland oat scones in the woodstove oven for them. The scones were a hit with the grandchildren and the platter was licked clean.

November 27—Seven degrees! Bundled up to milk my cow, then took a hot teakettle of water to thaw out the chicken's water. While the men hauled several loads of newly purchased calves to the ranch, I made a batch of whole wheat cinnamon rolls.

More bawling again, as more than 100 head wail for *maaaaa-ma* and more snow fell during the night.

November 30—A clear, bright 10-degree morning as I went out to chore and milk the cow. The new calves were still bawling out in the feedlot. Each day grows shorter now; by 3:30 the sun has slid down behind the cold Wallowas, and that familiar, bitter chill steals in for the night.

On Monday night, Doug, Steve and I attended a computer class at the Enterprise High School. Steve, who has had college classes, whizzed through just fine, but Doug and I have decided we are definitely not of the computer generation. The young fellow who taught the class knew the ins and outs of the machines and made it look easy. However, trying to absorb that much information into our minds... well, it just didn't compute!

Storing cattle records on disks would be nice, but if such a machine were to be purchased, one would have to be able to press the right button or it would all be a loss. Then there is the danger that the computer might win! Like a friend told about. After purchasing one, he said, "I worked all through the night on the thing, and by morning I was reduced to a puddle on the floor at monster's feet!"

December 1—10 degrees and a frosty fog enveloped Prairie Creek. Thick hoarfrost transformed the willows, weeds and grasses into works of winter art.

Walking out to chore, I kept thinking about the "hands on" class in computers and decided it takes "hands on" to break ice for the cattle to drink, "hands on" to milk the cow, fork her hay; and so much of a successful operation depends on the hired "hand" who tends the livestock; one who cares about their daily condition and sees what needs to be done to improve upon or possibly avert a problem by thinking on his feet. We may live in an age of unending paper work, but the fact remains it is cowboy who faithfully tends the cattle, in all kinds of weather, on a day-to-day basis that makes or breaks the operation. One of the reasons many large operations fail is simply because they have lost that personal contact that family-run operations have. The computer is a tool, but that tool can be only as successful as the man in the field doing the work. Records on paper are sometimes deceiving and conditions may be entirely different in the corral.

Thick hoarfrost covered the tips of Startch's black winter coat. Signed up my 4-H club for another year. Thirty members again.

December 2—A rosy-hued sunrise welcomed a new day. I watched it from the chicken's pen while feeding and packing water to them. The thermometer under the clothesline read nine degrees, but it was such a busy day I didn't notice the cold.

Spent the day picking up a Santa Claus suit at the Fire Department and selling beef gift certificates for the CattleWomen at the Bank of Wallowa County in Joseph. From there to Cloverleaf Hall to meet "Santa" (Jim Blankenship) and give him his clothes!

My 4-H'ers appeared on schedule to take photos of children sitting on Santa's lap. This is our annual money-raising event. Again Cloverleaf Hall was transformed into a holiday bazaar. Homemade fudge, quilts, soap, wooden reindeer, aprons, potholders, hand-knitted sweaters, fragrant fir bough wreaths tied with pretty ribbon, and all manner of hand-crafted items. Out in the kitchen, the Imnaha Grange ladies served up home-made soup, chili, sandwiches and delectable pies.

At 7 p.m. we closed shop after a very successful picture-taking session.

December 3—Today is the opening of the second season of the antlerless Alder Slope controlled elk hunt. So it was out of bed at 5:30 to go the Slope, where I met son Todd, who drove me in his pickup and before sunrise, until we spotted the herd. Just as the sun lit up Ruby Peak on that clear morning, my dry cow elk lay dying in a stubblefield.

I had mixed feelings about shooting her then, though I know the herd must be thinned down. The area can't support those numbers. Depredation to stored winter hay is just one of the problems, but it bothered me, seeing that beautiful animal there and knowing she wouldn't live to see another Alder Slope day.

Later, after the meat was hung, the feeling passed and we now look forward to some excellent winter meat. Late choring that morning, then into Enterprise to pick up the Santa photos and return to Cloverleaf to hand them out to those who had purchased them.

For supper we enjoyed fried elk heart, potatoes, biscuits and gravy. A stick-to-the-ribs meal for a cold winter night.

After chores the next morning, some friends and I decided to check out the cross-country skiing on upper Alder Slope. We abandoned the skiing, but did hike up to the old black marble quarry, where the snow was quite deep. It was an invigorating hike on a lovely, clear day.

From the waterfall we could see the valley spread out below like a large relief map, colored in shades of December. The sun slipped behind the tallest peak before 2 p.m. and the air turned bitterly cold.

We were able to stay relatively warm, because we practically ran back down the steep road. Numerous snowshoe rabbit, elk and deer trails criss-crossed in front of us and led off into the woods.

After a hot shower I donned a dress, and Doug and I attended the County Chamber of Commerce annual banquet, held this year at the Wallowa Lake Lodge. We enjoyed a great meal, served up by chef Horst Meyer and his kitchen staff. The rustic lodge still retains its old-time charm and a cheery fire crackled in the massive stone fireplace.

Inside the dining room, the tables were set with cloth placemats and colorful green napkins. Long tables held steaming soup, freshly-baked rolls, three kinds of salads; an adjoining table held the entrees. Such delectables! Then, if you had room left, there was yet another table covered with pumpkin and apple pies.

Annual community service awards were given and door prizes won by those lucky enough to have a colored dot under their placemats. Several of us came home with a pretty basketful of Christmas goodies.

December 5—Up early again, doing chores, so as to leave by 8 a.m. with a car full of CattleWomen to help serve breakfast at the Wolfe Ranch sale in Wallowa. We had a great time and all went smoothly, thanks to head chefs Bryan Wolfe and Jack Coleman. I just imagine, in the background, Bryan's wife, Lou Ann, had a lot to do with the planning.

We served more than 300 people hot biscuits, ham, hash browns and gravy. At 12:30 Bill Lefty began his sing-song chant, and 125 bulls and 350 females were sold to the highest bidder.

Home to catch up on the ranch. This evening, my two daughters, several grandchildren and I attended the Eugene Ballet performance of "The Nutcracker." That's Wallowa County! One minute you are at a cattle sale, and the next attending the ballet!

The live performance was given at the Enterprise High School gym, the only place big enough to put on such a production. The tickets were sold out before the doors opened.

December 6—What a week we've had! No sooner had Thanksgiving marched off the calendar than, in rapid-fire succession, the days held us to so many events, was hard to keep track.

Stopped to look at the calendar and realized that, at this rate, it will soon be Christmas. The pace, lately, resembles that of August.

December 9—Everything encased in ice, after an all-night storm of freezing rain followed by fog. Doing chores, slipping on frozen cow pies kept me alert! Let's warm up a bit and return to late summer.

December 13—The wind blows out of the north and the temperature is over 40 degrees this morning! Our cows, which have been left in the hills, are on their slow way into Prairie Creek. Yesterday Ben and Doug, with much difficulty, rounded up the spring calvers and headed them toward the valley. It was late last evening when they finally corraled them for the night at Circle M.

Due to an unseasonable thaw, the back roads have no "bottom" and the cattle had pretty tough going. Doug reports the good news that melting snows have penetrated the dry hill land. There is still plenty of dry feed and we have been supplementing with protein blocks, but one of these days it will snow again and freeze; then it wouldn't be too pleasant trailing cattle in a blizzard. It will take lots of stored hay and silage to sustain these pregnant cows through the winter, not to mention the man-hours to feed them.

Have enjoyed being busy writing Christmas letters to far-away relatives and friends. Unlike our children, who have their Christmas decorations up, we haven't. Maybe this weekend we can go hunting for just the right tree. We cut and wrapped the front quarters and loin of my cow elk for the freezer. Our cats and the puppy are feasting on the scraps.

Last Thursday, daughter Ramona and I attended the CattleWomen's annual Christmas party-meeting at Marian Birkmaier's Walker Lane home. Such a variety of yummy snack foods, and we exchanged gifts. My contribution was a freshly baked loaf of sourdough bread, which Rhea Lathrop took home.

Marian's house was decorated for the holidays and we enjoyed the view out her windows of the snowy mountains that rise abruptly beyond the town of Joseph. Birkmaier cattle grazed the stubblefield in the foreground.

December 14—The snow began with a fine sifting in the wind, then grew to soft, downy flakes, until the frozen earth lay hidden under a white coverlet. Much better weather for feeding cattle. We finished cutting and wrapping my elk tonight.

December 15—One below zero in our frozen, silent world! Had breakfast dishes and chores over with before sunup. What a sight, the morning sunlight streaming through frosted willows.

Baked a blueberry-huckleberry cake. Doug to the hills to check on things at Salmon Creek, back with a pretty, little fir tree from the woods. Placed the angel on the treetop, then fixed supper before we drove to Imnaha to attend the school Christmas program.

A brightly-lit Christmas tree and students' drawings covered the walls in the two-room schoolhouse. First through eighth grades, prompted by teacher Char Williams and aide Pat Stein, staged an around-the-world Christmas pageant. The room overflowed with proud parents, grandparents, uncles and aunts. They watched a series of skits that portrayed Christmas customs from Hawaii to Germany.

As usual, the children were adorable and each scene change was accomplished simply by tearing off a large sheet of butcher paper, which revealed an appropriate backdrop. Soon a hush fell over the children and Santa Claus came bustling down the aisle with a bagful of treats for them. Near the tree, a long table, laden with traditional Christmas treats from around the world, tempted us all.

December 16—Zero degrees again as a beautiful, clear day dawned. December's sharp cold seems to paint mountain peaks in a deeper shade of pink than at any other time of year. The violet morning sky resembles a Christmas card scene.

Spent the day on Alder Slope tending grandchildren while their moms drove to Lewiston to meet granddaughter Tammy's plane. She will be spending the holidays with her family. The children and I spent a lot of time reading books and playing with two-year-olds' toys! I did manage to bake a loaf of sourdough bread to take to a dinner party that night.

After the mothers returned safely with Tammy, Doug and I attended the dinner at Melvin and Mary Lou Brink's lovely ranch home. Christmas seems to be the one time of year we neighbors ever take time to visit. We all had such a great time, and wondered why we don't get together more often.

December 17—Two below zero, with winter not officially here yet. Put a big kettle of clam chowder to simmer on the woodstove before driving to town to pick up a VCR, so we could view a video of the "Wallowa Story." Carlton Conkey and his fiancee, Dorothy, from Walla Walla, drove over with the video, which is in its final stage of production. Carlton has been trying to complete the project before Christmas.

I served the clam chowder, after which our committee viewed the "Story" and approved, with a few minor changes. Hopefully now the video will soon be available to anyone wishing to purchase one. Proceeds will benefit the Wallowa County Museum.

That night we met with cattlemen and cattlewomen friends at Mack and Marian Birkmaier's Walker Lane home. 'Tis the season to be jolly. Earlier in the evening I attended a cantata at the Baptist Church in Enterprise, where I was joined by an entire pewful of grandchildren! Daughter Jackie's voice mingled with the others as they sang songs of praise and Christmas joy.

December 18—The days grow even shorter and cattle feeding becomes routine. We enjoyed a roast beef supper with daughter Ramona and her family this evening.

December 19—Cloudy and warmer as a storm approaches from the coast. Doug delivered six bags of potatoes to the Elks' Christmas basket program this morning, then purchased more calves at the livestock auction. I sent off the last Christmas cards, put a stewing hen to cook on the woodstove, and made gingerbread cookies to hang on the tree.

The haunted cabin on the left is located inside the rail fence that encloses the cow pasture, where a milk cow grazes in the morning light. The Minam River flows in front of the cabins. Photo by Duane Rueb.

This evening, daughter Ramona and granddaughters Tammy and Carrie joined me at an old-fashioned "Village Christmas" in our small town of Joseph. Main Street glittered with cheery lights and merchants kept their doors open until 9 p.m. for the Christmas shoppers. It was fun walking from shop to shop and I was able to purchase gifts for everyone left on my list.

We found colorful posters at the Art Angle, collectibles at Harshman's Country Store, saddle blankets at Bud's Hardware, and mittens at Soft Winds apparel; then treated ourselves to a piece of homemade fudge at Eagle Mt. Gallery. At the Sports Corral I found just the right size wranglers and outfits for my small cowboys and cowgirls.

Shopping was relaxed, the selection very good, and the proprietors in the Christmas spirit.

December 20—Gingerbread boys decorate the Christmas tree; outside the window, it is 13 degrees with snow in the forecast. The predicted snow didn't materialize and by nightfall all the clouds had disappeared; the wind died and a moon-washed stillness flooded over Prairie Creek. The mountains fairly glowed in moonlight.

It is the time of long nights and short days, and Christmas is only five days away.

December 21—The Winter Solstice begins, and it snowed during the night. It is hard to get up in the mornings now. Instead, I am wont to burrow like a hibernating animal; but, once I'm up fixing breakfast on the wood stove and out in the cold to milk the cow and tend the livestock, I am back to normal.

Did some last minute shopping for Christmas dinner and made a batch of peanut brittle to give for gifts.

December 22—Eighteen degrees, partly cloudy, and bitterly cold and windy. Stinging particles of dry snow blew in my face as I chored. Snow "smoke" swirled across roof tops of barns and sheds. A cold day for Steve and Ben, who are down at the chutes worming cattle.

We had several friends over for dinner tonight. Baked Doug's large steelhead in the oven; made sourdough bread sticks, a large tossed salad and a "from scratch" lemon pie. We enjoyed the meal and friendship by candlelight.

December 23—More snow fell during the night. Baked Christmas stollens, which are German fruit-nut yeast breads, to give away for Christmas gifts. Intermittent snow showers and sunlight; at one point it was snowing through sunshine! Diamonds and crystals sparkled in the air!

Feeling a little housebound, my puppy and I went for a walk around the ranch. Everywhere lay calendar winter scenes, especially along the creek: frozen waterfalls, open patches of water, ice panes resembling broken glass piled along the banks, and tracks of small, wild creatures criss-cross and tell stories in the snow.

A glorious full moon rose tonight. I watched it grow through the Christmas tree lights outside our picture window. A celestial ornament! Glowing softly from afar…until a thin, dark horizontal-shaped cloud covered the bottom half. Moon glow lit up the clouds after it disappeared into a solid cloud bank.

December 24—A brilliant star shines in the east! I watched it out the kitchen window as all the other stars faded from the morning sky.

Finished my Christmas baking, loaded it all into the car and played Santa Claus, delivering gifts to friends and relatives. I always look forward to stopping long enough at each home to visit.

Doug and I spend a quiet Christmas Eve alone, opening our gifts and enjoying the night. Snowing softly outside, cozy and warm inside. Oh Holy Night! Peace be with the world tonight!

December 25—Still snowing and very cold. Out to give the animals their Christmas breakfast.

Began preparations for Christmas dinner for 17. Prime rib roasting slowly in the oven, raspberry pie baked by 9 o'clock. Yeast rolls rising, two salads made, and peeling potatoes when the first family arrived.

Soon our house was overflowing with children, grandchildren, and the cheery voices of Christmas! When everyone was seated son-in-law Bill said the blessing. It is always somewhat emotionally overwhelming to have one's family around, all healthy safe and close. We have so much to be thankful for. The little cousins growing up so fast; soon they will have families of their own.

After everyone left and the house restored to a reasonable semblance of order, I relaxed and contemplated Christmas. Christmas is what we make it. I have decided not to get into a frenzy over the season anymore and that makes the whole experience more worthwhile. True, it does take a lot of planning, but many things, not really necessary, can be dropped. The important thing is to enjoy family and friends and not lose sight of the true meaning of Christmas.

December 26—Six below zero this morning. We could tell last night it would be colder this morning. That certain "feel" was in the air. Hard to keep warm while choring. The sky is cobalt blue and brilliant sunshine floods across freshly fallen snow.

Took another winter walk today, down the county road, then turned up a back road to Echo Canyon. At the top of the hill, I cut across Hough's field and came to Locke's and Hough's irrigation ditch. I heard a loud crack, followed by another. Looking into the ditch, I saw strips of ice on both sides of the open water.

As it warmed under the sun's rays, the water caused little wisps of steam to waver over the water's surface. The contracting and releasing created patterns along the crystal-strewn edges of ice. Little amoeba-like movements grew and shrank under the ice, as the melting and thawing took place. By sundown the freezing would resume and soon the entire ditch would be frozen over.

My puppy found a coyote's track, so we followed its trail, which wandered hither and yon. We saw where it sniffed a mouse in a snow tunnel, explored a squirrel's den, wriggled under a fence, then drank from the ditch, before exploring more, and finally heading up hill to a rock pile where we lost its tracks. The air was freezing cold, but my blood was warmed by the walk. By 3 the winter sun had disappeared behind the cold Wallowas.

December 27—A wind blew away a gray day and my chores were lessened; my milk cow Startch is now officially dry. As life's tempo slows, I actually find time to file recipes, work on photograph album, and embroider blocks on the state flower quilt. Winter pastimes.

We had Ben, his wife, Jackie, and their children over for dinner during the holidays. It was nice to visit and get to know their family better.

December 28—The temperature hovered around zero, and when the sun rose over a brilliant white world, I decided it was time to go skiing. Taking two of my older grandchildren with me, we drove to the nearby Ferguson Ridge Ski area, only 15 minutes from our ranch. The snow was perfect and the exercise great.

December 29—The temperature dipped to three below and then the skies clouded and a freezing wind began to blow. Felt sorry for the animals, all huddled up against the stinging cold. The carpenters who are constructing Imnaha's first church called. They are beginning the bell tower and need the bell that Doug has restored for the church.

More snow, adding to what was already on the ground. My 4-H Sourdough Shutterbugs enjoyed their annual ice skating party on Boucher's frozen pond. The Prairie Creek wind roared on into the night.

December 30—We listened to a weather report on our local KWVR radio station and learned that the season's worst storm had missed us. Mountain passes were blocked by heavy snowfall and blizzard conditions on all sides, but for some reason Wallowa County was spared. All traffic was stopped in Baker and Pendleton. Travel through the Blues was halted, as was access to La Grande. Oblivious to stormy conditions elsewhere, Wallowa County proceeded as usual, except when a neighbor or relative called saying they were stranded somewhere. A few locals barely got through before the roads were closed, and listening to their stories made us glad we stayed put in the valley.

Only a slight breeze blew that morning and it was 20 degrees when Doug delivered the bell to Imnaha, ringing it loudly as he left the ranch in the pickup. Went skiing again, meeting the grandchildren on the slopes. Great snow-laden clouds moved slowly across the sky, and the air was pure and fresh.

It was snowing lightly that night as Doug and I drove to meet family for dinner at the newly renovated Wallowa Lake Lodge. A blazing fire in the rock fireplace was comforting as we walked in to the lodge and waited to be seated in the dining room. Soon we were enjoying some of chef Horst Meyer's excellent cuisine amid the rustic surroundings of the historic lodge.

December 31—10 degrees, no wind in a cloudy sky that threatened more snow.

Baked a ham, rolls and raisin cream pie, and invited Prairie Creek neighbors Max and Dorothy Gorsline over for dinner. Later, we stacked the dishes in the sink and retreated to the living room, where I showed slides of our past mountain trips. Once again we relived those adventuresome pack trips to McCully Creek basin and other scenic camps.

Without a drop of alcohol, we managed to have a relaxing evening, visiting until 11:30, at which time our company left, having exhausted their tall tales about people, deceased or still living, who lived, or live, in our valley. Such characters they were, and are, ourselves included. As the old year left us, we "old fogies" called it a day…er night, and wished everyone a happy new year.

*Doug and Janie Tippett pan for gold at Doty's Ravine in the Sierra foothills.
The can on the fire? Hobo coffee.*

1989

January 1—On this New Year's Day, our porch thermometer registered a balmy 20 degrees. Blue patches in a cloudy sky as I went out to feed the animals their New Year's breakfast. Took down the old calendar and printed, in red, birthdays and anniversaries to remember on the new one. It got sunnier and prettier as the day progressed, so by afternoon I Was headed to the ski area to meet friends for some cross-country skiing.

We followed a recently completed ski trail into the woods and up a steep ridge. It proved to be a real workout, but worth every herringbone stride, because at the top we were treated to a breathtaking view of the valley below. We had skied to the top of the ski run!

But how were we to get down off that mountain? You guessed it: telemark skiers we weren't, we simply took off our light skis and walked, until we found a lower trail that led into the woods again. The snowy woods sparkled in sunlight and we sometimes fell in the soft snow as we glissaded, not so gracefully, down the hill.

January 2—After chores and watching the Rose parade on TV, I couldn't wait to hit the ski slopes again, this time riding the T-bar with my friend Ruby Zollman. About 15 years ago, several of us "over 40" gals decided to take up skiing. Of that group, very few continue to pursue the sport. Those of us who still stick with it are much more cautious than our younger counterparts, but we have just as much fun.

Returned to the ranch to bake an apple crisp for a potato meeting Doug had scheduled here.

January 3—Weather warmer today, and then the fog rolled in. Granddaughter Tammy was stranded in Seattle, her flight to Sacramento having been canceled. Luckily, another flight left for San Francisco and she rode with some people to Davis, and made it to her college by 7 the next morning to register for winter term. We all put in some anxious moments until she arrived safely.

Dismantled the Christmas tree, and put away the decorations that make the season jolly. Now the house looks dull and lifeless. Attended a

4-H leaders' meeting at the Cloud 9 Bakery in Enterprise at noon. We planned another busy year, one that will be in full swing before we know it. Time waits for no one. We are already into 1989 and the new year has begun!

January 7—After doing chores, I picked up one of my older grand-sons, Shawn, and we went skiing up on "Fergie," an affectionate short-ening of the name Ferguson Ridge Ski area. It was a lovely day and the view at the top of the T-bar lift breathtaking. The air was crisp-cold and the snow perfect. We had a great day of skiing before I returned to pack for a two weeks' vacation, as we will plan to stay with relatives in California during our annual trek south.

January 9—I am writing this from the 10th floor of the Red Lion/Lloyd Center in Portland. I can look out over the rain-soaked city and see tall pine trees swaying in the wind in a small park below my window; hear unfamiliar sounds, like the traffic's din, the occasional wail of a siren.

My country eyes take in the slow-moving gray clouds, skyscrapers, people walking under umbrellas and three sea gulls soaring and dipping over all. The MAX light-rail clatters by every so often and cars zoom-varoom in all directions; everyone bent on going "somewhere" in a hurry. The city exudes energy. Except for the sea gulls!

Doug and I are here attending the potato conference, along with other potato growers from Wallowa County. After our hair-raising trip of yesterday, we finally arrived safely in Portland. Having traveled on icy, snow-slick roads to Elgin, we encountered a full-scale blizzard and heavy, drifting snow. We stopped briefly in La Grande and decided to go on over the Blues. Visibility was limited to the car ahead of us and we were sprayed regularly with flying snow from passing trucks.

Descending Cabbage Hill, mercifully the snow turned to slush and finally to rain. My fingernails were permanently embedded in the door handle! We spent the night in The Dalles and hydroplaned into Portland in a heavy rainstorm.

January 12—Hello again. Here is me on the 22nd floor of Bally's in Reno, Nevada, the biggest little city in the world. Or it used to be. Now it really is a big city, one that sprawls out and encompasses this high desert basin that lies at the base of the eastern slopes of the Sierra Nevadas.

Yesterday morning we rode up through the snow-covered mountains on a bus with my mother and her husband to spend a night among the glitter of Reno. Much of the time, however, is spent pounding on the typewriter that my husband so patiently packed on and off the bus and into hotels.

What an office I have! I can look out and across to the high snowy Sierra's ramparts, or down on a large pond of water that seems to be home to hundreds of ducks of some sort. From this dizzying height, the birds appear to be very small, but swim in formations that change and form patterns when viewed from above.

I like seeing them, because in the bright glitter of the lights and man-made jets that roar down out of the skies to land at the airport, also in my line of vision, I find a semblance of peace and order. Peace amid a world that has gone mad! Reno and the surrounding mountains have been transformed into a playground and the look in the eyes of the people who inhabit these places disturbs me.

The potato conference ended Thursday and we packed our bags and headed down I-5 to Woodburn where we visited Aunt Amey, then down through the Willamette Valley to Roseburg. The sun came out and it was a lovely drive. We arrived at the Matthews ranch around 3:30 p.m. The rolling oak hills and quiet country atmosphere was most welcome after the hubbub of Portland.

The late afternoon sun spread its soft yellow light upon the pale, green hillsides, and the tinkling sound of sheep bells was heard as the sheep grazed. Wallowa County, lying under a deep blanket of snow, seemed non-existent. Carolee whomped up a super supper featuring thick, juicy Longhorn-Shorthorn-cross steaks.

January 13—We left this morning in a rainstorm. It is Friday the 13th, a fact I have tried not to dwell on all this long day.

We had been treated to breakfast by our hosts at a little restaurant along the North Fork of the Umpqua, before heading out in pouring rain toward Ashland. While sipping clam chowder in Ashland we listened in on local conversations concerning travel of the Siskiyous, and how we would be required to chain up. They were right! We slowly made our way up the summit of the snowy Siskiyous and started down the other side, where slush turned to rain and some pavement became visible.

Doug took the chains off and we zoomed down I-5 to Weed, where we rested before continuing our long trip to Auburn. As the slanted rays of Northern California sunlight faded into dusk, we pulled into the cow town of Red Bluff. We ate our supper farther on down the line in Marysville and arrived at sister Mary Ann's around 10 p.m.

Thank goodness, Friday the 13th was nearly over, and we were safe.

January 14—Mary Ann and I began the day with an early morning walk, a walk so refreshing that we kept it up every morning of our stay.

We watched the mists form in the American River Canyon below us, and wondered about all the new subdivisions that now cover the once-beautiful oak-studded hills, remembering patches of baby blue eyes that once bloomed there in the spring.

All in the name of progress? Around us such affluence. Three and sometimes four cars, parked in driveways of enormous homes, all with a view, dominating the hills.

We watched the sunrise over the Sierra and walked back to have breakfast with Doug. Auburn is in the heart of the Gold Rush country, and reminders of that '49ers era are everywhere.

Mary Ann took us to the old fruit packing sheds in Newcastle, where many young people earned their summer wages during my youth. Today the old sheds are occupied by small specialty shops and a restaurant, where we ate a delightful lunch, before browsing around like tourists; and I was able to dig out some original editions books in an antique store to purchase and end this run-on sentence!

January 15—Mary Ann and I took our usual three-mile walk before sunup. A great way to start the day, especially since I don't have any ranch chores on vacation. Her deck overlooks the American River. Tall digger pines and several varieties of oak trees grow on the steep canyon side all the way to the river. Different woodland birds come to the bird feeder on the deck railing. From the dining table we can look across country into neighboring El Dorado County with its hills covered with manzanita, chaparral and toyon berry.

We packed a lunch and drove to Thermalands, which is east of my hometown of Lincoln. Our friends, the Vineyards, were branding calves. It was a beautiful, sunny day in the Placer County foothills as we visited old friends and my brother and wife who were helping with the branding. The Vineyards have been in the cattle business for several generations, holding onto their properties while around them many have succumbed to tempting prices offered by developers. These ranchers had a bunch of long, modern cows, used top quality bulls and had an impressive calf crop.

It was a novelty seeing green grass, even though it was a bit washy this time of year. They, like us, feed hay, only not as much.

We stopped to visit Lila, my old 4-H leader, on the way out. Same old Lila, living in the same wonderful old house. A four-story affair that has the high ceilings, ornate wood carvings, porch pillars and stands tall in a land that is ever-changing. Lila's country garden is still intact and the venison stew she was cooking for the branding crew smelled the same as when I was a girl!

Thank goodness for people like the Vineyards, who have stuck with agriculture all these years and preserved a way of life and a means of making a living by growing food for the masses…masses who have no idea how, where, or why that food is grown. Bud's two strong sons carry on the tradition and, from the looks of things, will for some time to come.

We drove to the nearby Manzanita Cemetery, where my father sleeps. I was happy to see that this area has not changed. Ageless oaks, calm witnesses, guard the headstones, some of which date back to the middle 1800s. On to Doty's Ravine near the old ranch of my childhood, we hiked over a hill to the creek, where we built a fire on a gravel bar.

Doug brewed coffee in an empty coffee can with a baling wire handle over the fire, and we ate our sandwiches. Then Doug tried his hand at gold panning and came up with an impressive amount of "color." Later we walked over to brother Jim's ranch and looked at his new Polled Hereford bull.

January 17—Frosty this morning under a crisp, clear sky. Since I brought along some of my trusty sourdough starter, I whipped up a batch of sourdough hotcakes and invited more relatives for breakfast. I fried rocky mountain oysters from yesterday's branding and scrambled eggs. We had a good old Wallowa County breakfast in Placer County.

Then Mary Ann, our guide, drove sister Caroline and me to El Dorado County to the old mining camp at Rattlesnake Bar. Doug had gone off to Doty's Ravine again, smitten with "gold fever." Driving to the end of a remote road, we walked two miles to a lovely spot called Wild Goose Flats.

Several hundred honkers, feeding on the green hillside, flew up at our approach. Below lay an expanse of blue, low water; the back waters of Folsom Dam, or now lake. Dormant, bare-limbed oak trees added their dark character to the landscape. Due to a three-year drought, Folsom Lake is very low. Here on the North Fork of the American River, below its junction with the Middle Fork, just above Whiskey Bar, lies Rattlesnake Bar, whose historic mining camp and nearby diggings are emerging water-logged.

Mining at the bar was exhausted in 1850-51 because the claims were so situated that they could not be worked by natural water. The Camp-Tent City was founded in 1840 on the banks of the American River. Annual floods forced the inhabitants to locate on a higher flat. More about Rattlesnake Bar next time. It was a most fascinating place. Meanwhile, I finish typing this in a setting that is alien to my country heart.

January 19—Mary Ann and I kept up our daily morning walks, sometimes leaving the house well before dawn, a lovely time to stroll the quiet streets of River View Drive neighborhood.

This morning Doug and I visited my grandson Bart, who attends a school for exceptional children in Newcastle, which is only minutes away from Auburn. It was an emotional experience for me. Bart was born with many handicaps that happened as a result of unforeseen circumstances during his mother's pregnancy. Until two years ago, Bart lived with his parents, who raised this brave little boy in spite of doctor's predictions that he would not live to see his first birthday.

Today Bart is nearly 17, having overcome physical as well as mental handicaps that would have done other children in. Life for him will always be limited, but Bart is a survivor. He stays in a private home nearby and commutes daily to his school. As Doug and I waited for the buses to unload students who are bused from all over Placer County to this special place, we saw children mostly in wheelchairs or stumbling along in walkers as they were helped off specially built buses with elevators by their smiling aides.

Hidden Ravine School is a cheerful place, and it was sunny and warm on that beautiful morning. My heart went out to the children as well as the aides, who were such sincere, caring people. Smiles on the children's faces were heart-warming. They were all so obviously eager to get to school!

Bart's bus was late and we had already met his teacher, Donna, whom my daughter, Ramona, and her husband, Charley, had told us to look for. I first glimpsed his light brown, curly hair through the window of the bus and then couldn't hold back the tears. It had been almost two years since we'd seen him. There was "Bopper," a family nickname given him.

A recent illness had taken its toll, but he was bouncing back like always. Frail, pale and thin, with a tenacity to life that is somewhat of a miracle, he laughed his deep lower laugh, took my arm and led us to his classroom. He hung up his small pack and jacket and went to sit in a chair where some music was coming from a tape player. Bart still loves his music.

We visited and observed the therapy sessions going on all around us, and marveled at the facilities and highly skilled teachers, all of whom seem to enjoy their work as well as the children. After a while the teacher suggested that we might take Bart for a walk on the nearby nature trails, which we did. So, hanging onto my arm, this exceptional grandson went hiking with his grandma. Maybe he couldn't hike like his other strong cousins, along a high Wallowa trail, but it was wonderful just the same.

We walked among wild red toyon berries, tall Digger pines and oak trees, then over a wooden bridge. Bart did well, stopping every so often to look at the trees, the sky, feel the warmth of the sunshine or listen to a bird's song. Reaching the end of one path, he didn't want to turn around, but finally did, and we took another fork in the trail. His light brown curls shone in the sunlight. He could have been any one of the other grandchildren there beside me.

Doug followed behind and took a picture of us walking together. Bart was visibly tired when we returned, whereupon he sat again in his favorite chair, smiling and listening to the music, which is his life. He looked content and has accepted his lot. We bid him goodbye and I gave him a hug and with a lump in my throat growing by the minute, left.

As we walked out of the room, Donna remarked that she could tell I was Bart's grandmother, I cried just like his mother! Now I know how hard it must have been for his family when they moved to Oregon, so far away from their beloved Bart.

We then drove down to the American River, crossed the bridge and drove up the winding road toward Coloma, turned at Pilot Hill and took the road to Rattlesnake Bar. I wanted to show Doug the area that my two sisters and I had visited earlier. It was a balmy 75 degrees and we didn't need a jacket.

We had packed a lunch and intended to investigate the gold mining diggings most of the day. Near an old foundation of some sort of mining operation, we ate our lunch. Earlier we had discovered several darkened mine tunnels. Bright green mosses covered huge old rocks and dark green ferns spilled out of dark crevasses. It was a lovely spot. This time I remembered my camera and did a lot of photographing.

The geese on the opposite hillside were feeding. I found the quartz vein again that had been exposed by the high water and dug out a specimen. We could easily have succumbed to gold fever here. Every time we'd pick up a rock, we'd imagine a gold nugget might be lying under it.

Returning to Lower Auburn (Old Town), which has been restored and is now a series of antique shops and Chinese restaurants, we purchased a cast-iron skillet for Mary Ann and browsed around before returning to the house. That evening we returned to Old Town once more and treated Mary Ann to a Chinese dinner at the Shanghai restaurant. What a delicious, authentic meal. It tasted so good, especially after whetting our appetites in the gold fields.

January 20—Almost a full moon shone as Mary Ann and I walked our two miles this morning. A slight, mild wind blew a few wispy clouds away. We met several other women out walking and exchanged good mornings. Then we were all invited over to Mary Ann's neighbor's for breakfast. Paul outdid himself and proceeded to fill us up on his specialty: buckwheat pancakes.

Mary Ann doesn't have a TV, so we watched a bit of the inauguration of President Bush. Sunlight streamed into the room while we ate and another golden California day began. Paul, by the way, is an avid reader of Agri-Times. He shares my sister's copy.

Later on, Doug and I drove to Nevada City and met friends for lunch at a place called "Lotsa Pasta," where we gorged ourselves on ravioli and freshly baked french bread. Glad I took that morning walk. Afterward we took a tour of the fire-ravaged oak hills around Rough 'N Ready and Lake Wildwood. A miracle the whole area didn't go up in flames. Blackened woods looked like scenes from the pages of a mystery novel.

We returned via busy Highway 49, which used to be a lazy, relaxing drive through the Gold Rush country. Not now. It is a buzzing thoroughfare filled with vehicles whizzing along at frightening speeds. Commuters mostly, living in out-of-the-way places like Penn Valley, who must then drive "49" to the freeway and down to Sacramento, where most of the employment is. It seems to me they take their lives in their hands each time they drive. But guess that is "life in the fast lane" and most appear to have accepted their lot.

That evening, sitting in the living room of my childhood chum, Sandra, and her husband, Fred, we gazed down from their high ridge-top home that overlooks the entire Sacramento Valley. Each year the ever-encroaching mass of humanity crawls closer and fills the empty fields, until now, one solid mass of light glitters in the night.

January 21—Today my youngest sister, Kathryn, took us to the Roseville Auction. When I was a young girl the Roseville Auction was a place we children went with daddy when he hauled down a cull cow or Guernsey hull calves to sell. As the years went by, a type of flea market emerged, along with the usual livestock sale held every Saturday. One could purchase a booth and sell just about anything. The idea grew and today the Roseville Auction sprawls out to accommodate several acres of booths, barns, buildings and parking lots that contain the most incredible sight imaginable. The auction is, to put it mildly, an experience. It is a melting pot of Americana. People of every nationality come there, to buy, sell, trade, visit, eat and enjoy.

It was 70-plus degrees as we strolled along through a maze that defies description. The place was colorful, noisy and very entertaining. It was, I imagined, like market places in Europe might look. The wonderful aroma of ethnic foods drifted out over all and lunch time found us shopping around for just the one we preferred. It was a difficult choice, but we finally agreed on Greek gyros, being prepared by a middle-aged, smiling Greek fellow.

What appeared to be a ground mixture of meat, herbs and seasonings was slowly cooking on a vertical rotating spit. The happy fellow cut off slices of this wonderful-smelling meat and slapped it into a freshly made pita bread, adding cucumbers, onions, tomatoes and a special sauce, before handing the dripping sandwiches to us. We sat in the sun, watched the people go by and enjoyed our gyros.

Earlier we had wandered through the fresh fruit and vegetable section. Nearly an acre of fresh, tree-ripened oranges, lemons, grapefruit, polished apples, kiwi fruit, broccoli, cauliflower, green peppers, nuts, honey, huge wheels of cheese, artichokes, avocados, garlic, potatoes and dried fruit. We purchased a big bag of kiwi fruit and eight lemons for $1. We tasted free samples of sweet tangerines and navel oranges while Kathryn purchased her week's supply of fresh produce.

I was able to find Mary Ann a trifle bowl for $3 and grabbed it just in time — the women next to me was reaching for it. An old man was selling copper boilers, butter churns, wagon wheels, school bells, iron frying pans and other quality antiques. Everywhere, babies in backpacks or strollers pushed by young parents, dogs on leashes, older people, and people from every walk of life. Many Vietnamese, who purchased their chickens and rabbits live, then took them home to butcher. We peeked into the livestock sales ring briefly, but didn't stay for the sale. There was still so much to see.

That afternoon we drove out to Roseville and headed for Folsom, then took historic Highway 50 to White Rock. It is here my cousins have been engaged in cattle ranching for several generations. Their ancestors settled the area in the 1800s. The Wilsons and the Smiths are among the last of the pioneer families left at White Rock. The old, red brick three-story house survives, as does a windmill, barns and corrals that stand amid miles of lonely, tree-less hills. The first green grass was beginning to appear, late in starting due to the fall drought. Out of sight, just over the hill, things are changing.

New subdivisions and huge industrial parks are appearing. But here, the Smith and Wilson cattle continued to graze while sunlight glinted off a meandering stream. We were saddened to hear cousin Edna Smith had recently suffered a disabling stroke and was in the Folsom hospital. A book could be written about this woman, who, at nearly 86 years of age, was living out the final chapter of her long and active life.

Cousin Aggie fixed us a wonderful dinner and we talked about old times, mostly about Memorial Day picnics years ago, when relatives from miles around converged on this very ranch. Mary Ann and I remember the homemade root beer, hand-cranked ice cream, fried chicken and the uncles and cousins playing baseball. The picnics have continued all these year, but due to distances, I have been absent. Perhaps next Memorial Day I will return.

January 22—Left Doug in front of niece Lori and husband Tom's TV set on this Super Bowl Sunday, while Mary Ann, Kathryn, Clive and I hiked to Horseshoe Bar on the American River. It is peaceful there, but a bit depressing owing to the ruination of the land. Black, water-logged Digger pine stumps, erosion and an unnatural look of what used to be the shoreline of Folsom Lake now harbors the flotsam and jetsam of too many people's litter. Because of the recent drought, low water marks now expose the once beautiful banks of the river, before the dam.

January 23—While typing my column this morning, I can look across the American River Canyon to the fog shrouded ridges of El Dorado County. A fine, drippy rain fell during the night and continues to do so, bringing much needed moisture to drought-ridden California. During our nearly two-week stay, this is the first day that it hasn't been clear and sunny.

The river below the deck is lost in swirling mists, and one of Mary Ann's cats sits beneath the bird feeder, loudly scolded by a dozen or so noisy blue jays perched in a nearby live oak. Because I was so fascinated with Rattlesnake Bar, I must finish describing that early-day gold mining area.

Around 1853 the mining camp-town of Rattlesnake Bar was home to the notorious Rattlesnake Dick, a character who could, and did, fill a book. In addition to the usual stores, hotels and express office, the bar boasted a theater. The devastating 1862 American River flood swept away most of the bridge constructed in the early gold rush years. Toll fees proved lucrative: 50 cents for one person, $5 for one horse and a wagon, $1 for each additional horse. The new Rattlesnake bridge was built in 1862 and replaced two foot suspension bridges that connected Rattlesnake Bar with Wild Goose Flat, which is where we hiked. The old bridge abutments were still visible, because the waters of Folsom Lake were so low as to expose them again.

Water brought by the Bear River Ditch Company in 1853 was used by a Mr. Qua to begin sluicing operations, and he quickly made $30,000. Mining began to decline around 1855, although it was reported that the dirt still paid $10 to the wheelbarrow load. The bar, normally under Folsom Lake, is today visible due to drought conditions. Because the water has receded, the old diggings are exposed again.

We spent a lot of time poking around Wild Goose Flat on that sunny morning. Not a soul around on Martin Luther King Monday, save for the soft babble of wild geese that flew up from the flat to cavort in the river below. Huge oaks, open-armed to the sky, devoid of leaves, created beautiful scenes everywhere. An old homestead site on the flat was all that was left there. A lone century plant bloomed next to an olive tree, which was loaded with tiny black olives. A citrus tree of some sort had survived along with a working windmill. Beginnings of green grass appeared under the dull gray, dormant star thistle.

Ditches dug by the Chinese were in evidence everywhere. It appeared that these ditches were built to divert spring run-off into holding ponds that were used to sluice the dirt below. Manzanita, with its smooth, dark red bark and shiny green leaves, was scattered about that land of decomposed granite, quartz deposits and red dirt. Gold country!

Having returned on the 18th via the bus from Reno, we began a week of visiting relatives and seeing more country. Hectic, but relaxing to us, because the weather was like California gold. Meanwhile, calls from home reported three feet of snow, with higher drifts in some spots. Son Steve called and said snow was drifting so high that he could walk over the chicken-wire fence. And that is a high fence!

January 23—A fine, misty rain fell as I walked this morning. Mary Ann had gone to work, so I walked alone along streets with names like Poet Smith Drive and Mary Jane Avenue.

People were out walking their house dogs: all kinds of people with all kinds of dogs. The dogs matched the personalities of their owners. One woman, dressed in the latest designer-fashion raincoat, led a white poodle, dressed in a similar raincoat. It was a drippy doggy morning, and the only rain we encountered during our entire stay.

Sister Caroline came for lunch with her grandson Jeremy. It was fun visiting her and watching the antics of little Jeremy, who made me homesick for my grandchildren. Baked sourdough biscuits to go with Mary Ann's clam chowder for supper and invited neighbor Paul to share our meal. Now he knows those biscuits he reads about are for real.

January 24—This morning we visited my wonderful 80-year-old uncle who lives in Rio Linda, a suburb of Sacramento. John lives alone in the sturdy four-story house that my grandpa Wilson built. Surrounded now by schools, subdivisions, fast-food mini marts, gas stations and suburbia, it still has dignity. The pomegranate tree is still in the yard.

Dear Uncle Johnny, recovering from a broken wrist, entertained us with yarns of early-day El Dorado County. This white-haired, tall man, who still is a song writer, piano player, historian and writer, is my favorite uncle.

After our visit with Uncle Johnny in Rio Linda, we were by some miracle able to re-enter the freeway and get ourselves to Davis, home of UC Davis where my oldest granddaughter is a student. The sun was shining and a brisk north wind blew as we walked onto this campus where some 23,000 students are pursuing their higher education.

Bikes whizzed by everywhere, some students walked and parking was a problem. We finally left our car in a "no parking" zone and met Tammy, who gave us a grand tour of the campus. Well, part of it. The university has grown to such gigantic proportions that seeing it all in just one day would be impossible.

Tamym suggested we eat lunch at a place called A.J. Bumps, which was located in downtown Davis. It turned out to be a good choice and we enjoyed our gourmet sandwiches and visiting with Tammy. Old photos of UCD, when it was a "cow college," adorned the walls, and I remembered my father talking about the "Cal Aggies" way back then.

I was surprised to see that North and South halls were still standing. We used to stay in these dorms during 4-H conferences when I was a young girl. After lunch we took a brief ride out of town to Cassidy Lane, where our family lived for 13 years. I didn't recognize the area, it has changed so. Because the wind blew away the smog and fog, we were able to see the Coast Range mountains, mountains that were once a sight I loved, before realizing a lifelong dream to move to the mountains of Wallowa County.

We drove past the Fairfield School where three of my children once attended, and noticed a modern school replaces the old one-room wooden structure. That evening we met my brother Jim and his wife, Joyce, for dinner at what used to be known as the "Ground Cow" near Penryn. We had a nice visit with them before stopping by to visit old acquaintances Joan and Phil Oakes in Loomis. Their children grew up with mine during the early years and it was interesting hearing about the interim of their lives that spanned 20 years.

Cattle on Prairie Creek in Wallowa County wait patiently for their daily ration of silage and hay.

February 1—As frigid arctic air moves down on us from Alaska, I brace myself for a cold night. The wood box is full, thanks to Doug, who split enough wood to last until he returns Friday from the Washington potato conference. Once again I write from my warm country kitchen, having returned safely from our trip south and an absence of three weeks.

Because we arrived home to Prairie Creek in the dark, we were surprised the next morning as we looked out to see huge drifts encircling the house. Another drift has grown so high it covers the garden fence. My puppy, who was ecstatic at my return, loves the snow and frolics and rolls around in the white fluff in pure enjoyment.

My grandchildren were also happy to see grandma back, especially 2-and-a-half-year-old James, who spent all day Monday at grandma's house. What a day we had, sledding, lighting a fire in the sheepherder's wagon stove and pretending we were herding sheep and camping, a favorite pastime for both James and me. He especially likes to cook the camp meal and listen to stories from grandma, told in the snug confines of the old herder's wagon.

On Tuesday two other grandchildren, Rowdy and Chelsie, spent the day, as they were recovering from bad colds and their parents drove to La Grande to watch older brother Chad compete in a district FFA creed speaking and parliamentary procedure competition. So all is back to normal, albeit a little snowy, and Ben and Steve continue to feed the hungry cattle, a job that takes up most of every day. I am back to haying the milk cows, feeding the horses and tending my chickens, which continue to lay eggs despite the bitter cold.

February 2—There was a short blizzard here that piled snow even higher on the drifts caused by earlier winds. I baked an apple pie today for grandson Shawn's 15th birthday, and decided to brave the storm and deliver it. The warm, fragrant steam from the pie was comforting as I drove through the blizzard. Deciding to stay overnight, I helped with Shawn's birthday dinner.

The next morning, with the temperature at zero and fine snow sifting down, I drove back to the ranch in time to do morning chores. After stoking up the fire and cooking some breakfast, I realized my flu was really taking hold. An especially bad bug this year. I think the bugs are becoming more resistant to modern medicine and becoming hardier. I decided not to fight it with anything other than home remedies. Most of our family already has had the malady or still has a touch of sickness.

Daughter Lori called from Wyoming and reported a chilly minus 27 degrees in Thermopolis. By afternoon our weather cleared and the thermometer plummeted. And that official groundhog, somewhere back east, didn't see his shadow!

This evening daughter Ramona called. Her family lives near the banks of Prairie Creek before it enters the town of Enterprise and becomes the Wallowa River. She had watched fascinated as their indoor-outdoor thermometer dropped from zero to minus 19 in less than 15 minutes. I notice that ice has formed on the inside of our double-paned windows and heavy frost covers the threshold on our front door.

Thank goodness, Doug returned a day early from Moses Lake due to the extreme cold.

February 3—Our county seat town of Enterprise reports a low of 29 degrees below zero and therefore has the distinction of being the coldest spot in Oregon today. Daughter Jackie calls later in the day and reports a balmy zero at Imnaha.

Because Steve has been out of commission all week due to a knee injury, Ben, who until today has been doing the feeding by himself, struggles, along with Doug, to start trucks, tractors and pickups. They have balked because of the frigid weather. While the cattle bawl, most of the feeding is done with Ben's truck, a process that takes much longer as there are so many cattle to feed.

Meanwhile, predictions are for more of same. Diamond-like crystals hang suspended in sunlight as the severe cold creates its own rare beauty that is both lovely and terrible, soft and harsh and deadly dangerous.

When the day ended, the sun sank behind the silent, cold Wallowas and the temperature sank with it.

February 4—This morning it is clear, still and 32 below. Looking outside, the sunlight is deceiving. That frigid air will freeze the skin and chill the lungs instantly. Gradually, my laying hens stop laying. Their egg production has been dropping daily, down to three eggs, then none.

We keep the wood cookstove, fireplace and baseboard heaters going night and day. I feel sorry for our fall calves. They shake their heads and I wonder if some will have frozen ears this spring. Also, I miss the little birds. There is no birdsong. Where have the juncos gone? But the hawks are hardy. I see them perched in the tall cottonwoods or flying over the frozen meadows in search of mice.

One of my Alder Slope neighbors, Guy McCormack, died today. This winter has seen the passing of many Wallowa County old-timers, like my friend Betty Cornwell's husband, Ken. To everything a season, and a reason, and the inhabitants who continue to live here seem to be made of the same stuff as the pioneers who settled the Wallowa country. In fact, many of us would rather contend with natural phenomenon here than man-made dilemmas that exist "outside."

In my thinking, it is easier to co-exist with nature than with man, or at least man that has become alien to country living and never suffers physically, but becomes such an emotional cripple he destroys himself. One has only to travel out of the valley to realize this, and put things in their proper perspective.

It is a time to cook hot oatmeal, embroider, read, poke and feed the fires, and baby the flu with steaming cups of soup and tea. I finished reading three excellent books and have only 22 squares left to embroider on the state flower quilt.

February 5—Son Ken, wife, Annie, and their three children arrived to take showers. Their pipes have been frozen for several days. Rowdy and Chelsie's 4-H ewes have picked this cold time to lamb and the family stays up nights bringing newborn, wet lambs into the house to be dried off with a hair blow dryer. It works and mothers and babies are doing fine.

February 6—Minus 18 this morning, and so brilliantly gorgeous outside that I wanted to get out and do some photography. But my flu discouraged that project.

February 7—Dave Nelson, our local radio announcer, reports an overnight low in Enterprise of minus 22 degrees; here on Prairie Creek, at 6 a.m. it is minus 18. Our cattle and horses stand motionless in a frozen world, waiting patiently for their daily ration of hay. Not a breath of wind stirs, thank goodness, and when the sun finally makes its appearance over the eastern hills, Prairie Creek is suddenly transformed into such a brilliant white, glittering landscape; it hurts the eyes to look at it.

For nearly a week now we have been experiencing severe cold and all the agonies that go with it. We in Wallowa County, however, seem more adjusted to this than other areas such as Pendleton, Spokane or the Willamette Valley. So what if rigs don't start and pipes freeze? That has been the story of winter life in the Wallowas for years. During the past few winters, however, we in the valley have been lulled into almost believing that maybe winters like our old-timers talk about will never come again. This winter is bringing us back to reality.

The winter of '88-89 will long be remembered by our generation to fuel stories told to our grandchildren, perhaps exaggerating a bit as memories dim during future, milder winters.

February 9—It was only 17 below this morning, and the blue-sky, sunshiney days marched on, seemingly without end. Startch, Daisy and May are beginning to "spring" in the dead of winter, their bellies swollen with calf.

The funeral for my Alder Slope neighbor and friend, Guy McCormack, was today. He was laid to rest on this incredibly cold, beautiful winter day. He is one of many Wallowa County old-timers who won't see another Wallowa County springtime. I like to remember Guy that day, last fall; I took him a freshly baked loaf of sourdough bread when he wasn't feeling well. He hadn't been eating, and the bread had really helped, he said.

A group of Guy's friends and relatives visited in the sunshine outside Bollman's Funeral Home, before slowly dissolving and going on about their business. From the hill above Enterprise, Guy's grave will overlook his beloved Alder Slope, where he was born January 17, 1910.

Above the Slope lies Murray Gap, named after Guy's mother's family, the Murrays, early settlers who emigrated from Quebec, Canada, and homesteaded on the wild, forested slopes of Ruby Peak. All that remains of the old place are some lilacs, which have run wild, a few fruit trees and several large poplars that mark the spot in a clearing.

In the fall, the mule deer like to eat the few apples that hang from the trees there. Thanks to hardy pioneers like the Murrays, we who follow have life much easier.

February 10—Really warmed up today—minus 4 and the ninth straight day of below-zero temperatures. Using the good lemons we purchased in California, I made another lemon pie for son-in-law Bill's birthday.

Doug and I left the ranch about 6 p.m. to drive to Wallowa Lake, which is now frozen thick enough for local ice skaters to play on. As we pulled into the lodge parking area, we noticed the formation of a high ice sculpture, and a thin stream of water still sprayed out the top of the fountain.

Inside the Wallowa Lake Lodge, a log blazed in the massive stone fireplace and people, clad in Scottish tartans, clustered around to warm themselves and visit. We had all come to celebrate the birthday of the Scot poet, Robert Burns. It was, almost, like being in Scotland. The festivities began with the Highland Fling, danced by several pretty young local lassies. Retiring to the dining room, we were welcomed by Millie Fraser, who has spent days organizing this annual event for our county.

With flourish, ceremony, and piping of the bagpipes, the haggis is carried in on a platter by chefs Horst Meyer and Bruce Malone, followed by a toast and "Speil to the Haggis." Ron Peterson, owner of the Blue Willow Sausage Kitchen, said that although this haggis was not quite authentic, it did contain beef, pork, herbs, steel-cut oats and just a bit of liver. It was actually cooked in the sheep's stomach lining. Whatever! Ron, who is an artist when it comes to these things, did a superb job, and the concoction was marvelous.

The staff at the Wallowa Lake Lodge served mashed potatoes and rutabagas, salad, rolls and their version of Scot's trifle. The dining room overflowed; all tickets had been sold. My friend Scotty expounded on the immortal memory of Robert Burns, whom she said was a beloved poet of the common man. There were toasts and more toasts and poetry, such as "To a Mouse and to a Louse," recited by Scotty and Ralph Swinehart. Then Ron Peterson gave his rendition of "The Haggis of Private McPhee."

My favorites were the songs of love, such as "My heart was once as blithe and free," and "My Luve's like a Red, Red Rose," sung by Suzanne Peterson in a hauntingly beautiful voice. June Bombaci and Katch Josephy sang a light-hearted medley that included "Corn Rigs and Barley Rigs" and "Bonnie Leslie."

The program ended with everyone well-toasted, full of haggis, standing, holding hands and singing the familiar Auld Lang Syne before stepping out into the frigid Wallowa County night and crunching through the snow to our cars. A wonderful evening that brought out the Scot in all of us.

February 11—We could scarcely believe our eyes when we saw that it was 10 degrees above zero.

I took grandson Buck and daughter Jackie skiing that day at Ferguson Ridge. Mona Lee and I didn't ski as I was still getting over the flu. We spent the morning in the warming shack, looking out the sunny window to the ski slopes and watching Buck's progress.

Later I took them home and did some photographing in the canyons. No lack of subjects: the partially constructed church, Imnaha's first, with its handsome bell and tower, and the wooden cross in darkened contrast to brilliant blue sky and snow-dusted rims; the frozen Imnaha with its thin channel spilling out over ice floes of the purest blue. Horses, cattle and a few baby calves were beginning to appear.

I stopped at the Riverside Cafe to visit old-timers Jim Dorrance and Ferm Warnock. We exhausted the subjects of winter weather, state of affairs on the river and the good ol' days. Ferm and Jim are a wealth of information on early Wallowa County history, and I could have visited all night. But it was getting late and already the winter sun had slipped behind canyon walls, before I started the 30-mile drive back up on top to Prairie Creek.

February 12—Zero again and felt almost like spring, so I potted an amaryllis bulb, a geranium and some narcissus. My kitchen looks like a greenhouse and some Imnaha pussy willows are beginning to open in a little vase on our kitchen table.

February 15—It was just before sunup when Mr. Coyote disappeared into his den near a rock pile on the eastern hill on this zero-degree morning. Moments later, the high Wallowa peaks that rim this valley blushed with a ruby glow, and another beautiful winter morning began on Prairie Creek. Severe cold often is accompanied by breathtaking beauty, and we might as well enjoy it, for soon the frost will leave the ground, leaving barn lots and back roads turning to slush, followed by weeks of MUD.

But for now the fields and feeding lots are frozen solid and appear clean, as the cattle slick up their hay and silage, leaving nary a stem. A large flock of wild mallard ducks has discovered the silage. After the big yellow truck augers the tempting mixture onto the snow, they

Big plastic bags contain the smell of summer—fodder that provides for hungry livestock during the long, cold Wallowa County winters.

suddenly appear. When the cattle jostle and move about, they take to the skies, resembling a wavering, dark-beaded necklace against the winter-white landscape. Weaving and changing formation, they re-group and gracefully land, before gorging themselves on the fragrant silage.

As is so often the case with wild things, these ducks were depending on what we feed our domestic livestock for their survival during this severe winter.

I cooked up a kettle full of oatmeal for my laying hens. Chester, the banty rooster, discovered the hot mixture first and chuckled his "come and get it" call. Those hens really made fast work of that mush. By the time I got back to the house my nose and cheeks were numb. Warmed up by the cookstove before going back out to feed the milk cows and the horses their hay.

Clipped colorful pictures of fruit, flowers and vegetables from the seed catalogs to make valentines for my 13 grandchildren. This may seem a bit "corny," but the children love them and one can use creative thinking to compose verses: *I carrot for you, peas be my Valentine, you are the apple of my eye, I'm just nuts about you.* Just heard on the news that Wallowa County is the coldest spot in Oregon, a distinction we would just as soon share with other parts of the country. Made a lemon pie for son Todd's pie-a-month birthday present.

My youngest granddaughter, sweet baby Adele Marie, celebrated her first birthday on Alder Slope. It was a happy time for relatives and friends, and recorded on video, which we viewed on the VCR on TV before the party was over. What a world we live in these days. Being able to capture on permanent record these precious childhood moments is one of the modern inventions that will benefit mankind.

Creating that sense of belonging, it seems to me, is a far cheaper method of assuring that the next generation will mature into responsible adults, than producing neglected castaways who turn to drugs and become a threat to society. We, as parents and grandparents, have a big responsibility, one that could keep our prisons empty if we spent as much time on our children's values as we do at our jobs.

Guess I'd better step down from my soap box and continue with this column. I had ordered a pair of handmade, fur-lined leather moccasins from Cheryl Cox of Imnaha for Adele's gift. Cheryl, who is a modern-day pioneer gal, makes her own soap, bakes bread, cans and dries all her own food, and lives a simple, uncluttered life along the banks of Sheep Creek, just upstream from where it empties into the Imnaha. She and cowboy husband Barry are typical of the new generation of young people who are making homes here in our isolated country. They seem to be made of the same stuff as our early settlers.

February 16—Just to let us know the winter wasn't over yet, it dipped to one below zero. I poked wood to the stove and cooked up a kettle of soup. Because son Steve is now laid up for a year with a back injury, well need to look for another hand. One of the hazards of ranching involves the heavy lifting required, such as feeding hay bales. We sincerely hope Steve will recover from this bit of bad luck.

Working on the CattleWomen's scrapbooks, pasting, clipping and sorting through a three-year accumulation of material. After four days I finished. It made me tired just to read of all the activities we'd participated in during that time.

February 17—23 degrees! I treated my pregnant milk cows to a mineral block I had won as a door prize at the cattlemen's convention in Baker.

February 18—Our low was 28 degrees; the warmest morning yet. The barn lots are melting and slushy manure appears around the feeders. Time to don hip boots.

Doug and I drove to Enterprise High School and watched 15-year-old grandson Chad, who had won a seed in the district wrestling finals. He had to wrestle varsity opponents, but succeeded in winning a fourth place in the tournament. All this grandmother really cared about was that Chad escaped without injury. Although this competitive grandson is my pride and joy, his wild escapades give me more gray hairs.

February 19—It was 30 degrees when we awoke to a fine, wet snow falling that resembled rain. Because we are short of help, Doug canceled his trip to Salem to attend the quarterly cattlemen's meeting.

On Monday, President's Day, I went for a two-mile walk down our country road with my puppy. Alabaster clouds with gray bellies floated in an azure sky. Birds sang, and water oozed from snowbanks and flowed in rivulets through the fields. Cows and yearlings soaked up the sun and steam rose from the pavement.

It was so refreshing to get out of the house and feel free and clean after such a siege of cold. Split a wheelbarrow full of wood, and gathered two eggs from the laying hens, who have decided to lay again. Great drifts still rim our yard, but the primroses growing next to the house have emerged. Strawberry and raspberry patches sleep under their blanket of insulating snow.

Yesterday two-year-old James and I played all day. First we drove to frozen-over Wallowa Lake and fed the deer. Then we drove around looking at the blue-iced fountains, some of which have grown to gigantic proportions this winter. We seemingly had the park to ourselves; just us and the deer.

Returned to the ranch where we ate lunch in the sheepherder wagon. Then I pulled James in the sled over the hill and down along the creek, which is still iced-over. I showed James the "owl tree" and pointed out tracks in the snow, made by muskrats, ducks and weasels. Several hawks flew over and two cawing crows looked down at us. We returned via the milk cow's pasture and paused to rest on a stack of hay and played with the barn cats. James and I look forward to these times. It is an age where we can both communicate.

February 22—An angry wind roars across the melting surfaces of Prairie Creek. After a silent, cloud-shadowed night, the wind, born in the south, began sweeping over the fields, blowing hay, twigs and leaves before it. The decayed brown leaves, set free by thaw, dance and skip along in a sort of last farewell, before lodging somewhere to nurture the earth that once nourished them.

The wind is warm, our first chinook of the season. There were puddles of water around the hay feeder when I forked breakfast to my milk cows. After a week of above zero temperatures, there is a different "feel" to the air. I think the back of Old Man Winter is broken. Not to say we won't experience blizzards or more freezing weather, but the severe cold is behind us.

Yesterday Chester flew to the top of the snow-filled chicken yard fence, flapped his wings and crowed. And our first new baby calves appeared in their snow-covered world night before last. Doug, using the dozer blade on the small Cat, cleared paths in the lower pasture so the cows will have some protection while calving.

March 1—March marched right on into our valley like the proverbial lamb, bringing with it a calm, beautiful morning. I whipped up a batch of sourdough hotcakes on the Monarch range for the benefit of our guest, Renee Warriner, Oregon's IFYE (International 4-H Youth Exchange) delegate to the Netherlands. Doug, still in Salem with son Steve to meet with a specialist on Steven's back problem, called to check on things here. Meanwhile, Renee helped with my barn chores, and got a kick out of pitching hay to the milk cows and feeding the horses and chickens.

While waiting for a potato grower to call and arrive to look at our seed, I worked on my column. After the buyer arrived and Ben took him to our cellars, Renee and I drove to Enterprise, where we ran some errands before meeting daughter Ramona at the "Country Place" for lunch. While eating we were entertained by the antics of many ducks cavorting about in a small open space of water beginning to appear at one end of frozen Pete's Pond.

Afterward we continued on to Wallowa Lake to do some sightseeing. The frozen surface of the lake was beginning to show large irregular cracks in the ice. We saw many deer. None had horns. Then we realized it was now that time of year when bucks shed their antlers. Some of those big does were, in fact, bucks. We parked the pickup and went for a short walk, at which time March changed its fickle mind and began to snow.

When we returned to the ranch, the snow was really piling up again; as the wood box was empty, I split a wheelbarrow full of wood. Baby calves were coming thick and fast in the lower field, natch! Those cows knew a storm was coming! Sledded a sack of chicken feed to the chicken house and gathered the eggs.

That evening Renee and I attended a 4-H leaders' banquet at the Elks lodge. After a prime rib dinner, Renee showed her slides and gave a most interesting talk on her six-month visit to the Netherlands. This 21-year-old miss, of Dutch descent herself, captivated her audience as she enthusiastically described her stay with various host families, and her observations of life in the Netherlands.

One thing she said that impressed me was that the family unit in Holland was very close. For instance, meals were a big thing and all members were most always present. TV and radio were turned off while the family simply visited and enjoyed one another. If a member was late; they thought nothing of waiting an hour before starting the meal. Birthdays also were big events and the celebration of them went on all day long.

The Dutch are very social, innovative, smart and extremely friendly, Renee said. She has made lifelong friends there and would like one day to return and visit her host families. To illustrate their innovative thinking, the Dutch came up with the idea to build huge dikes, drain portions of the Zider Zee and thus reclaim new land on which to raise crops like seed potatoes.

This land, not more than 50 years old, is being homesteaded. One farm Renee visited raised cattle, and the owners didn't castrate bulls. They were all raised until they were three-year-olds before being slaughtered for food. These animals were kept in stalls all their lives, and stood on slatted floors. Their manure was drained out beneath them and eventually marketed by the farmer in the form of commercial fertilizer. Renee said the farmers were just as proud of their manure business as they were of the animals.

As we stepped out of the Elks lodge into that March night, we were immediately plunged back into winter, and several inches of new snow covered the town in a soft, white blanket. During our absence, Doug had returned safely from Salem, and we all went to bed as March acted more like a lion than this morning's calm lamb.

March 2—While doing chores, I noticed that Daisy, one of my Guernsey milk cows, was close to calving. A freezing wind began to blow and the loose snow swirled across the fields, obliterating the landscape. Extremely cold arctic air began pushing down on us once again. Renee had an appointment at the local radio station for an interview and I began typing up my column.

That afternoon Doug and I had a dental appointment in Enterprise, and when we returned, Daisy had already calved. Ben carried the chilled calf into the shed and when Renee and I went down to shake out some straw around the newborn, Daisy got extremely upset...and charged right at me! Looking like "Flo" in a Jerry Palen cartoon predicament, wearing hip boots, holding a pitchfork, I beat a hasty retreat. I could feel that cow's breath in my hip pocket.

Needless to say, we left mom and babe alone.

That night the temperature dropped and we awoke to a nine below zero morning. When I went out before daylight to check on Daisy's calf, it was dead and frozen stiff. In her nervous condition it appeared Daisy had tromped on her baby. Or else, motherhood at this time in her life was not what she wanted. The cow was still on the tear and acting "ringy" while I fed and watered her. Luckily I was later able to calm her down enough to let an orphan calf nurse and milk her.

Doug had left again, this time to deliver our feedlot cattle to C&B Livestock in Hermiston. He would stay over for the sale the next day. Meanwhile, back at the ranch, Ben and I saw to the calving of the main herd, which was shelling out calves right and left in 10 inches of new, blowing snow and freezing weather. At the height of yesterday's blizzard, six calves were born and the calving shed was full.

March 3—Our thermometer registered zero degrees as the sun burst over the hill this morning, transforming our landscape into a dazzling panorama of purest white. Drifts that had melted down were now higher than ever. The huge one near the garden has completely covered the fence. Giant icicles hung from eaves of all the ranch buildings and sunlight glittered through them like quartz crystals.

Ben and Jim chipped away at barn doors to free them of ice, and fed the long lines of hungry cattle. In spite of bitter cold weather, we have managed to save our calves. They certainly must be tough little critters to survive being born on Prairie Creek this winter.

Renee left around mid-morning to drive back to her home in Lebanon, after presenting a final program at our local Rotary Club. I really enjoyed having this young person stay here, and it was an interesting experience for her as well.

Baked a raspberry pie for son Todd's pie-a-month birthday gift, and a raisin-cream pie for Doug, who will return tomorrow.

March 4—Daughter Jackie and children spent the night, and this morning we all drove to Ferguson Ridge and went skiing. Already in good shape, after having wrestled with Daisy and her adopted calf all morning. We had fried chicken and packed a picnic basket before heading for a day on the ski slopes.

Snow from the storm lay thickly on the tree branches and created a Christmas card effect. Nine-year-old Buck, his mom and grandma had a great day on the T-bar. The snow was incredible. Perfect, in fact, with just enough soft, dry powder to make for great skiing. Views from on top were far-reaching and spread out before us like a winter wonderland.

Rancher Mike Hanley signs a copy of his book, Owyhee Trails, *for Ruth Nutting of Heppner, Oregon. Mike is from the Jordan Valley country in Southeast Oregon.*

It was back to the barn when I returned, then warming up colostrum to feed a weak calf born in yesterday's storm. Ben worked into the night with the calving cows. What would we do without him? Doug returned around 9 o'clock, having purchased a bull at the sale.

March 5—Gray overcast and 20 degrees, which felt like a tropical heat wave. That Sunday morning began with a calf coming breach, so Doug called our local cowboy-poet-vet, Fred Bornstedt, who immediately came to the rescue.

Meanwhile, at the barn, Daisy and I had reached a truce of sorts and things were going pretty smoothly. It was late afternoon when a moaning chinook wind came blowing across the valley. Its warm breath as if by magic melted the icicles and reduced the snowbanks again.

March 6—The chinook's breath has changed the face of Prairie Creek—the sound of running water, the sight of bare ground, and a rainbow sprouted from the earth's warm mists.

March 7—Last night, donned in hip boots and carrying a flashlight, I tromped around our watery cow pasture to check on the Guernsey milk cow May, who is close to calving. I could see the spotlight's bright beam sweeping across the lower field as Doug checked the main herd from his pickup. After covering the entire pasture, I spotted May under some ancient willows, chewing her cud.

What began as a cloudy, dull, drippy day, soon turned into a cloud-spangled, blue-sky afternoon. Our snow continues to recede as May grows bigger and bigger. Daisy's adopted bull calf has begun to bloom, and my hens have laid five eggs!

I made posters for our upcoming bull sale and drove to Enterprise to have copies made of the sale order. An incredible panorama of sunshine and cloud shadow marched across the snowfields, and on Prairie Creek it has melted the huge snow banks down enough so we can see the bottom pole on our yard fence for the first time all winter. It feels so much like spring that I ordered my baby chicks.

The men brought me another calf, taken from a big-teated cow this evening. The little heifer wasn't hungry enough to nurse, so waited until morning.

Attended a CPR training class at the local hospital tonight. After practicing on "Resusci Annie," I feel more confident about saving someone, if the need ever arises.

March 8—Out early to check May, who still hasn't calved. After wrestling the heifer calf to get it to nurse Daisy, I was covered with mud. In the shower to wash off corral no. 5!

Met daughter Ramona at "A Country Place" on Pete's Pond for lunch, before we drove back to clean her house for a CattleWomen's meeting scheduled there tomorrow. Ramona scrubbed and vacuumed, while I washed windows. The house fairly gleamed by late afternoon, and I drove home to rest up a bit before doing chores.

The new little heifer simply walked into where Daisy was stanchioned and began to nurse. Hooray!

Finished the evening with a meeting of our Wallowa Valley Arts Council. A busy spring season lies just around the corner.

March 9—A very mild morning, another chinook blowing, a warm rain falling, and snow-melt running everywhere. The two calves nursing well on Daisy, and May still hanging in there. Baked a peach pie for grandson Shawn's pie-a-month birthday present, gathered up materials for CattleWomen's meeting and drove to daughter Ramona's.

The area we know as Prairie Creek, which includes the upper, middle and lower Prairie Creek country, was a sight I'll never forget. Snow melted so rapidly that small rivers formed in every swale, then gathered momentum and rushed across the county roads. Flat, low-lying areas turned into instant lakes.

Baby calves stood on higher ground with water lapping at their feet. Meanwhile, floating overhead, the clouds were almost impossible to describe, like lofty mountain ranges in the sky, billowing alabaster, contrasted with dark gray and purple where a water spout suddenly fell from above.

The soft, warm breath of the chinook blew like a hot fan across the land; snow drifts evaporated before my eyes. Sunshine would burst through a glorious show of clouds and the rays would stream down onto a red barn or a lovely pastoral scene. The clouds moved along in a sort of symphonic rhythm, as if an unseen conductor orchestrated this phenomenon. Trees and power lines whipped and lashed about.

All the wild ducks and geese loved the landscape's sudden transformation into an immense wetland. Birds sang wildly, *spring, spring,* and flew about delirious with joy at seeing earth again; the snow is leaving.

The hills, just yesterday covered with snow, were swept as if a giant vacuum cleaner sucked off all but a few rib-like white streaks on their dull brown sides. Bubbling, foaming, yellow-brown, snow-ice melt flowed like a living thing across the fields, smelling of manure, earth, rotten leaves and grasses.

I had to drive very slowly, as the waters were rushing across our roads with such force they were washing whole sections away. The flood that originated on the land we call Prairie Creek had not, as yet, reached the creek of the same name.

I stopped at Eggleson Corner and started down Highway 82 to Ramona's, expecting Prairie Creek here to be a raging torrent, but it was only a bit roily and muddy, and not high. I crossed the wooden bridge and pulled into the yard. About that time, water from the surrounding fields had created its own river and was swirling under and around their deck, bubbling up in the garage.

"How high's the water, mamma?"

Meanwhile, the creek was beginning to look angry and the Cattle-Women arrived. I took a shovel and tried, to no avail, to divert the water. The weather alternated between periods of rain, wild winds and sunshine. It was incredibly warm.

After the meeting ended, the ladies all drove safely back across the bridge, and I tended to the children while Ramona and Liza were successful in digging a ditch to divert the flooding of the garage. While the gals worked in the rainstorm, they heard a loud crash and looked up to see a wall of water, the combined melting of all three Prairie Creek areas, come rushing down the creek.

The sound turned out to be the tearing and loosening of an entire fence line that had been holding limbs and other debris behind it. At that point the creek was transformed into a river on a rampage, but by some miracle the bridge held.

The frothy, coffee-colored flood raced on down toward Enterprise, spilling out onto the low-lying meadows and changing the course of the stream. I drove alongside it to Enterprise to pick up a prescription for son-in-law Charley, who was laid up with an infected leg. The sight that greeted me in Enterprise was a nightmare.

All that swirling, dark water covered the streets, which were now rushing rivers. It continued to rain, a warm tropical rain. A bluebird sky played peek-a-boo now and then between water spouts dumping their contents on Upper Prairie Creek. A low meadow area east of the town continued to fill with dirty, debris-filled floodwater, in which a few white ducks bobbed happily about amid the flotsam, seemingly oblivious to any threat of danger.

As the raging creek turned river, the Wallowa River, as it is called after it enters Enterprise, hurled itself along, jamming debris against bridge abutments, plugging culverts, then simply overflowing, moving as one body across town in its haste to follow the natural course of its flow. The flood lapped at homes; fish and muskrats entered people's patios, children dip-netted trout in their back yards, and the people stood in doorways, helpless, as water poured out or in.

I put my car in low gear and swam it to the drug store. As it turned out I was to make two more trips into town to transport stranded grand-children.

On the last trip, grandson Shawn said, "Don't drive over the bridge, grandma!" and I braked just in time to see the roadway that joined the bridge abutment cave in.

We were able to jump the chasm onto the bridge, which still held, and get the children over. Leaving Liza's car stranded on the other side, I took her family, along with another granddaughter, home to spend the night. Shortly after this the water rushed over the bridge, causing it to fall off one of its cement abutments.

After one more hair-raising trip through Enterprise, we made it safely to high-and-dry Alder Slope. Later, I was able to take a back road home via the Hurricane Creek, Joseph, and Imnaha highways, and onto Tenderfoot Valley Road, which was also under water.

At 9 p.m. I went out to let the calves nurse May, just in time for another cloudburst to send rain pounding down on the tin roof of the cow shed. Then, all was quiet. The wind ceased, the last cloud moved on, stars blinked in a clean rain-washed sky. An owl *hoo-hoo*-ed from high up on a limb of the old cottonwood.

March 10—Golden sunshine streamed from brilliant, blue skies this morning, and on this lovely morning our friend and neighbor Dorothy Gorsline passed away. Never more will Dorothy suffer, and the very day seemed to rejoice in this.

The flood waters receded, leaving fence lines draped with grasses and debris, and gravel bars, river rock and silt deposited upon the floodplain. Phone calls began mobilizing action to replace the bridge over Prairie Creek with a higher, stouter one, and Enterprise residents were out assessing the flood damage and attempting to dry out their water-logged homes.

Meanwhile, Prairie Creek (the land) is swept clear of ice and snow except for occasional patches that remain on the shaded "norths." It will take many man-hours to repair the damage done to our county roads, but already road crews are out tackling the worst areas this morning.

Baked a large loaf of sourdough bread for Max Gorsline's family.

March 11—The mild morning began partially clear, and a warm wind continues to dry things out. One of the first returning robins hopped into my line of vision through the kitchen window, eyeing with anticipation our new raspberry patch for future meals. The barn lots are a sea of mud, a yearly condition we ranchers must live with and accept for quite a while. A yellow primrose is bursting into bloom alongside our house.

This afternoon Ramona, daughter-in-law Liza, and children accompanied me to the OK Theater to attend the production of "The Fisherman and His Wife," the Missoula Children's Theater's annual treat to our area. This company travels from town to town in the Northwest, auditioning local children, who are then cast in various roles, and practice after school for one week before presenting the play.

Sixty-three Wallowa County children participated in this year's production, and granddaughter Carrie, along with several of her friends, had landed bit parts. The audience was filled with proud grandparents captivated, naturally, by the acting of their offspring.

On the way home I stopped by the Blue Willow Sausage Kitchen to pick up my elk sausage. Daisy seems happy with her two calves, and my hens laid seven eggs today.

March 12—Another glorious day. The earth smell of spring is in the air. Fixed sausage gravy and biscuits for breakfast, did my chores, packed a light lunch and then left with our hiking group for Big Sheep Creek canyon near the Imnaha. This being our first hike of the season, we were all rarin' to go.

Traveling along Little Sheep Creek for 25 miles, we noticed it was running full of snowmelt, and cows with their newborn calves basked in sunlight amid new greening on the canyon sides. After delivering 150 potatoes to daughter Jackie's for the upcoming cow chip, lottery, and baked potato feed at the Imnaha School, we turned onto a rocky dirt road that crossed a bridge over Little Sheep Creek, then drove to the Courthouse Ranch, where we parked our Jeep in the yard.

After visiting briefly with Anne Borgerding, we began our trek. This ranch, now owned by Don Buhler, resembles a scene from the pages of a Western novel. High rims tower above Big Sheep Creek, which rushes along through the middle of the canyon of the same name.

Lots of early history here, when large, early-day sheep outfits inhabited the area. Walking along, we watched calves being born right before our eyes. Others, only hours old, romped around in the warm sunshine or curled up asleep. Such a wonderful place to calve out cows.

Newborns, the placenta still clinging to them, staggered unsteadily to their feet to suckle full udders before they were even dry. This is the stuff of life: birth, death, winter, spring and everlasting life. Thank goodness for these rural areas, where one's faith can be renewed in the eternal and the Master's handiwork is always in evidence.

We visited cowboys Eric and Don before continuing our lovely, long walk. Leaving the calving cows behind, we then marveled at greening canyon walls, where pine trees marched up the draws and joined the snowline on top. The Divide country stretched high to our west, a vast tableland of grass that would provide summer range for the cattle.

To the south lay the Marr Flat grazing area, another sea of summer grass that is kept productive by the controlled grazing of cattle whose grazing stimulates grass growth, not to mention the benefits of manure that nurtures the soil. In much the same way, herds of buffalo used to nurture our Western prairies before man nearly exterminated them.

We walked past dormant hackberry, thornbrush, sumac, and wild rose with shriveled red hips still clinging to the bushes. Under the brown tufts of bunch grass, the new green was beginning to appear along with the cheatgrass that lay like a carpet on the creek bottoms.

In a sunny, sheltered nook alongside the road, we searched for and found the first yellow waxy buttercups. Fueled by the air of "early springness" we seemed to derive energy from the canyon. Choosing a sheltered spot to escape a breeze that had suddenly sprung up, we ate our lunches.

Too early for rattlesnakes to be about, or so we told ourselves, and we joked about my yard sale straw hat that kept blowing off my head. Scotty solved the problem by punching two holes in it with a stick and tying a scarf around under my chin. We startled a small covey of chukars and then crossed another wooden bridge, and before we knew it we had reached the Soderblooms' cabin. We had walked nearly seven miles!

Resting up a bit before the long hike out, it was nearly dark in the canyon of the Big Sheep when we at last reached the parked Jeep. I was late doing chores that night, and after a long, steamy tub bath, fixed some supper, thus ending a perfect day.

March 13—Today was our bull sale, held before the Enterprise Auction Market sale, and this afternoon Doug and I attended Dorothy's funeral. In juxtaposition to yesterday, a freezing March wind blew mini blizzards across the valley.

An overflow crowd showed up for Dorothy's service, and filled Bollman's Funeral Parlour with flowers. Lester Wells, long-time friend of the family, spoke fondly of Dorothy, and many members of the Imnaha Christian Fellowship were there to pay their last respects.

We all shivered in the biting wind as we stood outside, waiting for the casket to be carried to the hearse. A snow squall all but obscured Ruby Peak, the mountain that dominates the town of Enterprise. A dark blue curtain of sky hung in the west as the long funeral procession slowly made its way up the hill to the Enterprise Cemetery.

A snow storm, waiting in the wings behind that curtain, began to empty itself on the mourners gathered around the grave. Snowflakes swirled down and covered the blue casket as Lester Wells concluded the graveside service. Rosemary Green tossed a basketful of flowers over the casket. Pink and yellow petals fell softly, like the snow.

March changed its mind nearly immediately, and the sun was shining by the time we drove to the church for dinner. We partook of a delicious meal, prepared by the church ladies and members of the Imnaha Christian Fellowship.

And so life goes on. I couldn't help but notice a sweet, innocent baby girl asleep in the arms of Phyllis Dotson, Dorothy's friend and neighbor. The wonder of a new child. Birth, death, youth, old age, winter, spring. The baby girl's name was Emily.

This purebred Gelbvieh bull calf was born during a storm in Wallowa County, but is cozy and warm in a straw-filled stall on the Mt. Joseph Cattle Company Ranch, near Enterprise.

March 14—It snowed last night, a wet spring snow that rapidly soaked into the earth. Brief periods of clearing toward afternoon, in the wake of a blustery north wind. Played with my little buddy, James, this afternoon.

We constructed a bow for his arrow, out of a green willow limb. Each year toy manufacturers come up with more new plastic contraptions for children to amuse themselves with; but little boys will always love sticks, and anything made out of them, like fishing poles or bows and arrows.

Only 16 squares left to embroider on the state flower quilt.

March 15—Cloudy, ground frozen, 20 degrees. Ice formed on the puddles, so we got a break from the mud. We are about halfway through with calving and my Guernsey, May, still hasn't done anything. Maybe she's going to call the whole thing off.

Baked Italian Easter bread in a paper sack, which turned out to be fun as well as delicious.

Doug and I met daughter Ramona and husband Charley at the makeshift footbridge this evening, and we drove to the OK Theatre to attend the Montana Repertory Theatre production of "The Rainmaker." The play, very entertaining, was a comedy about a farmer and his two sons and daughter in a drought year. We in the valley are very fortunate to have live theater brought to us by our Wallowa Valley Arts Council.

March 16—Cloudy and cold with snow in the forecast. Worked all morning on the purebred Simmental registration forms. By afternoon, it began to rain before turning to snow. It was a wild and windy evening when Doug and I left to attend the Imnaha School's Cow Chip Lottery and baked potato feed. Snow blew in front of us as we drove down Tenderfoot Valley Road to the Imnaha highway.

As the elevation lowered below Sheep Creek Hill, the snow became a fine rain, and then a mere drizzle by the time we arrived. A small plot on the school lawn had been roped off and marked with wooden stakes. A yearling steer grazed inside the enclosure. A steer chip lottery?

Squares could be purchased for $2.50, and the purchaser's name written on the square, which was drawn on a large poster board. When the steer was so moved, the spot would then be determined by charting on the board and the marked stakes in the steer's enclosure. The lucky square would determine the winner's prize of $100.

While everyone waited for the steer to let the chips fall where they may, we ate a baked potato with all these different, yummy toppings. Proceeds, after the $100, of the lottery would be donated to the Jack and Harriet Finch Memorial Scholarship Fund, to remember these beloved former Imnaha school teachers. Money raised from the baked potato feed would help finance the annual end of school field trip for grades 1-8 of the Imnaha school.

Meanwhile, the steer, content to graze the lawn, or buck and play as he saw the children doing next to him, was not cooperating. It was quite dark when we left, and the steer hadn't! We later learned that Thelma Buchanan won the $100, and generously donated it back to the scholarship fund.

Returning out "on top," we found that the storm had ceased and the snowy roads already melted.

March 17—Forgot to wear green on this St. Patrick's Day, so naturally got pinched by husband, who remembers these things.

Took granddaughter Chelsie to lunch at the "Country Place" for her annual birthday treat. We ate and visited at a small table for two, watching the snow storms come and go over the mountains. Afterward Chelsie purchased a bag of fish food, which she fed to the hungry trout, who competed with ducks, geese and black swans for their meal.

Home to start an elk stew simmering in the dutch oven for supper, and tend to my cows and calves before Doug and I drove to Joseph High

School to watch grandsons Buck and Rowdy wrestle in a tournament. Can these really be my dear little boys? Turn around and they are competing in school sports; turn around again and they're in college. What next?

March 18—Doug's nephew, Mike, arrived late last night, to spend the weekend with us. He was here when May finally decided to calve. Without further ado she simply laid down in the pasture and produced a big red bull calf, which was soon up nursing.

Mike and I drove up to the Ferguson Ridge ski area for a look-see. The mild weather had taken its toll and things were melting, leaving the place deserted on this Saturday.

Driving home, we ran into a blizzard that erupted out of the March clouds. Stoked up the fire and enjoyed the aroma of roasting chicken in the oven, while we played a long game of scrabble. Mike, a bachelor, really appreciated a bit of home cooking.

March 19—Snowed through the night. Mixed up a batch of health food muffins for breakfast, full of grated carrots, apples, oat bran, raisins and nuts.

Invited son-in-law Charley over for supper tonight, as his family is California-bound to pick up their daughter at college for spring break.

March 20—The first day of SPRING! And what a day, with nary a cloud, bright, clean, sunshine, birdsong and no wind. Turned Daisy out with two calves and let May in the barn to milk her out. By nightfall a gauzy layer of clouds separated just enough for a big, brilliant moon to swim into view. The weather is changing.

March 21—A warm spring rain awakens the sleeping native blue grass, and a faint tinge of green begins to spread across the land. My sister Mary Ann is visiting this week in the Northwest so, after doing chores, she and I took a tour of Wallowa Lake.

The surface ice was beginning to break up, creating interesting patterns of open water. Reflected in those sky-blue strands of open water were puzzle pieces of snow-covered Bonneville and Chief Joseph Mountains. We went crazy taking pictures. The park was deserted, except for the deer, and was a new experience for Mary Ann, who had seen it only during tourist season.

We met Doug at Kohlhepp's Kitchen in Joseph for lunch, then drove to Eggleson Corner, parked our car and hiked along Prairie Creek, through the fields to daughter Ramona's house, which is still inaccessible from the highway because of bridge construction.

Intermittent snow and rain showers did a number over the mountains, which were in full view during our trek. Mary Ann took several panoramic shots to piece together when they were printed. The moon, one day away from full, sailed across a spring sky, and a brisk wind turned Pete's Pond to a frothy glow as we treated Mary Ann to dinner at the "Country Place" that evening.

March 22—Worked all day on my column, then invited Charley, still batching, over for elk steaks, sourdough biscuits, mashed potatoes and gravy...the works. We topped it off with a gooseberry pie that Mary Ann had baked.

March 23—Since May is producing so much milk, I put another calf on her.

Wrote an article for California Cattlemen's magazine, a labor of love, a profile on my cousin, Edna Smith, who passed away in January of this year. She would have been 86 this month. Edna was an inspiration to all who knew her and a rancher all of her life. Her pleasure was her work, and her work was her pleasure; the only way to fly!

March 27—Cool and cloudy, with the snow line returning to upper Prairie Creek. Our crew began sorting and loading seed potatoes in preparation for shipping tomorrow.

March 28—It was snowing when we got up this morning. Our world turned white again with wet spring snow. Orange-breasted robins decorated the bare-limbed, snow-covered apple tree. Fluffed up in the cold, they, too, wonder what happened to spring. The grass appears to receive a magic ingredient from spring snow and when it melts, as it quickly does, a brighter shade of green lies underneath.

Our first load of seed potatoes left the county today. Between writing this column and cleaning house, I baked an old-fashioned devil's food cake for daughter-in-law Liza's birthday dinner here tonight.

By late afternoon I was knee-deep in beef enchiladas and chile rellenos. It had been such fun searching through my foreign cooking recipes to create a south-of-the-border meal. There were 12 of us around the supper table that night, enjoying our Mexican feast. The children, both young and old, never tire of lighting the candles on the cake, which are often re-lit for the benefit of the younger ones.

After supper I walked out into the night to let May in the barn to nurse her calves.

March 29—A good two inches of snow on the ground, and it continued to come down most of the day, as small blizzards swept down off the mountains and across Prairie Creek. It was pretty miserable for our potato crew.

March 30—The morning dawned clear, with brilliant mountain snowfields gleaming above all. By mid-morning a chill wind began to blow and soon high clouds blotted out the sun. A pot of beans and leftover Easter ham simmered on the wood range all day.

March 31—The month of March goes out like a lion whose roar is full of swirling snow flakes, so laden with moisture that when they hit the window panes the water drips down like rain. Wet snow piled up and became pretty sloppy by the time I went out to chore.

Tonight I tended grandchildren while daughters helped out with a junior art festival at the Joseph Civic Center. The stars appeared in a cold, clear sky, and it was frosty-cold when I returned to the ranch.

April 1—Greeting me in the kitchen this morning my husband informed me that my favorite cow, Startch, was on her back, all four feet pointed skyward, in a ditch! This I believed until a slow grin spread from ear to ear! April fooled...again.

The ground was frozen and a biting wind blew as I chored. After cleaning house, I attended a junior art show sponsored by our Wallowa Valley Arts Council. My mind is still boggled at such an exhibit of youthful talent. Wallowa County young people outdid themselves. There were watercolors, drawings, oils, oil washes, basketry, photography, murals, and computer art.

What a feather in Doris Woempner's cap, as she had given birth to the idea of a junior art show and chairmanned it. All media were presented and displayed well. A most impressive show.

April 2—No surprise; we'd heard the storm in the night. By 6 a.m., daylight savings time, a good six inches of snow had fallen. A frozen yellow sun glowed through the cloud layer as it rose over the eastern hill.

Out in the cow barn, the wind-driven snow had sifted through cracks in the door, creating interesting patterns on the walls. After finishing our chores, Doug and I decided we'd had enough of snow on the ground, so we drove to Imnaha for a change of scenery. We left the snow-line behind about halfway down; last night's storm appeared to have been pretty widespread. Little Sheep Creek splashed happily along the roadside on its way to join the Imnaha River.

Reaching warmer climes, we were cheered by misty-yellow weeping willows and bright, spring-green wild gooseberries appearing on the canyon hills. The ground was saturated from the recent heavy rains and the hillsides had greened up noticeably.

While eating lunch at the Riverside Cafe, we missed seeing the familiar smiling face of old-timer Jim Dorrance, whom we learned now resides in a La Grande rest home. In the dining room that looks out over the river, Jim's big chair was vacant, and the many-forked mule deer buck that Jim bagged years ago on the Snake River stared down at us from the wall. We all miss you, Jim.

Afterward we drove downriver, where Doug tried his luck at steelhead fishing. While I read a good book, Doug hooked a nice one, but it wasn't a "keeper," having no clipped fin, so it was turned loose to spawn and provide for future fishing.

Nearby hillsides and draws were decorated with the lovely white blossoms of the sarvis berry. We drove slowly past the Imnaha gardens, savoring the sight of yellow daffodils and purple crocus. We noted that Inez Meyers and Ferm Warnock already had their gardens tilled. On the way home we stopped for ice cream at the cafe.

Imnaha is a "place in the heart" for those who live there, and for us who visit. The small settlement consists of a tavern-store, cafe-gas pump, tiny post office and a 1st-8th grade schoolhouse. Just up the road a piece stands Imnaha's first church, the building still under construction on land donated by long-time resident A.L. Duckett. The progress of the church depends on funds, which are limited. Many local residents have contributed to the church building fund and soon the dream of completing their church will be a reality.

As we left the cafe I noticed a poster on the bulletin board: *Lost Dog, Wanted: 3 legs, blind in one eye, missing right ear, tail broken, recently castrated. Answers to the name of LUCKY.*

We drove back up "on top" and into winter again, started a fire and went out to do the evening chores.

April 3—Gorgeous morning, which began when a white light flowed softly over the snowy Wallowas at sunup. I ran up to the top of our hill to capture the fine early light on film.

More snow fell overnight, which lately seems to be a nightly occurrence. Attended a noon 4-H leaders meeting at the Cloud 9 Bakery in Enterprise.

April 4—Because many ranchers are still in the midst of calving season, I thought Agri-Times readers would like to hear about a couple of calving incidents that were recently experienced by two Wallowa County gals.

It seems Rod and Linda Childers, of the Blue Ridge Cattle Company, had this cow in labor, which wasn't too happy with the world in general and became even less happy when Rod and Linda showed up to discover she was having trouble calving. When it became apparent the cow couldn't complete the birthing process without human help, Rod attempted to drive her to the corral on his horse. After a few near-miss charges from the cow, the horse said, "No way Jose," and refused to have anything more to do with the irate mother-to-be.

The couple returned to the pickup, pulling a gooseneck trailer that they parked near the cow. Further enraged, the cow charged the truck, dented a door, and resisted all attempts to be loaded. She was, at the point, one mad cow, ready to charge anything that moved.

She had blood in her eyes when Linda, using a bit of cow logic, climbed onto the trailer, held her jacket over the tailgate and shook it at the cow! The infuriated bovine came rushing, like a wounded rhino, at the jacket, which Linda dangled just ahead of her. Whereupon the cow flew furiously into the trailer in pursuit of the jacket. Rod slammed the gate and they headed to town and the nearest vet.

All turned out well for both cow and calf, until it was time to load her up for the trip home. No one could get that ornery cow into the trailer until, once again, Linda came to the rescue, waving her jacket. It worked like a charm!

Then there was Denny Dawson, another Prairie Creek rancher, who held a prolapsed uterus in her arms while hubby Jim summoned the vet. I've heard of ranch wives left holding the bag, so to speak, but not a cow's uterus, the cow intact! This story has a happy ending, in that both cow and calf survived the ordeal, as did Denny. Good work!

Like Linda says, there are days when ranch wives want to turn in their resignation; but they don't, and what would the fellows do without 'em?

This is the first morning in quite awhile we haven't awakened to see snow lying on the ground. Not yet anyway. A biting wind blows and the air feels heavy with more of the white stuff, as it continues to snow over the mountains. All this wouldn't be so bad, except that the calendar insists it's spring. We in Wallowa County know this doesn't mean warm, sunny days, just more unsettled March-like weather continuing on through April and May. At least we're receiving much-needed moisture, and for that we are thankful.

Easter Sunday dawned warm and cloudy before the sun's rays melted away the clouds, revealing an incredible blue dome of sky. Cooked a batch of sourdough hotcakes on the wood range, then mixed up the starter to bake bread for Easter dinner. Out to chore before returning to the kitchen to put a huge ham to roast slowly in the oven and bake a raspberry pie. Yesterday I'd baked an apple pie and made a big potato salad.

It was a happy morning with birds singing, ham and pie sending out delicious smells, and the arrival of grandchildren. Young James wore a T-shirt which said it all: DON'T WORRY, BE HAPPY! The house overflowed with colored eggs, and baskets of Easter bunny grass. There were around 23 of us, give or take a few who arrived late due to cattle-feeding chores.

Being such a pretty day, for a change, some even ate outside. The boy cousins got into a rousing game of football on the lawn and the little ones ran interference. After pie and ice cream the children locked up the dogs, so they wouldn't eat the eggs, hid Easter eggs around the yard, and staged several hunts.

April 5—Cold and windy outside, so decided to bake an oatmeal cake using a recipe from Judy Wandschneider's new cook book, *Cookies and Conversation*. The cake contained so many good ingredients: whole wheat, flour, honey, nuts, coconut, butter, eggs, milk and oatmeal. The honey gave it a wonderfully moist texture that was delicious.

No new snow, but still very cold with a raw wind blowing off the mountains, which continue to spawn snow storms. Shook out clean straw, hooked up the heat lamp and washed and the baby chicken feeders. All is ready for the new chicks when they arrive. Baked two loaves of oat bran, whole wheat bread to go with a hearty beef-vegetable soup for supper.

Attended a meeting of our Wallowa Valley Arts Council this evening. We are in the midst of planning our seventh annual Festival of Arts, which is scheduled for the end of the month. In addition to a fine art show, the cowboy poets will be coming to town and there will be a good western dance band for Saturday night's shindig. Lots of local volunteer effort goes into this event, which grows larger each year.

April 6—A beautiful spring-like day, incredibly warm. I have another calf to feed at the barn, a little thing whose heifer-mother didn't have enough milk.

Picked up my baby chicks at the Grain Growers feed store this morning: 25 Cornish-cross fryers and 25 Rhode Island Red pullets. Got carried away with "spring fever" and purchased my vegetable seeds as well. It was a nice warm day to receive the day-old chicks. They were soon running around in their clean quarters, drinking water and eating, a pastime they will continue non-stop for days. So fast will they grow that some of the Cornish-cross fryers will be ready to butcher at six weeks.

Ben and his sons are harrowing our fields, which always gives them a cleaner look, spreading the manure around and stimulating grass growth.

A colorful sunset flamed and died as I did chores, so I took a walk down Tenderfoot Valley Road. Clouds, edged in salmon-pink and shot with golden rays, resembled an artist's brush strokes, and the sky was his pallet of living color. Dark, bare-limbed, ancient willows and snowy mountain peaks etched themselves against the canvas sky.

April 7—Cloudy at dawn, but warm sunshine later in the morning. Very busy as spring chores increase daily. My typewriter, on the kitchen table, doesn't get used as often now, and I look longingly at it in passing.

The warmth has brought up purple crocus and the first red-green furls of rhubarb. Cleaned out flower beds and raked willow limbs in the yard, which is beginning to dry out some now. The snow-line has fled to the timber on upper Prairie Creek.

Each day the green deepens and the grass grows. Out on Salmon Creek the elk appear in large numbers, grazing the new grass just beginning to grow. Understandably, the ranchers are very upset over this because they are feeding expensive hay to their cattle while elk graze their future spring-summer range before the cattle are even turned out. Hopefully, ranchers can work with Fish and Wildlife people and, perhaps, hire someone to "herd" elk off private lands.

The elk much prefer grazed-over areas, where cattle have run, to forested areas where livestock grazing is not allowed. In effect, the cattle rancher supports these elk herds and isn't given any compensation for doing so. Maybe we should be in the business of raising elk instead of beef. McDonald's could sell elk burgers and people would ask, "Where's the beef?"

April 8—Cloudy, cool and windy; warmed up by afternoon. After chores I drove to Alder slope to care for grandchildren while mom helped with the 4-H radio auction, an all-day money-raising event that netted our county 4-H program a nice sum.

Wondering who had received the highest bid on my sourdough bread sticks, I later learned my own husband had purchased them. Items such as a flat of Wilmer and Mary Cook's raspberries, Gale Johnson's homemade huckleberry jam, and Edna Bornstedt's pie-a-month for a year sold very well.

April 9—Baby chicks and new calves growing like weeds, and the laying hens are up to 10 eggs a day. The banty rooster, Chester, crows at the beginning of every new day, and we should, too, for every day we are alive is a good one.

April 10—It was cloudy and cold when Startch, the big Simmental-Holstein cow, calved this morning. Her calf is a spittin' image of May's big red bull. The sire, a red bally Simmental, must be pretty potent.

The baby chicks are sprouting wing feathers.

Worked all morning on publicity releases for our Wallowa Valley Festival of Arts. Ben hauled our older bulls to the hills today, while Doug went out to check fences and chase elk away. Late for supper, he didn't return from Salmon Creek until nearly dark. It seems snowmobilers left gates open this winter and several head of horses and a mule were roaming around in our neighbors' fields. Since the road out in that country is not open for winter travel, it was the earliest Doug could get out there with a pickup.

April 11—Beautiful, clear morning and frosty cold. Let Startch in the barn and May's two calves helped with the milking! Our thoughts this morning are with son Steve, who is undergoing back surgery.

Ben and Jim drove the fall calves to the corrals and separated cows from calves. Now the bawling begins and early tomorrow morning we head the cows to the hills.

Fried chicken for supper, then went out to deal with Starch's huge udder. The barn cats are in heaven; fresh milk again!

April 12—Finished chores just as the dawn sky blushed faintly pink. Clear as a bell and unbelievably warm. There must be some mistake. Usually, Mike McFetridge and I trailing cows to the hills brings on a snow storm.

Saddled my mare, packed fried chicken and a bottle of water into my saddle bags, and climbed aboard for a long day. Ben and Doug, mounted on Hondas, helped drive the cows away from their calves. We got them on a dead run and kept them moving pretty fast so they couldn't look back at their bawling calves. After much urging and yelling, we drove the milling cows into the four corners, headed them north, and began the 16-mile ride to the Dorrance corrals, where the herd would bed for the night.

After the cows lined out pretty good along the gravel Crow Creek road, Ben and Doug returned to the valley ranch and potato cellar. It was an incredible day, neither hot nor cold, and no wind. Buttercups began to appear like spilled patches of sunlight upon the hills.

The creeks were running, fed by melting snowbanks that lay high up in the shaded draws. Mallard ducks were pairing up and numerous hawks circled lazily overhead, some nesting already in willows alongside the road. The earth smelled of spring, the air so fresh and pure. We drank in big gulps of it. The cows soon quit their bawling and settled down to a nice steady gait.

Noon came, and Mike and I ate our lunches in the saddle, riding along as the herd wanted to keep traveling. By now motherhood was completely out of their minds and those cows were envisioning acres of rolling, bunch grass range. No more stale winter hay. We rode slowly past the remains of old homesteads, like the Warnock place and alongside Crow Creek we approached the hand-hewn log cabin on the old Dorrance place.

Having been in the saddle for 16 miles, I was a bit stiff-legged when I dismounted to open the corral gate near the old "pink" barn. By then the cows, too, were showing signs of weariness and willingly trailed in. Mike, at 80-plus years, looked as spry as ever. Quite an old hand.

Doug soon appeared with a truck load of hay, which was scattered around for the cows. Mike and I unsaddled our horses and turned them into a small pasture along Crow Creek.

Meanwhile, back at the ranch, we did our chores before attending the Enterprise FFA barbecue and auction at the high school. We were relieved to hear that Steve came through his operation just fine and expects to be home in a week.

We enjoyed a Jim Probert pit barbecue beef dinner, then bid on items offered for sale by FFA members, which had been constructed in their shop classes. Sturdy metal and wooden feeders, gate fasteners, picnic tables, wooden clocks and many other beautiful wooden items were auctioned off by Roger Nedrow, local auctioneer. Proceeds would help finance the chapter's annual California field trip.

April 13—Up before dawn to chore and fix lunch, and then Doug drove Mike and me out to Crow Creek. Another absolutely gorgeous morning: two in a row! A little frost on the green grass meadows quickly turned to dew. Sparkling Crow Creek glinted in sunlight as Mike waded across to drive our horses into a corral. We were soon saddled up and driving the cows, which eagerly took off toward Dorrance grade. Doug drove on ahead to put out salt and check fences.

The road was dry and a cloud of dust hung in the still morning air above the cattle; all we could see of the bunch were backs and heads. The hill ground appeared moist and the grass was growing. Several large snow banks remained on the shaded norths of Dorrance Gulch amid a stand of ponderosa pine. Meadow larks sang to us as we climbed the grade and Lorelei Cannon stopped to chat on her way out to herd the elk away from private lands. That new breed of horse, called Honda, was riding in the back of her pickup.

Reaching the top of the grade, we turned to look back at the distant Wallowa range, whose snow-covered peaks shimmered with white light. The cows, nearing their destination, took off toward Dry Salmon, which was wet! Nearby snowbanks, uphill from us in a stand of aspen, sent trickles of water down to fill the creek. And everywhere, buttercups! Never have we seen them so thick.

Mike and I rode along, silent most of the time, savoring the solitude of the rolling hills. Near the corrals at the Johnson place we spotted a jack rabbit, his long ears pinned tightly against his body so Mike's dog Sam wouldn't spot him. The ploy worked and the rabbit escaped detection. Rarely do we see rabbits in these hills, except for an occasional cottontail.

As the miles rolled slowly on, Mike, who was born on Elk Mountain, related many interesting tales of his youth. All too soon we topped the rise near Greenwood Butte and turned the cattle into the Butte Creek pasture. The count at the gate: 118 head. The cows immediately went to grazing, catching a bite of old grass with the new. Their calves are only a memory now.

As Mike and I rode back to the Johnson corrals, we were able to view the distant Wallowas and absorb the miles of peaceful quiet, broken only by the steady clip-clop of our horses' hooves. At the corral we ate our lunches while waiting for Doug to pick us up.

Back in the valley in time to clean up, pick up neighbor Ardis Klages, meet Betty Van and Trudy at Safeway, and drive with them to attend our monthly CattleWomen's meeting at Marilyn Johnson's in Wallowa. Home to chore and deal with milk cows and baby chicks before joining friend Bud and Ruby Zollman for supper at Tony's Shell in Joseph, after which I made it, albeit a little late, to a photo club meeting at Eagle Mountain Gallery. Needless to say, I had no trouble sleeping that night.

April 14—Mild and warm, with high cirrus clouds and no wind. Son Steve is progressing satisfactorily, but faces a long, slow recovery period. The weaned calves have bawled themselves hoarse and are beginning to settle down.

Charley Phillips is ready to throw his loop to heel a calf during a branding on Big Sheep Creek.

Our potato crew continues to ship seed out of the county on most days. Local veterinarian Sam Morgan arrived after lunch to Bangs vaccinate heifers. Seventy degrees today and so warm, my daffodils have burst into golden blooms.

Baked a batch of sourdough bread sticks for Doug, who, after all, paid $16 for them at the recent 4-H radio auction. They went good with the elk steaks we had for supper.

April 15—A beautiful, clear, frostless morning, and each day sees the spring greens deepen in color. Three calves are now nursing Startch, after I acquired another calf from an older cow that Doug plans to sell. After chores I invited friend Grace Bartlett to drive down to Big Sheep Creek with me while I photographed a branding.

Sarvis berry created white sprays against the greening canyon sides, and new shiny bright leaves appeared on alder, cottonwood and willow. A few clouds had formed—their dark shadows moved slowly across rimrocks—and Big Sheep Creek ran full of snowmelt as we drove about four miles up a dirt road to where the cattle were corraled. When we arrived, cowboys were putting several cows through the chutes to ear tag them. Baby calves separated from cows were bawling for mamas, and the cows likewise.

My son-in-law and son were there as were other hands from around

Wallowa County cowboys brand calves on Big Sheep Creek. The ranch is owned by the Mt. Joseph Cattle Company.

the county. It was a picture setting there along the creek, surrounded by rimrock canyon country, ponderosa pine and a large meadow. Border collie cow dogs roamed everywhere and youngsters twirling their own little lariats ran in and among the baby calves.

After a branding fire was blazing, syringes filled, and brands heated, the cowboys mounted their horses and began to heel the calves. Making it look easy, they roped a calf by its hind feet, dallied to their saddle horn, then drug it to a waiting ground crew who branded, castrated, vaccinated and dehorned the calf.

It was over so quickly, the calf scarcely knew what happened. Four cowboys roped and a large ground crew was always ready to finish the job. It is always such a pleasure to watch good cow horses work. They must be able to back up and hold the rope taut while the ground crews complete their task. No timed event here, no rodeo, just practical work.

Most modern-day ranchers use chutes to work their calves, but many Wallowa County outfits still rely heavily on the horse and the old ways, to get the job done. There is an art to working cattle and Eastern Oregon is proud of the fact that it has some real cowboys left, even in an age when they are referred to as a "vanishing breed." And from the looks of the young ones coming on, the "Old West" will continue to live for some time to come.

As we ate our lunch, grandson James joined us in the pickup, after which we left, taking small James with us. Anne Borgerding, assisted by daughter Ramona, daughter-in-law Liza and neighbor Bonnie Marks, prepared a big dinner at the ranch house for the branding crew.

Driving out, we noticed the yellow cascade of blooms on the forsythia, and that Imnaha's rhubarb was ready to pick. Meanwhile, back at the ranch. James was quite taken with grandma's baby chicks and we spent a good deal of time down at the calving shed, sitting among them. He was a tired little buckaroo when mom picked him up that evening.

April 16—Cloudy and threatening rain, which we sorely need. After chores, I hoed the flower beds and strawberry patch. 'Tis the season of weeds again.

Doug and I treated ourselves to dinner at the Gold Room restaurant in the old Chief Joseph Hotel. All weekend the establishment had been celebrating the opening under new management. The branding crew had danced until the early morning hours to live music at the Cowboy Bar, and reported quite a turnout. Shades of Chief Joseph Days!

The place recently had undergone a facelift. We were happy to see Erma Tippett there, looking just as charming as ever. Years ago Erma owned the Gold Room, and she and the old hotel have seen lots of history being made in the county. With its hand-carved wooden signs out front, the hotel is a landmark and continues to lend a colorful air to the town of Joseph.

April 17—It is so nice to be able to hang clothes on the line after such a long winter. Dryers are nice, but nothing beats the fresh air smell on clean clothes.

Picked up biographies on cowboy poets from veterinarian Fred Bornstedt this morning so I can write articles for local newspapers. Then I stopped by 4-H'er Cory Miller's house to watch some of his Bobwhite quail hatch from their tiny eggs. They were just minute little balls of soft feathers, and went right to running around the minute they pecked their way out of the egg.

Cory had them in his bedroom and transferred them from the incubator to the brooder after they hatched. He is using the project for both school science and 4-H.

Doug left for Salem to pick up son Steve, who is being released from the hospital after his back surgery. I made two banana cream pies: one for grandson Shawn's and another for son Todd's pie-a-month birthday gifts.

Attended the annual meeting of the Alder Slope Pipeline Association this evening at Wilmer and Mary Cook's place. Aside from the business of maintenance, discussing leaks, and various improvements, the meeting is a chance for neighbors to get together and visit. It was voted to lower the assessment. How refreshing in an age when everything else is rising. After a most productive meeting, we munched on Mary's homemade cookies.

A light sprinkling of rain fell as I drove home, and a moon grows, like the spring grows, and sailed between rain clouds.

April 18—Very busy all this week working on publicity for our annual Festival of Arts. The day began with a beautiful, warm, clear morning and a few thunderheads beginning to build over the mountains. Took grandson Chad a video copy of the "Wallowa Story" for his 15th birthday today.

An amaryllis bulb that has been growing near my kitchen sink finally opened into a deep red bloom today. Lovely flowers feed the soul, and in this day and age we do need to feed the soul often.

A dry wind began around noon. We really need more moisture.

Baked a sourdough chocolate cake for granddaughter Carrie's 12th birthday, which also is today. I dropped it off on the way to attend a panel discussion on the needs of our local hospital. The rural health care issue is one that affects us all in Eastern Oregon. After several brain storming sessions, many excellent suggestions were brought to the forefront, written down and voted on. It was generally agreed we need a well-staffed facility. Now, all we have to do is fund it.

On the way home I stopped to have a taste of birthday cake. Doug had returned with Steve, who is a bit sore but glad to be home.

April 19—Bright and sunny. Even though the usual thunderheads build, nothing materializes in the way of rain. Am irrigating flowers and rhubarb because things are very dry.

The huge old Prairie Creek willows are beginning to leaf out. Always a miracle of sorts to see green everywhere we look. The old apple tree is bursting with buds and the robins are beginning to build nests everywhere.

Haven't lost a single baby chick. They just keep eating and eating.

Attended a planning meeting of our Wallowa Valley Arts Council this evening, where we went over last-minute details of the festival.

April 20—The crew loaded four semi trucks of seed potatoes at our cellars on this warm, sunny day. Cleaned out the vegetable garden, pulled up stakes, and tossed out withered sunflower stalks. Baked a gooseberry pie to use up frozen berries, for all too soon the bushes will be bearing again. Hot, dry winds continue. We all wonder about irrigating so soon. Phone rings constantly with coordinating potato trucks. The full "spring" moon rose tonight before disappearing behind dark clouds.

April 21—A fine misty rain falling this morning. Just what we needed. Several of us CattleWomen served 80 senior citizens dinner at the Joseph Civic Center at noon. A fierce wind developed, and black clouds boiled up, thunder cracked, and soon it began to hail. Then, across the greening fields, a rainbow sprouted. Mother Nature to the rescue.

April 22—A light skift of snow melts into spring-green grass, and the snowline appears to be up near Max Gorsline's place this morning. After days of winter white and early spring brown, we are always in awe of the seasonal change around us, so refreshing to the eye.

My chicks continue to grow and baby calves frolic around in the lower field. On my way to town this morning, I noticed around 30 head of mule deer grazing an alfalfa field. They, too, crave something green.

On the way home I stopped at the Harley Tucker arena in Joseph to watch the riding trials being performed by the 1989 Chief Joseph Days court. Already another year has passed, and tonight a new queen will be chosen. It was cold, windy and spitting rain as the girls completed their maneuvers on horseback. The spectators held their breath as each girl came flying at breakneck speed around the arena for their run-ins. Waving with one hand, reining their horse with the other, they raced at terrifying speeds and smiled to boot. They will be required to perform this act at each rodeo performance. Daughter Jackie, herself a former court member, helped judge the riding trials.

I gathered up my grandchildren and brought them home to warm up and eat lunch. After chores that evening, I attended, as a member of the press, the queen coronation dinner at the Joseph Civic Center. It was raining and the mountains were obscured by misty clouds. Long tables, decorated with cowboy boots full of flowers, and colorful balloons greeted a large crowd that began to arrive at the annual affair.

Several former court members attended, among them the 1949 Chief Joseph Days court: Queen Beverly (Oliver) Graham and two of her princesses, Marian (Mawhin) Birkmaier and Ruby (Mallon) Zollman. Still looking young and charming, and wearing the same blouses they wore on the 1949 court, their beauty has obviously endured the test of time.

After a delicious prime rib dinner, there followed a program emceed by Tom Swanson that included reports by the Chief Joseph Days rodeo and Indian events committees. Plans for this year's Indian dances, tepee encampment and parade are under way and, according to chairpersons Ralph Swinehart and Millie Frazier, promise to be bigger and better than ever.

Henry Kinsley and the Hell's Canyon Band played so people could dance and, at 10 p.m., during an impressive ceremony, the 1989 Chief Joseph Days queen was crowned by the 1988 queen, Chantay Jett. Queen Heather Williamson and her princesses, Jill Stilson and Shawna DeVault, teary-eyed for the moment, now face a busy year as they represent one of the most popular rodeos in the Pacific Northwest.

April 23—Gorgeous morning, with clear, rain-washed skies and Wallowa Mountain snowfields dazzled by sunlight. Giant, cottony clouds began to form and soon dark horizons appeared out north, and we wondered if it was raining in the hill country.

Hoeing in the strawberry patch when Liza showed up with the two little ones. Grandma would watch them while mom and dad helped with another branding on Big Sheep Creek today. I made it through the day, and also renewed my respect for mothers of small children. How, I wondered, did I ever get anything done?

When my grandchildren are here, I don't attempt to do anything else. To small James I am the epitome of a "pal." In his childish eyes, there is simply nothing grandma can't do. How could I resist any request from this small person, who holds me in such high esteem? He is so innocent, sincere and endearing, I melt just looking at him.

Adele, at a year, is grandma's dolly and, because she is still at the carrying stage, we did everything with baby sister on my hip. We picnicked in the yard, walked down to see the baby chicks several times, played in the sheepherder wagon, read books, gathered eggs, and the day disappeared.

That evening when mom showed up, James was branding! After having roped and tied a big teddy bear, he would take the fireplace poker and "brand" Teddy. Then he roped my foot while I fed Adele in the high chair.

My returning daughter and daughter-in-law took one look at me, and commented that my eyes had that glazed look. The house was upside down, crumbs, toys and "branding" stuff lay everywhere. But oh, what fun those children had. I fixed supper and collapsed into a chair to rest briefly before tackling the chores. Motherhood, I decided, is definitely for the young.

April 24—Twenty-nine degrees. Frost whitens the green grass this morning as Doug leaves for Hermiston to sell some yearlings that have wintered in a feedlot there. The cattle will be sorted, some sold, and the remainder hauled home. It began to cloud up after he left.

We will begin trailing cows and calves to the hills in two days, and somehow sandwich in the Art Festival, which begins the following day.

A steady, cold rain began by late afternoon. I built a fire in the wood cook stove and finished typing my weekly column. Our crew loaded four trucks of seed potatoes at our cellars today.

April 25—Gusty winds blow wild-looking clouds across the valley. The ever-changing mountains alternate between light and dark, appearing and disappearing between shifting veils of mist that resemble thin gray curtains. The stiff breeze bends and exercises the grasses, grooming them. Trees sway in the fresh, cold air; it is around 35 degrees.

Sunlight streams through the picture window until, without warning, a passing cloud empties itself of sleet-like rain that quickly turns to curtains of snow, slanted in the wind: a blizzard. The horses run to a pasture corner, turning their rumps to the storm.

The cloud moves on, replaced by more sunshine, and the scene repeats all day long. Hope things improve before we start the cows and calves on their long drive to summer range tomorrow. So strong was the wind, I found it difficult to stand upright when I went out to do evening chores. New, green willow leaves littered the barn lot.

Baked a batch of chocolate chip cookies to fill the empty cookie jar. At the sink, doing dishes, I watched new storms come and go over Mt. Howard and Bonneville Mountain. By late evening the wind had lain down and the skies were beginning to clear. It was nearly 10 p.m. when I heard the rumble of our cattle truck coming down the road. Doug had returned safely with a load of yearlings.

April 26—A big semi-truck-trailer arrived this morning to deliver the remainder of our yearlings. I went down to open corral gates for the driver. The first animal off the truck was Startch's yearling heifer. Covered with manure and mud, she seemed happy to be home.

"Spread with Ed" Jones is fertilizing our fields today. Ben and Jim sorting cattle, so we can start the drive tomorrow. It is traditionally a very busy time of year for Wallowa County.

Raining off and on all afternoon, as Doug hauled two loads of cows and newborn calves to the hills, and Ben and Jim branded heifers at the chutes. Rain drummed on the roof when we went to bed.

April 27—Morning arrived early—5 a.m. I went out to chore in the still, damp dawn, while Doug fixed breakfast. I put together a lunch, then put on layers of warm clothing, a slicker, chaps, hat and warm gloves. Old hand Mike McFetridge and I had the same problem: we were wearing so much clothing, we could hardly climb into the saddle.

Ben and Doug helped us round up the cows and calves in the lower fields, and without too much difficulty, finally got them lined out onto the road. Thus began a LONG day for the three of us, one that wouldn't end until the herd reached the bed ground at East Crow.

The Joseph school bus slowly made its way through our trailing cows and calves, and near the four corners a big fertilizer truck waited patiently until most of the cattle passed before proceeding down the road. No traffic on the gravel lane that borders Klages' property, but we encountered a problem when the herd strayed into an open field where the fence was down.

Ben rode on ahead to help Doug, while Mike and I rode drag, which meant urging the smaller calves on, a constant job. Several of these babies would be pretty footsore by trail's end. Cows in the lead would miss their calves and come bawling back to find them.

On a short stretch of pavement, a calf suddenly turned around and headed back to the ranch, with me in hot pursuit. I finally got him turned and drove him back to the rear of the herd, which was nearing the Blue Ridge Cattle Company ranch. A cold, misty rain began to fall as the cattle lined out along the Crow Creek gravel road.

Doug left on his Honda to return to the ranch, leaving Ben in the lead and Mike and me bringing up the rear. The cattle were strung out for quite a ways as we started up Crow Creek Pass. Mike and I kept after the calves as we slowly plodded along.

The cold became more intense and we were glad for layers of clothing and our slickers. A freezing wind accompanied by sleet and more rain greeted us as we climbed the long hill, and rain dripped off our hat brims.

As we reached the top of the pass the sleet diminished somewhat. Before us stretched the endless rolling hills, the long winding road and the cold, gray day. Gone were the buttercups and snow banks...and sunshine. At noon we ate our lunches in the saddle, still using willow sticks to prod the calves along.

Briefly I visited with son-in-law Charley, who was hauling Mt. Joseph Cattle Company yearlings to grass. The yearly exodus has begun; McClarans were also trucking cattle to summer range. Must admit the inside of a truck cab would have felt better than the saddle today, but Mike and I wouldn't miss riding for the world. The cows would mosey along, resting or grazing and drinking when they came to water.

Doug appeared and we were able to warm ourselves briefly in the pickup. Then back in the saddle to finish our job. We made it to the holding pasture at East Crow around 5 p.m. I climbed down off my mare to push the last bunch of tired calves through the gate, then unsaddled and turned my horse loose with the herd.

Along the trail several calves had crawled through fences and had to be retrieved. Once I climbed a fence, caught a calf by a hind leg and pushed it back under the fence. Unbeknownst to us, a small calf had lain down under some thorn brush, hidden from view, as we rode off without it. Mack Birkmaier, driving by, informed us about the missing calf. Doug had driven back, roped it and brought it back to the herd.

Back at the ranch we did chores, then cleaned up and made it to the Enterprise FFA parent-member banquet by 6:30. My face was red from being subjected to the cold wind all day. A large crowd enjoyed a delicious roast beef dinner served by the FFA girls.

I was very proud of my two grandsons, Shawn and Chad, who are greenhand chapter members. Chad, who won the Initial Greenhand Award, looked so much like his father at that age. Looking around I noticed many third generation FFA members in the audience. A very well-organized program followed, which was conducted by the FFA members in a business-like manner that displayed poise, public speaking ability and leadership skills. As usual, I was especially proud of most of the top award winners, as they were members of my Sourdough Shutterbugs 4-H Club.

Driving home we noticed lights on in the calving shed: Ben's day not over yet; he'd had to haul a heifer into the vet for a C-section.

April 28—Again I chored in the gray light of dawn, then back to the kitchen where Doug had cooked up a batch of sourdough hot cakes on the wood stove. Mike and I enjoyed a good stick-to-the ribs breakfast before we rode out with Ben to East Crow.

Not as cold this morning, although still cool, as a chill breeze blew across the green hills, rippling the puddles of water in the road. Mike and I agreed it was hard to leave the cozy, warm pickup and catch and saddle our horses, but we did. Our horses munched oats while we saddled up and soon we were gathering the herd into one bunch.

It was a lovely sight, seeing the cows and calves trailing out onto the winding road in the early morning light, that filtered down between the green hills and running creek. The cattle traveled much easier, the calves mostly trail-broken by now. However, we still had to prod the tail-enders. Sunlight and shadow dappled the landscape, and Mike spotted a

Chad Nash, left, winner of the initial Greenhand Award, stands with his cousin Shawn Phillips. The boys are members of the Enterprise FFA chapter.

returning salmon splashing up the shallow creek.

We let the cattle rest where Crow Creek meanders near an old log cabin near the Dorrance Place. Later, as we rode up the grade, we noticed the first golden blooms of the balsamroot, and looking back we could only see the Wallowas for a fleeting second, as they swam in dark purple-gray clouds.

The last calf reached the top by 1 o'clock and Doug soon appeared in the pickup. Mike and I gratefully took advantage of the opportunity to eat our lunches in the warm cab. After Doug drove on ahead to put out salt, I walked about three miles to keep warm; chaps flapping, spurs jingling, using a whip to keep the stragglers going.

More miles over rough, rocky places, until finally, we reached the Deadman pasture and turned the herd through the gate. While riding over another hill to Salmon Creek, I noticed scattered patches of blue bells, vase flowers, bird bills, pink phlox and sweet fennel. Heavy clouds hung like a gray canopy overhead, and the wind blew with a moaning sound as we rode into the corral to unsaddle and turn the horses loose.

Because we would be coming back in a week or so to brand, we left the horses there.

After the long ride back to the valley ranch, chores, and a hot bath, I donned denim skirt and blouse, and Doug and I made it to the artists' reception at the Joseph Civic Center. Our Art Festival had begun.

When we walked through the door, it was like entering another world. The quality of the artwork was incredible and beautifully displayed. Crowds of people arrived to view bronzes, oils, pine needle basketry, pottery, photography and water colors. Many pieces came from all over the Northwest, but the majority was done by local artists. Twelve quick-draw artists completed a piece of work in one hour's time and it later was sold during a silent auction.

Around 9 p.m. I began to fade. Long days and short nights were beginning to take their toll.

April 29—Mike McFetridge called around 6 a.m. to report that some-one had called telling him another calf had been found on the road. A good neighbor had tied the calf up and delivered it to Jim Probert's place, where Doug picked it up. Mike and I will never live this down.

As a warm sun rose over the hills, it melted the heavy frost that lay along the bottoms. Chester crowed—time to get up. The happy morning suddenly wasn't, however, when I went out to the barn lot to find my Guernsey milk cow May dead. She had appeared healthy last evening, but this morning, apparently, she was the victim of frothy bloat.

As she lay with all four feet stuck out, her calf stood nearby bawling, so I drove him into the barn, where Startch accepted a fourth calf. It is hard to believe May is gone. I had raised her from a calf.

Later, our friends from Lakeview, Sunny and Alice Hancock, arrived. We met them, along with Max Gorsline, at Pete's Pond for supper before attending the Cowboy Poetry Gathering at Cloverleaf Hall. The program, arranged by Leigh Juve, broke all records for attendance and proved to be another hit here in the county.

Leigh and her decorating committee had outdone themselves. Blue-dyed sheets with western scenes painted on them provided a colorful backdrop. A cow's skull, chaps, wagon wheels, spurs, bits and bridles decorated the hall. Lovely freshly picked tulips and lilacs from Hermiston were arranged in Olaf's pottery vases.

Promptly at 7 p.m., master of ceremonies Fred Bornstedt opened the program by singing one of his original songs, and the line-up of poets that followed was impressive, including Leon Flick, from Plush; Scott McClaran and Sam Loftus, from Imnaha; Dan and Carol Jarvis, from Joseph; Jennifer Isley, from Burns; and Sunny Hancock, from Lakeview. Mike Hale and Imnaha cowhands Greg Krolick and Chuck Gibson provided old-fashioned foot stompin' music between poets.

The show was professionally carried off by Bornstedt, who had composed limericks for each poet's introduction, which added to the total merriment of the evening. Young third generation cattleman Scott McClaran, who had become a father for the third time only days before, kept the audience entertained reciting poems he had written about AUMs and Forest Service restrictions, and how they relate to cattle ranching in Wallowa County.

Sunny Hancock recited a poem about a turkey using crutches, and Jennifer Isley presented a poem about "Them Durned Wire Gates," which many of us gals in the audience appreciated. Carol Jarvis brought a few tears to our eyes when she talked about her grandson in a poem she wrote after he asked, "Grandma, what does a cowboy do?"

Carol's husband, Dan, wearing high topped boots with undercut heels, recited poems he'd written that reflected his own life riding the western ranges. Sam Loftus brought down the house when he took out his teeth, much to the horror of wife, Laura, to recite "The Saga of the Bad Brahma Bull!" Leon Flick, standing on a table, wore slippers that resembled two horned Hereford bulls, and used them as props while reciting a humorous poem about two slippers—'er ,bulls—getting into a fight.

More music from the Imnaha cowboys; more hilarious, nostalgic, humorous poems that so honestly reflected the life of a cowboy. The stuff of poets...in the hearts of cowboys. It was all there, the hard work, the pathos, and the humor that sustains them through the long days in the saddle.

The show was deserving of national billing. It told the cowboy's story, as only he can tell it. Fred Bornstedt wrote a song that he says is being recorded soon. A song, he says, that is a rebuttal to Waylon and Willy's song "The Last Cowboy." Fred's song, titled "Waylon and Willy Are Wrong," tells how the cowboy is still alive and well, at least in Eastern Oregon.

Finally, Fred asked everyone to stand and sing the first verse of "Home on the Range," a fitting end to a marvelous program. Leigh's committee was instantly in motion, and soon more than 600 chairs were moved so Scotty Alexander and the North Santiam Band could play, and people could dance; and kick up their heels they did, until the wee morning hours. Wallowa County loves good western music.

Meanwhile, just off the kitchen, Mike Kurtz and his crew barbecued-

Leon Flick   Fred Bornstedt   Sonny Hancock

Carol Jarvis   Dan Jarvis   Scott McClaran

Cowboy poets.

on-a-stick way into the night, until it sold out. The marinated beef (tri-tip) was served with cold asparagus, sauce and fresh pineapple chunks.

Doug, Max and I folded around midnight. Another smashing success for our Arts Council. Kudos to all who worked so hard to pull it off.

April 30—The morning was beautiful, as had the entire weekend been. Birds sang, hawks were nesting in the willows, tulips were red in a row alongside the house, chicks growing each day, and a few new baby calves still coming in the lower pasture.

Later I went to the art show in Joseph to pick up my photographs and, while there, helped count the people's choice votes. The award went to Austin Barton's beautiful bronze Indian, titled "Winds of Autumn."

Barton's own story was interesting. At the age of two weeks, he was packed into Hells Canyon by mule, as his grandfather's wealth came from a gold mine there. After his parents were married, they took the job of caring for the first elk herd brought into Wallowa County.

Barton grew up in Joseph, on the edge of the wilderness, working on ranches, trapping, hunting, logging and breaking horses. He was the seventh son in the family. After World War II he returned to the Wallowa Valley to begin his own family. A back injury in Hells Canyon forced him to change professions and allowed him to follow a strong desire to become an artist. He received his formal art training in Portland.

Today, Barton is a full-time sculptor, who also works on his ranch in Southwestern Washington, where he has raised registered cattle for the past 25 years.

Returned to the ranch to mow our law; the first time this year.

May 1—Spring is now full blown! This afternoon I drove up on Alder Slope to visit my grandchildren. As I pulled the little ones up the road in their wagon, the grass appeared an iridescent green, and a snowy peak would occasionally peek through the clouds, its ramparts caught in moving mists that snagged in draws and swirled around the timbered slopes.

The children picked dandelions and loved being outside. Horses, calves, and lambs kicked up their heels at spring, like the children, rejoicing in the day.

The mill whistle blew at four, and I knew son Todd was on the job at Boise Cascade in Joseph. His shift would last until midnight.

May 3—A late calf was born dead, so Ben skinned it and placed the hide on one of Startch's four calves. Now I was able to milk for the house without stealing from the calves.

May 4—Early this morning, Lockes' cattle trailed past our place on their way to summer range in the hills. It was almost hot, like a summer's day.

Doug cleaned out the chicken house, a yearly undesirable job, but necessary, as I will move the chicks up there in a day or two.

May 5—Wilmer and Mary Cook stopped by with a new variety of raspberry and a cherry plum tree for us to plant. All over the valley ranchers and farmers are frantically busy, planting their spring crops, fertilizing, repairing fences, cleaning ditches, trailing cattle, branding, and setting out irrigation pipe. The work never all gets done. And we wives learn to live through this "fever" that spurs our men to stretch each day, make it longer, so they can catch up.

We invited Max Gorsline to supper. I had baked an apple pie, made sourdough biscuits, and a pot roast was in the oven.

Leaving the men to finish eating and visit, I drove to Enterprise to listen to a talk given by a local fellow who took six months out of his middle-age life to hike the 2,200-mile-long Appalachia Trail. Living a dream he held for 40 years, he told of experiences along the trail, which stretched from Georgia to Maine, ending at Mt. Katahdin. This just goes to prove nothing is impossible if one has enough desire and determination.

May 6—Burning with a summer-like intensity, a glaring, hot sun rose over green fields this morning. After chores, while Ben and Doug worked the yearling steers and heifers in the corrals, I moved my growing chicks to the chicken pen. Using our little Luv pickup to transport the birds, I first caught the pullets and placed them in a cardboard box on the front seat.

As I was driving from the calving shed to the chicken yard gate, those squawking Rhode Islands escaped their box and begin to fly around inside the cab. One red pullet perched on the steering wheel, while another lit on the dash. I brushed one off the gear shift and it flew to sit on my shoulder! Feathers flew, but somehow we made it to the chicken yard, where I turned them loose into a clean, grassy area.

Shaking out clean straw in the chicken house, I placed water and feed there before going back for a load of fryers. Luckily those plump Cornish-cross meat birds lacked the agility of the pullets, merely crouching stupidly in the box. It was a hot morning and, the odor of chicken overpowering inside the pickup, I seriously contemplated not raising chickens next spring.

Just time to wash my hands before helping Ben and Doug move the yearlings to a rented pasture on the old Estes place. Returned home to a hot shower, I attended the Joseph Junior Rodeo and watched several of my grandchildren perform. The pee wee events were run that day and they ranged from mutton riding to goat tail-tying.

As usual, it was highly entertaining watching Wallowa County's miniature cowboys and cow-girls perform. I took lots of photos.

May 7—Brilliant sunshine makes the dandelions look like drops of shimmering gold amid the sea of steamy, wet, intensely green grass. The chickens are happy with their new quarters. I went out to milk Startch for house milk, then let the three calves nurse.

A pair of honkers are nesting across the way near an irrigation ditch. My tulips are intensely red in the sunlight, and the first strawberries are blooming in the patch. The heat of the sun burned a hole in the morning sky, and by late morning cotton ball clouds floated overhead, causing dark, dramatic shadows to sweep across the fields and hills.

We could do with more rain.

Returned to the Joseph Junior Rodeo today, to watch the juniors and seniors do their stuff. Aside from some anxious moments when grandson Rowdy was stepped on by a steer in the riding event, all went well and Chad and Shawn managed a second place in the cowhide race.

Neighbor Willie Locke started up his wheel line irrigation.this morning, while the Houghs, worked their field across the road, plowing until well after dark.

May 8—In the middle of the night, thunder pealed in the distance and the horizon lit up briefly with heat lightning before the rain came.

May 9—Very busy writing and taking numerous photographs for various projects in the county. Seems like everyone is putting together a slide show and my pictures are in demand. Really keeps me hopping to sandwich ranch work chores, grandmotherhood, and domestic work between these tasks. The days aren't long enough.

This morning I made it to Cloverleaf Hall to attend a tour organized by members of our local timber industry. As a member of the press, I rode along in a bus out the long Zumwalt road to Buckhorn Lookout, where the local CattleWomen were set up to serve lunch. No restaurant could duplicate the view, not to mention the cuisine, that greeted tour members that day.

Below lay the canyons of the Snake and Imnaha, stretching on for as far as the eye could see—miles upon miles of unpeopled places. The ridges unfolded into each other in many shades of springtime green. Wildflowers such as pink phlox, in variations of white to bright pink, lay like a carpet. Although a stiff breeze blew, it wasn't uncomfortable.

I was amazed to learn while visiting an 83-year-old local woman, that she was looking upon the scene for the first time. She said her men folks had been there from time to time, but she always stayed home to cook a meal or tend the children.

Dappled sunlight and shadow fell on the benches as tour officials talk about managing our natural resources. I took photos and made notes, and then we drove to Cold Springs Ridge Road where we viewed the damaged timber within the confines of the largest forest fire in Oregon last year, the Tepee Butte fire.

Our long-awaited rain began to fall around 9 p.m., a good, warm rain. Just what the country needed.

May 10—Our rain gauge measured more than an inch of precious moisture this morning. I went around picking up night crawlers, which were everywhere, and put them in a coffee can of dirt for fish bait. I can dream, can't I?

By 10 I was attending a town hall meeting at Cloverleaf Hall, filled with loggers, ranchers, businessmen, timber industry leaders, Forest Service, housewives and politicians. Most of those there were people whose livelihoods directly or indirectly depended on a healthy timber industry. I took more notes as the crowd waited, hoping to hear some solutions to problems created during the aftermath of the Tepee Butte burn. It seems agriculture or timber is facing a crisis of one kind or another every day.

We listened to explanations of comprehensive management plan impact statements in accordance with rules governed by the Hells Canyon National Recreation Area. When it was over, the people walked out into their rainy world carrying yellow ribbons that would fly from their hats and cars, showing solidarity to their cause. There's no escaping the fact that to accomplish anything these days, and in the days to come, we must all become involved.

Later that afternoon, between rain showers, I managed to take several shots of Max Gorsline's 1916 steam tractor for an article. Misty clouds clung to the mountain sides and Max had fired up the old tractor, belching smoke, for the benefit of my camera. There it stood, like a behemoth of the past, painted and restored to its original splendor. I could feel the warmth of its innards as the fire had heated the water to create steam.

Max, who is an artist when it comes to restoring old machinery, has a special knack for tractors. The old tractor looked indestructible and remains a marvel of man's early ingenuity. Truly a labor of love.

May 11—Cloudy, cold and whiskers on the mountains. Periods of sunlight illuminate the brilliant greens of the surrounding fields and hills. Our old apple tree is a shower of pink and white blossoms.

Daughter Ramona and I were on our way by mid-morning to meet Ilene Potter at the bottom of Sheep Creek Hill, after which we proceeded to Imnaha to attend our monthly CattleWomen's meeting. The meeting was preceded by a delicious potluck lunch at the home of Bonnie Marks.

Little Sheep Creek was full with snow melt and rain runoff. The recent moisture greened up the canyons and golden balsam root glowed on hillsides. We noticed A.L. Duckett had already set out quite a number of cabbage plants. The partly constructed church stood nearby, sporting new windows that beamed in the morning light.

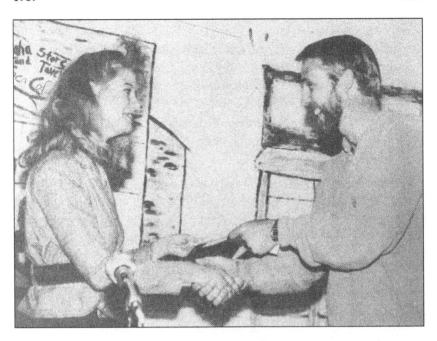

Tina Bauquet, the only graduating eighth grader at the Imnaha School, receives her diploma from Mike McCulloch, Joseph School principal.

Gorgeous fleecy clouds floated over Imnaha and the pioneer cemetery was sprinkled with the blooming white narcissus. The sweet scent of lilac and locust tree blooms hung in the air, and Imnaha's old-fashioned gardens were abloom with honeysuckle and violets that had escaped their beds. New gardens were up and the river was higher than we'd seen it in years, carrying snowmelt of the high country to join the Snake, then the Columbia, and thence to the Pacific.

On the way home we stopped at Borgerding's on Big Sheep Creek to pick up grandson James. Anne had been watching him while mom helped ride. Big Sheep Creek, too, was high as the snow continued to come out of the high country.

That evening after chores and supper, I drove the 30 miles back down to the Imnaha canyons to attend the annual end-of-school program. Grades 1-8 staged a show centering around the theme "Hee-Haw," presenting a selection of skits, jokes and songs, which were hilarious.

Teacher Char Williams, who is full of energy, wit and enthusiasm, was aided by several mothers who helped with rehearsals and props. The stage backdrop consisted of dyed sheets on which were painted scenes of "downtown Imnaha." Students, who assumed roles of various members of the community, acted out a typical day at Imnaha. It was a riot.

Little girls dressed as local ladies coming into the store for coffee and local gossip. Buck Matthews and Luke Royes, walking bowlegged, outfitted in cowboy togs, strolled in as Bill and Clyde, and discussed the affairs of the day over a cup of coffee.

A typical "Hee-Haw" question: One student asked another, "How would the Forest Service put out a kitchen fire?"

"That's easy," replied the other.

"They'd start a backfire in the living room!"

Imnaha resident Lloyd Doss, formerly of the "Sons of the Pioneers," accompanied the children as they sang a Western song. The one graduating 8th grader, Tina Bauquet, was presented her diploma by Joseph School Principal Mike McCulloch.

Just as the sky turned pink with sunset colors, the children raced outside, and under the direction of their teacher, who joined in, they danced a lively Virginia reel. Pam Royes and Chuck Gibson provided live guitar music of "Turkey in the Straw." These were happy children, seemingly oblivious to the cares of the "outside." Happiness sparkled in their eyes as they swung their partners and clapped to the music.

"Only in Imnaha," commented a young mother next to me.

Homemade pies evaporated as cowboys ate three or more slices. Hugs from my own grandchildren before driving home in the twilight. As usual, feeling a little better about the world, at least this small corner of it.

May 12—Twenty-five degrees, clear, with heavy frost. Loading the last of the seed potatoes out this week.

May 13—Frosty, clear, sunny. Two Imnaha grandchildren spent the night, but had to leave early because Buck was to help his dad brand today.

May 14—Mother's Day dawned clear and sunny. Received many nice cards and gifts from my family, including a new camera case from Doug.

This morning two friends and I hiked up on the mountain and went morel mushroom hunting. We found enough for all of us along old logging roads. The forest wildflowers are gorgeous, and included larkspur, goldenrod, calypso, Indian paintbrush, and wild strawberry.

Finding the first morel is always exciting. They were so camouflaged, it was hard to spot them right off, but we soon got an eye for them.

By noon, huge billowy thunder clouds formed overhead as we ate our lunches high on the East Moraine overlooking Wallowa Lake. Later, in my kitchen, I dredged the morels in flour, sauteed them in butter, and froze them on a cookie sheet. When they were frozen, I packed them into plastic bags to store in the freezer.

That evening Doug treated me to one of Russell's famous hamburgers at the Lake. Several other local people had the same idea; the popular eating place was packed.

May 15—Up at 5 a.m. to fix breakfast, do chores, make lunches, and head out to the hills with Ben and Doug for a long day of sorting cattle on Salmon Creek. After catching and saddling our horses, we rode through the west pasture and up into Deadman to gather the cows and calves we had recently trailed out.

After driving them into a small field and into a corner where they were to be held, Doug and Ben began to sort. Mike and I kept the herd together while Doug and Ben cut out purple tags, yellow tags, drys and heifers. After each bunch was sorted, they were driven to separate pastures, a slow process that seemingly went on for hours, as all cows had to be paired with their calves.

Different bulls would be turned into breed different bunches of cows, and a "heifer bull" turned in with some heifers. At one point Mike joked, "If they sorted down to two head, we might have trouble holding them!" With the wisdom of years in the saddle, this 81-year-old hand can still put in a good day's work.

Taking a 15-minute lunch break, we stretched out in the shade of the old log barn to eat and rest before climbing back into the saddle to continue sorting. The remaining cattle were driven across the road into a large pasture. Then we rode up the meadow and brought in several pairs and some yearlings, sorted them four ways.

It was after 6 p.m. when we finally drove a few cattle to the creek pasture, unsaddled our horses, turned them loose in the horse pasture and headed for the valley ranch. Cooked supper and did chores and to bed, another long day ahead tomorrow.

May 16—Out in the dawn to chore, then fix breakfast and lunch before Mike, Ben and I drive out to Salmon Creek, where we catch and saddle our horses, load them into the cattle truck and drive to Butte Creek. Ben helps us gather the fall calvers and head them onto the road, before leaving to repair fence. Mike and I begin the long drive to Circle M where the cows will bed for the night.

It is the beginning of a three-day drive that will eventually trail the cows to their high moraine pasture for summer and fall calving. It is frosty and a chill breeze blows over the lonely hill country. We have 118 cows, already sleek from spring grazing, and it turns even colder as we approach the top of Dorrance Grade, but we are somewhat sheltered the wind further down by large banks alongside the road.

Here we ate our lunches on horseback while stopping briefly to visit with Jim Mackin of C&B, and Mack Birkmaier's family. The cows were nearly to the "pink barn" along Crow Creek before we caught up to them. We finally arrived at Circle M, corralled the herd, turned our horses in another corral and drove home.

After doing chores Doug and I attended a prime rib dinner at the recently renovated Camas Room in the Wallowa Lake Lodge. The occasion was to honor and present owners of brand boards whose brands had been used in the past to decorate the lodge.

This was an early CowBelle project when Rita Reavis was president and Opal Tippett was secretary, many years ago, and both Rita and Opal were present. Opal, being the oldest one there, received in addition to her husband's brand a free dinner. One by one, each brand owner got up and gave an interesting history of their brand. Many old-time cowmen's brands were lined up on the wall, like Jay Dobbin, Jidge Tippett, Stubblefields, and many more.

When we walked out into the night it was raining, a steady, soaking rain, and the cattlemen were happy.

May 17—Up at the usual 5 a.m. to chore before Ben drove Mike and me out to the corraled cows at Circle M. As Ben disappeared toward Salmon Creek to repair fence, Mike and I caught and saddled our horses, then drove the herd out onto the road toward the valley.

The cows grazed their way along the grassy Crow Creek road as the long, silent miles passed by. When we reached the top of Crow Creek Pass, the wind kicked up and it became pretty chilly. For the third day in a row, we ate our lunches on horseback.

Arriving at the valley ranch around 4, we were met by Doug, who arrived pulling a sprayer with a tractor. We drove 20 head at a time into a smaller pen and treated them for lice. After turning the cows loose in the lane to graze until dark, we rode over the hill, unsaddled and turned our horses loose in the horse pasture, and called it a day.

May 18—The snow line is at Gorsline's and it appears to be snowing off and on over the mountains. Very cold and windy, the ground still muddy from last night's rain. By 6:30, Mike and I are riding over the hill to meet Ben and let the cows out into the lane and begin our cold morning drive.

Clad in long johns, down jacket, slicker, hat, chaps and wool scarf, I was still cold, as a freezing wind blew off the mountains and snow showers continued in the direction we were headed. I asked 81-year-old Mike how he kept his uncovered ears warm. He replied that after the first freeze of the winter, they turn numb and don't bother him.

My Border Collie pup, who until yesterday simply followed at my horse's heels, spent all day watching Mike's experienced dog work, and decided to do the same. I was so proud of her.

Approaching the elk fence gate, our teeth chattering in the freezing wind, we could see a snowstorm just above us on the east moraine. But, due to the exertion of having to push cows uphill into a snowstorm, which they didn't want to do, we warmed up considerably. My pup saved the day several times by getting after some cows holed up in thick timber.

Halfway up the side of a mountain, it began to snow, and we were suddenly riding through a winter forest. The hot bodies of the cattle sent steam rising into the cold air. It was quite a sight seeing the colorful cattle being driven through evergreen thickets and grassy slopes covered with snow.

The bright yellow of our slickers stood out vividly as we rode through the woods. When we finally reached the top of the lake hill, we looked down to see thousands of golden balsamroot wildflowers blooming on the hillside next to the lake. The waters of the Wallowa Lake were frothy as the wind-whipped whitecaps beat against the shore.

Again we had to urge the cows down an old wagon road, which they continually tried climbing out of. After much yelling and hard riding on an incredibly steep hillside, we drove them to their water supply and left them. We rode back up on top again and Doug was waiting in the pickup.

Exchanging a pack saddle for a riding saddle on my mare, Ben and Doug loaded salt on her, and Ben, riding his horse and leading the "pack" mare. rode down to the salt ground. At the elk fence gate we loaded Mike's horse, then drove back in the cattle truck to the lake side and picked up Ben and the two horses.

It was well after noon when we were joined by son Steve and Mike's wife, Joyce, at Kohlhepp's Kitchen in Joseph, where we ate ravenously of hamburgers and savored the warmth of being indoors. One more job accomplished. These cows will begin calving in mid-August and will be trailed home before it snows this fall.

After a hot shower, I drove to Enterprise to a book signing reception for Shannon Applegate, who wrote the book *Skookum*. While driving into town I noticed a late heifer calving in one of our fields. I climbed the fence to remove the placenta from the calf's head, so it wouldn't suffocate.

As I was washing my hands at the Bookloft, I met Shannon, who proved to be a most interesting young woman. She had taken 17 years to research and write this book about the interesting lives of the Applegate descendants, of which there are many living here in our valley, including one of my daughters-in-law.

"Skookum" is the story of a famous Oregon pioneer family's history and I had enjoyed reading it, so it was fun to meet the author. That night, a nearly full moon was swallowed up by dark clouds.

May 19—Clear and 25 degrees, and a heavy frost. Clouds formed by mid-morning above gleaming white snowfields and green Prairie Creek. Could have slept all morning, but rose to meet the challenge of another day. We shipped out the last of the seed potatoes today.

Watched the grandchildren a while, then baked a strawberry-rhubarb pie for grandson Shawn's pie-a-month gift. The full May moon rose over Sheep Creek Hill as I brought my bedding plants in for the night. It is supposed to freeze again!

May 20—Slept in until 6. Luxury! Twenty-five degrees again, ice forming on the sprinklers.

Baked another strawberry-rhubarb pie, this one for son Todd's pie-a-month, and as always, I had to make one for my husband, lest he feel slighted. Doug is plowing the potato field in preparation for planting seed.

Returning from the field where I'd driven Doug to the tractor, a glorious sunset flamed. Glowing like a giant coal in a pale, apricot sky, the sun sank behind the dark blue mountains around 8:15.

As spring days lengthen, the last rays of light linger over Prairie Creek even after the slopes have long been in mountain shadow.

May 21—Cloudy and cool, looks like it could rain. Hiked on a field trip near Minam with a history group. We ate our lunches along the river and enjoyed seeing many wildflowers, including the bright blue Camas, which was a mainstay of the Nez Perce diet.

Doug had roto-tilled the garden spot in my absence. Soon be time to plant the vegetables. Set out my bedding plants and hoed in the new raspberry patch.

May 22—A warm, dry day, and a strong wind blew into the evening. After milking my cow and doing some house work, I heated a kettle of water and chopped the heads off the heaviest of the fryers.

Was plucking feathers when daughter-in-law Liza came over with James and Adele to help. We finished butchering and dressing the first fryers by noon, "aided" by the grandchildren. Our crew cut seed today in preparation for planting seed potatoes.

May 23—At 9:30 a.m. it is snowing! Snowing on apple blossoms, snowing on lilacs and snapdragons and the petunias I transplanted two days ago.

Doug and his crew were to begin planting seed potatoes this morning, but that was postponed. The seed is cut, fertilizer ready to apply, and the ground prepared, but Mother Nature decided the ground needed moisture. She was right, and no matter what form it takes, we'll not question it. The snow was short-lived and soon replaced by cold rain.

On this gray, cold morning a pot of beans simmers on the wood cook stove. The aroma creates a homey, warm feeling that counteracts the gloomy day. Next to me, as I write, a cluster of fragrant lavender lilacs reposes in an old purple glass cream bottle. Because I am somewhat behind again on my column, due to working cattle last week, I try to skip over several days and return to the present.

May 24—Spent the day watching grandchildren while mom and dad did some cowboyin'. It was still cold when our crew began planting seed today. To do chores, I bundled the babies up in the wheelbarrow and tucked blankets around them. I wheeled them from the chicken pen to the cow shed. They thought it was great fun.

Baked a yummy gingerbread cake using a recipe from Judy Wand-schneider's cookbook. Canceled a short trip daughter Ramona and I planned to take to California for a Memorial Day family picnic. How could I leave the ranch in the spring?

May 25—Frost sparkles on green fields this morning. Down in the cow barn, mama kitty is giving birth to four kittens in the manger. Having made the decision to call off a planned trip to California to attend a Memorial Day get-together with relatives, decided to butcher the remaining fryers, and was soon plucking feathers.

While I was thusly engaged a fancy car drove in. Luckily, Doug was in the shop, as I was in the middle of entrails, gizzards, hearts, livers and naked birds and definitely wasn't in the mood to socialize.

By noon I had them all dressed, packaged and in the freezer. Dark clouds raced over the valley as hundreds of small yellow canaries flew in to feed on dandelion puffs. Planted two rows of peas and a row of radishes in the garden. As I worked, a large flock of sea gulls lit in Hough's newly planted grain field, while several large black crows harassed them. Through it all walked Nermal, the orange tomcat, which really created a ruckus!

May 26—So, on this day instead of leaving for the California reunion, I began a 16-hour workday.

Daughter Ramona, who was to accompany me, was on the potato planting crew, while I would help with the branding. It was up to a frosty morning at 5 a.m. to chore outside, then fix breakfast and gather food to cook out on Salmon Creek. By 7 we pulled out, saddle horses loaded into the truck and me driving a pickup with the cattle sprayer in back.

Arriving at Salmon Creek, we mounted our horses and each took off in a different direction to bring in cows and calves. A fresh morning breeze stirred the air and fleecy clouds floated in an azure sky. I rode through lupine, balsamroot, purple larkspur, pink geranium, owl clover, Indian paintbrush and mule ears.

Noxious weeds, says Doug. He is chairman of our local weed control.

The lush ocean of bunch grass moved in undulating waves over the hills. This immense rolling hill land is also home to elk, hawks, owls, squirrels, coyotes, badger, mule deer, not to mention songbirds like the meadowlark and bluebird. I might mention that our owls aren't spotted; they are the big horned owls that inhabit our old barns.

The thornbrush that lines the creek was covered with white blooms. As I rode to the top of a hill to look on the other side for cattle, I could smell spring in the air as my mare's hooves bruised the grasses and wildflowers, releasing the fresh scent of earth and growing things.

A sudden loud crack broke my reverie and my mare jumped sideways. I shook my fist at a retreating jet. How dare he break the sound barrier over these peaceful hills. The rude interruption was soon forgotten as I gazed in wonder at the scene below. From the hilltop, I could see the winding course of Salmon Creek, tucked between the hills, lined with thornbrush and willow, meandering through a long, green, wildflower-sprinkled meadow.

Overhead, floating clouds cast moving shadows across green hills. In the distance rose the snow-covered escarpments of the high Wallowas. The log barn, corrals and house stood at the north end of the meadow. I could see Doug gathering a bunch of cattle far below, and on the hill opposite, I spotted a bigger bunch, and so descended the steep hill and crossed the creek.

I helped Doug drive his bunch through a gate before riding up to gather the ones I'd seen. The cattle felt good and suddenly began to run...past the gate and up a draw. I spurred my mare and took after the lead. A horse rushed past. Doug to the rescue!

The cattle took off up another hill while some brushed up in an aspen thicket. We finally got them going back, and Ben was at the gate to head them in. Ben and I took the main bunch to the corrals, and Doug brought in a smaller bunch. Already we were nearly worn out and the day's work hadn't yet begun. Ben and Doug sorted, while I held the cattle in a corner. While the men did some ear tagging, I dug a fire pit, and soon a branding fire was blazing.

By this time it was past noon, so I opened some Dinty Moore stew and heated it on the branding fire in a dutch oven. We ate on the tailgate of the pickup. This would be the last food we'd eat until after 9 that night. Ben and Doug wrestled the calf chute off the truck and positioned it next to the wooden chute, while I went to the creek for water in which to put the mountain oysters.

Then I entered the long wooden chute and began pushing calves, two by two, into a squeeze chute that fed into a calf table. While Ben and Doug branded, vaccinated, ear tagged, dewlapped, castrated and tattooed the purebreds, I tried to avoid getting kicked by the lightning quick feet of those big calves. I devised my own system after a while, and all went smoothly. I twisted so many tails that I developed muscles where I didn't have any before.

When the pen emptied of calves, I ran more in. The smell of scorched hair and smoke from the fire mingled with the incessant bawling of cows and calves. The afternoon wore on and thankfully it remained cool.

Between the wooden sides of the chute I gazed longingly out at the new green leaves on the willows bordering the creek. When the first bunch was worked, we ran the cows in, sprayed them, and turned them on the hill. Then horseback again to bring in another bunch, and repeat the long process. I could tell by the sun it was getting late. When we finished the second bunch, and after they were turned out in the meadow, we mounted up without a minute's rest and gathered some dry cows and bulls across the road.

As evening descended on the Salmon Creek hill country, we were still riding, clattering over rocky scab rock, as we brought in the unwilling bulls. We drove the bulls with different bunches of cows and sprayed the drys. It was dusk when we rode back the length of the meadow. I glanced up to see two young hawks staring down at me from a nest of sticks in a thornbrush thicket. They seemed to say,"What's with all the ruckus today?"

After pushing a few cows to the creek pasture, we rode wearily back to the corrals, unsaddled and turned the horses loose. Almost fell asleep driving the long miles home to the valley ranch.

Startch, with a swollen udder, was waiting at the barn door. I gathered eggs, still wearing boots and spurs. Doug was frying mountain oysters and making Bannock in the kitchen. If Ramona and I had left for California, we would have been sleeping on a Greyhound as it sped through the dark Nevada desert.

Oh well, just another day on a ranch.

May 27—A new mountain snowfall gleams through openings in the clouds, and what clouds. Lofty mountains themselves, billowing and constantly changing form.

Fried one of the first fresh fryers; cooked mashed potatoes, milk gravy, buttermilk biscuits and creamed corn. We enjoyed a good home-cooked meal again, after either eating on horseback or a late-night rushed meal. When the cook is cowboy'in, she doesn't do much cooking.

May 28—Gray morning, the rain mixed with pellets of sleet and hail. Breakfast of ground elk, eggs, biscuits and strawberry jam. Starch swished her "switch" in my face while I was milking her this morning. Not a good way to start the day.

A warm fire in wood stove feels good. We had several visitors over this Memorial Day weekend.

May 29—Bright sunlight shining through east living room window is short-lived as dark clouds roll over Prairie Creek and empty over the mountains. The big Memorial Day get-together of my relatives will be today in White Rock, California, where they will gather and visit graves of our pioneer ancestors.

It hailed around mid-morning for about 15 minutes, leaving the ground white with hailstones. Other than the need for moisture, is the need for rest, and our farmer-rancher husbands rest when it rains. It is the only time in the spring they do.

Our calendar says this is Memorial Day "Observed," although traditionally, it is the 30th. At any rate, it has been a cold, rainy holiday for those who are visiting Wallowa Lake during this opening weekend of tourist season.

Meanwhile, back at the ranch, the spring work goes on, as always, for those of us making our living from the land.

May 30—Now that the holiday is over, the weather clears and Enterprise reports a chilly 29 degrees, the lowest temperature in the U.S. Here on Prairie Creek, it is a bit warmer. Ground fog burns off quickly as the earth's warm mists linger over Hough's newly planted field. Low clouds entangle themselves among the snowy peaks and then lift to expose a brilliant new snowfall.

A glorious, fresh, rainwashed morning, full of birdsong. Picked up grandson James, who went with me to the Alder Slope Nursery to purchase cabbage, tomato and other bedding plants for the yard and gardens. Must always restrain myself at Pam and Randy Slinker's beautiful nursery, or I'd buy a truckload of plants and flowers.

Bearing morel mushrooms, fresh asparagus, roast chicken and rice-shrimp salad, we drove up to Aunt Amey's cabin at Wallowa Lake to eat supper with her and Bernice. The West Fork of the Wallowa River tumbled full of high mountain snowmelt, rushing past the cabin window as we visited and enjoyed our meal.

May 31—As May prepares to leave us, a gorgeous, clear, bright sunny morning ensues. After hauling a wheelbarrow of aged manure from the barnyard, I planted the tomatoes alongside the south end of the house.

Our potato planting crew is out in the field again. Butchered the last of the fryers, mowed the lawn, and began planting the vegetable garden. Tomorrow we finish branding the calves in the hills, about 100 head.

June 1—June arrived like a beautiful song; by 5:00 a.m. it seemed as though all the birds on Prairie Creek had joined the chorus. The musicians just busted out all over, from Chester in the chicken pen to the smallest canary in the willows.

After chores, I gathered up the large fry pan and food to cook a noon meal out on Salmon Creek, as it was time to finish the branding in the hills. Friends Scotty and Max Gorsline drove out with us to help. Doug, Ben and I were soon riding across the vast rolling hill country gathering in around 100 pairs. After an hour or two we finally got them corraled and began sorting cows from calves.

The branding fire blazed and we were hard at it. Once again I pushed calves up the chute, until Max relieved me and I helped work the chute gate with Scotty. At noon I fried hamburgers in the long-handled frying pan over the branding fire. We laid the food out on the tailgate and ate hungrily.

The long, hot, noisy, dusty afternoon wore on, with Max and I taking turns pushing calves up the chute. Thunderheads boiled up over the mountains as the men sprayed the cattle, and turned cows back with calves.

As they finished, Scotty and I walked up the meadow to check on the baby hawks and owls before driving home. That night, Doug treated his "crew" to dinner at Kohlhepp's Kitchen in Joseph, and it was after 9 p.m. when we returned to the house and the mess of branding gear strewn all over.

We were then visited by son Steve and fiancée, who wanted to discuss wedding plans! I was too tired to contribute much. Steve said they were planning a "simple" wedding, but from experience in these matters, I knew what that meant.

I took a long, hot tub bath and concentrated on taking one day at a time to get through the busy days ahead.

June 5—Nearly every afternoon large thunderheads build over the mountains, only to dissipate by evening. The hills where our cattle are grazing summer range are very dry, and in Wallowa County we rely heavily on June rains, especially on that bunch grass range.

My garden is planted and the sprinkler is going this morning. I usually don't irrigate the garden this early, but at this rate the seeds won't germinate without moisture.

June 13—Overcast, but no rain in sight. June continues to be hot and dry. Although the valley remains lush and green, due to irrigation, the hill country and high plateaus are dangerously dry. Somehow, the spring work always seems to be accomplished; seed potatoes are in the ground, calves branded, fall calvers moved, garden planted, and all my fryers are in the freezer.

June 20—With the first day of summer less than 24 hours away, a cold, brisk wind blows over Prairie Creek and a new snowfall dusts the high Wallowas.

It is such a busy season for everyone. At present, Wallowa County is hosting the state Grange convention and Grange folks are everywhere. What a wonderful group of people they are. Our local granges have planned for months for this sudden influx of visitors, and the welcome mat is out.

Last evening I attended a Grange program at the Enterprise High School gym. A skit depicting the theme of this year's convention, "Climb

every mountain," was acted out by several women. Printed in the program
were the words to the song:

Climb every mountain,
Search high and low,
Follow every bi-way,
Every path you know.

Climb every mountain,
Ford every stream,
Follow every rainbow,
Till you find your dream.

A dream that will need,
all the love you can give,
Every day of your life
For as long as you live!

A fitting theme, I thought, that expresses the feeling of many of us
who choose to live here amid the beauty of Northeastern Oregon, even
though living here means hard work and sacrifice.

Cowboy poet and "cow doc" Fred Bornstedt entertained with his
self-composed ballads that, as he explained, let the audience peek into
the heart of the cowboy.

Blue Mountain Fiddlers Don Norton, Charles Trump, Don Foster,
Vadna Norton and Loretta Foster played some foot tappin' music, which
was followed by Imnaha cowboy poet Sam Loftus, who kept the Grangers
well-entertained with homespun humor.

A local square dance group, "The Alpine Twirlers," danced to the
calling of Jean Stubblefield. The state Grange president and his wife even
joined in.

In a closing tribute to Northeastern Oregon country, conducted by
John Fine of Portland, whose roots are in Wallowa County, I recognized
several of my slides as they were projected onto a large screen accompanied by a narrative and the strains of "Climb Every Mountain."

The world shrank as I visited the woman next to me, who was from
Portland. Although they weren't agricultural people now, she said, her
husband had once operated an Iowa farm. She had several grandchildren
there who were, she said,"being raised in the Grange tradition."

As I looked around the audience, my heart was warmed by these
people. Grangers have long been the backbone of our rural American way

of life and, when everyone stood to sing the "Star Spangled Banner," they did so with pride. These people brought to mind some of my California relatives, many of whom have been life-long members of Grange.

Tomorrow at 5 a.m. we local CattleWomen will begin preparing to serve breakfast to the Grangers at Cloverleaf Hall.

June 27—Haying time already. The fragrant meadow grasses quiver and fall to the swather, before coming to rest in pretty patterns that wind in rows over the low hills. And now, this afternoon, the raked windrows march away to the mountains through my kitchen window, and Willie Locke's baler spits out soft, round bales that send late afternoon shadows over the shorn fields.

Somehow, we have survived a very busy weekend that saw a wedding performed on our lawn, a Beef Council meeting, a grandson's birthday, another wedding in Waitsburg, Washington, and Aunt Opal Tippett's 90th birthday party!

Son Steve planned the wedding here, and the rest of us carried out his plans, which included a pit barbecue to follow the ceremony. So, last Friday, friends and relatives descended on our ranch and the wedding went off without a hitch. In fact, it was really quite lovely.

Intermittent rainstorms the evening before had made us all a bit nervous, but by Friday evening Mother Nature put on a show of her own that included hanging dark, dramatic clouds over the pastoral setting of Prairie Creek.

The old-fashioned roses that cling to the bunkhouse were a profusion of yellow blossoms, and the raspberry and strawberry patches were all freshly hoed and weeded. Twenty-five bales of straw were placed on the lawn for wedding guests to sit on, and the ceremony was performed under a willow tree, with the snow-streaked Wallowas providing a scenic backdrop.

The children, especially, had fun. They trooped in and out of the house, ate wedding cake in the sheepherder's wagon, and ran out to the barn to see the baby kittens.

The next morning we heard a cow bawling. Poor Startch had been shut in all night. Apparently the children had forgotten to latch the barn door and my milk cow walked in and closed the door behind her! Or something. Anyway, my milking parlour was spattered from wall to wall with nervous cow!

The chosen wedding date conflicted with grandson James' third birthday, and I was able to escape long enough to have waffles, straw-berries and whipped cream that morning on Alder Slope with my little pal. Then it was down to Cloverleaf Hall to hurriedly take some photos at the Oregon Beef Council meeting before returning to the wedding preparations.

Daughter Lori and husband Tom had arrived that morning, having driven straight through from Thermopolis, Wyoming. Thanks to lots of good help from our grown children, Doug and I survived the evening and spent the next morning cleaning straw off the lawn and living room carpet, not to mention scrubbing pots and kettles.

By 11 a.m. we were on our way to Waitsburg to attend the wedding of Doug's niece, Kim Miller. Son Steve and bride Jo would also attend the wedding before departing for an 11-day honeymoon on the Oregon coast.

Upon arriving in Waitsburg, we were told by the bride's mother, Sharon, that Waitsburg loves a wedding, and that is a fact! The church wedding was peachy: peach colored satin dresses on the pretty brides-maids, peach candles burned in ornate candelabras, peach bow ties and cumberbunds on the groomsmen, and peach ribbons festooning the pews. The reception featured peach colored mints and, not to be outshone, the peaches-and-cream complexion of the lovely and radiant blonde bride.

And what a reception. Music, food, a bubble machine, and such gaiety to wake up the sleepy, Saturday atmosphere of that small town on a hot, late-June evening. Waitsburg, with its lovely tree-lined streets and interesting older homes, is surrounded by rich agricultural land, rolling grain and pea fields, and everywhere the lovely patterns created by fallow field and sky.

These earth tone watercolor textures are woven into the folds of the hills. Colorful roses were blooming in Dixie, a peaceful little town we passed through on the way to Waitsburg. We returned home around midnight Saturday night to a blissful night's sleep. Here in our own country, June is the time of blooming wild roses, brilliant fireweed, and the sweet-scented syringa, which decorates the woods with a white shower of mock orange.

Around noon on Sunday, we delivered potatoes to "Russell's" at the lake and ordered hamburgers and fries, natch…beef and taters. Then we drove to Enterprise and attended Aunt Opal's 90th birthday party. This grand little lady, with hardly a wrinkle on her face, greeted her large family and many friends, many of whom had traveled long distances to be with her on her special day.

Opal, with husband, Charley, reared her family out on Pine Creek, traveling to and from town in a horse-drawn wagon. Because trips to town were few and far between, she made do like others of her era, and survives to tell us her interesting stories. Although most of her generation are gone, Opal remains in excellent health, a tribute to hard work, and years of "doing" for her family.

July 4—Here we are into July, and where did June go? Was it only a dream? Why do the longest days pass by so quickly? Perhaps it is because we are so busy "making hay while the sun shines," a cliche that accurately describes our Wallowa County summers.

We had our annual gathering of the clan for our family fun 4th of July picnic, complete with fire crackers. Our children, big and small, love the old-fashioned kind of 4th of July, with hand-cranked ice cream, watermelon, home-grown chicken, and barbecued hamburgers. There were roughly 25 of us, and if this large family becomes even more prolific, we'll have to rent the Liberty Grange Hall. Once again the sheepherder wagon serves as a spare bedroom for summer visitors; the grandchildren, especially, look forward to sleeping there.

After the picnic we gathered in the living room and watched a video of Steve and Jo's wedding. Liza, who had filmed the entire ceremony, also got in some candid shots, which were most entertaining. After the last sparkler died from each child's packet of fireworks, the dog came out of hiding and the horses relaxed.

July 5—Drove to Alder Slope to pick up my pie cherries at McCormacks, which were grown on the Grande Ronde River. Came home and began pitting them.

Daughter Ramona invited me to lunch at a small deli called "Mountain Brew," which is located near Wallowa Lake. And what a quiet, restful treat it was. Granddaughter Tammy works at the small eatery, which specializes in freshly ground gourmet coffees, deli sandwiches, freshly baked croissants, and delectable desserts, like rhubarb coffee cake and chocolate dipping cookies.

We ordered Italian soda with our sandwiches and ate outside on a shaded deck that borders peaceful, scented pines, watching the antics of a friendly chipmunk scampering about, waiting for a crumb to fall his way. "Mountain Brew" is off the beaten track, away from tourist traffic, and we found it a most pleasant respite from a busy summer day. A yearling mule deer buck, his new antlers in soft velvet, greeted us as we left. I returned to the cherries with renewed vigor, and soon had them in the freezer.

The valley hay is going up beautifully, with no rain damage, although the lack of moisture has cattlemen worried as to how late summer conditions will affect already dry range land.

July 10—Today, daughter Ramona and daughter-in-law Liza helped me cater a large wedding reception at the Joseph Community center. We cooked 90 pounds of baron of beef, made fruit, tossed salads, baked rolls, and served around 200 people. It was a lot of work, but turned out nice.

At 1 p.m. we took a break and watched the re-enactment of the Great Joseph Bank Robbery, just beginning its summer run. Every Wednesday and Saturday through Labor Day, for the benefit of visitors and tourists, this western drama is staged by various local cowboys.

The actors come riding into town, tie their horses to a hitching rack and proceed to rob the old bank, which now houses the Wallowa County Museum. A fellow driving a horse-drawn hack clatters up the street and deposits three young damsels, one of who is a dance hall girl. Several old cowhands stroll along the sidewalk and the sound of hammering, coming from a man repairing a wagon wheel, echoes along with the clip-clop of horses hooves.

There is an air of expectancy in the hot afternoon. All seems peaceful until gun fire erupts from the bank. A girl screams. The sleepy town atmosphere of Joseph is shattered. One man falls "dead," while another tumbles from a nearby roof. Meanwhile an escaping robber makes his galloping retreat down Main Street.

Then the taped words blare over the loudspeaker, continuing "The rest of the Story." One of the robbers served his time, and eventually became vice-president of the very bank he helped rob.

Bullet holes in the old bank door testify to the validity of the story. The small mountain town of Joseph, normally pretty quiet, really comes to life during tourist season. The lofty Wallowas look down on a growing artists colony, whose shops line Main Street.

Even the proprietor of Bud's True Value Hardware takes time out from selling fishing licenses, tack and plumbing supplies to portray a bank robber. If you work in a Joseph store on bank robbery days, and are not dressed western, you could be fined. Singing in the streets is provided by three local gals who entertain with old-time ballads. Joseph is also gearing up for its annual Chief Joseph Days celebration, which takes place on the last weekend of July.

Meanwhile, in the outlying agricultural areas that surround the small town, ranchers and farmers are frantically busy haying and irrigating or riding herd on their livestock. Their work goes on, mostly hidden from tourist's eyes. Ranchers, many of whom work seven days a week, rarely come to watch the goings-on in town, except for Chief Joseph Days. Then they come from the hills and canyons to watch the big parade and attend the rodeo, and visit their neighbors.

Two women who fill the dual roles of ranch wife and writer attend the Fishtrap Writers Conference. Janie Tippett, left, sits beside Alice Warnock, from Baker.

The garden is thriving, and soon the zucchini will be ready. We look forward to eating outside in our pretty yard during long summer evenings. Hay lays in the fields in all shapes and sizes, from round bales to Hank Bird's huge, loose stacks. Already the irrigation is going over the first, hayed-over fields, as we hope for a good second cutting.

July 11—Each day now "Tucker's Mare" melts away on the mountain; the snow shape of a horse grows smaller as summer progresses.

Here on Prairie Creek, the haying continues, and the long stacks begin to appear across the valley. While the rural areas are busy haying, a typical summer weekend ensues in other parts of the county. This weekend included a wide variety of events that seemed to happen simultaneously.

Those of us who arose early and drove to a hill south of Enterprise Friday morning were privileged to watch several colorful hot air balloons being launched into a flawless morning sky. Driving toward the sight, I was startled by the sudden appearance over a hill of an enormous balloon, in many shades of purple. We photographers had a field day.

When I arrived at the scene, some balloons were already airborne, while others were being readied for take off, laying in colorful profusion in the field. It was a breath-taking sight as each one lifted slowly off the ground and drifted into the clear blue sky. The clarity of the morning, the snow-clad Wallowas, and the brilliantly colored balloons created quite a sight.

Soon all of them were up, splashes of brilliant color dotting the sky as I drove home. Cattle in the fields looked startled and wondered about the unfamiliar objects in their midst.

As summer temperatures begin to soar, it means constant irrigating for our seed potatoes, hay fields, pastures, not to mention my gardens, lawns and flowers. I was especially busy organizing chores and house work, so as to be able to attend the second annual "Fishtrap" Writers Conference at Wallowa Lake, which is also this weekend.

In addition to the writers' conference, my priority, the town of Enterprise, was celebrating its annual Crazy Daze with sidewalk sales and a parade. Our CattleWomen were cooking the "perfect cheeseburger" on the courthouse lawn Friday evening. And, at the Alpine Meadows Golf Course, the Elks' 28th annual golf tournament was in progress.

Then, on Saturday night the county's bachelor doctor married his beautiful Kathleen. There was a Baptist church anniversary, two funerals, and if you happened to be in Imnaha, a yard sale. So you get the picture. When summer makes its appearance, which locals say is the month of July, everything happens...at once!

As if that weren't enough, more than 800 jazz fans congregated near the shores of beautiful Wallowa Lake and listened to "Jazz at The Lake" on Sunday afternoon. Meanwhile, for daughter Ramona and me, "Fishtrap" was our big happening. We wouldn't have missed it for the world.

Driving to Wallowa Lake, we noticed the pretty white syringa blooming along the shoreline and dotting the moraine above. The air was scented with the cloying sweetness that only the syringa possesses. We picked up our packets at the registration desk and, by reading name tags, began meeting literary people from New York, Texas, Idaho, Washington and all over the U.S.

We talked to publishers, journalist, novelists, librarians, teachers, poets and readers. What would writers do without readers? The conversations were very stimulating, and for those of us in the writing community it was wonderful. As the conversations flowed, so did the exchange of ideas.

We sat in on a panel discussion conducted by some of the most well-known names in contemporary literature. The next morning, we returned to Fishtrap for breakfast, eaten outside in the morning sunshine, amid an informal, relaxed atmosphere, an atmosphere that prevailed during the three-day conference.

The weather, and the setting, couldn't have been more lovely. Some visitors were curious as to why the name "Fishtrap." We explained: The tripods, made of sticks, that were used to hold the Nez Perce fish traps were called Wallowas, hence "Fishtrap."

There were some native Americans on Saturday's panel. They read samples of their work, which was incredibly beautiful and sensitive to a way of life that has been forever lost.

Driving to pick up Ramona the next morning, I could see that purple hot air balloon drifting over Prairie Creek. The prevailing winds seemed to be carrying them a different direction than yesterday. I couldn't help but notice the look on a lone bull's face, ears pricked upward, as he watched the big balloon sail overhead. Nearby, a palomino mare and colt ran around the field, wondering, too, about the unaccustomed sight.

At breakfast, I enjoyed visiting friend Alice Warnock, who is also doing some writing. She and husband, Dan, old-time cattle ranchers in the Sumpter Valley, just celebrated their 60th wedding anniversary. Because one of the topics of discussion on Saturday's panel concerned "The Landscape as Character," many interesting ideas were brought out.

In the midst of this discussion, Alice, speaking from her heart, with years of experience, told how her family felt about the land. From a rancher's point of view, she explained how they manage and care for it. This small, older woman, speaking softly, told how they rotated pastures, managed trees, and how they lived in harmony with their land, which was, in fact, their livelihood.

Those of us in agriculture were very proud of Alice that day, as her words echoed the sentiments of many others present. In an age where battle lines are being drawn between preservationists and agriculturalist, this little lady brought about understanding.

It is only through such understanding, on both sides, that we will survive these difficult times, and hopefully join forces and do what is best for the land, for what is left is precious, and its stewardship will continue to be the most important issue in all of our futures, and more importantly, the futures of our children's children. For it is for them we must make the intelligent decisions that will best shape the future. We must be open-minded, listen, and educate.

Writers play a significant role in that education by providing the power of the written word. We are in an era of great change and hopefully, common sense will prevail. Congressman Les AuCoin, who, motivated by early exposure to good writing and supported the 12th Young Writers Program this year, was on hand at Fishtrap to welcome the ten winners of this year's contest. AuCoin told how good writing literally changed his life.

"Good writing produces clear thinking and sustains our culture," said AuCoin, adding that we must promote good writing, because children are growing up in a different world now, a world of visual aids and sounds, not written words. The ten young writers would be participating in a week-long workshop taught by professional writers. AuCoin started the fund raising with $1,000 contribution, and hopes to establish an endowment for its continuation.

It was fun visiting with the young writers, who were from high schools all over the state. We listened to readings from various poets, like William Stafford, and enjoyed the readings of Craig Lesley, who read from his recently published novel *Riversong*. One chapter in his book, entitled "Dug Bar," uses Wallowa County as a background for this fictional story about a Nez Perce Indian named Danny Kachiah.

Home late the second night in a row, then back up for Sunday breakfast and more good conversation and meeting new people. The final discussion, moderated by Montana's Lois Welch, concerned the topics of boundaries between fiction and non-fiction, and the writer, reporting and recording. Also on that panel were Herbert Mitgang, cultural correspondent at the New York Times, a novelist, and playwright; Alvin Josephy, author of numerous books on Nez Perce history, who was associate editor of Time Magazine and editor of American Heritage, who lives part of each year in Joseph; and Jonathan Nicholas, daily columnist for The Oregonian, who is originally from Wales.

The conference closed with remarks from Marc Jaffe, of Houghton Mifflin in New York, and Oregon's own William Stafford. We ate lunch outside again and, not wanting to spoil the magic of "Fishtrap," left without saying goodbye, just, "See you next year."

Meanwhile, as they say, back at the ranch, I plunged myself back into the rhythm of ranch life by cooking supper for my husband, who had spent the weekend haying.

July 14—It was up to a beautiful summer morning to meet my Sourdough Shutterbug 4-H'ers at the Grange Hall, from where we drove to the Hurricane Creek trailhead. Carrying day packs loaded with cameras and lunches, we began hiking up a wooded path that quickly took us to a fork in the trail to Falls Creek. Taking the cutoff, we were soon walking on what was left of an enormous snowbank, under which Falls Creek flowed after tumbling down a steep rock gash in the mountain. We photographed the falls, which ran full of snowmelt as a result of rapidly disappearing snowbanks that dotted the peaks above.

At the base of the falls, just before the foaming waters entered a cavernous snow tunnel, a rainbow formed in the sunlit mists. Refreshed by the sight, and cooled by mists and spray, we descended to intercept the main trail again. The morning warmed quickly, and the trail wound above blue-green pools that lay in a gentle stretch of the creek. Unable to resist the temptation, we took off our shoes and socks and waded into the icy creek. Even though our feet turned numb with cold, it invigorated us and made hiking easier as we continued up the trail, which overlooks white-water rapids and wanders through woodsy places.

We walked through an old slide area and broke out into a wildflower-strewn meadow, where blue alpine forget-me-nots and red-orange Indian paintbrush nodded in the breeze. After crossing Deadman Creek, we looked up to see several water falls spilling down, singing the song of the Wallowas. As we reached the trembling aspen thicket that grows below the gorge, near the confluence of Slick Rock Creek, we noticed many of the trees were lying flat. It was as if the weight of winter snows had pushed them over.

We climbed the steep switchback trail and peered down upon the awesome gorge carved by water and time. A few more steps took us around a bend to where Slick Rock Creek plunges in a series of waterfalls, from one terraced rock garden to another. Climbing to the second terrace, we picked a cool spot to eat our lunches. By then it was nearly noon. As spray from the falls drifted over us, we gazed upon magnificent scenery in all directions.

The water warmed as it flowed down over the hot mountain rock, and was just right for a shower. We couldn't wait to stand under the falls, which we did with our shoes off and our clothes on. As we suspected, that Friday was one of the hottest days yet, and the experience was heavenly. We also proved great subjects for photos and took turns photographing each other under the cascading falls.

A lone wispy cloud appeared over the Hurricane Divide, followed by another, until huge, cottony thunderheads tilled the eastern sky. Cooled off. wearing wet clothes, we began descending the terrace to the main trail for our return. We soon reached another fork in the trail, which took us to an old abandoned log cabin, built years ago by a sheepherder. We walked very carefully across a fallen tree that spanned Hurricane Creek, and, after more picture-taking, we returned to the blue-green pools, bordered by white sand bars.

Dried off and warm again, we decided to jump in for a swim. Into the icy-cold creek we plunged. A few youngsters had swim suits, but the rest of us wore our clothes. The current was strong in places and the cold took our breath away, but we had a great time and, as always, I felt like a kid again. Young people seem to rejuvenate me.

We walked barefoot along the warm sand bars and left our footprints next to those of elk, deer and birds. We caught two grasshoppers for Jeff, who then caught two dolly garden trout with his fishing pole. It was a magical place, no pop cans, no litter, and aside from a lone fisherman, we were the creek's only human inhabitants.

It continued to cloud up and the cobalt blue skies were gone by the time we arrived home.

July 15—Overcast and cool, and it began to rain lightly as we drove a herd of fall heifer calvers down off the high moraine pasture. Yesterday's heat wave was only a memory. We had trucked our horses to the bottom of the moraine, unloaded them there, and ridden to a high field where we had cut out several heifers from a neighbor's herd of cows and calves. The water supply where the cattle were pastured was beginning to dry up, so we'd had to trail the herd down to the ranch.

What a view we had from those high slopes of the moraine. Aspen trees fluttered in the breeze, wildflower scent filled the air, the Seven Devil Mountains rose off to the east across Hell's canyon, while below lay the fertile checkerboard fields of hay, grain and grazing livestock. Great cloud shadows moved silently over the landscape.

After leaving the pasture, we had to drive the cattle through a field of yellow-blossom sweet clover that grew saddle-horn-high. At one point we lost our heifers in the yellow mass, but managed to keep track of them by following a cloud of yellow pollen that hovered above the herd.

When we emerged from that sea of yellow clover, we found ourselves near an open gate, which the cattle had to pass through to get onto the road home. However, a pack of baying hounds, tied to dog houses, stopped the heifers in their tracks. After much "persuasion" the lead cautiously stepped through, whereupon the rest followed. After we turned the heifers into a hayed-over field with plenty of water, I rode over the hill, unsaddled my mare and fixed lunch.

I picked up grandson James, who will be in my care for the next two days.

July 16—We slept in the sheepherder wagon, a special treat for three-year-old James, and I kept my promise to take him fishing in the nearby creek. Digging worms in the vegetable garden proved to be far more productive, and fun, than fishing, for my small grandson.

Tonight, my thoughts turn to my oldest grandsons and their friends, who are spending two nights in the wilderness on their own. As it turned out, I needn't have worried; they had a grand time, even hiked to the top of Ruby Peak and reported the flag we placed there last summer was still flying.

One of the greatest gifts a parent or grandparent can give a child is appreciation for the great outdoors. Lessons learned there will help young people grow spiritually and physically, and thus become better prepared to meet the challenges of an increasingly complex world.

July 17—The lettuce wilts in the midday sun and the garden grows frantically, as if it knows the season is short. Daily afternoon thunderheads form over the mountains, making the heat seem even more intense.

July 18—Awoke to another beautiful summer morning. Doug is out early in the potato field, astride his big home-constructed, three-wheeled rouging machine. As he cruises slowly up and down the long rows, he can view potato plants and note any that are diseased or stressed.

Because the summer months are so full, I have turned Starch's three calves out with her, thus eliminating the morning chore of bringing the milk cow into the barn and let the calves nurse; not to mention milking for the house milk. The barn cats, however, have moved to the carport and miss their daily bowl of warm milk. We, too, miss having the real thing. That stuff in plastic cartons can't compare to whole milk.

My mornings are spent tending to the chickens, hoeing in the garden while it's cool, watering, and accomplishing myriad small chores. Take care of the little things, and the big things will take care of themselves, or so they say. The system seems to work well for me because I must be organized to the teeth to "steal" time to write.

We are enjoying the first garden leaf lettuce; piling it on sandwiches and eating healthful salads. Everything, it seems, is on the brink of harvesting: raspberries, gooseberries, strawberries, zucchini. 'Tis the season of plenty.

We ate outside this evening in the cool of our yard. At sunset we heard the gabbling of many geese and soon at least 13 small families of honkers came winging low to land in our neighbor's field. Probably the maiden flight for the spring hatch, and how happy they were. We could see their long-necked heads bobbing up and down in the midst of the tall grass, which grows near an irrigation ditch.

Farmers' fields provide the perfect habitat for wild geese, and the honkers especially love Prairie Creek. We were amused watching the youngsters practice their awkward flying. Later, as the full summer moon appeared over the dry hills, its golden light glinted off the irrigation waters and I could still hear "goose music." A few silvery clouds floated in an otherwise mild summer sky.

July 19—A few lingering clouds, warm, turning hot by mid-morning. Picked the first tender young beets and cooked them with their tops for lunch. A large Grain Growers truck drove in to pick up one of our ailing tractors to be repaired.

Drove to Joseph this afternoon to sit with our Wallowa Valley Photo Club's photography exhibit, which is on display at the Eagle Mountain Gallery through Chief Joseph Days. Just as I arrived, the re-enactment of the Bank Robbery was about to begin, and a large group of tourists stood behind a roped off area to view the portrayal of this real-life drama.

As Chief Joseph Days draws near, the small mountain town of Joseph takes on a western flavor. Herb and Jessie Owens can be seen driving their team of horses, pulling a buggy up Main Street; locals, dressed in early-day garb, sit in chairs along the sidewalks, sewing or discussing the affairs of the day. Merchants join in the fun and an early-day atmosphere prevails. It is almost like stepping back in to the late 1800s.

In some ways Wallowa County has progressed to meet modern standards, while in other, more charming ways, time here appears to have stood still. Ranchers and farmers still work from dawn till dusk, the loggers work at all hours, the mills operate all night long and, in the remote areas, some women still cook on wood stoves and manage without electricity. They live simply, much as our ancestors did.

Wallowa County combines the best of two worlds, which is the charm and uniqueness of the place. The magnificent scenery of the surrounding countryside enhances the total feeling of the area and is an omnipresent part of the whole.

It was interesting meeting people from other states who wandered in to view our photo exhibit. It's amazing how so many people travel such long distances to see our valley. Recently I read an 1897 edition of a Union newspaper, wherein the editor described in flowery phrases the virtues of Wallowa County. It was a land of unlimited natural resources, he said, a healthful climate prevailed, and the business and farming opportunities were endless.

It sounded like our present-day Chamber of Commerce. Interesting to note that the population in 1897 was 6,000, whereas today it is only around 7,500, nearly a century later. The long articles were full of interesting observations and descriptions of the entire county. Wallowa Lake, then referred to as Silver Lake, was already a popular spot for visitors, and Lostine and Wallowa were booming towns, as was the county seat of Enterprise.

July 20—Darting from moonlit clouds, zig-zags of lightning flashed in the mid-summer night's sky, and thunder rolled down the valley last night about 10:30. A small amount of rain fell before all was still again.

The air is cleansed this morning, and only a few leftover clouds hover over the mountains. It made being outside pleasant, and I weeded the vegetable garden until I finished.

At night now, we turn the white mule, Maud, and my mare, Cal, into the machinery yard to graze down the high grasses. Maud has learned to unhook the horseshoe latch on my garden gate, after which she wreaks havoc amid my vegetables. Nipping the tops of corn stalks, rolling on cabbages, she was found the other morning looking guilty with a mouthful of tender beets. Thanks to her, my peas and beans are well thinned. but the garden is hardy and survives the mule, and I've since learned to wire the gate shut.

Our neighbors, the Heptons, inform us they are missing two sows that are due to farrow any day, so we are looking for two very large pigs that may be somewhere on our property.

Attended a meeting of our Wallowa Valley Photo club at the Eagle Mountain Gallery in Joseph this evening. Our newly formed club has produced a black and white photo calendar that features our photographers and depicts scenes of Wallowa County. We have already sold enough of the 1990 calendars to pay for the printing.

July 21—Helped CattleWomen serve nearly 100 senior citizens dinner today at the Joseph Community center. We were busy!

July 22—Up early making preparations to leave on a back-pack trip up Hurricane Creek with daughter Ramona and three of my grandchildren. Shouldering our packs, we were soon hiking up the Hurricane Creek trail, a first for all except me. The three grandchildren were also members of my 4-H photography club who were unable to participate in the last hike. One of the purposes of the outing was to take pictures to enter in the upcoming Wallowa County Fair.

Wild strawberries grew in profusion along the trail and were just beginning to ripen, so we stopped often to pick the bright red, flavorful berries. We made camp at a pretty spot I had picked out on our last hike. It was near the creek, at the edge of a meadow, and afforded a view of 10,000-foot Sacajawea. Across the creek loomed the rugged high talus slopes of the Hurricane Divide. A few trees had conveniently fallen across Hurricane Creek and therefore provided us access to the camp.

After gathering firewood and eating our lunches, we walked up the trail to Slick Rock, where we photographed the gorge and falls. There were many people using the back country that Saturday, and we visited with a 62-year-old woman who was on her way to climb Sacajawea! Later that afternoon we met one of our local doctors, Dr. Lowell Euhus, who, with a younger doctor, had just climbed Sacajawea. They had reached the summit at 1 p.m.

We in Wallowa County are so fortunate to have access in our own backyards, so to speak, to this wonderful back country. Unfortunately, many who have lived here all their lives have never seen it.

July 23—Daughter Ramona, the grandchildren and I cooked our supper over a small campfire, and roasted marshmallows. Cousins Chelsea and Carrie remained around the fire, singing songs they had learned at 4-H camp, while the rest of us crawled into our sleeping bags and watched the flickering glow of the campfire dance among fir and spruce. That elusive alpine bird that sings with a flute-like voice sang one last song, before stars, big and brilliant, began to appear, until the heavens glittered in a dazzling display of twinkling bodies.

Gazing up into a nighttime sky always makes us Earth-bound souls feel tiny and insignificant, but especially so in July, in the Wallowas. I made my bed at the edge of the meadow, next to a stunted fir and a large False Hellebore (skunk cabbage) plant.

Sometime around midnight, a silent moon rose over the high, eastern ridge. Fir trees stood outlined in charcoal on the ridge top, their dark outlines etched against the golden moon. The stars paled and seemed to disappear as the meadow slowly filled with moonglow. The moonlight illuminated the high ramparts of Sacajawea Mountain, and her naked sides pulsed with soft light.

Around 4:30, birdsong erupted from the surrounding forest and the water sounds of the creek intensified. A pine squirrel scurried up the trunk of a nearby tree and began to breakfast on pine cones. The moon continued its journey, or the Earth spun on its axis, or whatever is supposed to happen, and by 5:30, I was up for the day watching the high summits of Sacajawea become fired with gold!

Our meadow, still in shade, stayed cool. I built a fire, went to the creek for water, and ate a breakfast of hard-boiled egg, canned peaches and blueberry cake. The rest of crew snoozed away in their sleeping bags

Later that morning, we packed up and headed down the trail. While stopping to rest at the blue-green pools, five Hurricane Creek llamas, led by some friends, passed us on the trail. The llamas packed all their camp gear for a two-night stay in the wilderness.

July 24—Back to ranch living, while attempting to keep up the frantic pace of a typical Wallowa County summer. But little did we know the summer of '89 would top 'em all,. As the weather grew hotter, the forest became drier, and each day we worried about lightning storms. The hot breath of daily afternoon winds blew across the valley, worsening the situation. Our tinder-dry forests were accidents waiting to happen. Clouds appeared, only to disappear, and no rain fell.

The summer squash began to ripen and I dug the first red potatoes to go with fresh peas. Doug and Ben hauled in the drys from the hills and sold them at our local auction. The prices were unreal! One large Simmental cow brought nearly $800.

I made strawberry and raspberry freezer jam, and froze gooseberries. A construction crew began building our new potato storage. The 80-acre seed potato crop grew, bloomed and headed toward a September harvest.

Visiting Nez Perce began to set up tepees along the creek near the Joseph rodeo grounds, as Chief Joseph Days drew near. The seed potato inspector from OSU arrived to inspect our Wallowa County fields.

July 26—Noticeably cooler, and a few clouds formed overnight.

Around 10:30, as I drove to Enterprise to meet several friends for lunch at A Country Place On Pete's Pond, a terrific thunderstorm was brewing. Soon, lightning zing-zapped down into the dry forested slopes of the Wallowas, thunder rolled across the valley, and it began to rain. The ducks, swimming on the pond, were obviously happy, as the first heavy drops made split-splats on the surface of the water. Blue-white flashes continued to sizzle across the sky with alarming frequency, and we worried about the fires.

It was during this time, east of Joseph, near the canal road that leads to Salt Creek Summit, on Wing Ridge, that a very large lightning strike ignited the first that would become the "Canal Fire," and grow to a 23,560 acre monster that I would watch for days through my kitchen window. The fire would become the top priority fire in the U.S. Two other fires of major proportions also started during this storm. The 8,000-acre Summit fire and the 610-acre Lookout fire near Hat Point, both in the National Recreation Area.

Driving home I could see a fire burning on a high ridge, up the Hurricane Creek canyon, the smoke from it boiling up and growing as I watched. As a result of that terrible storm, more than 100 fires began in Wallowa County alone.

That evening, we could see the glow of flames from the Hurricane Creek blaze, which was, thankfully, extinguished in a few days. We later learned there were lightning starts at Indian Village in the Zumwalt country and another on Elk Mountain. We worried about the fires all night.

July 27—It dawned bright and sunny, and Ben and Doug and I drove 43 head of heifers to a pasture on upper Prairie Creek. The morning coolness was short-lived, and by mid-morning waves of heat rose from the field. Looking up Hurricane Creek, we noticed the fire seemed smaller and only a few wisps of smoke remained as aerial attacks continued. Due to the steepness of the terrain, it was the only way to fight that fire.

Later, after unsaddling my mare, I glanced toward Ferguson Ridge, to see a big cloud of smoke come boiling up over the mountain. Before my eyes, two ridges over, the smoke rolled and mushroomed, advancing like a living thing as the dry, resinous material exploded.

It was a frightening experience. Old-timers here were aware of the situation, and some said if a fire ever started on the mountain, there would be no stopping it. By evening the fire was completely out of control and heading north toward Prairie Creek. The "Canal Fire" was born.

July 28—Today is the Chief Joseph Days Kiddie Parade. I always look forward to visiting and photographing the beautiful native American Indian children, who dress in their colorful beaded, buckskin and feathered outfits for the occasion. Wallowa County's children are also on parade, reflecting the regional occupations of their parents. Little loggers, mill workers, ranchers, packers and guides, artists and even future Joseph Days courts, riding stick horses.

Rabbits, geese, ducks, cats, dogs and even calves pant in the July heat, accompanying their young owners, playing a variety of roles. This upcoming generation of Wallowa County citizens would appear to possess the essential qualities it takes to survive here. What a wonderful crop of youngsters.

Unfortunately, unless conditions change, many of these youngsters, reaching adulthood, will be unable to find jobs in the county and be forced to move elsewhere. And one of the county's most precious resources will have been lost.

July 29—Another breathlessly hot morning. The Canal Fire continues to grow, and billowing clouds of smoke from other fires erupt all around us. It is hard to concentrate on anything else. Doug and I hauled my appaloosa mare "Cal" to the Indian encampment, where I left her with Soy Redthunder, of the Colville Nez Perce, who would ride her in the parade.

After Doug, Max Gorsline and I partook of a cowboy breakfast, served outside, we found a place to watch the parade. Hundreds of people lined both sides of Main Street and leading the procession, carrying the proud Soy Redthunder and wearing a beaded breast-collar, was my cow pony.

The Chief Joseph Days parade, famous for its fine horse flesh, was honored this year to have Oregon Governor Neil Goldschmidt riding on a wagon seat next to Cy and Creighton Kooch. The beautifully harnessed Springwater Clydesdales pulled the shiny wagon down the street with class.

The Blue Mountain Boys shot up the town, spooking horses and terrifying children. The '59ers made an impressive entry, having ridden over the mountains, camping along the way, to join the festivities. The highlight of the parade, however, was the growing number of Native Americans, dressed in their finery and displaying a proud heritage.

And, hour by hour, the smoke increased as the fires grew. After the parade, we escaped the heat and retired to the coolness of our shaded lawn for a family picnic. While, on the mountain, fueled by an accumulation of downed limbs and trees that have lain undisturbed for more than 70 years, the wildfire raged.

Cinders and ashes soon began to sift down upon Prairie Creek, and the hot winds died down somewhat. Two other major fires burning out of control near Hat Point, along with the Idaho fires, added to an already smoke-filled valley.

By evening it was both beautiful and terrible here on Prairie Creek as we sat on the lawn watching the smoke clouds pick up the evening light. Still feeling uneasy, we drove to the rodeo grounds and attended the Saturday night performance. Record-breaking crowds filled the stands, and 300 people were turned away.

Horses bucked and cowboys rode, and announcer Bob Tallman spoke about what was on the minds of us who live here, the fires, and hoped for the safety of family members involved in firefighting efforts. Ashes and cinders continued to fall on the rodeo as the blood-red sun sank over the smoky blue Wallowas.

July 30—The sleeping fires, held at bay in the morning coolness, left a layer of smoke hovering over the McCully Creek Basin country.

Checking the fall calvers on the way to the Sunday cowboy breakfast in Joseph, we discovered a newly born calf had fallen into an irrigation ditch. None the worse for the experience, mom licked him off, and just minutes later he began to nuzzle around for his first warm meal.

We met Max Gorsline in the breakfast line, which was beginning to lengthen considerably, due to three busloads of Indian firefighters who had been flown in from Arizona. After breakfasting on buffalo burger, grilled outside, and/or steak, pancakes, juice, coffee, milk and eggs, they would be assigned to the fire lines. Clad in yellow fire-retardant shirts, they created a colorful addition to the Chief Joseph Days event, and were interesting to talk to.

This high-mountain valley was quite a change from their Arizona country, they agreed, and this wasn't your ordinary breakfast. While eating our buffalo burger breakfast, Doug and I enjoyed a pleasant visit with Mike and Jill Thorne. The senator, along with his wife, who was scheduling the governor's itinerary, were relaxing in Wallowa Country's laid-back hospitality. Meanwhile, the governor took his turn flipping pancakes, before partaking of a Wallowa County cowboy breakfast himself.

Jill Thorne, a farmer's wife also, visited with me about combining several roles, as so many of us modern women do these days. We compared notes until, on schedule, they left to catch their plane, which would fly them to the Eastern Oregon community of Monument.

It is only because Jill believes so strongly in the future of agriculture that she spends the time in Salem, which she would rather spend on their Eastern Oregon ranch. Both she and the senator have endeavored to put Wallowa County back on the map and have championed the rights of the Eastern Oregon country, a vast country that is as diverse as it is beautiful, lonely as it is hospitable, and relatively little known to those in the western part of the state, except during tourist season.

Returning to the ranch, we nervously look up at the advancing Canal fire. Son Ken was out in the thick of it, protecting private property with his skidder, as were other local loggers. Meanwhile, concern was mounting for the safety of cattle grazing the Divide and Sheep Creek ranges. Cowboys were being summoned to ride in these areas and move cattle, many of which could be in danger of being trapped between fires.

By afternoon, the Canal fire worsened and the air was heavy with smoke, with even more boiling up on the eastern horizon, as the Summit and Lookout fires had merged. These enormous fires, all in the Hells

Canyon National Recreation Area, have been fanned by merciless afternoon winds, threatening the Memaloose guard station and burning
down one of the old Marks cow camp cabins, south of Freezeout.

Our sky was full of helicopters and airplanes that had to abandon
aerial attacks due to turbulence and intense heat from the fire on Ferguson
Ridge. The fire was creating its own storm on the mountain.

After catching up on the irrigating and berry-picking, Doug and I attended the finals of the Chief Joseph Days Rodeo. During the events, Bob
Tallman announced that anyone living east of Ferguson Ridge should go
home and make preparations to evacuate. Several people left the stands,
along with the local Search and Rescue, which was also summoned.

The extremely hot, dry winds increased and the fire raced over Ferguson Ridge and headed toward upper Prairie Creek with spot fires
breaking out below the main fire. The smoke over Sheep Creek Hill was
so thick, visibility was cut to zero. It looked like the entire county was
on fire.

By evening a command post had been set up at the Cleve Coppin
ranch on upper Prairie Creek. Responding to a plea for food, I made up
a batch of sandwiches for the local volunteer firefighters who would be
protecting homes situated in the forests directly below the path of the
fire. The fire became even more spectacular at nightfall, as a red glow lit
the ridgetop and fireworks displays shot into the night, falling down the
mountain like fire falls, shooting burning embers out over the Prairie.

Doug and other ranchers filled cattle sprayers and water tanks, put
pumps in creeks, and prepared to wet down homes, next to, and in, the
timberline areas. Ranchers wet down their haystacks and put sprinklers
on their shake roofs. It was a long night for the inhabitants of upper
Prairie Creek.

As Chief Joseph Days ended, hundreds of firefighters arrived to
replace the tourists and rodeo visitors.

August 17—There is a sharp autumn coolness in the morning air.
The garden slackens its frantic growth and the Prairie Creek pastures
have reached their peak, as far as nutritive value is concerned. The steady
march of time now turns toward winter.

Ice formed on windshields yesterday morning as temperatures dove
to the low 30s. Golden grain ripens in the fields and second cuttings lay
in windrows. Our terrible forest fires are contained, Chief Joseph Days
is history, as are the annual Stockgrowers-CattleWomen's doin's. One
event just melted into another until we suddenly realized, like we do
every year, that our brief, beautiful summer is nearly over!

Through it all, the raspberries ripened profusely and required daily picking. Somehow I managed to steal time between fair and CattleWomen activities to fill the freezer with jam and berries.

August 23—Trails of mist follow the mountains, and the rain, which has been soaking the valley in a drought-breaker for the past two days, continues to fall. The clouds lifted briefly yesterday afternoon to reveal the season's first snowfall. On August 22nd!

The parched earth is refreshed and the once-dry hills appear tinged with a spring-like green. Some second cuttings lie in drenched fields, and ripening grains begin to lodge. The soil is saturated, the creeks and rivers running full of earth-colored waters. Streams flowing down out of the burn carry ashes and soot mixed with mud.

It appears our first fall storm has arrived a little earlier than years past. And, thank goodness, the fire season is over. Seasoned tamarack snaps merrily in the wood cook stove, providing just the right degree of warmth and coziness for early autumn. Spent this day cooking and baking as our family is planning a 20th anniversary surprise for daughter Ramona and husband, Charley. The original intent was to pitch a wall tent on their recently purchased grazing land, but due to soggy weather conditions we are letting them use the motor home.

A plump chicken roasts slowly in the oven, a raspberry pie cools on the table, and the aroma of freshly baked french bread lingers in my kitchen as I type this. Am also in the middle of trying out a new recipe for chicken enchiladas, one that requires lots of "from scratch" preparation. But when the weather is such, it is fun, after a summer of outside activities, to cook and bake and stay indoors.

Wearing boots and raincoat, I ventured forth this morning into my soggy flower beds and picked an enormous bouquet, which I have placed in an old white enamel coffee pot. Pink cosmos, Shasta daisies, blue bachelor buttons, snapdragons in white, pink and yellow, poppies, and one newly opened orange-red gladioli create an explosion of color, warming my heart on this gray day.

Digging through old scrapbooks, I finally came up with wedding pictures of the couple. Other members of our family who are collaborating on the surprise arrived to decorate the motorhome. Before the rest of us schemers partook of the good meal, we sent the surprised anniversary couple off to their hill-top retreat, complete with satin sheets, flowers and a gourmet meal. And still it rained, and rained, and rained!

At this writing, 3.78 inches have fallen during the past 72 hours.

August 24—It rained steadily all night, and we thought about the anniversary couple and hoped the motor home wouldn't develop leaks. It did, but they stuck it out until the wee hours of the morning before driving home.

More than two inches of rain fell over a 24-hour period, breaking local records. The snow level remained constant at 6,000 feet, and mornings were cool enough to warrant a fire in the wood cookstove.

The prairie fields and the bare, brown hills accepted the deep watering like a sponge; Prairie Creek ran bank-full.

August 25—Skies began to clear and our local radio station reported 3.78 inches of rain had fallen in the past 72 hours! This in a county where the average annual rainfall is around 14 inches.

A bird concert erupted from the willows and the sun streamed down between clouds, bathing the earth in a tropical steaminess that revived gardens and flowers, and turned pastures lush green.

Baked two apple pies, washed clothes and hung them out to dry. The Rhode Island Red pullets laid their first small, brown eggs.

By evening all of the clouds lifted above the mountains, exposing a bright, fresh blanket of snow.

August 26—We awake to a brilliant, rain-washed morning. High snow fields contrast with green, growing things. Apples ripen on the gnarled old tree, green tomatoes hang heavy on the plants, sunflower buds turn toward the sun, and the zucchini goes wild.

Enjoyed interviewing old-timer Oakley Johnson this morning for an article on Hell's Canyon Mule Days. Oakley, a retired sheep rancher on Snake River, lives with wife Marjorie in a tidy house in Joseph. Colorful petunias, marigolds and lobelia explode from weedless flower beds that border a well-kept lawn.

I could have visited with Oakley all day. Such fascinating tales he weaves, of mules packing sheep camp to the summer range along steep canyon trails. Oakley produced a cardboard box of old black and white prints of scenes right out of the pages of history: the Snake River boat "Idaho" that carried sacks of wool to Lewiston, or a mule carrying a disc into a ranch.

"Hardest thing to pack," said Oakley, "was a horse-drawn mower."

My next stop was Alder Slope to visit Max Walker, chairman of Mule Days, to pick up information I needed for the other Mule Days grand marshal, Hazel Fleet. Hazel also spent her early years along the Snake.

Returning home I began writing articles about two very interesting lives.

August 28—Doug and his crew began ag-bagging 90 acres of rain-damaged second cutting we purchased from a neighbor for silage. All over the valley, second cuttings turn blacker by the day, the grains losing their golden color and beginning to sprout or turn mildewy. The drought was broken, but not without exacting a price from the farmer.

While Jim and Don rouged seed potatoes, the construction crew raised the trusses on the new storage. This new building obstructs my kitchen-window view of the neighbor's house and barn. I will miss seeing the Lockes' friendly lights glimmer across snowy fields on winter nights.

August 29—The mountains are shrouded in clouds that rumble with thunder, and a dampness born of rain prevails. Summer is over and the past two weeks have been more characteristic of September than late August.

Patches of snow remain on the Wallowas, and more rain is likely, dampening hopes of further August pack trips in to the mountains. Even our annual trek into the Horse Ranch was canceled, because school has begun, and that means football practice for some of my Sourdough Shutterbugs. In fact, my grandsons say their first game is tomorrow.

August 30—Drove to Wallowa Lake, to pick up the slide-tape program "Wallowa Story," which has been shown at the park amphitheater all summer to record-breaking crowds. As it is the last day of August, the summer tourists were mostly absent and the lake was returning to its autumn calmness. Labor Day campers will begin to arrive today, however.

September 1—The tractor-drawn chopper eats its way down the windrows of newly mown second-cutting meadow grass, the fragrant green chop spewing forth into the bed of a silage truck alongside. Back and forth, up and down the field, until that truck is filled.

Another truck takes its place and the full one roars off to the bagger, where the green chop is mechanically stuffed into a large "Ag Bag" made of double thickness plastic. These long, shiny-white bags, filled with fresh chop, will ferment, turn to silage and be fed on cold winter mornings to our fall calvers.

The bright, shiny tin roof on the new potato storage glares at me through my kitchen window. Hopefully, the structure will be completed in time for the harvest.

In the meantime, I loaded our mini-motor home for a 2-1/2-day camp-out. The wind began to blow and rain clouds formed a threatening cluster over the mountains. I dug potatoes and carrots in the garden, made lists, crossed them off and, due to a delay in the silage making operation, didn't get under way until after 7 p.m.

Ranch work seems to go on and on, and we would never get away unless we just did it, so we left; me in the Luv pickup, following Doug who drove the motorhome. We headed up Salt Creek Summit in the shortening daylight hours, past the burn, on down Gumboat Creek, and soon found a secluded camp spot on the upper Imnaha.

It was after 9, and visions of sizzling steaks over campfire coals had long-since faded, so we opted for tomato sandwiches and glasses of milk. The river's song was the last sound I remember before dropping into a blissful sleep.

September 2—Doug was up bright and early, and left in the dawn to go grouse hunting, while I snuggled deeper into our warm sleeping bags. Such earned luxury! Later I stood looking out the door of our camper to see the Imnaha! We were parked just above the river and the fresh morning-smell of rain-dampened ponderosa pine forests filled my senses. The ranch work and life's recent cares melted away.

After kindling a fire using dead spruce boughs, I walked down an embankment to the river for water, then sat on a rock in a patch of brief sunshine. Doug returned, grouse-less, and we grilled the steaks we'd planned for last night's supper, enjoying an unhurried, relaxed breakfast.

I washed my face in cold river water until it tingled, then read a good book and caught up on my daily journal. Doug went upriver to do some exploring.

This year's Labor Day holiday was a far cry from last year's experience. No bees, wasps, intense heat, or dry forests; no air filled with forest fire smoke. Instead, the upriver grass is green, the air fresh and clean, the weather cool and cloudy, and here, at least, the grouse are scarce, the chipmunks active, and the huckleberries gone.

Soothing sounds of the river calms my summer-jangled nerves, narrows my world to this place, an Eden far-removed from civilization. Civilized man needs to visit his natural environment once in a while, so he can return to the man-made environment and cope. He can store this peace in his mind's eye to provide stability and reason in a man-made world that is growing madder by the day. Solitude heals, helps us grow, renews faith in ourselves and allows us to think clearly, and put things in proper perspective.

On the Imnaha in the fall, there is no TV to report destruction and violence, the phone doesn't ring, the appliances don't hum, and modern civilization is far removed. Demands here are simple and basic: hunger and sleep.

A badger ambles into camp, then sees us and scrambles down the river bank. A woodpecker eats insects that have crawled into holes in a nearby tree, and the river runs north!

After setting sourdough biscuits to rise, we drive up toward Halfway and turn onto an old road where huckleberries, turning red now, glint like fire in patches of sunlight as the skies begin to clear. Purple-blue wild asters grow in profusion along the roads. We drive through a maze of old logging roads that lead us onto a ridge that affords an awesome view of the rugged breaks of Hells Canyon.

Cloud shadows dot the miles of unpeopled places below. Hazy mountains of the Salmon River country appear faint blue in the distance. The scene is like a dream, and as brief, as Doug turns the corner into a forested area where the road forks with a lesser-used one.

Doug chose the dimmer of the two roads, which soon forked again. We find ourselves on a mere cow trail that eventually dead-ends on a steep, grassy hillside. Everywhere the bright berries of the mountain ash made an orange splash. We eventually found ourselves on a deeply rutted, muddy road, skirting a ridge, bumping through boggy springs, and winding around trembling aspen thickets.

We noticed that the range was greening up and the stock ponds were full. Fat cows and calves looked content. The forests need the grazing animals, and the animals need the forests, and man needs them both. After a couple of hours I wondered out loud where we were.

To which hubby replied, "Don't you know where we are?"

"Do you?" says I. Silence as we continued to follow these old logging roads that lace Wallowa County's outback, until we hit upon a road that led to the familiar McGraw area. Nary a grouse did we see, or a grouse hunter, but Doug pointed out the spot where he'd seen a six-point bull elk this morning.

Returning to our cozy, riverside camp, we grilled more steaks and baked the sourdough biscuits, and we had to agree, it just don't get any better than this.

September 5—Cloudy, windy and cold, as the men continued to make silage. Electricity was hooked up in the new potato storage building, and I spent the morning canning 31 jars of sauerkraut.

September 6—The cucumber vines and squash plants look a bit tattered due to a frost. Last night, picked what green beans were left and started a crock of sweet pickles going with the few cucumbers I could salvage. Cucumbers are "iffy" in our high mountain valley. The good ones come from the Imnaha gardeners.

My wildflower patch is such a joy this fall. Seven varieties all blooming at once! Cosmos, petunias, marigold and snapdragons, revitalized by the rain and enjoying the coolness of autumn, have turned more vivid each day. Bright red geraniums in granite ware pots bloom on the picnic table; and alongside the house, the brilliant orange of the Chinese lanterns.

Indian summer is colorful and the air is wonderful. If only it would last! The nights are cold now, and the harvest moon grows. Bow hunters stalk our woods and fields, and sometimes we see bull elk and buck deer antlers protruding from the hack of a passing pickup.

My kitchen smells of autumn. Pickled beets, plum jam, apple sauce, sweet pickles, apple pies, homemade bread and sauerkraut. It is the season of plenty, but there are never enough hours in the day to preserve that plenty.

Instead of working on my weekly column, like I should be, I devoted my day to three-year-old James. He so loves it here on the ranch. I let him feed the chickens and gather eggs. Then we caught grasshoppers.

My small grandson laughed and laughed at the sight of his grandmother on her hands and knees, throwing an old sweater on the ground to catch a grasshopper. Laughter erupted, uninhibited again, when the hopper spat "tobacco juice" on my hand. Sometimes it takes a small child to teach us how to laugh. Laughter is the best medicine and in today's world we need to laugh more, and not lose that child-like spontaneity.

Anyway, James and I were the better for it, and the day just got better and better. We loaded the jar of grasshoppers and a fishing pole into the car and drove to a nearby irrigation ditch, where the water spills over a wooden flume into a foamy pool. A big rainbow trout, waiting under a rock, took James' grasshopper, finally, after nibbling away for about 15 minutes.

We put another tobacco-spitting grasshopper on the hook and this time the fish swallowed bait and hook! We had quite a time landing the trout, and Patrick McManus would love to write about it, but between the two of us we captured our prize. We returned victorious to the kitchen sink, where James was even further amazed to find the grasshopper in the fish's innards!

And so the column was a few days late, but time spent with a child is never lost. They grow up so fast, and like the beautiful fall, change and move on to another season. How I love the fall, especially September. It is my birthday month, and also my husband's, for we are but a day apart. We celebrated our birthdays by treating ourselves to a dinner at the Wallowa Lake Lodge, where we were joined by our good friends Bud and Ruby Zollman.

We dined in the recently refurbished Camas Room, which still retains the old lodge's charm. We splurged and ordered shrimp-stuffed trout, which was delicious. The evening eyed the pain of growing another year older! Afterward, we still had time to get in on the tail-end of a football game in Enterprise and watch grandsons Chad and Shawn play. And the Savages won.

September 9—Somewhere, just at sunrise, from the folds of the hill land that separates us from the Imnaha canyon country, a coyote chorus erupts into the frosty, morning air. What is Mr. Coyote saying? Will there be an early winter, and what kind of winter will it be?

Old-timer Jess Earl, when he used to live on the Imnaha, used to say the severity of the winter could be determined by the black stripe on the fuzzy caterpillars, and if they were going uphill or downhill. I've already forgotten which way meant what, but I haven't forgotten Jess Earl. He was as much a part of the Imnaha as the fall-fuzzy caterpillars.

I took five grandchildren to watch the Hells Canyon Mule Days parade in Enterprise, today. Later, as we watched the events from the grandstands, I though of what a far cry this year's Mule Days was from the very first one, when riders gee-hawed their animals around the poles, and mules balked and bucked. Most mules had never been to town before.

There were 31 entries in the trail class this year, and the polished, well-trained mules performed beautifully. The long-eared animals were obviously well-loved by their owners, who are a dedicated and fun-loving group of people.

Wallowa County is losing its biggest Mule Days supporter. The only chairman the growing event has ever known, Max Walker, is moving to a ranch in Union. Knowing Max, he'll still help out with next year's show.

September 10—This week I helped trail some steers and heifers from a rented pasture on upper Prairie Creek to the main ranch, where they were shipped out the next day to a Hermiston feedlot. After camping on the upper Imnaha until noon on Labor Day, we returned to the ranch, where I began baking potatoes for our CattleWomen's steak feed. An enterprising young businessman by the name of Bob Wolfe from Hermiston, donated all the wonderful, delicious potatoes for our Labor Day steak feed this year. Bob recently won the highest honor bestowed on an FFA member, agri-businessman of the year. Under the name of Bob Wolfe Company, he markets corn and potatoes in his area.

The Labor Day steak feed is a tradition in Wallowa County, and has grown from modest beginnings when the CowBelles cooked and served a dinner years ago after the fall feeder sale. Part of that tradition was Imnaha tomatoes, cucumbers, and cabbage made into slaw. Although there was no coleslaw for CattleWomen to make, Bonnie Marks of Imnaha donated very tasty, crisp cucumbers, and there were sliced tomatoes, warm rolls, watermelon slices and the nutritious grilled steaks to go with those famous potatoes.

Steak and taters. The fuel that keeps Wallowa County's ranching families going. Diets come and go, but hard-working ranchers need REAL FOOD. After delivering the potatoes I picked up my little buddy James, and he joined Doug and me for the dinner at the sale yard. The auction had just ended, but I showed James where the animals had been sold, then took him out to where they were loading out the cattle into big semi-truck-trailer rigs. He was all eyes.

It was a beautiful, warm evening, with old-timers, newcomers and townspeople mingling to enjoy visits, and the CattleWomen's great meal. And for the first time in more than 13 years, this Cattlewoman and her husband didn't serve baked potatoes in the serving line. Having been chairman of the steak feed in the past, I didn't even feel guilty.

September 11—A dirty cloud of grain dust hovers over the harvester as it threshes our neighbor's barley crop, leaving rows of stubblefield in its wake. Ancient trucks, laden with grain, often driven by women, slowly make their precarious way to the Grain Growers' elevators. Harvest time is here.

Our seed potato digging will commence next week, weather permitting. The phone has been ringing with workers wanting to know what day we'll start and others asking if they can glean the fields after digging, to gather their winter potato supply. The silage is curing in the long Ag Bags for winter feed, and the second cutting of meadow hay has been baled and stacked.

After all that rain, the weather has been warm and dry enough to accomplish these fall jobs. The woodshed is stacked full of seasoned tamarack, waiting to be split into cookstove-sized pieces. That way we can be warmed twice; once when we split the wood and haul it to the wood box, and again by its warmth in the fire.

September 15—Awoke to the sounds of a Prairie Creek dawn: my mare chomping grass on the lawn outside our bedroom window (a gate had been left open last evening), the wailing of a coyote on the eastern hill, and Hough's Angus cattle bawling in the field across the road. Country sounds. And they all meant something, though I don't know what the coyote was trying to communicate. Maybe he was telling me to get up and put the mare and mule in their pasture before they got out onto the road; which I should have, and didn't. And they did!

Leaving bacon frying on the stove, I jogged down Tenderfoot Valley road to see if I could spot the errant white mule and her companion, my appaloosa mare. Nary a sign. After fixing Doug's breakfast, I left in the pickup to track them down. No luck. Returning to the house I looked through my binoculars to see them trotting up Echo Canyon, which lies northeast of our house, toward the coyote's hill.

A rosy glow preceded the sun, which was just spilling over Echo Canyon Hill when I began to drive the two animals home. Maud, the white mule, kicked up her heels in the fresh, fall morning air. as if to say thanks for the lark, it was fun. Last night it was so warm we slept with our bedroom windows open all night. The mornings have been frostless for so long, it seems as though the season has changed its mind and headed back toward summer.

My giant sunflowers hang heavy with huge, golden blooms, and the tallest plant measures more than 12 feet. By the front door, morning glories show off their "glory in the morning." Last spring I purchased a packet of the "Heavenly Blue" variety. Remembering the long rows of them I used to raise as a 19-year-old mother of two, I eagerly awaited the first blooms.

Finally they began to bloom, but instead of Heavenly Blue, a mixture of red, purple and white variegated flowers unfurled each morning. Then last week amid the vari-colored blooms, there appeared a large Heavenly Blue! I considered about writing the seed company, but thought better of it. The breathtaking beauty of the lovely, delicate, sky blue morning glory stands out amid the lesser ones. It is like life somehow; which isn't all heavenly blue, far from it, but the special flower, or experience, nourishes the soul of man, and provides hope.

Our seed potato harvest has begun. Yesterday the first load of potatoes was unloaded into our new storage here on the ranch, and I helped sort out rocks and dirt alongside our cellar crew.

I returned last week from Portland where I attended the 1989 National Beef Cook-Off. It was an experience we Oregon CattleWomen will never forget. Twenty-four Wallowa County CattleWomen helped stage the three-day event at the Red Lion at Lloyd Center.

It was dark and raining when I left early Sunday morning to drive to

Pendleton, where I had arranged to meet C. Belle Probert, with whom I rode to Portland. C. Belle, a Prairie Creek neighbor and CattleWoman, had been attending the Pendleton Round-Up with husband, Jim. Other Wallowa County CattleWomen were already in Portland.

As we walked into the lobby of the Red Lion, we were greeted by Sally Bowerman, serving on the hospitality committee, who presented me with a red rose for being a member of the press.

Lugging my trusty camera and notebooks I began "absorbing" that most ambitious undertaking, so I could write about it for three newspapers. Only trouble was, there was too much to absorb. It was an exhausting schedule. At all hours, up and down the hall of the Red Lion, foot-weary Oregon CattleWomen hurried and scurried, performing myriad tasks that staggered the imagination. It's a good thing we ate beef every day, or our strength would have ebbed.

C. Belle and I picked up our pre-registration packets and settled in on the eighth floor where we could look down on Portland's Oktoberfest in the park below. I walked across the street to Lloyd Center to purchase batteries for my camera and returned just in time to depart, along with 800 or more, who were being bused to the Masonic Temple for the opening reception.

The mild Western Oregon weather was incredible, with lovely clouds billowing up in a pure blue sky. Contestants and press from other states were most impressed by the autumnal clarity of the skies. No smog. After trudging up several flights of stairs (no one showed us the elevator) we entered an enormous hall that had been transformed into an early western town. At a "saloon" we found Marian Birkmaier, Wallowa County CattleWoman from way out on Crow Creek, dressed as a dance hall girl, feathers and all, serving Sioux City Sarsaparilla.

Assisting her were Mike Hanley and his pretty wife, Judi, from Jordan Valley. Judi, too, fit the part, and Mike, who looks like he stepped out of the pages of a western novel, added an authentic touch. The sarsaparilla, bottled in dark bottles, tasted like mild root beer. Wagon wheels, corn stalks and a blacksmith shop front added a nostalgic charm. And then we glimpsed the gigantic hall. Tables, set to accommodate 900, with red-checked tablecloths and pots of white mums for centerpieces.

Running around snapping pictures, I noticed a CattleWoman's California name tag. Came to find out she and her daughter were from my home town of Lincoln, people I knew and who knew my family! Virginia Allen and her mother and I visited about Placer County and "our people" in the middle of Portland.

Gerda Hyde, right, chairman of the hospitality committee at the National Beef Cook-Off in Portland, serves an ice cream cone to Florence Howell.

C. Belle Probert, left, and Janie Tippett at the opening reception of the National Beef Cook-Off.

Jeanette Knott, who is president of the Oregon CattleWomen, has a motto, "If it is to be, it is up to me!" That opening reception certainly reflected Jeanette's expertise and attention to detail. Bob Smith, Oregon congressman, gave a short "welcome to the West" address, as did Jeanette Barthle, president of the American National CattleWomen, Inc.

Music provided by "Country Pride" served as background music for the meal, which was served buffet-style from four locations to approximately 900 people. The mouth-watering menu included prime rib with a salmon complement, scalloped potatoes, three creative salads, hard rolls, huge, colorful fresh fruit trays and cheeses. Desserts were choices of spice, carrot or blueberry cake. Contestants and guests from all 50 states were heard to comment that it was one of the best meals they had ever eaten prepared for so large a crowd.

Baxter Black, ex-veterinarian turned cowboy-poet-philosopher, donated his services as emcee and introduced the 64 contestants from 50 states. However, Baxter, being such a friendly cuss, got so carried away visiting each contestant that the evening melted away and the event's chairpersons were tearing their hair out. To no avail Judy Wortman motioned for him to speed up the process. Finally, after sending Mike Hanley out on stage to give Baxter the "word, things sped up considerably. But it was too late for Baxter's own entertainment, which was canceled.

The "Dancing Cowboys," a western swing group from La Grande, performed on the stage to the delight of the audience, who clapped and stomped their feet to the familiar western hoedowns. It was late when we returned to our hotel room. It had been a long day.

Gerda Hyde, CattleWoman from Chiloquin, did a super job as hospitality chairman. She and her committee met airplanes and welcomed contestants from all over the U.S. All during the cook-off, Gerda and her crew made sure everyone was welcomed, and that welcome was extended all three days. Gerda saw to it that the hospitality room was stocked with coffee, tea, fresh fruits and in the mornings there were rolls and bagels and cream cheese. During the day she served up hundreds of ice cream cones in many delicious flavors. A familiar sight throughout the cook-off were members of the media, the Japanese delegation, Cattlemen and CattleWomen and contestants, all licking ice cream cones.

Adjacent to the hospitality room a country store was set up under the direction of Bernice McGee, CattleWoman from Riley, Oregon. Here one could purchase T-shirts, cookoff aprons, stuffed cows and other country what-nots. Carolee and Lee Perkins, from Joseph, set up a mini-Eagle Mountain Gallery with everything from Ted Juve Pottery to

Valley Bronze sculpture. Hawk Hyde, well-known rancher-author from Chiloquin, and Mike Hanley, Jordan Valley rancher-author, were kept busy autographing and selling their books.

On Monday members of the media, contestants and all manner of cook-off helpers were bused to the Coleman ranch in Molalla for a real taste of western hospitality. Steve and Cathy Coleman and their children opened up their ranch for tours, a barbecue and a rodeo.

During the one-hour bus ride to Molalla our tour guide was none other than Wallowa County's on Duke Lathrop from Lostine. Aided by Sharon Beck, from Alicel in Union County, Duke gave interesting info on Portland and Oregon in general for the benefit of people visiting from other states. Those of us from way out in Eastern Oregon cattle country got a kick out of one of Duke's remarks. He said he was from way out in Wallowa County, where some people lived so far out in the sticks they had to own their own tomcat.

September 29—Up early on this bright fall morning, as Doug and I prepare to pack into McCully Creek Basin for the opening weekend of deer season. Leaving our potato harvest crews working in the field and cellar, we haul our saddle horses and pack animals to Max Gorsline's place on upper Prairie Creek.

I didn't purchase a hunting license this year. There is still elk in our freezer and one deer would be sufficient. My job on this hunt would be camp cook, a role I enjoy. Actually it was nice not to pack a rifle and all the gear associated with hunting, and a lot less cumber-some. It is always a wonder to me why most men seem to need an excuse to pack into the mountains. Why does it always have to be bird, fishing or big game season, when really, most hunters and fisher-men go for the get-away-from-it-all-feeling anyway?

After we loaded our gear onto the pack animals, I bridled my mare, cinched her up and climbed aboard. We wouldn't get out of the saddle for eight miles of steep mountain riding. Leaving the valley below out of sight, out of mind, we rode up the dirt road past Max's place and soon entered the timbered slopes under the burn. As the day warmed the soft horses and mule began to sweat. The smell of pine and fir was pleasant and the grass at that elevation was green.

Max's buddy "Mel," a man of few words, forged on ahead. Max commented as how Mel might fall off a little on this trip, but guessed it wouldn't hurt him none. Occasionally we glimpsed Chief Joseph Mountain through the trees and the checkerboard valley below. This fall, instead of threading our way through viney Alder and fallen logs, a fire road made the going easier.

At the top of a ridge we rode into the burn. Before us stretched a scene of devastation, charred, lifeless forest. It was an eerie place filled with a deep, black silence. Presently we reached the McCully Creek trailhead and began the steep climb to the basin. McCully Creek splashed over fallen, blackened trees, singing its happy song. The only happy thing in an otherwise bleak environment.

With welcome relief we rode into color again, although we could still see the path the fire had taken on the opposite side of the mountain. The trail followed the creek's course to a golden meadow filled with straw-colored grasses and yellowing scrub willow. Our horses' hooves sank in boggy places where springs seeped and formed little water courses that flowed into McCully Creek. The creek became smaller as we neared its source.

Evidence from the August snowfall was all around in uneven patterns that had formed in patches of soft earth, like a spring thaw. We came upon a large cougar track and no fresh deer sign. Several jays screamed at us, but other than that the basin appeared pretty lifeless.

After the trail ended, Doug led on into spruce thickets, across more boggy meadows and finally to our old camp near the ruins of the Mc-Cully cabin. Above loomed the familiar landmark of Aneroid Peak. On the southeast rim castle-like spires jutted into the blue sky. The creek wandered through a frosted meadow downhill from the cabin.

Deep snows and wild winds of winter had done little to change the camp from when we visited last fall. Short fir trees threatened to engulf the log cabin, and the log we used to lay our saddles on was still there. Mel hunted a shady spot under a tree and laid down and went to sleep.

Maud, the white mule, shed of her pack, found a soft sandy place to indulge in several luxurious rolls. After the horses and pack animals were hobbled, we set up our tent and started a fire around 4 p.m. A few clouds began to form and float off toward the valley, a wind sprang up, softly at first. Mel offered little assistance when it came to helping Max figure out his new tent, but among the three of them the tent was pitched.

Refreshed after a short nap, I peeled potatoes and began to fry them with onion over the cooking fire. As the sun disappeared behind Aneroid Mountain, it turned cold and the fire felt good. The smell of wood smoke mingled with the frying potatoes and onion, and camp was home.

From my kitchen I could look up at a large snowbank that lay curled under a high rim. Little feathers of new snow clung to the rocks under the peak. From its birthplace in the basin above, the creek tumbled down in a waterfall to wind through our meadow. The dark, castle-like turrets to the southeast stood stark against the darkening skyline.

I broiled lamb chops on a grill over the coals. After supper we built up the fire and sat around telling tall tales while darkness seeped into the basin along with strong gusts of wind that blew pine needles to the ground.

By 8 p.m. the wind increased and powerful gusts swept down off the mountain. After I mixed up a bowl of sourdough hot cake batter for breakfast, we joked about who was going to sleep with the mixture to keep it warm. Doug finally placed it carefully in one of the pack boxes, covered it with the wooden lid and tarped down everything so the wind wouldn't carry off our kitchen.

As the few stars quickly disappeared under a cloud layer and the windy gusts became even more frequent, we all opted to go to bed. Mel, who had already been asleep for some time, blissfully snoozed away in Max's tent.

Doug and I sacked into our comfy sleeping bags just as a terrific blast of wind tore at our tent. It huffed and puffed and flapped until around 1:30 a.m. when we heard the first rain drops. Just before dawn the wind ceased and I slept. Doug got up to tend to the horses and start a fire.

September 30—As I stepped out into a misty mountain morning, I glanced above camp to see a sprinkling of new snow. Clouds of foggy mists swirled away to expose our white mule and the dark shapes of the horses, whose bodies contrasted with the golden grasses and yellow willows. It was a scene right out of Alaska.

I joined Max and Doug around the fire. Because of poor visibility the men gave up on a morning hunt. Mel slept in while I mixed up the sourdoughs and baked them on a hot grill over the fire. When we finished breakfast Mel staggered sleepily out of Max's tent, wolfed down six hotcakes and retired once more to the warmth of the tent.

The fog lifted to expose threatening rain clouds and the smell of snow was in the air. It got colder as the temperature dropped. We were huddled around the fire, and Max was in the middle of a story when all of a sudden we looked up to see Max's gray mare, Dusty, take off on a frightened course that led her straight up toward the old mine. Behind her a long dark object followed in hot pursuit. Airborne, it followed her, then hit the ground and jumped high into the air. At first we thought it was a cougar after her. As it turned out a cougar had spooked her and the terrified mare lunged forward, dragging the log she had been tied to with her.

As she thundered up into a rock slide, turned and headed back down toward camp, the log had been reduced to a mere stump. Doug set his cup of coffee down on a flat rock and ran to head her off. I hid behind a large tree so the flying stump wouldn't knock me out when she went flying by. The mare clattered into camp between the wood pile and the fire. In doing so, her long tether rope caught on a scrub fir and held fast.

She stood trembling long enough for Doug to untie the stump. And can you believe the coffee wasn't even spilled, the grub boxes weren't broken and Mel didn't even get shook up? Not me, I was shaking like a trembling aspen leaf, just thinking of what might have been. A bitter chill settled over the basin, Mel took another nap, and it began to rain, turning to sleet.

We decided the deer hunt was over, packed up and headed down the trail. Two hunters verified our suspicion about the cougar that spooked Max's mare. Wet and cold we arrived back at Max's place around 4 p.m. We all agreed the trip had been an experience, and not all bad. Mel just wagged his tail.

October 1—Dawned cloudy and cool, with no frost. McCully Creek drainages lay under misty clouds and I was thankful we were not still camped up there this morning. Cooked breakfast on the wood cook stove, packed a lunch and Doug and I headed for the hill country to check cows, fences, and look for fencing material. Doug was hoping a mule deer buck might just happen to stand in the way.

The hills were unbelievably green for October. Warm fall rains, followed by mild Indian summer weather, had carpeted our summer-dry hills with a new growth of grass. High on a ridge above Dorrance Grade, in a patch of morning sunlight, stood 10 does and fawns. We drove through the silent, rolling hills, which consist of a high, grassy plateau criss-crossed with rockjack fences, laced with creeks, and dotted with rock piles and stock ponds.

The creeks have names: Wet Salmon, Alder, Pine, Dry Salmon, Butte. They feed into Chesnimnus, which joins Crow Creek and becomes Joseph Creek. How I love creeks, and their names. Summer and fall range to Wallowa County's famous beef cattle. Our cows and their spring calves were all fat and sassy. From our Butte Creek pasture we could see the misty-covered Wallowas in the distance.

By the time we reached the ranch on Wet Salmon, we had seen 23 head of deer and around 30 elk! Doug unloaded Maud, the white mule, and turned her loose to run with two horses in a large pasture.

After visiting briefly with some deer hunters, we drove across Pine

Creek to Zumwalt, passing by the old one-room school house keeping its lonely vigil in a lonely country. We drove by the Steen ranch and noticed several deer camps on the way to Buckhorn. Several hunters had deer hanging, but many didn't.

The air was crisp and cool and a breeze was blowing some of the clouds way by the time we stopped for lunch near Cemetery ridge. The vastness of the Snake and Imnaha canyons spread out before us. Doug had driven down the old wagon road to Eureka Bar. Not more than trail when last I rode it; we had taken the cattle down to winter range in the fall of '78.

Far below we could see the small house at Horse Creek and the bright ribbon of the Imnaha flowing north through its deep-carved canyon. Golden grasses waved in the breeze at Spain Saddle, as Doug showed me where the old Dobbin supply cabin once stood. It was here that the cattle were turned down the steep slope toward Tully Creek, before being trailed Cow Creek and on up to the permit land that went with the Dug Bar ranch.

Inching our way down to another bench, so we could turn around, we saw the Snake winding through cavernous canyons. Timbered draws arched down the canyons and harbored deer, elk, bear, grouse and other wildlife.

Back up "on top" we drove through miles of the 1988 Tepee Butte burn, rich has been seeded with wheat and grass seed. At one point I had Doug p the pickup; I couldn't believe my eyes. Yellow star thistle growing in r forests! The scourge of California. We picked all we could find in that area so it wouldn't re-seed.

Looking for poles we drove out toward Coyote and by the time we reached Crow Creek, it was nearly dark. We could see the soft gas lights glow from the windows of Mack and Marian Birkmaiers' house along the creek. If there were any bucks out for the evening, it was already too dark to shoot. While I held the flashlight, Doug changed a flat tire on the dirt road near Klages'. It was nearly 9 p.m. when we reached home, and the weekend deer hunt was over.

October 2—The potato crew in the field by 8 a.m. Rained during the night, but not enough to halt the harvest. Later in the morning low clouds lifted to expose a new snowfall on the Wallowas. Our camp site on McCully Creek would be pretty wintery this morning.

Spent most of the day with my grandchildren before catching up on my housework. Picked up windfall apples and made a batch of apple-sauce; and covered plants as it is supposed to freeze tonight.

October 3—Up early to fix breakfast. It did freeze, but the flowers next to the house were spared. A few stringy clouds wreath the snow-covered mountains, which contrast with the brilliant green valley.

Picked up our frozen pork at Jerry's market in Joseph, then home to more housework; gathered eggs, picked a panful of strawberries and a few confused raspberries that are bearing again. Dug a hill of yellow Finn potatoes, along with carrots and beets to go with a lamb roast for supper.

Doug purchased a 4-H lamb and hog at the fair auction this summer. What a treat to have the winter supply of meat in the freezer. We really don't need venison. Daughter Ramona, who works on the digger, reported they got out 11 loads today, and it was her birthday.

October 4—A blue-gold Indian summer morning. Fresh pork sausage for breakfast seasoned with home grown sage and herbs. Found it hard to concentrate on my weekly column, so when Grace Bartlett and Cressie Green stopped by to get eggs on their way to Imnaha, I went with them.

We drove downriver to Inez Meyers' place on that lovely fall day. Cressie, who hadn't been to Imnaha for more than a year, commented all the way down about the beauty of the rimrocks and what a wonderful place it was for children to play. Sumac, just beginning to redden, glowed in sunlight. Little Sheep Creek sparkled with a clarity that is characteristic of October. Golden aspen and cottonwood leaves floated down the creek.

Imnaha's first church, which is still under construction, stood proud under high rims. The old cast-iron bell waits in the bell tower to ring up and down the canyon and call people to worship. The new cross outlined against the clear, blue sky. As we passed the Imnaha store with its two wooden Indians out front, we noticed a flatbed truck parked there with five deer antlers displayed on it. Buck hunting appears better in the canyon country than "on top."

Inez's old-fashioned yard was bursting with fall color, as were her gardens. Tomatoes hung red-ripe on the vines, zinnias bloomed, late corn ripened, huge banana and Hubbard squashes peeked between trailing vines. Cucumbers, shiny green and red bell peppers, bright orange pumpkins, and apples, plums and walnuts. A smiling Inez came out to greet us.

Alongside her house bloomed delicate blue windflowers, foxglove, violets, mums, dahlias and several varieties of ground cover. From an immense walnut tree hung the scales she used to weigh her vegetables. Inez's small house seemed dwarfed by the surrounding canyon and the

Imnaha running by. We visited a while before gathering our produce. While talking about rattlesnake experiences Inez told how she had killed one in her basement and how the snakes like to lie among the squash vines. But Inez is used to canyon living and these are just things that are dealt with, no big deal.

We drove home bearing the famous Imnaha baking squash, which our valley season is too short for, and cucumbers, peppers, tomatoes and enough windfall apples to make apple butter.

Things are changing on the Imnaha. Naomi Doss is retiring as post-mistress and Bonnie Marks will take her place. A.L. Duckett, just turned 95, has moved into a trailer house and leased out his house. He will spend the winter in Bend with a relative. A.L.'s once-brilliant, colorful, bounti-ful gardens already belong to the past, but we will always remember his sauerkraut and bulging canning cellar, where he preserved "summer in a jar." A.L. reaped rich harvests sown by love.

Jim Dorrance has been long gone from the Riverside Cafe and resides now in a nursing home in Enterprise. The winds of change blow, the old-timers fading away and the new ones taking their place, and the Imnaha rolls on into eternity.

October 14—As the last row of seed potatoes rolled their way up the chain to pass by the gals on the digger, a mighty cheer rang across the field. The harvest was over! Meanwhile, I was busy planning a menu and doing grocery shopping for the harvest party to be held in our shop Monday evening.

On Sunday I attended an all-day photography workshop, sponsored by our local photo club, at the Wallowa Lake Lodge. Armed with tripod, camera, lunch and a warm jacket, I left early to help set up for the workshop.

Out of a clear morning sky the full harvest moon shone down upon Prairie Creek's frosty fields. It was 15 degrees. The seed potatoes went into storage just in time. Wallowa Lake, reflecting moon glow, appeared silent, cold and lovely during off-tourist season. Inside the old lodge a cheery fire blazed in the large, stone fireplace and I could hear Sunday morning voices in the kitchen.

Shortly Jon Kepley and wife, Kay, walked downstairs where Sharon Rowbury and I joined them for a visit while they ate breakfast in the Camas Room. Following an informal get-acquainted class where we learned about different kinds of camera equipment, used for Jon's "mood" photography, we strode forth into the frosty morning and wandered along the river bank, near where the water empties into the lake.

The sun took a long time making its appearance on that cold morning, but when it spilled over the high mountain ridge and filtered through the red and gold colored leaves near the river, it was worth the wait. Under Jon's expert tutelage we photographed October's colors at the lake: rocks, running water, minute flowers and weeds hidden in meadow grasses, as well as leaves.

We must have created quite a picture ourselves: hoods over our heads to block out the side light, poised in a variety of undignified positions over camera and tripod. Kepley, who used second-hand or home-made gear to accomplish his "meadow-diving" techniques, was a most interesting instructor.

At noon, on the way into the lodge to eat our "brown bag" lunches (and warm up), we were side-tracked by the pond, where we spent another half-hour photographing an elusive rainbow in the fountain's spray, ice-encrusted grass and pine needles floating on water. The afternoon was spent viewing Kepley's slides, which depicted his own visual discoveries. The lovely images were made in natural light, he said, with attitude priority and patient mode, macro focusing and, among other things, tripod, wife, gumshoes, raingear, eyepatch, scissors and round file, on Kodachrome film. His slides were truly an inspiration.

At 7 that evening we were treated to more slides: beautiful dual images of scenes around the Pacific Northwest, accompanied by soft music. Mood photography. Kepley records images and creates a mood, he ways. He doesn't just photograph nouns, or the obvious, and his photography evokes strong feelings for the natural world around us. A world that many never see. Driving home in the cold moonlight I knew my flowers would be done for by morning.

October 16—Fifteen degrees again, and except for the geraniums I brought inside, all else is blackened by frost. Clear, crisp October morn. Golden tamarack, also called western Larch, glows against the evergreens on Wallowa slopes.

Spent this day cooking for our harvest dinner. It being so cold I kept the old Monarch fired up to cook a huge kettle of beans and ham hocks, and boiled up enough potatoes for a humongous salad. In the wood stove oven I baked deep-dish apple pies as fast as I could peel the apples. Using the electric ovens in our kitchen and trailer I prepared 30 pounds of roast beef in cast iron dutch ovens.

This year I purchased french bread; simply ran out of steam to bake it myself. Daughter Jackie appeared to help and by 5 p.m. all was baked, cooked and put together. Daughters Ramona and Annie arrived with granddaughters to help decorate the tables with Indian corn, pumpkin and funny-shaped potatoes we had saved on the digger for the occasion.

By 6 our seed potato crews and their families converged on our shop, which Jim, Doug and Ben had spent the day cleaning; in short order, more than 50 healthy appetites demolished my food.

Ramona and Annie entertained us with a hilarious skit they had spent all day putting together. Dressed as "potatoes" made of gunny sacks filled with cotton and pillows, they appeared as "Doug's Darlin' Diggers." With Annie on guitar they sang a song they had composed which told the story of their experiences on the digger during potato harvest. Their "act" brought down the house, 'er... shop, and put everyone in a good mood. Their unique outfits included potato chip earrings and french fries strung into necklaces. It would have been a tough act to follow in any talent show.

October 17—An early phone call from high school teacher Gail Murphy in Monument, Oregon, began my day. Was I still planning to drive to Monument and give a presentation to her writing class tomorrow?

"Looking forward to it," I replied, then wondered how was I going to clean up after the harvest supper and do all that needed doing that day, which included a going-away open house for our neighbors, driving into town to take in, and pick up, our car (which wouldn't start) to the garage to be worked on, and still have time to put together a slide show presentation and talk.

Somehow the day disappeared and all was accomplished, except when Doug and I went to pick up our car. It still wouldn't start. The kindly man at Milligan Motors came to our rescue and loaned us a car to make the trip to Monument. On the way into Enterprise I first heard the news about the San Francisco earthquake and our troubles seemed small indeed.

October 18—We were up and gone in the pre-dawn on that clear, cold morning, to drive to Monument, which our map showed to be 22 miles from Long Creek. We made it as far as Lostine, where we were finishing breakfast just at sunup. Frost covered the Grande Ronde valley and wisps of misty vapors followed the river.

As Doug drove the long, quiet road toward Ukiah, I jotted down some notes. Perhaps, I thought, I could talk to Gail's students about the importance of being observant. Many of us look, but don't see the world around us.

And because I am fascinated with creeks and how they got their names, I began writing down creeks: Jordan, Bear, Meadow, Burnt Corral,

Tybow Canyon, Camas, Rancheria, Bear Willow, Lane, Cable, Wilkins, Five-mile, N.F. John Day River, W.F. Meadow Brook, Granite, Barnes, M.F. John Day, Pine, Pass, Long, Shaws, Paul, Little Basin, Cottonwood, E.F. Deer, N.F. John Day River.

By the time we arrived in Monument I had recorded 26 creeks and rivers. Just think of the writing material contained in the histories of those creeks. Other Eastern Oregon trademarks included range cattle, abandoned homesteads, deer, elk, porcupine, coyote, crows, hawks, small logging towns and their inhabitants, old-timers and real cowboys, not the TV versions, who wear the fancy hats, and boots that never see dust, mud or manure.

You can read their stories in their faces, where the years of being out in all kinds of weather has written it all down. Driving through this vast country, I reflected on how much of our west is still relatively unpeopled; cattle and timber country. And the ones who do inhabit these areas share a common bond, sacrificing many of life's amenities for the privilege of living where their heart is.

As we drove down the final winding road from Long Creek to the small community of Monument, we noticed the beautiful rock formations amid October's color. Rustic old barns and remote cattle ranches were tucked into the folds of the canyons. We wondered about the lives of those hard-working ranching families who lived so far out in that rugged country.

Situated along a bend of the John Day River, near the North Fork, lay the small community of Monument (population 185). We drove past older homes that sat back from tree-lined streets to the school, where directly across the street, Cora Stubblefield, postmistress, was getting ready to close the post office at noon. I was scheduled to give my talk around 12:15, so we ate lunch at the high school cafeteria, where the aroma of freshly-baked peach cobbler permeated the school.

Even as I looked upon the sincere, young faces of Miss Murphy's high school English class, I didn't know what I would say to them. Then suddenly, the words came without hesitation. I tried reaching them on an individual basis. That was what I most wanted to convey; that each one of them was unique and in their own special way had something to offer the world.

I had learned that most of Monument's students belonged to hard-working families who lived far out on remote cattle ranches that lay scattered among the juniper and sagebrush hills. I wanted to impress upon these young people that they should be proud of their heritage. That wherever they went, they would always remember Monument.

The very silence of the land would help shape them as writers, if they chose to write. The character of the land would become their character; it would happen without their knowing it. To be writers they must read, read, read, and write, write, write; and pretty soon it would happen. And to pay attention to Miss Murphy, a teacher who inspires as well as teaches. In an age when most news seems to be bad news, I felt it was the modern writer's responsibility to write about positive happenings that could, in turn, help bring love, faith and some goodness back to a troubled world.

After showing a few slides of Wallowa County that I had hurriedly put together the night before, I turned on "The Wallowa Story," the automatic 45-minutes slide-tape program that our history group had produced for a centennial project in 1987. It was nearly 2 p.m. when I finished. Monument was playing Long Creek that afternoon in volleyball, and we were told there weren't enough students to make up an eight-man football team.

Doug and I retired to Gail's house, where we rested before picking apples that grew in an adjacent orchard near the John Day River. Those apples were crisp and sweet and tasted like October. The scene from Gail's kitchen window was pastoral: the river making a turn, a long green meadow dotted with grazing sheep, all backgrounded by the canyon country that surrounds the small community of Monument. There was a warm, lazy, hazy feel to the town, which seemed as quiet as the country.

That evening Gail and daughter Katie took us to supper where we were joined by Clyde Cavender and her husband, long-time Monument residents and avid readers of Agri-Times. We ate in the town's only cafe, and because most of Monument's citizenry was still in Long Creek, we had the place to ourselves.

Fascinated with Clyde's name, I asked her why she had been so named, to which she explained how her uncle "Clyde" had delivered her as a baby. Clyde, who is involved in the local home extension club, had been responsible for organizing my presentation to the community that night.

Because the Grange hall was just across from the cafe, we walked while Doug drove the car over and helped set up the projector. One of the men split some kindling in a wood shed room that opened off the back of the hall, and soon a blazing fire crackled in the old pot-bellied stove.

Meanwhile, in the kitchen, women of the community prepared coffee and punch and set up a dessert tableful of cakes and cookies. We met some very interesting people, including Cora Stubblefield, who had written me a fan letter several years ago. Cora has been Monument's postmistress for 30 years.

We also met Bud and Osie Engle, and Darrel and Oleta Farrens. Darrel, a 76-year-young cowboy who rides for a 1,300-cow outfit, said he has been a buckaroo since 1933, and was born just 30 miles from Monument. Darrel continues to ride nearly every day and the healthful life style must agree with him because he looks great.

The people were warm and friendly and enjoyed watching the "Wallowa Story." I expressed the hope that someone would be inspired to put together a history of Monument's rich heritage.

October 19—It was just breaking daylight when we pulled out of Monument and headed down along the John Day River toward Kimberly. We were amazed to see acres of fruit growing there along the river: well-kept apricot, peach, pear and apple orchards. We had been told earlier that pickers are brought in and fruit is shipped out of Kimberly.

We enjoyed the peaceful morning drive along the beautiful John Day River and passed the Fossil Beds National Monument. The place wasn't open that early and we had to be in Baker for a bull sale by noon. We saw many mule deer grazing the bottoms or drinking from the river near Dayville, and we stopped in Mt. Vernon for pancakes at the "Wounded Buffalo" before continuing on through John Day.

Leaving Prairie City we climbed 5,280-foot Dixie Pass and took the Austin turnoff to Sumpter and arrived in Baker by 11:30 a.m. Following directions in our sale catalog. We found the Thomas Angus Ranch, where Baker County CattleWoman Martha Jane Jacobs and her crew were just serving up hamburgers to a large sale crowd.

The Thomas family, in the ranching business for 40 years, has consistently improved the quality of its Angus cattle. Their sale is run efficiently and the cattle offered are bred for top performance. It seemed as though half of Wallowa County was there and many of them purchased bulls and some females.

After Doug purchased a young bull, we stayed until the sale ended and partook of a delicious roast beef meal, compliments of the Thomas family and served up by Martha Jane and her "happy helpers," who really know how to put on a real western feed. We even visited with Don and Lois Hough, who live across from us on Prairie Creek. Pretty bad when we ranchers get so busy we have to attend a bull sale in another county to visit our neighbors.

As dark clouds hovered over the mountains and the wind began to blow, everyone seemed to sense our long Indian summer was coming to an end. Now that the potatoes are safely in storage, we must concentrate on the cattle. Fall calves to brand and work, bulls to haul in from the hills, and it will soon be time to bring the cows and fall calves down off the moraine.

November and winter and snow are just around the corner.

October 21—Windy and cloudy this morning, rained during the night, and a fresh blanket of snow covers the mountain tops. Doug hauling bulls in from the hills to put with our fall calvers. As I peeled apples to bake an apple crisp, angry clouds began spilling more snow over the mountains and the temperature took a dive.

The Prairie Creek wind blew fiercely as Andy and Kris Barr delivered our new bull that Doug had purchased at the Thomas Angus sale in Baker. We were invited to dinner at "A Country Place on Pete's Pond" with some friends. After enjoying a good meal and visit, we stepped outside to see it was pouring down rain, and the ducks on the pond were happy!

A brisk wind blew enough clouds away at daylight to expose the snow-clad Wallowas. October snow seems brighter somehow, perhaps due to contrasting dark blue slopes splashed with golden tamarack. Baked another apple crisp (using up the windfalls) to take to 4-H family appreciation night potluck. Planted iris bulbs given to me by a friend.

I was very surprised and touched to receive a special "Friend of 4-H" award during the program tonight. Afterward, daughter Ramona and I went to see "Dead Poets Society," which was playing at the OK Theatre.

Later, as I write in my daily journal, the fire in the wood cook stove slowly dies, the teakettle sputters and is silent, the clock ticks away the hours, and the lonely Prairie Creek wind blows on into the night.

October 23—A brilliant "cowboys warning" sunrise this morning. Autumn winds blow away October's color. The sunburst, between painted clouds, disappears, not to appear again. and our cowboys brand one bunch of fall calves on this wet, stormy day.

This evening, as I cleaned mountain oysters, the wind finally laid down and a steady rain drummed on the roof.

October 24—That time of year already: out early to hay the milk cows and calves. The coyotes must have been practicing for a concert, as their yips and yowls came echoing across the hills on this cold, clear morning. Frost sparkled over the prairie and the thermometer registered 23 degrees. Early sunlight transformed cottonwoods to gold and another layer of snow gleamed off the high peaks.

Stricken with "photographer's fever" I drove to upper Prairie Creek where I tried to capture the golden color against the fresh snowfall. Everywhere there was beauty: old weathered barns, split rail fences, creeks full of floating, colorful leaves and reflections of trees; aspen, tamarack, blue, gold, white mountains with just enough clouds moving in to make it interesting.

Must make the most of this subject material, as the days dwindle down.

October 25—Fixed Doug's favorite cold weather breakfast on the wood cookstove: sourdough hotcakes with mountain oysters and scrambled eggs. Cloudy and cold, yesterday's beauty only a memory, threatening rain, and the mountains wreathed in autumn mists. Overnight the snow line lowered to upper Prairie Creek.

Split and hauled wood to fill the wood box and stopped typing my column so I could play when the grandchildren came to visit. They came bouncing into my morning like two lively chipmunks. We had a great day! We built a tepee in the living room, then pretended to go fishing and hunting (for bears mostly), played the piano, cut out pictures from catalogs, painted, and fixed lunch to eat in the tepee (a blanket over a card table).

They would rest I read and rocked them; but sleep they wouldn't, just too exciting being at grandma's house to waste on sleep. Tried to finish typing my column that evening, but grandma could scarcely keep her eyes open.

October 26—Twenty-five degrees and clear with heavy frost. Frozen puddles in our lane shattered like glass when the men came to work. I donned layers of clothing as Ben, Doug and I would gather and trail the cows and fall calves off the high pasture this morning. Peering through a small opening in the frosted windshield of our old stock truck, we chugged off to Wallowa Lake with our saddle horses loaded in the back.

From the road, we spied a bunch of cows grazing near the farthest fence line corner. So I got out to start them on foot, to save riding all that way after them. My boots (not made for walking) slipped and slid on the steep, frozen hill, but cows and calves took off in the right direction and soon Ben caught up leading my mare, which I then rode.

The exertion had warmed me up and the cattle were moving well along parallel trails. Above, etched against the morning skyline, stood six deer, including one four-point buck, staring down at us. When I had time to look below, the lake reflected in its calm morning waters the snow-covered Chief Joseph mountain. The air was pure October, the kind you drink, not breathe: fresh, cold and pure.

Doug, who had driven up toward the head of the lake and unloaded his horse, was gathering cows and calves on the timbered side of the moraine. As Ben and I pushed two bunches up onto the old wagon road, a few wind clouds formed and the ground beneath our horses' hooves rang in frozen cadence. Steam from the cattle's bodies hung in the air and, just before we reached the top, the welcome morning sun streamed over the ridge.

The view on top was breath-taking: The Seven Devils range in Idaho, the patchwork farm lands below, and the rolling hill land beyond. While I rode the high ridge looking for scattered cattle, Ben rode off in another direction and soon Doug brought his bunch down out of the timber. We all converged with cattle about the same time, near the elk fence gate, where we waited for another herd of cattle to go on down the road and be corraled before letting ours out. We had quite a time getting everything "mothered up," but eventually we started the cows and calves down the road toward home.

As we approached the alfalfa field where we would pasture them, threatening clouds formed over the mountains and already it looked stormy where we had just been. A cold wind had began to blow and we turned the cattle into the field and rode on home; it was nearly 2 p.m. when we ate lunch in our warm kitchen.

That evening I joined our photography members for a dinner-meeting at Vali's Alpine Delicatessen at Wallowa lake. We celebrated our first year, electing officers and enjoying dinner prepared by Mike Vali and served by wife, Maggie: chicken paprikash and homemade rolls and noodles. Yum.

October 27—It was raining when I drove home from the lake last night. When it became silent in the night, we knew it was snowing. This morning Prairie Creek is covered with a soft, white coverlet of the valley's first snowfall of the season.

Shuffling through the spring-like snow to feed the cows, my dog thought it great fun to romp and roll in the stuff, but I'm not ready for winter yet.

October 28—In the midst of a full-scale blizzard, driving our four-wheel drive Luv pickup. I slowly made my way into Joseph. Huge flakes of snow swirled and flew into the windshield, making it difficult to see the road ahead. Phyllis Johnson had called last evening to ask a favor: did

I have any poems about a ranch wife that could be read at her parents' funeral, scheduled for 11 this morning?

While searching through my library, I came across what I was looking for in a book of poems written by Betty Cornwell, upper Prairie Creek poetess and neighbor. The book, entitled *Build Me a Bridge,* contained the poem "Requiem for a Farm Woman." So touching were the words, I could not hold back the tears while reading it.

After delivering the book and some eggs to Chandler's Bed, Bread and Trail Inn, I returned to the ranch. The wet, spring-like snow was melting as I joined a long line of people waiting to enter the Enterprise Christian Church for the funeral of Chester and Mildred Hafer, who lost their lives in a tragic auto accident this week. The front of the church overflowed with flowers, and two pine caskets, covered with pine boughs, stood below the altar. Chester's hat sat atop his casket while over Mildred's cavorted ceramic children. The couple had celebrated their 50th wedding anniversary when all the children were here this summer, although their official date would have been in November.

The Hafers had lived as full-time ranchers way out north on what is known as Eden Bench. Local veterinarian and cowboy poet Fred Bornstedt sang a western ballad to begin the service, which was performed by Lester Wells. A poem, written by another local cowboy poet, Dan Jarvis, was read to honor Chester, and was followed by "Requiem For a Farm Woman" for Mildred.

It seemed especially fitting that both song and poems were composed locally. And a small community draws closer somehow, when all can share in their neighbor's sorrow. I wish I could have driven out north to the Eden Cemetery for the burial, but my day wouldn't allow it. Chester and Mildred have returned to their Eden, an Eden that looks down to Troy, over to Paradise, Lost Prairie, Flora and Promise. Names of real places, where real people live in Wallowa County.

While I grocery shopped, I marveled at all the convenience foods that fill the shelves of our local supermarket. It would seem no one cooks anymore.

Elk hunters were beginning to invade the area, stocking up their camp provisions. Ben and Doug had been back riding the snowy moraine, looking for a missing cow and calf most of the day. By evening the temperature took a dive again so I cooked supper on the wood cookstove: elk steak, potatoes, creamed corn, tomatoes...cold weather fare. It had begun to snow heavily by 8:30, as I drove Doug up to the elk fence gate to bring home the stock truck he used to haul horses there today.

Requiem for a Farm Woman
by Betty Cornwell

Down through the years
  she rode the wind
    with a reckless faith
Spurning the catcalls
of the warm and wise
  she picked a coral-bell
    While the dinner burned...
Who... who's to judge the legacy she left
  the too-poor land,
    a shambled house,
      fences down.
Children scattered who would not return,
  Yet...
    in the hayloft a black cat
holding a mouse stares out expectantly.
Chickens wander disconsolately in the
  barn lot.
A giant pig, standing in the feed trough
  aims its china-eyes
    towards the house.
The neighbors come to make amends.
  (luckily it is sale day)
The cow is loaded in a truck.
  The sheep are herded down the road.
  Seven geese waddle down the stream.
A great owl hoots his sad lament.
    Yet somewhere
in the near-by woods
the bluebells and the yellow bells
all raise their fragrant heads
    and chime
in one ecstatic
  symphony.

October 29—Twenty-nine degrees, snowed most of the night, a good four inches of white stuff lies under dull, gray skies. Elk hunters should have good trackin' snow. The McFetridges drove a bunch of heifers by our ranch this morning. A scene being repeated all over the country this time of year. In fact Ben and Doug are moving some of our heifers from upper Prairie Creek to the ranch this morning.

The snowy mountains seem so close and harbor that familiar chill. Picked apples in a friend's orchard today, as it is supposed to freeze hard tonight. I plan on using the apples to make a batch of apple cider. Doug drove out to the hill ranch to repair more fence where elk have torn them down again, and reported some cattle had gotten out.

October 30—Although we have returned to standard time, we continue to rise before daybreak. This morning the mountains blush with pale, pink alpenglow and it is a clear, cold 12 degrees. After breakfast and chores, Doug and I left for the hills to put the loose cattle back in and repair more fence. When we found the heifers grazing along the road, I got out and drove them back on foot toward Salmon Creek where they had gotten out.

While Doug went on ahead in the pickup to repair fence, I enjoyed my walk in the frosty hills. The heifers were nearing their pasture when something spooked them and they plowed through the opposite fence! Now Doug had more fence to fix. Feeling like Flo in a Palen cartoon, I broke the news...and there was no tree to climb.

We drove the long miles home, loaded potatoes into the van, and traveled 30 miles to Imnaha to deliver them to Phyllis at the Riverside Cafe, where we then ate lunch. After a short drive downriver, we drove part way up the newly-improved road to Hat Point. Red sumac and yellowing cotton wood melted into blue distant canyons and snow-dusted rim rock.

Returned to Prairie Creek, gathered the eggs, and tried to rest up for the long night ahead, as Doug and I would man the hay station at Minam during the 9 to 2 shift. It was frosty cold again as we arrived to relieve Pat and Ray at the makeshift shelter along the Minam River. A gas-powered generator hummed noisily, providing light inside the tarp-covered, wooden frame. A metal stove held a hot fire, bales of straw and a crude, wooden bench provided a place to sit. A coffee pot, containing very strong "cowboy coffee," boiled away on the stove.

Outside, stacks of hay and straw were available for hunters to purchase. In an effort to control the spread of noxious weeds, no outside hay would be allowed into the county. Although I brought along a good book, it was hard to concentrate. We alternately froze and roasted, depending on which side was turned toward the stove. The long, cold watch wore on and by 2 a.m. the coffee was chewable and we were ready to relinquish our duties to Steve and Van, who showed up on schedule.

It was turning into one of those long days and short nights, as we drove home, got three hours of shut-eye, then greeted the day, which included branding and working 100 fall calves we'd recently trailed off the moraine. It was a chilly 15 degrees as we drove cows and calves down the road to the corrals and sorted them. I spent the day at the chute, vaccinating while Ben branded and did the rest, while Jim pushed the big calves into the chute and Doug sprayed the cows.

After Doug hauled a cow to a missing calf, we broke for lunch and took a brief nap until hubby awoke and said "you gonna sleep all day?" So it was back to the chute until 4:30 when Doug took over my job. Weary, dirty and cold I warmed up leftover elk stew and biscuits. After washing up the syringes I headed for bed.

October comes to an end tomorrow, and witches, ghosts and goblins will be about, as it will be Halloween.

November 1—Doug left early for the hills to check on elk hunters. General bull elk (first season) and cow season (Zumwalt) begins this morning. It is a mere 12 degrees.

Turning on our local KWVR radio station, I hear all kinds of news: it is Marian Birkmaier's birthday, there is no school because of elk season, and the regular radio announcer, Dave Nelson, is elk hunting. So Lee Perkins was loose in the studio. Lee can make even bad news sound good. And when he sang happy birthday to Marian, way out on Crow Creek, well: it was something.

I tried calling to wish her the same, but the single-wire phone line that drapes itself over leaning posts and trees to the end of that 30-mile line was already humming with others who were doing same. As I tore October from the calendar, I noticed a quote written at the bottom of November: *No fruits, No flowers, No leaves, No birds, November*—Thomas Hood.

I breathe in the fresh, cold air as I walk out in the frozen morning to feed the new bull, a steer, and the milk cows and calves. Then I carry a tea kettle of hot water to the chicken pen to thaw out their water.

Later in the morning, after loading up pails and sacks full of windfall apples, Grace and I head for Imnaha to press apple cider. Even at lower elevations it is brisk and cold, but we soon warm up cranking the old grinder and pressing the clear, golden juice from the cold apples. Daughter Jackie has arranged for us to use a neighbor's press, which is a very old one; well-made and sturdy.

We take turns washing the apples, feeding them into the grinder, and turning the crank. Crunch, grind, and soon the wooden-slatted bucket below is filled with ground-up apples. Some juice has already made its way out onto the wooden trough and trickles into a pan. The ground apples are covered with a wooden lid that fastens to the press. We crank down on the press and the juice really flows now. It is fun, even though it turns out to be hard work.

The pulp is spread out on the garden and the process repeated until all the apples are gone. The juice is poured into plastic and glass gallon jars, ready to freeze for winter. And while we work, the lovely canyons of the Imnaha surround us, still wearing their fall colors. We took time out to eat our lunches and sample the fresh, cold cider, then back to washin', grindin' and pressin'...until we finished with 13 gallons of delicious cider.

The sun disappears behind canyon rims early now, and on Prairie Creek it slides down the back sides of Twin Peaks around 4 p.m. While some hunters encountered good luck, others didn't see hide nor hair of any elk. Among the lucky ones were a son-in-law and grandson, who each filled cow tags.

November 2—Cold, clear, frozen 18-degree morning when Doug left for the hills to clean out stock ponds with the cat. Cloudy and warmer by nightfall.

November 3—No frost, due to clouds; much warmer air moving into the valley. Spent the morning baking pies for various members of the family. Still using up those apples! Also made a banana cream pie for grandson Shawn's pie-a-month birthday gift.

Delivered the pies and took some potatoes to Aunt Opal in Enterprise.

November 4—Doug returned from the hills with all sorts of elk tails...'er, tales. Didn't know if I should believe them. They seemed more preposterous with each telling. We invited Max Gorsline down for supper tonight and I found out those stories were, indeed, factual!

Earlier, I had baked a pumpkin pie from our Halloween jack-o'-lantern. All day heavenly smells wafted from the old Monarch. Apple sauce bubbling away, mingled with the lingering spice of pumpkin pie; then there was the wild yeast aroma of sourdough biscuits baking, and pork chops sizzling. I mashed the potatoes, made milk gravy, and put together a carrot and raisin salad.

Max and Doug, who had spent the day outside, appreciated the cold weather fare, which was fun to prepare. Cooking isn't work when it is creative.

November 5—Dark, overcast, and gloomy with very little frost; the barn lot muddy enough to wear rubber boots. Put fresh, clean straw in the pullet's nest and scattered a little wheat around for them to scratch and peck. This makes them sing and be happy, as well as provide a variety to their diet of laying mash.

Followed Doug out to the hills (he drove a big flat bed truck) to bring in the caterpillar tractor. The roads were muddy due to recent heavy rains, which apparently missed us in the valley. We visited briefly with a hunter who had just filled his cow elk tag.

A cold, bone-chilling wind blew across the brown November hills as Doug loaded up the tractor and we started for home.

November 6—Mike McFetridge arrived early with his horse to drive to the hills with Doug and Ben, and begin weaning the spring calves. I spent the day caring for grandchildren and catching up, so Doug and I can get away for the cattlemen's convention.

November 7—Bundled up the children and they helped grandma with the chores. It was windy and cold when the crew headed for the hills again to haul in more calves. Our corrals are full of bawling babies. The sound is one continuous roar! Thank goodness the cows are out on Salmon Creek.

After the children were gone, I got busy on my column so it could be mailed before we left for Portland in the morning.

November 8—It was dark, cloudy, and a frosty 32 degrees when we packed up and left for the big city, leaving the bawling calves behind. We made it as far as Lostine before we got hungry and stopped for breakfast at the Lostine Tavern. We always know we will get a good breakfast there and be served hash browns from our own potatoes.

The Lovells do a fine job of managing the place, and we get a kick out of their signs: Ewe Joint, Fleece Room (Lovell is a sheep shearer, among other things), and it is the only "gathering place" in town. An old-timer who frequents the place always pays for the coffee of the first person through the door each morning, and that happened to be us. Whoever else comes in thereafter does the honors of keeping everyone's cup full. The regulars began drifting in, discussing and cussing the affairs of the day.

The main topic of conversation that morning was local neighbor-rancher Bill Wolfe, who recently suffered a heart attack. Everyone voiced concern and hoped for Bill's speedy recovery. Small towns are like that, and that is nice. Thank God for Lostine.

It was pleasantly mild as we drove over the Blues, which we were surprised to see devoid of snow. Our own snow-clad Wallowas faded in memory as we sped along the Columbia and stopped for lunch at The Dalles.

It was windy in the Gorge, which was gorgeous with fall color, and the skies were filled with clamoring honkers. It began to rain as we flew past Multnomah Falls, and I glimpsed a gauzy spray of white water cascading down into brilliant autumn yellow. No doubt about it, the western side of our state is still beautiful in November, where maples contrast with the evergreens.

We reined up at the Holiday Inn at the Portland Airport, and carried our bags to the second floor. A far cry from the 14th floor of the Red Lion, but nice. After settling in, Doug attended an early meeting while I walked around the lobby and looked down on a huge indoor fountain from which water spilled from graduated levels to form a center piece for a Spanish patio or court yard. Next to the fountain was an indoor swimming pool in which two children were happily splashing about.

One of the convention speakers, James Spawn, executive secretary of the American Gelbvieh Association, needed a ride to a reception we had also been invited to, to honor Dianne Snedaker of Ketchum Advertising in San Francisco. So, shortly, Mr. Spawn and Doug and I were driving over the Willamette River to find the Portland Advertising Museum, where the reception was scheduled for 5:30.

We found the Portland advertising museum to be a very fascinating place. Mick Scott, executive secretary for the Oregon Cattlemen's Association, a major contributor to the museum, showed us around. The large room was filled with dated advertising memorabilia, such as an old wooden barber pole, Burma Shave signs, a 1760 edition of Benjamin Franklin's newspaper, Philip Morris and Lucky Strike ads and continuously playing black and white movie ads.

The museum provided an appropriate place for Dianne Snedaker's reception. While Diane, president of Ketchum Advertising, enlightened us on how producers' check-off dollars are being spent to promote beef, we nibbled on delicious appetizers prepared by the gals in the Oregon Cattlemen's Association office.

And for the next couple of days, we country folks, who are used to being outside, would spend all of our time indoors, except for crossing over to the trade show. And be well-fed on our product, which was prepared in many delicious ways. Everyone obviously enjoyed the tempting continental breakfast, compliments of trade show exhibitors, where ranchers could relax and renew old acquaintances around informal tables.

It was a well-organized convention and lots of work went into hammering out resolutions that would benefit the industry. The lineup of speakers ranged from a special assistant to the president to Bobbie Gee, who brought the convention to a rousing close with her keynote speech about the power of image.

Next time you run into Union County rancher Bob Beck, you might ask him if he's changed his image yet. Actually, it might be more interesting to ask wife, Sharon.

November 11—Refreshed by the Willamette Valley's colorful autumn foliage, we sped along in the flow of I-5 traffic to Salem. Rain threatened, but never materialized. Every so often I caught a fleeting glimpse of an old barn in juxtaposition to urban sprawl.

After a brief visit with a daughter and new grandson, we returned home on Sunday.

November 13—Up early this morning to move the fall calves and their mamas back to the ranch, where they will spend the winter eating silage and hay. As soon as the cows were moved. Doug, having missed out on the first two days of his bull elk hunt, headed out to Salmon Creek. I know this must seem like a whopper of a hunting story, but he just happened on a herd of 250 elk, which several other hunters had surrounded, when this bull came running toward him. And on his own place yet!

To make a long story short, he was back in two hours with a big grin and meat in the pot. Which just goes to prove elk hunting is 95 percent luck and five percent skill.

November 14—A light snow fell during the night and a freezing wind blows across the white prairie this morning. Doug recorded weaning weights on our spring calves, which averaged more than 700 pounds, with a few going as high as 850. Spent the day typing articles on the convention and doing chores.

November 15—As the dawn sky blushes pink. I fix breakfast early, so Doug can leave for the Divide to receive 107 head of weaned calves he has purchased. After chores, I baked a mincemeat pie, then spent most of the day behind the typewriter, which seems to be a permanent fixture on our kitchen table.

November 16—Clad in overalls and "Flo's" boots, I walked out our lane to mail my column on the way to the corrals where I pushed those 107 calves through the chute. Thawing snow made the holding pens slippery and muddy as Doug and Ben branded and vaccinated. Save for a brief sleet storm, the weather held until we finished before noon; nice, because I was able to attend our monthly CattleWomen's meeting in Enterprise.

Returned home in the early darkness to gather eggs and begin supper of fried elk heart. Spent the evening on the phone organizing Thanksgiving dinner. Counting babies, we'll have 21. Pouring rain by bedtime. Stayed awake most of the night planning where I would put that many people and how much to cook. When sleep finally came I had a nightmare about everyone coming and no food was prepared.

November 17—Shuffled through the snow to chore. The rain had turned to snow during the night. Brief sunbursts send shafts of light through openings in a gun-metal sky, and frozen slush begins to slide off tin roofs. The mountains are hidden in autumn mists, and above in the cold November sky, I hear the honkers, lost in the fog.

November 18—"Fog frost" covers every inanimate object, and the phantom-like Wallowas appear and disappear in swirling mists. Fallen leaves become objects of beauty, encrusted in crystals.

Began the day with a hearty breakfast of oat bran muffins, sausage, eggs and fresh-squeezed grapefruit juice. Got a kick out of reading a May 1936 issue of The Country Home (originally established in 1877 as Farm and Fireside). A friend gave us this yellowed magazine, which contained articles with titles like "Flip-a-switch farming," "Grandma Spunk," "Hail to Cholesterol," and "Keeping up with the Country Woman."

1936 was a time when electricity was being extended to the rural areas. I would have been three years old, but don't remember electricity coming to our foothill ranch until much later. The ads were wonderful. You could purchase a dependable 1-1/2-ton stake Dodge truck (6 cyl) for $690, while others proclaimed: "Goodbye to gray hairs (test it free, by sending a single lock snipped from your hair); see results first. No risk, just mail coupon."

Or how about a Maytag multi-motor washing machine, with a simple, dependable, in-built gasoline engine designed for a woman to operate? In fact, states the ad, most farm women prefer these. How times have changed, yet the need for some things never changes, and on the last page, in the very last column, was the following poem written by Nellie R. Nesselroade of West Virginia:

Late fall visitors to Wallowa Lake State Park have a chance to hand feed the big bucks.

HOME
Nellie R. Nesselroade

Clean hearth, a glowing fire, a sparkling windowpane;
Blast of wind in the tree-tops, a dash of beating rain;
Fresh-baked loaf, a pitcher of milk, a bowl on the table wait;
Children's heads at the window sill;
Father comes through the gate.

And in far-flung rural America, scattered across the land, it was the farm family HOME that cemented this nation. Unfortunately that cement foundation is crumbling because the homes are crumbling. A return to HOME, as described in Nellie's simple poem, regardless of where one lived, would eliminate the need for building larger jails.

Thanksgiving has come and gone in our home, and I sincerely hope those around our bountiful table will always keep HOME alive in their hearts, and be thankful for family, friends and their faith in God.

December 3—Walking on a path of crusted snow to feed and water the chickens, pail of water in one hand, can of wheat in the other, I hear a rush of feathered wings. Looking up I see a large V of honkers flying low into the rising sun. As sunlight burst through pink-tinged clouds, one goose sounds a clarion call; immediately, the V shifts, changing course, winging in a wide circle against the snowy mountains. Long necks stretched, gracefully undulating wings catch the new sun's rays.

The sight made my morning, a prayer to Prairie Creek provided by the geese, and blessed by the December morning sun. It has been a busy week. A week of company, cooking, cleaning, and caring for my family. And now that Thanksgiving is over, it would seem we must immediately concentrate on Christmas. Christmas decorations go up earlier every year; to get us in the Christmas spirit? Really, we should be in the Christmas spirit all year, not just during the holidays.

I was counting up the people on my Christmas list last evening, and each year it seems to grow, what with the addition of children and extended family. Reading the December newsletter sent out by the Joseph schools, I came across the following paragraph, which I feel warrants a wider audience: *In years to come, kids will forget most of the toys you bought them. But they'll never forget the gifts you gave of yourself. As Jesse Jackson says, 'Children need your PRESENCE more than your PRESENTS.'*

My sentiments exactly. So this year, as in the past, I will dedicate more of my time to grandchildren. Besides, if you want to stay "forever young," surround yourself with young people; they have so much to offer and your presence is so important, if only as a good listener.

Most mornings the temperature hovers between 6 and 12, and climbs higher during the day, before plunging downward as the short daylight hours fade by 4 p.m. The ground is frozen and waterways no longer gurgle with song, but lay stilled in ice. Once again it is time to chop holes in frozen ponds and ditches, so cattle can drink. And from dawn until dark, seven days a week, the cattle must be fed.

After darkness settles in, there are long evenings to read by the fire. Winter is a restful time, a time for enjoying the warmth of home; it is also a time for baking, trying out new recipes, and enjoying the canned fruits of summer's labor that line the cupboard shelves. December means Christmas bazaars and holiday open houses.

This past weekend, the Hand Crafters Guild put on its annual holiday bazaar. Cloverleaf Hall was filled with homemade fudge, handmade quilts and rugs, dough art, wooden toys, hand-knitted sweaters, fragrant pine bough wreaths, fruit cakes, a lighted Christmas tree, Santa Claus and sticky candy canes. In years past, my 4-H Shutterbugs have taken photos of children sitting on Santa's lap, but this year our Wallowa Valley Photo Club took over the project.

Tom Swanson made the perfect Santa, with his own white beard and mustache. Molly Murrill and I began the picture taking sessions, enjoying the wide-eyed children who, so seriously, told Santa what they wished for Christmas. Members of the Imnaha Grange took over the kitchen and served roast beef dinners, soup'n sandwiches, and generous wedges of homemade pie.

The town of Enterprise, the Wallowa County seat, looks like the North Pole. Windows are decorated with "cotton ball snow" and fir forests, Santa's reindeer pulling a sleigh, and tiny Christmas bells that chime a tune in the frosty air. The gazebo on the courthouse lawn sports brightly lighted decorations, and a large decorated Christmas tree stands on west Main Street. Christmas carols float out over the town, which fairly glitters with lights. And the mountains, wrapped in winter snow, look down on it all as another season rolls around.

Joseph, too, is festive. Harshman's Store, a homey place to shop, is heated with a wood stove, and the fragrance of freshly-brewed gourmet coffee fills the place. The Harshmans have just about anything you'd want and then some. Doll houses, dolls, books, jewelry, teddy bears, as well as old-fashioned country store items too numerous to mention.

Next door, Donna Butterfield's Art Angle provides more gift-giving ideas, such as a variety of colorful posters that suit any taste. You can even have the posters framed there, or frame them yourself. On up the street Bud's Hardware caters to hunters, fishermen, housewives, and cowboys who often come in just to see Bud and Ruby's smiling faces.

Missy Marshall's wildflower shop is a sight to behold and lovely beyond description. Gorgeous dried flower wreaths adorn the walls and you can buy a sassafras broom. A large Christmas tree and a one-horse open sleigh occupies the front of the shop. A toy train runs around and around a snowy track in the window of the Eagle Mountain Gallery across the street, and inside, wares, such as Ted Juve pottery, paintings, bronzes, and umpteen different flavors of fudge, tempt the shopper.

The Snooks have just about anything in the line of western wear for the entire family in their Sports Corral, and between the other shops up and down the street there is no reason to shop out of the county. Goodness, I'm beginning to sound like the local Chamber of Commerce, but small towns need all the help they can get these days.

Winter, unfortunately, is also a time of sickness. I was reading the Stratford's Edition of a very old copy of *The Modern Home Cook Book* and *Family Physician* today, and came across this bit of advice. HOW PEOPLE GET SICK was the heading, and here are the contents:

Eating too much and too fast; swallowing imperfectly masticated food; using too much fluid at meals; drinking poisonous whiskey and other intoxicating drinks; repeatedly using poison as medicines; keeping late hours at night, and sleeping late in the morning; wearing clothing too tight; wearing thin shoes; neglecting to wash the body sufficiently to keep the pores open; exchanging the warm clothes worn in a warm room during the day for costumes and exposure incident to evening parties; compressing the stomach to gratify a vain and foolish passion for dress; keeping up constant excitement; fretting the mind with borrowed troubles; swallowing quack nostrums for every imaginary ill; taking meals at irregular intervals, and on and on...

Happy holidays, and for goodness sake, don't get sick!

December 4—Even though it seems a bit warmer this morning, the roads are glazed with black ice and the inevitable accidents have been reported due to the slick driving conditions. By noon, moisture dripped off roof tops and trees. The neck of an elk simmers in a kettle on the stove; it will be ground up and used for mincemeat. Cleaned six dozen eggs to deliver in town. Typed out "CattleWomen's Corner" for the Chieftain.

Ran errands in town, which included leaving a negative at Photo Express for Christmas cards. As usual, I wait until December to do this! Doug working on a stock-watering system that won't freeze, and we hope it will eliminate the need to chop ice all winter. My daughter's family had a guest recently from California during elk season. It so happened I had baked an apple pie for grandson Shawn's pie-a-month. Ernie was still there at the time and helped Shawn eat his pie (three large wedges).

Last week my daughter received a letter from Ernie pleading for "mom's" apple pie recipe, which he claimed was the best he'd ever eaten. So in response to that request I sent the following recipe, which I here share with all the young cooks who say "I can't bake pies." Of course you can, and here's how:

Prairie Creek Apple Pie

Be in a happy, baking mood; use fresh, tart cooking apples or make do with what you have at hand. While peeling apples, cultivate cheerful thoughts: think of the happiness your pie will bring to the recipient, and concentrate on peeling the entire apple without breaking the peel. Don't bother coring apples, simply cut slices off around the core into a large bowl. Add sugar to taste, depending on sweetness of apples. Sprinkle over with a bit of flour and some fresh, ground cinnamon. Let stand while you make the crust, thusly:

Place in bowl approximately 2 cups unbleached flour, though the amount depends on the size of pie plate or pan. Add a dash of salt, then some shortening, but don't ever use the same amount, just go by feel. Cut shortening in with two table knives, then use fingers to lightly mix.

When this feels right (not too short, nor too floury) sprinkle very cold water over the mixture with your hands, like we used to do sprinkling clothes during the bygone days of ironing. Now take a fork and toss the mixture lightly, until moistened just right; right being defined as feeling right.

After baking 3,000 pies, you will know RIGHT. Shape the dough lightly (never knead or work the dough) into a round ball, flattening the edges as you press it onto a lightly floured board. With the floured rolling pin or mason jar, lightly roll out into a round to accommodate the pie plate.

Fold in half and place in plate, then unfold and press into the bottom. Now heap the apples which have been "juicing" in the bowl. They should be soaked in a nice cinnamony juice. Roll out the top crust, the same as bottom. Dot apples with butter (absolutely no substitute), place the top crust over, and moisten the rim of the bottom crust with cream.

Pinch edges together, flute or press with fork, trim, and make cinnamon rounds for the children with left-over dough.

Brush top crust with cream, mark with "A" for apple, your brand, or whatever strikes your creative fancy. Bake 425 for 15 min, then (depending on your oven) 400 for a half-hour, and finish out the hour at 350. Cool on a pie rack and enjoy warm with ice cream.

The secret ingredient, of course, for creating tasty pies, growing lovely flowers, raising happy children or bringing peace to those around you, is LOVE. Everybody and everything responds in a positive way to LOVE. When I was but a young housewife, a kindly, elderly lady by the name of "Mom" Ayers offered this bit of advice when I asked for her bread recipe:

"The bread will turn out OK if you follow the recipe," she said, "but if you put love into it, the loaf will turn out so much better." Whenever I bake bread I think of "Mom." Even though she has been gone for years, her words will never be forgotten.

Blustery winds send snow squalls sweeping over the mountains as dark clouds race over the valley. Listening to the wind whistling and blowing decaying leaves about the yard, I browned chunks of elk in the cast iron dutch oven, added carrots, onion, cabbage, canned tomatoes and soon supper was simmering on the wood cookstove.

December 5—Just a touch of frost this morning. I was just finishing the chores when a brilliant, warm sun broke through gilded clouds to burnish Prairie Creek in copper light.

Leafed through an old, tattered recipe book to find my mince meat recipe: 5 bowls of apples, 3 bowls of meat; the ingredients measured in bowls. The spicy, vinegary, apple smell permeated my kitchen all day.

December 6—No snow left on the ground now and the white line has retreated to upper Prairie Creek. Heavy frost glitters over the landscape as I drive to care for grandchildren while their mom goes shopping.

December 7—Clouds edged in pink lace at sunrise as we begin another day of feeding cattle, a never-ending job. Ben starts up the big tractor and pulls the loaded hay wagon up on the hill where the cows wait for their breakfast. Later in the day they will be fed silage, which is augured out onto the frozen ground.

Began some serious housecleaning as the CattleWomen's Christmas party/meeting will be held here next week. Doug finished cutting up the last quarter of his elk tonight.

December 8—After chores, I loaded up card tables and delivered them to various local banks for our CattleWomen selling beef gift certificates. This yearly Christmas promotion takes lots of volunteer help and, thanks to the gals who gave of their time during this busy season, we had a successful day.

My shift was at First Interstate, where I found everyone congenial and helpful. Attended a book signing at the Bookloft where Jerry Gildermeister, of Bear Wallow Publishing Company, appeared with their recent book entitled *Around the Cat's Back*.

The book, beautifully done, with illustrations by Don Gray and Gildermeister's photography, centers around the childhood experiences of Daisy and Caroline Wasson, who came west with their parents in 1885 to homestead on what we call the Divide. This area, not too far from our ranch, hasn't changed much since those early years. It is still a lonely, beautiful land situated between Big Sheep and Little Sheep creeks. A long grassy. ridge named the "Cat's Back" stretches across the high Divide, and it is here where the story unfolds.

Hank Bird's long, loose stacks of hay add a nostalgic charm to the fertile pastures east of Joseph. Several ranchers in the valley put up hay this way. It's fed in the winter on the snow with a farmhand and tractor.

Told through the eyes of a little girl whose diary was used in the book, one glimpses a life both beautiful and harsh, happy and tragic, and not unlike life today where winters are still long and cold, and spring comes late. It is fortunate that this small girl's diary was kept and preserved, and even more fortunate that my friend, historian Grace Bartlett, brought the diary to the attention of a publisher who has preserved this valuable history in book form.

December 9—The long December dawn seems to take all morning; by the time the sun finally comes over the hills, chores are done and it feels more like noon. Just enough of a light skift of snow fell during the night to turn our lane white.

Dragged the Christmas decorations out of the closet and began to scatter a bit of Christmas gaiety around the house.

Short daylight ends and Prairie Creek sleeps silent—wrapped in the cold of a long moon-washed December night. We head now toward the winter solstice, after which the days will begin to lengthen.

December 10—A weak winter sun penetrates cold, grey clouds as the cattle patiently wait for their hay and silage. The temperature hovers around 20 degrees as my faithful dog and several cats follow along while I complete my round of morning chores. A bitter wind begins to blow tapioca-like sleet, which soon turns to dry flakes of snow.

We drive in and out of snow flurries on the way to Enterprise to purchase Christmas trees from the FFA chapter. After delivering a Christmas tree to the Alder Slope grandchildren, we were treated to a home-cooked chicken dinner. It was fascinating watching the mini-snowstorms sweep down off the mountain, from within the warm house. Cotton balls, shot with sunlight, dancing in the wind. The snow held no moisture, and what there was seemed to evaporate in the wind and dry cold.

December 11—Six degrees at 6 a.m. and the dawn light reveals a clear sky. Oatmeal bubbles on the wood cook stove to warm us before we venturing out to feed the livestock. My frosted cows are glad to see me, as are the three "pee wee" calves that eagerly slick up their barley. Afterwards I help Doug and Ben drive the feedlot calves into the corral; they will be shipped to a Hermiston feed lot this morning.

A nasty flu bug with its resulting infections is reaching epidemic proportions in the county. Why does sickness always have to appear during the holidays, just when everyone has so much to do? Our family is having its share of whatever is going around and this grandma does the usual worrying, which does no good at all.

Somehow got my column typed as the short afternoon disappeared and moon appeared, glowing high above a lavender horizon. The snowy mountains were already reflecting cold moon glow when I gathered the eggs before they should freeze. The wood cook stove has "eaten" an unbelievable amount of wood today; such an appetite that Monarch has! Cooked a pot of seafood chowder for supper, which hit the spot on this cold night.

December 12—The "bug" has made the rounds and now it is my turn. Sleeping in until 6:45, I awake to the sounds of Doug in the kitchen, stirring up sourdough hotcakes. A scatter of pale pink clouds float like silk scarves in the dawn sky as I gaze out at the new day. A jet draws a straight line through the soft filmy shapes. The jet appears as an interloper, its contrail's color out of place in the morning sky, and the straight line spoils the soft, natural lines of the clouds.

The lemon-colored moon lingers over Ruby Peak until after 7, glowing and pulsing above the snowy mountains in the violet sky. It is 7 degrees, which is probably among the coldest temps in the state this morning. Began to write Christmas card letters, trying to take it easy, but somehow there is always work to be done.

Finished the day by decorating our Christmas tree. Outside tonight the full December moon turns Prairie Creek back into day.

December 13—Concentrated on making our house look Christmasy for the CattleWomen's meeting/party here tomorrow. Between this obligation and cooking for more than 150 people Saturday night at the Civic Center, my mind reels with details. I simply don't have time to be sick!

Stratas of dark clouds veil the moon's face this evening. It warmed up to 40 degrees by afternoon and the ground even began to thaw.

December 14—Another beautiful day; clear, sunny, and almost warm. With the help of two daughters, a granddaughter, and neighbor Ardis Klages, I made it through the day. Our Christmas meeting/party was great fun.

Everyone brought a plate of holiday goodies and a gift for the gift exchange. The gifts were placed in the middle of the floor and everyone given a number. Number 1 chose her gift first and opened it, then number 2 could either choose a gift from the pile or number one's gift. And so it went. I had baked a loaf of sourdough bread as a gift, and it was passed around to most everyone there until it was claimed by the final recipient.

Rose Glaus' hand-crocheted Christmas tree made the rounds too. We had a merry time and seemed to benefit from the spirit of the season. After chores that evening, Doug and I attended the Wallowa Valley Photo Club's monthly meeting, where we were privileged to view a a slide presentation given by the Rotary German exchange student, Jens Meiners. His slides were marvelous, but the real treat for us was visiting with Jens later. This 16-year-old educated us on his country and his people more than any newspaper or T.V. ever could; it was real.

December 15—Still attempting to ignore a nasty sinus infection, I concentrated on tomorrow night's turkey dinner for all those people. By nightfall I had the beginnings of the desserts under control, and lists lying all over the place to remind me what to do.

Instead of spending the evening gathering up what was on those lists, I curled up on the living room sofa with two visiting grandchildren and watched "Rudolph the Red-nosed Reindeer."

December 16—Another incredible day, weather-wise and other-wise. By 8:30, thanks to Doug, the van was loaded with food and utensils and I was on by way to Joseph, where I would spend the day cooking. My . ever-faithful friend, Scotty, was with me.

Various members of my family appeared and disappeared all through the day and by 6 p.m. we were ready with roast turkey, ham, dressing, gravy, rolls, salads and desserts for more than 150 people.

After 8:30, leaving a clean kitchen behind us, two granddaughters and I took a tour of the beautifully lighted homes in Joseph before driving home. It had, indeed, been a long day.

December 17—A light skiff of snow lays on the ground, while left-over clouds linger in an otherwise blue sky. After putting away the effects of last night's cooking and tending to my chickens, I returned to the Christmas card list. Then a friend called to invite us to an impromptu brunch. So, after Doug finished the morning feeding, we joined our friends and partook of a most elegant feast.

Pat, who claimed she had "just thrown the meal together," served a sausage-egg casserole, freshly baked Christmas breads, hot fruit compote, orange juice and coffee. What a treat, especially after our day of waiting on people yesterday.

That evening Doug and I attended the Wallowa County Christmas Cantata, held at the Baptist church on the hill above Enterprise. We were met in the lobby by grandchildren who had saved us a seat. Good thing, as the church was overflowing with people.

We relaxed and listened to the beautiful Christmas story unfold along with the familiar carols sung by local people. The program ended with "Silent Night" and a candlelight ceremony. It was all so peaceful and made us aware once more, of the true meaning of Christmas.

December 18—After sunup, which occurs shortly before 8 o'clock, a few wispy clouds give way to bright, golden sunshine. Because we haven't had any snow or moisture of any kind for days, the air is ex-tremely dry. Mailed some last minute Christmas packages and cards. The flu bug continues to plague various members of our family as well as several of our friends.

December 19—After breakfasting on Doug's sourdough pancakes, I felt somewhat better. A nasty sinus infection has taken its toll on my stamina. Ordered a 15-pound prime rib roast for Christmas dinner. Hopefully, that delicious cut of beef will satisfy 20 healthy appetites!

Somehow I managed to get four pages of words typed for my column, before sitting down after supper to make sense out of it. Clear, cold and windy tonight.

December 20—Another clear, cold morning. By afternoon it was so mild it felt more like December in California than in Northeastern Oregon. A knock on the door brought us a lovely poinsettia delivered by the local flower shop; a gift from Doug's sister Betty, who lives in

Clarkston, Washington. The bright red plant brightened up the day considerably.

Cows on the hill begin bawling when they hear the silage truck's motor start up. Such violence on the national scene these days! Here in our far-away valley, the news is hard to visualize. Perhaps because we are so wrapped up in our own lives, and those of our families, we are too busy to comprehend such life on the "outside," but when we read a newspaper or turn on the TV, we know that the "other world" exists.

At a time when all the world should seek peace on earth and good-will toward men, it always seems like such a shame, especially during Christmas.

December 21—Winter has officially arrived. The winter solstice, which our dictionary defines as "the time of year when the sun is at its greatest distance from the celestial equator, and seems to pause before returning on its course." Here on Prairie Creek it is so mild, it feels more like the first day of autumn, with crisp mornings and warm afternoons.

But the colorless landscape makes a winter statement. Normally covered with blue-white snow that transforms piles of junk into objects of beauty, our ranch seems strange and bare. There is an air of expectancy as the land waits for a seasonal change that does not come.

The livestock don't complain; no mud, no snow, but warm sunshine for taking afternoon naps, and plenty of feed. Our young Simmental bulls cavort around their pen as though it were spring. Alongside the house, yellow primroses bloom. My pullets sing and lay huge, brown eggs. Chester the banty rooster flies to the top of chicken wire pen, crows loudly, then flies down to hunt and peck under the apple tree... until my dog discovers he is out and sends him scurrying back to the safety of the pen.

One of my older grandsons helped grandma run errands today. We drove high above Alder Slope, under the snowy mountains, to Harold McLaughlin's place, where I purchased some bread boards for Christmas presents. I always enjoy visiting Harold, listening to him talk about wood. This gentle man, who so loves working with interesting grains and pretty patterns in wood, turns rough boards into works of art that would make the trees proud. Each piece he creates reflects this craftsman's love of wood. Upon leaving Harold presented me with a wooden Kleenex box, which came in handy at the moment.

In the farm house, Hope, Harold's wife, spends countless hours piecing together homemade quilts that are much in demand. It is good to see people working with their hands and hearts, keeping alive traditions

This is the Monarch range that reigns in the Tippett kitchen.

and trades, in an age when nearly everything is made on an assembly line or belongs to the "plastic generation." The love, pride and durability are lost in mass production. Price tags can't really be put on Harold and Hope's labor; it is priceless.

This evening we drove to Imnaha to attend the annual school Christmas program. The small school room was cramped as tightly as a sardine can, with standing room only. The program is always looked forward to by the relatives, the community and the children. As long as school marm Char Williams can hold out, I suppose it will continue to be a tradition on Imnaha.

The children themselves reflect values taught in a one-room school, where students go out into the world armed with more than an education. They learn about life early and the canyon country is imprinted forever on their character. Living on Imnaha isn't easy. Many families barely eke out an existence, but the canyon children are one of the area's assets and the locals are very proud of them. When young Luke stands alone on stage and plays a Christmas carol on his harmonica, everyone there is touched, or when Sarah's fingers search out a tune on the piano, and Fox and Breeze recite poetry they have written themselves, everyone there is proud.

Coughs punctuated memorized lines during the play, as the flu flew to Imnaha as well. A precious toy fairy (my granddaughter), looking pale and sick, delivered her practiced part and my heart went out to her and several others, who I know weren't feeling well. The children were so determined to make the play a success in spite of all odds. But during the ending, where the children sang together on stage, several were missing. I found my little one sprinkled with fairy dust, not sparkling, but lying on a pillow in the back room. She and the other ailing children were taken home just as the roof fairly shook with thundering hooves! Santa had arrived on Imnaha.

Lately there is much ado about the changes occurring along the Imnaha. It seems to me one of the most scenic attractions on the river is its special breed of inhabitants, who choose to live there year-around, where living is far from easy, and who have, for generations, created that special touch which is the Imnaha. Their beautiful gardens, orchards, hay fields, pastures and cattle ranches are as much a part of the scenic quality of the area as the wild side.

They have made a life here, and perhaps many of their children would hope to, also. The Imnaha needs these people as much as the people need the river. They feed each other. And their bountiful gardens and beef cattle feed many more "on top." Because of families like the

Warnocks, the Markses, the Johnsons and other pioneer names up and down the river, the Imnaha is what it is today. The history of the early settlers provides hope for the future. Imnaha's children are living proof that this future is worth saving.

If the Imnaha had never been settled, it would, indeed, be a place to preserve as "wild and scenic," but that is not the case here. This special "place in the heart," for those who live there and those who visit, exudes a charm all its own, one created by the inhabitants. Remove them and the charm is gone. Even the pioneer cemetery that overlooks the tiny settlement, is about as wild and scenic as anything could get. May those resting there convey a lesson in courage to the present generation.

December 22—Both grandma and Imnaha's small fairy had to call upon the doctor today. Hopefully we will be on the mend by Christmas day. Day after day of sunshine, with no moisture in sight.

December 23—Met several people in Joseph doing last minute Christmas shopping. At least when we wait until the last hour, we do it! Fell asleep planning Christmas dinner for 20.

December 24—Spent the day baking Christmas yeast breads and traditional stollens. As Doug and I delivered the baked goods to various homes scattered around the valley, a brilliant star shone in the west. Surely it was the Christmas star!

December 25—No white Christmas this year, the only white in the form of frost. Sunlight streamed in the windows and warmed our Christmas feast. Our hearts were warmed as well by the presence of so many family members. Christmases come and go, but this one seemed special somehow. Perhaps as we grow older, we learn to appreciate each day for what it is.

December 26—The dry, frozen ground is covered with frost on this six-degree morning. Doug has gone to the hills to check on the cows and chop ice in the ponds so they can drink. Wrote several thank you's, thereby bringing to an end any further commitments to Christmas.

December 27—A soft, white band of fog curled around the base of the mountains then disappeared by late morning. The snow, on the south face of the mountain, visible from my kitchen window, has evaporated to the point where "Tucker's Mare," the snowy shape of a horse, is appearing. This "spring" phenomenon shouldn't be taking place now!

Helped drive some of our heifers home from a rented pasture along the Imnaha highway this morning. My job was to follow in the car with the blinkers on and warn the logging trucks. For some unexplainable reason I have been unable to shake my illness, which seems to hang on indefinitely.

December 28—A fine sifting of snow builds up on the yard fence, slowly transforming colorless shapes into clean, white lines. It is 12 degrees, and the snow falls into the afternoon. December 29 One day fades into another, and I am still sick, unusual for me.

December 30—Gray clouds melt into blue sky by mid-morning; warm sunshine, dripping and melting. Is this December?

Around 3 p.m. I hear whistling and look out on the road to see a herd of cattle being driven by my son Ken and grandsons, who are bringing their cows home. Once more the snow on the hills quietly disappears. As the sun goes down out of sight, the cold brings the young cowboys in to warm by the fire and drink steaming cups of hot cocoa and marshmallows.

Awoke in the night to find I was suffering a severe allergic reaction to the medicine I'd been taking for a sinus infection. You'd a thought I had the measles!

December 31—As the final hours of 1989 slip away I am unaware of much else, other than wanting to feel well again.

Happy Holidays—and the best to you and yours in 1990!

Jake, Josh, and hidden behind, Mona Lee, swing out across Little Sheep Creek in the canyons of the Imnaha.

1990

January 1—Another year has ended, a new decade has begun; good-bye to the '80s and hello '90s. Watched the Rose Bowl parade on TV. All those healthy people cavorting about in 75-degree weather in Pasadena!

Life, formerly in my control, has suddenly gone out of control. I am covered with a red mass of itching rash. My world has shrunk to the sofa, from which I barely lift my head. Thank goodness for my husband, who, in addition to his responsibilities, is also performing mine. My one accomplishment today was to take down the Christmas tree.

January 2—Looked outside this morning to a white-out. Snow flakes beating against the window panes as daylight seeped into Prairie Creek. I could see soft, feathery drifts, sculpted by the wind, taking shape around the yard.

It is time to bring the cows home from the hills. Doug and Ben disappear into the white void. Jim, back after an arm injury, is able to do the feeding here. Due to the storm, the cows will follow the pickup load of hay and it won't be necessary to drive them on horseback. By afternoon the cows were corraled and fed hay in the holding pasture at East Crow, where they would bed for the night.

January 3—It is 6 below zero and a freezing wind blows. Quickly it warms to 17 and somewhere, out on the Crow Creek road, Ben is on his way home with the cows, who shouldn't need much persuasion to to return to the valley for the remainder of the winter.

More snow on the way. My appetite, absent for days, has returned. Hungry for something besides soup, I fix a meal of elk steak, milk gravy and potatoes for supper.

January 4—We have been for some time planning to head south on our annual trek to California today, but now remain uncertain as to our departure. High winds, periods of blue sky and sunshine. My pullets continue to lay an incredible amount of eggs!

January 5—Doug and I make the decision to leave. Still plagued with a rash and a return of the sinus infection, I pack. In less than an hour we are gone. Driving as far as Lostine, we stop for a good breakfast at the Lostine Tavern. We are cheered by a visit with Bill Wolfe, who is looking much improved.

The morning is clear-cold and bright sunshine follows us to La Grande. As we head through Ladd Canyon, a white banner of snow blows across the pavement and the wind chill plummets to minus 6. I try not to think of being stranded and sick out in this somewhere.

A foggy winter gloom stays with us until we wind our way up into the lovely Owyhees, where the sun suddenly comes bursting forth and the Oregon high desert stretches before us. My spirits soar and I feel better for the first time in days. Definitely not what the doctor ordered, but working better than what was prescribed.

We spent the night in Winnemucca, Nevada.

January 6—It was a gray, cold morning when we left Winnemucca behind and hit the long, straight desert highway that stretches south through sagebrush and alkali, bordering shimmering Humboldt sink.

Speeding along in our modern car, I try to envision plodding oxen and emigrants making their painful way across this inhospitable land. Then I look again upon the desert and see beauty; muted tawny earth colors, sulfur yellow, alkali white and snow white, gleaming on soft distant hills. Sage green mixes in a desert pallet where sunlight spears clouds and filters onto snow-frosted mountains. Deep purple, distant blues, and rusted reds. Cattle, horses, and abandoned cars, all eventually claimed by the vastness and absorbed by the desert.

After a stop in Lovelock, we take a cutoff to Fallon through miles of sickly yellow, sun-baked flats. Fallon, once a cattle community, is now being edged out by the ever-changing scene of modern development; resembling, in a way, the outskirts of Reno.

While eating lunch in the Nugget's Prospector room, we can't help eavesdropping on two elderly ranch women in the next booth, who talk about the changing face of Fallon. How they must lock their doors now, about high speed wrecks and drinking drivers, and newcomers; how they don't know anyone in the store anymore. The story is the same all over rural America, and is bewildering to the natives who worked so hard to settle an area and create a peaceful community.

We make it to Reno, where the surrounding blue skies disappear and are replaced by a layer of smog that envelopes the city. The "Biggest Little City in the World" is now simply a city, with city problems. We watch a huge jet full of fun-seekers land at the airport.

While Doug gasses up our van I watch fascinated as a family erupts from a small station wagon. One by one, three large boys, one small girl and one small boy climb out the back. Then I watch in disbelief as a huge black dog crawls out. Inside I can see a small mother busy rearranging suitcases, blankets and clothes, so everyone can get back in.

The children run into a nearby convenience store for snacks. The tall, well-fed husband stretches before he and his family pile back into their mini-station wagon. The dog and the children appear happy. They are family, albeit a little squashed, but still a family, traveling somewhere for the weekend. My faith in humankind is lifted.

Not wishing to battle a Reno Saturday night, we opt to head over the mountainous Sierra to our Auburn destination. The summit over Donner Pass is free of ice and snow, and we glimpse long lift lines at Boreal Ridge, where there is sufficient snow for skiing. It is a beautiful drive in a warm afternoon and the miles flash by as we descend the western side of the Sierra Nevada (the range of light) and cross over the Placer County line and near the land of my youth.

As daylight hours fade away, hazy clouds roll up from the Sacramento Valley. There is a feeling of rain in the air as we enter the sprawling, foothill city of Auburn.

January 7—Auburn, California—It is 62 degrees. A warm soaking rain began to fall on the dry foothills last evening. A soft, gentle rain creates a dampness very unlike our dry, high altitude cold, and although the temperatures are mild, we find ourselves chilled.

It is good to see my relatives again. My mother's apartment is within walking distance, so we go there for lunch and, because of the rainy weather, pass the afternoon playing endless games of Scrabble and Trivial Pursuit. This year's persimmon crop was good, apparently, and everyone we visit offers us a treat baked from this delicious fruit. We've had cookies, cake, bread or simply eaten them plain. Sometimes called "The fruit of the gods," this bright orange fruit can be used to create a moist, flavorful product that improves with age.

My mother, nearing her 80th birthday, gave us a private showing of the results of her latest watercolor painting class. She and my stepfather, Bill, appear to be in the midst of a second childhood; we found them into aerobics, low fat diets and looking fit as we'd ever seen them! My health steadily improved, and I began taking walks around the Sky View Ridge neighborhood.

Mom and Bill treated us to lunch at a place called "The Headquarters

House," an enormous building constructed with massive wooden beams, with fireplaces and separate intimate dining rooms that look out on Auburn. Through huge glass windows we looked out on hills covered with digger pine and granite oaks. These hills are gradually being covered with houses; not your ordinary home, however, but mostly the $200,000 and up variety, which spring up like mushrooms after the rain.

In secret ravines, where once stood tent cities during the gold rush era, or hastily constructed wooden structures later destroyed by fires, now stand substantial homes, with fireproof roofs, built according to many codes and accompanied by $12,000 building permits! Between the starthistle and mistletoe-laden oaks, alongside digger pine, red-barked manzanita and Toyon berry, appears the cement sidewalk.

The natural environment looks confused and frightened in an un-natural world. A world of overnight landscaping, perfectly groomed; blooming rose gardens and transplanted exotic plants not native to Placer County. Asphalt has replaced blooming baby blue eyes and the golden California poppy; purple lupine used to cover the hills in springtime, nodding their heads alongside Johnny-Jump-ups, scrambled eggs and blue bells.

Dormant seeds will not sprout and bloom in March and April this spring, having been scraped away by giant bulldozer blades, laying bare granite, leaf mold, grass and top soil; cement poured over all. Sterile. Leaf mold, dry grass, trees, brush, which stored precious moisture, replaced by water-proof surfaces that shed water…water that now must run off into man-made drains, controlled, not drunk by the earth.

January 8—Beautiful morning with blue "petticoats" appearing between rain clouds. Slept till 7. Such luxury.

While getting my hair cut at a little shop down the street, I was most entertained by the hairdresser as she snipped off my locks. She said she lived in Forest Hill, a mountain community above Auburn. Her husband worked weekdays in San Francisco and returned to Forest Hill on weekends.

After hearing her second-hand account of the earthquake, I listened to her "bear experience." It seems, partly because of drought years, the bear's food supply has been somewhat limited; so the bears quickly found out they could move in with the human population and find life easier than they'd ever known.

Although she never glimpsed Bruin but once, on a moonlight night, she waged an ongoing war with this elusive beast. She would nail the chicken house door shut, only to have it torn open the next morning and be shy one more hen. This went on until her chicken population dwindled to three nervous survivors. Then, when her prized Nubian nanny milk goat was carried off into the woods one night, bleating frantically, that did it! The government trapper was summoned and the bear dispatched.

I was surprised to be given a senior citizen's discount at the hairdresser's. Even with the discount, the same haircut in Wallowa County would have cost $3 less, but I doubt if they could have matched the story-telling.

As Los Angeles and the huge Bay area population relocate themselves in these once lovely foothills, they bring with them their population problems. Where will it end? What will happen to minds unable to see God's creations as they were meant to be? Hopefully, areas will remain where a child in the year 2000 can look upon a blue bell, hear water running, smell damp leaf mold, feel grass growing, and experience SPRING in the foothills.

Everyone needs this bonding to earth, and the ones who need it the most aren't aware of that need. There is order in nature, chaos in civilization and to maintain any semblance of order in civilization, we must understand order in nature. Nature teaches us to simplify, be patient, be reverent and learn from past mistakes, and most importantly, work with her, not against her.

As I looked out over the countryside, I thought of these things. The food was wonderful and featured certified Angus beef, which interested us, being beef raisers.

Here we are, I thought, in this "pleasant rut," created by a system of beliefs in which the present generation is trapped. Something is wrong. Perhaps it is because our very planet is not happy. Food for thought. I guess vacations are good, in that in traveling around the country you gain new perspectives on life in general, and have more time to think.

After lunch, Mom and Bill showed us around some of the new housing developments. Like Falcon Crest, where once indeed hawks swept down to light on rocky crag and digger pine. Today, however, they fly over tiny bits of land left in the canyon and the names of their species are given to streets: Peregrine, Eagles Nest, Condor, Buzzard's Roost.

The very charm that must have attracted these people to build here in the first place has been replaced by mansion-style homes unique in design, alike in luxury. And they all use water, precious water that even now runs off into drains instead of soaking into the hills beneath. As far as the eye can see advances this crush of humanity marching ever closer, consuming the Mother Lode. In Placer County, the livestock person is among the endangered species.

Recent headlines in a local paper portray the dilemma of a fourth generation cattleman, standing helplessly by as his habitat and that of his cattle diminishes.

January 9—We eat breakfast as pockets of morning mist form in the American River canyon just below my sister's deck. Doug off to pan for gold; me to write my column, pounding out the words on the trusty portable typewriter I brought along for this purpose. As I type, I can look off toward the El Dorado hills and temporarily forget about the advancement of homes happening just one block from here.

From time to time, I take breaks from the typewriter to walk out on the deck and gaze down toward the river. Surprised to see two liquid eyes staring up at me, I see a black tail doe and her yearling fawn, browsing among the live oaks and digger pine. When the outside temperature reaches 70 degrees, I sit outside in the sunshine to correct my column.

Wallowa County seems far away indeed, out of mind, but still very much in my heart.

January 11—Through sliding glass doors a dark evergreen etches itself against a persimmon sunrise as we visit with Mary Ann before she leaves for work. These days of relaxation and being far-removed from former obligations are having a positive effect on my health, which is steadily improving.

Doug is gone for the day attending a livestock sale in Fallon, so I walk down the hill to my mother's for lunch. Afterward I walk with my stepfather to a nearby park, then meet mom and walk back to Riverview. The walking is bringing back my strength.

Many varieties of flowers bloom here in Auburn, due, we suppose, to the unseasonable warmth. It is 70 degrees this afternoon, and among the flowers we saw were California poppies, snapdragons, roses, alyssum, painted daisies and pansies blooming along our route. And everywhere, bright orange berries of the pyracantha, upon which bushes hundreds of robins and cedar waxwings were becoming drunk.

January 12—Steady, warm rains, which began last evening, are causing some flooding in Sacramento. Calling home we learn the weather is so mild in Wallowa County that the frost has gone out of the ground, and Ben and Jim must now contend with mud while feeding the cattle!

Feeling domestic, I decide to tackle the remainder of my sister's fall apple crop, which is on the verge of rotting away. After stewing up a large kettle of applesauce, I baked several with walnuts, cinnamon and honey. I had invited mom and Bill for lunch, after which we passed the rainy day by playing more Scrabble and Trivial Pursuit.

The pouring rain persisted as we all drove out Highway 49 for dinner at the Great Wall, where we enjoyed delicious Oriental cuisine. In the deluge, we stopped on the way home to grocery shop at a brand new Belle Aire market. What a place!

Newly planted primroses, loving the rain, bloomed in colorful profusion in long brick planters that graced the entrance. Search lights shone through the rain-drenched blackness, attracting people by the score to the grand opening. The immense vegetable/fruit section was extremely colorful and contained every conceivable variety imaginable, in and out of season.

There was a post office within the store, as well as a complete bakery, catering service, and cooked ethnic foods you could take out or eat there. And the fish counter...every kind of shell fish and fresh fish imaginable. Judging from the prices, Californians spend a lot of their dollars on food; that is, if they have anything left from house payments!

As we sloshed out to the car with the modest makin's for tomorrow's soup, rain gutters ran like rivers everywhere. As it continued to rain on into the night, we would later learn that Grass Valley, to the northeast, would receive eight inches in eight days! Just what the country needs.

January 13—More rain. Cozy and warm inside; a perfect day to cook up a kettle of soup for my three sisters, who would be here for lunch. However, sister Caroline couldn't make it; she was down with the flu. We would only be three.

Visiting, catching up on our lives, dipping crusty chunks of french bread into our tasty soup, we enjoyed each other's company. The skies cleared up enough in the afternoon for us to take a long walk around the neighborhood. Ironically, the streets seemed to be named for us: Mary Jane and Caroline, which connected to Poet Smith! All we needed was Kathryn.

We returned to a warm oak fire in the fireplace and sipped peppermint tea and listened to soft music on the stereo. The years rolled back and we were kids again. Except there was no stereo then or nice house. We were raised without material things but had it all, the "all" being 240 acres of creeks, meadows, hills, woods land hayfields. As our family grew, so did the herd of registered Guernseys that provided the income for us to live.

In those early years the foothills were sparsely settled, and virtually everyone who lived among the folds of those hills made their living from the land. Small dairies and fruit orchards mostly. Today grand homes dominate the hills; everyone wants a view. And the livestock consists of "pets" that range from goats to horses, who mostly live miserable lives attempting to graze amid starthistle-choked lots.

Doug returned from the rain-dampened Roseville auction with lemons, tangerines and fresh pineapple. And so the pleasant, unhurried days passed, the rain eventually ceasing and sunlight streaming through the American River canyon's mists and blue skies prevailed, bringing a familiar, cold January crispness. We were treated royally, and invited to visit and dine with many friends and relatives. We, in turn, invited all to visit our valley so we could return the hospitality.

January 16—The rain returned along with windy gusts that caused digger pines to swish their limbs in furious sweeps. And in the nearby Sierra, the skiers were ecstatic. The snow line eventually lowered to Applegate, just above Auburn. In between typing on my column, I decide to bake a lemon pie, using those wonderful fresh lemons. Perusing Mary Ann's cookbooks, I came across this interesting recipe for "Old Fashion Lemon Pie":

Ingredients: 1 cup water [should be sugar, see page 290], 1 1/2 cup flour, 2 cups water, 1/2 cup fresh lemon juice, and 3 egg yolks, slightly beaten. The meringue called for 3 stiff egg whites, 1/2 teaspoon salt, 1/2 tablespoon lemon juice, and 6 tablespoons sugar.

There were no further ingredient directions, as it was assumed one knew how to make meringue. Mix sugar and flour in sauce pan. Add water and lemon juice. Cook until slightly thick. Add egg yolks, cook until thick. Cool. Pour into baked pie shell. Cover with meringue, bake until delicate brown, serve cool.

You will notice, in this "old fashion" recipe, it is taken for granted that the cook understands basic cooking; otherwise, one would have a disaster when adding the egg yolks, which should be mixed with a little of the cooked mixture before being stirred, slowly, into the custard!

The absence of cornstarch and the fact that you cook the lemon juice with the water/flour mixture, instead of adding it later, is interesting, but the result is delicious: a tart, delicate, lemony flavor persists that is less sweet than most recipes, and the texture of the filling is firm. Feeling creative, I decorated the meringue with thin slices of fresh orange.

Doug, meanwhile, had spent the day browsing around an enormous antique emporium (now housed in Roseville's former J.C. Penney store). He returned with all manner of tools and interesting items. That evening we invited Paul, a neighbor across the street and an avid reader of Agri-

Times, over for lemon pie. It is always interesting to visit people everywhere who read this newspaper.

January 19—After the usual sad farewells, we packed up and headed north, following Highway 65 to Northern California towns like Chico, Red Bluff and Redding. Brilliant, rain-washed blue skies greeted us that morning. Little roadside stands, like the red barn, tempted us to purchase bags of fresh oranges, walnuts, pecans and dried fruit bars. We munched our way north, eating a variety of fruits and nuts for which California is famous.

Mt. Shasta, covered with fresh snow, gleamed in sunlight as we ate a bowl of clam chowder and looked out of glass windows in a small restaurant in Dunsmuir. The 14,000-foot volcanic mountain soared skyward for miles as we continued north on the great I-5 corridor and crossed over the Siskyous to OREGON!

It was nearing 6 p.m. when we pulled into the Matthews' yard, off Garden Valley Highway in Roseburg, to spend the night.

January 20—Very foggy and 32 degrees. A heavy frost covers Carolee's geraniums and we can barely see several mules standing under misty oaks. The dog barked all night and this morning we find out why. He had a coon treed up the hill!

We treated our friends to breakfast at a restaurant along the foggy Umpqua River. That afternoon, heading west to Reedsport, we stopped to see a herd of Roosevelt elk grazing near the road. We spent the night in Florence, a small coastal town near the sand dunes.

The sun was just sinking into the restless Pacific when we walked out for a first glimpse of the Oregon coast. That evening we enjoyed a memorable meal at the Windward Inn...live piano music, a fire crackling in a stone fireplace and seafood. It was good to be back in Oregon and we would be home in less than a week.

January 21—After eating breakfast this morning, just ahead of a busload of high school wrestlers, we left Florence and headed up 101 north along the Oregon coast. We drove in and out of foggy little seaside places with names like Cape Perpetua, Devil's Elbow, and Heceta Head. Brief sunlight greeted us as we neared the ocean side village of Yachats. I wanted to photograph the picturesque houses perched on the hill above the small settlement, but Yachats was muted in fog. Perhaps the mists would have enhanced the picture; at any rate, some day I would like to return to Yachats with my camera.

Farther north, Doug turned up a steep gravel road that commanded a wide view of the ocean and ended up at Yaquina Head lighthouse. From here we could watch the long, blue-green waves splash off wet rocks that formed a cliff below. Spewing salty froth and roaring with mighty energy, the breakers finally spent themselves and trickled back to sea.

Their shiny, dark bodies glistening with wet, several seals swam in foamy waters and slithered up onto rocks to watch us. The lonely cry of sea gulls, salt spray, ocean breeze, blooming yellow broom, sandy beaches littered with kelp and driftwood, the lighthouse's beacon sending messages to ships far out on the undulating horizon; all these describe the spectacular Oregon coast, but mere words fail.

Farther up 101 we stop the car to walk a lonely stretch of beach, and presently come to where a little stream empties into the ocean. As the tide ebbs and flows, pulled by unseen forces, the little creek runs in; fresh water, born high in the Siuslaw forests, mingles with the salty Pacific.

Farther north still, we stop for lunch at a tiny cafe that appears to hang suspended over a cliff and offers a splendid view of the pounding surf below. The shoreline is visible for miles in a southerly direction and the northern beach ends in a small cove above which appears a few scattered cliff-side dwellings. Wind- and water-carved rocks provide a backstop for waves that crash and hurl themselves near the inlet. What first appears to be numerous swimming seals proves, upon closer inspection, to be floating kelp!

Amused by a couple of fun-loving ducks bobbing up and down in the foamy water, we waited for the waitress to bring our lunch. Our table, warmed by comforting sunlight that streamed through a huge glass window, provided a pleasant place to rest from traveling. A brisk wind blew flecks of yellow foam across to the inlet and a man and his dog walked the cove, beachcombing.

We enjoyed the view considerably more than the food, which left much to be desired. Perhaps the cook was having a bad day but it was to be the worst meal of the trip. North of Lincoln City we took Highway 18 to Grand Ronde Valley Junction, then on to Salem where we spent the night visiting relatives.

January 22—It is raining when we leave Salem and drive north to Woodburn, where we have breakfast at the Country Club with Aunt Amey. Optimistic golfers, due to a brief period of sunshine, were hitting the rain-soaked green. Swept along in a steady flow of traffic and rain water, we speed along I-5 into Portland, take the Jantzen Beach exit and find ourselves in front of the Red Lion/Columbia River where a familiar sign greets us: "Welcome Oregon Potato Growers."

A misty rainbow arches over west Portland as we settle into our room in the riverside wing. After a delicious buffet lunch in the Red Lion, I retire to the room to catch up on some writing while Doug attends meetings. That evening, with other potato conferees, we walk out onto a misty, rain-soaked deck that leads down a gangplank over the river to board a large sternwheeler.

It is warm and cozy inside and we choose a table on the middle deck that looks out across the river to misty city lights that border the shore. It is quite an experience, being out in the middle of a river at night, listening to live music and dining on board. We watch fascinated as a section of bridge swings open to allow the sternwheeler to pass, before swinging back into position.

We walk out on the deck, wet with rain and mist, to where wooden paddle wheels churn the water and create soft splashing sounds and leaving a long wake behind the boat. Enormous ships, in whose holds are transported goods to the Orient and other exotic ports, are docked along the shore. There is something mysterious about these giant hulks, perhaps because they travel far across the sea to strange places most of us will never see.

As the rain increases, I pull my hooded coat over my head and, sipping a cup of hot chocolate, step out onto the deck to "experience" the river. Little wavelets dance across the water's surface, and the wind and rain on my face feels good. In due time we turn around and head downstream back to the Red Lion's boat ramp, where we once more enter the creature comfort world of the motel.

January 23—After attending the opening session and doing some photo journalism, it was back to the room to pound on the typewriter; deadline time again! Oblivious to most else, I work on my column until noon, at which time I join Doug and other potato growers for a luncheon in the Riverside Room.

Full length glass windows look out on the Columbia River. Huge chandeliers hang from the ceiling, and tables set with so much silver, we wonder what to use! Colorful cloth napkins, stuffed decoratively in water goblets, and plates filled with chicken salad-filled croissants, fruit slices, and potato salad wait for us. Over lunch, Doug and I enjoy the company of some Hermiston folks.

Back to the room to resume working on my column. By late afternoon, I am feeling the need for some exercise, so I walk across the street to a large shopping center, hike the length of it, then enter a large outdoor store. Here I browse and dream about backpacking and camping, and

leaf through endless books on how to do it all. If I were from the city
and wanted to go off into the mountains, I would need six mules to carry
all the paraphernalia recommended therein!

Returning through the mall, I ran into the old Jantzen Beach merry-
go-round and had an uncontrollable urge to ride. If there had been a
grandchild there I would have. The walk refreshed me for the banquet
that evening, which was also held in the Riverside room.

Seated with other Wallowa County delegates and two from Klamath
County, we chowed down on filet mignon, baked potato, hard-crusted
rolls, salad, broccoli and a frozen mousse topped with whipped cream
and chocolate sprinkles. Good thing I'd gone for that walk!

The real treat of the evening was listening to the guest speaker, Pat
Leimbach, a farm wife and columnist from Vermilion, Ohio. I had been
looking forward to her talk, having read her columns and one of her
books. She was all I'd hoped and then some. This middle-aged woman
wowed the potato growers, especially the wives, who could relate to her
humorously-told, often pathetic experiences. She'd been there!

Visiting with Pat afterward, I learned she has been writing a column
for 25 years, and each week she is going to quit! How I know the feeling.
We both agreed: somehow we just keep on writing. It is almost like a
disease. What impressed me most about Pat was that in spite of great
sadness, the loss of a son, she was able to look again at life, after a time
and the birth of a granddaughter, and see the good...and the humorous.

Humor: The number one ingredient for survival of the farm wife.
Amen!

January 24—It was cold and foggy when we left Portland, the kind
of cold that chills to the bone. We made it safely home by 9, finding only
scattered, dirty patches of snow and evidence of former high winds. My
dog came from the shop to greet us and one by one the cats returned to
hover around the back porch door.

I hope readers have figured out that the 1 cup of water listed in the
ingredients for the "Old Fashion" lemon pie [on page 286] should read 1
cup sugar! I wouldn't have caught the error myself, had I not used the
recipe in the column to make a pie for the CattleWomen's/Stockgrowers
potluck last Sunday. As I said, one must understand basic cooking.

January 25—We both slept in this morning; tired, I suppose, from
traveling, and returning to the inevitable "mountain" of mail that accu-
mulates when one is gone. It seems a waste of trees to provide enough
paper for all the junk mail that comes to all of us these days!

Looking outside to our familiar, yet strangely unfamiliar world, we see the wind has stripped off the dry raspberry leaves, and the canes stick through patches of dirty snow. The thermometer on the car-port registered 25 degrees when we arrived home last night.

Once again our bodies must adjust to the dry cold. A wind that arrived in the middle of the night moans in a lonely way around the house. Sifting "snow dust" sweeps across the prairie, creating a scene from the frozen arctic. We can't see our familiar mountains for the blowing snow, yet it is not snowing. And on our porch...eggs! In our absence the family simply couldn't keep up with those prolific pullets! They kept up their production because January was so mild.

I attempt to create order out of chaos but accomplish little, partly because the phone rings all morning and into the afternoon. The word is out: we are home. By evening I've made a stab at reestablishing a long-lost routine, if, on a ranch, there is such a thing. A pot roast cooks in the cast-iron dutch oven and our calendar, on into February and March, is filling up. A granddaughter calls from Imnaha asking "granma" to make a special angel food cake for her birthday. Other grandchildren call. It is so good to hear their young voices. We are anxious about a grandson in Wyoming who has been hospitalized with pneumonia. But most of the calls now concern our seed potato business. By nightfall the barometer takes a plunge and it begins to snow.

January 26—Baked a batch of low cholesterol bran muffins for breakfast, and served them with high cholesterol scrambled eggs. It occurs to me some cholesterol could be created by all the stress of worrying about what is safe to eat.

Here on the ranch we continue to eat nutritious, wholesome foods, which include eggs, meat and milk. In Wallowa County there are many 90- and even 100-year-olds, who provide living proof that these much-maligned farm products can't be all that bad for you. What they didn't eat in their growing-up years was junk food, but real food, grown on the farm and not wrapped in plastic or served in an aluminum can.

Bundled up against the cold, blowing snow to tend the chickens, I am glad the landscape is painted white again; this is more like January should be. Spent the morning cleaning dozens of eggs to deliver to customers in town. Every afternoon, as the old yellow truck lumbers up the hill, the cows begin to bawl when they smell the silage wafted in the air. The aromatic scent of fermented summer is rather pleasing on a cold winter day. And in other pastures, our spring calvers' bellies are swollen with new life as calving season nears.

January 27—A happy day! We celebrated the birthday of an 8-year-old granddaughter, letting her know we are so glad she was born. Wishing all children were so lucky. She frosted her own cake and we lit the candles several times so all the little ones present could take turns blowing them out. Seeing such happiness reflected in children's eyes has got to be one of life's greatest joys.

As I make a pot of clam chowder for supper, snow falls softly outside, floating down, adding more inches to what has fallen during the past two days. The snow, so dry and powdery, is carried off in the wind to settle in drifts.

The house tonight seems strangely quiet after the birthday day, missing the the chatter of young voices. I settle into a chair by the fire and absorb myself in a good book.

January 28—Wild, erratic winds continue to blow loose snow across Prairie Creek in great white gusts. We invited a friend over for chicken dinner, which included freshly-baked sourdough bread and apple pie. After feeding cattle, the Imnaha family joined us to spend Super Bowl Sunday.

Meanwhile, all day the cold wind blew snow around in three directions while the '49ers trounced the Broncos. Backcountry roads became drifted and at times there were "white outs" where nothing could be seen but swirling snow. That night, fresh snow flakes fluttered against our windows, creating patterns that clung to the panes. Around 9:30 p.m. I could see the blinking lights on the snow plow making its slow way up Sheep Creek Hill in the storm.

January 29—The winter storms continue. Snowing, blowing and drifting. Tough on livestock. Our cows broke down a fence around the haystack last night. It is most difficult feeding loose hay in high wind, as it only scatters and blows against the fence rows.

Busy at the typewriter this morning, pounding out CattleWomen's Corner and an article on the Oregon potato conference, and my column. Doug is braiding a set of reins he'll donate to a silent auction to be held at our Stockgrowers/CattleWomen's potluck this coming Sunday. We welcome a brief warm spell, free from wind, before the storm returns, worse than ever.

Sleet and snow fly before the wind and the drifts continue to build.

January 30—As this first month of 1990 disappears it is partially clear, and the wind has laid down. Tended the chickens and split some wood. The day was taken up caring for two young grandchildren who "helped" grandma bake lemon pies for birthday pie-a-month gifts. One pie ended the 12 months for a grandson and began 12 months for a son-in-law.

For the first time in a long while, bright stars glitter in a cold, blue-black sky and snow light brightens Prairie Creek tonight.

January 31—The dreaded cold month of January is nearly over, only this year, the bitter cold (20-30 below) didn't materialize…yet!

The two grandchildren spent the night and were delighted with their breakfast pancakes, which we baked in shapes of animals. In the bright, still sunshiney afternoon, we built a snowman, complete with carrot nose, stick arms and a scarf, after which the house became a soggy mess of gloves, boots and melting kids. We sure had fun.

February 1—As bright sunshine greeted our morning, I was wishing I didn't have so much inside work and could be outside cross-country skiing. By afternoon the familiar dark clouds reappeared, along with the wind.

Helped a grandson celebrate his 16th birthday tonight. Lots of birthdays. When one has 14 grandchildren and seven children, they roll around with increasing frequency.

February 2—Gray, cloudy and windy. It will have to clear up considerably today if the groundhog wants to see his shadow, at least here on Prairie Creek. Began work on that "yearly headache," the income tax. Temperatures remain in the low 30s, far above normal for this time of year.

We enjoyed visiting with neighbors at the annual groundhog supper tonight at the Joseph Civic Center. In addition to groundhog (sausage) we had pancakes, cooked up by the Joseph Chamber's menfolk, assisted by the women folk. Proceeds from the dinner help fund Chief Joseph Days in July. Three pretty young misses, all members of the 1990 C.J.D's court, helped with the meal.

February 3—Great clouds of snow boil up from the McCully Creek drainages as wild winds hurl against ridges, loosening and sending snow flying in white banners over the mountains and down below timberline to the valley's edge. And on the high peaks, the erratic winds blow with such fury the entire mountain chain dissolves in a white, shifting veil.

How must it be up there, in such a furious gale, with no protection from the elements? Where last summer we watched in awe as forest fire smoke from the destructive Canal fire raced toward the prairie, we see billowing "snow smoke" blow through the burn. Although here on

Prairie Creek the temperature is warmer than Hermiston this morning, the scene created by loose snow blowing across the landscape does not a picture of warmth paint!

Walking out to feed and water the chickens, I can barely stand upright, and the wind-driven snow stings my cheeks. Our eastern hills are a sight to behold, as the wind comes sweeping down over them, blowing the snow in giant waves that resemble foaming ocean breakers. The waves spill down upon Locke's field, exposing ice-covered ditches that glint steel-gray through sifting snow.

The wind is all-consuming; moaning, howling, incessant, with occasional wild gusts rattling doors and windows. Our horses stand with their backs to the onslaught, tails blown between their hind legs, ears laid back, looking uncomfortable, yet displaying that enduring animal patience to foul weather.

And on this prescribed day, Max and Millie were married. Doug called Max this morning, and asked if the wind was blowing up there, to which Max replied, "I don't know but there's sure a lot of snow going past the house!" If we thought the storm was bad here, we found it as nothing to upper Prairie Creek as we drove up there to attend the wedding. It was practically a "white out" and large drifts were forming across Liberty Road.

The wind fairly took our breath away before we entered the large, comfortable home of Don and Rosemary Green, where the ceremony was to be performed. As the angry wind roared and sifted snow over the fields, swirling around the house and obscuring the close-by Wallowas, Max and Millie repeated their wedding vows. The warmth and love that flowed inside could have melted the cold outside, because everyone was so happy for the deserving couple.

To sleep that night with the dull roar of the ever-present wind.

February 4—Stillness. Absolute stillness. And crystal clear skies with only a few low-lying clouds wreathing the mountains. The wind and snow gods are at rest. The sky appears polished and clean, scrubbed by wind and snow.

Bull buyers beginning to come around and look at our sale bulls. Busy all day cooking and baking. A lemon pie for the Stockgrowers/CattleWomen's potluck tonight, sourdough bread, to be donated to a silent auction, and an elk stew, which simmers in the dutch oven. I would much rather be out in such a lovely day, but it is afternoon by the time I finish preparing all this food. I managed to get in a mile or so of walking down our country road before we left.

After a delicious potluck came a successful silent auction, where my bread sold for $10 (to my husband), then resold to a woman who wanted it, also, for another $10. Doug's reins brought in $62, while proceeds from other items swelled our memorial scholarship fund, and we had fun doing it.

We were treated to a slide program presented by one of our local doctors. Dr. Lowell Euhus has attained a goal he set for himself, and that was to visit every lake in our high Wallowa mountains. This experienced back packer transported us to summer, and we too were able to see those lovely lakes, scattered throughout the Eagle Cap Wilderness, through his camera lens. Dr. Euhus' beautiful slides inspired us to make an effort to see more of our own "back yard," so to speak.

It was 25 degrees when we drove home to a moonlit, starlit Prairie Creek... with no wind!

February 5—Cloudy, cold, 10 degrees. The familiar wind beginning to rise. A repeat of last week's weather pattern seems inevitable as a series of new storms blow inland off the Pacific and make their way over the Cascades to Eastern Oregon. A good time to "hole up," catch up on reading and writing. Try to anyway. Never really catch up. Always something comes up on a ranch.

February 6—Another inch of snow fell during the night. I leave, driving icy roads, to run errands in Enterprise before staying with grandchildren while mom attends to some work.

Large icicles hang from the eaves, tinkling and melting as sudden breezes blow off the mountain. Sunshine sparkles through them before they fall and splinter onto the thawing ground. It is great entertainment for the children and me. From the warmth of the kitchen we watch little snow flurries whirl across the mountains, then disappear in a sudden burst of sunlight. The weather is very fickle today.

Grace and I attend an entertaining performance entitled "Horse Sense" at the OK Theatre tonight. Two "cowboy" performers sang and played a medley of old western songs, like "Streets of Laredo," "When the bloom is on the sage," "Bury me not on the lone prairie"... the ageless old-time cowboy ballads that have been around for years, but not heard much anymore. These two talented performers played the fiddle, banjo, mandolin. guitar and spoons, then threw in some cowboy poetry, spiced with humor. It was a most pleasant way to spend a cold winter evening.

Driving home a pale, muted light shone from a three quarter moon, which was veiled in snow clouds. The mountains stood ghostly still in moonglow. their dark evergreen slopes contrasting with the high country; locked in deep winter silence tonight.

After leaving Grace off at her house, I passed by the rows of logs. stacked, waiting for processing at the Boise Cascade mill, and the silent snow covered Harley Tucker Memorial Arena. Then through deserted Joseph and on out the Imnaha highway to Prairie Creek. Little new lambs lay curled next to their mothers in the snow. I arrived home. having never passed a single vehicle on this cold February night.

February 7—Snow falls softly in the gray light of dawn, and when the sun finally penetrates the clouds, looking more like a glowing lemon suspended above the eastern hills, a small patch of blue appears overhead. It is 18 degrees when I go out to chore. The three pregnant milk cows appear to be wintering well, and should begin calving next month. My dog, a constant companion, tumbles down snow drifts and rolls in the white stuff; she enjoys winter.

One more week I manage to juggle housework, demands from my family and sneak time to pound on the typewriter, which is a permanent fixture on our kitchen table. Ranch kitchen tables seem to be the hub of what's going on at the moment. Ours, like most, displays any number of items, depending on the season.

The wind and blowing snow return, so I build up the fire, water the horses, split wood, and in the early storm-brought darkness decide to bake an apple pie. This takes my mind away from wondering about Doug, who is driving home alone from a cattlemen's meeting in Portland on this wild night. Much later, he makes it home safely, just in time... the access to our valley was closed shortly afterward.

Winter seems to be arriving later than most years.

March I—March comes in like a soft, sunny lamb. The morning starts frosty but soon melts and gives way to an incredible day. By 8:30 I have cooked breakfast, done chores, baked a mincemeat pie. washed the dishes and made lunches.

Doug takes off for Imnaha with Max to go steelhead fishing, while some friends and I drive to Minam. Here we shoulder our day packs and walk down along the river to where the old Smith toll bridge used to cross the Minam. After finding the site, we soon locate the old wagon road, which takes off up Smith Mountain, named for A.C. Smith, an early pioneer settler known then as "The mountain man of the Wallowas."

This dim road climbs a steep hillside, wet now in spring thaw. After more than 100 years, lots of brush and trees grow in the road, but we manage to follow its rock-strewn route and begin a steep, diagonal accent to the top of Smith Mountain. We pass a lone buttercup, blooming bright yellow in the soggy, sun-warmed earth. After much huffing and puffing we reach a saddle, walk out into a high ridge, and try to envision a team of horses plodding its way up or down that steep, narrow road, pulling a wagon load of fright or passengers. At one time this was the only access to the valley, but because people objected to the toll road, other routes were established.

On top we tromped through deep snow, under which the characteristic red soil of Smith Mountain oozed and melted in the warm sun. Ridge after ridge appeared ahead and finally we came to an old spring where immigrants stopped to water their teams and refresh themselves. Water is still scarce on Smith Mountain. We paused under a very old pine tree, a tree that must have witnessed history, the very settling of the Wallowa country.

Near here we walked to a rocky point, sat down and drank in the air, and view. We could see far below to the Minam River, winding around to join the Wallowa. The route to the "outside," modern Highway 82, disappears up the canyon, and so does the railroad track that changed the way of life here. The changes 100 years have brought in transportation. From wagon road to highway and today we think nothing of the 60-mile drive to La Grande.

We ate our lunches and watched a bald eagle fly along the Minam River and begin to spiral upward in a beautiful, graceful way. Circling near us, searching with his eyes, he soared higher and higher, until we lost him to the deep blue sky.

March 4—It began to snow this morning. White, feathery flakes landed softly on brown grass and muddy earth. After feeding cattle and doing chores, Doug and I drove up to Vali's at Wallowa Lake for continental breakfast.

Great storm clouds hovered over the Wallowas and broken patches of thin ice lay at both ends of the lake. The calm, open water in between mirrored snowy Chief Joseph Mountain, and herds of mule deer grazed the steep east moraine. Back at the ranch I thawed out some colostrum milk in a bottle to feed a small twin calf (mom decided she only wanted one).

March 6—A heavy frost covered the fields, but the day soon warmed and cows were dropping baby calves everywhere. Meanwhile, our cellar crew was busy sorting and shipping seed potatoes. After supper, stepping outside to get a breath of air, I heard wild geese calling, and then there they were, a flying V across the face of the growing spring moon.

March 7—This morning began when a shocking pink sunrise projected a golden light across the snowy Wallowa summits. After three milk cows, one twin calf, three yearlings, two horses, 30 chickens, one dog and four cats had their breakfast, I fixed ours. Another hour of doing dishes, washing clothes and odds and ends of housework later, I was typing out my column.

At the sound of the door bell, I opened the back porch door to see a smiling gentleman who said he was an avid fan of Janie's Journal, not a traveling salesman. I invited him and his wife, who was sitting in the car, to come in and get warm around the wood stove. Long johns were drying in back of the stove and the house seemed suddenly cluttered, but no matter, they are ranchers, too, from over in Union County. They understand our lives. And it was nice to meet and visit.

March 8—Last night we had four grandchildren around the supper table. I always enjoy cooking for a large family, but had almost forgotten how much growing children can eat. The older two spent the night and I sent them off to school with sourdough waffles under their belts.

Two horned owls *hoo-hoo*-ed in the willow trees, which meant it would snow soon. They were right! Large, feathery flakes stuck to our windows this morning, creating pretty patterns. The March mini-blizzard soon marched off across the mountains, and a warm sun melted the snow.

This afternoon I attended our monthly CattleWomen's meeting in Enterprise and in the evening our photo club met in Joseph. We were treated to a demonstration by Joy Klages, wife of master photographer Walter Klages. Over the years, Joy's behind-the-scenes work merits recognition as an art form all its own.

March 9—It was 19 degrees when the sun came up in a clear blue sky and Daisy, our Guernsey milk cow, freshened. Soon her pretty Simmental/cross heifer calf was up and nursing. More robins appeared and a northern flicker began to drum away on a potato piler. Excedrin headache number 3!

Scotty came out this afternoon and we walked up and down Tenderfoot Valley Road. Tonight Doug took a cow into the vet for a Cesarean section. The calf was upside down and backward. Mother and baby survived just fine.

March 10—After the usual morning chores, Doug and I attended a meeting in Enterprise of the Oregon Lands Coalition, a grass roots organization representing timber and agriculture; a voice in the wilderness, speaking of wilderness issues and the future of man and the wilderness.

The battle over how to manage our precious natural resources here in the Northwest will go on for the rest of our lifetimes as well as our children's.

Meanwhile, while the people spoke of these things, Mother Nature was at work outside and we walked out of the high school multipurpose room into a white world filled with thickly falling flakes. The soft, spring snow clung to everything, soon bending branches under the weight of it.

Home to thaw out more colostrum milk for two chilled calves born in the storm. It wasn't long before Prairie Creek resembled Jackson Hole, Wyoming, and the landscape returned to winter.

March 11—Awoke to look out at a frozen fairy land. Large drifts covered the front yard, snow lay on the pole fences, "whipped cream" topped every object in the yard, frozen snow and ice cornices hung suspended from roof tops. Long icicles glittered in the rising sun. It was cold and still.

Crunched through deep powder snow to feed, then took my camera to photograph the winter scene. As it turned out, the storm dumped the most snow of the winter! Prairie Creek was a work of winter art. New little calves shivered in the cold, but managed to survive.

By noon Scotty and I were cross-country skiing on Alder Slope; first time on skis all winter! Low clouds covered the mountains and the temperature remained cold enough to hold the snow. It was great to be out sliding and gliding over the fields, then making the vigorous trips up hill to glide smoothly down. The distant hills appeared purple and white, and the Seven Devils wore a veil of snow clouds. The air was wonderful.

Back home in time to chore, after which I baked a batch of whole wheat biscuits to go with the elk roast that had been simmering along with parsnips, carrots and onions all afternoon. A brilliant full moon illuminates our snowy landscape.

March 12—The temperature took a nose dive overnight; 10 degrees this morning, very still and clear.

March 14—Things went somewhat better this morning: that is, compared to yesterday. Could be because it was the 13th. Who knows? Anyway, yesterday was the day my milk cow Startch decided to calve. Shortly after daylight, I looked out our bedroom window to see her tail out, looking like she had already calved, hopefully in the straw I had shook out for her.

The porch thermometer registered 11 degrees as I ran out to have a look-see. There was the calf, stuck in an ice-crusted, manurey mud hole, the sort of goopy stuff that builds up around hay feeders. The big black baldy calf lay partially submerged in the ooze. Chilled and wheezing, its nose barely above the icy mud, it lay shivering in the cold.

Grabbing the calf by one hind leg, I pulled it out of its dire predicament and laid it on the bed of straw, then ran back to get Doug's help in loading it into the pickup and taking it to the house. We laid the calf, icy mud and all, onto an old rug in front of the wood cookstove. The house began to smell like essence of springtime barnyard as I sponged the filthy calf with warm water and rubbed it all over to warm it. As the mud came off, I could see it was a nice heifer calf. What a way to come into the world.

Meanwhile, one of our hired men called, saying one of his own cows had calved in the night and his wife had the chilled calf in their bathtub; he wanted to know if we had any colostrum to spare to feed it. So I went out to drive Startch into the barn, milked out some of her first milk for his calf, after which I milked a bottle full for Startch's calf. The big heifer, feeling like life wasn't so bad after all, warmed up, inhaled the bottle of milk and began to stand up. So we took her back out to mom, leaving her lying in a fresh pile of hay in the sunshine.

Then it was time to finish the rest of my chores before returning to face my filthy floor. A half bottle of Pine Sol later, plus washing overalls, rags and rugs, the house was reasonably clean and smelled much better. It was 10:30 before I finally sat down to eat some breakfast. The men had long gone off to the cellars to ship seed potatoes.

The calf slept in the warm sunshine until late afternoon. Later we took her into the barn and I ran Startch in so the calf could nurse. That way, I could let the bottle baby twin I'd been feeding for over a week, nurse too. The twin took right to the cow but the heifer was so tall, she kept o'ershooting her mark to find the milk supply. Frustrating. I finally milked some into the bottle and fed her that way. It had already been a long day.

March 15—We have a new puppy. Shy at first, the little border collie soon warmed up to us and now feels happily at home here. The refuse of winter (bones and sticks) will be gnawed on and dragged about the yard. Clothes will no longer be safe hanging on the line, and the cats will live in terror for a while. But there is something about a puppy that evokes happiness, and of course there is always hope that he will turn out to be a good stock dog.

Startch's calf is growing like a bad weed, and so is the adopted twin; however, I continue to milk more than a gallon after the calves have nursed their fill. Hopefully, there will soon be another calf to relieve the cow milker of her morning and night chore.

Doug off to Hermiston to ship our feedlot yearlings, while I remain on the ranch to tend chores and clean house. It is also my job to be by the phone and direct potato truck drivers to our cellars. This sunny, clear day is causing the snow to melt, again.

March 16—The sun coming through the living room window was so warm, I didn't bother to start a fire in the wood cookstove this morning. We are more than halfway through calving.

March 17—Two Imnaha grandchildren spent the night. This morning I fixed us all a big breakfast before going out to chore. No frost!

When the chores were finished, I took the children to nearby Wallowa Lake State Park and let them feed apples to the deer. It was very quiet up there, not much activity during the winter season, and the deer gratefully crunched on the apples.

That afternoon the children and I, along with other family members, watched the first performance of "Snow White" at the OK Theatre. Each year the Missoula Children's Theatre comes to Wallowa County, then casts over 50 local children in various roles for the play. Because granddaughter Carrie was one of the seven dwarfs, we got there early to get a good seat. It is truly amazing, how, in just one week, this musical comes together. As in years past, it was quite a production.

March 18—Continued warm with no frost. Saved the first of Startch's milk for house milk this morning. Could hardly wait to bake a raisin-rice-custard pudding, which turned out to be delicious.

Friends from Roseburg stopped by to spend the night on their way to Imnaha. I prepared a supper of elk steaks, homemade french bread, and salads to go with the yummy pudding.

March 19—Warm and cloudy. Up early to finish chores, before cooking sourdough waffles for our guests, after which they left for Imnaha to visit a son and his family. Warmed up into the 60s today.

March 20—The season's first thunderstorm rolled down the valley last night. This first day of spring really feels as though the change is taking place. Other signs indicate spring has arrived; the first purple crocuses have appeared alongside the house, and the familiar odoriferous essence of barnlot floats on the breeze!

More than 20 calves were born this past weekend. Startch's new heifer now frolics in a balmy 60 degrees. Once more I settle into a spring routine of milking the cow, haying the horse, tending the chickens and caring for the calves: twice a day, seven days a week. If I do go somewhere during the day, Startch will be bawling at the barn door if I'm late.

It is great to have real milk again, and fun to bake custard puddings, pour cream on our cereal, or simply drink tall, cold glasses of it. Our cats and dogs and chickens are in heaven, as there is always an excess. This year I am trying my hand at making yogurt, and we enjoy homemade ice cream, butter, milk gravy, and then, of course, whipped cream on everything.

Then I must work extra hard, like feeding the cow and doing the actual milking, to work off all those calories. As the spring work becomes even more physical, this never poses a problem. With gardening and yard work just around the corner, not to mention more adventurous treks into our scenic back country, I can usually hold my own, and I will need the nutrition provided by milk products.

March 21—We drove to Imnaha this afternoon to visit family and go fishing. From our daughter's yard we looked up Big Sheep canyon and counted 70 head of elk grazing under the high rim! Apricots were in full bloom and everyone is keeping their fingers crossed that a frost won't ruin the crop like it did last year. Such a joy to see yellow forsythia and the first sarvisberry in bloom. Hundreds of baby calves basked in sunshine, and all along the river gardeners were working up their soil and preparing to plant.

While Doug tried to coax a wary steelhead to take his bait, we walked along the river and watched little lambs frolicking in green grass. The sights and smells of springtime. Later we watched as the grandchildren took turns riding a Welsh pony around a corral. Lucky children.

After a nice supper, topped off with hand-cranked ice cream, we returned "on top." It was nearly dark and Startch was about to shove in the barn door. Pale cool stars blinked above me as I walked to the chicken house and gathered the eggs. I could hear my pullets and Chester, the banty rooster, shuffling around on the roost, settling down for the night.

March 22—The robins sing a spring song; spring has officially arrived. I walk out the lane to mail my column, a weekly ritual that becomes increasingly difficult as spring progresses.

Baked an applesauce cake using a recipe found, written in pencil, tucked into a rusty coffee can in one of our old cabins in the hills. This never-fail cake calls for home-canned applesauce, and when I use this recipe, I always wonder who wrote it. Was it a bachelor or a rancher's wife, who learned to "make do" in those lonely hills?

My mother always says: "Children are forever!" And today, it seemed, in one way or another, I was involved with all seven of ours.

Shipping more seed potatoes this morning as the busy days march on by.

Anyway, back to this morning. Snowing. but much warmer with patches of blue showing overhead. Cooked oatmeal and ate breakfast first, before going out to face the "moosic." As expected, Startch is waiting at the barn door for her calf. She has this enormous udder full of milk. Here we go again. So, clad in my "Flo" boots, I let the big cow into the barn, lock her in the stanchion, then struggle with the hobbles, which are finally slipped into their maximum slot because the swollen udder keeps her legs so far apart.

I let the little twin in and she immediately goes to nursing. Not so the big, Simmental/Holstein-cross heifer. She simply stands there nuzzling her mother's flank; her head a good foot above the "calf-a-teria. where milk is literally running from mom's teats. I give the calla taste, my milking some into my hand, which gets her all excited, but she still can't find the faucet. She is so large I can't straddle her. so I push from behind, and use one hand to tilt her head down under the teat. No luck. Pretty soon both of us are exhausted. Then I see a possible solution. I flank her, placing her gently onto the floor. beneath the dripping teat. And in this relaxed position I place the teat in her mouth. *Voila.* Success!

Meanwhile, on the other side, happily wagging her tail, the twin slurps down her breakfast. What a pair. I sink wearily down on the milk stool and watch. After the calves are through, I still must deal with that udder, which is still bulging. The cow's rear teats, especially, pose a problem, as they are extremely short when she first freshens. I must use two fingers.

Several minutes later, I emerge from under the cow with a bucket full of colostrum milk, which I will freeze for future weak, chilled or motherless calves. Because we've used up last year's supply, it is either now or never. Without the cooperation of Startch, I couldn't accomplish this. She patiently waits until I finish, snow melting off her flank and sticky colostrum running down my arm. I grease her udder with bag balm to prevent chapping caused by cold weather, and finally let the poor cow out.

With each passing year, my bones protest louder during this first week of Startch's freshening. I wonder, do those who are now three generations away from living on the farm ever think about what goes on behind the scenes? Do they ever wonder how their carton of milk or that nicely wrapped package of beef comes to them in the supermarket?

Perhaps one day, we, too, will simply go to the store and purchase our meat, milk and eggs there. Will there be enough future ranchers who will want to go through all of this, year after year, to feed the rest of the world? I hope so.

March 23—Snowing, 32 degrees, with a good two inches on the ground and a heavy wet snow continuing to fall. Took granddaughter Chelsie to lunch at "A Country Place on Pete's Pond," an annual birthday treat from grandma. While seated at a table for two on the glassed-in deck, we watched the snow fall on the pond, where the many ducks dove and fed.

Meanwhile, large trout swirled around beneath us and a muskrat swam by, followed by two graceful white swans. Suddenly, several Canadian honkers landed on the surface of the pond, sending up a spray of water and honking loudly. What a show. It was hard to concentrate on our clam chowder.

Afterward I took Chelsie home with me and, because she loves to bake, I showed her how to make a raspberry pie. Very patiently, my 11-year-old miss worked at weaving a lattice crust for the top of the pie. Soon the red juice began to bubble between the crusts and, when her parents and brothers arrived to pick her up that evening, that beautiful pie was reduced to one slice.

March 24—Cold, foggy, 30 degrees and the ground is again frozen. It would appear we are back to winter again. I still can't believe it. I CLEANED OUT MY REFRIGERATOR! Inspired by an ad on our local radio station, something about an extension class being offered, entitled "The care and fitness of your refrigerator," I actually accomplished this messy chore.

After Doug found a plastic bag in the vegetable bin that contained some sort of unidentifiable black goo, I decided the old icebox was trying to tell me something. So, while our potato crew loaded more seed, I dealt with the innards of the fridge. Those who know me are amazed at what this long-suffering appliance must put up with. And I must say, it was amazing when the contents were all placed on the kitchen table.

After discarding anything not easily identified, I removed each shelf and gave it a baking soda bath, and felt an enormous sense of accomplishment. Now my refrigerator was fit. And maybe it was just my imagination, but I could have sworn I heard it hum "Thanks."

March 25—Ten degrees, clear, with lingering snow or heavy frost covering the brown fields. Started the day, as usual, cooking breakfast, then going out to chore. Startch's warm udder warms my cold hands, and the barn cats sit in a half circle meowing for their breakfast as streams of steaming milk fill the pail.

After cleaning our carport, I gave Scotty a call to see if she wanted to hike along Wallowa Lake. With light lunches in day packs, we drove up to the old lodge and parked the car. It was a winter scene among the snow-frosted evergreens, the late morning sunlight causing soft swooshes of sound as the white stuff slithered off the laden branches and sifted silently down. Swish, as huge branches of tall pines returned to their original position after releasing a burden of snow.

In shady places it was cold and we walked briskly to keep warm. Blue jays scolded, mule deer wandered around looking for a handout, and the great icy-blue ice fountain sparkled in rainbow prisms while a thin spray of water erupted from its depths. The recent storm had plastered snow on tree trunks and covered chokecherry bushes along the shore, smothering them in cotton balls. The calm waters on the lake's surface reflected the lovely snow-lit face of Chief Joseph Mountain; wild mallard ducks paddled nearby, then took off quacking to seek refuge by the far shore.

We met very little traffic and only three other people out walking. As we walked the 4-and-a-half miles to the foot of the lake, the day began to warm and we feasted our eyes on a sight many tourists would never see: the clear, cold lake, framed by leafless aspen, blue-white mountains rising straight up, snowclad, brilliant in sunlight. One could almost feel the grinding, glacial action that formed this lovely lake, and in the quiet noon, see a Nez Perce encampment along the shore, drying their fish on racks in the sun.

Returning to the car after a nine-mile walk, the cold had lost its grip and everything was melting. Back at the ranch I stopped by the calving pasture where we watched a heifer in labor. After a little assistance from Doug, who drove the young cow into the corral, everything came out all right.

After chores I cranked up a hatch of homemade ice cream, then prepared barbecued beef for sandwiches, which we transported to a daughter's family to share for supper.

March 26—After sourdough hot cakes, it was out to chore and thus began another day. Typed up "CattleWomen's Corner" for our local paper, finished some correspondence, hung out two loads of wash, swept the floors, and answered telephone calls all morning concerning potatoes and bulls.

Purchased my vegetable garden seeds at the feed store when I was there picking up chicken feed this afternoon. After grocery shopping I returned home to gather eggs, bring in the wash, milk the cow and let the calves nurse, hay the cows and fix supper. Just an ordinary day on the ranch.

The overnight low was 21 this morning, much warmer than yesterday, but we fear the Imnaha apricot crop may have been ruined by the low temperatures.

March 27—Sunup now occurs shortly after 6 a.m. on these frosty mornings. Worked on my column, trying to sandwich in a 2 p.m. meeting, a weekly egg delivery and company for supper. The company was family and it was fun to have grandchildren around the table. I fixed the Korean beef stir-fry recipe that appeared recently in Agri-Times. Delicious and easy to prepare.

March 28—Breakfast over, chores finished, back in the house by 7:30. A gorgeous morning. It was so warm we didn't build a fire. Doug and the potato crew are loading a semi-load of seed potatoes at the Joseph cellars. Spent most of the morning baking. A lemon pie for son-in-law Bill's pie-a-month present, and a sour cream-raisin pie for Doug, because I must bake him one before any other pie goes out the door! Unfortunately, connections for transporting the lemon pie to Imnaha never happened, so another son-in-law's family "kidnapped" the pie.

Sitting at my typewriter the first of every week, beginning another column, I wonder, is the effort worthwhile? Then in my mail, a letter arrives, like the one received yesterday from Gladys Jeffries of rural Colfax, Washington.

I am now 80, but well and active, and anxious to get out and into yard cleaning, spading and getting ready for a garden," writes Gladys. *"Oh how I'd love to drop in for a long visit with you by your range in your kitchen!* She goes on to to say she married a farmer and lives about halfway between her two grandparents' homesteads, and is interested in reading about Wallowa County because she attended kindergarten and first grade in Enterprise when her father was a cattle rancher there, until failing health forced him to give up ranching.

Gladys recalls early memories of going camping somewhere near Wallowa Lake in a wagon. *We had to cross a little creek or river and the water was up to the bed of the wagon and we kids were so scared.* She has an old photo of the outing and their tears show in the picture how frightened they were crossing the stream.

It was pretty slim pickin's after daddy died. I know what it is to not have water in the house, or bathtubs or toilets. I've heated water on the range and washed by hand...still do a lot! she writes. Gladys treasures the days she used to herd the cattle for her daddy. Riding her pony, she herded cattle along roads and railroads that ran through the middle of their farm. She and her sister rode their pony 2-and-a-half miles to a country school, where, she says, *there were about 30 to 35 pupils and one teacher I loved.*

She taught school herself for three years before she married her farmer boy and together reared a girl and two boys.

We have never known riches, writes Gladys, *but we are rich...three loving kids, four loving teenage granddaughters, we have our home, we are debt-free, we are able to do our work.* That sort of sums up how many readers of Agri-Times still live, and it is gratifying. Gladys ends by saying, *Janie, I can just see you feeding chickens, cows etc...I've been there. Stay well and keep writing.*

This is a sample of the many letters I've received in the past, and therefore conclude, perhaps the effort is worthwhile.

March 29—Another clear, warm, sunny day. After morning chores I drove to Alder Slope and joined the two younger grandchildren and their mom for a picnic on their place. We walked through patches of buttercups atop a high ridge and sat in an open, grassy hillside to eat our lunch. The mountains seemed so close in that "Sound of Music" setting. The world, with all its trials, seemed to melt away on such a day, in such a place.

Later, I drove farther up the slope to Harold McLaughlin's place and loaded up a bookcase I'd purchased. The Seven Devils in Idaho were plainly visible from the McLaughlins' ranch, as was the valley below. Harold and wife, Hope, are like Gladys Jeffries and her husband; they are rich in the things that really matter.

That evening at the Joseph Methodist Church, along with other contemporaries, I attended a literary reading presented by Kim Stafford. Sitting there in that quiet, beautiful church, listening to Kim's story-telling and songs, many written about our area, I realized again how lucky we are to live here.

March 30—Three semis of seed potatoes left our cellars. Company arrived from Kennewick, Washington, and Doug and I attended the Grain Growers annual dinner meeting tonight at Cloverleaf Hall.

March 31—March went out like a soft, little lamb. Gorgeous morning, filled with bird song and the gabbling of wild geese beginning to pair up and prepare to nest. Farmers' and ranchers' fields provide excellent habitat for nesting waterfowl and we like that.

April 1—So occupied with "spring things" we forgot about it being April Fool's Day. A lovely sunset closed the curtain on this day.

April 2—I always enjoy the quiet, cool time before sunrise on these April morns. The two youngest grandchildren were here most of the day. We picnicked in the yard, played house in the old sheepherder wagon and spent most of the day outside. A spring moon grows in a clear. cool sky tonight.

April 3—Just a touch of frost this morning as the magic of springtime spreads over the land. Between chores and other numerous projects, I spent most of the day writing.

Several of us local writers are working on a local encyclopedia that we hope will be published by Christmas. The project is being funded by a grant received from the Oregon State Library by the Northwest Writing Institute of Lewis and Clark College. The project, "Writing about Home in Oregon Libraries," allows three communities in Oregon to participate, and ours, Toledo's and Hood River's were selected.

April 4—The clear, dry, almost hot days continue. Even though there was a heavy frost this morning, it warmed up quickly. I've had to irrigate the daffodils and tulips alongside the house. Cleaned up the vegetable garden: it is now ready to till, but too early to plant.

April 5—Very busy day.

April 6—Four semis of seed potatoes were loaded out at our Joseph cellars today. A long day for our crew. Unseasonably warm. Now we are deep irrigating the shade trees in the yard.

April 7—After chores and loading more seed potatoes. Doug and I attended another meeting of the Oregon Lands Coalition. Three hours of speakers painting a gloomy picture for the future of timber and agriculture in our area. It seems now is the time to tell our story. Apparently this story hasn't been properly understood by the masses who live in urban areas, and who consume food and fiber produced in places like Northeastern Oregon.

Dark clouds boiled up over the valley and shed a few scattered showers, but overall, contributed little in the way of moisture.

April 8—A couple of friends and I headed for the hills after morning chores, just to roam around and see how that country fared through the winter. As we walked up the meadow on Wet Salmon Creek, our horses ran up to greet us, mane and tails flying in the wind, looking like wild horses, having wintered there. What a life!

Many varieties of blooming wildflowers, including yellow bells and birdbills, and the bright splash of an occasional blue bell gladdened our hearts as we walked along. On the skyline of a long ridge, more than 100 head of elk lingered, ogling our grass! In the thornbrush along the creek, hawks and owls nesting. From fence posts and rockjacks erupted the full-throated melody of the meadowlark. The song of the hills.

Yellow cous bloomed on the rocky hillsides; we dug some and peeled the bulbs and ate them. The Nez Perce used to dry this bulb and then pound it into a sort of meal, which was then baked. The ponds built by ranchers draw the wildlife to this otherwise arid area. And they were all full with feeding and nesting mallards happily taking up residence there. Ranchers have always been conservationists; every day is Earth Day for them.

April 9—Twenty degrees with a hard frost. A typically busy Monday with many phone calls. Ran errands in town and tended to details related to several projects. Ended up at the Cloud 9 Bakery for lunch, where I attended a 4-H executive meeting.

Another meeting tonight, when the Alder Slope Pipeline Association conducted its annual meeting. I always enjoy this chance to visit by Alder Slope neighbors, as well as tending to business of irrigation water.

Because we weaned our fall calves today, the bawling is rather intense tonight.

April 10—A wondrous sight greeted me this morning. Leaving Doug in the kitchen to fix sourdough hotcakes, I went out in the dark at 5 a.m. to water and feed the chickens. A full moon, glowing with soft, yellow light, was beginning to slip between the area of Chief Joseph Mountain and Twin peaks. I stood there in the chicken pen, watching it disappear over the snowy Wallowas.

In the quiet coolness of dawn the robins began their song, and Chester the banty rooster answered with his cock-a-doodle-do! A soft light glowed above where the moon had been, and a single bright star hovered over the eastern hill divide as dawn stole softly over Prairie Creek. The dewy earth smelled of greening grass. The cows and calves began to sound off with their own symphony as a pink glow lit the eastern sky.

How much most of us miss when we stay in bed. I could see the white face of my milk cow coming toward me from the dark pasture. The large cow ambled into the barn and let the two calves nurse, and then I milked her out. It was just beginning to break daylight as I walked into the kitchen with the pail of milk.

Soon, 82 years young Mike McFetridge and I were trailing the fall calving cows to the hills, leaving the bawling calves behind. We would trail them to the old Dorrance place out on Crow Creek where they would spend the night. Snowbanks, usually present this time of year, were noticeably scarce. Buttercups bloomed in profusion with patches of gold all along the route.

Mike and I made the long, dusty miles disappear by visiting about the "good old days" and comparing what we would do to improve on the state of the present days, and we had most of life's problems solved by the time we reached the Circle M corrals. Here we let the cattle rest while we ate our lunches.

Farther down Crow Creek we encountered a large, orange sign, "Construction Next 3 Miles," then another one, "Federal Highway Project." Highway? Out there? Our horses and cows shied at the enormous new, shiny tin culvert that stuck out at either end, buried beneath a mound of freshly moved gravel, under which flowed the tiny creek.

Gone was the cool grassy area along the road where trailing cattle could drink at the creek, graze and rest. So much money being spent. What was wrong with the way it was? We wondered about this and then saw the huge, ugly gouge in the hillside where earth was scooped for the fill. Stakes in the rocky hillside indicate more changes in the road. Why? Progress?

Doug had driven out to meet us as we drove the 106 head of cows into the corrals. We'd ridden 17 miles in seven hours. Home to do chores, then the boss took his cowgirls to Joseph for a hamburger. Tomorrow we resume trailing the cows to their summer range.

April 11—Up before dawn on this cloudy, warm morning. Out to chore while Doug dealt with the sourdough hotcakes and made my lunch. Another day in the saddle for Mike and me. Mike ate breakfast with us and soon we were in the pickup, traveling out the long Crow Creek road to where the cows had spent the night. A light sprinkling of rain dashed against the windshield, then ceased as we drove out from under a dark cloud. It was so dry, the dust wasn't even dampened. At that early hour, the greening hills appeared somber and quiet. A golden eagle, perched on a fence post, flew off at our approach.

At the pink barn corrals, our cows were anxious to hit the trail. Our horses were caught, grained, curried and saddled, and soon we were mounted up, driving the herd to water. Doug drove on ahead to put out salt. The cows took off up the gulch; the leaders knew the way to summer range.

Meadowlark melody filled the air and the road was dusty. At the top of the grade, the vast undulating hill land stretched before us. The high plateau, bunch grass cow country, has been maintained and managed for the past 100 years by some of the best stewards of the land: ranchers. Hard working ranchers who have built ponds in an otherwise arid land to capture and store water.

Not only do these watering places provide drinking water for their cattle, but for the vast herds of elk that also call the area home. Contrary to popular belief, deer and elk were scarce, and even non-existent in this land, when the first cattlemen brought their herds in to graze. Elk were later introduced, the herds grew, and thanks to the grazed range land created by the cattle, elk now prefer that forage to any other.

Now the numbers of elk are reaching proportions that are far greater than the habitat will support, not to mention the impact it has on the cattle's grazing needs. Many times when an area looks overgrazed, it is because the elk have eaten the new shoots of spring grass down before the cattle were ever turned out.

Dry Salmon Creek was wet...only time of the year it would be! Yellow bells and pink grass widows waved in the breeze, and the silence of the hills engulfed us. We separated the herd just beyond where the old Dry Salmon Creek school house used to stand, Mike driving half of the cows on ahead while I stayed with the rear bunch.

When Mike reached the Pine Creek road, he headed his cows up toward Wet Salmon, then helped turn mine toward Butte Creek. After my bunch lined out pretty good, he returned to his cows. We would turn the split herd into two pastures—Mike's bunch in the Red Barn pasture and mine to Butte Creek. Riding along with my dog and my cows, I began to sing.

It was such a beautiful day and the hills were alive with springtime! Looking back I could see Mike driving his bunch out of sight over a hill. Little dots on the horizon, heading east. My cows grazed the succulent green grass alongside the road, and the fresh scent of bruised grass smelled wonderful. As we neared our destination I was glad to see Doug had left the gate open. I counted 55 cows as they filed in...then I had to struggle with that "durned wire gate."

I led my horse to a bank and waited for Doug and Mike to appear.

After loading my mare and dog, we were soon rattling down the long, dusty road to the valley ranch. A road we had spent the past two days riding horseback.

April 12—Another unseasonably warm morning. CattleWomen's meeting at noon, then grocery shopping and home to chores before Doug and I returned to town to attend the Enterprise FFA banquet at the high school.

Three hundred people enjoyed roast beef, mashed potatoes, gravy and green beans, topped off with strawberry shortcake. As this most impressive program, run entirely by the Future Farmers of America, unfolded, I reconfirmed my conviction that Wallowa County's most precious resource is its youth. What poise and proficiency these boys and girls possessed.

April 13—Another rain-less day. Although the country is turning green, it is desperately in need of moisture. We need a real frog-strangler!

As she would be riding this morning, mom left my two youngest grandchildren off early. The two sleepy-eyed tots were bundled up and put into a wheelbarrow, then grandma wheeled them from chicken pen to horses to milk cow barn. Two-year-old Adele sat in the wheelbarrow, wrapped in her blanket, while 3-year-old James "helped" grandma milk the cow. He finally succeeded in aiming a few squirts into the pail.

Played with the children all morning, fixed lunch, boiled up three dozen eggs to color Easter eggs, and by afternoon four more grandchildren arrived to join in the egg coloring venture. Such fun we had! All the eggs, as well as the children's hands and faces, were soon all brightly colored.

Another thunder storm threatens. No rain. The young cousins played in the sheepherder's wagon, hid Easter eggs and had numerous "hunts" on the lawn. That evening young James and nine-year-old Buck sat on milk stools on either side of my milk cow. Both pulled teats, then glanced under the cow at each other's progress.

"Think I'm getting the hang of it," said Buck.

"Me too," said James.

Grandma was most amused and Startch, the milk cow, was the epitome of patience!

April 14—Having exhausted themselves yesterday, all the children slept in. I had the cow milked and the chores finished before they sleepily appeared for sourdough waffles. Daughter Jackie left to judge the Chief Joseph Days court riding trials and the rest of us attended an estate auction at Cloverleaf Hall. A large crowd was assembled and stayed until the last item was sold. Wallowa County loves country auctions.

I left for home earlier to boil potatoes for a potato salad for Easter Sunday tomorrow. After chores were finished, I attended the queen's coronation dinner at the Joseph Civic Center. We took notes and photos of the program, and at 10 p.m. the queen was announced.

Amid tears of joy and hugs from parents, grandparents and friends, Vixen Radford, Enterprise, was crowned queen of the 1990 Chief Joseph Days. Vickie Roundy of Joseph, and Nicole Jones of Imnaha will be her princesses.

April 15—A bright, hot sun rose in a clear sky, burning with a summer-like heat. Can this be April? After chores I hurriedly put the potato salad together, placed a ham in the oven, and drove 30 miles to attend an Easter cantata service at the Imnaha school, which suffices as a church until the church is finished.

New, green, shiny leaves on the cottonwoods. Little Sheep Creek running bank to bank with snow melt. The canyons "April lovely," but also in need of rain. Little girls, wearing frothy pastel dresses, looked like spring flowers as they played on the grassy playground. The singing cantata was very beautiful and the audience was so touched by the Easter story, it was hard to hold back the tears.

Back "on top" to change clothes, load the food, and head up to the top of Sheep Creek hill to a branding. Here son Ken was working his spring calves. A family affair, soon everyone from the littlest cowboy and cowgirl to the oldest was hanging onto a rope with a struggling calf at the other end. Daddies roped and held the calves while moms and older sons branded, vaccinated and marked the calves. By late afternoon 100 calves were worked and the kids were covered with dirt and still smiling!

Around 1 p.m. we had stopped for a picnic fit for a king. Roast turkey, ham, salads and cupcakes. The lofty Wallowas were all in view from the high rolling divide that separates the canyon from the valley. The children put on another egg hunt with the already worn-out eggs, and a great time was had by all. Who says big, corporate ranching is the thing of the future? Family-owned and run ranches are still the most efficient...and they still exist!

April 16—During these days of summer-like weather, it is hard to believe this is only the middle of April. Overnight daffodils burst into bloom, lasted but a few days, then withered in the heat. Great clouds of dust hover over the tractors in the fields and follow the cattle trucks rumbling along our back country roads. The grass has a good start and the valley appears green, but thirsts for rain, which is desperately needed to ensure growth, especially in our hills and canyons.

April 16—Another bright sunrise in a clear sky. Grass appears to be surviving on morning dew. Some of the native forbs growing on the high ridges wilt under the midday sun.

After a busy day, Doug and I attended an "IRS dinner" at the Joseph Civic Center. Proceeds benefit the "Poor" Joseph Melodrama, which will be staged in Joseph all during the summer to entertain tourists. Local people have been cast in various roles of this "hiss and boo" production. Joseph is regressing to the old-time western town with its reenactment of the Great Joseph Bank Robbery and now a melodrama. What next?

Members of the community appeared in their grubbies; nothing left after taxes! The menu featured Coney Island Special and chili. Prizes were given for the most appropriate attire. From the looks of them, several citizens didn't have much before taxes! Bale twine served as belts; shirts and jeans with holes worn in them, and barefoot! Our work clothes fit the occasion quite well.

April 17—After a hardy breakfast of mountain oysters, scrambled eggs and toast, I greeted this day, which would be a lulu! Chores finished, which always includes milking the cow, I made myself a sack lunch and tucked it, along with a bottle of water, into my saddle bags. Presently Mike McFetridge arrived with his horse and dog, and we were off across the hill to the west end of the ranch to corral a young bunch of fall calvers.

After Ben finished feeding he joined us on his horse, and we turned the cows out onto the road and headed them up toward Echo Canyon. Before Doug left for the potato cellar, he had given Ben a map he'd drawn to show where the cattle were to be driven. So armed with this "map," we started off with our cows, trailing them up into new country neither Ben nor I had ever been in. Thank goodness old-timer Mike was along, as he had rented pasture there years ago and was somewhat familiar with this vast, treeless grassland that lays east of our ranch.

Numerous ranchers have leased this range in the past. It contains good feed, but relies on sufficient moisture to grow the grass and fill the stockponds. If the ponds are dry, the grass can't be utilized. This high plateau, sometimes referred to as the end of the great Palouse Prairie, also includes the country known as the Three Lakes area. In the early days, homesteads dotted these hills.

As we rode along, Mike enlightened us as to who homesteaded each place. Mike also said that at one time vast herds of sheep grazed these grassy hills. The sheep were owned by Pete Beaudoin, a well-known early day rancher. Beaudoin's old home place lies north of ours and the old Beaudoin barn is still in use today, owned by the Don Houghs.

After leaving an old abandoned county road, we headed eastward. At last, I was finally able to see that mysterious country that lies beyond the eastern hills visible from our living room window; that high open divide separates prairie from canyon.

We drove the cows down and across a stream of water, which flows out of Kinney Lake, then veered northeast up another hill. The country seemed to go on forever; natural grass-land, stretching northward as far as we could see. It resembled our Salmon Creek range. To the southwest rose the Wallowas, their snow-covered peaks scraping the clear, blue sky. Tree-less, the country rolled onto the horizon.

Looking north we followed with our eyes the course of Pine Tree Gulch, and sure enough, like Mike had told us, there stood a pine tree. We topped the cows out onto a high ridge, then trailed them down to a pond. While the cattle watered up, Mike and Ben consulted as to where we were.

According to the "map" we were supposed to be traveling in an easterly direction toward the head of Hayden Creek. Mike assured us we were on the right track. So, over hill and dale, passing more ponds and climbing more ridges, we finally stumbled onto Hayden Creek running down a winding, deep gulch, or draw, where a well-defined trail followed the little creek's course.

Here the country took on a different look. We were suddenly in rocky canyon country and riding high on the breaks of the Imnaha. We pushed those tired cows down past blooming sarvis and gooseberry, rode under interesting rock formations and eventually came to a wire gate. Driving the cattle through and closing the gate, we looked again at the "map" feeling like Lewis and Clark.

Ben determined we were supposed to turn the cattle off the trail and head up a steep draw, which we did, and came to a dry pond bordered by aspen trees. Because there was no water there, we continued to push the tired cows uphill onto a long bench thick with bunch grass. We rested our horses while the cows grazed, and looked down upon the winding course of Little Sheep Creek far below where the Imnaha road follows the canyon.

We continued to urge the cattle around the steep canyonside, until we found a pond that contained water. Leaving the cows there we rode up yet another steep draw to a high, grassy ridgetop. It was by then 2 p.m.; time for lunch.

From our vantage point we could look eastward to the shining Seven Devils range in Idaho and southwest to our own Wallowas. Due south lay the other high grassy plateau known as the Divide. We rode over several ridges covered with prairie wildflowers, a sight I shall always hold dear in my heart. Riding toward home, we joked about having to find our way with a map and a bunch of cows, and even though we were tired, it would be a day to remember.

Having shipped potatoes, the rest of the crew was working the fall calves at the chutes when we rode by. Huge thunderheads formed over the mountains and we prayed for rain. By evening the clouds had melted away and there was no rain. I kept thinking about those stock ponds in that wide grassy country thirsting for moisture.

April 18—Another warm day, no morning frost. Milked and strained a gallon of house milk, and washed out the milk pail, a task that is becoming almost as familiar as brushing my teeth.

Busy day, typing out my column, running errands, writing for our writing project, and cooking. After chores were over for the evening and supper fixed, I drove to the Enterprise library to attend a meeting with the writer-in-residence of Lewis and Clark College and our writing group.

April 19—By mid-morning it was as hot as a summer day. After chores, I drove to a Zumwalt stock pond, where I was joined by several other CattleWomen and members of our local Stockgrowers as well as people representing the press, Oregon Department of Fish and Wildlife, Extension Service, and the Tree of Life Nursery.

We all pitched in and planted trees, built a fence to protect them from livestock and by late afternoon, had completed an "experimental plot" that we hope will provide habitat for songbirds, game birds and raptors.

Livestock will benefit as well because the trees shade the water, and it should be cooler and cleaner. Everyone involved in the project felt good about it.

In an era when so much emphasis is put on the environment, it seems to me action speaks louder than words. And it was gratifying to work alongside people from different walks of life who all care enough about the environment to do something about it.

April 20—Our long dry spell finally broke around midnight. A warm, gentle rain began to fall and continued this morning through a bright pink sunrise. The mist seemed to relax the dry, stressed grasses, allowing spring to resume.

Leaving the barn door open so I could enjoy a sudden spring rainbow, I milked my cow. What a picture! Daisy, the Guernsey cow, and her heifer calf encircled in the pastel-colored air. I wished for my camera. The rainbow quickly faded along with my hopes for a "rainbow cows" print.

Treated granddaughter Carrie to lunch today at "A Country Place on Pete's Pond," her birthday present. I also had the two younger grandchildren, who so love to feed the fish and watch the swans and ducks. A pair of swans showed off their babies (cygnets) for us. After eating our lunch on the glassed-in deck, I let the children feed the giant trout that swirl close to shore to practically eat out of their hands.

Home to put the little ones down for a nap and prepare a fruit and cheese tray for the opening reception of our annual Wallowa Valley Festival of Arts, which is this evening. After daddy picked up the children, I milked my cow and let the calves nurse, then Doug and I left for the Joseph Civic Center to attend the artists' reception.

A large crowd was already viewing the beautiful and interesting works of art, including bronzes, oil and watercolor paintings, blown glass, pine needle baskets, jewelry, wood sculpture and photography. Art Council members outdid themselves on the hors d'oeuvres, and there was sparkling punch and a wine-tasting. As if that weren't enough, there was live music.

The popular quick-draw drew lots of artists who completed a piece of work in only one hour, which was then sold at a silent auction. A lovely watercolor painted by Native American Anderson Benally topped the sale at $1,001.

April 21—Rain, wonderful rain. The mountains are wreathed in clouds, exactly how April should look. Sunny and Alice Hancock of Lakeview arrived this afternoon. Sunny, a well-known cowboy poet, will perform tonight as part of our Art Festival. We always enjoy having Sunny and Alice for guests, and we spent the remainder of the afternoon catching up.

As usual, Cloverleaf Hall was packed with people who had been looking forward all year to this performance. In addition to Sunny, the performers included Imnaha cowboy Sam Loftus; Dan and Carol Jarvis of Joseph; Jennifer Isley of Lakeview; Leon Flick of Plush; Fred Bornstedt of Enterprise; Scott McClaran of Imnaha; and Craig Nichols of Joseph.

It was quite a gathering of poets, and Sam Loftus had composed a poem to introduce each one. Local Stockgrowers president Van Van Blaricom recited a poem about "old hands," then introduced Harley Caudle of Lostine, Wallowa County's own "Old Hand," who won the contest at Haines on the 4th of July, 1988. Van said he'd written the poem one night by kerosene lantern light, when the power was off for a few days this past winter on his Prairie Creek ranch.

Cowboys and cowgirls whirled around the floor to the music of the McKenzie River Band. We four older cowhands and cowgals were home in bed before midnight, however.

April 22—Up early to chore, so we could all meet with more friends for breakfast at the Lil' Homestead in Joseph. What a treat. Over a country-style breakfast we laughed a lot over some good cow dog jokes interspersed with the sort of tall tales that just seem to erupt when this group gets together. We bade Sunny and Alice goodbye and headed back to the ranch.

Due to the continuing rain our valley is now a brilliant shade of green and many of the flowering trees are beginning to bloom. It is a beautiful time. This afternoon I picked up the four photos I'd entered in the art show.

Having watched this event grow over the years to its present prestigious status, I marvel again at the volunteer hours that go into pulling off this event. The eighth annual Arts Festival is now history. Art feeds the soul of man.

April 23—Still raining, the grass is fairly leapin' up. Four more loads of seed potatoes shipped out today. Worked most of the day at the typewriter, taking time out to bake a batch of hermit cookies using an old recipe that called for spices, honey, and lots of raisins and nuts. Yum!

As the clouds lifted periodically, we could see a new snowfall on the Wallowas. White snow above and green grass below, quite a contrast. All the willows sport shiny new leaves, and the red tulips have unfurled. Robins build nests in the apple trees and Canadian honkers are nesting along the creek.

A bright burst of sunlight pierced dark clouds this evening, bathing Prairie Creek in a golden light. It intensified the green fields and freshly tilled soil, a beautiful moment in time.

April 24—"Whiskers" on the mountain this morning. A cold prairie wind blows off the snowfields. Baked a gooseberry pie for son-in-law

Bill's pie-a-month.

The fertilizer "swamp buggy" bounces over our hay fields this morning. Spring fever has taken hold of the farmers. The days will never be long enough to get all the work done.

April 25—Thirty degrees and thick clouds over the mountains, the higher slopes frosted with new snow. April is the last month with "R" in it, so Doug dug the horseradish, which we will grind with white vinegar to use on roast and such.

Baked another gooseberry pie, this one for Doug, who reminded me HE likes gooseberry pie, too.

April 26—The two younger grandchildren were here most of the day. Mom riding again. It was so cold outside, we did inside things.

April 27—Out to chore in a cold rain/snow mixture. The valley continues to soak up the much-needed moisture.

Attended to a myriad of errands and chores all this day, while a pot of homemade vegetable/beef soup simmered on the wood cookstove. Baked a skillet of cornbread to go with the soup for supper.

April 28—Snowing on our green grass again, just a skift here, but upper Prairie Creek looks like a Christmas card. Spent all day in the kitchen cooking. Invited family for supper. The aroma of sourdough bread mingled with freshly baked apple pie. A pot roast cooked slowly in the wood stove oven as big, fat flakes of snow fell outside and began to turn our world white again.

We enjoyed the food and the company. It had been fun preparing the meal, which provided a way to pass a snowy Saturday. After supper I sloshed out through the snow to chore, leaving the grandchildren and my daughter to do the dishes.

April 29—Looked outside at daybreak to see a good six inches of snow on the ground, with the white stuff still coming down!

Apple blossom pink, red tulips, green grass, brown cows and white snow! April snow; soft, feathery flakes covering up springtime! But that's OK. A thirsty land accepts moisture in any form, for it brings the continuing assurance of a green spring.

Leafed-out willow limbs droop under the weight of wet, spring snow, and it is heaped on top of the picnic table and the fence posts look like ice-cream cones.

April 30—Twenty degrees with a heavy frost, but an incredible morning to look upon. Clear, washed skies, sunlight, brilliant, white snow fields on the mountains, equally brilliant, green prairie: frost melting rapidly under the warmth of the sun. Spent most of this day writing and catching up on household duties, because in the morning we start cows and spring calves to the hills.

May 1—Another beautiful morning; frosty, crisp, and cool. Up at daylight to chore. After catching and saddling my mare, I was soon helping drive our cows and calves out of the lower field and onto the road to their summer range. The long road stretched ahead into an equally long day.

At first my job was to ride ahead, shutting gates and blocking holes. Six wire gates later, plus chasing cows and calves out of one field where there was no gate, the herd was at last strung out along the Crow Creek road. When Steve rode ahead to get his lunch I rode back to help Ben push the tail-end calves, which always become foot sore about mid-way. A great deal of patience is required at this time.

Around noon we let the herd rest and ate our lunches. By late afternoon the calves were flagging, not to mention the cowboys and cowgirl, so we let them rest again. Finally that last calf trailed into the pasture. Doug appeared in the truck; we unsaddled, turned the horses in with the cattle at East Crow and headed back to the valley.

Meanwhile, back at the ranch (as they say). I learned that Startch became a grandma this morning. Her own first calf heifer gave birth to a beautiful, black baldy heifer calf, which I named May. Wearily I dragged myself out to chore, gathered the eggs and checked on little May, who was frisking around the pasture, feeling fresh as the first day of May. After treating his cowgirl to a steak at the Lil' Homestead in Joseph, Doug drove home and she was nearly asleep when she hit the pillow. Another day in the saddle tomorrow.

May 2—Cloudy, with a fine misty rain falling. Much warmer, great for the grass, and nice and cool for trailing cattle. Milked a gallon of house milk and let the calves nurse. Fixed breakfast, made lunches and soon we were heading out to East Crow.

The cows were scattered and most of the calves were lying down. The hills were so green in the morning cool, the pond was full and the little creek ran through the bottom of the field. I put on my long yellow slicker, caught and saddled my mare, and soon the three of us were bunching up the herd to head them out onto the road again.

It was a picturesque scene: those cattle flowing from several directions, up and over the green hills to form one bunch, a splash of yellow slicker, cowboys and cowgirl yelling to get the cows moving, the bawling calves, the smell of springtime and growing things in the misty green morning.

A chill wind sprang up by mid-morning and the temperature dropped as a fine rain began, soaking into the green hills. The herd traveled right along in the cool. Soon we were headed up Dorrance Gulch, the cows and calves strung out ahead for half-mile or so. Patches of pink phlox and yellow balsam root began to appear along our route.

Halfway up the hill I got on my horse and walked behind some of the tired little calves until we reached the top where we let the hen rest and the lead drift. We ate lunch there, shivering in a cold breeze that blew across the open Zumwalt range.

The road was muddy here and the little calves traveled easier as we resumed our way along Dry Salmon Creek, but they were soon sore-footed again as they tiptoed across some recent rock fill put on the road by the county road department.

When the cows and calves filed into the Deadman pasture, mammas put down their heads and began to graze and the babies laid down. It had been a long walk.

May 3—Awakened early by the phone which rings at all hours — potatoes and bulls! A clear, blue sky and a warm sun greeted this day. A Wallowa County springtime is nothing short of spectacular, and well worth the long winter wait.

After chores I relaxed by playing the piano for about half an hour, it worked wonders. Once again white billowy clouds form and sail over the green valley, and the morning is filled with birdsong—blackbirds, meadowlarks, killdeer, rails and hawks. All happy about this day.

While immersed in some serious housecleaning, I found it hard to keep from being distracted by the cloud shadows floating silently across the green hills: light green and dark green patterns, matching the clouds overhead.

Into Enterprise to pick up a granddaughter after school, who will be spending the night here. Carrie helped with the grocery shopping and cooking supper as we had invited two more grandchildren, two 16-year old grandsons, who brought along a friend.

May 4—Sun-up in a clear, blue sky, not a single cloud and the day promises to be unusually warm. Tended to a myriad of chores and household duties early, so some friends and I could spend the day hiking.

We had decided to walk over the hill east of us and check our cattle pastured in the Hayden Creek area. It turned out to be quite a long day.

James Nash, 3, makes his first ride in the mutton-riding event at the Joseph Junior Rodeo.

After walking the area thoroughly, checking on the cows, and returning, Scotty's pedometer registered 16 and three quarter miles!

We had sunburned noses, even under hats, from being out in that tree-less high divide all day. I must confess it was a bit difficult to walk out to the barn and chore, and harder to fry trout for supper, but I got no sympathy from my husband, who thinks hiking is a waste of time!

Memories of that "feeling of freedom" while tromping around those springtime hills made the effort worthwhile. It is called LIVING!

May 5—Sunup by 6:30 in a clear sky with the promise of another unseasonably hot day. Just setting breakfast on the table when I looked out the window to see some of our yearlings ambling down the road. Interruptions such as this are routine on a ranch.

Loosened up my hiking muscles, running them in the corral. Doug repaired the fence before eating his breakfast, which had been "on hold" in the oven. Milked the cow, cleaned eggs, delivered them, then attended another one of those fascinating auctions.

The morning warmed rapidly, it was hot, really, as a large crowd gathered to peruse the offerings that were piled all over the yard. There were several items I wanted, books mainly, but I wouldn't be able to stay until they were sold. The scene was colorful; the home, situated on the outskirts of small-town Joseph, faced green fields. Apple trees in bloom served as racks for old-fashioned jewelry, which hung sparkling and glittering from branches in the sunlight.

An interesting library of old, original edition books lined several bookcases; used household items; an organ; a beautiful rocking chair; and all the cluttered effects of a family's lifetime. The chanting auctioneer while friends and neighbors visited; another reason to attend an auction.

Memories must go along with each household item, to create even more stories in a different home. Many will end up in yard sales, passed from owner to owner, but that is the way of it. As is so often the case, the widow was moving to a small apartment and had to get rid of a lifetime's accumulation.

A large griddle that cooked many a hotcake for her family; lovingly embroidered pillow cases; faded patchwork quilts; dishes, fancy and plain; pots and pans; garden tools. "Things" accumulated over the years until there comes a time they aren't needed anymore. Sooner or later, it happens to all of us.

I left around noon, as this was also the day of the Joseph Junior Rodeo, and this grandma had eight grandchildren entered. They ranged in age from 3 to 16. So, armed with a jug of lemonade and a bag of hermit cookies and, of course, my camera, I was soon sitting in the stands surrounded by family.

Poised to get an action shot of the mutton riding event, I was really surprised when I saw my own 3-year-old grandson in the camera lens. No one told me he was going to ride a wild sheep! But ride he did, a grin spread across his little face, hat falling off, until he was dumped in the dirt, not the least upset. My baby!

Daddy wiped the dirt out of one eye and he was soon entered in the goat-tail tying and the dummy steer roping. Having watched the older ones perform last year, many of these little ones couldn't wait for their turn. Since this was pee wee day, the two Imnaha grandchildren were in many events that lasted into the afternoon. Mona rode a sheep and Buck ended up placing in roping and barrel racing.

Regardless if they won or lost, grandma was proud. And thankful no one was injured. No wonder it felt hot today; the high was 80 degrees!

May 6—Cloudy and cold, with a cold wind blowing! What a change from yesterday. A few hardy souls, relatives mostly, shivered and chattered under blankets in the rodeo grandstand from I until 6 today, as the older grandchildren had their turn.

Chelsie, Carrie, Rowdy, Chad and Shawn did their thing. Some rode steers, while others galloped the length of the arena, took a rope from their partner, which was attached to a cowhide, dallied around the saddle horn, and took off for the finish line on a dead run...with the partner riding on the cowhide, eating dust! The two 16-year-olds won the buckles in that exciting event.

It was hard trying to keep up with them all. I drove home, still shivering from the cold. Milked my cow, warmed up supper and took a hot bath before I finally warmed up.

May 7—Spring snow again! Nearly obscuring the apple blossoms; occasional blades of green grass protrude above the soft white stuff this morning. It is 27 degrees! A good thing I didn't set out the tomato plants.

Melting by mid-morning and partly sunny, but still cold. Snowed again this afternoon. Doug brought me another calf. Now I'll have three calves on Startch, and won't have to milk her twice a day. Hoo-rah!

Our weaned fall calves have been trucked to a rented pasture in Wallowa, in the lower valley. Cows, along with their spring calves, have been trailed to the hills; the only cattle left here on the main ranch are a few young bulls, some purebreds that will be AI'd, and my milk cow herd.

Ben's glad. It's been a long winter of feeding cattle.

May 8—Twenty-six degrees, cloudy and cool. Sunday's fierce wind storm dried up the mud puddles. The new calf nursed lustily this morning. Spent most of this day writing my column.

May 9—Beautiful clear day, heavy frost, 20 degrees, brilliant sunshine. Doug off to Baker to see about buying a used truck. All set to begin working on several manuscripts for our local encyclopedia, but the nice day beckoned.

Soon two friends joined me and we were driving on top of the Divide, which lies southeast of our ranch. We ate our lunches on the Cat's Back and gazed down toward Big Sheep and Coyote canyons. Later we glimpsed mountain bluebirds, coyotes, and several deer. The grass is looking good everywhere this spring and the dirt road was passable due to Sunday's wind storm.

Wildflowers fluttered in the breeze. The views of the Seven Devil Mountains in Idaho and the Wallowas were incredible from that high divide. It was a golden balsamroot, blue sky, white cloud day.

Returning home in time to chore, I grabbed a quick bite to eat on the way to pick up Grace, stopped by the Flower Shop to pick up a lovely pink begonia Mother's Day remembrance from the "Wyoming kids," and actually made it to the Enterprise library where we met with our writing group. What a day!

May 10—Up and at 'em. Chores, breakfast, housework, then to Enterprise and up on the hill to the cemetery to attend a graveside service of one of Doug's relatives. It was a perfectly lovely morning.

The Wallowas rising above green Alder Slope lent a peacefulness to the otherwise sad occasion. Colorful flowers, touching words, a quiet time for introspection as life closes in on all of us. Times like this we realize anew just how precious each day is. How short our time here.

Doug was late, having hauled a load of bulls to the vet to be semen tested. After grocery shopping I attended our monthly CattleWomen's meeting at the Cloud 9 Bakery. Home to unload the groceries, gather eggs, let the calves nurse the cow, and leave by 5:30 to attend the Imnaha school program, held along with the annual Cow Chip lottery. A 30-mile drive.

The cow, Betsy, that used to be my son Ken's family cow, named Rosie, was contentedly grazing in a fenced-in enclosure on the school lawn. Everyone was anxiously waiting for her to do "her thing," which was to deposit her "chip," hopefully on their lucky square. Only she wasn't. The program began on schedule inside the school house.

Just after it commenced, school marm Char Williams announced, "The cow went," whereupon all the children dashed outside. A winner was determined and money left over was donated to a memorial scholarship.

After everyone settled back down again we enjoyed watching the 1st through 8th grades of the two-room school present a slice of Americana like you'll never see anywhere. Like 95-year-old A.L. Duckett, who sat in the front row, said: "Entertainment like this couldn't be bought."

The community and proud relatives cheered each child's performance. A play entitled "Pecos Bill," adapted from the book of the same name, was wonderfully cast. Stage props and costumes were terrifically creative. And Pecos Bill lived again!

May 11—Up early to fix breakfast, milk the cow, make lunches, and plant my tomato plants, before Mike McFetridge, Ben, Doug and I head to the hills to sort cattle. While Doug puts out salt, Ben, Mike and I ride our horses up to the pasture known as Deadman, to gather in the bunch of cows and calves we trailed out last week.

From a fold in the hills two golden eagles and a mess of ravens fly off at our approach. Suspecting something has died, we ride over to investigate and discover the carcass of a calf. The head and the rib cage, nearly picked clean, were all that remained. As Ben removed the ear tag to identify the calf, our horses snorted and shied away from the carcass.

At this point the weather was pleasant, with a few clouds floating around. A beautiful day in the hills. The native bunch grass was sprinkled with lupine, yarrow, balsam root, phlox and an occasional blue haze of camas that grew in the soggy, boggy areas. Great, silent cloud shadows drifted over the Zumwalt hills.

As we rode, huge clouds with purple bellies began to build over us and a cool breeze began to blow. While Mike checked the far corner of the pasture, I gathered in several drys, moving them toward those Ben was bunching together in the bottom. One of the calvy cows looked as if she could calve most any minute!

All in one bunch, we drove the herd under that vast big sky, across those green grassy hills, it created a cowman's dream. This is what it's all about, and makes up for the long winter of cold and mud. Finally we drove the cattle through a wire gate and held them in a corner of a small holding pasture where the sorting would take place.

May 12—Cloudy and cold, the mountains are wrapped in low clouds. While delivering eggs in Joseph this morning, I stopped to pick up a bleeding heart plant that a kindly lady had started for me. This thoughtful woman remembered me saying I wanted one once. I brought the plant home and transplanted it by the front door. Bleeding hearts conjure up visions of old-fashioned gardens, and the blooms add a special touch to fresh-cut bouquets.

Doug and Ben branded the few calves left here on the ranch this morning, including my milk cow's calves. Doug loaned our cattle truck to a local group hauling a load of newspapers to the recycling center in La Grande.

This evening I joined a daughter and a granddaughter at the local theater where we watched the movie "Driving Miss Daisy." Amid the trash being produced in Hollywood these days, it is refreshing to see a movie such as this. A simple theme and truly great acting. We need more like them.

May 13—After chores and because it was Mother's Day, Doug took me to breakfast at Kohlhepp's Kitchen in Joseph. Later we ran into Max and Millie, who were also eating out this morning.

One thing led to another, and on the spur of the moment we agreed to meet later and go mushrooming. So even though the day was cool and threatening rain, we took off for the nearby woods. The four of us had a great time tromping around, enjoying the spring rain smell of the forests and even finding a few morels.

"Look, here's one, and there's another!" It was like being a child again hunting Easter eggs. Shafts of occasional sunlight streamed through evergreen and tamarack before the dark woods' coolness returned. Once we heard a ruffed grouse drum on a log, and several hawks screeched in the sky above.

The forest floor was carpeted with yellow and lavender violets. The lovely orchid-like pink calypso (lady slipper) appeared in mossy places. The ground was damp from recent snows, and imprints of many deer and elk tracks laced the game trails. After all that walking, our Mother's Day breakfast began to wear off and we were hungry. That's when Millie produced a tailgate picnic, which tasted so good out there in that fresh air. What a wonderful way to spend Mother's Day.

Back home to chore, soak the morels in salt water, answer phone calls from our children, then meet Max and Millie at the Lil' Homestead for supper. We gals really got treated royally today. It was raining and cold when we returned to Prairie Creek.

May 14—Slept in until 6:30 because I heard rain in the night and knew we wouldn't be branding today on Salmon Creek. Not only had it rained, but a new skift of snow lay on the ground. A good day to concentrate on my writing projects.

Mud puddles bordered in white, melting snow, in odd shapes, hang suspended from the barn's tin roof. So far it promises to be a wonderful feed year. The growing grasses have turned a brilliant shade of green. Where only yesterday we walked in woods hunting morel mushrooms, there is this morning a blanket of spring snow. Underneath lie the yellow and lavender woods violet and the delicate, pink calypso; while the morel waits for another warm spell to poke through the forest floor.

Drifting past my kitchen window, blown in the wind, apple blossom is hard to distinguish from snowflake! Pink and white blossoms, faded now, scatter among raspberry canes and snow flakes melt on contact with green grass blades.

Yesterday was Mother's Day, and as the matriarch of seven children, not to mention a growing number of grandchildren, the day seems to grow more significant each year. As always my heart is warmed anew by the fact that all of them remembered mom in their own, special way.

Colorful azaleas, begonias, lilacs and peonies were delivered. Lovely cards bearing personal sentiments arrived in the mailbox, one little one thrust a loving message scribbled on paper into my hand, and then there were phone calls from a son and little ones: "Happy Mother's Day, grandma." Just about the sweetest words there are!

May 15—Rained again last night and snowed a bit too, by the looks of things. Had the two youngest grandchildren today. We made "cow" cookies with ceramic molds, using sugar cookie dough. Flour all over the kitchen and a little dough here and there. The children loved it, and the cookies turned out great.

It hailed during a brief thunder storm, covering our lawn with little balls of ice. I went out to chore after the children were gone, and found a small black-baldy bull calf bawling hungrily in the box stall. Ben had hauled the half-starved calf in from the hills. Its mother had dried up due to an infection. Startch now has four calves on her!

A lovely, mild evening. Hopefully we can brand tomorrow.

May 16—Up early to begin this incredible day. After chores and getting ready to go, including loading lunches and branding supplies into the pickups, we left. Scotty wanted to get in on the action again this year so she rode with me.

It was a gorgeous morning in the hills, partial sunshine and cloud cover. Much warmer than the past few days have been. Dorrance grade was so muddy I had to put the pickup in four-wheel-drive. Soon Ben, Steve and I were riding out of the corrals to gather in the cows and calves. The recent coolness and moisture preserved the wildflowers, which are now in the lupine/balsam root stage of blue and gold.

More than 100 calves later we finished the branding and the men ran the cows through to be treated for lice. That's when it happened—Too many cows crowded into a small holding pen came crashing through! One whole section of the corral was reduced to splinters in about five seconds. It began to rain about that time, as we all pitched in to rebuild the thing.

We gals pulled out nails, straightened them, and held boards while they were nailed back up. Scotty even helped dig a deep hole to place a railroad tie. An hour later the job was finished and then all those cows had to be run through! It was 7 p.m. when we mounted our horses and drove the cows and calves out on the road; then, while Ben put the horses away, Scotty and I, on foot, drove the herd to the Johnson pasture.

A few miles down the road later, we were all pretty tired when the last calf passed through the gate, but the day hadn't ended yet. As we drove the long miles home, a fuchsia-colored sunset backgrounded the vast Zumwalt hill country.

By the time I dealt with Startch at the barn, it had been a 16-hour day!

May 17—After arising early on this beautiful spring morning, I did chores, then returned to the kitchen to partake of mountain oysters and scrambled eggs prepared by my husband. Thus fortified we were soon on our way to the hills to finish the branding. Steve decided to stay in the valley and begin working up the potato field for planting. Scotty, still looking tired but a good sport, showed up for another day and rode out with me again.

We arrived at Salmon Creek just as Ben and Doug were catching the horses. The distant Wallowas were quite a sight from those high, rolling hills, and the bunch grass stirred in the breeze like waves in an ocean of grass.

Ben and I were driving a bunch of cows and calves toward the gate when suddenly a coyote ran between us. He then turned and sat on his haunches as he looked us over before trotting out of sight over the next hill.

The cattle were corraled, separated, and thus began another long day. However, things went much more smoothly today and the corral held. By 4:30 we were finished. We mounted our horses, drove the cattle up to Deadman, rode back down to the corrals, unsaddled and turned the horses loose. How they love it out there in those hills. Only trouble is we can't leave them. They'd get so fat we couldn't cinch them up.

Back home to the chores, always the chores, twice a day. The newest orphan calf is doing well and glad to have milk and a mama. After Doug treated us to dinner at the Lil' Homestead restaurant in Joseph, I hit the hay at 8:30.

May 18—Slept in until 6:30. What luxury. Another beautiful morning. Doug and Ben to the hills to turn bulls with cows. Cooked breakfast, did my outside chores, hung out three loads of wash, cleaned eight dozen eggs and, because I was the only one left on the ranch, I dealt with bull buyers.

Ended up helping drive our bulls into a corral to be sorted and then driving them back to the pasture, on foot! Visions of resting up today faded with each passing hour. Made lists, delivered eggs in Joseph, then to Enterprise to shop for groceries and cross errands off the lists.

The numerous varieties of flowering peach, plum and crab apple trees scattered throughout the country are especially lovely this spring. Our meal tonight originated from field and forest: elk hamburger in a meatloaf and morel mushrooms.

May 19—Cloudy, cold, warming as the day progressed. Had the two younger grandchildren most of the day. They "helped" grandma prepare a fresh strawberry pie. Doug's sister, Betty, from Clarkston, Washington, along with a daughter and two granddaughters, visited this morning. My house was a shambles, but we visited out in the yard, which was pleasant.

Large thunderheads began to build over the valley and by afternoon we had some showers. During this time daughter Jackie showed up with bowls of rising sourdough bread dough under her arms. Could she use my oven? Hers was on the blink. Soon, every bread pan in the house held bread that was baking or rising. Two more grandchildren ran around, in and out of the house.

Doug returned, rested a bit, then roto-tilled my garden. We sampled the fresh bread and eventually everyone left, taking children with them, and by evening Doug and I ate a roast chicken dinner topped off by strawberry pie.

May 21—The month of May marches on... Cloudy, drippy, raining, yet so warm we leave windows and doors open. Whole wheat hotcakes and eggs for breakfast. The wet weather is slowing preparation of the potato fields for planting. Ben and Doug ear-tagging the fall replacement heifers.

Turned in several manuscripts to the library for our writing project this afternoon. And so goes Janie's Journal. Are you sure this isn't becoming boring?

May 22—A warm Prairie Creek wind ripples through the grasses and echoes around the buildings in a lonely, moaning sort of way. Huge May clouds boil up over the mountains, threatening more rain.

Native grasses are luxuriant, cattle have been turned out on summer range, calves branded, fences repaired... my garden is roto-tilled, waiting to be planted. The lawn has been mowed... several times. June waits in the wings of a busy summer. What kind of summer will it be?

The last load of seed potatoes was shipped from our cellars this morning, and the rented ground is worked and ready to plant our potato seed tomorrow. While the planting crew works in the field, cowboys and cowgirl will start the three-day drive to bring the fall calving bunch of cows in from the hills, where they will be turned into the high moraine pastures to utilize the lush feed there all summer. These cows will begin dropping their calves in August.

May 28—A wonderful, warm, soaking rain penetrates the already, moist earth. What a blessing to the country! Our potato crew finished planting the tuber-unit russets, having worked in the field until late Saturday evening.

Sunday evening, just as the rain commenced, I began to plant my garden. A row of peas later, and I was rained out. My milk cow was dripping wet and full of lush, green grass when I let her into the barn this morning. Wallowa County's livestock is in good shape this spring, what with such an abundance of grass.

On this Memorial Day, in all the many cemeteries scattered about the county, people will place flowers on graves of their loved ones. These bouquets should stay fresh this year, due to the coolness brought about by the rain.

Wallowa County's cemeteries hold the hidden secret of its wonderful history, much of which ended with the death of many an early settler. Some of these cemeteries are very picturesque. Prairie Creek cemetery, for instance, is on a knoll under the east moraine of Wallowa Lake, seemingly dwarfed by the mountain known as Chief Joseph. Below the clustered, fenced-in headstones sprawls the prairie itself, a colorful patchwork of farmland and pastures.

This is the place known as Prairie Creek, which is divided into areas: upper, lower and middle. Prairie Creek, in addition to being a cemetery, was also known as a school, which used to sit on upper Prairie Creek. Then of course there is the creek. As the mountains empty themselves of winter, as they are doing now, Prairie Creek tumbles full of snowmelt. As all the little drainages swell it, along with run-off irrigation water from Wallowa Lake, it becomes a more impressive stream by the time it enters the city limits of Enterprise and becomes the Wallowa River.

How did I get from cemeteries to rivers? Easy, they are both favorite subjects. Wallowa County's first permanent white settler, William Mc-Cormack, is buried in the Alder Slope pioneer cemetery, where his and other early settlers' gravestones repose under the protection of Ruby Peak. The rich, black loam soil here drew some of the first settlers to the county in the 1870s. The town of Alder, at one time, was bigger than Enterprise.

Many other lovely, old pioneer cemeteries dot the back country, like the one tucked away at Promise, where at this time the lilacs, gone wild, bloom in purple profusion. There is the Bramlet cemetery in the lower valley, and the Flora cemetery, where wildflowers lift their colorful heads in and among the headstones. High on a hill above the county seat lies the Enterprise Cemetery, and others with haunting names like Lost

Prairie, Eden, Paradise. The narcissus bloom among the graves at the Imnaha pioneer cemetery at the bridge.

Then there are all those lonely graves of two or three family members, or even just one soul. Some have been fenced-in by descendants, and they are scattered all over the hills and canyons. Some are marked, others not. Cattle, deer and elk graze around them, wildflowers bloom upon them in the spring, and deep snow covers them in winter.

Those who have made their mark on Wallowa County history are remembered today. I think of many old friends who have passed on. Somehow their spirit lingers, perhaps in a remembered saying, or a lovingly hand-carved boot jack, or a photograph, or just a special time recalled in memory.

I also remember my father's grave in the pastoral Manzanita pioneer cemetery in Placer County, California; the quiet oak-shaded cemetery at Latrobe, where many of my pioneer ancestors are buried; the hilltop in El Dorado County where my grandparents and great-grandparents are buried, among the lonely hills they helped settle, now consumed by the creeping cancer of Sacramento's urban sprawl.

It is a melancholy day. The rain, the grayness, the remembering... but yesterday was different. We had a family picnic at Imnaha and, although skies were cloudy, the day was warm and pleasant and we ate outside amid incredibly green canyons and rimrocks, Little Sheep Creek roaring past us, full of snowmelt and trout.

The grandchildren caught salmon flies and used them for bait to catch wriggling rainbow, which they proudly held up for grandma to see. The "herd" of happy children took turns flinging themselves out over the creek on a tire swing, suspended from a tall poplar along the bank. Such wild, free abandon of youth, just let out of school!

The summer stretches ahead and being a canyon kid is pretty wonderful. We gorged ourselves on fried chicken, potato casserole, lasagne, ham, salads, hand-cranked ice cream, homemade cinnamon rolls and strawberry pie.

June 5—Tucker's Mare, the snow-shape of a horse, has been covered by successive snowfalls these past weeks but is beginning to reappear. The first sunshine to stay around for a while this morning. However short-lived it may be, as thunderheads continue to build over the mountains, we welcome it.

Yesterday was mostly cloudy and cool, but nice enough to accomplish some long-delayed yard work. I mowed the lawn by stages. It seems the older I become, the longer this job takes, or maybe it's because we now have one of those fancy new mowers you must empty of grass clippings every so often. The bag is heavy and I was having to empty the thing every two minutes. Because our lawn resembled a hay field, perhaps a swather would have been more practical!

Our potato crews are now working from dawn til dark planting 120 acres of seed potatoes. While Doug and his crew plant spuds I concentrate on my vegetable garden and the yard. Last evening I planted the last row in the garden; a good feeling. It has been so rainy and wet this past week, nothing could be planted; still we don't complain. Beautiful springs are the result of rain, and what a springtime we are having.

June is bustin' out all over. All over the Prairie and the hills, over the canyons and valleys. Only the high alpine regions remain locked in winter, and the high mountain lakes still frozen over. School is out for my grandchildren and they are rarin' to go on promised camping trips. So is grandma.

It was a chilly 33 degrees this morning, barely above freezing my tomato plants and geraniums, but that's just part of gardening in our high mountain valley. Best accept it and not fret. Mother Nature knows best.

Only because I spent this entire morning outside, can I now sit down inside at the typewriter and concentrate on my column. Having exhausted myself physically, I am much more mentally alert to face the task. I enjoyed transplanting blue Lobelia in granite ware pots, weeding raspberries, hoeing around the tomatoes, and planting nasturtiums.

Just simply being out in this lovely morning was a real pleasure, especially when one can glance up any-time and see those glorious mountains.

June 13—Above the chirpings of a pair of parent robins carrying worms to their young, above the sound of songbirds in the ancient willows, I hear the faint whine of machinery that is carrying the cut potato seed over a conveyor and up into a waiting truck. Through the open screen door I can also hear our horses blowing through their noses as horses often do. Then there is the sound of a tractor and loader bucket dumping cull seed into a truck.

There is very little traffic along our road these quiet June mornings; maybe an occasional rancher rumbling past in a truck, his saddle horse in the back. Mostly, though, it is just our potato crews driving to the fields with trucks loaded with cut potato seed and returning with empty trucks to the cellar here to be reloaded. Out in the fields, about five miles distant, a tractor pulls the potato planter slowly up and down the rows.

They are well into the second field now and, if the weather holds, probably will finish by the weekend. Hough's black cattle graze contentedly across the road to the east of our ranch, among incredibly green pastures. All of Wallowa County is incredibly green because of the continuing showery weather pattern.

June is like life: sunshine, shadow, sunshine, shadow. Among the rolling open hills late spring varieties of wildflowers are having their turn at blooming. One of the showiest is the hot pink wild geranium.

Resident wild geese and ducks have long since hatched off their young amid a most wonderful local habitat, what with all the grass and such an abundance of full ponds and creeks. My garden is up. Well, the radishes, onions, lettuces, peas and spinach are. The squash, corn and beans seem to be waiting for mornings warmer than 37 degrees.

The bleeding heart plant by the front door is growing well, as is the sky blue flax, which is also a gift from a friend. The colorful pansies love our coolish spring, as does the bright orange Oriental poppy. My tomato plants are in a holding pattern. I cover them each night, which protects them, but they want warmth!

Strawberry, raspberry and gooseberry flourish, and rhubarb is enjoying one of the best springs in a long while. I have been using this succulent red pie plant in cakes as well as pies.

The milk cow Startch continues to produce enough milk for her assortment of calves and our house as well. Various grandchildren have been teaching one of her little orphans to lead, and Buck has named him Pecos. He is becoming a regular pet, having been mauled and hauled around the lawn these past weeks.

June 23—The longest day of the year has come and gone. And the first day summer was *really* summer. Our thermometer recorded 00 degrees, which is pretty warm for this high mountain valley. There is a different feel to the air now. The nights are mild and things are really beginning to grow. Our summers are akin to the short Alaskan summer, where long daylight causes vegetables to grow to gigantic proportions even though the growing season is short.

Given a wet spring like we've had this year, and now the warmth, the county should have a record-breaking hay crop. Our meadow hay was nearly shoulder high before Doug laid it down today with the swather. The freshly mown hay always looks so pretty out my kitchen window as it lays in fallen rows marching toward the mountains. And the smell! That, mingled with clover blossom scent on a dew-spangled June morning, is what my grandchildren would describe as "the ultimate!"

Our neighbor, Willie Locke, already has his hay baled in those soft, pretty, round bales. The shadows they cast in the evening and morning against the green field create a beautiful scene. Wallowa County ranchers, who are also farmers, are frantically busy now. Even though the days have lengthened, they are never long enough. These tired, sunburned men can be seen in their fields at dawn with a shovel, flood irrigating their fields, and again as the last light of day fades they are still "chasing water." During the day they are busy with other ranch work.

Sometimes I think it is a sort of relaxation for them before, and after, a hot day of work to be out in their quiet, lovely fields.

And then there are the pipe changers, children mostly, although every year it becomes more and more difficult to find youngsters who are willing to commit themselves to this task. So there are women, and men, doing that also.

The ranch wife doesn't see much of her husband these busy days, and communication is limited. They do appear at meal times because, like the tractors they drive and the horses they ride, they need fuel. Because the daylight hours are long, they get very little rest. They make hay while the sun shines.

Here on our ranch there are so many directions to go of a morning: irrigating, ag bagging, potato fields, cattle, haying. Because we have cattle scattered around on several ranges, it makes a full-time job for Ben to move, salt, check, fix fence and retrieve wandering cows that have gotten into the neighbor's herd, or vice versa.

Just yesterday we did some back-riding to pick up 16 head of fall calvers that were missed on Saturday. Eighty-three-year-old Mike McFetridge, one of the oldest working cowhands in the U.S., went along to help. Mike, who is still one of the best hands I know, is entered in the "Old Hand" contest at Haines this year. Mike is in his element when he is riding some high grassy divide, pushing a bunch of cows, and he sure looks at home in the saddle.

I always know when it is haying season. There is a constant banging away at something in the shop. Used farm equipment never runs smoothly, and new implements don't either. Haying time is synonymous with repairing. Parts time. Daily talks with the parts man at the local co-op. "Do you have a whatchamacallit for the doohickey?"

Every day is an experience in living. Each one a challenge. The secret to survival: take one day at a time, capitalize on what the day has to offer, make the best of it.

My tomato plants have taken off, After a slow start, the garden is flourishing, along with the weeds. I did manage to weed the whole thing the other morning. But already the new crop is appearing. The lawn could be mowed every three days. June is fast disappearing and July looms.

Already we are getting the usual summer phone calls. "Hi. Remember us? We haven't seen you in 17 years. Just thought we'd come by for a visit, as we happen to be in the area."

"Sure," we'd say, "we'd love to see you."

My husband is haying. Twenty pounds of cherries need pitting for the freezer, this column must get in the mailbox by noon, and those weeds just keep growing in the garden. But one thing about company: it makes us feel pretty lucky as we stop to look at our lifestyle as seen through a visitor's eyes.

Plus, we *need* to stop and rest and look at *our* world once in a while.

In the midst of this workaholic schedule there aren't too many free days to escape the merry-go-round. So out of sheer desperation, I create one. Such a day was last Sunday.

I had heard that some of our backcountry trails were opening up. I could envision water tumbling down from rapidly melting snow. Roaring white falls, high mountain meadows. The yen to be one of the first in the high country after a long winter was too much to resist. Besides, two grandsons were champing the bit.

Soon we were off, lunches in our daypacks, leaving the trailhead. Aneroid Lake, read the sign, 6 miles. All uphill! The day was beginning to warm, but the trail was mostly in shade, winding in and out of ferny, wet places, and always in our ears the roar of falls and rushing water. We would follow the East Fork of the Wallowa River to its headwaters.

How wonderful it felt to climb higher: the solitude, the air, the view of Wallowa Lake below, the woodsy smell, the pale green aspen leaves rustling in the breeze. And such waterfalls, white flashing and roaring falls at every bend or seen through the trees. Pink lady slippers appeared alongside the trail, along with other wildflowers like the woods violets. As the trail crossed under a large rock slide a Pika (rock rabbit) scolded us.

We walked through high alpine meadows covered with a blue mist of forget-me-nots, and lush new grasses. Birdsong. Everything here was happy! Noon came and went. The boys had gone ahead. Grandma walking slowly, savoring the mountain springtime, listening, smelling, seeing. Water running everywhere, trickling down from snowy peaks, flooding meadows, the sound of water running, in the "land of Winding Waters."

Clouds formed and moved swiftly overhead. The air was cool. The streams ran pure, cold, unpolluted and unbelievably clear. There were no tourists and no mosquitoes, both of which would take over in a matter of days. The boys, having made it to Roger Lake and thinking it was Aneroid, had stayed there. So by the time I reached them and finally made it to Aneroid, it was 2:30 and time for me to eat lunch.

The last mile in we trudged through deep snow on the trail. Huge snow banks hung out over the lake and dripped into the water. The lake was blue-green and full, snowmelt flowing in a swift stream from the high ramparts under Tenderfoot Pass and emptying into the lake. We glimpsed high waterfalls falling down and disappearing into snow, then reappearing below.

The scenery was awesome, magnificent. We were the only inhabitants, and what appeared to be some of the first visitors this spring, although we found horse tracks in the snow. There at 7,500 feet the pussy willows were just coming out and the buttercups bloomed in the meadow.

Lots of history here, like old Silvertip's cabin, which still stands. But that is a story in itself, and there are at least three versions. All interesting.

The lake itself was once called Anna Royal Lake, because the first white woman to visit it was named Anna Royal. A man by the name of Hoffman Phillips named it Aneroid in 1898.

July 10—Doug and I returned from a 10-day vacation that took us first to Thermopolis, Wyoming, and home by way of Auburn, California. In Wyoming we visited a daughter and her family, and in California we helped celebrate my mother's 80th birthday. The trip was long and mostly hot, but we have many wonderful memories that are stories in themselves, but that will have to wait.

Upon returning to the ranch at Prairie Creek, where record-breaking heat was scorching the garden, flowers and lawn, not to mention 150 acres of seed potatoes, we were at once immersed in the rhythm of ranch life. Doug climbed almost immediately onto the tractor and baled hay until midnight.

It was good to be home, work and all. As on previous travels about the country, not one place appealed to us more than Wallowa County. How lucky we are. Ben, aided by Jim, Steve and Charley, had carried on admirably. Hay had been cut, raked, baled and stacked; more hay laid down, and irrigating continued around the clock. The seed potatoes were growing like mad.

What would we do without capable hired men? The very existence of all forms of agriculture depends on these unsung heroes of the land. Ours are exceptional. Ben has worked on our ranch a long time. He knows what must be done and he does it.

There are halls of fame for cowboys, but we need one for the hired man. The faithful hired man who more often than not never realizes the dream of one day owning a place of his own is responsible for the success of many an operation. He is a fence builder, cowboy, mechanic, irrigator, farmer, jack-of-all-trades fellow who keeps a ranch going. And nowadays these guys are few and far between.

During our absence, 20-year-old granddaughter Tamara kept my garden alive, watered the flowers and newly planted maple tree in the yard, gathered eggs, watered and fed chickens, collected mail, and managed to work at two jobs besides. Pretty neat gal!

It is still hard to believe we managed to leave for that long, especially in the middle of haying, but leave we did, and returned to find our Wallowa summer busy and in full progress.

July 11—It is 95 today. Records are breaking all over the Northwest for this time of year. Mercifully, nights cool off on Prairie Creek. All over the valley it is haying time. Such frantic activity in spite of, and because of, the heat. No sooner does this heaviest hay crop in years fall to the mower than it is dry enough to bale. Due to such a heavy crop, breakdowns are frequent and delays common. Sweat-soaked shirts cling to backs of men and boys who wearily trudge into ranch kitchens, fuel themselves, and rest briefly before returning to the hot fields.

A sight many tourists never see reposes in these hay fields: a peaceful, pastoral scene of hay in different forms of storage for the winter. On Prairie Creek we have them all: Hank Bird's long, loose stacks; Willie Locke's soft, round bales; our conventional bales; up the road, those large, square bales; across the road, Don Hough's "bread loaf" loose stacks cast shadows in the early morning and late evening. Haying is an art, performed by the men of the land. Wallowa County's livestock will eat well this winter!

Stooping to pull weeds for 2-and-a-half hours in my vegetable garden until darkness forced me to quit last evening, my vacationed muscles are protesting. But my mind is more at ease, because now I can see my vegetables: row of corn, carrots' ferny tops, beautiful red-veined beet tops, swiss chard, onions, beans, potatoes, sunflowers; rows curving in a graceful sort of way.

My young grandchildren will be proud. All that we planted and replanted came up, grew, and thrives, owing to warm nights and days. Already lettuce is ready for the table, as are onions, radishes, swiss chard, along with the first tiny beets, cooked with their tops.

By 9:30 this morning I was attending a Fishtrap workshop on oral history! Workshops had been going all week, but because we were gone, I'd been unable to participate. The workshops were held at the Joseph Elementary School. My historian/writer/friend Grace Bartlett was there.

It was most interesting and very enlightening to find out what should be done to correctly compile oral histories. The way Grace and I have recorded local history paled in comparison. Nevertheless, there may come a time in my life when I can concentrate on such things, and the procedures learned at the workshop will be invaluable.

The workshop was taught by a most competent woman from Washington State University, Laurie Mercier, who has worked under Sue Armitage, who is doing marvelous things with histories of pioneer and other famous and not-so-famous women.

At noon I rushed home to feed the haying and irrigating crews, and then to Enterprise to stock up on groceries and spend precious little time with two younger grandchildren, who missed grandma so much. While their mom shopped, we had a milkshake and caught up on their two- and four-year-old worlds. We communicate, these two and I, in a special way understood universally by grandmothers.

Then it was home to leave supper on the table for Doug and make it to our photo club meeting, which was brief so some of us could be at the Methodist camp at Wallowa Lake by 8 p.m. to watch the movie "Heartland," which was being shown as part of Fishtrap. It was hot and, as always, I was feeling more than a little guilty about leaving my husband baling in the field and couldn't see the film.

Elinore Pruitt Stewart wrote a book, *Letters of a Woman Homesteader*, Houghton Mifflin, wherein are presented the true to life letters of a woman homesteader in Burnt Fork, Wyoming, in 1909. Stewart's book provided the basis for the film "Heartland." The film had been aired on public TV, but I missed it.

Although the story takes place in 1909, I was surprised by the resemblance to my own life in Eastern Oregon today. We need more films like this that portray ranching as it really is. Sad to say, the film, produced in part by grants and contributions, is still being paid for. The cost of production was the better part of $1 million and no one is making money from it.

This true to life film shatters the Zane Grey image of the West and comes as close to the real West of today as it did in 1909. The actors, local people from around a small town in Montana, are real. The calf being born is real, as is the baby born around the Judith Basin country at the time the film was shot. The film crew and actors slept in their makeup and clothes to be ready when a calf would be born in the barn.

Annick Smith answered questions about the filming that were very interesting to the audience of Fishtrap.

In the film the woman milks a cow, tends her garden, chickens, cooks for her man, cares for her little girl, plows, washes clothes in wash tubs and wrings them out with a portable wringer, bakes bread on a Monarch wood range...and you are there, in a cabin that is not built by Hollywood but is actually an authentic log house.

The photography is superb, the cast great, and the script real. There are branding scenes and butchering hog scenes that are authentic, performed by actors who know what it is all about. Heartland touched my heart, as it will those who live next to the land. Meeting and listening to producer Annick Smith was a treat of a lifetime and introduced me to another creative art form, filmmaking. If only I had a million dollars!

July 12—Lovely, mountain morning. A thunderstorm has refreshed the land and brought cooler temperatures. Mowed the lawn and weeded the flower beds. What a joy my wildflower patch is. I started to weed it and then found I was pulling up some little wildings, so I simply left it alone.

Golden California poppies bloom among blue Bachelor buttons, baby blue eyes and daisies. Grass and weeds blend into the overall wild look. It is a place where I can dream and refresh my spirit.

Hurriedly I finish up the ranch and household chores so I can attend the Fishtrap writers' conference by 4:30 p.m. How I've hungered for this "feeding" of the mind. Nourishment to the soul. Talking and listening to writers, the most interesting group of people I have ever known. Kindred spirits. Rapport with bookworms who digest the written word to hone their own writing skills. How wonderful it is to talk about books with those who write them.

It was hot when I drove up to Wallowa Lake. I savored the sweet mock orange scent of the wild syringa that blooms profusely along the shore and on the moraine.

It was a pleasant surprise to renew old acquaintances, such as rancher wives and writers Alice Warnock from Baker City and Helen Cowan, who drove by herself from Riley, in Harney County. Then to see the now familiar faces of well-known writers from west of the Rockies, and New York publisher Marc Jaffe from Houghton Mifflin Company.

That evening, after listening to writers read at an opening session, we enjoyed a most delicious dinner, eating outside in an informal atmosphere. Here we were joined by the park deer, a mule deer doe and her tiny spotted fawn that ambled across the meadow nearby. The bucks, sporting new velvet antlers, proved to be a novelty to the visitors.

Afterward we listened to Rich Wandschneider's welcoming address, which set the tone for the conference, and listened to readings by such literary greats as Ursula Le Guin, William Kittredge, and Terry Tempest Williams.

Returning home that night I could hear the thump-chunk of the baler—my husband, in the field, baling until midnight.

July 14—Up early to finish mowing the lawn, irrigating gardens and flowers, and sprucing up the yard for a wedding reception to be here in a week! Leaving Doug's breakfast on the stove, along with a note, I delivered eggs to Chandler's Bed and Breakfast on the way through Joseph to the lake to attend another day of Fishtrap.

The hot, dry days continue, and the searing high-altitude heat is cooking the valley, forests, hills and canyons. It seems breathlessly hot. I ate my breakfast outside at Fishtrap, visiting and meeting more interesting people. More readings and audience response. A discussion developed around the theme of the conference: "Patterns."

Molly Gloss, who came as an unknown to Fishtrap the first year, was there this year as the well-known author of *The Jump-Off Creek*. Molly read passages from her new book, which will be a science fiction novel.

That evening three of us ranch wives attended what is called "Jazz at the Lake." We were given box lunches at Fishtrap, which we took to the shores of Wallowa Lake to listen to the jazz and eat our fried chicken.

We went for the experience; jazz is not our kind of music. We received the experience! Jazzy people (around 1,000 strong), howling dogs on leashes, frisbee-throwing children, food concessions, heat, intense heat, loud music, and people dancing around to the beat (when there was one), people reposing on blankets, draped on lawn chairs, or wandering around dodging flying frisbees.

The sober, snow-less Wallowa looked down on part of this and trembled. Personally, I would much rather listen to—without the company of 1,000 souls—Kim Stafford's "Half a Song." It just seems more in keeping with the place. I think I've slipped over the mountain to that stage in life referred to as the "older generation."

Anyway, we ranch wives-writers took it all in as we enjoyed the box lunch, even though we couldn't visit over the loud music. When a burning sun sank in back of the mountain known as Chief Joseph, a delicious coolness wafted across the lake and refreshed us, and we left before the concert was over.

Returning to Fishtrap we partook of a reception for the fellowship recipients and listened to their readings. One of the "fellows" was a young mother of two, a marionberry-sugarbeet rancher's wife from Amity, Oregon. And she could write. She wrote about her life on the farm with such grace and feeling that it brought a tear to my eyes. Another kindred spirit.

July 15—Same as yesterday; up to eat breakfast at Fishtrap. Feeling guilty about leaving my husband home to do the work. The morning session had to do with the now and new West, with audience participation. Somehow we got onto the Marlboro man and couldn't get off the subject.

My daughter Ramona, mother of four and rancher's wife, ended it by saying she was married to the Marlboro man, only he didn't smoke and changed diapers on the children! That shot down the myth of the West right there, and ended that.

Actually some of us here in the West have been writing about our "real" West for quite some time. Unfortunately, our audience has been limited to our kind. I hope, as Marc Jaffe put it so well, we can "get this show on the road!"

July 17—Stick tripods that once held Nez Perce fish traps were called Wallowas, and Wallowa is now the name of a town, county, lake, chain of mountains, state park, and numerous businesses that lie within this remote corner of Northeastern Oregon.

Now in its third year, that writers' conference known as "Fishtrap Gathering" has just ended. Have attended Fishtrap since it began. The gathering brings together writers from all over the U.S. who listen to readings, exchange ideas, participate in panel discussions, and talk a lot about writing west of the Rockies.

It is an exciting, high energy time for us. The expressed feelings of deep thinkers gives us much to chew on. And this ranch wife/writer's head is swimming! It is hard to concentrate on much else.

July 16—We awoke to find the weather had cooled somewhat. Fixed the usual big breakfast for my husband, after he came into the kitchen from changing the wheel line. I have this system down pat now. I push the toast down in the toaster and break the egg in the pan when I hear the sound of his Honda.

Alone, the massive job of keeping the lawns, gardens, berries and flowers watered is enough during our hot summer. I have learned to appreciate anew the wonderful snowpack in our mountains during the winter, for it assures a green, irrigated valley in summer.

Although I have turned the milk cow out with three calves, I still tend to the chickens. So much of my time was, and still is, spent outside, especially since a wedding reception for a son and his new bride is scheduled for this weekend.

In between seemingly endless yard work, I type out CattleWomen's Corner for our local newspaper, make long lists and begin crossing off each task as I come to it, prioritizing as I go. Somehow I managed to keep meals on the table for my hard-working husband at odd hours of the day or night, answer the ever-present phone, and try to stay cool.

Each time I looked at the new raspberry patch, I averted my eyes. The bushes were loaded with ripening fruit.

Wallowa summers are volunteer times. Year after year, each of us ranch women seems to take on these time-consuming tasks to make our communities a better place to live, and to keep programs like 4-H and FFA going to benefit our grandchildren.

Fair time is nearly here. Need I say more?

July 17—Concentrated most of the day on my column, or at least made a vain attempt to do so. The phone rang off the hook! Each caller wanted me to do something for him or her.

July 18—Up early, as usual, fixing breakfast, doing housework, then off with more big lists to town by 8:30. Company coming—time to stock up on groceries.

My errands took longer as our county filled up with tourists. Long lines at the check-out stand, no place to park. Nine months of the year we inhabitants of the valley sometimes take our peacefulness for granted. Then tourist season rolls around.

I had promised the two younger grandchildren they could come to grandma's house and spend the night in the sheepherder's wagon, and this grandma tries never to break a promise. That evening I took the two little ones fishing in a nearby creek.

Four-year-old James caught a large rainbow trout by letting his line drift under a bridge. We were all so excited we jumped up and down and hollered right there in the road.

That night, while Doug baled late again, we lit a candle in the old sheepherder's wagon and told stories and watched the stars out the window. These two will grow up all too soon, and I want them to know about fishing and telling stories by candlelight and grandma.

July 19—I left the sleeping children in bed and began my day early. When they finally came, barefooted and tumbling into the kitchen in their pajamas, I stopped what I was doing to cuddle them. What could be more important than cuddling sleepy babies?

After breakfast we walked down to the cow pasture and caught the orphan calf "Pecos" and led him up to the lawn, where the children brushed and led him around most of the morning. Hopefully Pecos will be gentle enough to be led in the Chief Joseph Days kiddie parade.

A large semi-load of mine salt had managed to negotiate our narrow lane, with help from Doug's brother Biden, and soon a sweaty crew spent the entire morning unloading large chunks of salt by hand to store in the salt house. This salt is divided two ways and supplies the needs for two ranches. At noon I prepared lunch for our crew, who joined Biden and son Casey on our lawn to eat under a cool shade tree.

After the grandchildren left for home, I began preparing for the visit of a daughter and 14-month-old grandson who would be arriving around 4 a.m. in La Grande to spend two weeks with us. I couldn't wait to hear about 16-year-old grandson Chad's experiences in Washington. DC, while he had been attending an FFA leadership conference.

Our first cutting of hay is all baled! My salvation is the vegetable garden. I love hoeing, weeding and just being there in the cool of evening, like one of the plants, growing, maturing, responding to sunlight, air and earth. Solace—the fruits of my labor.

Wearily to bed: body and mind at ease. And for the first time in days my husband sleeps before midnight. , At 2 a.m. the alarm goes off—time to drive to La Grande and pick up Linda and baby Jordan. After Doug leaves, I can't sleep. I read.

At 4:15 the phone rings. It is Doug, 60 miles away, at the unlighted, deserted bus depot. The bus is late. At 6 a.m., they drive in safe and sound.

July 24—A rainy breeze chases clouds over Prairie Creek, thunder echoes off Chief Joseph Mountain, and lightning shreds the purple sky. It is time for Hin-mah-too-ya-let-kekt. It is the season of fire, when lightning-caused sleepers doze, only to awaken and become full-fledged forest fires.

Overhead I hear the rotor noise of a helicopter heading in the direction of Hells Canyon to check on one of several fires ignited during last night's storm. But this summer, unlike last July, there is a cooling, soaking rain, which lessens the danger of fire in our mountains and canyons.

Two 16-year-old grandsons are backpacking into the heart of the Eagle Cap Wilderness. Looking up toward Twin Peaks this morning, I see nothing but dark purple clouds cloaking the Wallowas. Westward, under Twin Peaks, lies Francis Lake, a magical spot where the ice-blue lake is rimmed on the east by steep talus and mudstone scree slopes, and gained by a nine-mile trail via the Lostine canyon.

How I envy them. I can see, in my mind's eye, the snow-shapes above the lake, of a whale, a buffalo, and the profile of a girl's face. I try to picture the boys huddled under a lean-to made from a tarp, the mountain storm pouring down, the thunder booming like it does at that high altitude. But then again, maybe they are catching fish. After all, that is the best fishing, when the rain knocks the bugs down into the lake.

Two batches of apricot-pineapple jam repose on the table as I pound on my portable Smith Corona. Granddaughters Chelsie and Mona Lee are at this minute taking the last batch of chocolate chip cookies out of the oven.

The phone never stops ringing here in my kitchen-office. Would I be able to work at the food both during the too-quickly approaching county fair? Could I be available, again, to photograph the market animals for the buyers' cards at the FFA/ 4-H fat stock auction? Could I ride my horse and carry the banner in the CattleWomen's Chief Joseph Days parade entry? Did I remember to write CattleWomen's Corner column for the local weekly paper? Did I purchase the officers' gifts for the annual CattleWomen's luncheon meeting?

Then there are the grandchildren, who would all like to spend the entire summer at grandma and grandpa's. "Could we come over and fish the creek and sleep in the sheepherder's wagon?" Sure. They, after all, our priority.

Last Saturday we held the wedding reception on our lawn for a son and his bride. It was wonderful and emotional, as it always is, for mothers of the groom, and this one was also the official photographer, caterer of a meal, and watcher of grandchildren, all time-consuming roles.

Other than the photographer forgetting to take her camera to the church, all went well. Doug and I began counting grandchildren after this wedding and one of a similar nature last spring. Eighteen! A rather startling revelation. Ranging in age from 20 to 14 months, they are all precious.

The first cutting of hay has been put up without getting rained on. The potato inspectors were here yesterday for the first field inspections of our 150 acres of seed potatoes. One of our hired men called in sick.

Doug has been putting in 16-hour days. I see him only briefly at meals or else we communicate with notes left on the telephone. The "vanishing" rancher isn't. He is real. He is here, in the Wallowa Valley. He is in his fields, with his herds of cattle, sitting at his desk, inundated with paper work, trying to remain calm in a world that is changing, trying to hold together not only his livelihood, but his way of life. A way of life that follows the old values, where family is important, where the dignity of work is important, where independence is important.

And if the less than three percent of the U.S. now engaged in agricultural pursuits can make it through these next few years, perhaps they can continue to feed the world, a world that is growing more complex and further away from these aforementioned values each year...values that western ranch families hold dear, and know in their hearts could just possibly be the only hope for the future of an America that is hungry for food to not only nourish their bodies, but their souls as well.

Down off the soap box, and back to my daily journal...

August 1—My feet got cold walking barefoot through dew-laden grasses to turn the sprinkler on in my vegetable garden early this morning. August! From now on summer will wane. There is a new freshness to our high mountain valley this morning, and there could be frost any night now. A refreshing coolness, wafted on the morning breeze, tells me fall will soon be here.

From a distance the mountains have a purplish tinge to them. In fact, the whole area, as described by a visiting artist from Sligo, Ireland, appears alizarin crimson (a shade of oil paint) in August. I think of him now and understand. Perhaps the heat creates the effect, but it is real.

Chief Joseph Days has just ended. Our small town of Joseph reeled under the impact of thousands of people for nearly a week, some of whom came from all over the U.S. to participate in the annual celebration. The town never slept.

And by Sunday store proprietors and Chief Joseph Days volunteers, of whom there were many, were weary of it all: the carnival, the bright lights, the cars, the people, the night life, the socializing, the cowboy breakfast, the rodeos, Indian dances, friendship feast, parades and heat!

But out of town. only a few miles away, on places like Prairie Creek, it was as though the event never occurred. Ranchers and farmers continued with their work and in the coolness of evening the wild geese flew in with their young (just learning to fly) and landed in our neighbor's fields to feed. Goose music filled the air. and still does. The geese like it here and we like the geese.

As on other ranches, our irrigating continues around the clock. Doug gave our hired man the weekend off, which meant double duty for him. When he wasn't cultivating potatoes or changing wheel lines, he was off on his Honda, shovel over his shoulder, to flood irrigate the lower fields.

Then there are the fall calvers, already beginning to calve on the moraine. Meanwhile, this ranch wife/mother/grandmother attempted to captain the ship and create some semblance of order on the home front. This was accomplished, after a fashion, by wearing a multitude of hats, most of which determined at a moment's notice. Some of the hats were rearranged in midstream, and some didn't fit, but I wore them anyway.

Somehow I managed to keep afloat during a week I didn't have time to keep notes on and emerge none the worse for wear. Actually, I envied my husband, hard work and all, for he could concentrate on one job at a time, while I sometimes had 10 going at once.

I admit it. I failed. After all it is human to err, but I did not sink the ship! The very afternoon that Fishtrap Writer's conference ended, I slipped out of my writer's role and returned to the more familiar one of grandmother, as Doug and I drove to Alder Slope to help celebrate the birthday of a new granddaughter.

After being absent so long, it was catch-up time. The weather continued to be intensely hot, often in the 90s, with no relief in sight. During the coolness of evening, I weeded my garden until dark. listening to the thump-chunk of the baler as Doug baled hay until midnight—again.

August 16—At sunup I am reading a newspaper account of a fire in the Eagle Cap Wilderness area. Fires all have names—this one is called the Elk Creek Fire. The facts are printed coldly in the column, meaningless to many; not to me.

The fire, according to the article, grew to about 35 acres Tuesday, and is burning in alpine fir north of Mule Peak, east of Burger Pass. It was not known when the fire would be contained or controlled.

As daylight spreads over the green prairie, the morning coolness of the irrigated bottoms mingles with the drier, warmer air of the summer-scorched hill to the east. The Wallowas to the south and west have seemingly vanished from the landscape. In their place, a blue-gray haze, as smoke from the Elk Creek Fire hangs, unmoving, in the mid-August morning. Elk Creek, another place in my heart, where not so many years ago I lived in a tent for 20 days during hunting season as the elk camp cook for Red's Wallowa Horse Ranch's deluxe camp.

That Elk Creek hunting camp was 19 miles up the Minam River trail from the horse ranch. We rode in horseback from Moss Springs, pulling a pack string a distance of nearly 30 miles, picking up the dude hunters at the horse ranch, where they had been flown in with their gear. It was during the last week in October, at the tail end of a beautiful Indian summer when we came into the upper Minam. I remember the trail, carpeted with the fallen golden needles of the tamarack.

Our horses' and mules' hoofbeats were silenced by the needles, which had fallen during a windstorm. I remember the ever-present sound of the river and the fall smell of the woods. There is something about the high country in autumn that can't be put into words.

In a large wall tent at Elk Creek on the Minam, I baked sourdough bread, pies and cobblers in a small wood stove oven on a daily basis. The crisp, cold fall weather whet everyone's appetite, and the city-bred hunters ate that food like it was going out of style.

I carried water from the Minam, built my cooking fire each morning, and began the day with sourdough hotcakes that were consumed as fast as I could fix them. When the men were all out hunting during the day, I made friends with blue jays and chipmunks, and watched as glorious sunset clouds swirl overhead and witnessed similar clouds at sunrise. I "tuned in" to the sound of the river, the season of fall on the upper Minam, and fell in love with the frosty meadow, the creek flowing into the Minam, the lovely, tall trees, the pure air, the birds, and the peacefulness of it all.

On Halloween night a blizzard erupted over the upper Minam country and snow fell all through the night. The next morning it was below zero and my bucket of kitchen water was frozen solid.

The work was hard, and sometimes uncomfortable, but I loved it. And now, as this Wallowa summer madness grips those of us who are trapped into it, as this season of frantic activity winds down, I think again of Elk Creek as I read this news article, and I am sad. Perhaps the fire didn't get down to the camp area, but the high country under Mule Peak will be charred, and 35 acres is a big area when you consider chipmunks, trees and blue jays.

Later, over breakfast, I turned the page of the newspaper. Under obituaries: Herb Owens, 75, a Joseph rancher and member of the Rodeo Hall of Fame in Colorado Springs, Colorado, died Saturday, August 11, 1990, at St. Mary Medical Center in Walla Walla, Washington.

More statistics.

Doug and I attended our friend Herb's funeral yesterday, which was followed by the burial service at the Prairie Creek cemetery, only a few miles south of our ranch. What can one say? How to remember him?

Herb helped us drive cattle, drove potato trucks, put up silage in the ag bagger, drove tractors in our fields, broke my cow horse to harness and to pull a buggy, polished an old ornate stove part I wanted to make a bookend out of. Herb gave to his friends just a little bit extra, and he loaned me some books to read, written about the Horse Heaven Hills in Washington State, where he was reared. He loved horses and worked with them all his life.

At the funeral, the song "Empty Saddles in the Old Corral" was played and all of his many descendants were very moved, as were those who knew him. A granddaughter read a moving tribute to her grandfather and a grandson read a letter written by Herb describing how it was to grow up in the Horse Heaven Hills.

Looking down, Herb wrote, *I could see one thousand head of wild horses running in those rolling, grassy hills.* He told about the draws, the creeks, the wildflowers, and painted a realistic word picture in that place in time. And in doing so he left a wonderful legacy to his children and those who follow. A legacy that will be forever cherished by his descendants for years to come.

It is Thursday: Chieftain day. Our weekly newspaper arrives with another obituary: James Dorrance, born September 28, 1900, on Crow Creek, was the oldest of eight children of William and Minnie F. Tinsley Dorrance. He attended school on Crow Creek and worked with his dad until 1927.

That year, Jim moved with his bride to Christmas Creek Ranch on the Snake River, where two children were born. They sold the ranch in 1942, and for the next 30 years Jim worked on cattle ranches in Nevada. He returned home to Wallowa County in 1972, where he lived with his daughter on Imnaha. Jim was a friend to all who knew him, and his advice was sought on many things, including the training of horses and just about everything pertaining to cattle ranching.

Jim died August 7 and our life has been so busy we didn't know about it until we read it in the paper today. I have written many times about Jim in columns. He was the official greeter for years to one and all at the Riverside Cafe in Imnaha. He was also the dishwasher, a job he said no one challenged.

When he became too crippled with arthritis to wash dishes, he sat in his wheelchair, reminiscing about the past and giving advice on the future. Jim's heart, however, was always far off somewhere in Battle

Mountain, Nevada, where he buckarooed for so many years. The obituary says his cremains will be scattered over Battle Mountain. That is good. Jim will rest in "the place" in his heart.

When Doug and I were driving from Salt Lake City last month, en route to California from Wyoming, we drove through Battle Mountain because we had been talking about Jim and this, his country. And there in that small, dusty, dying desert cowtown we purchased a postcard in a little, dusty grocery store, addressed it to Jim Dorrance, c/o Wallowa Nursing Home, Enterprise, Oregon, and wrote a little greeting on it to Jim, saying we were thinking of him.

When we returned we got so busy with our lives, as usual, that we thought we didn't have time to go by and see if Jim got the card or find out how he was. Now it is too late. Such is life and death and summer— brief, inevitable and busy. There should be a lesson there somewhere and Jim, if he were alive, could put it into finer words than I, and use fewer words to do so.

This column will arrive on the editor's desk two days past the dead-line this week. Yesterday and the day before, when I should have been typing away at my kitchen table, were spent doing other things, including visiting with friends who dropped in.

After attending Herb's funeral, it somehow brought home to me that visiting friends while they are still around to visit was far more important than doing my column. I realize this is hard on editors and those putting together the paper, but the staff at Agri-Times is extra special and, I think, somehow they will forgive me.

August 22—Today was the first day since this unreal summer began, that I had one entire day to myself. How I savored it! Up at dawn, listen-ing to Prairie Creek awaken, sipping a cup of Pero, I wrote, uninterrupted, until 10 a.m.

Because Doug is attending the quarterly cattlemen's meetings in Ontario, I didn't have to fix the usual big breakfast. In fact, I nearly forgot my own! By mid-morning I was out in the yard drinking in the beauty of my wildflower patch. Due to our recent rainy, cool weather pattern, the varicolored blooms are brilliant and incredibly lovely.

I walked among the vegetables, which are lush and growing so in-tensely. For instance, there is this one pumpkin vine which is taking over the garden. Already it has conquered the turnips, crossed the cabbage line of defense, and is advancing on the corn. A thunderstorm blew my sunflowers over onto the cabbage and turnips, so I can't even walk up and down rows now. I need a machete to chop my way through this jungle...but it is wonderful.

The cabbages shaded by the fallen sunflowers are not splitting open this year, instead holding until I have time to make sauerkraut. And this morning, one of the fallen sunflowers is blooming. It's a volunteer from last year, and now the largest one in the garden. Its golden head peeks through the row of Early Sunglow corn Corn which, if it doesn't freeze soon (knock on wood), will mature on Prairie Creek this summer. It isn't every year we have corn or beans, but the grandchildren and I have picked the first crop already.

Gardens have personalities. And mine provides so much pleasure that it isn't work at all. Just when I thought they were tapering off, a whole new crop of raspberries has decided to come on. And due to the coolness, some are as big as my thumb, so I join the birds and pick more for my bulging freezer. Surely someone will use them in this large family, and I can't bear to see anything go to waste.

This new raspberry patch has attracted a host of different birds to feast on the berries, and it also provides cover for them. I enjoy watching them through my kitchen window. Jenny wren has returned, perching on the fence and cocking her little head at me. Such a joy to see her.

The two dogs and I went for a walk along our country road. Nerma, the tomcat, brought up the rear. I listened to the sounds of Prairie Creek: sprinklers irrigating the fields, cattle bawling, the far-off barking of a dog, and the sharp report of a cock pheasant's call, the blackbirds flocking together for fall, the distant sound of Willie Locke's Honda in the field, the scream of a hawk, and the calls of killdeer, meadowlark and robin.

The sun burst forth; the earth and grasses sparkled and were refreshed because of rain and coolness. The sun felt warm and pleasant, not searing hot like summer. Light slanted in a different direction and fell softly, not harshly. I can feel the season's change. My favorite time nears.

My oldest daughter and a granddaughter are on their way home from an extended trip to England and Scotland. Their plane landed in San Francisco yesterday. In their absence I have thought about them, reading and re-reading their postcards from those far-away places which I will most likely never visit. It will be fun to hear of their adventures in person.

I peeled, sliced and froze a box of peaches a daughter brought me from Imnaha. I wrote letters to relatives, answered fan mail, and reduced the tall stack of correspondence a little. I photographed my wildflowers and this evening's sunset, and I fixed my two meals from the garden.

I boiled fresh cabbage with a bit of leftover ham, stir-fried zucchini, tomatoes, onions, and topped the whole with cheddar cheese. Wonderful! My dessert: fresh raspberries picked from the patch.

What a summer. Every year we say, "Let's just go into the mountains!" but of course we can't, or think we can't. Then it starts... weddings, Chief Joseph Days, family reunions, CattleWomen and Stockgrowers doin's, grandchildren's birthdays, canning, freezing, putting food by for winter, irrigating, community involvement, fair time, and company (if only we had time to enjoy them).

Summer is stressful and should be relaxing; well, a little bit anyway, but Wallowa County has to make hay while the sun shines: in haste, before the snow flies. Some of us who live here all year-round look forward to winter. I am one. Winter gives us time to rest up for another summer, each of which seems to become crazier than the last, or maybe it's simply my imagination.

But perhaps we should just go to the mountains.

Anyway, this writer/ranch wife, plus two more tired ranch wives and my old pal Scotty, now in her 70s, leave next Tuesday for the Wallowa Horse Ranch in the Minam wilderness. From Moss Springs, east of Cove, we'll follow the Little Minam River, climb a long hog's back, and drop down to the guest ranch situated along the Minam River, a distance of eight miles,

We'll stay two days and two nights, eat home-cooked food, swim (maybe) in the Minam, rest and relax. R and R! And hike back out, carrying our sleeping bags and packs. Because we didn't get to go last August, I am really looking forward to this annual trek.

September 1—Two grandsons have already started football practice, and others are scurrying around with their mothers, buying school clothes.

School! It began on the 29th. Summer is over.

We really enjoyed having my three sisters here. One sister, Mary Ann, brought her grandson Josh, who was reared in the city. After one week of "Mainstream Wallowa County," Josh was a different kid. What a change it must have been for him: eating sourdough hotcakes, sleeping in the sheepherder wagon, gathering eggs, riding horses, going on hikes, staying on Imnaha with a cousin, going fishing, experiencing our county fair (without a carnival!) and meeting all of his country cousins on their home turf. Surely an experience he'll remember all of his days.

Sister Caroline slept in the mini-motorhome, which was parked next to the sheepherder wagon where M.A. and Josh took up residence.

Kathryn opted for the spare bedroom in the house. Because they were here during "Fair Week," there wasn't time to do much else, but we did anyway.

Time and space does not permit me to tell of the schedule we kept, but we did it all and our energy held. Well, theirs did. Mine flagged, for various reasons I'll not go into.

At 4:30 one morning, I got everyone up to go on a hike up the hill opposite our ranch to watch the sunrise. At 4 a.m. I was out hanging clothes on the line and watching the nearly full moon disappear over the mountains.

Soon we were off, crossing the damp, hayed-over field, walking through dew-laden grasses that brushed our faces, and getting ourselves wet. We climbed up a dry cow-trail, following a draw to the top of the eastern hill land that divides prairie from canyon.

The summer's heat, held at bay by the dawn, would soon pound down upon us. The smell of morning dew on sage and summer-brown grasses, the pungent odor of late-blooming lupine, the stillness before daylight. Turning around we could see the first pink light flood the Wallowas.

As we walked toward the rising sun, we listened for the whir of wings...and heard them, the waterfowl leaving the pond to fly to the irrigated fields below to feed. Suddenly the air was filled with the sound of rushing wings and faint honking...goose music.

The sun burst over the Idaho/Oregon border and burned with intense heat, even at that early hour. We hiked a large circle, returning to the ranch by way of Echo Canyon. The August sun was hot and merciless, and it was 8 a.m. when we got to the house to find Doug had left a note: "I fixed breakfast already." Pretty neat husband.

Then another day volunteering at the fair. The sisters prepared dinner that evening and we hiked the east moraine to watch the full moon rise over Hells Canyon of the Snake River. We sat there on top as the silent moon slowly appeared, listening to the meadowlark's song and watching upper Prairie Creek go to sleep at our feet. It was all a soothing balm to my spirit after such a long, hot day.

Tomorrow would bring another hot day at the fair, but I had taken time to savor summer with my sisters, watching the beginning and ending of this wonderful day.

Verda McLain of Dayton, Washington, sent me a collection of poems and sayings she got from the walls of Dingle's Store there in Dayton. Vera says Mrs. Dingle is in her 90s now. How I would like to meet her, as

Completing their year on the 4-H court at the Wallowa County Fair are, from left, ShanRae Hook, Jody Alford, and Jessica Olsen.

well as Verda. The following are a few of the sayings she sent me from "Dingles of Dayton."

Happiness is the mosaic of life made up of many kind acts throughout a busy day. Ideally, we would all be happier if we could do only those things for which we seem best suited. Life, how-ever, is far from ideal. The secret of happiness is not in doing what one likes, but in liking what one has to do.

It's the little things that matter,
That add up in the end
To the priceless, thrilling magic
Found only in a friend!

September 6—Accessible only by plane, horseback or hiking, The Horse Ranch on the Minam River is a relaxing place to visit. Formerly known as Red's Wallowa Horse Ranch, the place is managed now by Cal and Betsy Henry of High Country Outfitters of Joseph, Oregon.

Tucked in the heart of the Minam Wilderness, it is the place to go if you seek a wilderness experience. No phones to bother you: delicious home-cooked meals; friendly, courteous staff; and rustic, comfortable accommodations. Log cabins with showers and fireplaces are situated

A surprised Travis Jones holds the prestigious Jidge Tippett Memorial trophy presented by the Wallowa County CattleWomen to the outstanding beef project at the Wallowa County Fair. Travis is a 4-H member from Wallowa. His sister, Teah, won the trophy last year.

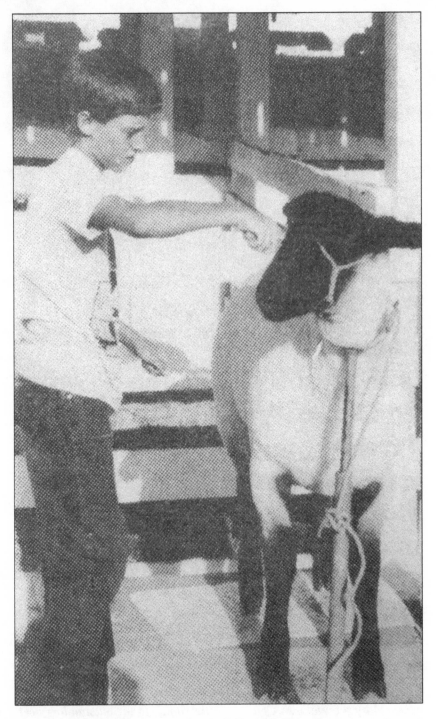

Rory Johnson, Wallowa, gives his Suffolk a final bit of grooming. Rory is the son of John and Amy Johnson, and is a 4-H member.

Grand champion market steer at the Wallowa County Fair was shown by Chad Nash, member of the Enterprise FFA. The steer is a Simmental cross.

Shawn Phillips, Enterprise FFA, shows his Simmental cross steer that was named FFA reserve champion market steer.

James Nash, 4, waits with his sister, Adele, 2, for the Pee Wee showmanship class at the Wallowa County Fair. All participants were awarded a blue ribbon, a dollar bill, and a chocolate sucker shaped like a sheep. This class is the most popular with the audience of any at the fair.

Josh Cool, grandson of Bill and Edna Cool of Prairie Creek, exhibits a prize cabbage. He helped his grandmother plant her garden this spring.

Tisha Stangel, 12, of Enterprise, is ready to show her half-paint, half-Appaloosa gelding, "Alleba," in the 4-H horse show. Tisha is a member of the Rambling Riders 4-H Club. The daughter of Joe and Mary Stangel, she also has other 4-H projects in photography, sewing, and cooking.

Helen Jones, Scotty Doyle, and Linde Irwin pause along the eight-mile trek to Red's Horse Ranch. They're resting on a bridge that spans the Little Minam River near the halfway mark.

along the peaceful Minam River.

The place is managed in such a way that it doesn't disturb the wilderness surrounding it, but rather blends into the total feeling of the area. All who visit there love it and come under the spell of the place. It is wonderful to have retreats like this where older people who can't hike or ride on horseback can be flown in and experience wilderness.

Hopefully this unique ranch will be allowed to continue to operate for these reasons. People who live amid the hustle and bustle of today's modern world need to experience this type of setting. There is talk of shutting down this wonderful place because of new wilderness restrictions.

September 20—It was love at first sight. Astride my cow horse, waiting for the long Chief Joseph parade to begin, I spotted her. This fellow was riding her up and down the street and her long, floppy ears rose and fell with each clip clop. Nothing seemed to bother her much.

I was attracted to the classy look of her: the pretty head; sleek, brown body; black mane and tail; the refinement of good breeding. I didn't know her name but she looked to be quite young, just a baby really. I asked her rider how old she was.

"Comin' three," he replied. "She is the mule to be raffled off at Mule Days in September."

A banner flapped behind the saddle and hung down cross her rump. *Hell's Canyon Mule Days,* it read. Seemingly oblivious to the crowds of people lined up on either side of Joseph's main street, she walked right out, just like a well broke mule. I was very impressed.

Along with hundreds of other hopefuls, I later purchased a ticket from the Mule Days committee on a chance to win her. My eyes followed her down the street as the little molly mule and her rider disappeared into the melee of the parade.

As our CattleWomen's group rode on down the parade route, all I could think about was that little molly mule. I envisioned myself riding her along the Crow Creek road behind a bunch of cows, or she and I climbing a steep mountain trail. I could imagine her braying as I stepped out of a tent in the backcountry, or appeared out the kitchen door in the morning to feed her.

She would be my friend, as well as a mode of transportation as I grew older. She had her whole life ahead of her. And more than that, there was something about this little mule that spoke to me. At the time I couldn't put my finger on it, but I never told anyone, nor did I forget her.

Rozanne Adams, of Joseph, rides "Big Bertha," the 16.2 hands mare mule owned by Gene Marr, of Imnaha, who stands next to the mule.

Alfie, love at first sight.

July melted into August, on came September, and soon it was time for Hell's Canyon Mule Days in Enterprise. From several western states they came: mules, mule fanciers, mule trainers and spectators, most of whom hoped to win my little molly mule.

Again I saw her being ridden down the main street of Enterprise in the Mule Days parade. I photographed her. Then Doug and I, and daughter Lori and family, who had arrived the day before from Wyoming, drove to Waitsburg, Washington, to attend a wedding.

Returning on Sunday, Doug and I stopped at the fairgrounds to watch the mule and horse auction and grab a hamburger for lunch. During the sale they held the drawing for my mule.

I didn't win her.

But a fellow by the name of Don McKinney of Elgin did, and he ordered the mule sold.

She was ridden, under saddle, into the auction area. Again, I photographed her. She was wearing a hackamore and appeared to be bothered about something. But I didn't pay much attention to her behavior; my heart was racing.

Before I really knew what was happening, I began to bid. I just kept raising my hand and soon the auctioneer cried, "Sold!"

She was mine. For $1,000. Oh my gosh! I looked back at Doug.

"Now whatcha gonna do?" he asked.

Yeh, I thought. *Now what?*

Then a nice lady, Betty Prock from Milton-Freewater, came up to me in the grandstand and said, "Oh, I'm so glad you bought Alfie." And she told me how she had bottle fed the baby mule and how special she was, and how happy I had her now. It was meant to be.

Ken and Betty Prock raise good mules, and they cared about who Alfie went to. Cared enough that if she didn't sell for $1,000 they would have bought her back from the Chamber of Commerce, which had purchased the mule from them earlier in the year.

Well-known mule and horse trainer Fred Talbott, of Hermiston, had started her, and Noel Wright, of Enterprise, had ridden her in the parades this summer. Alfie's story was starting to unfold.

For as long as I can remember, I have wanted a mule like Alfie. Convincing my husband of this seemed all but impossible, so I didn't bring the subject up. Now I had to discuss it...I owned Alfie!

So on that September 9th, my 57th birthday, I wrote out a check, paid for my purchase, obtained the brand inspection certificate, and drove with Doug home to the ranch on Prairie Creek. Doug helped me put the racks on the tailgate of the truck so I could drive back into the fairgrounds to bring home my mule.

When I walked into the arena to get her, she was striking and kicking the fence; she wanted out of that place, a place where she had been prodded, poked, teased and looked at curiously by hundreds of people all weekend. A kind, young lady who understood mules led her to the loading dock, whereupon the little mule walked calmly in and was tied securely by her halter rope. A new halter and lead rope were in the deal—nice.

The clanging and banging it took to get the endgate in didn't phase Alfie, who simply stood there until we finished. Driving along Highway 82 that borders Prairie Creek, she began to bray loudly and move around quite a bit in the pickup truck. Perhaps she was wondering what would be happening next in her life.

Rolling down the window, I called her name and she settled down. Soon we were home, where Doug unloaded her. Her ears went all floppy and she was turned in to a small lot with my cow horse. Alfie liked her new home.

The days since then have been spent winning Alfie's trust. She does bray when I appear out the door of a morning, because she knows she'll soon be munching her ration of horse feed. She also knows when I go into the garden in the evening to pick fresh corn that she will have another treat. Alfie loves corn husks.

There is still much to do to convince Alfie that no one is going to poke her, but we'll keep working on that. And one of these days, maybe this writer will be riding her little molly mule down the Crow Creek road pushing a bunch of cows toward the valley. Who knows? And perhaps my husband will understand why Alfie is now part of our family.

September 22—Seed potato harvest has begun, and this place will be hopping until all those spuds are out of the ground and stored in two cellars. My kitchen office is the hub of communication. It is here I take calls from people who want to work in the fields or in the cellars. I receive calls from our hired help and coordinate work schedules, relay messages about ordering parts, and answer myriad questions concerning seed potatoes.

Yesterday I cowboy'd. We gathered and moved pairs of cows and calves off the east moraine of Wallowa Lake to another pasture on Prairie Creek. Faithful "old hand" Mike McFetridge, 83, along with son-in-law Charley and I got the job done by 1 o'clock. A welcome thunder shower cleansed the dusty air and refreshed us as we rode.

Still, we have no frost! The garden continues to bear. Cosmos, nasturtiums, petunias, snapdragons and wildflowers are so lovely it is impossible to describe their beauty.

My friend Elane Dickenson, who writes for our local paper, enjoys digging into the old issues of the Chieftain and writes an interesting "Out of the Past" section. I note in this week's paper her discovery of September 26, 1940, this jewel:

Editorial—Untimely frosts late in the spring, any time in the summer and early in the fall keep farmers and gardeners guessing in Wallowa County. This season (1940) has been one of those rare periods when potatoes, squash, tomatoes, corn and beans have turned brown and rusty from old age instead of blackened by frost.

A comparison: 1939, a hard frost, August 7, ruined gardens; 1938, a record, the first killing frost held off until October 14!

Don't know how much longer our first killing frost will hold off here on Prairie Creek, but in the meantime we are enjoying corn on the cob and green beans, and the pumpkins are turning orange. Normally I don't even plant pumpkins, but a friend gave me some seed and I planted it late.

And the squash! Zucchini, anyone?

The young Northwood maple I planted this spring is turning color now. Sunlight gleams through its reddened foliage. The "Heavenly Blue" morning glory seed I planted by the front door is, in fact, "Heavenly Blue" this year; no red and white seed mixed in like last year. Only two twining vines survived the hot summer, and yesterday was a "two morning glory morning." Mostly though, just one bloom greets me as its lovely sky-blue petals unfurl in the warmth of the morning sun.

Alfie, my mule, brays for her morning feed and attention. The hens continue to lay big brown eggs, and Chester, who is no spring chicken anymore, looks after his harem...'er, flock, and crows just at daylight like a young rooster.

Our new raspberry patch is now a "forest" where the latest batch of kittens has grown up. Having been well protected from dogs and children, these "raspberry kittens" are finally taming down enough to be petted.

I am bottle feeding an orphan calf at the barn now. Apparently its mama died this summer and, when we gathered the other day, we found it bravely following the herd, looking rather forlorn. The little brown heifer calf now follows me around and gratefully munches calf manna between bottle feedings.

My days are so full: cooking, grandchildren, putting food by for the winter. The sauerkraut is canned, the eight-day sweet pickles are put up, I apple-sauced every apple I could find, jams and berries fill the freezer, and soon it will be hunting season, which means mincemeat-making time again.

How I love the fall and the smells associated with it. They are good for the soul, as well as the body, and bring nostalgic reminders of grandma's kitchen. Actually, this is the way of life for us. Microwave cookery and instant food doesn't appeal to me at this point. We'll continue to enjoy the wholesome food, cooked from scratch, that we raise. No shortcuts. Cooking is a joy.

September 27—The rain of last evening has cleansed the air and refreshed Prairie Creek. There are mud puddles in the lane. The two younger grandchildren were here for a while this morning, and then, because more help was needed on the potato digger, I spent the remainder of the day picking dirt clods and rocks out of hundreds of potatoes. A hard and dirty job, accomplished while standing on a clanging, banging, swaying, jerking digger, by five women, working as fast as our hands can fly over the moving chain in front of us.

While a big John Deere pulls the enormous digger up and down the long rows of potatoes, truck load after truck load of seed rumbles off to our cellars. At day's end, two crews on the diggers descend the monster machines and return to their homes. For me it is time to feed the calf, hay the mule and horse, gather eggs, and fix a supper of cold chicken, corn on the cob, and garden veggies.

I then clean the two gallons of strawberries the children and I picked this morning, and make a batch of jam. Later, soaking in the tub, I remember my column isn't in the mail yet, and I'm too tired to write anyway.

September 28—An absolutely gorgeous morning. So mild last night we slept with the windows open to the fresh fall air. The "boss" says I'm not needed on the digger today, so after morning chores I sit myself down in front of the Smith Corona and begin.

I wanted to write about gathering cattle on the moraine last week (10 hours in the saddle) and the wonderful hike Scotty and I took last Saturday to LeGore Lake (Oregon's highest) and back the same day, but I promised my husband strawberry shortcake, and after a day in that potato field, he deserves one.

October 3—Dark storm clouds swirl over the Wallowas. Misty fingers reach downward and snag the canyons. Howard, Bonneville, Ruby, and Chief Joseph mountains all wear white this morning. Sometime in the night, the first snow fell in the high country.

A cold wind blows over Prairie Creek, and the "raspberry forest," as seen from my kitchen window, sways and tosses its green leaves in wild abandon. The Northwood maple's brilliant leaves cling tenaciously to the young tree, and the last golden cooking apple falls to the ground. Autumn has arrived.

It was 32 degrees yesterday morning and the squash plants, although blackened a bit, are loaded with zucchini and crookneck. Floating in the wind, the cosmos create a picture of moving color, pink and white against the irrigated field and dry hills beyond. The profusion of wildflowers continues to bloom. I will pick a big bouquet to give to daughter Ramona today, as it is her birthday.

The Marshall ever-bearing strawberries keep coming on and the robins have disappeared, so we get them all now. The solitary morning glory blooms on a daily basis, but unfurls now in the afternoon rather than in the morning.

The gals and guy working on our two potato diggers are bundled up against the cold this morning. It is no picnic for them to brave blowing dust and bitter cold as they do the hard but necessary work of sorting dirt clods from potatoes. They are a tough lot, and without them we wouldn't finish the harvest.

Daughter Jackie is on the crew this year, and because she didn't have time to both work and can two boxes of tomatoes, I canned them for her yesterday.

How I love to can. Such satisfaction, preserving the wonderful bounty of our local gardens. Using leftover tomatoes, I made a batch of fresh salsa, adding peppers, onions and spices. Found an old-fashioned recipe for bread and butter pickles and utilized the last cucumbers that had grown a bit too large. My kitchen still smells wonderful.

Although Doug and I didn't buy deer tags this fall, various menfolk of our large family did. Consequently, two sons, one son-in-law and two grandsons got their bucks on opening weekend, and we were given some delicious fresh liver.

One night for supper I fixed Basque potatoes to go with the venison liver. Ideally this dish should be prepared in deer camp, but if you can't be there, the kitchen will have to do.

Saute a handful of onion, a finely chopped garlic clove, and a little parsley in a bit of oil in a cast iron skillet. Add and brown sliced raw potatoes. Add a little water and cover for a while. That's all there is to it. Wonderful! For a main dish, you could add crisp bacon or chopped ham.

Yesterday I pulled all the yellow keeping onions to dry them for winter use, then picked the last green beans. I cooked up more beets to pickle and brought in a wheelbarrow of squash. Those big zucchini are good to fill with meat and bake with fresh tomato salsa and cheese. Yum!

You can tell our appetites are sharpening with the return of cooler weather. My mule Alfie brays the minute I enter the garden, anticipating her daily treat of corn husks. The Early Sunglow corn is still flavorful, although some ears are becoming a bit too mature.

Last Saturday morning, opening of mule deer season, I was up at 4:30 a.m. to do the chores, fix breakfast, pack a lunch, and be off with five of my hiking friends to hit the high trail to LeGore again. The parking area at the Hurricane Creek trailhead was full of deer hunters' vehicles, but most of the hunters were on the Hurricane Creek trail, not where we were going.

It was a crisp fall morning. Clear skies prevailed and autumn was painting the high country chokecherry-aspen-willow yellow and huckleberry-ninebark-wine red. Last Saturday, two of us hiked all the way to LeGore Lake and back in one day. Today we would attempt to climb Sawtooth Peak.

Up and up we climbed on one of the steepest trails in the Wallowas, scrambling over rocks, pulling ourselves up over the hardest parts, using our walking sticks for support. I had my father's walking stick. Daddy loved this area and now his wonderful worn stick would return to Hurricane Creek. It was like taking him along on the hike.

A mile up the trail: boom, boom, boom…deer hunters. Then silence. Presently, walking down the trail, we encountered a hunter, nearly played out, packing his buck. We congratulated him on his deer and continued on. He was a real hunter and had earned that buck.

Far below the trail, where water fell over rocks and flowed between the jungle of willow and scrub fir, we spotted a hunting camp on a small frosted meadow under the awesome Hurricane Divide. Two tiny backpack tents were pitched near the stream, and two hunters and a boy bent over nearby, skinning a big mulie.

What a spot. They seemed dwarfed by the setting around them. Twin Peaks loomed high above and we glimpsed gleaming water spilling down over black rock below LeGore Lake. We entered a trembling aspen thicket and crossed a cold stream before beginning the steepest part of the climb.

One foot in front of the other, slowly gaining altitude with each step. The sky above was a deep azure blue and contrasted with the hazy valley far below.

Arriving at the old mine site, we traversed around to the right on a game trail that led upward over loose scree to a high ridge top. At 1 p.m. we ate lunch there, sitting on a log and staring up at 9,174-foot Sawtooth Peak.

Originally we had hoped to climb Sawtooth and write our names in the register there, but the short autumn day wasn't going to give us time. One member of our party had already opted to return. Not used to the altitude, she felt like she was getting into more than she could handle. Now we were four.

After a brief rest, we walked over another boulder-strewn ridge to gaze down into Little Granite, a tumble of rock slides with a basin at the bottom. The view of the valley far below took our breath away. Slowly we made our way ever-upward toward Sawtooth.

We came to a high mountain meadow where water seeped from underground springs to form tiny streams. No sign of human habitation here, and no hunters. We were high in the very heart of the Wallowas, and obviously in the home of the Rocky Mountain sheep, as their beds and signs were all around.

We traversed a rock slide and came to the high basin that lies north of LeGore Lake, under Sawtooth. The air was thin and still, and the sun warm upon us in an incredibly blue sky. Silence ruled the basin. This was a special place, gained by hard exertion and worth every step of the way.

Here we rested, while one more member of our group opted to return to the trailhead, not wanting to hike in the dark. The three of us lingered, photographed, and savored the fleeting moments of that September day.

Reluctantly we said goodbye to the golden meadow, the bright and clear stream that flowed seemingly off the edge of the world, and old, weathered Sawtooth, which we vowed to climb another time.

We made our way slowly down an enormous jumble of boulders. The small furry Pikas, rock rabbits, scolded us as we made our precarious way over the rock slide. We gained the tiny basin below and came upon a patch of brilliant blue Gentians beside the stream, their lovely petals already closing for the night; the sun had long since sunk over the Hurricane Divide.

Down below, far from the trail, we could see the curl of smoke from the solitary campfire. How tempted we were to join the hunters and spend the night. We could smell and taste venison liver frying with onions, feel the warmth of their fire, hear the nearby stream tumbling by, and see the moon beginning to appear over Miner's Basin.

Sacajawea's barren summits began to flow in moon-light as the last light faded and darkness engulfed the canyon. It was nearly 8 p.m. when we reached Fall's Creek below the falls, and we took from the ice cold creek the bottles of orange mineral water we had cached there that morning.

October 12—Another new snowfall in the mountains this morning. Looks like it's getting serious this time.

Made another batch of crab apple jelly, typed out my column, cooked a chicken dinner and after supper nearly fell asleep listening to our local radio station's broadcast of the Enterprise Savages playing the Grant Union Prospectors at John Day.

So many miles for our boys to travel, two of my grandsons included.

October 13—Up early to fix breakfast, do chores, and put on long johns under cold weather riding gear. It's raining when we pick up Mike McFetridge and his horse, and drive to the elk fence gate at the lower end of the east moraine. We notice the snowline is now around the 4,500-foot level and the middle-slope evergreens on Mt. Howard's sides are frosted white.

Doug hauled hay to 18 pair of cows and calves yesterday, and they waited there by the gate for another handout today. We unloaded our saddle horses and Doug returned to the potato cellar while Mike and I began to drive the pairs to a lower field on upper Prairie Creek.

It was on the verge of snowing but, thank goodness, we had no wind. The cattle traveled right along in the rain and our yellow slickers kept us reasonably dry. Rain dropped down off our hat brims as we rode along.

It began to rain pretty good as we drove the small herd by one of our potato fields. We waved to the crews on the diggers as we passed. Turning the cows and calves down a narrow grassy lane, we opened a gate and drove them in with some other pairs. The sun came out as Mike and I rode across the fields to our truck.

Home just in time to get my column in the mail and fix lunch. Later I peeled some of those smaller pears that Mary Cook gave me, and made a delicious pear pie in the wood cookstove oven. Doug was late returning from the potato cellar. Our crew finished another field today. One more to go.

Somehow, we managed to drive to Enterprise and attend the Chamber of Commerce dinner. It was relaxing to visit friends and eat a nice meal out for a change.

October 14—Raining. Slept in until nearly 6:45. More snow in the mountains this morning. The fall colors are slow to appear here in the valley. Willows and cottonwoods are still green in most places. Even though a gentle rain continued to fall, two of my friends and I decided to hike a canyon trail down toward Imnaha.

Here we found a scattering of autumn color and, even in the rain, it wasn't as cold as "on top." Dressed for cold, the exertion of walking soon warmed our blood. We ate lunch under the canopy of several canyon trees and enjoyed ourselves very much. Beats watching football on TV.

Because winter appears to have taken over the high country, our hikes might be confined to the warmer canyons from now on. We saw a variety of wildlife in the rain: chukar, deer, hawks, and a large horned owl that looked down at us from an ancient cottonwood. Later, by the fire, we sipped orange cappuccino and ate pear pie.

Doug, home from checking on cattle and deer hunters in the hills, reported it was raining pretty hard there also. That is good. The country really needs a good soaking. It rained on into the night and I curled up with a good book by the old Monarch and read.

October 15—Cold and cloudy, threatening snow or rain. After feeding my mule, as well as the "raspberry kittens," chickens, and cows, I peeled more of the little pears and baked another pear pie, this one for 16-year-old grandson Shawn, who recently broke his ankle in two places. Because he has to be in a cast for six weeks, I thought a pie would cheer him up.

Taking the warm pie from the oven, I drove to upper Prairie Creek and, while mom took Shawn to the hospital, I took care of grandson Bart. When Shawn returned with his wet cast on, he said the doctor had asked him if he'd received any sympathy from the family. "My grandma baked me a pear pie," he said. That's what grandmas are for.

Delivered eggs and arranged publicity for a museum benefit, then returned to my kitchen to peel the remainder of those little pears and start some pear butter to cooking. How I love the smell of spices and pears simmering together in the crock pot. After 24 hours it is thick and ready to can.

Warmer, with partial clearing. The potato crew is readying the last cellar for storage, as all others are filled. It will be a relief to have all those spuds out of the ground. Then there are cows to trail in from the hills, spring calves to wean, more cows and calves to be driven from the high moraine, fall calves to brand...Ranch work follows the seasons as they roll.

October 16—Soft, fat flakes of snow dance in the wind. Although the snow isn't sticking here, it is on upper Prairie Creek. Brief glimpses of mountains paint a winter scene between snow flurries. It is cold, and will become colder by nightfall. Our faithful, hardy potato crew is working in the last field today. If all goes well, they should finish tomorrow.

Looking out at the cold, thinking of the gals on the diggers, I feel a bit guilty in my warm kitchen. Taking from the oven a batch of peanut butter granola cookies, hearing the seasoned tamarack pop in the wood cookstove, smelling pear butter simmering, mingling with the baking cookies, typing this column…when suddenly, in they come!

It is lunch time and they are frozen. Some put their feet up on the open oven door, others group around the fire's cozy warmth and eat their lunches. I offer freshly baked cookies and don't feel quite so guilty.

Doug informs me that the harvest party and dinner will be this Friday in our shop. Guess I'd better get this column out and begin planning for that. Around 60 people will be coming for dinner.

October 17—A pack of serenading coyotes breaks the frosty silence of early morning. The porch thermometer registers a chilly 20 degrees, but the low meadows along the water courses appear much colder. Prairie Creek is white with October frost.

A homey warmth radiates from the old Monarch as I prepare breakfast. Sausage sizzles in the iron skillet next to sunny-side-up eggs. Thick pear butter is spread on slices of whole wheat toast. I carry a tea kettle of hot water to the chicken pen to thaw out the the waterer, then out to the barn to throw some meadow hay to the milk cows and calves. Alfie, my mule, waits not-too-patiently for her breakfast. The "raspberry kittens" tag along, always underfoot now, seeking affection and food.

My kitchen is soon full of women potato workers, all waiting where it is warm until the ground thaws out enough to dig. They will finish today. We catch an occasional glimpse of snow-clad mountains as they appear through bursts of weak sunlight that burn away misty clouds cloaking their high peaks.

At noon, daughter Ramona and I drive grandson Bart to La Grande to catch a ride there and return to school in Salem. La Grande is 60 miles distant from Prairie Creek, and a nice drive. I especially enjoy traveling the Minam canyon when October paints the canyon autumn colors.

After leaving Minam Hill, we drive down across Cricket Flat and encounter a wild wind storm that stays with us the rest of the day. After a rendezvous with a kindly woman from Baker City who will deliver Bart to Salem, Ramona and I duck out of the wind into a charming little place on Main Street called the "Fickle Fox" to eat lunch.

A big storm moving in, so we hurry home. Dark clouds boil up and the wind blows even harder. Back in Wallowa County the wind has uncovered the mountains, and their pure whiteness contrasts with the dark, purple sky. Driving by the potato field, I could see our faithful crew still hard at work in that bitterly cold wind. As the two diggers chugged down the final rows, I could bet the gals were very thankful the harvest would soon be over.

Due to the storm, our power was off for three hours this evening. I lit candles and an oil lamp, cooked supper on the Monarch, and enjoyed the quiet. There is something to be said for silence. No appliances humming, no TV; even the muffled roar of the wind was somehow soothing.

After supper, we read by lamp light and were just heading for bed when the electricity came on.

October 18—Willow leaves and limbs are strewn about the yard this morning, and new storms sweep over the Wallowas, dumping even more snow. It has warmed to 40 degrees.

Made several phone calls arranging for CattleWomen to serve at the senior meal site tomorrow. Then began peeling apples and baking deep-dish apple pies for the harvest party in our shop tomorrow evening.

More phone calls break the monotony of peeling apples. One amusing one from Dottie Britton, county 4-H Extension agent. She was in jail! Would I bail her out? After I pledged a sum of $10 that would be donated to the local cancer fund, Dottie thanked me and hoped other 4-H leaders would be able to come up with enough to bail her out.

Suddenly it was quiet. The wind laid down, and it began to rain. Now that the potatoes are out of the ground, let it rain.

Fresh venison steaks and baked potatoes for supper, topped off with lemon cream pie made from a 100-year-old recipe. In the mail today, a card from my mother and her husband, Bill, from Massachusetts. They are enjoying a New England autumn.

The photo postcard showed the Housatonic River flowing between the southern Berkshire mountains. Flaming maples blazed among evergreens along the river bank.

October 19—Cold, windy, frosty. I was busy from the minute my feet hit the floor in the morning until I crawled wearily into bed at night. The harvest party!

Soon, 35 pounds of top sirloin was roasting in three dutch ovens. I put together a humongous potato salad, baked two pumpkin pies, set a large canning kettle full of beans and ham hocks on the Monarch to simmer all day, and gathered up paper plates, napkins and silverware for 60 people.

Meanwhile, it took five men to clean out our shop. By noon they had it pretty well under control and I invited them all in for sample slices of roast beef on hoagie buns. After demolishing what was left of the lemon cream pie, they continued on with the ranch work.

Daughter Jackie arrived to help with the long loaves of french bread, and soon Brenda and her daughter, Julie, appeared to help set the tables and decorate them with autumn leaves and Indian corn. Grandchildren Buck and Mona, from Imnaha, also helped carry things out to the shop.

By 6:30 we had a shop full of potato crew and their families. We carried out and served the hot food to a grateful group of people. A pot of cowboy coffee simmered on the shop's wood stove, and the place was cozy and warm.

Meanwhile, the temperature outside plunged rapidly. As everyone was finishing the last crumbs of pie and ice cream, Scotty stood up and presented a humorous account of this year's harvest, much to the amusement of the crew. She then presented Doug with a "spud phone" and a potato "man," which had been cleverly fashioned by Rose Glaus.

Scotty has worked for Doug for more than 15 years, and despite her age she continues to be one of our best workers.

October 20—Eighteen degrees. Heavy frost. Clear, crisp, cold. Slept in until 6:30, then wearily stumbled out of bed to fix breakfast. My thoughtful husband suggested we eat in Joseph. All right!

Back to the ranch to carry in all that stuff from the shop, hang out a wash, and scrub kettles. That evening Doug and I treated ourselves to barbecued beef ribs at the Elks, after which I brought home two grandchildren who would spend the night.

Grandma and her two little ones "camped" in front of the fireplace and bedded down in sleeping bags. After reading many books, telling numerous hunting stories, drinking endless glasses of water, eating grandma's cookies, and making subsequent trips to the bathroom, we finally slept.

In the morning four-year-old James said, "Get up, grandma, time to go duck hunting!"

Doug left with several menfolk of the family to go steelhead fishing on Imnaha, and the children and I "pretended camping" until time for Sunday school. It was raining and cold. Good weather for ducks!

After church we drove to Alder Slope and enjoyed Sunday dinner with family. The men returned after dark from fishing, all smiles. The weather must have been good for steelhead because they brought home two nice ones. Fish barbecue tomorrow night.

October 28—This Sunday just wasn't my day! Perhaps it was due to the time change; surely an extra hour of sleep couldn't have made that much difference. I was cooking oatmeal on the stove and going back and forth from the kitchen to the front room window, watching a bright pink sunrise, when my dog began to bark. She was standing outside the open gate to the chicken pen, where some "varmit" had recently created havoc in the midst of my otherwise placid hens.

Chester strutted back and forth, feathers ruffled, squawking *buc, buc, buc, ba—uck!* One hen was chewed up beyond recognition, while another one was found dead between the chicken pen and the barn. Why the gate was open remains a mystery, and whatever critter did the dastardly deed made its escape before I arrived.

When I went out to feed Alfie I heard the strange yelping of a solitary coyote behind the barn. Then I noticed my mare stretched out prone on the grass, obviously in misery, with what appeared to be a severe case of colic.

When Doug and I were hauling the mare into the vet, the coyote was heading toward the milk cow's pasture. Could this be the culprit of the chicken pen? Our veterinarian didn't paint a very rosy future for my mare...in fact, he didn't paint any future; and as we left, I sadly gave her a last loving pat.

On the way home I thought about all those miles we'd both traveled behind a bunch of cows, and I wasn't feeling exactly cheerful when four of my grandchildren showed up. Things got better after a wonderful afternoon of "playing camping" under the card table.

After their parents picked up the children I was attempting to restore some semblance of order to our living room, and while carrying a card table downstairs, it happened! My feet suddenly went out from under me and I came down, full force (card table and all) onto my tailbone. Ouch!

October 30—The unusually warm wind continued. More elk hunters drove into the ranch, parked their trailer, then went looking for a likely place in the woods to camp.

The cowboys worked the last bunch of fall calves and, after lunch, Sandra and Fred drove in. After they unloaded a box of persimmons and apples, our porch resembled a California fruit stand. Other hunters had given us kiwis and strawberries.

That afternoon I baked two pumpkin pies, all the while visiting with Sandra in the kitchen. Lots of conversation went into those pies! That evening I almost forgot my sore tailbone as Sandra, Fred, Doug and I laughed and visited over a home-cooked steak dinner.

October 31—Up early to find Doug already in the kitchen frying mountain oysters and scrambling eggs. After doing the chores, I made a big lunch and soon the two men and I were off to the hills to bag a cow elk, leaving Sandra snuggled in a warm bed.

Around 9 a.m. I couldn't help smiling to myself at the absurdity of the situation: sore tailbone, sitting here in this remote corner of Eastern Oregon, miles from home in cold and pouring rain that seemed more on the verge of snow, looking for a phantom herd of elk!

To make a long, wet, cold hunting story short, we returned with two nice cow elk. The men were nearly frozen to death, all icy blood and mud from gutting out two elk in a snow storm.

November 1—We all piled into the van and drove to Cow Creek on the lower Imnaha for steelhead fishing. Although the fish weren't biting that day, the gorge was gorgeous. Chukar hunting was excellent and we bagged enough for a meal.

A light shower erupted about a mile down the trail and we huddled under a rock, waiting for it to ease, when a misty rainbow appeared above us. A sudden burst of sunlight struck sumac and poison oak leaves, the brilliant red and orange colors glistened against the rock formations of the gorge.

On the drive out along the long, winding road that hugs the rim rocks of the Imnaha canyon, we counted 58 deer grazing in the golden light of evening between the Cow Creek bridge and the store at Imnaha.

November 3—Friendships are priceless. All friends are wonderful, but there is something very special about old friends, childhood chums, the ones you've grown up with and keep in touch with over a long period of time. Such a friend is Sandra. She and husband Fred left this morning after spending a week here on the ranch with us.

Anyone who visits us is immediately immersed in our lifestyle, so we continued on with what had to be done each day and they loved it. Sandra and Fred arrived the night before opening morning of elk season, while branding the fall calves was taking place.

For a warm send-off I cooked sourdough huckleberry hotcakes on the wood range for breakfast. Just as they were leaving, Sandra asked

Doug to take a picture of the two of us in front of the old Monarch. Both of us blinked back tears.

Suddenly, 39 years rolled back, and I was matron of honor at her wedding. It was a simple ceremony performed in her home. Suits were the style of the day then, and we both wore one. Sandra's was navy blue, and mine turquoise. The straight skirts were ankle length. Sandra, a year older than I, looked lovely and happy. At 18, I was already married and a young mother of a baby girl.

Thirty-nine years later, my friend still looks lovely and happy. Sandra and Fred celebrated their anniversary with us last Saturday night. Long after Sandra and Fred left, that familiar empty feeling that always appears after someone dear leaves just wouldn't go away.

Busy with daily life here on the ranch, childhood memories came flooding back...Sandra and I taking long walks together in the foothills of northern California, where we grew up. Sharing secrets, talking and dreaming of what we wanted to be when we "grew up," swimming in Doty's Ravine on hot summer days, stealing apples from Wally Allen's apple orchard across the creek, and playing house on Indian Rock.

Canning acorns, collecting butterflies, playing the clarinet in the high school band, remembering the pretty white formal Sandra wore when she was homecoming queen... me borrowing it a year later, when I was queen. Our days were filled with simple pleasures.

Then we graduated, and entered that world we talked about. We grew up. We are still growing up. And we have remained friends over the span of years. Now, as our own children and grandchildren grow up, we compare notes and wonder what the future holds for them. The pendulum swings and our hopes and desires are centered around them.

November 5—There was a heavy frost as I fed my mule and surviving chickens. Then, I eased myself into the car and delivered a projector and slide tape program, "The Wallowa Story," to the Flying Arrow Resort at Wallowa Lake, to be shown at an Elderhostel program that evening.

Meanwhile, our cowboys, minus this cowgirl and her horse, moved the fall calvers and calves to the ranch from upper Prairie Creek. The good news that Monday concerned my mare. She was going to live!

In fact, Doug hauled her home that very afternoon. The cowboys, plus three visiting elk hunters, branded and worked the first bunch of calves, while I prepared lunch. Soon an assortment of men filled my kitchen and the hunting tales that precede elk season fairly flew!

Tamaracks, growing on the slopes of the Wallowas, glowed golden among the evergreens. A warmish, late October wind blew, and elk hunters began to arrive in our county.

November 13—Gusting winds rattled around Prairie Creek all night and continued on into the morning. Swirling leaves pile up by the back door. "The raspberry kittens" huddle together for warmth on an old rug next to a wheelbarrow full of split wood.

Alfie the mule loves the wind. Head held high, she races after me as I walk to the barn carrying two suckle bottles full of warm milk replacer for the orphan calves. A "cowboy's sunrise," brilliant against the dull November hills, tells us rain is on the way. So does the wind.

Doug and I up early to accomplish what has to be done before we depart at noon for Portland and the Cattlemen's/CattleWomen's convention. Hopefully, tomorrow morning at this time Doug and I will be participating in a school Beef Blitz at Portland's Thomas Junior High with teacher Jan Preedy and her students.

Armed with map, lesson plans and tri-tip recipe ingredients provided by the Oregon Beef Council, we will attempt to find Thomas Junior High. Not an easy task for us country folks. However, if Jan and her junior high classes had to find Zumwalt, it would definitely be a problem!

That is what the Beef Blitz is all about. After we leave, hopefully these city students will not only have tasted our beef recipes, but tasted our way of life as well, and we theirs. For if we expect the students of Thomas Junior High to understand our way of life, we must make an attempt to understand theirs as well.

Piled on the table around my typewriter this morning, in addition to various cooking utensils needed for the demos, are samples of items manufactured from cattle by-products. This is a learning experience for us as well, because it is easy to forget that so many of the products we humans use every day come from the cow.

Beef is a remarkable, renewable resource. In fact, the pharmaceutical and textile industries, along with the butcher, baker and candlestick maker, would all be out of work if it weren't for the cow. An amazing thing about the cow: she keeps on giving...long after she is dead.

So, in my growing pile on the table are marshmallows, crayons, a toothbrush, film, glue, perfume, shoe grease, soap, phonograph records, a ceramic cow, and a band-aid...all manufactured from beef by-products. The American National CattleWomen have printed an informative brochure entitled *When is a cow more than a cow?* containing answers such as *when it's a meal, when it's a household, when it's a pharmacy* and *when it gets us there.*

Doug and I will demonstrate beef recipes in the classroom, and at the same time visit informally with the students. We will take this opportunity to show them pictures of our working cattle ranch and point out on a map where we live. We will be eager to know more about them— how they live and how they perceive our world. Often we perceive their world, but how can we really know unless we talk on a one-to-one basis?

Twenty schools in Portland have requested the CattleWomen and Cattlemen participate in the school blitz program. This is only a drop in the bucket. If city schools all over the U.S. could instigate such a movement, it would help bring about more understanding and help bridge that country-city gap.

A rancher standing in front of a class of Portland students is real, and so are those young people in Jan Preedy's junior high class. Wish us luck, and I'll report how it went…that is, if we can find Thomas Junior High School.

November 20—A fresh snowfall blankets Prairie Creek this morning, and the newly weaned calves are "in concert" down in the corrals. Alfie kicks up her heels, leaving a trail of flying snow behind her. The young molly mule still follows me each morning and evening to the calving shed, hoping for an affectionate pat.

Returned safely from Portland, we find ourselves once again in the rhythm of ranch living. Thanksgiving is only two days away and, at last count, 23 will be around our table this year. I should say tables, for we shall have to bring in saw horses and plywood to make our seating space. Our family helps with food preparation, and everyone loves to come to grandma and grandpa's.

But first, before I start baking those pumpkin and mincemeat pies, this column must get to the mailbox. Thanks to the efficient staff at the Oregon Beef Council office, Doug and I actually found Thomas Junior High School, even though it was some 20 miles from the Red Lion at Lloyd Center.

With Doug driving and yours truly reading directions, we were soon one with the flow of early morning traffic, speeding along the Sunset Highway to Hillsboro. For us country folks, the sights here, although different from what we are used to, were nevertheless fascinating.

The sky was cloudy with tiny patches of blue peeking through a moving, misty fog that curled around the meadows and low-lying areas of the suburbs. Ahead of us car lights poured like a twinkling river from a tunnel, curving downhill, heading into Portland. The morning commute.

Brilliant maples, their colors varying from yellow to deep orange/red, flamed along the highway. Evergreens mixed into the palette of color and appeared almost surreal through the fog. We turned off Shute Road and drove through a lovely, landscaped park of some sort, adjacent to a wild woodland. I made a mental note to tell the students at Thomas Junior High what a nice area they lived in.

We were met by a smiling Jan Preedy, who was already in her class-room. Jan made a pot of coffee, and offered us fresh apple juice and we soon felt right at home. "The kitchen is yours," she said as we hung our charts and arranged our demo equipment.

By 8 a.m. we were ready to roll with the first of four classes. Doug and I introduced ourselves, showed the students on an Oregon map where we lived, and began preparing beef tri-tip recipes.

Soon the kitchen smelled of broiling, herb-rubbed tri-tip roast and while the 30-minute cooking time elapsed, we talked about beef by-products and showed the students items we'd brought from home. They were amazed to learn that 99 percent of a cow is used for something.

While Doug demonstrated cutting a pocket in another beef tri-tip, I made a dressing to stuff inside, which contained herb-seasoned croutons, jack cheese, cilantro, egg, green onion and lime juice. This cilantro-stuffed tri-tip roast was later given to a very pleased Jan Preedy to take home.

The most interesting part of the school beef blitz was the question and answer period, when we learned more about the students themselves. Doug and I took turns answering questions about ranch life in faraway Eastern Oregon.

One student wanted to know if Doug went to an office each day to work; whereupon Doug thought a minute, then replied, "Well yes, sort of, but the office is in our home." Several students' fathers were at that moment hunting elk in Wallowa County. We asked what the students did for recreation.

"We go to the shopping malls," was one answer; "watch TV," another. Even though they were near to rural areas, their experiences in agricul-ture were limited. One boy had shown a hog at the PI, which is held close by at the Washington County Fairgrounds. The students didn't know what FFA stood for, as Thomas Junior High had no vocational ag program.

We let the students pass around photos depicting scenes of our ranch life, family, and Wallowa County. They seemed very interested and the pictures prompted more questions. When the herb-rubbed tri-tip roast was done, Doug demonstrated how to slice across the grain, and then those students devoured every scrap of that delicious beef.

Jan Preedy, 20 years a teacher, was reared on a Washington wheat farm.

During our second presentation, Jan filmed us with a video camera. At noon she treated us to a bowl of soup in the teacher's room, after which we returned to the classroom for two more demos. We learned much about the junior high students' lifestyles during those four classes. For instance, we found out many young people were responsible for the family cooking and they served beef several times a week.

As we left, Jan Preedy gave us a jug of homemade apple cider to take home. She and her husband have a small apple orchard. A combined total of 1,500 students in 60 classes at 20 schools were "blitzed" that Wednesday by Oregon CattleWomen and Cattlemen.

Returning to the hotel, we were unable to exit Highway 26 due to a traffic snarl and ended up downtown, which proved to be educational. For me, that is. Doug wanted to get over a bridge, any bridge, and return to East Portland. Meanwhile, I gawked at the city.

Two policemen on horseback clattered along the sidewalk. Flaming maples grew from small squares of dirt surrounded by concrete sidewalks, their leaves floating to the pavement. There was no smog, bright sunlight shining on the city, which was a living thing, going about its business on a bright November day.

A small, stooped white-haired lady, carrying a large brown shopping bag, made her slow, deliberate way across the street. The younger generation passed her by, unnoticed. Businessmen, clad in suits, carried umbrellas in case of rain. Immaculate women stepped out of Nordstrom's with large hats and shiny high-heels, resembling skinny mannequins escaping shop windows.

Overhead, prosperous Portland's highrises gleamed in the afternoon sun, their thousands of glass windows sparkling clean. The sound of horns honking...the song of the city. At last we found a bridge from which we could see the Red Lion's grinning face. We drove by the twin green glass towers that form the entrance to the new convention center.

A siren wailed; a young boy, a middle aged couple, and a balding man ran to catch a Tri-Met bus. We made it back to the Red Lion and entered the plush creature-comfort world of the hotel, rising silently to the fifth floor in a glass elevator that afforded a view of the city. All of a sudden, we were tireder than if we'd been working cattle. Guess the city isn't for us.

The convention lasted until Saturday. We, along with Wallowa County's large delegation, attended all the events. Too much to report here, but one of the highlights for me was meeting Jane Lindgren, American National CattleWomen president from Joliet, Montana.

Jane opened her talk with the following words, which say it all; and make those of us in the cattle industry proud:

I like American National CattleWomen. I like the way you come in assorted sizes...short, tall and medium. I like the way you come in assorted colors—blonde, brunette and in between.

I like your simplicity. I like your sincerity. I like the way you can wrangle cattle, make crafts or a quilt to donate...and then buy back for a fund raising project.

I like your friendly smiles and happy laughter. I like your compassion, caring, quiet manners and strong dignity. I like the pride you take in your husbands, and the support you give our industry.

I like cattlemen with their broad smiles on their work-worn faces. I like tall cowboy hats, and worn cowboy boots.

I like your children. They stand straight and tall, they have self-reliance, they respect the land, they pray at night, they respect mankind.

CattleWomen are as pretty in blue jeans as they are in the highest fashions. I like CattleWomen because they are helpful, because you know how to get things done.

I like CattleWomen because your homes radiate warmth, the smell of homemade bread and delicious beef roast.

I like CattleWomen for their charm, gentleness, and their courage to fight for what is right. I sure do like CattleWomen.

November 20—Thanksgiving day dawned warm for November, with only a touch of frost feathering the brown grasses along the bottoms. Skies were dull and overcast until a warm wind opened up spaces for the sun to stream through. Lucky for the many grandchildren here that day, as they were able to play outside, thereby allowing grown-ups a chance to visit.

After feeding various livestock their morning meal, I prepared to stuff two large turkeys with homemade bread dressing. What produces more traditional Thanksgiving memories than the delicious smell of onions and celery simmering in butter? As this is poured over a large bowl of cubed bread, the sage and parsley picked fresh from the garden is mixed in along with seasoning and a little broth. Finally, a couple of eggs to hold it together, as grandma used to say. The aroma is Thanksgiving!

As the steam begins to rise over the bubbling giblets, to which more celery and onions have been added, the long-awaited meal materializes. Soon the tantalizing aroma of roast turkey mingles with the other familiar odors, and the family begins to arrive. Little ones take from coat pockets pieces of paper on which they have drawn Thanksgiving wishes for grandma. These are proudly displayed on the refrigerator door.

Daughter Jackie and her family arrive bearing bowls of rising yeast dough and proceed to fill all of my pans with wheat rolls. We actually found seating space for our brood, all 22 of them. Everyone was quiet while we gave thanks for our abundant family, food, health, and way of life.

It was truly a wonderful Thanksgiving, in spite of the effort involved in feeding that many people. Most importantly we hope the occasion will become a precious memory for our children, whom we hope will carry this established tradition onto their young. Families and their traditions are important. The strength of them just could provide the saving grace for America's troubled future.

The weaned calves, settled down now, have ceased their bawling and turned their attentions to eating. The short winter days have arrived and the most recent snowfall covers the frozen ground.

As I write, a new storm materializes; blowing snow swirls past the window and sifts down upon the old snow. The wood cookstove gulps wood, the tea kettle sings, and Prairie Creek seems cut off from the rest of the world as brief daylight fades. Soon I will walk down the road to the calving shed and feed the orphan calf.

It is a major production just to go outside now. We would be chilled to the bone if we weren't dressed properly. This means overalls, warm scarf, gloves, boots, and jacket. Our mud room, or back porch, is a mixture of boots, a sack of calf milk replacer, veterinary supplies, hay that clings to us as we feed livestock and then falls on the floor, dirty gloves and dripping jackets.

Cloudy November skies contribute to spectacular sunrises and sunsets. Last evening while I was choring, a large flock of wild geese caught my eye. Etched against a persimmon sky, their feathered bodies formed a wavering V that pierced the brilliant sunset.

Honking of wild geese is a melancholy sound, perhaps because it signals the long winter ahead. I stepped out of the calving shed to find the sunset's flame had gone out, but the white and blue mountains glowed cold and somber, bathed in lemon light.

Winter has its advantages. Long, snowy evenings are good for the mind; that is if you are a reader. That long-anticipated stack of books piled by my bedstand can now be devoured. On days when it is cold outside but warm and cozy inside, I attempt to clean out my desk drawers.

I say attempt, because my work is never very productive. I soon find myself reading old letters that I've kept for years and can't bear to part with. Like some I found yesterday, written by my grandmother a year before she passed away. She was well over 100 when she painfully typed them out. Her hands hurting with arthritis, she still felt the need to communicate to a granddaughter 800 miles away in Oregon.

I am taken back in time to her last years, and realize just how precious life is, how short a time we have on earth. Reading her letters gives me a sense of continuity. My life goes on, perhaps where hers left off, for I have a feeling there were many experiences in my life grandma would have liked to have shared.

Watching my children mature, and their children, who are ever-changing, I can better understand grandma, and admire her even more for the way she looked at and accepted life.

A basket full of ripe persimmons shares the kitchen table with my typewriter, reminding me to bake a batch of cookies. For those of you who are lucky enough to come by some ripe persimmons, here is a recipe from my grandmother's old cookbook.

Persimmon Cookies

- 1/2 cup butter
- 1 cup chopped nuts
- 1 egg
- 2 cups flour
- 1/2 teaspoon cinnamon
- 1/2 teaspoon cloves
- 1 cup sugar
- 1 to 2 cups raisins
- 1 cup persimmon pulp
- 1 teaspoon soda
- 1/2 teaspoon nutmeg

Cream the butter and sugar in bowl. Add nuts and raisins; mix well. Beat egg. Stir in persimmon pulp. Add to butter mixture and stir until mixed. Add remaining ingredients; mix well. Drop from teaspoon onto greased baking sheet. Bake in preheated 350-degree oven for 10 to 15 minutes. Yields 3 dozen.

While I type the final copy of this column, listening for the timer to go off so I can take the first fragrant batch of persimmon cookies from the oven, I'll also be thinking of my friend Sandra and her husband, Fred, who gave us the beautiful orange fruit.

November 29—I took a Christmas tree that Doug had cut for us down to the bazaar, where other members of our Wallowa Valley Photo Club met to decorate it. The tree would provide a backdrop for taking photos of children with Santa Claus.

Cloverleaf Hall bustled with activity, transformed into an old-time Christmas. Artsy-crafty wares were colorfully arranged on tables; homemade candies, cookies, fruit breads, lovely handmade aprons, knitted sweaters, pine needle baskets, mop dolls, stick horses and stick mules, ceramics, leather crafts, paintings, and fragrant pine bough wreaths.

Delicious smells wafted from the kitchen where the ladies of the Imnaha Grange were beginning to cook tomorrow's soup. Imnaha cooks are noted for their pies, and a long refrigerated case displayed mouth-watering pies of every description. After the trees was decorated, we turned on the lights and were pleased, knowing Santa and the children would be, too.

November 30—A frigid breeze blew snow into small drifts as I chored. We gave the orphan calf to granddaughter Carrie, so I no longer walk down to the calving shed twice a day with a bottle. The "raspberry kittens" still follow me to hay the milk cows and feed Alfie and my mare, then accompany me into the chicken house to water and feed the hens and Chester.

Later that morning I was off to Joseph where I sold beef gift certificates in the Bank of Wallowa County until 12:30, at which time I drove over icy roads to Cloverleaf Hall and the bazaar. I spent what was left of that day photographing children with Santa Claus.

This year we had the added attraction of Mrs. Santa, who passed out candy canes and charmed the children. She had made her own dress and cap. Very colorful. Several of the children commented that they'd always wondered where Mrs. Santa Claus was.

It is a priceless experience to witness remarks made to Santa by children. One small, smiling girl looked adoringly up into old St. Nick's bewhiskered face and said: "Remember when I was four, and I didn't like you? But now I love you!" Others came clutching handwritten Christmas lists, which Santa seriously studied.

Cloverleaf Hall was filled with the spirit of Christmas. At 4, I was relieved of my photo-taking duties and able to enjoy a roast beef dinner cooked by the Imnaha Grange ladies. Long tables off the kitchen were decorated with pine boughs, red ribbons and candy canes.

The Wallowa County Old Time Fiddlers assembled and began to play. There was warmth and laughter as neighbors came from miles around to visit and do some of their Christmas shopping at the bazaar. Some folks from out north near Flora reported they had six-foot drifts, but that hadn't stopped them from coming to town.

I arrived home well after dark to feed my animals and rest up for another day of photographing.

December 1—Eight degrees this morning, our lowest reading yet. I was up by 6 a.m. doing chores in the cold moon-lit dawn. After a hardy breakfast (remembering yesterday, when I didn't have time to eat lunch) I drove once more to Cloverleaf Hall for another long day of shooting.

By 11:30 a.m. it began to snow, and by afternoon had worked itself into a full-scale blizzard. Santa cut his visit short and returned to the North Pole, so at 3:30 I was loading Christmas tree, rocking chair, table, stool, tripod, camera and other paraphernalia into the pickup before heading home over snowy, slick roads to Prairie Creek.

I worried about Doug, gone for two days, driving over the Blue

Mountains in the blizzard. Two grandchildren arrived to spend the night. As I was reading them a bedtime story, Doug drove in.

December 2—Pretty snowflake patterns are plastered against the window panes this morning due to a wind that swirled snow around in the night; 20 degrees, much warmer than yesterday. The children even built a small snow-man before mom picked them up.

Rested up today, curled up with a good book. By 4:30 the full December moon was already high in the sky. Doug drove out to the hills to check our cattle, and reported roads nearly drifted in. The cows would have to be trailed in by the end of the week.

Awoke at 12:30 a.m. unable to sleep. Looking out the living room window I could see bare willow limbs casting moving shadows on the snowy, moonlit lawn. Prairie Creek glittered in snow light and the entire Wallowa chain stood out in sharp relief.

December 4—Hurricane force winds that roared to life during the night have thankfully subsided. Overhead, a great opening of blue sky appears this December afternoon. Over the mountains, shrouded in snow curtains, dark purple clouds spew more snow. Prairie Creek temperatures have moderated and occasionally a few drops of rain splatter against a window pane.

During the height of this morning's storm, our neighbors' hay stack caught fire and burned. Fortunately their buildings were spared as the wind was from the south. In nearby Joseph there was more damage. A roof blew off the grade school building, a few windows were shattered, and garbage cans flew everywhere.

In the aftermath here on Prairie Creek, our ranch resembles a moonscape; snow lies in sculptured dirt-blasted drifts. Most of the snow evaporated in the fierce breath of the wind. And through it all Wallowa Countians go about their business as usual. Here, too, ranch life must go on.

Ben, Doug and Charley loaded two semi-loads of weaned calves, which began their long trip to Hermiston this morning, to spend the winter growing out in warmer climes. There is always the daily feeding of cattle left behind. Silage and hay must be fed to the cows and fall calves, and the young bulls are fed twice a day.

Meanwhile, out in the open Salmon Creek hill country, our cows are undoubtedly ready to come home.

Looking out the window to the east, I can see my oldest son driving his cows in from fall range for the winter. The long line of cattle drifts down the gravel road through the fold in the hills known as Echo Canyon.

Two cowboys on horseback and two dogs bring up the rear. It must be cold in the saddle today, as a leftover wind whispers through the hill country that divides prairie from canyon.

Baked squash pies this afternoon, making two small ones for visiting grandchildren. The annual Handcrafters' Bazaar last Friday and Saturday really brought Christmas into focus. Christmas! We just finished the Thanksgiving leftovers.

December 6—Gray, misty rain fell all day, turning to snow by evening. This morning clean snow-covered Prairie Creek blinks in bright sunlight. Snowscapes are more pleasing to the eye than rainy ones. They lift one's spirit.

December 7—Only 10 degrees when I arose to a dark, cold dawn to cook sausage gravy over hash browns, Doug's favorite breakfast (next to sourdough hotcakes). The ice in the ditches is pretty thick now, so am chopping holes so the horses and mule can drink.

December 8—Made myself sit down and begin writing Christmas card letters. Then I baked a double batch of persimmon cookies to store in the freezer. Emory Crawford of Milton-Freewater stopped by for a visit and left us a box of Granny Smith apples. We had to talk about our mules, of course.

December 9—After Doug treated me to breakfast at Kohlhepp's Kitchen in Joseph, where we were joined by daughter Ramona and son-in-law Charley, we drove to the hills with a load of protein blocks.

The hills, unlike the valley, were spattered with patches of snow, except for southern slopes, and ridges, which were bare and covered with a goodly amount of bunch grass. Since the weather had moderated somewhat and plenty of grass remains, Doug decided to leave cows and heifers there a while longer.

As we neared the old Dorrance place, where for many months road building or road changing or whatever has been taking place, it was a relief to see the federal highway project appeared to be completed, even if it has left the area looking strange.

Along both sides of the road, an unnatural shade of green jumped out of the landscape. The only other reminder of the construction was a solitary outhouse…also green. Thank goodness the road changers hadn't gone beyond Dorrance Gulch and up into the Salmon Creek country.

There we found drifted snow piled up along the roads. Some drifts near the fences had been carved by wind into frozen ocean-like waves, stilled in silence. The air was snow-clean, pure, fresh. The sun was warm and a slight breeze moved golden bunch grass. Hawks and ravens owned the hills. They were the only visible wildlife that day, but we could see evidence of porcupines that had been feeding in thornbrush thickets.

A snow plow had recently opened up a road near Deadman. Here Doug unloaded the first of the protein blocks, which we put out in four locations. He also chopped holes in the frozen ponds so cattle could drink.

We bounced over that vast hill range in the 4x4 pickup, never seeing another human or another vehicle. Just acres of rolling hill land, under a cobalt sky, stretching to the distant Wallowas in the south and the Seven Devils range to the east. The cattle, wearing winter coats, looked healthy and eagerly approached the protein supplement. They slurped and licked the palatable blocks, which contain molasses in addition to minerals.

The landscape made a winter statement. All around us were wind-swept ridges, golden bunch grasses, scab rock, frozen creeks and ponds, coyote tracks and limitless space. How I love the hills, even in December.

Most winters, the cattle would have long since been trailed to the valley and fed until May, but they have been allowed to stay longer due to an exceptional grass year. Of course, a heavy snowfall could change all that, and Doug drives out on a daily basis to check the cattle and break ice for stock water.

Driving along I wondered at the miles of fence—rockjack-stay-stay-stay-stay-rockjack-stay—and renewed my respect for the fence-builders. Most of the four-strand barbed wire has been patched and re-patched many times over the years, but, like the hills, the fences endure. Made from materials at hand, the rocks and split tamarack from the nearby forests, the fences fit into the character of the hills.

That evening, I prepared a vegetable tray and we joined neighbors at Wallowa Lake for a delicious roast beef supper. Good conversation with good friends helped get us into the Christmas spirit.

Granddaughter Tamara (Tammy) is home from college for the holidays. She's a 20-year-old junior at Cal Poly in San Luis Obispo, California. She brought me a copy of Ag Circle, a student newspaper published by Agricultural Communicators of Tomorrow. One of Tamara's articles made the front page. Naturally, grandma is proud.

The headline, "Mill Grinds its Way to the Top," begins the story that tells how Cal Poly has two types of dining halls on campus. One supplies nutrition to the students and the other takes care of all the livestock. The feed mill, built in 1950, is the biggest university feed mill in 11 Western states.

This young reporter writes that the mill is unusual in that it produces poultry, swine and beef rations in the same mill. Last year, $1 million worth of feed was sold with a profit margin large enough to cover expenses and salaries, though it does not sell to outside sources beyond Poly. The mill buys up some of the grain crops produced by the Crops Department.

Tamara's roommate, and friend since kindergarten days, Meredith Rehrman, writes about Ag in the Classroom. She says California's Ag in the Classroom has already been acknowledged as one of the most successful educational programs in the nation.

"It has succeeded in partnering agriculture and education, public and private sectors, and a variety of resources and activities." The program began in 1980 to address the problem of agricultural illiteracy in America.

Meredith reports that less than two percent of the total American population make a living on a farm or ranch, and this has had an overwhelming impact on society. She says "a large percentage of Americans do not recognize the relationship between agriculture and the American lifestyle." Most people have a preconceived idea of what agriculture is, but they need to see the reality.

Her article also says, "We needed Ag in the Classroom twenty years ago...and people today need facts; they need them presented as farmers, ranchers and ag industry leaders would present them, in their own way; they need to see what agriculturalists do and why."

Meredith says the program, which sponsors close to 20 projects, is funded by individuals, organizations, foundations and businesses that also want to help promote these goals and activities. Last year's fundraising efforts brought more than $200,000.

Isn't it encouraging to know that we have young people from rural backgrounds who care about the future of agriculture? I was impressed with their knowledge and enthusiasm to be involved in reporting these important issues. Perhaps the future is in good hands, if the students at other ag colleges are as competent as those at Cal Poly.

December 11—We greeted a dark, frozen dawn. New snow crunched underfoot as I chored. Doug and Ben branded and worked some heifers down at the chutes, coming inside every so often to thaw out.

December 12—11 degrees. A few rosy clouds tinted the eastern horizon before daylight. When the sun spilled over the edge of the world, Prairie Creek glittered like a thousand diamonds. It was a sausage gravy and potatoes morning.

Returning some books to my friend Linde Irwin, who with husband, Pat, lives in a log home they have been building at timberline on upper Prairie Creek, was like driving through a Christmas card.

Blue sky contrasted with Chief Joseph Mountain's brilliant snow fields, dark evergreens, their boughs laden with snow, covered the slopes; long lines of cattle eating hay scattered on snowy pastures; old weathered barns, snowy country lanes, split rail fences and frozen ponds all came to life under the brightness of a December sun.

December 13—Mixed up the sourdough before cooking breakfast this morning. A freshly baked loaf of bread is my annual contribution to the CattleWomen's gift exchange, and our local group will meet at noon today. Although bitterly cold outside, it was warm and Christmasy inside Marian Birkmaier's house.

Our CattleWomen's meeting was short, so we could enjoy the holiday treats we had brought and open our gifts. The latest "thing" making the rounds at gift exchanges is to give each person a number. Number one chooses a package and opens it for all to see and exclaim over. Number two has a choice. She can choose number one's gift or an unopened one.

This procedure creates hilarious dilemmas, as gifts are shifted around and owned briefly by all, until the last person has her turn. Betty Van kept everyone in suspense before deciding on the sourdough bread, much to Elaine Morse's chagrin.

That evening Doug and I attended an open house hosted by our photo club president. More goodies and another one of those gift exchanges, after which we enjoyed Alan Klages' beautiful slides.

Our Wallowa Valley towns are decorated with such a variety of colorful Christmas lighting this year, it is fun to drive around and enjoy them after dark. Even though this small winter population in the corner of Northeastern Oregon must brave the cold, their hearts are warm with the spirit of Christmas.

December 14—The thermometer under the clothes line registered a chilly six degrees when I went out to chore. Breath from my milk cows hung in the frosty air. Soon I was off to Enterprise to meet family at "A Country Place on Pete's Pond," where we celebrated daughter Jackie's birthday. We ate breakfast on the sunny, windowed deck that perches over a large frozen pond and watched many wild geese take to the air from a small patch of open water. What a treat seeing their graceful flight against snowy Ruby Peak. Noisy mallard ducks came to a skidding landing on the ice; steam hovered over the open water. Such are some of the winter sights tourists never see, but we are able to enjoy.

After eating a hearty hot breakfast, we shared photos sent to us from my mother and her husband, who spent three weeks in the New England fall. We were amazed to see mom, at 80, paddling a canoe.

Later, home in my kitchen, Jackie and I began cooking for a dinner to be served to 158 people at Cloverleaf Hall tomorrow night. The rest of that day was spent in preparing for that meal, and by nightfall I was ready for bed.

December 15—Ruby Peak blushed pink as I chored this morning. I took time to enjoy the sight, which would give me an added lift to face the day. The temperature didn't rise much above 15 degrees all that day, as we transported our feast to Cloverleaf Hall.

By 6 p.m. we were ready and, thanks to good help from family and friends, everything went off without a hitch.

December 16—Concentrated on decorating our home for Christmas while Doug drove to the hills to check on the cows. Seems a lot warmer today at 20 degrees.

A large, fresh evergreen wreath, delivered to our door from sister Kathryn, now hangs above the fire-place. The nativity scene was carefully unwrapped and placed on the mantel and a new lighted angel graces the top of our tree. After Doug returned from the hills, we ate supper before attending a Christmas cantata at the Enterprise Baptist Church.

Daughter Ramona and her family rode in with us. When we walked into the church, there must have been more than 300 people and we had a time finding seats. A group of violinists (children, teenagers and adults) were playing Christmas carols when we arrived.

The church, with its high wooden beams, beamed with the warmth of the season. Soon the choir members came down the aisle, took their places and began to sing. Cowboys, teachers and housewives blended their voices in joyful sound.

Our local radio announcer, Dave Nelson, narrated the story of "Heaven's Child." Carole Troutman, whose lovely voice led the choir, was accompanied by Elizabeth Perry on the piano. Then the children took their places and their voices mingled with the adults'. Their joy was reflected in their voices and this grandma's heart was full.

Three of my grandchildren and one daughter were among the singers. Wallowa County's community Christmas Choir's cantata ended with the audience joining in the singing of "Silent Night." If only the whole world could have been there.

December 17—Mailed the last of our Christmas cards and began shopping for gifts. A freezing wind blew across Wallowa's winter wonderland today and snow spit against the wind shield as I drove home from Joseph.

December 18—Our Christmas tree is decorated with gingerbread men. The ice grows thicker as the shortest day of the year approaches, and by the time you read this, 1990 will soon be history.

Cowboys Ben and Charley left this morning to bring the remaining cattle in from the hills. It is definitely long johns weather as an arctic cold front is poised to blast an official winter greeting. The mountains are veiled behind thick snow clouds as small mini-blizzards swirl over the valleys and hills.

The old Monarch eats up stacks of split tamarack; the cattle eagerly await their daily meal of silage and hay; crows, hawks and an occasional owl light in the ancient bare-limbed willows. Once in a while we glimpse a few small birds, but most have gone south for the winter.

December 18—There is the smell of snow in a howling wind that arrived sometime in the night. Out to chore in the dark, windy dawn, chopping ice to water horses and mule, and carrying hot water to the chickens.

Our cows and heifers, trailed by the cowboys, make it to the Circle M corrals, along Crow Creek road by eyeing. Ben hauled a pickup load of hay and scattered it around for the cattle to eat tonight.

Outside, our Christmas tree winks its colored lights against the window; a friendly beacon along our lonely country road.

December 19—Up early to fix breakfast, after Doug starts a fire in the fireplace and wood stove. Look back in my journal and see that we didn't bring the cattle in from the hills until January 3rd last year. Only one day all winter did it get below zero, and on Christmas day 1989 it was 40 degrees.

Our cows make it to the valley by late afternoon, with no time to spare; a bitter cold front begins to move in.

Grandchildren here today and we baked gingerbread cookies. I let them cut out gingerbread men and animals with cookie cutters. There is flour and dough clinging to everything, but little ones so love making cookies. Afterward we colored scenes in a large coloring book and read stories.

After struggling with layers of clothes, mittens and boots, I took the children home. It is already 10 degrees. Due to the predicted cold, we hadn't planned to attend the Imnaha school's Christmas program tonight, but then granddaughter, Mona Lee calls. She really wants grandma and grandpa to come on down.

Crossing over Sheep Creek Hill, a thermometer in our car registers an outside temperature of 2 degrees. By the time we reach Little Sheep creek, dropping down into the canyon, it has gone back up to 11. At the little school, at the bridge of Imnaha, a chilly wind blows off the snow-covered rims.

Inside the two-room school house, things are happening! A gaily lit tree twinkles in one room, while a stage has been set up in the other, complete with a colorful hand-painted back drop created by mothers Anne Borgerding of Big Sheep Creek and Myrna Moore, who lives up Bear Gulch.

All 16 students of grades K-8 performed. They recited poems, sang songs, played instruments, and acted out two original plays written by school marm Char Williams. The one kindergarten student, Tye White, is a great-grandson of the late Jim Dorrance. Mrs. Williams says there are no first graders, but that there were two 8th graders this year. The small, Imnaha canyon community is very proud.

On stage, Luke again, a little taller, more posed now, plays his harmonica and mandolin. His little tow-headed sister, Hope, plays her violin with a determination beyond her years. Acting out the role of a little lady, as eye glasses loaned to her by her father keep falling off, is our little Miss Mona Lee. Brother Buck memorizes his lines in the next play acting out Jack-in-the-beanstalk.

After the children sing several songs, Santa makes his appearance, *ho-ho*-ing down the aisle with a bulging bag of goodies and oranges. Five-year-old Kirk walks up and says: "You aren't the same Santa I saw last night!"

It is easy to pick out the cowboy daddies, whose reddened faces tell they have been out riding in the cold all day. Hope and Luke's dad, Skip, tells me he has pushed the last of the cattle off the top today, bringing them down Camp Creek. He is still thawing out!

Even jolly old Santa walks with the gait of a cowboy. You see, cattle ranching is Imnaha's most important industry. A bonus to the world are the children raised in those families. Far removed from cities, they have learned to make their own fun and they possess a quality that is rare among young people today.

After eating homemade cookies and drinking some hot coffee, we drove the 30 miles home. It was zero degrees "on top" and Prairie Creek slept in cold winter silence.

December 20—A still, white chill settles over Prairie Creek. It is 12 below as I bundle up like an Eskimo to chore. Frost forms on my eyelashes and clings to the scarf, which I wear like a bandit to keep my nose from freezing. Each day the ice penetrates deeper, and the axe is needed to chop into water for the horses and mule. Electric stock tank heaters keep water thawed for the cattle. My chickens, who don't want to get out of bed of a morning, say it is just too cold! There is no warmth to the sun, just light.

The mountains swim in and out of a deep freeze fog pale, ghostly, re-sembling giant bergs in a frozen sea. Our rigs won't start; the neighbors are in the same fix. Huddled together for warmth, Prairie Creek's cattle wait to be fed. My neighbor, Linde, shows up with a stuffed turkey and a ham for me to bake. Their housewarming is tonight. Her oven isn't work-ing, and they have no water in the kitchen. We laugh a housewarming on the coldest night of the year!

The men struggle all day with the trucks and tractors, and finally all of the livestock are fed. The temperature will not rise above zero all day. Grandson Bart is here while mom works at Harshman's store in Joseph.

At noon I fix sourdough waffles to thaw out the frozen men, then bake a large loaf of sourdough bread for the housewarming tonight at Irwin's. Soon my kitchen smells like Christmas. A layer of cold fog obscures Mt. Howard and McCully Creek's drainages. It must be the vapor clouds that form when the waters of Wallowa Lake meet the cold sub-zero air.

A weak, winter sun slips over the mountain at 3:30 p.m. as frost and ice crystals form on the inside of windows, and a white frosty line comes in to cover the metal under the living room door. By 5:30 we are bundled up, hugging hot turkey and baked ham, while driving up to the Irwin's on Upper Prairie Creek.

When we arrive to their home at timberline, it is 22 below! Snow crunches under foot and trees crack in the cold. Inside the cozy new log house, with its high ceilings and sleeping loft, a huge fireplace blazes merrily as neighbors and friends gather to "warm" Linde and Pat's home. The huge peeled log beams reflect fire light, a large Christmas tree adds more warmth and cheer. Outside, snowlight and starlight glitter under the mountain, which looms close.

Around 10 p.m. we step out into the crack'in cold of a 26 below night, and drive home. An eerie, frozen silence engulfs Prairie Creek and we are thankful for flannel sheets.

December 21—Doug up early as usual, making the rounds of our three potato storages to check on the seed. All appears well.

It is still 26 below. The rivers and creeks are beginning to freeze from the bottom up. Looks as though we are experiencing one of those winters the Old Timers keep telling us about!

December 22—As the shortest day of the year dawns, our thermometer registers 22 below zero. At 5:30 a.m., cold stars, frozen in space, glitter in a silent firmament. Patterns of lacy frost decorate the inside of our windows.

A cookie-baking session scheduled for today for all of the cousins has been canceled. It is best everyone stay put at home and keep warm. The battle to get vehicles started and keep them running goes on.

Baked several traditional stollens (Christmas fruit breads) and delivered them hot from the oven to relatives and friends.

December 23—On the third day of Christmas my rue love said to me...chickens are not laying, song birds are not calling, and there is no partridge in the pear tree. Instead there is bitter cold, thick ice, cattle to feed, kinfolk to worry about traveling over slick roads, and wood to split.

Only 15 below this morning, and what a difference it makes. Clear, except for white fog veiling the Wallowas as steam escapes from Wallowa Lake. The milk cows walk slowly to their hay feeder—a steady *crunch, crunch* in the crusty snow. They watch with large, silent eyes rimmed by frosted lashes as I fork hay to them. Then they begin to munch like slow-moving machines, ingesting the cured meadow hay that smells of summer.

As the fog-shrouded December sun burns its way over the eastern hill, a trail of steam follows the ditch where the water flows out and freezes. In the early sunlight, glimpsed through leafless willows, the scene is reminiscent of Yellowstone. The "raspberry kittens" drink in the little patches of water. In the vapor they appear as cool cats!

Attended church with family this morning. Enjoyed the sermon, given by my son, filling in as the pastor was out of town.

December 24—Warmed up to minus five. I chopped ice to no avail this morning, as there is no more water in the ditch: nothing but solid ice. Ben and Doug moved the horses and mule to where they could drink from a heated stock tank. Later in the day, it began to snow softly as I made a kettle of clam chowder for our Christmas Eve supper. Also baked two loaves of french bread.

Son Steve and his family spent Christmas Eve with us and we exchanged gifts after supper. Outside the snow continued to fall, piling up on fences, trees, cattle and roof tops.

Peace on Earth and goodwill toward men from Prairie Creek.

December 25—Christmas morning begins with a minus 13 reading, but quickly warms to eight above. Gave the milk cows a little extra hay as a special Christmas treat, then shuffled through deep, powdery snow to water and feed the chickens.

Lee Perkins is loose in the local KWVR radio station this morning, having given Dave Nelson time off for Christmas. It is always entertaining to tune in to what Wallowa County residents are doing on Christmas day.

Big John Hillock said he was going cougar hunting after they opened gifts. Tiffany Garrett said her father, a fireman, was at the nursing home because the pipes had burst. Rosemary Green, on upper Prairie Creek, said they were enjoying a quiet Christmas in a winter wonderland.

Artist Tara Brice, who lives up on the mountain toward McCully Creek Basin, said she was simply enjoying her rustic surroundings "in paradise." Reta Thornburg, matriarch of five generations, said all five generations would be celebrating the holiday at her daughter's ranch high up on Alder Slope.

Lee called into people's homes from one end of the country to the other. There were cheery messages from Imnaha, Wallowa, Lostine, Flora at the north end, Wallowa Lake, Joseph and Enterprise. Families enjoyed togetherness or visited friends in this cold wilderness county, having a merry Christmas within their homes.

Lee even called here to see what middle Prairie Creek was doing. "Feeding animals, kneading bread and roasting a beef rib roast" was my reply.

We didn't dream of a white Christmas, we had one! As we partook of our traditional Christmas dinner, cotton ball-size snow flakes blew past the windows, driven by winds that would plug roads and create drifts all over Prairie Creek.

Ten of us enjoyed prime rib, mashed potatoes, gravy, homemade bread, and salad. While the snow piled up outside, we were merry inside; opening gifts, all talking at once, while youngsters raced around in a frenzy of holiday excitement. Our house fairly rang with joyful noises.

In the end, our family came and went safely, the best gift this mother and grandmother could receive.

December 26—A rose-tinted group of clouds formed on the horizon and it was three below zero as the stars faded one by one and Doug built the fire in the cookstove and fireplace. Weak sunlight glowed on a fresh snowscape and inspired me to do some photography. Also hoped to get in some cross-country skiing, as it actually warmed to 26 degrees, but had to get my column in the mail.

My daughters gave me a piece of glass art that has bluebirds painted on it. As it hangs in my kitchen window, the winter light plays with the colored glass and the bluebirds cheer me up with their promise of spring.

December 27—A south wind elevated our temperatures from minus one to 24 above. The drift next to the chicken pen is waist deep now, and I must break a new trail to water and feed the hens and Chester.

As Dave Turner drives in with his big back hoe to unplug one of our ditches, a blizzard engulfs Prairie Creek. Visibility is limited to about two feet as blowing snow swirls in from the north, but Dave hangs in there and gets the job done.

Now we hear another winter storm warning on the radio. More high winds and drifting snow.

December 28—Warmed from zero to 20 degrees, cloudy and overcast. No wind, as the predicted storm seems to have moved to the northeast of us. Blowing snow from yesterday's storm has filled country roads with drifted snow, and this morning the snow plows are busy.

Simmered a beef vegetable soup all day on the Monarch range. We were invited to a daughter and son-in-law's on upper Prairie Creek for supper, where we warmed up eating homemade enchiladas. We could tell by the ice forming on the windows that the second arctic deep freeze had arrived. It was minus 10 by the time we drove home.

December 29—Minus 28 with a 32 below reading reported on upper Prairie Creek. The warmest it got today was minus three. We are living on a frozen planet. The animals all receive plenty of feed and somehow survive.

Baked three loaves of whole wheat and oatmeal bread. No reason to drive into town for groceries when we can make do with what is on our shelves and in the freezer.

December 31—Spent this day preparing a meal for 14 friends and neighbors who will spend New Year's Eve with us. A once-in-a-Blue Moon full moon brightens Prairie Creek and helps us welcome 1991.

Linde Irwin skis along a lake with a mountain rising in front of her. Groomed Nordic ski trails offer great skiing at Anthony Lakes.

1991

January 6—A cold fog obscures the American River canyon, which yawns below Mary Ann's house here in Auburn, California. A thin sheet of ice that covers the wooden deck begins to melt as large drops of moisture fall from oak trees, digger pines and large camellia bushes.

Doug and I, having left Prairie Creek on Thursday, traveled to Winnemucca and arrived in Auburn late Friday evening. We brought granddaughter Tammy as far as Loyalton, where she was to catch a ride with a roommate back to college, then took Highway 49 through the rugged Sierra to Nevada City. After reaching elevations close to 7,000 feet, we zigzagged our way over miles of narrow mountain road traveling through picturesque little towns like Sierra City, Sierraville and Downieville.

At 5,400 feet, in the heart of the Sierra Nevada mountains, we stopped to rest at Bassett's Station, an old stage stop established in 1863. We learned that the place has also served as a telegraph station, logging camp and sawmill. It has grub-staked miners, boarded sheepherders and loggers, rested horses, bedded and fed wayfarers, and outfitted wilderness explorers. It was a quiet place, covered with snow and ice, but open, so we went in.

From here, we followed the North Yuba River, which wound its way through a rugged canyon strewn with boulders, many of which had obviously been moved by the gold seekers. After what seemed like hours, we arrived in Nevada City and took 49, that two-lane, white-knuckle highway, to Auburn.

A steady stream of car lights glared at us from the Friday night commute fleeing from city to foothills. By some miracle we made it to sister Mary Ann's where we rested before partaking of Oriental cuisine at the Great Wall.

Now on the sixth day of the New Year, I sleep in. Nothing needs me! No cows to feed, no chickens to worry about; even my husband has taken care of his own breakfast. So here I sit, in front of Mary Ann's electric soft-touch typewriter, in her office, looking over the American River canyon, which is studded with oak trees and digger pine. An occasional blue jay and several pigeons visit the bird feeder, and other than a black-tail deer searching for acorns near the deck, I am quite alone.

Yesterday morning the three of us drove above Auburn to escape the fog, and visited friends Sandra and Fred, who live on a high ridge northeast of here. Sandra and Fred live on Hubbard Road in an area that used to be referred to as Hubbardville, as the area was settled by Fred's family. Fred, who grew up in this rugged foothill country, has roots that twine a long way in Placer County's past.

Leaving Doug and Fred to visit, we gals—Sandra, Mary Ann and I—decided to take a hike down to Coon Creek, which flows through a steep canyon below their house. On the ridge top the fog had lifted, but cloudy skies prevailed. It was noticeably warmer as we followed a cow or horse path along the ridge to a point where we could view the oak-studded canyon that has been carved, over eons, by Coon and Dry Creeks, whose waters ultimately flow into Bear River.

Here we began our descent, following a game trail through dense oak woods. We walked among large granite outcroppings where bright green patches of ferns protruded from niches and crannies in the mossy rocks. The soft, wet, red clay-like soil of Placer County sank under our feet. The path was littered with the leaves of black oak as we walked under great toyon berry bushes laden with red fruit, barren Buckeye, and leafless white oaks, their branches bent and broken by the heavy, untimely snows in November.

Leafless poison oak limbs lined the trail and wild grape vines entwined themselves among the oaks. Massive digger pines grew along with Jeffry pine on the steep hillside. We smelled the woodsy, mossy leaf mold odor as we descended even farther into the canyon, and soon we heard the sound of falling water, and peeked through thick underbrush to see a waterfall cascading down rugged granite course cut by the creek.

In the red mud we saw signs of fox, coon, bear, deer and opossum. There were screaming blue jays in the digger pines. Near the creek bottom, decorating a large toyon bush, were six pair of mountain bluebirds. Their bright blue bodies darted through the air, startling and thrilling us. We watched them a long time, soaking in the beauty of the place as well.

It was quiet there in the canyon on that January Sunday, punctuated by the far-off baying of a hound that seemed to be on the trail of some varmint.

We returned, following the bank of an old PGE ditch that ended where an old wooden flume lay rotting in the hillside. Higher up we found another irrigation ditch, full of water. Here grew wild blackberries in profusion amid little springs that soaked the hillside.

Sandra told us wild turkeys were numerous here and she had photographed them in their yard. The hike warmed up our blood and proved very invigorating. As we sat in lawn chairs on the frosted lawn, I felt very far removed from Wallowa County in mind, but not in spirit.

Earlier, when I had called Sandra to say we'd be up, I mentioned going on a hike below her house, to which she replied, "Actually that was about the furthest thing from my mind." But now that we had done it, she had to agree the effort was all worthwhile.

When we returned to Mary Ann's, I set a sponge of sourdough to rise, as we had been invited to a niece's for supper and were supposed to bring a loaf of bread. Later, when we arrived at Lori and Tom's, I carried the rising sourdough under my arm. My wild Wallowa County yeast performed just fine in Lori's "Sunset Magazine" kitchen.

Out the window for as far as we could see in the cloudy night sky, twinkled the millions of lights of Sacramento's creeping suburbia, a growth that threatens to conquer the Sierra foothills. When I was a small girl, these hills were wild, full of birds and oak trees, and far off, at night, one might glimpse a light or two. And on those clear days, before smog, we could see the Marysville buttes.

My mother and Bill joined us for supper and, while we waited for the fragrant bread to come from the oven, we watched a video of a recently family wedding, wherein the California relatives were able to see all of their Oregon family, which seems to entertain families no end. Our Oregon bunch, whose lifestyles are quite the opposite of their California cousins, made for an attentive audience.

Entertaining in the captivating way of children was 3-and-a-half-year-old Kyle, who cared more about eating lasagne than watching his Oregon cousins.

January 7—It is raining and Californians are happy. They have been in the midst of a long drought, which makes any rain welcome. Great drops of moisture drip from digger pine, oak and sodden camellia bush, a steady patter that falls onto the deck.

M.A.'s office is a far cry from my kitchen one in the ranch house on Prairie Creek. A computer stares at me from an organized computer desk to my right. A sliding glass door leads to the rain-soaked deck and the trees beyond, which march down to the breaks of the American River canyon. Riverview Drive is quiet and gives no hint of the freeway and city, which are only minutes away.

On Saturday Doug and I drove, via the multi-laned freeway, to Roseville and thence to the Roseville auction and flea market. Even though it was the first day of fog, it was 45 degrees and not like the cold we were used to. This immense auction is filled with vendors, who spread their wares over acres of pavement.

Due to the cold, the lemonade concessions weren't doing too good a business, but we joined the crowds of people wandering around and through this maze of humanity and junk, looking at everything from iron kettles to bird cages. We didn't buy anything, except for a funny little noise maker that Doug had to have.

Then we strolled through the vegetable/fruit section, which was located under a huge roofed-over area. What a colorful place. Citrus fruits, pineapples, kiwi fruit, pomegranates, apples, and persimmons were all heaped upon long tables. Also heaped were fresh vegetables, brussel sprouts, cabbages, cauliflower and broccoli. Vendors hollered about the goodness of their products.

Beautiful, dark-eyed Spanish girls weighed out the produce. Portuguese and Italian Americans, all together in the great melting pot that is California. Salami, cheese, olives, dried fruit, honey, and long loaves of bread filled yet another area. Another building gave off the wonderful smells of ethnic cooking.

We walked into the livestock auction section to get warm, mainly, and compare cattle prices with those at home. I was amused to see a large man carrying a tiny kid goat in his jacket pocket, and next to him was a woman carrying a chicken under one arm and vegetables in another—a walking stew.

Outside were old farmers in old trucks, remnants of the foothill rural people who have somehow managed to survive suburbs. If my father was still alive, he would be one of them.

January 14—Auburn, California—Yesterday we made our yearly pilgrimage to French Creek. Doug likes the creek because he finds paydirt in the crevices near bedrock. My sisters and I love the place for its aesthetic and nostalgic qualities, and because it continues, by some miracle, to be one of the few unspoiled areas left in this part of the country.

The property, near the old settlement of Latrobe in the gently to steep rolling foothill country of El Dorado County, once belonged to our relatives. In the early days, 800 Mexican gold seekers established a large mining encampment on the same flat where the remains of a stone foundation can still be seen. The rock foundation is all that remains of the Smith house, which we sisters remember from the times when, as children, we attended annual Memorial Day picnics there.

Two aged black walnut trees have dropped their yearly crop of nuts on the dry grass beneath. Near the decomposing mortar that holds the stone foundation together, several clumps of narcissus struggle up through the thin granite soil. Owing to California's prolonged drought, they are not yet blooming and only the spiked, green leaves show through starthistle and filaree.

Below the house, which sat on a knoll across the creek, hangs the remains of a swinging bridge. Old rusted cables, resembling wild grape vines, dangle above the waters of the creek. Several frayed cables have bits of weathered wood attached to the strands, and the two ancient black oaks that anchor the bridge have grown over the wires in such a way as to make them appear as if they were growing out of the trees.

While Doug and Mary Ann's grandson, Josh, panned for gold near the old suspension bridge, we went for a walk up the creek. My youngest sister, Kathryn, joined us and we three looked for adventure. Right off, next to the water, we encountered a large, flat rock containing an Indian grinding hole. Native Americans used these holes in the rocks for thousands of years to grind acorns into a meal they then used to make bread.

We noticed many large moss-covered rocks along the deer trail we were following, and over the ever-present trickling of the small creek, we heard the happy sound of many song birds. Deer tracks laced the trails, and in one large cave-like rock we found a cougar's den—minus the cougar.

While searching for a remembered waterfall about a mile up the creek, we heard the faint sound of tumbling water. Approaching the area through thick oak brush and toyon berry, we were amazed to find, in addition to a small waterfall, a grotto, which appeared to have been carved over eons by the waters of French Creek.

There were sculpted hollows filled with the sweet, winter smell of wildness. Mirrored in the quiet pool were bare-limbed oaks whose rotting leaves filled the bottoms of the creek. We caught the silver movement of small fish darting under shadows of overhanging rocks. In deep, dark caverns, carved from solid rock, we could envision Indian women bringing their children here to bathe and to escape the summer's heat.

Returning along the opposite bank, we noticed and then followed a sort of trail that appeared to have been built up years ago with rocks. Perhaps after the Indians, Mexican miners used this same trail to travel to this special spot. At noon we spread blankets in the warm sunshine on the ground near the creek and ate our picnic lunch of tuna/egg sandwiches, persimmon cake and fresh fruit. Later, on the hill above us, we heard voices and soon a father and his young son came walking down to greet us.

It turned out they were related to the fellow we had gotten the key from to come in here. The man said he had been reared in the area, and he loved this spot so much he visited it almost every weekend. We mentioned the waterfall. He said he knew the place and then remarked that just recently there had been several cougar in the vicinity. In fact, four black tail bucks had been killed on the ridge above us by a big cat.

After spending most of the day on French Creek, we drove home by way of old town Folsom, where we stopped at a remembered ice cream parlor. In lieu of supper, we treated ourselves to the most outrageous ice cream cones we'd ever tasted. The cones had been dipped in chocolate and nuts.

This morning, after the fog faded from the American River canyon, Mary Ann took Doug and me on a tourist tour of the old high school turned Civic Center, and of the courthouse, which is Auburn's pride and joy. The remarkable old building, recently restored, is now in use like in years gone by. Great granite steps march upward to two outside entrances and into round, marbled halls with oaken window and door frames. We walked up three flights of stairs to several levels that held oaken court rooms.

Walking back to the car, we entered the open door of the Pioneer Methodist Church, built in 1852, one of the oldest buildings in Auburn. I wrote my name in the guest register, mentioning that my first-born, Ramona, was baptized there in 1952. The colors were brilliant as streaming sunlight poured through stained glass windows to brighten old oaken pews and altar.

So far, we've been having a very full, relaxing vacation. The weather has been incredibly mild, our hostess congenial and the food out of sight. On Tuesday we returned to where I was reared, in the Mt. Pleasant district of Placer County, and did some gold panning. The day was mild and sunny and, although the creek was mostly dry because of the prolonged drought, Doug was able to find some nice little nuggets in leftover potholes where the cattle drank.

Six deer tread softly past Doug as he panned, feeding on fallen acorns that litter the leafy forest floor. Turkey buzzards circled overhead. Something dead around? Perhaps our smoked oysters, cheese and crackers. Small tree frogs croaked in oak logs, and gray squirrels swirled through the dull winter woods, the color of blue smoke.

My brother Jim's cattle lay in the sunny meadow, chewing their cuds. The "mountain" of my youth, old "Big Top," only a small hill in reality, was visible over the meadow. Hidden among the 450 acres of woodland, meadow, creek and hills that was my home, are no less than 15 homes.

Doug built a small fire to ward off the creek's chill, and we ate our lunch there. The place, as always, has a dream-like quality to it, and although we could hear sounds all around of human habitation, it was a pleasant spot that evoked many childhood senses. As always, I felt my father's presence. He so loved these woods.

On Wednesday, taking my mother along, we visited a Simmental breeder in Elk Grove before stopping to see my uncle John, who lives in Rio Linda in the same old house that grandpa built in the early 1900s.

Uncle John, who at 82 still writes music and lyrics for entire musical productions, sat down at the same old piano he played when we were children. He brought to life some recent tunes he'd composed. On the wall above the piano, old photos of my great-grandfather Isaac and grandmother Eliza Wilson stared down at us. Isaac traveled west in a wagon train during the early migrations to California in the early 1800s. With his long heard and thin face, I thought he looked like Abraham Lincoln. Eliza had sad eyes.

On Thursday I spent the day creating a gourmet supper to which we invited my mother and husband Bill, and sister Caroline and her husband. It was fun planning and cooking the meal. For the main dish I concocted in the crockpot a Greek dish that featured beef shanks. Mary Ann's kitchen smelled of garlic and onion and bay leaf for days.

On the 11th two sisters accompanied Doug and me to the North Shore of Lake Tahoe, where we met up with an aunt and uncle who live on Tahoe's south shore. We ate lunch at the Hyatt House in Incline Village, but that's another story.

January 15—Foggy, damp and cold. Walked in fog down a steep hill to the Pacific Avenue apartment where my mother and husband Bill live. Found these two senior citizens on the floor doing aerobics! What seemed like rather vigorous exercises to me, they accomplished quite easily. This, in addition to walking and adhering to a healthful diet, has contributed to their youthful appearance.

Doug showed up later and the four of us played a game of Scrabble in which we were beaten badly. We treated the winners to lunch at a place called Chaos Cafe. We were amused at the cafe sign that read: "Life uncertain, eat dessert first!" Doug, not heeding this advice, waited until after his soup to partake of Chaos chocolate cake, which reposed in a puddle of hot raspberry sauce.

While we ate, the sun came out and burned off the fog. That evening Mary Ann. Doug and I drove to Nevada City, where we had been invited to supper with another relative. Nancy's home was lovely: soft carpets, formal dining room, huge plants and beautiful furniture. The table was set with candles, a lace tablecloth and cloth napkins, and all the dishes and silverware matched.

It was a far cry from one of our family meals on Prairie Creek. But then, Nancy's world is different from ours. She has lost two husbands, one in a car accident and the latest from a heart attack. None of her three children is married, so she has no grandchildren. When she visits us, she enjoys the chaos of family and the disarray that accompanies it, so it is good for us to enjoy her in her surroundings, lest we forget what we have, mismatched silverware and all.

After a delicious meal, we watched TV and, like all other Americans that night, wondered about the war, which was scheduled to be, or not to be, in a matter of minutes. As usual, we had eaten enough to be miserable, and around 3 a.m., after tossing and turning all night, the boysenberry pie made peace with the Peking chicken, and I slept.

It seems all of our relatives and friends are bent on outdoing themselves to impress us with their cooking. What a way to go.

January 16—When Mary Ann and I went for our early walk around the neighborhood this morning, it was so clear, we could see off to the valley, clear to Sacramento's millions of twinkling lights. A virtual sea of brilliance stretched from valley to foothills and northward toward Marysville and Yuba City.

Folsom Lake, a mere puddle of its former self, shone pale in the dawn light. As a cool, fresh breeze blew from the northeast, I wondered about all that humanity and its need for water, and California going into its fifth year of drought.

Later, taking mom with us, Doug and I drove over to White Rock to spend the day with our cousins, the Smiths and the Mehrtens on their ranch. Subdivision after subdivision crept outward from Folsom, threatening to engulf the once lonely hills and displace the old ranching operations. Today the ranches' former names grace the estates.

The old Smith ranch continues to survive despite this wave of "progress" that seems to be sweeping the El Dorado Hills. We bounce along a narrow, chuck-holed country road until it turns into a dirt track, and there, off in the distance, we see the familiar brick home. The barns, corrals and creek are the same. A couple of windmills dot the first field, and cattle graze the faint green that has just begun to show beneath the dry grass.

The frantic harking of several Catahoula cattle dogs announces our arrival and soon we are greeted by cousins Sue and Aggie. We comment on the dogs, and Sue says the fiercest, Catman, is the "catch and hold" variety.

"Sure makes it easy to treat a calf," she says. "Catman catches and holds the animal without biting it."

Sue said her husband, Chuck, was horseback, moving some dry cows to another field. Her saddled horse was in the corral and she took off to join the cowboys, saying "Be back in about three hours; know you'll stay for supper."

"Yep," we said, eating again. I wished I could have ridden off with Sue, because our own country is covered with snow and riding is limited to spring, summer and fall. It would feel good to be on a horse again...and to work off some of this food!

We were joined by another cousin, George, for lunch in the old three-story ranch house, after which we visited while picking pecans from a yard tree laden with nuts. Then mom and I visited more while cracking pecans. Doug had not been able to resist the lure of French Creek, which is close by, and had succumbed to gold fever.

Thus engaged, we first heard the news that U.S. forces had attacked Iraq. As President Bush came on TV with his address to the nation, explaining about the war, the Smith cattle grazed and the old windmills slowly turned; meadow larks, mockingbirds, crows and robins vied for their prime time at White Rock, while across the Mediterranean, things were not so peaceful.

Our coffee can filled up with cracked pecan meats, the cowboys returned, and Aggie served one of her famous meals at the old oak table. We sat there in the same chairs that have seated generations before us, talking of things like generations before us, listening to George and Chuck tell stories of times gone by.

There was much laughter, interspersed with "Please pass the bread and jam," "Well, I guess there is room for berry pie," "Remember those Memorial Day picnics?"

I felt cousin Edna's presence there in the old house, even though she passed on two years ago. The wall above the table was hung with tributes to this remarkable woman who devoted her life to the cattle industry, her community and her church. If the world were made up of Ednas and these, her people, there would be no need for war and such.

We marveled over Sue's bridle bit collection, which covered an entire wall. Antiques filled the old three-story house, and many of them served a useful purpose. In juxtaposition, the modern homes just over the hill looked cold and unfriendly, hastily constructed and solely for greed, not need, as many were not even occupied.

January 17—Despite news of war, we can't be too sad. It is a lovely day, clear, bright with sunshine that streams through Mary Ann's sliding glass doors for breakfast. Doug said today was "returning to your roots day."

First I took him to the Gold Hill area, where I lived from 1951 to 1956. Hidden in rolling foothill country dotted with oak trees, creeks and blackberry thickets, was the tiny, falling-down house, obviously deserted for some time. Blackberry vines trailed into the back porch. The once-beautiful pear orchard was reduced to four scraggly trees, and two new homes occupied the front pasture.

My old garden spot was gone to weeds, the clothesline sagged, and the rusted cattle barn seemed about to succumb to time. I remembered washing clothes in the wringer washer and hanging up all those diapers, canning 300 quarts of peaches, pears and apricots, milking a cow, raising a garden, helping fit show cattle, and not knowing how to drive a car.

Could 40 years have really gone by so quickly?

We drove up another remembered road to where I used to walk as a child to visit my girlfriend Sandra. Where once Sandra's family's modest home stood was now a brick mansion, which rambled over the same knoll, its 20 rooms looking like a castle. We were to learn this was only a weekend retreat for a couple who lived in San Francisco.

Another road led to the one-room Fruitvale school house, where I attended first grade, walking the three miles both ways each day from Clovertop Ranch, where my father managed a purebred Guernsey dairy.

That evening we enjoyed another of mom's delicious meals, after which Bill and I went for a long walk around the neighborhood to digest all that food.

January 18—Another sunny morning as we walk over to neighbor Paul's for his special buckwheat pancakes and sausage. Paul, who is a faithful reader of Mary Ann's copy of *Agri-Times*, enjoys seeing us each year, and we him.

Doug is becoming hooked on antiques and spends lots of time in lower Auburn, where he makes daily trips to see what treasures he can turn up. Today he came back with an oxen shoe and a rare cornstick pan.

At noon we treated mom and Bill to Mexican food in Colfax, where Doug was in heaven. We were surrounded by antiques. They hung from the ceiling and covered the walls. We liked to have never got Doug out of there!

January 19—A refreshing south wind blew away the valley fog and smog as Mary Ann, her friend and I drove to Sutter County. The air, so clear, we could see the distant outline of the Sierras to the east and the Coast Range to the west.

Mount Lassen reared its snowy dome above the northern horizon, and as we approached the Sutter Buttes, we could see their oak-covered sidehills rising abruptly from the valley floor. Because Doug opted to help my brother Jim cut wood and later get in some gold panning, and because it was such a nice day, I decided to accompany Mary Ann's group to the Graylodge Wildlife Refuge.

This huge waterfowl preserve stretches over acres of canals, open ponds and swamps, providing habitat and protection for all manner of Northern California wildlife. And of course large flocks of geese and ducks, as well as shore birds, winter here.

After discussing at length whether we should eat before or after hiking around the preserve, the final vote was unanimous: we'd eat before and after. Then we walked the trails, using binoculars to identify different species of waterfowl.

This, I decided, was a great way for Californians to spend a peaceful day away from their crowded city environments and noise pollution. Not that there wasn't noise there, but somehow those sounds were more soothing.

As we walked that maze of trails that wandered by ponds, waterways and swamps, we heard the gurglings of unseen water birds, ducks, grebes, mud hens and geese. Once, off in the distance, we spotted a group of sandhill cranes, the unmistakable sound of their calling coming to us over the swamps.

In the sky a huge flock of Canada geese banked to the west and flew slowly toward us. Growing from a black blur to a well-defined body of wild honkers, they settled gracefully onto a nearby pond. We heard the splashes of muskrat and other water animals scurrying off the banks.

Always present, swaying with the windy tules, the red-winged black birds sang. Their liquid notes bubbled together, forming a January concert. Lesser Yellow legs searched near the shore for food, sticking their long bills into the mud to feed. As we walked along we could feel, see and hear the beauty of that vast watery retreat.

On our first walk we thrilled to the sight of thousands of snow geese, babbling softly, resembling the background noise of a crowd of people. A plane flew overhead and suddenly, alarmed, that great white wave of fluttering feathers took off.

The south wind swept them into air currents and they scattered into the sky, the distant Coast Range mountains providing a background for this mirage of white against blue. The snow geese circled in a sort of organized confusion, and then two by two, three by three, they fell like poplar leaves to the water. The soft gabbling resumed until another plane flew over, and the scene was repeated.

We ate our second lunch on a picnic table under some ancient eucalyptus trees, in full view of the nearby Sutter Buttes. After another walk around the refuge, we left Graylodge. A blood-red sunset created a startling backdrop for dark, bare-limbed oaks as we traveled a back road home.

January 20—The nice weather continued, as did our enjoyment of friends, relatives and food. My, what meals!

January 21—We took Mary Ann, our guide, and drove to Forest Hill, then to the old mining town of Yankee Jim's, and down a steep dirt road to the bottom of Shirttail Creek canyon. we drove up the opposite side of the canyon to Iowa Hill, another gold mining town. We read on a historical plaque that this town burned down three times and was rebuilt twice. Gold was discovered there in 1853 and by 1856 weekly production was estimated at $100,000. The total value of gold produced up to 1880 was placed at $20 million.

Everywhere, on either side of the road, was evidence of hydraulic mining. Today, all that remains of Iowa Hill is a store, post office and tavern, all in one. As we headed off Iowa Hill and drove the narrow, twisting mountainous road to the Middle Fork of the American River, we were glad to arrive safely at a small picnic area near the Iowa Hill Bridge.

Here, along the river, we ate our lunch on a 70-degree day. Was this really January? Green grass poked through the banks of the middle fork, along with toyon berry, manzanita oak and pine. Doug did some gold panning while I photographed.

We returned via another winding road to Colfax, then took old Highway 40 down again to the canyon of the North Fork, crossed the bridge and stopped to rest. Bay laurel, madrone, and red bud grew here. The water was very low in the river, but the red granite soil was damp, due to the one day of rain.

That night we took Mary Ann to the grand opening of a Mongolian restaurant. Our last night in Auburn. We will head home on the morrow.

January 22—Winnemucca, Nevada—As we head north and return to Wallowa County, wonderful memories of this vacation flash back before becoming fodder for future reminiscing. It is mind-boggling to think we actually did all these things I've recorded in my journal during our brief stay in Auburn.

Each Monday I would type out my column and slip it into the mail slot that opens into Mary Ann's hallway. After trying gamely, at my family's insistence, to type copy on various "modern conveniences," I turned once more to my faithful portable Smith-Corona, which seems to know me. These others fought me and, even though they obliterated errors, I spent more time correcting than creating.

So, while Doug tries to win at the Winner's Inn here in Winnemucca this evening, I resist the urge to attend "Dances with Wolves," playing at the local theater, or to watch TV's "Lonesome Dove," and, instead, concentrate on "Janie's Journal."

January 23—Sand, sage and sky stretched ahead of us as we headed north through Nevada. After spending the night in Winnemucca, we made it safely home to Prairie Creek.

Spent the evening sorting through mail, which was piled high on the kitchen table. We found most of the snow gone, except where deep drifts had been. Ice. however, was everywhere, especially in the meadows, where creeks overflowed, and along ditches where water flowed out and froze.

Although it had warmed somewhat, it was still very cold. Everything appeared normal. The raspberry kittys ran to greet us; the cattle, horses and mule were in good shape; the chickens alive. But something was missing. My faithful dog was absent. No wet nose to nuzzle my hand, no adoring eyes, no wagging tail. Freckles had been run over while we were gone. I hoped she hadn't suffered.

We were also saddened to hear our neighbor Hubert Rosser had passed away. I will always remember the twinkle in his eyes and miss being able to give him zucchini.

The next morning I walked down to see Alfie, my mule. She came on the run to see me, *hee-haw*-ing all the way.

January 27—And now we are back in the swing of ranch life. Soon it will be time to ship seed potatoes, and the swollen bellies of our cows tell us calving time is near. My grandchildren were so happy to see me, and I had two of the younger ones here all day Friday. We were able to play on the haystack with the kittys and take a walk, as it was a warm, sunny day.

Last Saturday I made a sourdough chocolate cake for a granddaughter who lives on Imnaha, and we delivered the cake to the birthday girl on Camp Creek. There were signs of spring in the canyons, as new baby calves are already being born.

That night Doug and I joined friends and attended a crab feed at the local Elks Lodge, then danced 'til nearly midnight.

The next morning after breakfast, I was joined by rancher-wives-neighbors Betty and Linde for a four-mile hike through the hills east of us. The entire Wallowa chain, its snowfields shining in the morning sun, was visible from our vantage point. As we crunched through patches of snow and ice, we talked of many things, catching up on camaraderie. It's sure good to be home.

January 28—Snowing this morning. As a wind rises, great swirls of snow blow off the roof, smearing my kitchen view. The young maple tree shudders and bare raspberry canes writhe like coral, caught in the reef's current. Beyond that, my mountains have disappeared. The snow ceases, but the bitter wind continues.

A good day to stay inside and write "CattleWomen's Corner" and my column, to answer letters and bake a deep-dish apple pie. Cooking provides a diversion from the concentration of writing.

Leafing through a January issue of Farm Journal, I spot a colorful, mouth-watering photograph of a meal. Substituting lamb ribs for the pork roast shown, I prepare the remainder of the menu for supper. It turns out looking like the picture, and tastes wonderful. Spoon bread, sauteed carrots, and sauerkraut salad complement lamb as well as pork.

By evening the wind lies down, the sky clears, and a pale, yellow moon makes its steady way over the eastern hills.

January 29—Sourdough hot cakes for breakfast. Tended to the chickens and took a walk in the crisp, 10-degree morning. Earlier, the temperature had dipped to five below. Missing my friendly dog, who always followed along, I noticed that several of the raspberry kittys trailed behind me.

Baked a sourdough chocolate cake for son-in-law Bill's birthday. His wife Jackie had hinted that he sure would like one, and it was an easy birthday present.

Later, by afternoon, the wind came up again and we could see the waving "snow banners" of loose snow blowing across the high peaks.

Like most everyone, I suspect, Doug and I are working on our income tax... that time of year has rolled around again.

Since the sourdough is active, I bake a batch of biscuits to go with oxtail soup for supper. The moon appears again around 5 p.m., its golden body swimming in a skyscape of wintry purple and pink. Through binoculars I see the man in the moon.

The phone rings, granddaughter Carrie: "Are you looking at the moon, grandma?"

Regardless of war and unsettling conditions here at home, it is nice to know that the moon responds, as it always has, to the forces of nature, and comes up at the appointed hour to say to us, *Have faith. This too shall pass.*

Also nice that a granddaughter watches it.

Along these lines, I have just finished reading a book entitled *Trashing the Planet*, written by Dixy Lee Ray, wherein the author has put down in book form a long overdue assessment of the doomsday approach being handed to the public these days by some non-discriminating media supporters and other factions. She writes that we need to keep a sense of perspective, that this old earth has been through drastic climate changes and upheavals without any help from humans. As I watched an OPB TV program on "The Great Rift" last night, it reinforced what Dixy Lee Ray speaks about in her book. The earth, she says, will continue to change; it has never been stable for long.

She goes on to say: *Humans cannot live on earth without altering it, and without using natural resources. Our responsibility is to be good stewards of the environment and to remember that a well-tended garden is better than a neglected woodlot. It is demeaning beyond belief to consider mankind simply another species of animal, no better and no worse than wild beasts.*

Reading this book will enlighten those who would like to believe we are headed for doom. It is good for the mind to digest "the rest of the story," rather than accept everything we read in the newspapers and see on TV. It lets us think for ourselves and draw our own conclusions.

Off the soapbox. What I'm really trying to say is: don't become too serious about what you hear, and don't forget to watch the moon's silent beauty, which reminds us of these truths... without scaring us.

January 30—Since I was about a year or more behind in pasting clippings and photos into the CattleWomen scrapbooks, my neighbors Linde and Betty came to my rescue. I put a pot of seafood chowder to simmer on the wood cookstove and, after sipping soup for lunch, we spread out glue, scissors and scrapbooks, and went to work. Not only fun, but many hands made the work easier.

Such a busy organization we have. Re-reading all about our activities made us tired. We worked non-stop until 4:30, when we ran out of pages. Time to purchase another scrapbook!

The theme of our present CattleWomen's association is "Adapting to Change." Hopefully, some things never change, and we will keep alive traditions that have proved successful.

January 31—As January exits, this last day of the month dawns cloudy, and cold mists trail over the mountains.

After breakfast, I walk down to the horse pasture and chop a hole in the irrigation ditch for the animals to drink. The stock-tank heater went on the blink while we were gone. Horses, unlike cattle, can survive by eating snow, but the cold is so dry and there isn't much moisture in what's left of the snow to do much good. Using a heavy pick I chipped through three layers of ice to reach water. It was like uncovering different ice ages.

Grocery shopping during the winter is nice, in that we see neighbors and friends in the store, and have more time to visit. Unlike summer, when we are all so rushed and the unfamiliar faces of tourists fill the aisles.

For supper this evening we attended the Joseph Chamber of Commerce's groundhog dinner at the Civic Center. In addition to "groundhog" sausage, we had pancakes cooked over a large grill by several men of the community. The trio of lovely lasses who make up the 1991 Chief Joseph Days court waited on us hand and foot. Proceeds of the dinner will go toward funding the annual Chief Joseph Days celebration, which takes place the last weekend in July.

February 1—February flies in on the warm wings of a chinook. As the south wind moans over Prairie Creek, its soft breath melts the ice. After a hearty breakfast of sausage gravy over hashbrowns, I walked down to feed the horses and mule, then up to the chicken pen to water and feed the hens and Chester.

Because it was so warm, wind and all, Linde and I could not contain ourselves. We decided to hike over the eastern hill, down into the breaks of the Imnaha canyon, and come out on the Sheep Creek highway. After taking one car down to trail's end, we drove another to the jump-off place, where we began our walk.

We trudged over snow and ice, up and down hills, crossing a frozen creek that winds through pine tree gulch, and on up another snow-crusted hill. The south-facing slopes were blown pretty bare, with old grass exposed, but the norths were drifted and frozen. The furious wind on top of Sheep Creek Hill was luckily at our back. We were being blown along by the chinook.

The Wallowas, all icy white, were spectacular from on top, bathed in sunlight. Looking back, we saw the snow-covered hills gleaming like polished shards of glass lying in fields of golden grass.

As we entered the canyon at the head of Hayden Creek, we said goodbye to the view of the Wallowas, and also to the wind, and hello to the blue-white Seven Devils range in Idaho. High above us flew the hawks, riding the thermals, hang gliding; chukars whirred away around the bends, two mule deer watched us from a high trail, and magpies scolded in the leafless cottonwoods.

Typical of February, to lull us with a false spring before resuming with winter.

February 2—As the chinook continues, high gusts fairly shake the house and rattle windows. Snow melts before our eyes, and the ice patches begin to evaporate. My hens, deciding it must be spring, begin to lay big, brown eggs again. Three loads of wash flap on the clothesline and the primroses alongside the house are beginning to send out new green leaves that appear to grow from the old, decaying ones.

Baked an apple pie and delivered it hot from the oven to grandson Shawn, who is celebrating his 17th birthday. On the way home from upper Prairie Creek, it began to sprinkle rain, and great snow clouds formed and spilled their contents over the Wallowas.

Everywhere here on Prairie Creek, ditches overflow with muddy snowmelt, and lakes of melted ice pool in fields seeded to winter grain. Unsightly cow manure piles are exposed now, dotting pastures and fields wherever cattle are being wintered; the best recycling program ranchers have. When, in late spring, these piles of manure are broken and scattered by harrowing, they give back to the soil what the cattle have taken. A wonderful renewable resource that takes care of its own disposal and returns, as it should, to the earth. Each spring these animal wastes enrich and mulch the hay fields and pastures, helping the grass grow again.

February 3—Doug out early feeding silage to the cows and fall calves on the hill. The wind has ceased. Hoorah! And a hard frost halts temporarily the formation of MUD.

Son-in-law Charley and grandson Shawn here to hay and feed our fields full of cattle on this Sunday, which is always Ben's day off. A cold wind replaces the warm one and blows on into the night.

February 4—Cloudy and windy, but still warm for February. After chores I bake a pumpkin pie, using a pumpkin grown in my garden last fall. I had picked it, still a bit green, before the heavy frost, and while we were gone it ripened to a deep orange.

I tried a different recipe, as it's always fun to try out a new one. This one called for sweetened, condensed milk, and no sugar. After it was baked, a mixture of cream cheese flavored with orange and lemon juice was spread on top. The pie was very tasty and not as sweet as most recipes.

A lamb stew simmers on the Monarch as I pound away on my column, and outside, what news reporters are referring to as the "Pineapple Express" continues to melt away winter here on Prairie Creek.

February 5—Continuing mild days. This one partially clear, with intermittent sunlight. The Wallowas swim in and out of dark purple clouds. Only small glimpses of their snowy escarpments are exposed for any length of time. The air, cleansed by the wind these past few days, is fresh and pure this morning, wonderfully calm.

My friend Linde and I pack a lunch and drive up Little Sheep Creek to the home of Ilene and Lawrence Potter. On this lovely, spring-like morning we will clean their house. The Potters have lived here along the banks of Little Sheep Creek for 58 years. Ilene, nearly 84, feels the effects of age and caring for her husband, who isn't able to do much these days due to arthritis.

"Things just got kinda behind," says Ilene, apologizing for her house. "That's what neighbors are for," we say, and begin to dig in.

Outside, Little Sheep Creek races merrily between ice and snow-covered banks. The smell of pine, rotting ice and swampy meadow fills the air. Native blue grass is turning green, having been insulated under a blanket of snow all winter.

The small, old-fashioned house is filled with the accumulation of years of living, and was in need of dusting. Rugs needed vacuuming and windows needed washing. My vacuum cleaner roared to life, Linde turned into a clean machine of torn rags and soapy buckets and dirt, and dust fled before us.

Windows soon sparkled in sunlight, and the one in the dining room that looks up the creek's meadow to the mountains turned the scene into an oil painting view. Carpets and rugs were cleaned, knick-knacks dusted and returned to their proper places, and by lunch time the house was under control. Linde mopped the kitchen floor and then we sat down opposite that mountain-meadow view to eat our lunches and visit with a grateful pair of wonderful neighbors.

As we ate, we listened to Ilene and Lawrence tell us of the long-ago when there were horse-drawn wagons to haul them up from Imnaha to Joseph. Ilene, born at "The Bridge" on Imnaha, was reared on the upper Imnaha River.

Before we left, I photographed Ilene and Lawrence in front of their dining room window. They both had smiles on their faces, and so did Linde and I. What a wonderful way to spend a morning. Not work, really, when you are helping someone. Who knows, we may all be in that boat some day.

Walking into my own house, I looked at the windows and decided they, too, needed cleaning, so began scrubbing them. Then one thing led to another, and soon I was washing curtains, vacuuming rugs and dusting. Goodness, I must have a case of spring fever.

February 6—Another gorgeous morning, clear and a cold 20 degrees, which quickly warms. A perfect day to spend with grandchildren. Since most of them attend school now, I have only the two younger ones to play with on weekdays.

After photographing some local scenes for our photo club's 1992 color calendar, I picked up the children. We drove to Pete's Pond so I could photograph the ducks, swans and geese that were swimming in open water surrounded by ice.

The children were delighted with this, and the water fowl showed off for us. There were at least two pair of black swans, a pair of white swans, and numerous varieties of ducks and wild geese. We watched as groups of waterfowl flew in to land on the ice, then skidded along trying to put on their brakes.

Since it was nearly noon, we decided to eat a bite there. We munched our hamburgers sitting on the sunny, enclosed deck, where we could continue to watch the entertaining antics of the water birds. I let the children purchase small bags of duck feed, which they tossed out onto the pond. Huge trout swam lazily below in the murky depths. They appeared lethargic and never surfaced for the feed. Perhaps their metabolism slows down when they live under the ice all winter.

It got up to nearly 60 degrees by afternoon, which we spent outside pretending to camp and round up cattle. Later, we read books in the sheepherder wagon. The children were having such a good time they didn't want to go home.

February 7—Another beautiful day in Paradise, as they are fond of saying around here. Gone are memories of 32 below zero readings and days of bone-chilling cold. Like childbirth, the cold is soon forgotten, and when the sun warms our bones, we are lulled into thinking spring is nearly here. Almost.

Tonight Doug and I attended a live performance of the popular Neil Simon play "Last of the Red Hot Lovers." Our local OK Theater was packed with people, and the play was hilarious. Laughter, the best medicine, gave everyone there a lift.

February 8—Under wine-blush-tinted East Peak (boy. if that isn't descriptive!), the first faint outline of a horse known locally as "Tucker's Mare" slowly takes shape. Twenty degrees this morning when I walk down to throw hay to the horses and mule.

After tidying up the house, I went for a walk around our "country block," a distance of four miles or so. A lovely morning for such a walk. I enjoy seeing our neighboring ranches and their many old buildings that remind us of Prairie Creek's colorful past. Although there is some ice and snow left in the barrow pits alongside the road, the snow is mostly gone from the fields.

Was a guest with my husband at a Rotary Club luncheon meeting where the speaker is our friend Ron Baker, owner of C&B livestock in Hermiston. We have been selling cattle to Ron for many years, as well as using his good bulls. We did forgive the chef at the Elks for serving chicken, but it would have been more appropriate, we thought, since Ron talked about his natural, light beef, if we could have sampled some.

After supper this evening I made valentines for my own "herd" of grandchildren. After cutting out colorful pictures in magazines, I glue them to paper and write an appropriate valentine greeting for each child under them.

February 9—The chickens' drinking water isn't frozen this morning! In fact it is so mild I don't even build a fire in the cookstove. Doug left early for Hermiston where he will sort cattle we have in a feedlot there.

Everyone is wondering how long this false spring will last. It is so gorgeous today I can't stay in the house any longer than necessary, so I head over the eastern hill for my daily walk. The snow Linde and I tromped through last week is all but gone. The occasional remaining banks send muddy rivulets trickling down the hill. Looking close to the ground I see the first green buttercup leaves.

The first robins are arriving, Prairie Creek cattle sun themselves in the barren pastures and earlier I heard a few honkers fly over. The walk is refreshing and blows the cobwebs out of my mind. Star bright, frosty night.

February 10—Another beautiful morning, with heavy frost and no wind. Spring-signs everywhere, like the lilac bush beginning to bud...too soon. Fried trout (found some in the freezer) and sourdough hotcakes with raspberry jam for breakfast. (Eat your heart out, Paul!)

Baked a long loaf of sourdough french bread and made a lemon meringue pie to take to the Stockgrowers/CattleWomen's potluck tonight. If I don't quit describing food, Paul (who lives in Auburn) will book himself with the next freight on the stage into Wallowa County.

After lunch I took grandson Shawn skiing at the nearby Ferguson Ridge ski area. Leaving Shawn at the T-bar, I don cross-country skis and follow snowmobile tracks to the Canal road. The road, still covered with enough snow to make good skiing, is quiet, and I have the ski trail all to myself. Even though the sun is warm, the shady norths keep the snow from melting, and a pair of noisy blue jays keep me company.

That evening, Doug and I, armed with bread, pie, an armload of CattleWomen scrapbooks and our eating utensils, attend another one of those outrageous Wallowa County potlucks. This joint CattleWomen/Stockgrowers get-together always brings out the best in our country cooks.

Ken Knott, president of the Union County Cattlemen, was our speaker. He was accompanied to Wallowa County by his pretty wife, Jeanette. My bread brought $1 at the silent auction held to raise money for the scholarship fund, and every crumb of the lemon pie was eaten.

How was the bread, Ed?

February 11—A cloudy morning sky creates a brilliant salmon-colored sunrise, which happens as we eat our sausage-and-eggs breakfast. My hens got carried away and shelled out five eggs today.

Baked a pumpkin pie, using up the remains of the pumpkin from my fall garden, then worked the rest of the day on this weekly column.

February 12—Another warm morning with no frost, though cloudy and threatening rain. Doug off to a meeting in La Grande with other local ranchers to continue working on a solution to the ongoing rancher-sportsman-wildlife issues.

Ben, meanwhile, does the feeding every day except Sunday. As I've said, Ben is one in a million. When it comes to dependability and faithfulness, he is tops. No way could we have gone to California in January if it weren't for him. Behind every successful operation there is a top hand, and Ben deserves much of the credit here.

February 13—A silent snow fell during the night, a soft, wet spring snow that soaks quickly into the ground. Baked a loaf of Dakota bread today, a delicious, nutritious combination of whole wheat, white and rye flours, cottage cheese, honey, oatmeal, wheat germ and yeast. The round loaf comes from the oven fragrant, browned to perfection, and of course we have to sample the heel right away.

Spent more time labeling slides I will submit for possible use in our photo club's color calendar, which we hope to have printed before Memorial Day. Linde came down and we went for our daily hike. We hope to be in shape for mountain climbing when summer rolls around.

Four miles of tromping around the hills and we returned to cook supper for our husbands. Lamb roast, with parsnips, carrots, onions and potatoes cooked in the meat juices, with the Dakota bread.

February 14—Received a handmade valentine from my youngest grandchildren. One way to beat the commercialism of Valentine's Day is to make our own cards.

Birds in the willows are singing up a storm this morning. Doug is pruning the raspberry patch. My view of mountains and upper Prairie Creek is much improved.

From 11:30 until 1:30 we CattleWomen served a beef chili lunch at the Enterprise Les Schwab Tire Center. With the chili we served bread and cookies. It was such a warm, sunny day and a good crowd of folks showed up from miles around to eat chili and visit. Everyone talked about how warm the weather was for February.

Afterward, Linde and we hiked up the second moraine of Wallowa Lake. Each step brought to view a different perspective of the valley below and mountains above. The last of the snowbanks was melting in the bottom of a draw between the two moraines as we followed a cow trail to a high basin. Bonneville, then Mt. Howard came into view, and Chief Joseph Mountain seemed close enough to touch.

On top we looked down on frozen Wallowa Lake, but a gauzy mist veiled the mountains. Large cracks have appeared in the lake ice, creating pretty patterns. A chill wind began to blow the mist away as we headed back. Just as we left the basin, a lovely rainbow-colored sun dog lit up the clouds at either end of Chief Joseph Mountains.

Home to fix supper, soak in the tub, and make a 7 p.m. photo club meeting.

February 15—Cloudy and warm, with no frost when I fed the animals this morning. Doug and I joined neighbors Linde and Pat at Vali's at Wallowa Lake tonight for supper, then back here to watch "The Wallowa Story" and eat slices of lemon pie. A nice warm rain falls on into the night.

February 16—Ate early, fed livestock and left to pick up son Ken and wife, Annie, and their friend Loretta Johnson, then drove to Union where we spent the day watching the district wrestling tournament.

Grandson Chad won the championship for the 168-pound category. Although this grandma was very proud, as this win allows him to compete for the state title, she is even more proud of the way he helps his teammates and supports them before their matches. In other words, Chad is a nice person, and for that alone I would be proud.

To celebrate Chad's victory, his parents treated us to a delicious seafood dinner at Skipper's in La Grande.

February 17—Snow on the ground this morning. Doug out feeding silage early, while the ground is still frozen. The snow melts quickly and soaks into the ground, which is good.

Spent a lazy Sunday embroidering on my state flower quilt, which is only four squares from being completed. Sitting in the stands at the wrestling tournament, I finished Illinois.

Decided to invite daughter Ramona and her family for supper, and bravely tackled homemade tamales. A first for me. After doubling the recipe I had masa dough, filling, and coin husks all over the kitchen.

One hundred tamales later I began steaming the first batch. Soon those healthy appetites, three teenagers included, began eating tamales. I was glad to have doubled the recipe. The leftovers froze nicely in the freezer.

After viewing some slides of family camping trips, we called it a day. I dreamed about assembling tamales!

February 18—Heavy frost, well below 20 degrees. Thick layers of clouds hover over the Wallowas. Baked a batch of huckleberry oatbran muffins for breakfast.

Typed "CattleWomen's Corner" for our local paper, did more photo-journalism and typed a letter for Doug. The cowboys are sorting and culling some cows to sell at the sale today. Worked on my column, watched two grandchildren, and left at 3 to take granddaughter Carrie to audition for Cinderella.

Stew for supper with parsley dumplings, cooked in the cast iron dutch oven on the Monarch. Yum!

February 19—Snowed most of the night, a wet, spring-like snow that quickly melts into the ground. Doug leaves early for Salem, where he'll attend the Oregon Cattlemen's Association quarterly meeting.

Tended to my chores, ran errands in town, mailed a birthday gift to granddaughter Lacey in Wyoming, purchased Jack Evan's book *Powerful Rockey* at the Bookloft, and returned home to evening chores.

Then I drove up to share Linde's crackpot stew with her and husband, Pat, and munch warm sourdough bread. It was rosy and warm in the new log home, where a huge fire blazed merrily on the hearth. After giving Linde some of my sourdough starter, she is well on her way to becoming a good bread baker.

After eating, we were transported to Edinburgh Castle (via a video and VCR) to watch all the pomp of a Military Tattoo. It was almost like being there.

February 20—Accompanied by two good friends, I enjoyed a hike up Big Sheep Creek today. Armed with lunches in our day packs, we began our hike around 10 a.m. Although the morning was cloudy and threatening rain, the air wasn't cold. Leaving Linde's Jeep parked near a haystack, we began to walk up the creek, following a dirt road that led past several enclosures full of calving cows. Baby calves cavorted or dozed in the mild canyon air while mamas munched hay.

Four cowboys were busy ear-tagging, attending calving cows, and feeding, a never-ending job this time of year. Weary hands take turns checking cows round the clock, for as sure as cows are left alone, trouble appears, like a calf coming backward or a first-calf heifer needing assistance.

Big Sheep Creek has been fenced off from the cattle, which protects the riparian area from any damage that could result from tromping. In a time when ranchers are consistently being portrayed in the role of bad guys, examples such as these never find their way into the proper media channels.

These cattle drink from watering troughs instead of walking into the creek. After leaving the final bunch of cows behind, we gazed upward to see a reddish haze covering the canyon sides—goat weed. Leafless syringa, sarvis berry and dormant sumac grew there as well. Small patches of white-barked aspen grew in the golden grass-covered draws. Looking up, we could see cavernous caves, filled with fallen rim rocks, their dark depths contrasting with clouds that sailed overhead.

It began to sprinkle a bit, and great gray curtains of rain beginning at the top of lofty rims swept downward in the most incredible fashion. High above, snow-dusted rims loomed at the head of the canyon, while here on Big Sheep Creek the stream gurgled and flowed along banks beginning to show the first spring green.

Several mule deer leaped the road in front of us, then tripped lightly up the steep canyon side to rest on a bench and watch us. Chukars flew up at our approach and whirred around the next bend. Arriving at a brown-grass meadow along the creek, we found a sheltered cove where we pulled up the nearest rock and rested. We munched our lunch listening to the sound of water and entertained by returning robins that decorated a hackberry tree. We hiked up around one more bend before returning to the Jeep.

It rained all the way home, and we all felt good after hiking about 8-1/2 miles. After supper, I was off to another meeting of our photo club to select slides for our 1992 color calendar. The photo selected for April was mine: a branding scene on Big Sheep Creek, near where we had walked today. All of our members had submitted such outstanding slides, but we could only choose twelve photos. It was a difficult choice to make.

February 21—The rain ceased during the night, It was 30 degrees and a sheet of ice covered everything when I went out to feed the horses and mule.

CattleWomen's meeting at noon today at "A Country Place on Pete's Pond." After lunch we discussed the upcoming cooking school and planned many spring events. Some of the gals had just returned from the state quarterly meetings in Salem, and extension agent Arleigh Isley was present to update us on what is happening concerning the ongoing struggle for ranchers' rights as they pertain to water issues and grazing on public lands.

There seems to be a great deal of confusion these days about the definition of the word ecology. Arleigh had some good common sense answers to questions that concern all of us in the beef industry, and is very well-versed.

Three loads of wash dried on the line today. Ben, who returned from the hills this afternoon, reported conditions good out there, with all of the snow melted on the back roads. Doug returned safely, and late, from Salem.

February 22—Cloudy and cool, with partial clearing. After chores, went for a walk around our "country block," which took exactly one hour.

Picked up the youngest grandchildren, treated them to milk shakes at the Food Farm, then came home and played outside all afternoon. The children spent the night and slept with grandma, who didn't get too much sleep. Small arms flailed me in the face, and James fell off the bed.

February 23—The season's first calves were born today in mild, sunny weather. Can this be real? Fixed the children a good breakfast. Grandson Bart joined us while daddy helped sort calving cows. The children helped me rake limbs off the lawn. A heavy morning frost quickly melted and the temperature nearly hit 70 degrees.

February 25—Ice had formed over the ditches this morning when I went out to hay the two milk cows that have been moved from the main herd back to my charge again. They aren't due to freshen for a while yet.

February 26—Sun spilled onto our breakfast table as we ate and answered phone calls about seed potatoes. Our cellar crews are very busy loading out more semis of seed.

Spent the morning cleaning up winter's debris on the lawn, pulled old dead stems from the flower beds, and burned the raspberry prunings. Baked a loaf of Dakota bread, washed rugs, scrubbed floors, and put a stew hen on to simmer with rosemary, celery and onion for soup tonight.

Scotty came out from town and we went for a walk, then visited over a cup of tea. So warm and sunny I've had windows open all day airing out the house.

February 27—Another bright, clear day ensues as February leaves us. So warm this morning, an amaryllis bulb on my sink counter begins to bloom. Grandchildren again today. I was missing them. We walked down to a big irrigation ditch and did some "pretend" fishing.

While I was lifting a hot apple pie from the oven this evening, Max and Millie Gorsline stopped in for a visit. The smell of that pie helped persuade them to stay for supper, after which we enjoyed hearing about their recent trip to Mexico.

February 28—The shortest month of the year ends with another clear, flawless day. A frosty morning quickly warms and how long can this last?

Baked three loaves of whole wheat bread: one to eat, two for the freezer. A friend gave me some apples that have been stored all winter in a root cellar. so decided to can them. After peeling, slicing and packing the apples into jars, I poured a light sugar syrup over them and processed the jars in a boiling water bath.

Think of all those future apple pies, Shawn.

The war has ended. Our county, virtually covered with yellow ribbons and American flags, displays the patriotic feelings for our Wallowa County boys whose lives were interrupted by Operation Desert Storm.

March 1—The morning begins leaning more toward the lamb, but soon changes to a lion, in more ways than one. No sooner did the first semi load of seed potatoes begin to be shipped than it began to rain and blow. On upper Prairie Creek the rain soon turned to snow.

Canned seven more quarts of apple slices. Baked two pies. Delivered one pie to Cressie Green and the other one to grandson Rowdy, who is recovering from a broken ankle. Apple pie heals saddened hearts and broken bones.

Today will long be remembered as the day Ben got hurt. Everyone is just thankful it wasn't worse. Things had been going from bad to worse at the cellar anyway, and the last semi didn't get loaded until 6:30 that evening. Between the accident, a broken piler and the rain storm, everyone there was pretty well worn out.

It was an especially long day for Doug, who, after returning home from the cellar, had to go out and feed cattle, then get on the phone to line up someone to replace Ben...for a long time.

Since son Ken and son-in-law Charley each has his own cows to feed and calve out, not to mention full-time jobs, a schedule was finally worked out between them. It was late when Doug finally ate supper and got everything lined out so he could get away to attend the C& B sale in Hermiston tomorrow.

The rain was short-lived and a predicted snow storm passed to the north of us.

March 2—When Doug left for Hermiston this morning, that left me with calving cows, the phone, and my usual outside chores. A thin glaze of ice covered everything, but blustery winds on the warm side quickly melted it away. Several calves were born unassisted and Ken was here to feed, so the day passed uneventfully.

Linde and I checked the cows on our way in to Enterprise to attend a cooking school. Cloverleaf Hall, hub for community activities, was transformed into a culinary extravaganza. Local merchants, such as The Centennial House, had set up booths. Carolee Perkins was serving hot cappuccino and free samples of beer bread. Tempting flavors of fudge were displayed next to aromatic coffees. The Sports Corral had an attractive display of western wear, and Harshman's Store laid out some of its popular items on a long table.

Linde and I were hostesses, greeting people as they came in the door, giving them samples of barbecued tri-tip beef roast that had been grilled outside in the wind storm. A stage had been set up to accommodate Wayne Philen, who is the official Oregon Beef Council chef. Huge posters of mouth-watering beef dishes were displayed at the left of the stage.

Meanwhile, a March storm brewed outside. The wind increased, rain beat against the windows, and Wayne finished grilling 75 pounds of beef. While his stir-fry pan sent steam wafting into the air, Wayne presented a short slide show that illustrated how successfully the check-off dollars are working to promote beef.

Wayne, an imposing sight in his tall chef's hat and white jacket, is quite the showman as he flips the contents of his pans into the air with wild abandon. When his peanut oil caught fire, he calmly remarked that in such a situation one needn't call 911—unless the curtains burst into flames.

"Just put a lid on the pan," he said, "and if you smell hair burning, you're too close to the fire."

The combined smells of teriyaki sauce, sesame oil, green-yellow-red peppers, onion, beef and zucchini permeated the hall. Philen sliced onions with lightning-quick chops, in time to a quick-witted commentary. When some stir-fry veggies fell to the floor, Philen commented, "That's one for the queen, as they say in England."

More entertainment as he pinched seasoning between his fingers and threw some directly into the pan, then tossed some over his shoulder, to show how it's done in France and Germany. The chef then prepared an herb-rubbed-stuffed roast that was later given as a door prize. The delicious light beef was donated by Ron Baker of C&B Livestock in Hermiston, and the recipes were handed out to people who were just dying to go home and try out Wayne's techniques in their own kitchens.

Afterward we CattleWomen served cookies, answered questions concerning beef, and returned to our country homes. Meanwhile, the rain cloud passed on to the east and the winds rested. Linde and I drove home under a gorgeous yellow moon that floated between gilt-edged clouds in a rain-washed sky. Prairie Creek appeared bright as day, and the snowy mountains glowed in moonlight.

Doug was already home in bed, and the cows were all OK.

March 3—Today we had rain, wind and rainbows. Trees have blown over, our neighbor's wheel lines have escaped their fields, and some are still rolling around the back roads!

High winds nearly knocks me over when I go out to chore. Then more rain. My hens are all ruffled up in the chicken house as wind whistles through broken window panes. Charley and Shawn arrive to feed the cattle. I thaw out colostrum milk to feed the twins, as their mother is drying up due to retaining her afterbirth.

March 4—At the moment, March can't make up its mind whether its weather should be mild or mean. Wild, blustery winds that have been blowing mild air around in furious gusts for the past two days have temporarily laid down to rest. A warm March rain soaks into the ground, which has been dried out by the fierce winds, and the snowline has retreated to the upper slopes of the mountains as the month comes in with its proverbial lion lamb weather.

Calves are coming thick and fast now, and our pasture is dotted with babies, which arrive in all colors. The mother to the twins retained her placenta, and as a result isn't able to produce enough milk for them now. So here I go again, feeding bottle babies. Unfortunately, my milk cows haven't freshened yet, or I could be grafting the twins on them.

The 25 Barred Plymouth Rock pullets will be here the 13th, at which time I will be surrogate mother to baby chicks as well. We are now loading out semis of seed potatoes on a daily basis. Our crews work out in the rain and wind, doing a job that must be done. The weather turned nasty the first day we shipped. Wouldn't you know that up until then, one gorgeous day after another elapsed, causing us to wonder if March were going to pass us by.

Our reliable hired man Ben met with an unfortunate accident while loading potatoes last week, and as a result will be laid up for a while. Son Ken is helping feed until Ben gets back on his feet. Ranching is hazardous to your health, but what isn't these days?

March 5—Frost lays thick under cloudy skies as I walk down to feed the twins their bottles of milk replacer. Snow falling in the nearby mountains as I look out my kitchen window and peel apples for two pies.

After lunch I give one pie to friend Grace and take the other one over to Ben, who is still feeling pretty bad. Then Grace and I visit neighbor Betty Cornwell, known locally as the poetess of upper Prairie Creek. After watching "The Bear," a beautifully filmed movie, five years in the making, produced by a French film company, on Betty's VCR, we savored decadent slices of vanilla cream pie with strawberries and whipped cream.

After which, I had to return home to fix supper. My heart wasn't in it. I was so impressed with the photography in the film, I went out and purchased a copy of "The Bear" for our family, so they could enjoy it also.

Worked on my column, then drove Doug into the cellar so he could bring a truck home.

March 6—The ground is white with snow, the result of a storm that swept through during the night. Doug up early, as usual, checking those cows closest to calving. I do my morning chores, walking from horse pasture to calving shed, to cow barn, to chicken pen. In the middle of typing, I stop to help Doug and Ken drive cows into a corral where the ones heaviest in calf will be sorted and put in the calving field.

Snow flies thick and fast past the window as I peel the last of the apples to make yet another pie. Fed cold cowboys Doug and Ken a noon meal of steak, fried potatoes and homemade whole wheat bread. By the time the men polished off the rest of the sponge cake and custard, bright sunshine was melting the snow and water began to pour off the roof.

Delivered the pie to the friend on Alder Slope who gave me the apples, then ran errands in town before returning to check cows and fix supper. As it clears off tonight, the temperature drops.

March 7—Bright sunshine and a frosty 20 degrees. Too nice to stay inside. Before picking up a bummer lamb, Linde and I hike up Alder Slope to Sheep Ridge. Snow clouds roll in as the sky begins to spit snow, but our exertion keeps us warm. The snow isn't as deep as we'd expected and so the going is fairly easy. The view from the top of the ridge is splendid.

We practically run all the way down the trail and return to our car. Driving past Hope and Harold McLaughlin's place located high on Alder Slope, we stop to visit. I always enjoy seeing this couple's creative work, from Harold's wonderful woodworking projects of picnic tables, bookcases, stools, picture frames and folding tables, to Hope's lovely handmade quilts and rugs.

Hope is at her large loom weaving colorful rag rugs. She takes us upstairs to see her new quilt-making sewing machine and frame. Samples of her creative quilts hang everywhere, all sewed with a patchwork flow and skill. One beautiful, commemorative quilt, still in the process of being sewn, spells out the words, "God Bless America, Land That I Love, Desert Storm 1991." The words aren't visible unless one stands back away from the quilt to read the message. As Hope sews, she can look out windows to the valley spread out below, or watch the sunrise over the Seven Devils mountains in Idaho. Other windows look out on Ruby Peak and up Sheep Ridge, where Linde and I had just climbed.

At son Ken's, daughter-in-law Annie meets us with the bummer lamb, which Linde names "Orphan Annie." I think of Roger Pond as I try to keep a bleating lamb from jumping out of a box on my lap as we drive home.

March 8—Another beautiful sunrise over frosty Prairie Creek. Clean sheets flutter on the line, the chores are finished, and I follow Doug in the Luv pickup as he tows a large potato piler into our cellars. With blinking lights flashing, I drive slowly and savor the morning, noticing our neighbor's baby calves and lambs.

Son Ken still doing the feeding, as it will be some time before Ben returns to work. The potato shipping crew hard at it again today. I can see Ken saddling a horse, to drive a cow in that needs help calving.

I place some huckleberry bran muffins in his pickup so he can have something to munch on as he drives to Alder Slope to check his own cows. This is a busy time for cowboys.

March 9—Windy all night and continuing on into this morning. Doug left at 3:45 a.m. to drive to Hermiston to sort cattle we have there in a feedlot.

I fight the howling wind and make my round of chores, checking calving cows all day. Turned the cow, whose calf Ken pulled yesterday, out with the others. My two milk cows are beginning to swell in their bellies. Soon I'll be milking again.

Invite families of strong sons over for supper, to have help in case a calf needs pulling. With Doug gone I don't relish being alone with a herd of pregnant cows.

Spent the day preparing a Mexican feast, a family favorite. Also baked a big, round loaf of sheepherders' bread in my dutch oven. The dough is powerful! It lifted that cast iron lid right up off the kettle! Grandchildren here are impressed. Of course we have to trim off the baked crusts that formed over the sides, and sample some with real butter.

Meanwhile, son Ken having a time with two cows calving at once. The cow that hasn't calved yet is claiming the other cow's calf. Tonight two sons help pull a calf before supper. By using the lure of food, I had plenty of help, and everything was under control when Doug returned late to find all of us watching "The Bear" on our VCR.

Ran across the following poem in the Joseph/Imnaha school news, and thought it deserved a wider audience. The author is unknown, and it is titled "Success."

Success doesn't mean that you've won great wealth.
That you strove all your life for gain,
That you hurried and worried and ruined your health.
Success such as that is vain.

But the good that you've done with the chance that you had
That you aided a man in distress.
That you spread good cheer and made others glad
That, my friend, is true success.

Not always crowned with a laurel wreath,
Nor placed in the hall of fame,
Success to the man in the place beneath,
is in playing an honest game.

With eyes to see and a heart to know.
To bring others happiness
It isn't the clothes, it's the inner glow,
That tells of true success.

March 11—Hey, the squirrels are out!

Harbingers of spring: little, hungry, brown, furry rodents that pop out of their holes in March to scurry around madly in search of food.

Everything around here is coming up calves and potatoes. When we aren't shipping seed, we are calving: that is, the cows are. Our lives rotate around a bovine maternity ward, potato trucks, pilers, drivers, workers, and incessant telephone calls to coordinate same. With Ben much improved, but still laid up, every member of the family gets into the act.

When Doug had to drive to Hermiston last week to sort our cattle there, I invited a son, son-in-law, and their families for supper so I would have strong hands "on hand" in case a calf needed pulling. The plan worked, and although Charley and Todd didn't finish pulling a big calf in time to eat with us, there were plenty of enchiladas left…and cherry pie.

Son Ken has been doing the feeding during the week, so Charley and Shawn take the Sunday shift. Son Steve is foreman of the potato cellar and I ride herd here. Doug goes all the time, checking cows on the night shift, trouble-shooting each operation, and keeping us all in line. So far none of us has gotten fired!

Lately there has been snow on the ground every morning, which usually melts by afternoon. But we can't complain too much about our weather. Compared to most Marches, this one has been pretty mild…so far.

March 18—Springtime is always welcome, it is especially slow in the high, mountain valleys here in our part of the Northwest. After long months of looking at a white landscape, or one that is colorless, greenness creates a sort of seasonal magic. That magic is beginning to happen here on Prairie Creek. And on the hills, the first buttercups are bursting into bloom!

As life begins anew, spreading over our hills, canyons and valleys, it reminds us that life is eternal. Springtimes are forever, a time when old folks and youngsters shout for joy. It should be a time for us in between, too, who think we are too busy, to take time to enjoy the season.

Doug and I took time to enjoy yesterday, although at one point my husband thought he didn't have that time. Somehow, it all worked out and we were able to get together with neighbors and celebrate St. Patrick's Day.

After much laughter, corn beef and cabbage, Irish soda bread, apple cheesecake, bagpipe music, kilts, green balloons, and good cheer, and more good cheer, we came home to calving cows and evening chores and went to sleep with visions of shamrocks dancing in our heads.

March 25—It is snowing... again! Soft, spring snow that melts within hours after the warm sun burns through wet clouds. Baby calves lie snuggled amid curving rows of hay scattered over the field for the cows to eat. Tummies full of milk, mamas close by, and a warm March sun make their snow-covered bodies steam. In the calving shed, my two-week-old Barred Plymouth Rock pullets are already beginning to feather out in their heated wooden box.

The phantom Wallowas appear through white mists, robins decorate bare willow limbs, and chirp, chirp, chirp. Mallard ducks fly in and out down along the creek, loving the wet, snowy weather. And each time our snow melts, the grass takes on a deeper hue of green. There must be some magic ingredient in spring snow, a secret something that causes tulips to burst forth from under the ground, crocuses to push up, and that spring-fresh quality appear in the grasses.

For us skiers it is a wonderful time. Some time ago, Duane Schubert, owner of Anthony Lakes Ski Resort, extended an invitation for four of us to come on up, stay overnight, and go skiing. So, we did. We, meaning the old gang of ranch women who trekked into The Horse Ranch along the Minam River last summer; Helen, Scotty, Linde and yours truly.

The four of us left Wallowa County at dawn last Friday, and drove to North Powder, then up through that picturesque valley laced with split rail fences which forms a gateway to the Elkhorn mountains. We soon left the valley far below and ascended a good road that led up into the snowy high reaches.

Around 9 a.m. we reached our destination, the 1,100-foot Anthony Lakes ski area. The well-maintained road took us to the main lodge, where skiers were just beginning to arrive for a day of skiing fresh powder. Newly fallen snow blanketed the evergreens, and icicles hung from the eaves of the lodge. Everywhere we found smiling faces, cleanliness and order. The groomed downhill slopes looked inviting, but we were anticipating the groomed Nordic trails.

The girl at the ticket office gave us directions to our quarters, which were located above the shop where the snow groomers were parked. We climbed a wooden stairway, toting our duffels up to our apartment, which looked right out onto the mountains and downhill slopes. After settling in, we made lunches, stuffed them into our day packs, and skied right off the deck of our apartment to the Nordic trailhead. Big, fat flakes of snow drifted downward, but we were dressed warmly, and it was pleasant.

Real, groomed trails. None of us Wallowa Countians had ever been on a groomed Nordic trail. Heaven. In fact we hadn't even stayed in a real apartment at a ski area! We felt like a bunch of college girls during spring break. A large wooden sign with illustrated maps gave us several options we could take: a short loop, a medium one, or the most difficult. Of course, we chose the latter.

At first it appeared we had the trail to ourselves, as we took off down a gentle slope. Sunlight broke through snow clouds, casting shadows on the clean snow. It was incredibly quiet, every sound seemed muffled and we became one with the snowy woods. The trail followed the shore of a lake, and suddenly a mountain rose up in front of us. We glided around the lake, listening to the soft slush, slush of our cross-country skis on the snowy trail. It was like being in a dream world. Could this be for real?

We approached a fork in the trail and took the one to the right. Soon we began to climb a gentle hill that leveled out onto a snowy meadow. At noon we stopped on a level spot and sat down in the deep snow banks that lined the trail. Our posteriors sank down just enough to create perfect chairs. We munched our lunch and laughed a lot before resuming our cross-country trek through the very heart of the Elkhorns.

The sun continued to stream through the clouds as we climbed steeper hills, then began to ski down to the lake again. More laughter, when sometimes we didn't negotiate a turn and careened into deep drifts off the trail. We actually made it safely back to the trailhead and skied up to the lodge, where we rested and looked out the large glass windows, watching the colorful downhill skiers come zooming off the different runs.

After returning to our apartment for a cup of hot tea, we decided to have one more go at the ski trails, or else we would fall asleep. Linde and I, being the faster skiers, elected to take the same route, only in reverse. Helen and Scotty took the shorter loop. We quickly got into the familiar slide and glide, loving every minute of it.

When we returned to the apartment, Duane paid us a visit and was happy to find us enjoying ourselves. Mentioning that I thought the Nordic ski trails were Oregon's best-kept secret, I wondered why more people weren't using them, as we had met only a handful of people. Duane, wearing downhill ski boots, said he guessed he'd have to ski Nordic one day to see for himself.

Linde mixed hot mugs of Irish coffee with whipped cream, and we relaxed until time for supper. I had brought along some homemade bread loaves, baked earlier and frozen. Before baking, the dough was spread with corned beef, swiss cheese and sauerkraut. So all we had to do was pop the loaves into the microwave and *voila!*—supper. Helen fixed crisp veggies to go along with.

As evening descended, the mountain emptied of people, who all drove down to Baker City for the night. With the exception of a few employees, us gals and the people in the next apartment, the place was deserted. In spite of good intentions, all those miles of trail took their toll and we didn't make it up much past 8 p.m. After a hot shower, we called it a day.

Before climbing into my sleeping bag, I walked out onto the deck to drink in the mountain air and moonlit ski slopes. Linde, who was in charge of sleeping arrangements, separated those who snored, so the combined sound wouldn't be concentrated in one corner.

Scotty, our poet, composed a poem while Helen read a murder mystery. Scotty's poem:

Janie said, "Let's ski," and I said, "Friend, join in." So off to Anthony Lakes we traveled at dawn. The snow it was perfect, just like we wished. And up and down we went, Our skis, they just swished.

There was Janie and Helen, and of course, Linde too. The time was just right, 'cause the people were few. As we hit the trail we were a colorful bunch, A regular rainbow, and daypacks with lunch.

The trail it was super, the grooming just right; And thanks to Duane Schubert, We spend the night.

This skiing Nordic to be so bold, is Jim for the young, as well as the old. When you finish the trail at Anthony Lakes, Friend, you have what it takes.

My friend Scotty, in her 70th year, can ski with the best of them. Born in Scotland, she has the Scots' sense of humor and is a hard-working, fun-loving person. As a cold wind blew loose snow around in drifts, we curled up in our warm nest, like hibernating bears, and slept like babies.

The next morning we were up early, before anyone except for the snow groomers, hitting the ski trails again. Snowshoe rabbit prints in snow led the way along the lake and into the woods. Gray dawn gave way to misty morn, and cold fingers of mist curled around the peaks. A light snow was falling and we guessed it was around 10 or 15 degrees. Great for skiing.

Later we packed up and returned to Wallowa County, stopping along the Wallowa River to picnic, feeling like tourists in our own beautiful area. And now, as I write, our ski trip seems like a dream again.

April 1—There is a soft, gentle feel to the air. The morning sun radiates a comforting warmth. and that spells April. A warm spring rain waits in the wings of a cloud, and the robins are ecstatic.

Yesterday, Easter Sunday, one of our cows decided to calve, but the calf, in its haste to be born, presented only one foot. The other foot was twisted back just enough to cause problems. It was a big calf, complicating matters even more, so Doug hauled the cow into the vet, who gave up Easter Sunday morning with his family to bring a big bull calf into the world.

Perhaps because of her ordeal, mama cow decided motherhood wasn't for her, and indeed, showed more than a little animosity toward the object of her pain. Every time the calf tried to nurse, she butted him out of the way, then kicked him in the head. Fortunately, both the calf and Doug got the message.

The result was that yours truly has added another orphan to her brood. After thawing out some colostrum milk (courtesy of my milk cow) and bottle feeding the calf several times, he has forgotten mom, but he sure likes me. It was 2 in the afternoon before Doug finished the Sunday feeding so we could drive to Imnaha for a family picnic.

Up Camp Creek it was lovely. The canyons were greening, forsythia bursting into sprays of yellow blossoms, a brand new filly bucking and kicking in the sunshine, and the happy laughter of grandchildren hunting Easter eggs filled the air. After ham and potato salad, the children hit with a stick a piñata that hung from a locust tree branch in the yard.

Three-year-old Adele had first chance to break the candy-filled donkey. As the ages of the kids progressed, so did the strength of their swings, and soon the anticipated contents spilled onto the lawn. Then came the mad scramble to pick up their treats. And for country kids, who don't get much candy, it was really a treat.

Mona and Buck Matthews ride their ponies through Camp Creek.

We couldn't stay long because another cow was in labor. Returning to Prairie Creek, we found not one, but two new calves. Linde and husband Pat are visiting relatives in California this week, so I am lamb-sitting "Orphan Annie." the Dorset bummer lamb. The Barred Plymouth Rock pullets continue to grow at an alarming rate, and will soon outgrow their large wooden box.

On Saturday, leaving new hired hand Tom in charge of the ranch, Doug and I drove to Clarkston, Washington, to attend the golden wedding anniversary of Doug's brother, Jack, and wife of 50 years, Blanche. On the way over we spotted a herd of elk grazing the new green grass growing on the high benches that form the breaks of the Grande Ronde River. Trees were beginning to leaf out along Asotin's streets. Daffodils, tulips and Bleeding heart created a welcome sight for our winter-weary eyes.

In this day and age, when statisticians are telling us that the American family is an endangered institution, it is refreshing to see Jack and Blanche's family. This couple reared five children on a cattle ranch along Joseph Creek. Times were tough, work was hard, and Blanche didn't have the modern conveniences available to most of today's wives. The life must have agreed with them, because they are living proof that hard work never hurt anyone.

Jack's voice trailed off and Blanche blinked back tears of pride as their five grown children walked up and stood beside them, bringing along their spouses and children. It was impressive, and Blanche thanked all of them for bringing so much joy to her throughout the years. Isn't that just like a mother? We made the acquaintance of other couples from Jack and Blanche's era, which included more strong families.

My sister Mary Ann spent several days with us, having driven up from California during Easter week. It was fun having "Auntie" here, and making the rounds to see all of her nieces and nephews. One day we drove to Imnaha and up Camp Creek to visit our canyon family. Youngsters Buck and Mona rode their ponies for us, showing off their riding skills. Bareback, they rode along steep canyon trails, crossed Camp Creek, and raced down the meadow. What a special place for youngsters to grow up.

One morning Mary Ann and I met daughter Ramona at "A Country Place on Pete's Pond" for breakfast. The ice melted now on the pond, and the large resident population of wild geese were taking off and landing. Huge rainbow trout vied with the waterfowl for food pellets thrown by visitors.

Seated on the sunny deck in full view of Ruby Peak and connecting mountains, which reflected themselves in the waters of the pond, we watch the reflections create a wavering water color painting, stirred by swans, ducks and geese. Our waitress, Kim Tippett, is busy scurrying around to get our table ready. This place is a very popular dining spot in the Northwest, and used to be the site of an old mill pond. We laugh and visit and savor our breakfast. A treat for me was a waffle with Marionberries and whipped cream.

Afterward we "do" all the shops in Joseph and I feel like a tourist in my own town. Reality hits when I return to the bummer lamb, calves, chicks, cows and horses, not to mention a hungry husband. On the last evening of her visit, Mary Ann treated us to supper at Cactus Jack's, known locally as the Chief Joseph Hotel, Gold Room, Cowboy Bar, or whatever.

We decided to give the restaurant, under new management now, a try. Doug and I ordered the special, "all you can eat" beef ribs, served with homemade bread, salad and potatoes. The atmosphere is nice and the new owner gracious.

We stopped on the way home to visit Ramona and her family on upper Prairie Creek. A bright moon illuminated the mountains, and their steep, snowy slopes were bright as day.

We are still shipping seed potatoes, the cows continue to shell out the calves, and the snow on Prairie Creek is gone—until the next spring storm happens along. Ben is recuperating slowly and we have hired a temporary man to take his place.

On Friday, Doug hauled a load of our young bulls to the vet to be semen tested. I chose that day to gather a passel of grandchildren, take them to lunch at Pete's Pond, and bring them out to the ranch to color Easter eggs. It was quite a day.

After putting vinegar in six cups, and adding fizzy color tablets and water, the children were ready to get very creative and color eggs. In fact some of their creativity spilled onto the kitchen floor, their clothes, and their hands and faces. Boy, did we have fun!

Afterward they playing a rousing game of hide 'n seek, and calls of "you can't find me" rang out of closets, the sheepherder wagon, and downstairs. After scraping mud from the youngest one's shoes, and wiping faces and hands, I loaded the children up and delivered them home.

Actually, it was the day I'd promised to take granddaughter Chelsie and her friend Analise to lunch, an annual birthday present. As it turned out, it was the only day we could color eggs before Easter.

That night it was a weary grandma who climbed into bed. Six children plum tuckered her out, but something four-year-old James said made the effort worthwhile.

"Oh boy," he said "Every year we go to grandma's and color eggs."

Yes, James, this you can rely on: every year you can color eggs at grandma's. And how I wish every little boy in the world could say that.

April 9—Peering through cold, blowing snow, Mike and I could just barely make out the 140 cows that trailed ahead of us on the Crow Creek road. Ducking our heads so our hats would shield us somewhat from the icy blast of stinging snow and wind, we urged our horses on.

Snow began sticking to our yellow slickers. It sifted and blew wet under the collars of our jackets, and our cheeks burned. I glanced sideways at Mike. His face was red with cold and his eyes watered. Wispy gray hairs that escaped from under my hat were plastered to my cheekbones, and my nose and eyes watered. We were quite an outfit!

Our horses walked crookedly, attempting to turn their backs to the April storm. Crow Creek road, which only an hour earlier had been bathed in sunlight, soon turned into a scene from the arctic. The change occurred when great passing clouds began emptying tapioca-like sleet, followed by a few fluttering flakes of snow, which erupted into a swirling, blinding blizzard.

Snow fell on fields of waxy, yellow buttercups. It covered my Appaloosa mare with white spots to match her rump. The white stuff clung to "Sam," Mike's Border Collie dog, and painted our black and brown cows white as we rode on into a great white void.

Having weaned all the big fall calves these past two days, we'd driven mamas down the road on a dead run, leaving the valley and its bawling calves behind.

As we left this morning, an April rainbow framed the Wallowas and the air was mild, and a gentle breeze carried the scent of new grass. Mike and I were dressed warmly, with long-johns, jeans, chaps, slickers, down coats, scarves, warm gloves and hats. Good thing!

Five miles into the blizzard, Mike remarked, "This ain't gittin' any better quick!" I had to laugh. He was so right. Mike, in his 84th year, has been here before—many times. He grins and asks if I'm cold.

"Naw, just right," I lie, flashing a frozen smile. Lunch time comes and goes. It is too cold to take off gloves and eat cold sandwiches. The wind increases, blowing sheets of snow across the lonely hills. Visibility is limited to the side of the gravel road, and we know the cows are ahead of us only because we hear them.

In the distance, a truck motor. Doug! Soon we are in the warm cab, sipping hot chocolate and coffee, and eating sandwiches. Snow melts and drips off our hats and slickers. No matter, it beats the Waldorf Astoria. Nothing can equal that hot drink. After thawing out, it's back into wet saddles to complete 17 miles.

The herd moves right along and practically runs into the corrals by the old pink barn at the Dorrance place. We scatter hay for the cows, unsaddle our horses, turn them into a lot by the creek, and travel the long, winding road back to the valley.

Meanwhile, back at the ranch, the calves are still bawling: *Ma, Ma.* But mamas have forgotten motherhood. Visions of green grass, inspired by occasional bites along the way, helped them forget. After a long winter of eating hay, they crave green grass.

Yesterday Mike and I helped gather in the fall calving pairs, so they could be separated. After unsaddling my mare, I changed roles and began to cook supper. Two Nevada cowboys would be here by evening to spend the night and haul home six of 10 bulls they have purchased from us.

A cast-iron frypan full of sourdough biscuits began to rise and two chickens roasted slowly in the oven. I put together a salad, mashed potatoes, and stirred up a big kettle of giblet gravy. That morning I'd baked a raspberry pie. The cowboys from Fish Springs Ranch enjoyed their meal, especially after pulling a trailer for 12 hours. We invited daughter Ramona and son-in-law Charley and their family to join us. Charley used to manage the ranch at Fish Springs, so it was like old home week for them.

This morning it was up before dawn to fix sausage, eggs and sourdough waffles for the Nevada cowboys, fix myself a lunch, feed my assorted critters, which include two orphan calves, 25 baby chicks, a lamb, my milk cows and laying hens.

As I write this, drowsy from a hot tub bath, it is hard to keep my mind on these words. The column's deadline is fast approaching, and time slips away. Tomorrow morning I must arise, repeat this morning's chores, minus the lamb (friend Linde returned and retrieved "Annie"), after which Mike and I will drive out early to Crow Creek, saddle our horses and trail the cows the final leg of our journey.

Hopefully, the weatherman's predictions of more of same are wrong.

April 10—Morning comes. I burrow deeper under the covers for one more luxurious minute, then I'm up to fix breakfast and make lunches. Leaving Doug to finish sausage and eggs, I walk to the calving shed with two suckle bottles of milk re-placer for the orphan calves. After chores are finished, I return to the house before sunup. And the sun does come up, and shine gloriously across the frozen prairie until blue-gray-bellied clouds appear on all horizons. It is around 18 degrees, the ground frozen hard and the ditch in the horse pasture stilled in ice. Thankfully, there is no wind. Yet.

I drive the Luv pickup, while Mike and Doug follow in the diesel truck with stock racks. In the Luv's bed I haul out Doug's "horse," a three-wheeler that he will use to go around fences while Mike and I trail the cows. When we arrive at the corrals, our cows are waiting at the gate, anxious to hit the trail. We catch and saddle the horses, and soon Mike and I are heading the herd up Dorrance Gulch.

Blue-black clouds race over the steep hill behind us, swept along by a knife-edged breeze that carries that familiar smell of snow. Our horse's shod hooves clatter over frozen puddles, leaving chocolate-colored broken glass floating in yesterday's snow water. The cows seem to hurry. Do they know it will soon snow?

The breeze turns into a stinging wind, and Mike comments, "Ain't exactly a chinook, is it?"

"Nope."

Today I have a wool scarf wrapped under my hat, which helps. On top of the grade, we look across the rolling Zumwalt hill country and see curtains of snow showers march across the grasslands. Along Dry Salmon Creek bloom hundreds of buttercups. They too shiver in the icy wind. Even the meadowlarks' notes have a frozen ring.

Despite the harshness, I think the country is beautiful. The coyote-colored hills are now turning green. Last season's grass is the color that the country wears most of the time. Hill hues are tawny, like the wildlife that inhabits it. Elk, deer, hawks, ground squirrels, and coyotes.

Even Mike and I seem to blend in, I muse as we ride along—chaps, worn and brown; dusty, tan-colored hats; old coats, the color of elk; our roan horses reflecting red rocks and the snow-covered dirt road. Even our slickers, tied behind our saddles, are buttercup yellow.

At the Johnson pasture, we count out 70 head and split the herd, letting 70 more pass by. That is, we hope we do. I ride on ahead to get a more accurate count. Someone up there likes us, because even after a few head escape and run back into the Johnson pasture, I come up with 69. The boss says to divide the herd, and that's close enough.

We take the other half of the cows on down the cold trail to Butte Creek, where Doug has the gate open for us. Our hands, feet and noses are numb from the icy wind and we walk stiffly after dismounting. It has begun to snow and the wind sweeps down on us from the cold reaches of Red Hill.

Doug returns on his Honda, from fixing fence. He, too, looks cold, but doesn't admit it.

"Don't get cold on my horse," he says.

And now, back in my warm kitchen, sipping tea and soaking up the Monarch's warmth, I type this last sentence.

April 11—Baked a batch of bran muffins to go with bacon and eggs for breakfast. Snow on the ground this morning didn't melt, and scattered snow showers throughout the day added to it.

Neighbor Betty Van Blaricom here to ride with me to CattleWomen's meeting this afternoon. We pick up another neighbor, Ardis Klages, on the way. The meeting is held in the spacious home of Prairie Creek rancher Mary Ann Yost. We CattleWomen are glad to be together, compare notes, and visit. Spring ranch work allows little time for socializing. We talk about how the calving is going or about our grandchildren, about brandings and turn-out time. After a productive meeting we sip tea coffee, and eat angel food cake frosted with whipped cream and fresh strawberries.

Back home, I feed the orphan calves, gather eggs, and make homemade noodles to go with some broth and bits of meat left from the recent roast chicken dinner.

April 12—A clear, absolutely gorgeous day dawns. The air is warm and mild, birds sing, and a few white clouds float around in a cerulean sky. Linde calls. We can't stand the thought of staying in the house, so combine business and pleasure, and hike up Lightning Creek to deliver a message to Fred Bornstedt, who works for the Bellwether Ranch there.

The ranch, formerly owned by old-time movie actor Walter Brennan, is in steep canyon country. It is about a four-mile walk from the forks of Lightning Creek and Little Sheep to the ranch headquarters. The canyon air is sweet April, and the Sarvisberry and gooseberry bushes are leafed out already. Huge old cottonwoods along the creek show swollen buds, which are about to burst forth into pale green leaves. Overhanging rim rocks line the way, a gentle breeze stirs the Ponderosa pines that march up the draws, and water seeps from numerous springs along the old road. The ever-present sound of the creek is comforting, and chukars, pairing up now, whir away at our approach. Hawks scream and circle overhead, blue jays scold, and northern flickers *rat-a-tat-tat* in dead cottonwood snags.

We find Fred in his office at the rear of a horse barn. Cowhand Fred, in addition to being the Bellewether's resident veterinarian, is a renowned cowboy poet and composer of western songs. At yesterday's meeting we CattleWomen had agreed to bake pies for the annual Cowboy Poetry Gathering, which will be September 1st at Cloverleaf Hall in Enterprise.

Fred had asked me to bring the matter up at the meeting, and report back to him. Not only did we deliver the message, but we were treated to one of Fred's repertoire of songs. Shouldering his guitar in that unique style of his, Fred sang us a very humorous ballad before we left to hike back down the old road.

As we walked, we passed some Longhorn cattle, and a large bull with long horns bellowed out his own spring song, which echoed up and down Lightning Creek canyon. It was after lunch when we reached Linde's Jeep, parked at the Imnaha road, so we ate on the way out. Then I still had to grocery shop, pick up my framed photographs, which are entered in the upcoming Art Festival, and go to the bank before returning to the ranch.

Fed the calves, gathered eggs and prepared fried elk steak and potatoes for supper, after which I picked up friend Grace Bartlett and attended a slide show at the Bookloft, presented by inveterate hiker Bill George, age 76. The place was packed; by April, it seems, everyone thinks about getting back into the mountains. Bill's slides transported us there. They were wonderful, and contained a collection that spanned many years of hiking, mostly unmarked trails through the northern Wallowas.

April 13—As a bright sun burns its way into another clear April morning, the Wallowa snowfields gleam blinding white. Caught up on some housework and attempted to reduce a stack of letters that needed answering.

Tonight, as a member of the press, I attended the Chief Joseph Days queen coronation dinner and dance at the Joseph Civic Center, where the largest crowd ever turned out for the festivities. Each year three lovely hopefuls wait anxiously for the big moment, which happens around 10 p.m., and each year the girls seem to get prettier and prettier.

Jill Yost was crowned queen of the 1991 Chief Joseph court. Teah Jones of Enterprise and Dawnette Waters of Joseph will be her princesses. Any one of the three girls would have made a lovely queen.

Not too many years ago, while traveling down Red Hill, we came upon several cowboys and one cowgirl driving a large herd of cattle toward Chesnimnus Creek. It was probably the fall ride, and when I stopped to do some photographing I found the young girl sitting on the grassy hillside eating from a brown paper bag. Her horse grazed close by and she was sharing lunch with her dog. That girl was Jill Yost, and that's how always remember her. I remember her grandma Gladys, too, and know in my heart how proud she would have been of her granddaughter that night.

My own small granddaughter, Adele, too young to aspire to being a future queen, loves to dance. This little blonde three-year-old miss had been looking forward to the "Queen Dance" for days, and dance she did, nearly wearing grandma out as I stooped over to hold onto two tiny hands. But the look of joy glowing in Adele's pretty blue eyes made it all worthwhile. She wanted her brother to dance all night, but it was too late for little ones to be up, not to mention grandmas, so I took the children home, where we three shared a bed with Adele's doll.

April 15—After typing the final sentence in last week's column, I looked through my kitchen window into the mischievous eyes of three yearling Simmental bulls. When I raced outside, one frisky bull was cavorting around our raspberry patch, and two more were playing ring-around-the-rosy on the lawn. As I chased the raspberry bull out, his cloven hooves narrowly missed three tiny fir tree seedlings. Having survived grandchildren, the lawn mover, and now this, I guessed they were meant to live.

A wild wind came sweeping down off the nearby mountains, announcing a change in the weather, and the bulls, which obviously escaped via an open gate, were feeling good in the way animals often do before a storm. In dismay, I realized that all 20 head were out and having the time of their lives, having demolished a small hay pile by the horse pasture. Two bulls were taking turns rolling bales with their heads and were already halfway out the lane.

Things weren't much better at the barn, where my milk cows' hay is stacked. The young ruffians had bales strewn everywhere. Three more head of the big bouncing bulls were working on unloading a truckload of hay, while another one jumped an electric fence and was, at the moment, flirting with the two milk cows. Naturally, there wasn't a man around.

After blocking all the entrances to the yard and pretending false bravado, I shooed the errant bulls into one bunch and drove them toward the open gate. They bucked and kicked, and went on by, ending up at the cow barn again. Playfully butting bales, they tossed two into the air and split several more open.

Easing the escapees along the feeder, I threatened the bulls with their lives if they didn't go through the gate. They must have believed me, because they all bounced in, except for the one making advances to the milk cows. He was showing more than a little interest in the matrons, until I informed him they were already in calf (indeed, soon to deliver) and therefore he needn't get any wild ideas. The milk cows got into the act, and helped me run their suitor out, after which he ran out onto the country road, me in hot pursuit. Luckily, we have a panel gate entrance there, so I opened it and shooed the fellow in.

Fifteen minutes later Doug drove in.

April 19—We attended the 61st annual Enterprise FFA banquet, where this proud grandma watched her grandson Chad receive numerous honors as well as being installed the new president. Outgoing president was the 1991 Chief Joseph Days queen, Jill Yost.

Another chapter member, Vixen Radford, was 1990 Chief Joseph Days queen. Enterprise seems to have an unlimited supply of pretty blonde queens. Two charter members of the Enterprise FFA were present, and as vo-ag instructor Dick Boucher remarked, "Like begats like," because three generations of Wayne McFetridge's family are still actively involved in the chapter.

As we looked around we could see many families that fit that remark. The impressive program, run entirely by the FFA members themselves, is a tribute to Dick Boucher, who is retiring after 20 years as vo-ag instructor. A delicious roast beef dinner prepared by the Enterprise school cooks and served by FHA members was enjoyed by 250 people. As in the past, our Wallowa County CattleWomen donated beef gift certificates to help pay for the beef.

April 20—The annual Wallowa Valley Festival of Arts opening reception was tonight, as well as our newly formed Author's Playhouse, which will run both tonight and tomorrow night. I was involved in both events and entertained grandchildren all day today as well.

April 21—Fortunate enough to sit in on an art appreciation workshop presented by Madeline Janovec, today. As I listened in awe at how the story of man is told in the art he has left behind, I thought about life here in our corner of the Northwest. Then Madeline said something interesting about our area, how the whole country is focusing on our part of the world now. Artists here have a message.

"Something is happening," she said. "Perhaps, through all of this, the world can heal."

After son-in-law Bill finished feeding cattle, the family all rode out "on top" with me where we went first to see the art show in Joseph, where this grandma had been lucky enough to win some awards.

Then we drove to Enterprise and enjoyed a relaxing lunch at "A Country Place on Pete's Pond," after which we returned to the art show at the Civic Center to pick up my photo entries. Doug and daddy Bill returned from the Grande Ronde, towing a hay rake Doug had purchased at an auction at the Four-O Cattle Company there.

Carolee and I prepared a big pot of clam chowder for everyone before the Imnaha crew left for the canyons. What a week this has been!

April 22—Attended the new Imnaha church, which is not completed but finished enough to hold services. The small, close-knit settlement of Imnaha was still stunned and saddened by the death of one of its well-loved inhabitants, Rancher Warren Glaus, who was accidentally killed on night watch. While attending a baby calf, his pickup's emergency brakes failed and he was run over.

The building of Imnaha's first church had been a dream fulfilled for Warren. Coming from Montana, he and his family moved to Wallowa County several years back and purchased a ranch on the lower Imnaha. Things didn't go well for them. They lost the ranch and were plagued with one bit of bad luck after the other, but Warren loved the Imnaha. How he loved his canyons. Montana winters are long, and ranching near the Big Hole Valley, where temperatures drop below zero for days at a time, made the ranch at Corral Creek seem like paradise.

Several of Warren's close friends from Imnaha accompanied his wife, Rose, when Warren's body was transported back to Montana for burial, but his spirit remains on Imnaha, where it will dwell in the hearts of those who loved him. Warren's body rests now, next to an infant granddaughter, buried in a remote cemetery surrounded by Montana's natural grasslands and backgrounded by the majestic Continental Divide.

Having returned at midnight yesterday, Pat Stein shared their experiences with the Imnaha Christian Fellowship. Rose will return to Montana to live, as all of her children and grandchildren live there. She, too, will be missed. She and Warren both worked in the past on our potato crew. They were a pleasure to work with and we are better for having known both of them.

Seated next to my grandchildren, I felt Warren's presence in that long-awaited new church. Rainbow prisms danced on the unfinished floor as sunlight streamed through new etched glass windows. Tears trickled down onto the pages of new hymnals as we sang songs Warren so loved. It was as though the entire congregation could see Warren standing there singing. How he loved to sing, and praise the Lord!

My grandchildren had not one, but two grandmas that Sunday. It had been their job to ring the big cast-iron bell that hangs in the bell tower atop the church. From where I sat, I could see a small rope hanging down through a hole in the ceiling, so little hands could reach up to pull and ring the bell. The children sat between their two grandmas, singing songs so familiar they knew them by heart.

April 23—After attempting several times to begin typing this column, I've finally completed one sentence. Columnists, I've discovered, must be organized. To put it simply, they must organize their work so they can find time to write. Excuse me while I answer the phone.

As I was saying...Oh, yes, writers must organize their time. But even when work is finished and time allows for one to sit thyself down in front of the typewriter, mornings like this just happen. For instance, Hubby says, "Could you please type two copies of this lease agreement for me?"

"Sure, no problem," says I, and begin to type.

The ever-present phone rings. A potato grower wanting to know if he can pick up a load of seed today. That means I must give him the cellar phone number and locate Doug, who has vanished.

Phone again. Neighbor Van wants to know where he can send his film to be developed by the end of the week. I find him a mailer and set everything out for him to pick up.

Doug returns. I have him answer the potato grower's call.

Meanwhile, a Fuller Brush lady knocks at the back door, Van arrives for the mailer, the Fuller Brush lady departs (I don't need any brushes today) and brushes past Van, who asks if I would like a Mountain ash tree to plant in front of my kitchen window, so I can watch birds come to feed on the pretty orange berries. Sounds wonderful. And soon I am in Van's car, heading to a nearby field where several young ashes are growing. He digs one for me and we return to the house. I thank Van, take a shovel and dig a hole, plant the ash and return to the typewriter.

Then I remember that I must drive four FFA members to Elgin this evening for a dinner and meeting, and won't be here to cook supper for Doug. I put a kettle of beans on to cook.

And now, after losing my readers completely, I should get on with this column.

The past three days have been absolutely lovely. Mild "growing weather" has allowed grasses and weeds to jump up, tulips to bloom, and cattle ranchers to think about turn-out time.

Whenever local cowboys aren't trailing cattle along our back roads, they are branding and working calves in corrals scattered all over the country. Yesterday morning my son Ken moved his pairs up Echo Canyon to a field handy to corrals so he can brand before turning out to grass. It

Becky Thompson, 8, of Alder Slope, hugs a three-day-old quarter horse filly owned by Becky's aunt and uncle, Bill and Jackie Matthews, of Imnaha.

turned out to be a long day for him. Several smaller calves got sidetracked along the way and had to be retrieved and returned to mamas before he could call it a day.

We who live here in this beautiful area, although removed from the rest of the world by geographic barriers, are exposed to a great range of human experience, all expressed in various ways: a beautiful, inspiring painting; a hymn to a deceased loved one; or a poem about place.

April 28—The sky is thick with clouds, and dew replaces yesterday's frost. Central Oregon's limitless skies stretch before us as we take a two-lane blacktop that takes off into the sagebrush north of Madras. The country here reflects the drought years. Most creeks are dry, and the others barely running. The land has a beauty all its own, despite the dry conditions, and we find the silence and lack of traffic refreshing after the bustle of burgeoning Bend.

We pull up in front of Antelope's only store and purchase a cold drink. We guess the gal behind the counter is tired of inquiries as to the location of Rajneeshpuram, because she hands us a piece of cardboard that has pencil-scrawled directions to the Big Muddy.

We weren't interested in visiting this place, but were quite taken with Antelope itself. There was a rustic church and a small newspaper office, both built in the 1800s; across the street from the church, a local resident's yard was bursting with bright, blooming bulbs.

Heading toward Fossil, we climb and descend canyonlands ending in green creek bottoms. Rounding a bend, we stare up at this incredible series of gigantic rock formations, which appear to pierce the sky with jagged spires of color.

We spot a sign—"Trail of the Fossils"—so park our car at a marked trail head and take a quarter-mile, self-guided loop trail that leads us through an area which was once a lush, sub-tropical forest of sycamores, palms and cycads (whatever they were!). In this place, according to our brochure, alligators, rhinoceroses and titanotheres flourished in a warm, moist climate. It was a time of volcanoes too, and their spewing of lava, cinders and ash, loosened by heavy rains, produced vast mudflows which encased plant leaves and wood.

Over millions of years of time and the slow percolation of groundwater containing silica, mud, ash and other debris were cemented together to form these rocks, known today as the Clarno Palisades. Our brochure helped us identify fossils at marked spots along the trail, but it was hard for our minds to comprehend that length of time—40 million years, during which span both animal species and mountain ranges have come and gone. Man, by comparison, has been on earth a very short time.

We found an embedded tree limb and many leaf imprints among the ancient mudflow boulders. It was fun walking through a bit of Oregon's geologic history. Decisions made by modern man, who now dominates the earth, are altering the face of the land. It, along with animal species, which have taken millions of years to develop, now hang in the balance. Man, it seems, has a pretty awesome responsibility. Hopefully, common sense will win.

There were very few visitors to the Clarno Palisades on this Sunday. Across the road, a peaceful ranch nestled against the sagebrush hills, from whence came the call of chukars. All of which brought us back to the present. We drove on into the town of Fossil and parked in front of the Fossil Mercantile. It too, was like stepping back in time.

One could purchase most anything under that one roof. Yardage for sewing clothes, boots, jeans, groceries, drugs, or you could even get your hair cut! Mounted elk and deer heads stared down at us from above, and antiques of Fossil's past lined the shelves. We noticed that Fossil was celebrating its 1891-1991 Centennial.

Leaving Fossil behind, we soon proceeded through winding roller-coaster hills and greening grain fields to Arlington, where we entered the freeway along the Columbia. Unlike the friendly backroads, the freeway was all business, and we sped along with the flow of traffic until we exited at Echo. We pulled up in front of the Echo Hotel and Restaurant where we were soon partaking of the Sunday special: barbecued beef ribs. The place was packed and normally required reservations, but the waitress must have thought we looked hungry because she seated us right away.

As we crossed over the Wallowa County line, I honked my horn. No matter where we wander, we who live here are always glad to return.

April 29—Five of us Wallowa County CattleWomen have just returned from the American National CattleWomen Region V meeting in Bend. Oregon hosted the event this year, and Gerda Hyde of Chiloquin and Melinda Nevin of Dairy arranged the program.

Having agreed to leave in the wee hours of the morning, we pulled out of Enterprise around 3:45 a.m. The April moon sailed through dark cloudy skies overhead as we sped out of Wallowa County to La Grande, and then slowed down over the Blue Mountains—the road was covered with black ice.

We stretched our legs out of Pendleton, then continued along the Columbia River to Biggs Junction. Linde took the wheel as we headed south to Bend and asked directions to Sunriver, where the Oregon Beef Cookoff was just winding up. After locating the resort, we navigated a maze of roads until we eventually found the lodge, which is situated in the middle of Oregon's high desert.

Melinda Nevin gave us our registration packets, It was noon by this time, so we ordered bowls of clam chowder in an elegant dining area that looks out on what is referred to as "The Meadows." We, meaning Meleese, Linde, Marian and I, then returned to Bend, where we found our reserved room at the Riverhouse, a beautiful, sprawling motel situated on the banks of the boulder-strewn Deschutes River.

Five of us, Rhee having checked in yesterday, would share the one

Wallowa County CattleWomen at a conference in Bend included, from left, Linde Irwin, Meleese Cook, Janie Tippett, and Marian Birkmaier.

room, which contained two queen-size beds plus one roll-away bed. After unpacking, we rested up for the Region V reception.

And what a reception, held in the Big Deschutes Room where the dinner menu featured "A Taste Of Oregon." This culinary treat, prepared by the Riverhouse and coordinated by CattleWomen, caused our taste buds to run wild. Several dishes were prepared from recipes developed by Oregon Beef Council home economist Diane Byrne and her staff. The following buffet was spread before us. Naturally, we sampled everything...

Tossed green salad with dressing, beef and wild rice salad, curried beef pasta salad, Northwest salmon filet, tri-tip roast, "Pacific Rim marinated tri-tip," braised beef burgundy, "tender morsels of sirloin and fettuccine," broccoli and cauliflower with Tillamook cheese sauce, chef's potato, sourdough bread, Marionberry tarts, cheesecake with huckleberry sauce, and Riverhouse specialty coffee or hot tea!

We were impressed. The fun thing about Region V is that we were able to visit with CattleWomen from Colorado, Wyoming, Montana,

Idaho, Washington and Oregon, as well as representatives from the National CattleWomen. To make sure we did circulate and acquaint ourselves, we were given different colored tickets at each meal and told to sit at tables displaying our color.

We found a form in our registration packets that required us to write down the most preposterous lie we could conjure, and the most unbelievable story. At the beginning of each session these "true or false" stories were read, providing many a laugh.

Saturday morning Meleese, Linde and I were up at dawn for a hike around the area adjacent to The Riverhouse. Frost crunched under our feet as we walked along a golf course. The sky was crystal clear, and fears of a stormy day melted as a glorious desert sunrise broke over Bend. Quail called from nearby junipers, robins chirped, and a resident gaggle of wild geese flew upriver.

We returned to the Riverhouse for breakfast, which was thankfully light, after last night's feast. At the opening session, Oregon Cattle-women's President Ann D'Ewart, of Durkee, asked us to recite the American National CattleWomen's creed, which goes like this:

Believing that the livestock industry is of basic importance to world existence, we, the American National CattleWomen, dedicate ourselves to support it with our labor and finances; to promote it through information and publicity; to encourage its producers with our understanding and love; to do all in our power to instill in the coming generation the love of the land and life, the humility and awe before nature, and the hope and faith in the future that is inherent in Cattlemen.

My friend Linde, a relatively new CattleWoman, pointed out that lest we sometimes stray from this creed, it would be good perhaps to refer to it more often. The creed was written by Mrs. Willard Sobak, of Fairdale, North Dakota.

The highlight of Region V was a workshop presented by Donna Schmidt of the Beef Industry Council. Having grown up on a ranch, with a 4-H and FFA background, this dynamic little gal had us taking off our shoes, standing on chairs, and really listening to what she was saying. Her message had to do with body language and how we come across to others, how we communicate our different perspectives. In an age when ranchers are constantly in the media, Donna said, how we project is very important.

Lunch consisted of a beef cook-off winning salad recipe concocted of spinach, marinated beef strips, hazelnuts and tossed with a spicy-hot oriental dressing.

After lunch we rode buses to the nearby High Desert Museum, one of the West's finest museums. There was much to see. We watched a woman feed a porcupine in the outside exhibit, then walked along a path to where several otters were cavorting in a pool of water bordered by large, native rocks. It was feeding time there. too, and we watched a man feed the otters some small fish. Through an underground, glass viewing area, we were able to see the otters swim. A sign on the wall read, "If it can't be done in fun, otters won't do it."

Sometimes I think people should heed otters. Work can be enjoyable, if we choose to make it so.

As we strolled inside the museum, viewing the marvelous life-size recreations of a life that was. and still is, on some of Oregon's high desert, we were amazed at the authenticity of the scenes. We "experienced" early Indian camps and the old Oregon Trail, listening to wind whining across the desert, crickets chirping, wavering choruses of coyotes and, from the inside of a tattered covered wagon broken down along the trail, the pitiful wailing of an infant.

May 6—Finally, a carpet of green covers our valley. And finally, that unmistakable quality in the air that spells SPRING. It all begins in February, when the first sunny days appear, and everyone thinks winter is over. WRONG.

It ends when it snows on Memorial Day and we realize that this spring is like all the others before it in our high mountain valley. March, April and then May come and go, with a few spring-like days sandwiched between cold ones. Then suddenly, it's summer, and we are left wondering what happened. That season between winter and summer in Wallowa County can be bright, sunny, snowy, frosty, windy, or rainy; apple blossom white or balsamroot yellow. Oftentimes, all of the above may occur in the course of a single day. Old timers hereabouts tell us, "If you don't like the weather, wait around a few minutes and it'll change," and that about sums it up.

The tulips alongside the house have opened their brilliant red faces this morning, and the young Northwood maple is about to leaf out. The willows along the creek have that gauzy, pale green appearance, responding to last night's warm rain. Most of the primroses. and all of the pansies, however… winter-killed.

As usual, Mondays are hectic and already it is 5 p.m., time to do chores and start supper, and my column is only just begun. I will be helping trail cows and calves to the hills tomorrow, and the next day. No time to type.

This past weekend, parents, as well as grand-parents and other assorted relatives, sat through two days of the annual Joseph Junior Rodeo. This grandma had no less than eight young cowboys and cowgirls competing.

On Saturday we watched as our little ones came busting out of the chutes on wild sheep, tied ribbons on wiggling goat's tails, or tried their hand at dummy roping.

Sunday afternoon it was the turns of the juniors and seniors. Things got pretty exciting when a Brahma bull climbed out over the chute and began chasing everyone around the arena. Thanks to clowns J.D. Nobles and John Bailey, the mad bull was persuaded to return to his pen. I think both clowns probably broke track records accomplishing that feat.

From the looks of things, Wallowa County has a good supply of future cowboys and cowgirls.

May 7—The dawn sky is overcast as I open the barn door to let "Startch" in. When the big milk cow puts her head into the stanchion to eat her rolled barley, I push the wooden block in place so it will hold her there while the calves nurse. In no time at all, the three hungry calves have drained the large Holstein-Simmental's udder of milk.

As the calves grow stronger, it becomes an increasing struggle to pull them off the cow, then push and shove them through a small gate. After "bag balming" her teats to keep them from chapping, I turn Startch loose to join one of her grown daughters, who is about to drop her second calf.

After tossing the two cows some hay, I walk down to feed mule Alfie and the horses, before carrying a pail of water up to the laying hens and the half-grown Plymouth Rock pullets.

Back in the kitchen, Doug's sausage, eggs and sourdough pancakes are hot off the griddle, so we eat breakfast. I make two lunches while Doug saddles my mare, who seems to know a long ride is in store for us today. Linde arrives with her horse, as does old hand Mike McFetridge.

We three ride down to our cows and spring calves in the lower pasture, and find Ben waiting for us. Together, we gather the cattle and drive them out onto the road. Counting a bunch of yearling heifers, which Doug turns in, we have more than 300 head to take to grass.

Mike, 83, is happy, doing what he loves best. Linde and I are, too; this beats housework any day. Occasional rays of sunlight pierce dark clouds, and the glorious, gleaming, snowy Wallowas reign over a green valley as we begin our trek to the hills.

The cellar crew is shipping the last two loads of seed potatoes today. Doug, who has been helping drive the cattle on his Honda, returns to the ranch to feed the few cattle left behind. Slickers tied behind our saddles, the four of us begin the long ride to East Crow. Ben takes the lead so the cattle won't string out too far. Mike, Linde and I ride herd on the tail-enders.

Just as the last of the herd makes it through the four corners, one calf ducks under the fence and runs back to the pasture. We leave him behind. He will only slow things up and give us a late start. Then another calf comes down with a severe belly ache and, after straggling along for a mile or two, Mike says, "Enough of this." The old hand shakes out a loop, which he expertly dabs over the calf's head.

While I push the herd on, Mike and Linde tie the calf's legs with a leather thong and leave him alongside the road for Doug to bring out later. We pick up speed; that one bellyache calf was holding up the entire drive. The morning is cool, perfect for trailing cows and calves, and they move right along. We meet other cowboys and cowgals along the road, driving out to work cattle in the hills today. We visit them as they wind their slow way through our herd.

As we turn onto the gravel Crow Creek Road, another calf crawls under a weak fence and heads toward some cattle pastured on a hill. Opening a gate, Mike rides in and pursues our calf. Linde and I ride on, pushing the herd, and pretty soon, down the road, comes Mike, driving the calf ahead of him.

Cowboys come and cowboys go, but the experienced old hands like Mike McFetridge, Elzie Lewis and Clyde Simmons, to name a few here in Wallowa County, take these situations in stride. If a job needs doing, they just do it. No fanfare, no yelling, no big deal. Mike, wearing his perpetual grin, returns the calf to our herd.

Heading up Crow Creek pass, Mike and I joke about how, maybe... this time. it won't snow! And it doesn't, and is, in fact, surprisingly pleasant. The wind even forgets to blow. As we ride along, we notice a few faded buttercups reposing under the protection of several rockjacks; today's yellow color is the blooming cous, also called biscuitroot, whose edible root was one of the mainstays of the Nez Perce diet.

Many of the larger outfits now truck their cattle to grass. And today, it appears, they are all on the road. Five semi truck trailer loads make their way through our herd. We guess they must be heading to the old B&H on Chesnimnus Creek. Mt. Joseph Cattle Company is hauling out some yearlings, and Jack McClaran's cattle trucks pass through. Yost's are ahead of us, trailing their cows and calves to East Crow like us. Many of the older, family-owned ranches have been bought out by larger outfits. Times are a-changin'.

Adele Nash, 3, tries to tie a ribbon on her goat's tail in the Joseph Junior Rodeo.

Lane Bailey, son of John and Cindy Bailey, of Joseph, and great-grandson of the famous Harley Tucker, for whom the rodeo arena is named, stands by the bucking chutes, waiting his turn in the mutton riding event at the Joseph Junior Rodeo. Lane's grandmother and grandfather are Dave and Darlene Turner of Joseph.

We holler "Hey, babies," "Hey, cows" to keep the herd moving, but many begin to lag as the day warms and we shed our jackets. Soon it is noon, and we munch lunches on horseback. Doug appears in the pickup with water, coffee and hot chocolate, which really hits the spot. Despite recent damp conditions, the hills appear dry and a cloud of dust raises above the herd. A warm rain would be most welcome. Seems after we get snow or rain, a cold wind sucks all the moisture out of the ground.

It is nearly 5 p.m. when we push the last of the tired calves through the gate into the holding pasture at East Crow. We have already put in a 12-hour day, which isn't over yet. Wearily, we unsaddle our horses and turn them loose with the cattle.

Linde and I offer to ride in back of the pickup with the saddles, while Doug, Ben and Mike ride up front. It isn't cold, but dirt and dust from the gravel road stings our eyes. We laugh about our faces covered with dust. After all, we joke, we hired on to be tough.

At the ranch, Linde and Mike return home while Ben and I do the evening chores. Then the boss takes me to Kohlhepp's Kitchen for supper. My wind-burned face shows I've been horseback all day, but Joseph is still a cow town, and no one cares.

After a long, hot, tub bath: blissful sleep. Doug works in the shop until 11:30, building racks for his new pickup.

May 8—Up to greet a rainy, drippy dawn. It has rained all night by the looks of things, but a fine, warm rain. Just what the country needs. We layer on the clothes this morning. A warm rain can turn to snow or sleet out where we're going.

Wearing long yellow slickers, we catch and saddle our wet, shivering horses in the pasture on East Crow. This morning we must coordinate with other ranchers. Yosts have just driven their cows and calves out onto the road, so we must wait until they are a couple of miles ahead of us before we start ours.

Then, after we trail past the old Dorrance place, the Mt. Joseph bunch can start its 200 head of feeders back toward East Crow. Can you imagine the wreck we'd cause if we hadn't met these fellow ranchers along the road yesterday and did some communicating? Those yearlings would have created some excitement for sure.

It is Crow Creek's verdant spring. Willows are leafing out, and all the varied shades of green carpet the hills. Cattle country!

May 9—The past two days have been spent in the saddle. We've just finished trailing all the cows and spring calves to the hills.

Remember that unmistakable quality in the air I referred to on May 6th?

Yesterday it was, but today it isn't! Today is winter laid over spring. The wood cookstove feels real good as I type, and it appears to be snowing in the mountains. The picnic we planned for the CattleWomen today on Imnaha has been canceled. Yesterday's warm rains loosened the snows and, according to Mary Marks, who lives on the river, the Imnaha is really high. Today it will go down, I imagine, because it is c-o-l-d.

And wouldn't you know Startch would calve while I was gone? She gave birth to a big heifer calf that Sunday morning while we Cattlewomen were in Bend. After suffering a bout of milk fever, she is now fully recovered and letting three calves nurse. Last night I milked the first house milk, which is most welcome after that pale, store-bought stuff that comes in a plastic jug.

May 27—Today is Memorial Day (observed), says our calendar. Cold clouds hovered over our valley this morning, but by late afternoon a warm May shower ushered in rainbow season. As I type, the delicate colors of the bow intensify against a dark purple cloud and brilliant green hillside.

The rhubarb (pie plant) is ready for picking on Alder Slope. I drove up there this afternoon and, with the help of two grandchildren, picked a mess of red, crisp, juicy stalks. Now a strawberry-rhubarb pie produces luscious odors from the oven, the red juice bubbling through slits in the crust. This past week has been incredible! Aren't they all?

Monday, we loaded our saddle horses in the stock truck and drove out to the hills to sort cattle, an all-day job.

Doug and I left for Salem on Tuesday morning, where we visited a daughter and grandson, and spent the night.

Wednesday morning found us at the state Capitol for the release of the 1991-92 Oregon Blue Book, a story in itself.

Our trip to the state Capitol was very special. This whole thing came about after being notified by Secretary of State Phil Keisling that I had won the Blue Book cover contest. As Doug and I walked up the steps into the Capitol rotunda last Wednesday morning, we stood in awe at what we saw around us. Destroyed by fires in 1876 and 1935, the present state Capitol was built to endure.

The building contains reinforced steel and concrete with an exterior faced with white marble from Vermont. The rotunda and all of the lobbies are lined with polished rose travertine from Montana. The floor and stair cases are made of large squares of Phoenix Napoleon gray marble

Tippett ranch shown on the Blue Book cover.

from Missouri, with borders of radial black marble from Vermont. All window casings and doors are made of bronze, as are the doorknobs used throughout, which feature the state seal.

It is the fourth newest capitol in the U.S. A ceiling design of 33 stars symbolizes Oregon as the 33rd state in the Union. Surrounding the rotunda are four large, colorful murals illustrating historic events in Oregon history: Captain Gray at the mouth of the Columbia River in 1792; Lewis and Clark on their way to the Pacific in 1805; the first white women to cross the continent, welcomed by Dr. John McLoughlin in 1836; and the first wagon train migration in 1843.

On top of the Capitol dome stands the "Oregon Pioneer," representing the spirit of Oregon's early settlers. Cast in bronze and finished in gold leaf, it weighs 8.5 tons. Surrounded by all this wonderful stuff of which our great state was founded was (as my grandchildren say) "awesome." While awaiting a press conference, we were given a quick tour by a friendly volunteer woman.

I was impressed with the following inscription, written in large capital letters on the rotunda wall: *In the souls of its citizens will be found the likeness of the state which if they be unjust and tyrannical then will it reflect their vices but if they be lovers of righteousness confident in their liberties so will it be clean in justice, bold in freedom.*

We should all be proud of our heritage and do all in our power to ensure that "lovers of righteousness" outnumber the "unjust and tyrannical," for the sake of our descendants. I could not help but notice that our state was founded on agriculture, including timber, and other resources that come from the soil.

The 1991-92 Oregon Blue Book's cover represents agriculture, and for this reason, I was very proud to have entered the winning photograph. The cover scene is of our ranch here on Prairie Creek, and I had snapped the photo last July during haying time. In the foreground is the field of baled hay that Doug spent half the night baling. An old wooden silo rises against the moraine of Wallowa Lake, backgrounded by the snow-patched Wallowas.

Hopefully, this photograph will remind Oregon citizens of the important role cattle ranching plays in the very existence of our great state. Wallowa County is proud of its family-owned ranches that have been managed with loving care for several generations.

When we read in the newspapers these days about the trampling that cattle can do, we wish everyone could realize that the beautiful scene on the Oregon Blue Book's cover has had cattle on it for more than 100 years, cattle that continue to contribute to the fertility of the soil. After haying season, the field is pastured and used for a wintering ground where cattle are fed for five months or longer.

A real treat for me was meeting Doris Atkeson, widow of famous Oregon photographer Ray Atkeson, in whose memory the new Blue Book is dedicated. Doris is a warm, friendly lady, and I so enjoyed making her acquaintance. Doris and I were introduced at the 10 a.m. session of the House of Representatives, then at the floor of the Senate.

Doris and I received complimentary Blue Books autographed by the governor, secretary of state, and other state officials. It was a pleasure to meet project manager and editor Carole Anderson and her assistant, Jean Haliski, as well as associate editor Donnella Slayton and designer Dannie Chain. All real friendly people who worked so hard on the Blue Book, which is compiled and published by the secretary of state.

We made it home at midnight Wednesday, and Thursday morning, of course, found me back in the saddle, rounding up cows and calves to be branded—far out on Salmon Creek amid the quiet grassy hill country. We branded 124 calves, and returned to the hills on Friday to brand two more bunches.

Friday evening we attended a grandson's high school graduation.

On Saturday, Doug helped son Ken with his branding, while I photographed the wild and woolly event: no chutes, all the calves were headed and heeled, and some of the February calves were pretty good sizes. Strong grandsons helped wrestle the calves after they were roped. We finished in time to attend Bud and Ruby Zollman's 40th wedding anniversary party in Joseph.

I got up early on Sunday and began cooking chicken for the 40 people expected to attend friend Grace Bartlett's 80th birthday dinner at Hurricane Creek Grange Hall. Between Saturday's branding, picture taking, and anniversary party, I had managed to bake two loaves of sourdough bread and one loaf of wheat bread for Sunday's dinner. After delivering the food I returned to clean up my kitchen and mow our big lawn, which by this time was high enough to harvest a hay crop!

Today I am washing clothes, typing this column, and wondering what will happen next. Meanwhile, our new hired hand, Mike, is plowing fields that will soon be planted to seed potatoes.

I'll be back in saddle on Wednesday, when we start the fall calving cows from the hills to their high moraine summer pasture.

While I type on this Memorial Day, my thoughts are in the pioneer cemeteries in California where my father and grandmother are buried near other pioneer ancestors who have gone before them. I think about the big Memorial Day picnic at the Smith ranch, where they will be eating barbecued ribs and beans. Hopefully this tradition will be kept alive for future generations. Family get-togethers are important.

May 29—We were awake at dawn. I cooked sourdough pancakes for breakfast, put together a lunch, did my chores, and left with Mike and Ben in the cattle truck, our saddle horses in back, to drive to Butte Creek.

The hills are even lovelier than when we branded, with new wildflowers blooming and the grass grown higher. Clear and mostly sunny as we unload our horses at a dirt bank near the Butte Creek place. I am sleepy, having celebrated our friends Pat and Linde's wedding anniversary last night with a dinner at their log home, partaking of Linde's herbed roast leg of lamb and visiting until late.

Looking south, we see the distant snow-covered Wallowas as we gather the scattered cows and turn them onto the road. The men leave me trailing 70 head while they ride the Johnson pasture to gather the remaining 70 head. It is quiet and peaceful here, golden balsamroot and purple lupine sprinkles the hills with color. The rockjacks and old, weathered fences blend in with the landscape. Meadowlark songs fill the air and ground squirrels scurry into their holes when they hear us coming.

I let my cows mosey, grazing along the dirt road. When we reach the corrals at the corner of the Pine Creek road, Ben and Mike are just bringing their bunch through the gate. Good timing. Two bulls have gotten out, so Ben drives them back to their field and returns to load his horse in the truck.

Over three days, Mike and I will drive the 140 cows more than 35 miles to their summer pasture, where they will begin calving in mid-August. With lots of time to think while riding along, I remember the Dry Salmon Creek school, no longer there. Damp places along the creek are dotted with the deep blue color of camas. Clouds form overhead, a cold wind rises and, as we pass an old homestead, still standing, the ghosts of the past fill my imaginings.

Nearing the top of Dorrance grade, those clouds open up. We reach back and untie our slickers from our saddles. Water drips off our hat brims. We aren't cold, as it is a nice warm rain.

"A grass-making rain," says Mike.

On top, we stop to gaze at the far-off Wallowas, our destination. The mountains are bathed in sunlight beyond the curtain of rain. White, late-blooming Sarvisberry brightens the view. The cattle trail below us on the winding dirt road, and they must like the view, too, for they stop in the road, not wanting to leave the grassy hills. Can't say as I blame

May brings graduations and award ceremonies. These Enterprise FFA members won district proficiency awards. From left are Willie Zollman, Jill Yost, Chad Nash, Jessica Olsen, Kevin Melville, and Kurt Melville.

them. There's getting to be too much civilization up at the lake.

Ben drives through with the truck. He will repair fence on the moraine and return to pick us up. Noon has come and gone. We dig into our saddle bags and eat wet sandwiches as we push the unwilling cows down the grade. On a knoll, a patch of pretty pink phlox brightens our rain-soaked spirits. It matches the old, pink Dorrance barn, built in 1918.

The rain stops and sun comes streaming through a break in dark clouds. Chokecherry leaves glisten with raindrops. Everything here is happy. The creek chuckles as it winds its way through green, grassy bottoms; a pair of mallards swim below us; a weathered log cabin stands in the meadow, as it has for years. Ponderosa pine marches up steep hillside draws and the air is fresh and clean. I'll always remember Crow Creek this way.

Steam rises from our herd of colorful Simmental-cross cows. "Injun cattle," Doug calls them. We ride by the old Warnock homestead. One barn has collapsed, and the weathered gray buildings show their years of abandonment. More ghosts.

Near East Crow, a deafening clap of thunder rolls away over the hills. We see black clouds over the western hill. It begins to rain again.

We let the cattle graze the roadside at East Crow before corralling them for the night. Mike and I are unsaddling our horses when Ben arrives to take us home. No rest for me, however, as I must show the "Wallowa Story" to a tour group of senior citizens from Spokane tonight at Wallowa Lake Lodge. My face shows I've been in the saddle all day. I am weary and hungry, but the good meal and compliments of the group revive me. It is pouring down rain outside the Wallowa Lake Lodge and the fire in the fireplace feels wonderful.

Another tour from Portland joins us as I put on the 45-minute automatic slide-tape program and retreat to the back of the room to lean against the wall and rest. When it is over, our guests ask questions. They are very interested in local history and in our county, and say it must be wonderful to live here.

"Yes," I reply, neglecting to mention how hard we must work to have that privilege. As I carry my equipment out to the car and drive home, I realize most of the senior citizens tonight were close to my age!

How could I even consider retirement? I'm just beginning to live.

May 30—Cloudy and cold this morning. A freezing wind is blowing out on the Crow Creek road as Mike and I saddle our horses and begin trailing the cows to the valley. Even though we have layers of clothes under our slickers, it doesn't seem to help. We are cold in the face of occasional spitting rain and sleet, but mostly it is the chill wind that plagues us. At one point, we get off and lead our horses to keep warm, which seems to help.

Later, we're able to climb back in the saddle and survive the day. The mountains are obscured by cloud and mist, and we know new snow is falling lower down the slopes. We reach the Liberty Grange road, across from our ranch, where we let the cattle graze with a sigh of relief.

After a brief rest, I drive over and hold the cows in the lane while the men spray them. It is still cool on this last day of May, but the wind has thankfully laid down as Mike, Ben and I trail the cows the final leg of our three-day ride. Although the sun doesn't shine, it is much warmer.

We divide the herd after crossing the Imnaha highway—Doug appears on his horse, and we drive 40 head up to their high pasture on the east moraine of Wallowa Lake, then ride back down and load our horses in the truck to catch up with Mike and Ben. Doug leaves me and my horse to help drive the remaining 100 head over the top, while he drives around to the lake side to pick us up. It is 1:30 when we wearily finish getting the cows where they are supposed to be.

Doug treats us to hamburgers at "Russell's at the Lake," while the tourists stare. Guess we do look a sight in our chaps, spurs, rain- and dust-soaked hats, and weathered faces. Surrounded by tourists, we feel a little like an endangered species.

June 1—What a glorious day! So warm, it feels almost like summer. My garden is roto-tilled and waiting to be planted, our field crew is planting seed potatoes, my second milk cow has calved, Startch is mothering four calves, and the "raspberry kitties" are having kittens everywhere.

My house is a disaster, since I spent the last three days cowboyin', trailing the fall calvers into the valley and up to the moraine for the summer. Am behind on everything, but I missed getting out last week's column so I better get with it.

It is now Saturday afternoon. Our daughter, who lives in Wyoming, just called to say she, her husband and two children are loading the car—they will be here tomorrow. Meanwhile, our crew will be planting potatoes through the weekend, taking advantage of the good weather. The lawn needs mowing…again. I promised to take several grandchildren fishing, flowers need to be transplanted, and birthdays and graduations just keep filling our calendar. Oh well. What's new?

June 11—The sweet fragrance of lilac fills the air this morning. Freshened by a warm rain, the lacy lavender blooms are at their peak of beauty. Like the song…*June is bustin' out all over* in Wallowa County. A cool breeze sends a shower of apple blossoms drifting across the raspberry patch. Noisy swallows build nests under the eaves of the old chicken house, wild mallard ducks gather at dusk to nibble our neighbors' tender fields, ancient willow and cottonwood along the creeks have leafed out, and a meadow lark sings on the hill for the pure joy of it all.

Yesterday, the gleaming, snow-splotched Wallowas provided a startling contrast to our green and growing valley as they reared up toward an incredibly blue sky. We must enjoy these days, for all too soon it will be summer, when the snows melt, the hills dry up, and the sky loses its bright blue intensity.

Why is it that the most beautiful time is always the busiest on a ranch? Last evening Doug didn't return from the potato field until 9 to eat supper. It is virtually impossible to plan meals. He left this morning for the field at 5:30, returning around 7 for breakfast. Often I have the eggs ready to crack into the frypan when I hear his truck drive in. Other times, I don't start anything until I see the whites of his eyes.

The past three days have been so gorgeous it almost hurts to look at our valley, mountains, hills and canyons. Too much beauty to absorb. I want to hold on to it forever. The high mountain trails always call to me, but it's always worst when I'm in the midst of housework.

After a week of company, which included a three-year-old grandson and an eight-year-old granddaughter, I had some major house-cleaning chores. I dug in up to my elbows and got it over with by noon so I could go mushrooming with two friends. It was nearly 2 before we arrived at the trailhead on Alder Slope and began following an old pack and stock drive trail until we found the first morels. Recent hot weather had dried them up lower down the mountain.

As we climbed higher, the snow filled the trail in places until we were suddenly stopped by an enormous snow bridge that spanned not only the trail but a gushing stream that fell down a very steep gully. Lest we slip and lose our footing, we opted to rest and turn back.

The view, worth the climb, took us within a half-mile of Murray Gap, under Ruby Peak. Far below, the peaceful valley lay spread before us, the town of Enterprise surrounded by varied shades of green and brown that make up the fertile agricultural lands. The grassy hill country rolled eastward to meet the canyons of the Imnaha and Snake, and dark cloud shadows moving silently over this incredible patchwork panorama.

The trail led back through deep woods, where we spied the first delicate pink Calypsos (Lady Slippers) and the forest floor was carpeted with yellow Wood's violets. We heard everywhere the sound of running water, as snow melted and trickled down, seeping into springs and forming creeks.

All along the trail we noticed numerous elk signs and watched carefully, lest we come between a cow elk and her newborn calf.

A wonderful, vanilla-like scent escaped the bark of tall pines as the sun's warmth released the resinous material. The new, bright green needles of tamarack contrasted with the darker evergreens. Squirrels and chipmunks scurried around, and the birds were everywhere... especially many of a small bird whose minor-key notes resembled someone tuning a flute.

Mostly though, we savored the haunting and deep silence found only in the forest. Spring activities can be very unnerving, where moments of peace and quiet are rare. After returning from yesterday's jaunt, we feel ready to face the world again.

Last week was so hectic, what with company, the garden to plant, bedding plants to set out, large meals to prepare, not to mention that we are in the midst of planting more than 100 acres of seed potatoes. We all had a lively time chasing grandson Ryan around. Trying to keep track of this active, red-headed three-year-old was a real challenge.

My pullets got mixed up with the laying hens on a daily basis, and therefore had to be sorted constantly. Ryan's favorite activity was chasing grandma's chickens. My hens went from laying nine eggs a day to three, and they are just now beginning to calm down. His next favorite pastime was playing in an enormous mud puddle, which attracted him like gravity the minute he was out the door.

One cold and windy day, when rain kept everyone out of the potato field, Doug took us fishing at nearby Kinney Lake. Although it was muddy and cold, the catfish were biting. We ran into Elmer Storm, Wallowa County's famous fisherman, who was pulling in catfish right and left. Apparently we didn't have Elmer's "special touch," or something, because we weren't catching anything.

Elmer let the children reel in several catfish, so Lacey and Ryan thought he was pretty special. We managed to catch two but, thanks to Elmer, we had a good fish fry that evening for supper.

Before the Wyoming family left Saturday morning, I fixed sourdough waffles smothered with strawberries and whipped cream. Things were pretty quiet around here after they left, until small James arrived, having been promised an overnight with grandma to go fishing and sleep in the sheepherder wagon. I took James to Kinney Lake and, while the fisherman next to us pulled in fish after fish, we still couldn't catch anything. We just kept baiting our hook as those catfish sure learned to peel off our worms as slick as a whistle.

Just as James was beginning to think grandma didn't know anything about fishing—and, in fact, said so—a slight breeze rippled the surface of the lake, the sky became overcast, and *shwam-o*, we hooked a fish. As James reeled in a nice rainbow, his grandma resumed elevated status of fisherman again.

My "grandchildren fishing outfit" is really something. I use this old fly rod and reel, with a short leader tied to a fly line. A moth-eaten fly, with some black thread clinging to it, serves as a hook; no sinker. James found a rusty lure on the shores of Kinney Lake, so we tied that on.

We then thread a wiggling gob of night-crawlers over the tattered fly for bait, and cast this apparition over the lake, like a fly line, only it lands with a thunk instead of a light fly-like flip. It must have amused the fish as much as the fishermen to watch this silly grandma and her four-year-old grandson. Oh well, anything goes. More important than fishing gear is that we actually take time to go fishing.

June 18—It would seem Mother Nature has definitely decided this is not going to be a good year for vegetable gardens, not on Prairie Creek anyway. It didn't freeze this morning, but the past three have been pretty frosty. Although my garden was planted around June 1st, not much is visible except for a row of radishes, a few sunflowers, some scraggly peas and a spindly sprouting of corn. The cabbage plants have survived, but haven't grown any since being set out; too many cold nights.

On Saturday, our crew finished planting the last of the seed potatoes.

Ben laid out the sprinkler pipes in the hay fields, the "raspberry kitties" kittens have opened their eyes, and the two milk cows are raising six calves. Granddaughter Tammy is on her way home for the summer from college at Cal Poly. Tourists now walk Joseph's main street waiting for the Great Joseph Bank Robbery to happen, the campground at Wallowa Lake is filling up, and haying time is just around the corner on the ranches.

Last Tuesday, neighbor Pat and son-in-law Charley moved a big trailer house that has been blocking our view of Chief Joseph Mountain for years. Although it was quite an undertaking, they got the job done, and that night I cooked supper for everyone to celebrate the event. A lot more time is spent looking out the window these days, now that a whole new view has opened up.

I awoke in the middle of the night on Wednesday to witness the aurora borealis, or northern lights. Having read about the possibility of seeing this phenomenon, which came about because of a recent solar storm, I was rewarded and awed by this display of energy. Natural occurrences such as these, which are out of man's control, make man seem pretty piddling in comparison.

Unfortunately, one day last week, Doug disturbed a family of skunks that was taking up residence in a culvert. You guessed it. Three days later, our house still smells skunky, even after the offending clothes were washed and hung on the line for two days.

Last Thursday, for the second time in two months, our CattleWomen's meeting at the Joseph City Park was canceled because of cold weather. That evening, I attended our Wallowa Valley Photo Club meeting at Eagle Mountain Gallery in Joseph. Our new 1991 color calendars are hot off the press, and are they beautiful. Dave Jensen, well-known local photographer, showed us some slides he'd taken on a recent trip to Australia.

On Friday, which was pleasant for a change, the two youngest grandchildren spent the day, so we went to the park, after which I treated them to hamburgers at Russell's at the Lake. Ben's sons, Zack and Seth, are changing irrigation pipes for us now, and the familiar hum of Honda motors zooming around the ranch reminds us it is nearly summer.

Friends Bud and Ruby Zollman treated us to dinner Friday evening at Cactus Jack's in the old Chief Joseph Hotel. The prime rib was delicious, and it was fun visiting old friends.

On Father's Day I cooked dad a good meal, since he'd spent his day beating weeds to death with a weed eater. The garden might look sick, but weeds and grasses are flourishing.

Yesterday was our anniversary, so we decided to go out for supper. Monday nights, we found, aren't the best for choosing a good place to eat. We ended up at a local pizza parlor in Enterprise. While we were eating and reminiscing about our wedding day, a young man walked in off the street, plunked several coins in a jukebox, which, in turn, blared out the loudest rock 'n roll selections we'd ever heard. Since marriages that work must survive all sorts of experiences, we simply smiled and tried to see the humor in the situation.

The first of the newly planted seed potatoes are just peeking through the ground. Before we know it, summer will be over and potato digging time will be here. On a ranch, the work never ends.

June 20—The early morning dawned cloudy and cool. Looking out my kitchen window toward the mountains, I saw a patch of sunlight spilling low over the prairie. The snow-flanked Wallowas were partly exposed and the effect was pretty dramatic. Leaving breakfast dishes soaking, I grabbed my camera and headed toward the light. Got some nice shots of cattle and sheep grazing, running water, green fields, and shafts of sunlight against those glorious mountains.

Even at that early hour, our neighbors were already at work. I saw Juanita Waters, armed with her shovel, out flood-irrigating their pastures. Juanita, her husband Larry, and family drove by our place the other evening, going about five miles an hour. Larry was driving their team of mules hitched to a wagon. A nice change of pace, and just meant for Tenderfoot Valley Road.

The sun disappeared for the rest of the day, and I decided to bake a batch of cinnamon twists. I took a couple fresh from the oven out to Doug, who was working in the shop, for his approval. Later, granddaughters Tammy and Carrie and a friend, April, showed up to visit, and they, too, gave their approval to the twists.

In the afternoon, I weeded my vegetable garden using one of those old hand cultivators. They work better than aerobics to keep one in shape.

This being the first day of summer, the annual "Wallowa Mountain High" balloon rally began on the outskirts of Enterprise. I watched from our hill as the colorful hot air balloons ascended into the still morning air, which was thick with clouds.

Later that morning, a warm sun broke through, creating contrasting lights and darks. The air had that after-a-rain clarity that makes for good photographing. So, armed with my trusty Olympus OM-2, I drove to the foot of Wallowa Lake and hiked up the steep east moraine, which was covered with wildflowers: bright pink Clarkia, blue-purple lupine, golden yellow balsamroot, red Indian paintbrush, and many more I couldn't begin to identify.

The view was incredible: turquoise lake, the wildflowers, the moraine rising against the mountain known as Chief Joseph. It was easy to shoot the entire roll of slide film.

Returning to Joseph, I took daughter Ramona, who works at Harshman's Store, to lunch at a new deli across the street called the Racquet Club. We sat facing the street and ordered the special: turkey sandwich and spicy meatball soup. We enjoyed our meal, as well as a freshly picked vase of wildflowers that Katch Hobbs placed on our table.

Returning to the ranch, I found Doug and Mike building a temporary fence so the horses and mule could graze the high grass outside our yard. Now, as I type, Alfie watches me through the window.

On Saturday I rode up on the moraine with Doug to check our fall calvers, after which we drove out to Salmon Creek to check on cattle there. We found the hills still green, with a new crop of wildflowers sprinkled in the big fields. Wild, hot-pink geraniums dominated them. The cows are sleek and fat, and the calves are growing.

On Sunday, Noel Wright, the fellow who rode my molly mule in the local parades last summer, paid us a visit. And guess what? He put my saddle on Alfie and went for a ride. Then, it was my turn. Alfie and I have lots to learn, but she is a pleasure to ride and we have a busy summer ahead, full of riding. It should be fun.

June 24—There is much clanging and banging coming from the shop this morning. The men are readying machinery needed to put up silage in long, double-plastic "ag bags." Things quiet down again by noon after John Deere tractors, pulling the ag bagger and chopper, rumble out of our driveway to set up operations in a neighbor's alfalfa field. The weather is perfect for ag bagging: cool, overcast, threatening rain. Our cloudy days continue, but no one complains much. Our canyons, hills and valley will remain green that much longer, and the irrigation is more effective.

My clothes dry on the line this morning. There are bursts of warm sunshine now and then, along with a breeze. Oriental poppies alongside the house are blooming. It is time for Hin-mah-too-yah-lat-kehkt and, as I write, I can see dark clouds and hear distant rumbles over the Wallowas.

The rolling thunder draws closer; rain, and then hail, pelts down on the horses and mule. They stand with their backs to the strong wind, tails blown between their hind legs, heads down. Through the jets of blowing irrigation water spraying from sprinklers across the road in

Hough's field, I watch the black cattle run toward a corner fence and huddle together for protection. Windows and doors rattle, hail beats down on my poor garden, and I rush out to grab armsful of clothes from the line.

Normally, June is the month for wild roses, but the first day of summer has come and gone, and the delicate, pink wild rose is yet to bloom on Prairie Creek. The old-fashioned, small yellow bush rose that bloomed so profusely alongside the bunkhouse when we were married is just now beginning to bloom. The vegetable garden is holding its own, however, and consists of a row of sunflowers; some Walla Walla sweet onion plants; a small row of corn; and a scattering of peas, squashes, lettuce, beets and swiss chard.

The red potatoes haven't come through the ground yet, and I've replanted beans and carrots. The one success is the sweet peas growing like mad alongside the garden fence. After meeting my column's deadline last week, I grocery shopped in Enterprise, then stopped by the Bookloft. After viewing the lovely paintings and other artwork displayed in the adjoining Skylight Gallery, I sat at a small table and sipped a cup of cappuccino, visiting with another Prairie Creek seed potato wife and artist, Eileen Thiel.

Mary Swanson, the congenial proprietress of the Bookloft, makes the best specialty coffees around, which she serves in original Ted Juve pottery mugs. And Mary has books—wonderful books, my weakness. After such a hectic spring schedule, Eileen and I agreed it was fun to relax, until, all of a sudden, it was 4 o'clock!

We hurried home to our ranches to start supper. On the way home. driving along Hurricane Creek road. near the creek, a mule deer doe crossed in front of me Bouncing along behind was her tiny. spotted fawn. I stopped long enough to watch the graceful pair melt into the adjacent woods.

After marinating strips of round steak in a spicy sauce. I fixed fajitas for a quick supper.

June 25—Cloudy and cool. Irrigation continues, even though it rained during the night. Doug is out early of a morning, every morning, chasing water around with his shovel, while I wonder when he'll be in for breakfast.

I baked a sourdough chocolate cake for grandson James' fifth birthday. Grandma's cakes are becoming a tradition around here, especially sourdough chocolate.

While the cake was rising, I delivered the "Wallowa Story" slide tape program to Joseph for the recreation director of Wallowa Lake State Park to pick it up. The program will be presented all summer at the outdoor amphitheater, once a week, for the benefit of park visitors. Last year, more than 3,000 campers viewed the 45-minute history of Wallowa County.

June 26—Rained all night again, leaving a cloudy and cold day. Doug left this morning to attend the OSU seed potato lot trials at the Hermiston Experiment Station, so I picked up two grandchildren to keep me company. We "played" all day, and spent the night in the old sheepherder's wagon.

We climbed into the wagon under a wild rose sunset in the western sky, framed by gilded clouds. By 8:30 p.m. the last rays of the fading sun shot through dark clouds to light up the wildflower patch.

"Look," said James, "magic." And it truly was, as a bright, pink flowering wilding lit up like fireweed.

June 27—It was only 35 degrees as I slipped out of bed, away from the sleeping children still snuggled in warm sleeping bags, and tiptoed from the sheepherder wagon to the house.

The June sun rose in a cloudless sky, for a change, and the morning warmed considerably before the children emerged from their warm nest to walk bare-footed on the dewy grass to the back porch. After the children left, I missed their friendly chatter. We always have such fun when they visit.

Last night, we read stories by candle light and, before we went to sleep, we leaned out the window and said good night to Alfie the mule who, along with the horses, grazed nearby.

June 28—Because it's threatening rain again, I tend to inside chores, and bake a new dessert clipped from Sunset magazine: Rhubarb Cheesecake Pie. The rhubarb plants growing near our bunkhouse are lush with red stalks from the rain and cool weather, and should be used. After making a graham cracker crust, I filled it with rhubarb mixture, then a cheesecake filling, and topped with sour cream. The tasty, colorful pie looked just like the picture in the magazine.

Warm showers fall all day on an already damp Prairie Creek. I took a couple of prints I'd had enlarged up to the Art Angle to be matted, framed, and made gallery ready for a scheduled photo club show this month in Joseph.

June 29—If the weather had cooperated, I would have bee riding horseback to Aneroid Lake with grandson Rowdy and his friend Ryan this morning. But it was cloudy and dreary, and there were no mountains, just layers of mist clouds where they should have been.

In spite of the inclement weather this Saturday, the first Imnaha community rodeo was held at a local ranch along the river. Also, a Christian cowboys' group staged another one of its successful playdays at the Enterprise fairgrounds. During the barrel racing, the clouds opened up and a cold curtain of rain came in from the west. Undaunted, the cowboys and cowgirls simply moved inside the indoor arena and proceeded to enjoy themselves.

These two events provide an opportunity for local horse enthusiasts, many of whom are novices, to participate in a learning experience and have fun at the same time. While it poured outside, rain pelting down on the tin roof, little ones and big ones alike competed in all manner of events.

Three-year-old granddaughter Adele rode a little mule, no bigger than a minute, led by big brother James. Becky and James took turns on different horses. If a youngster didn't have a horse, a friend loaned him a mount. I don't know who was the proudest of Tyson and Tanya Blankenship, Grandma or Grandpa, as they rode their horses in all the events that day. In a day when real cowboys are becoming scarce, Jim Blankenship is making sure there will be some around for the future. Good job, Jim!

After one cloudburst, Imnaha went on with the rodeo, having taken refuge under a barn during the worst of the downpour. Because it is so much warmer in the canyons, they were able to resume after the rain ceased. Grandchildren Buck and Mona informed me by phone that evening that they had a great time. Buck was all-around winner and Mona took a second in pole bending. Even mom and dad competed.

June 30—I rode out with Doug to the hills to repair a section of fence between our place and a neighboring rancher's that had been torn down by bulls. A lovely day, mostly sunny, with big cottonball clouds casting silent moving shadows over wildflower-dappled hills.

We spent most of the day under the wide open sky on our summer range land. Our herd of heifers climbed the hill to our fence corner and formed a curious ring around us. Watching Doug build a rockjack fence was like watching an athlete. With the skill acquired after a lifetime of experience, with not a single wasted motion. he accomplished the rebuilding of a large section of fence. When he finished the wire was taught, the rockjacks stout, and the fence looked as though it had always stood there.

Building a fence is hard work: lifting large rocks for the rockjacks, stretching wire, and building a wire gate. The fence blended in with the landscape...weathered gray posts, with moss clinging to them; tamarack stays; rusted barb wire, mended and patched; the colored rocks, so abundant in the area; rusty nails pulled from the old fence posts and straightened. Only a few shiny, new staples were used and, before long, they too will succumb to the color of the hills. It seemed a wonderful way to savor the last day of June.

Coming home, along the Crow Creek road, we spied the first wild roses beginning to bloom.

July 1—Nary a cloud to mar the deep blue sky this first morning of July. The sun feels warm but the air is soft, like June...lingering. After a month of cloudy and rainy weather, the Wallowa Valley responds to the sun!

California poppies open their bright, orange petals in my wildflower patch. The garden, no longer stressed, begins to grow. Young robins, having left their nests, chirp among the raspberry bushes. Prairie Creek will remain incredibly green all summer, as irrigation water diverted from Wallowa Lake brims over ditches and flows out into meadow hayfields, where an occasional rainbow trout, trapped in the shallow ditches, ends up on our supper table.

The men managed to fill one Ag Bag between last week's rain showers. Today they wait for a part to be delivered via UPS so they can proceed with the field of first-cutting alfalfa. Making silage is like "storing summer in a bag," to sustain our fall calvers, when snow lies on the frozen ground next winter.

How I love our long hours of daylight. The sun goes down around 8:30 p.m. now, and it's light by 4 a.m.

Prairie Creek's population of song birds opens and closes each day with a concert. Early morning and late evening are my favorite times. A dusky wash of golden light falls across the prairie at eventide and the mornings are dewy and fresh.

July 2—Bill and Carolee Matthews, from Roseburg, trailing their two riding mules, stopped by to visit on their way down to Imnaha for a week's visit with their son's family. They brought us a bag of juicy-ripe cherries from the Willamette Valley. Today was the warmest one yet.

July 3—Pleasant morning, sunny and clear, promising another hot day. I'm out in my vegetable garden cultivating and weeding early to beat the heat, picking spinach so it will retain its crispness for salads.

Baked two rhubarb pies for our big 4th of July picnic here tomorrow. The men are closing up the second Ag Bag today. The thermometer on the clothesline post registers 80 degrees by late afternoon.

July 4—Cooler this morning. A few clouds dot the sky and provide a welcome break from the bright sun. Our blood isn't adjusted to heat yet.

The two younger grandchildren arrive early to help grandma prepare for around 30 people who will attend our family picnic. When our family gets together, it is always a crowd. It is still cool before the work begins, so the children and I dig worms, then hike through the chin-high hay field to an irrigation ditch to fish. We get only one bite, but the jaunt is fun.

Patchy shade under a giant cottonwood near a stream of running water is a pleasant place to be on a summer morning. Killdeer and red-winged blackbirds talk to us, wild roses trail into the ditch, and the sound of water soothes. Carrying Adele piggy back through the hay field provides some vigorous exercise for me, while James gamely follows, toting pole and bucket of worms. For lunch, we thaw out trout caught in Kinney Lake, and fry them.

The first relatives begin to arrive by late afternoon. As some are pipe changers, or on haying crews, or cultivating potatoes, 4th of July or not, ranch work dictates when they can get away. Son-in-law Charley trailed in around 8:30 p.m.

We had a marvelous time. I prepared teriyaki chicken and mixed up two freezer cans of french vanilla custard ice cream. Men and children did the cranking. There's no substitute for homemade ice cream. After the pans of chicken, Ramona's barbecued ribs, Annie's potato salad, and Jackie's sourdough rolls were consumed, we brought out those rhubarb pies to go with the ice cream.

The evening was perfect for eating outside. Cousins of all ages ran around, climbing trees and anticipating the fireworks. The children, impatient to set off their little packets of fireworks, couldn't wait for dark.

The first sparklers were lit around 9 p.m., and there followed loud bangs, shooting stars, and balls of fire, some of which hissed, spat and changed color. It was a wonderful family time taken to honor Independence Day, which is what it's all about.

July 8—It is haying time. Soft round bales begin to appear in Willie Locke's field up the road. From my kitchen window, I can watch the baler give birth to large rolled-up strands of cured hay.

Doug and Ben take turns swathing on our own hay, which falls fragrant and quivering in the field. It is a busy, lovely time, and the weather is cooperating. Long hours of sunshine, with just a slight afternoon breeze, cure the hay. It looks like most of the first cutting will go up in fine shape.

This morning the men are raking the hay into windrows, after which Doug will start baling. Hopefully he will take time to nap during the day, as he'll probably bale on into the night, for that is the best time, when dew glues bales together and holds the leaf.

In irrigated meadows, the air is drenched with clover blossom scent. Wild roses bloom along country roads in pink profusion. The hills are losing their spring green and now appear toasted, with patches of alizarin crimson, the color of mature grasses, zig-zagging through them. Lavender lupine paints Minam Canyon's red dirt with shades of purple. The old-fashioned rose that nearly conceals the south side of our bunkhouse has become a trailing, cascading mass of pale yellow blooms.

Icelandic poppies, bachelor buttons, sky-blue flax, and Shasta daisies are having their moment of glory in the wildflower patch, my pride and joy. The garden, weeded and growing, is my escape and relaxation. Bending low, plucking tiny weeds tangled in lettuce plants, I feel close to the earth, and derive great satisfaction watching that which I have seeded, grow. Gardens, like children, take lots of nurturing.

As summertime activity increases, it becomes more and more difficult to begin and finish this column. Then I remember correspondence from readers that arrives often in my mail box.

For example, this letter from Lila Betts, in North Carolina: *I don't know how many subscribers to Agri-Times live in North Carolina, but I do know that I am probably the most addicted to Janie's Journal. My good brother-in-law Kohler Betts, from Athena, has sent occasional clippings of your columns, and finally gave me a subscription.*

I know nothing about ranching or farming from experience, having lived in the South all my life in an urban environment. Then why is your column so fascinating to me? I suspect it has something to do with my admiration for my brother-in-law and his fine family, who have been Oregon wheat farmers for almost a century. Your descriptions of your ranch life are lovely. I can smell your sourdough bread, your apple pies, and all those dishes you remove from the Monarch. I am grateful to you for sharing your experiences with people like me.

She goes on to write that she and her husband planned to visit Kohler in early July and hoped to meet me. In the meantime, Kohler had arranged a luncheon date with all of us at Wallowa Lake Lodge during that time.

Unfortunately, Lila's husband was involved in an accident and their trip was canceled. Kohler phoned to tell me the luncheon date was off. Perhaps Lila and I can get together another time. In the meantime, she is one of the reasons I keep on writing. Lila ended her letter: *With anticipation...and many thanks for your part in enriching my life.*

Thank you, Lila, for giving mine purpose.

July 16—Rather coolish for a July morning. Ben is running the loader-stacker in our hay fields and the hay shed is filling up, a long stack of hay forming on the hill. The weather has been ideal for haying and the fragrant green bales evoke a sense of security against the long, cold winter ahead.

But now it is summer. Our brief, beautiful summer is flying by. Because we are all so busy "making hay while the sun shines," in more ways than one, it is disappearing even faster than usual. This past week was typical.

Included in my busy lifestyle was Fishtrap. For me, this writer's conference is a special event, a time to mingle with kindred spirits and talk about writing in the West. Actually, I live from Fishtrap to Fishtrap. Aside from participating in the "Gathering," this informal meeting of the minds, so to speak, nourishes my soul, and I'm sure others feel this way as well.

Doug is up early to change sprinklers in the potato field, then participates in what I refer to as a local Fishtrap gathering of men, at Kohlhepp's Kitchen in Joseph. These men, mostly farmers and ranchers, sit at a long table, eating biscuits and sausage gravy, doing a great deal of reminiscing about the "good old days."

These men keep local stories and legends alive. Without stories about our past, there would be no link to the present. Stories glue past to present, and turn the page into the future. Everyone, it seems, loves to listen to stories and this group of men sure loves to tell 'em.

As in past years, Marc Jaffe of Houghton Mifflin flew out from the east to attend our writers' gathering in the west. While visiting with Marc, I was flattered to learn that he had renewed his subscription to Agri-Times so he could keep track of "Janie's Journal." After the conference ended on Sunday afternoon, Marc drove out to the ranch and I introduced him to Doug, whereupon they talked seed potatoes and cattle. Marc said he had to see for himself if what I wrote about was real. His wife also wanted Marc to find out if Janie really did "all those things."

A series of workshops were held the week before the "Gathering." Each evening there were "open mikes" open to the public, where workshop participants read their assignments. Since I was free most evenings, I attended three of these "open mikes." One evening Larry Johnson, who taught a workshop on "Writing the Historical Documentary Film," showed three wonderful films he'd produced, one of which was on early gill netters along the Columbia River.

From this educational, historical study of early fishermen, we changed course in midstream and went from gillnetters to a presentation by the Angling and Literature workshop class, taught by Jim Hepworth. Students were to keep journals and conduct field research in nearby lakes and creeks, while studying works by Hemingway, Maclean and other poets or authors whose works reflected the diversity found in the subject of angling.

In spite of considerable opposition voiced by Eileen Thiel, the only woman in the class, that it was getting too late to pull this thing off, it was by this time past 10 p.m., their leader plunged into a dissertation about angling in the brown and blue depths of Big Sheep Creek.

After viewing three films, it was late and it left only a few of us dedicated "Fishtrappers" as an audience. The resulting presentation, pantomime, or what have you, was, to put it mildly, hilarious. Big Sheep Creek angling had its finest hour and the story became finer with the telling.

When it was over, Rich Wandschneider's dog was even crying, restlessly pacing the floor of the Wallowa Lake Camp. Perhaps all of this nonsense transpired because someone took a bite out of the sun that Thursday. At any rate there was something "fishy" going on and a definite personality of 1991 Fishtrap was beginning to emerge. Still laughing and wiping away tears, I found my car keys, put a sweater on to ward against the Wallowa mountain chill, and stepped out into total darkness to walk to my car, which was parked some distance away.

Remembering too late, as in years past, that I should have brought a flashlight to Fishtrap, I stumbled blindly past two white tepees, and aimed for a banner that was strung between two trees. Then it happened—I felt like a salmon caught in a gill-net. I evidently took a wrong turn and entered into dark, wet woods. I heard, then felt, a very large sprinkler making its *swish, swish* rounds of the area near the parking lot.

Holding my registration packet up to shield my face from the lashing rain, I stumbled blindly onward. After submitting to the now-familiar sprinkler two more times, I emerged, dripping, at my car.

Now, this isn't meant to be a fish story, but it is in keeping with Fishtrap's emerging personality. I wish I could have taken The Angling and Literature workshop. One of the assignments was to write a letter to Norman Maclean, author of "A River Runs Through It." I would have written: *Dear Norman; Having a wonderful time, wish you were here at Fishtrap, there is a river running through it!*

Norman Maclean, of course, died last year, so this didn't make any sense at all. I did purchase the book "A River Runs Through It" from Mary Swanson, who had her Bookloft set up in one of those tepees.

The next day, which was Friday, I took rancher and writer Helen Cowan, who was also here to attend Fishtrap, to cover a resource tour for Agri-Times. Armed with my camera and note pad, with Helen for company, I followed three bus loads of tour-goers over a large section of Wallowa County. I snapped pictures and jotted down notes for my article and, after eating lunch at the Lick Creek campground, some 30 miles distant, Helen and I returned in time for the opening buffet reception of Fishtrap.

It had been a hot day, and the coolness of the Wallowa Lake camp felt good. After listening to marvelous reading by Teresa Jordan, Primus St. John, and Ursula Le Guin, I drove home and crashed.

Saturday morning, I finished my ranch chores in time to make it up to the writers' conference for breakfast. Then followed a traditional view of Western history by Sue Armitage, which was interesting. We all haven't quite recovered yet from Patricia Limerick, who smashed most of the traditional myths of western history. That afternoon we listened to Shannon Applegate, Craig Lesley, and E. Gamoa.

After a barbecue that evening, we heard more readings by the Fishtrap fellows and relaxed with songs and readings by Rosalie Sorrels and Jim Haynen. The Gathering ended Sunday after lunch, but I didn't want it to.

While Marc Jaffe was here, sitting at our kitchen table, I took a raspberry cobbler, a deep dish apple pie, and a chocolate cake out of the freezer to thaw., because that evening a group of us local women were to take desserts to the Appaloosa Trail Ride encampment (450 strong) that was encamped on upper Prairie Creek. But that's another story.

July 22—Tucker's mare, the snow shape of a horse, visible from my kitchen window, has shrunk to a mere skeleton. In the shimmering, high-altitude heat of this July afternoon, the rump of the horse has separated from its shoulders and head.

Wallowa Valley ranchers are still frantically haying. They must work fast now, because the summer heat dries the swathed hay so rapidly. Many of them have finished their first cuttings, and again the long lines of sprinklers send out jets of water over the greening hay fields. Nez

376 trail riders, all on Appaloosa horses, ride on Prairie Creek, backgrounded by the Wallowa Mountains.

Perce Indians, representing several tribes, are setting up their tepees next to the Harley Tucker Memorial arena. Chief Joseph Days begins this week.

The Appaloosa riders completed their 100-mile trail ride out near Cold Springs Ridge. It created quite a picture seeing those 376 riders, all mounted on Appaloosas, strung out across the vastness of our country. This is the third running of this memorial ride, which starts here in Wallowa County. This famous ride attempts to reconstruct the historical retreat trail of the Wallowa Band of Nez Perce, led by young Chief Joseph.

After crossing the Snake River, in flood, with their women, children, horses and cattle, into Idaho, they followed the Lolo Trail into Montana, crossed the Bitterroots into the valley of the Big Hole and headed toward Yellowstone. The fleeing Nez Perce, pursued by General Howard, finally surrendered at the Bear Paw Mountains in Montana, as winter was coming on. It was a heroic flight, and the surviving Nez Perce had outwitted soldiers until then, and managed to flee although their ranks had diminished, and it was snowy and cold.

They were not too far from the Canadian border, but Chief Joseph was worried about his starving and cold children. The Appaloosa Horse Club sponsors the ride, which takes 14 years to complete each time. Locally, Dick Hammond, a long-time participant in previous rides, organized the route through Wallowa County. Quite an undertaking. Local rancher's wife Gladys Nobles headed up the kitchen crew with her family helping, and did the ordering and buying of enough food to feed more than 500 people for six days. Each year the ride completes a 100-mile segment of the trail. Twenty miles a day for five days.

Everyone must ride an Appaloosa horse. Riders come from all over the United States, and this year a couple flew here from New Zealand and rented horses.

Three people walked the 100 miles, including a man from Seattle named Matt, who has participated in numerous rides in the past. He wears a hat covered with pins from previous rides. That first night those 376 riders, along with their 376 horses, a kitchen crew, a camp crew, plus numerous tag-alongs that numbered more than 500 people altogether, encamped not far from our ranch in an aspen-pine fringed meadow under the east moraine of Wallowa Lake. Several of us local women were asked to bring desserts that Sunday evening, and as a result were able to experience this enormous undertaking for ourselves.

When we arrived, the riders were going through a long chow line and another line was forming for our cakes and pies. Meanwhile, local cowboy plus one cowgirl poets were performing on a large folding wooden dance floor that would be transported from camp to camp each night. People sat around the dance floor in lawn chairs.

As dusk descended over upper Prairie Creek, a Western dance band began to strum foot-stomping music, whereupon gals and their guys began a real hoe-down. The mountain, known as Chief Joseph, looked down on the goings-on. A crescent moon hung next to a blinking star over Mt. Joseph. In the long meadow horses were tied to picket lines, or penned in portable corrals. Tents, horse trailers, campers and motor homes of every description covered the meadow and tree-bordered edges. Certainly a far cry from the 1800s Nez Perce encampment. The moon disappeared over the mountain, taking the star with it. As we left the scene, I noticed a neighboring rancher's Angus bull looking curiously across the fence at this unbelievable spectacle.

Having been a rider in three segments of the second ride (1970, '72 and '73) I was amazed to see how the thing had grown.

The next morning I was up early, camera in hand, snapping pictures of all those horses and riders against our Wallowa Mountains. It took nearly an hour for that many to pass me. The route took them up Sheep Creek Hill and then north through the Three Lakes country, which lies just east of us.

It was all I could do to refrain from saddling my Appaloosa mare and joining them, but I had been gone attending Fishtrap for three days and my husband was haying and working so hard that I decided against it. But my mind was with them all that day and the rest of the week.

Then, one day, Grace Bartlett and I drove out in her Jeep and intercepted the trail ride between Thomason Meadows and Buckhorn, where I was able to shoot some historic slides of all those riders against canyons and wildflower strewn ridges. I also visited with Matt, the elderly gentleman who appeared in splendid shape and was enjoying the country immensely.

Meanwhile, back at the ranch, the work never ends. Seed potatoes to be rogued, irrigated, and cultivated. Aphid traps put out. Haying goes on and on…one more field left to bale. Irrigation around the clock.

I visit with Doug briefly, at meal times, and then he is gone. I keep busy irrigating the lawn, flower and vegetable gardens; cooking for a hard-working husband; keeping house; caring for grandchildren and writing. We are enjoying the first fresh vegetables from the garden now, and the gooseberries are beginning to ripen. The Barred Plymouth Rock pullets are laying their first small, brown eggs and their happy singing comes to me through the open window.

On Friday, three of us CattleWomen served the senior citizens meal in Joseph.

This evening, I take a walk down our country road and turn east up Echo Canyon. The invigorating jaunt will help get me in shape for a hike to LeGore Lake next week. I pass by brimming irrigation ditches, under cool willows, alongside wild daisies and delicate pink roses. Hough's "bread loaf" hay stacks give off a savory summer scent of cured hay.

As the sinking sun lowers in the west, a soft evening light bathes Prairie Creek, while the mountains, cool and blue, hide in shadow. A half moon waits to glow as daylight deserts the sky. I was soon atop a high rolling hill, climbing over a rock jack, heading toward a large man-made pond.

I was amazed to see so many varieties of wildflowers still blooming among the drying hills. The coolness of irrigated meadows below mixes with drier scents of toasted hills, a delicious breeze mingling the two as a golden sun slips over Sheep Ridge. I reach the pond as the sun's last rays hover over the surface of the water, mirroring perfectly the gnarled willows growing in the far end.

My lengthening shadow precedes me, keeping me company and alerting a flock of mallard ducks, which fly off at my approach. I gaze in all directions and see nothing save rolling hills and mountains, and think how it must have been for the Appaloosa riders. The sun disappears in a persimmon glow, meadowlarks sing a soothing evening song, and a hawk cries, sadly.

As I walk back toward the ranch, the moon begins to glow, phosphorescent, and follows me along a cow trail that parallels the steep grassy hill. While gazing at a patch of brilliant fire weed, I nearly stumble into a coyote den. And while "Jazz at the Lake" is playing near the shores of Wallowa Lake tonight, I enjoy "goose music on Prairie Creek," as a V of wild honkers flies overhead! Far below comes the steady thump, thump rhythm of a hay baler. My husband... baling into the night.

It was after dark when I returned to the house and re-read a letter I'd received that day from my sister Caroline.

"The grandkids are really growing," she writes. "Matthew sang to me on the phone the other night, *row, row, row the boat, life is down the stream*. I think sometimes he is right," says Caroline, and I agree.

July 24—Up at 4 a.m., I made myself a sandwich and stuffed it, along with my camera, into a day pack, and drove to Jerry's Market in Joseph to meet Maryann Deck of Walla Walla, whom I'd never seen before. Maryann had written earlier wanting me to lead her on a hike somewhere in the mountains off the beaten track. I'd suggested LeGore Lake, mentioning that it would be a pretty rugged hike.

So, by 5 a.m. Maryann (age 59) and I (nearly 58) began our adventure at the Hurricane Creek trailhead. It was warm and muggy, and the morning sky was thick with clouds. A breeze refreshed us as we climbed higher, and those clouds blushed pink before the sun appeared over Idaho's Seven Devils mountains.

As the morning progressed, the high peaks above us were fired with gold. Sacajawea, the highest mountain in the Wallowa chain, came into view, her snows rapidly receding in the July heat. Due to late spring rains, the trail was nearly grown over with lush grasses and chokecherry, syringa, gooseberries, wild roses, ferns and willows. Wild geranium, Indian paintbrush, forget-me-nots and cinquefoil bloomed in profusion.

Looking far above, toward our destination, we could see a tiny stream of water splashing down over barren cliffs from the lake. The red firebrick rock of Twin Peaks loomed high in the sky. Large snow banks clung to steep talus slopes, far above timber line.

We wound in and out of willows and aspen thickets, and then began climbing a high trail that switch-backed through a mountain mahogany patch before breaking out into a grove of trembling aspen. We crossed a stream rushing with whitewater, full of cold snowmelt, where colorful wildflowers nodded along the bank and drank the spray. It was refreshing and cool here, and we stopped to drink water and rest before resuming our steep climb ever higher.

Patches of alpine forget-me-nots created blue mists of color. Penstemon, in every shade of purple and blue, mingled with the biggest petals of sky-blue flax we'd ever seen. Presently we came to another cascading stream that spilled forth from under a high snowbank sculpted into interesting patterns by the melting. We followed the tumbling stream into a high basin, where above and to our left jagged talus and limestone spires gleamed in the morning sun. We stopped to rest along the stream in a meadow covered with pink alpine heather bells.

We gazed up at an enormous tumble of boulders, which we had yet to climb to reach another high basin. We drank more water and tried to eat a bite, but hordes of mosquitoes descended, so we moved on up a huge snow bank that paralleled the rock slide, then began scrambling on hands and knees over the jumble of boulders.

Huffing and puffing, we gained the second high mountain meadow, where water from melting snowbanks trickled down to form the stream we'd been following. The peak known as Sawtooth loomed high above, and alpine buttercups filled the basin, mostly white with yellow mixed in. It was absolutely lovely. We were now in the home of the Rocky Mountain sheep, as their wool was caught in the plants everywhere.

We tried resting once more, but were forced onward and upward by nature in the form of more swarming mosquitoes and a new threat: an impending thunder storm. After scrambling up a steep sheep trail which led through loose scree, we at last crossed through a high saddle just as dark thunderheads boiled overhead.

The narrow sheep trail eventually brought us to the lake, Oregon's highest! It was 11 a.m. Hurriedly we photographed, not wanting to be caught exposed far above timberline when the first lightning struck.

An enormous snowbank clung to the north slopes of the lake, mingling its melt with the turquoise waters of LeGore Lake. Water at the eastern end of the lake seeped underground, then appeared to spill in a little stream downward to join Falls Creek far below. We could look down at this dizzying height and see the town of Enterprise, the valley stretching clear to the Bitterroots.

Maryann proved to be a good hiker and we both felt elated at having accomplished what we'd set out to do. In our haste to get off the mountain, we glissaded like skiers down the loose scree slopes, just ahead of those threatening clouds. Already we could hear the far-off booming of thunder. We scrambled over the boulders and then I opted to sit down on the adjacent snow bank and slide the rest of the way to the bottom on the seat of my jeans.

I looked back to see Maryann following my trail, walking sideways.

Maryann Deck of Walla Walla made it to LeGore Lake.

By noon we were sitting on a log in the old log miner's cabin eating our lunch. It had begun to rain lightly, thunder rolling off the high peaks, and occasional strikes of lightning made bright flashes in the dark sky. The cabin was roofless, but gave us a sense of protection under the trees. We were wet by the time we reached the trailhead, but not cold. The memory of this high country adventure in July will remain with us forever.

I can still see the rushing wild whitewater, the brilliant wild flowers, and the blinding white snowbanks of God's country, with not a soul there but the two of us. I left Maryann at her car around 3 p.m. and we agreed to meet again for another hike. She said she had read about my liking to hike in her wheat farmer friend's Agri-Times.

This weekend is the Tippett family reunion, which will be followed by the Wallowa County Fair, and before we know it, summer will be over. Sure glad Maryann suggested that wonderful hike.

July 29—The tepees are gone now, their inhabitants headed home from the Indian encampment along the creek. In fact, our little hometown of Joseph appears strangely quiet this Monday after the big Chief Joseph Days celebration, which drew throngs of people here to attend parades, cowboy breakfasts, and Indian dance contests, not to mention four PRCA rodeo performances.

Driving past the deserted rodeo grounds I spotted Gilbert Marlin, standing alone among the litter deposited by all those rodeo spectators. Gilbert, last year's parade grand marshal, is in charge of the rodeo grounds. Perhaps, like me, he was wondering at the silence, and remembering the yelling and applause when Greg Oules of Chelan, Washington, made that spectacular ride on a spinning, sunfishing Brahma bull! Or seeing again our three lovely local cowgirls come flying around the arena at breakneck speed, waving to the crowd.

Doug and I had been there, surrounded by family and a host of grandchildren, watching the Sunday finals. When I stopped at Jerry's Market, Steve Isley was turning in more empty pop cans.

"Made $75 yesterday," he said.

Store proprietors looked weary, and were no doubt glad the big event was over for another year. As for me, I miss our Native Americans. On Sunday afternoon, I attended their traditional dances, which were held out on the grass of the high school football field. With the blue sky and white clouds overhead, and the mountains for a backdrop, the colorful attire of the different tribes was something to see. The drum beat gets into my blood, and I love watching the little children and the older people.

They have a real sense of family, and the children reflect all the love that is lavished on them. They are proud of their heritage, and that is good.

At one point they invited others to join them for a dance and I was one who took up the invitation. These visiting Indians are warm, friendly and sincere, and I, along with many others in our community, welcome them back and am glad to see them enjoying themselves.

Meanwhile, out in the rural areas of Wallowa County, ranchers worked on without interruption. Many of them didn't make it to any of the festivities because of haying and irrigating. July is a busy time!

July 30—Two farm wife readers of Agri-Times drove over from Walla Walla to chat in the shade of our lawn with me. I am sorry I didn't write down their names. Maybe they will forgive me; so many people look me up and I'm finding it more and more difficult to remember names. But I will always remember them. I suppose, when one writes a column such as mine, they should expect mail, visits and phone calls. This past week has been one of all three.

August 1—I had grandchildren here all day yesterday. We spent the night in the sheepherder's wagon, listening to the sound of rain on the roof as a thunderstorm made its way across Prairie Creek.

Today, I took three more grandchildren plus two of their friends on a hike up Chief Joseph trail. Although we were stopped about a mile up the trail by bridge construction, we had a great time. We returned to the West Fork of the Wallowa River, which was all rushing full of cold snowmelt, and ate our lunches under the blooming branches of wild syringa, whose scent filled the air with orange blossom sweetness.

On the way home, I took them to the head of Wallowa Lake where they all went swimming with their clothes on, and then I treated them to a snow cone at Russell's. I should have been home washing windows, as we are expecting company all weekend...but grandchildren are always first priority.

August 2—I had to double up to catch up, so I could finish house cleaning in time to make a lunch date with the Betts family. Kohler had called from Athena saying his sister-in-law, Lila, and her husband, Reeve, would fly out from South Carolina after all. Her husband was able to travel now, his broken ribs having mended.

So, by 1 p.m., I was sitting between Lila and her husband around a table at "A Country Place on Pete's Pond." The Betts family, Mr. and Mrs. Kohler Betts and a daughter from McMinnville, had joined us. A delightful visit with delightful people. Since I've never been any farther east than Woonsocket, South Dakota, or any farther south than Utah, it widened my world to visit with Lila, who talked about the Blue Ridge Parkway and the Linn Cove Viaduct.

Lila's husband, Dr. Reeve Betts, unlike his brother, Kohler, opted to be a doctor instead of a wheat farmer. The brothers resembled each other by the twinkle in their eyes. Lila and Reeve had flown to Olympia to visit her son, and then on to Athena to stay with Kohler and his family. Reeve said that when Agri-Times comes to them in Asheville, South Carolina, Lila just drops everything and sits down to read "Janie's Journal."

In today's mail I received my second letter from 91-year-old Blanche Strey of Lacey, Washington, who, with her husband, Bill, lived at what is known locally as "The Buttes," north of us here on Prairie Creek out in the hills. During the 1930s they operated a ranch there.

In 1937 Blanche, who wrote under the pen name of "Dorcas Jane," wrote a column for the Wallowa County Chieftain, which began as a recipe column. George Cheney, the editor back then, suggested she add a short homily, which became "Kitchen News—and a Ranch Woman's Views," by Dorcas Jane. Jane is Blanche's maternal grandmother's name. The column ran for the next seven years.

After receiving an earlier letter from Blanche, I had written to her expressing similarities in our names. My first name is Blanche, my mother's name, and my middle name is Jane. I, too, write a column, "CattleWomen's Corner," for the Chieftain, which contains beef recipes in addition to CattleWomen's ranch news. And, for the past seven years, I have written this column for Agri-Times.

Blanche, now a subscriber, is able to keep up with what she calls a letter from home, one that brings back memories of life on The Buttes that her 93-year-old husband, Bill, refers to as the happiest time of their lives.

Blanche writes, *Our house was farther up the draw. And is gone. It is possible that one of the buildings seen from the road may be a small one Bill moved from the Johnnie Neal place. Plans he had for this were never realized. We were told that our house was a part of the original homestead cabin built by a German settler.*

It was not the usual structure, the lumber having been tongue and grooved by hand. The kitchen and pantry and a bedroom off the back porch were shedded on later. They were of little consequence, but I've always felt the original cabin could have been of historical interest. We sold our ranch in October 1944. Bill's health was not good at the time and hired help was impossible to find.

With the exception of more fences and a much wider graveled road, the Buttes today probably haven't changed all that much. The vastness of the rolling hills still butts up against the Buttes, which can be seen from great distances and are named the Findley Buttes. The area is still lovely, albeit a bit lonely. Cattle graze the natural bunch grass range and the old homesteaders' buildings are rapidly disappearing.

Farther south, along what was once an old stage road, the remains of the stage stop Midway stand shakily against the severe Wallowa winters. Out north toward Zumwalt, the old school house succumbed last fall to a wild windstorm. It simply sagged into itself, like it was tired.

It was just wonderful to hear from Blanche, and I'm sure many others who lived in her era will be interested in reading this. Perhaps there will be some who remember her column. I can't wait to find time to go through some back issues of the Chieftain and read some for myself. Truly, one of the rewards of writing this column are the associations with people like the Betts family, Blanche Strey, and Maryann Deck. It renews one's faith in humankind to know there are such people out there; as long as they exist, our country can't be in too bad a shape. Good news never seems to make the papers!

After making it almost two years with not so much as a sniffle, I suddenly came down with a nasty summer cold/flu thing that nearly knocked me flat, and the day before the Tippett family reunion!

As I write, I am still trying to get enough strength back to carry on with summer, which continues at an alarming rate. Family reunions are great. I enjoy meeting people rarely seen, except on a yearly basis; but it would have been so much better if I'd felt up to par.

The raspberries continue to ripen, and I picked enough to make the first batch of jam. Linde came down and we picked gooseberries, after which I sent her home burdened with produce from my bountiful garden.

This year I planted some "Gold Rush Zucchini," and it is beginning to produce the prettiest yellow squash you ever laid eyes on. Doug will be thrilled. Actually, he didn't even know he was eating some last night for supper. The tender squash was disguised in the spaghetti sauce.

My garden, which had such a bad start, is literally bursting out of its rows. Sweet peas climb the fence, and an Armenian cucumber is trailing toward the potatoes. As usual, I plant without a plan, and now it is utter chaos…And absolutely wonderful.

August 4—Most headlines these days are bad, but here's a good one. Down along the Grande Ronde River lies the small settlement of Troy. When someone is in trouble there, neighbors pitch in and help. In this case, rancher Doug Mallory was stricken with a heart attack just when he was in the middle of haying. Mallory has since recovered, but while he was hospitalized, around 30 friends and relatives hauled and stacked his 300 tons of hay.

While Mallory spent his 48th birthday and his wedding anniversary in Spokane's Sacred Heart Hospital, neighboring rancher Robert Morris organized crews to deal with the hay. Thanks to his efforts, twelve trucks and five tractors arrived in a caravan to haul the bales, which had to be transported from Eden and Bartlett Benches to Troy to be unloaded and stacked in two barns. Knowing his neighbors cared must have helped in Mallory's recovery. He is home and doing well.

August 6—Already we are into August, which means reunions; the county fair; company, Stockgrowers, and CattleWomen's meetings; irrigating pastures and potato fields; putting food by for the winter; and, if there is any time left, going hiking in the mountains.

August 20—Maybe it's the sound blackbirds make when they flock together, or the angle at which the late August sunlight falls across my kitchen sink, or a sudden cool breeze stirring the dry hills, but it feels like fall this morning. And after our usual hot and hectic summer, seasonal change is most welcome.

Our county fair is history. How so many activities can be crammed into one week is unreal, but volunteers make it happen, manning the food booth, leading 4-H and being parents, giving of their precious time to make our country fair what it is.

"An American Tradition" was this year's fair theme, and it seems to me the greatest tradition of all is the generosity of local citizens, already so busy they can hardly squeeze in another activity, but always coming through to pull off another county fair. Like all grandmas, this one was very proud of all her many grandchildren's participation in 4-H and FFA project areas. It is gratifying to see this generation carrying on this great "American tradition."

This past weekend was the CattleWomen's and Stockgrowers' annual meetings. Pat Goggins, editor of *The Western Livestock Reporter*, flew out from Billings, Montana, to speak at the Stockgrowers' breakfast meeting. Pat is an inspirational speaker and a friend of the cattleman. His speech started by defining wealth.

"Wealth," he said, "is only a state of mind." He knew a fellow once, from a very wealthy family, who chose to live simply, in a little dugout built into the mountain. He grew a small garden and lived there in contentment.

One day, Pat was invited into this man's abode where his friend cooked him a fine meal prepared with the food he had raised. In the course of conversation, Pat asked him why he had decided to live like this, when he could have a much higher lifestyle.

His friend replied that he considered himself wealthy. He had everything he wanted there, in his garden, his peace and quiet.

"That man was wealthy," said Pat. "If a man has his health, he is wealthy," he said. "Wealth is only a state of mind." Amen!

Our CattleWomen's luncheon was held following the Stockgrowers' breakfast and meeting. We elected officers for the coming year, and now we CattleWomen will plunge ourselves into baking pies for the Cowboy Poetry Gathering to be held September 1st at Cloverleaf Hall in Enterprise.

Our Labor Day steak feed was the next day, culminating in the annual feeder cattle sale at the Enterprise Livestock Market. Doug and I attended the CattleWomen and Stockgrowers' steak feed at the local Elks Lodge on Saturday night, after which we danced for the first time in months.

The next morning, we loaded our mini-motor home with some food and sleeping bags, and headed for Oregon's high desert country in hopes of filling an antelope tag Doug was lucky enough to draw. I had risen early to type out "CattleWomen's Corner" for our local Chieftain newspaper, and we left it under the door of the paper's office on the way out of town.

After such a weekend, we were a bit weary. We made it to Lostine before we stopped and had one of those good sandwiches, as it was almost noon. We enjoy stopping at the Lostine Tavern to visit with local ranchers. The food is always good.

We stopped again along the Wallowa River in the Minam Canyon to take a nap before heading to La Grande.

The day warmed rapidly as we pulled into Baker City, then headed up over the 5,392-foot Dooley Mountain summit and down along the South Fork of Burnt River. Despite the burning August heat, it was a lovely drive. Fertile green bottomland meandered along the river.

Ranchers were in the middle of haying, and such a crop! Bright green alfalfa fields stopped short of dry sagebrush hills. Baled meadow hay dotted the willow-bordered water course. It was a peaceful, man-made beauty, developed and maintained by generations of ranchers who had obviously cared well for their lands, and had created this winding green valley. Weathered split rail fences zig-zagged alongside the roads. Rustic barns, outbuildings, and old ranch houses added their pastoral charm to the scene. Even if these ranchers were barely making ends meet, they were "wealthy."

*Rowdy Nash, of Enterprise, poses his grand champion 4-H market steer.
Rowdy won the all-around showmanship trophy for 4-H. His steer sold for
$1.70 a pound to Wallowa Valley Simmentals.*

*Winning a lion's share of the awards at the Wallowa County Fair were,
from left, Chelsie Nash, Rowdy Nash, and Analise Johnson, all of Enterprise.*

Shawn Phillips, of Enterprise, showed the grand champion FFA market steer. Shawn also won the all-around advanced beef showmanship award. His steer sold for $2.10 a pound to Doug McDaniel of Lostine.

LeeAnn Lathrop, of Enterprise, concentrates on showing her hog.

*Wearing a wide grin and holding a big trophy, Kyle Johnson, of Lostine,
shows the Jidge Tippett Memorial award presented by Wallowa County
CattleWomen to the outstanding beef project.*

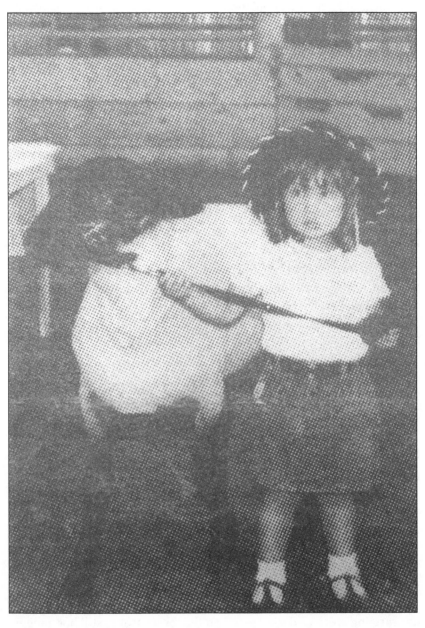

Little two-year old "Miss Katy" leads her lamb in the popular pee wee showmanship event at the Wallowa County Fair. Miss Katy is from Wallowa County's north end, near Flora.

Not many towns out there. The nearest thing to a town was the small settlement of Hereford, population 30, according to our map. Just before we drove through Hereford, Doug said, "A dollar on the first antelope."

"OK," I replied, and not five minutes later I spotted one—a lone buck, nibbling some rancher's freshly windrowed hay. Unfortunately, Hereford was not in the Beulah unit, which was Doug's hunt area.

By the time we drove past Unity Reservoir, great thunderheads were building up over the vast desert country. The reservoir drains into the South Fork of Burnt River, which heads somewhere up in the vicinity of Lookout Mountain near the Strawberry Mountain Wilderness area.

We pulled into Unity, population 300, where we were told at Stratton's store, the only store, that they didn't have any drinking water. Although our mini-motor home's tank was full, the pump wasn't working, so...no water. We finally found water at a nearby motel, where Doug filled our bucket at an outside faucet.

We stopped briefly at a place called "The Waterhole," which appeared to be the only restaurant in town, where I had a tall glass of iced tea. I asked the pleasant waitress about the antelope situation, to which she replied: "Our elk are down, so are the deer. The antelope? They are thick!"

We rumbled out of town following a dusty back road that led through a forest grazing allotment. Expecting to see antelope, we saw only cattle, looking good despite poor grazing conditions due to drought. Many cattle were already grazing the irrigated bottoms.

Evening descended as we wandered the sagebrush-bordered roads in the heat and dust, and we began to see plenty of deer, but they weren't playing with the antelope! Nary a one of these creatures did we see.

Somewhat delayed after taking a wrong turn, we finally pulled into a remembered camp spot along-side East Camp Creek. The picnic table, green grass, and tall ponderosa pines felt like home after that long, hot drive. It was 7 p.m. While I cooked corn on the cob, fried pork chops, and sliced some tomatoes, Doug fiddled with the water pump and got it working.

After supper, we munched zucchini chocolate cake and listened to the gurgling creek as darkness fell on the forest. It was still hot, muggy and cloudy. After washing the dishes and mixing the sourdough, we went to bed. A sudden wind sprang up and the tall pines swayed overhead. Lightning lit up the dark woods and a gentle rain fell on the motor home roof. The brief desert storm cleared the air, the stars fell, and a delicious coolness replaced the heat.

I awakened from a deep sleep, my bed moving through the woods. Doug, at the wheel, was on his way in search of his antelope. Sleepily I dressed as our swaying motor home negotiated the gravelled, sagebrush-bordered road that would take us toward Ironside. Soon I was awake enough to look for Doug's buck.

Changing from my former role as camp cook to that of guide and "spotter of game," I spied just at daylight something white behind a large sagebrush that turned out to be the white rump of a lone antelope. Looking through my binoculars, I gazed in wonderment. Lined up with the antelope was what looked like a gray wolf, but must have been a coyote. And, even better—the antelope was a buck.

Doug didn't take time to look; he took my word for it and pulled on down the road out of sight of the coyote/wolf and antelope, then parked in a wide spot alongside the road. Leaving me to witness a spectacular desert sunrise, he disappeared over a hill. A half-hour later, he was back, a nice buck strapped to his pack board.

We returned to camp, hung the buck in a tree, and I cooked sourdough hotcakes, ham and eggs, while Doug skinned his antelope. The sun was just coming out from under a cloud bank and the carcass cooled quickly there along the creek. After enjoying a quiet breakfast at our picnic table, we wrapped the buck in a game bag, placed him on top of the motor home, and took off for Jerry's Market. Stopping only once, in Baker City, we made it to Joseph by 1:30 p.m.

Meanwhile, back at the ranch, the zucchini had got out of hand! I spent the afternoon dealing with myriad zucchini and raspberries, not to mention 33 pullet eggs laid in our absence.

August 21—Spent the morning on some photojournalism assignments, which included publicity on the Cowboy Poetry Gathering and the CattleWomen's Labor Day steak feed. Tended to my sweet pickles and froze some Hermiston sweet corn that Doug brought back from Les Marks'. I enjoyed grandson Bart's company here while his mom worked.

Daughter Jackie stopped by with tomatoes and cucumbers from her Imnaha garden. So I made salsa, started a crock of nine-day sweet pickles and pickled peppers. Then called grandchildren, who were waiting to hear if "Pappa Doug" shot his antelope.

The evenings are cool and peaceful on Prairie Creek. Cows graze contentedly across the road, sustaining the calves growing in their bellies while making milk for the calves at their sides. Raspberries and zucchini ripen. Wild honkers land in the irrigated fields to feed at dusk. I love to sit outside and be a part of this special time as the days dwindle.

August 22—Cloudy and cool. Very refreshing change. Potato inspection today in our fields. Won't see Doug until evening. Mowed the lawn, which is ready to "hay" again. Son Todd and his family here to borrow sleeping bags for a camping trip. The children all excited. Son Ken borrowing our stock truck to haul horses to the trailhead up Lostine. They will pack into Brownie Basin and Chimney Lake.

I drive to Wallowa Lake State Park to pick up the projector with the "Wallowa Story" slide-tape program, which the recreation director, Mr. Goodgame, says was shown to a record crowd this summer.

Baby calves have been appearing in our leased moraine pasture for some time now, as the fall calving cows continue to calve. I pick more raspberries and make more jam. A warm summer rain soaked me as I picked this evening. It felt good.

August 23—A chorus of yelping coyote pups awakened me from a sound sleep at dawn. Friend Linde calls—it is her birthday. She wants to climb Ruby Peak, but I can't. The cabbage is ready to make sauerkraut, the green beans need picking, my husband is working long hours and needs a cook. I bake a carrot cake for Linde's birthday, using my own fresh carrots and a recipe out of my "Joy of Gardening" cookbook.

After a busy day, I delivered two of my framed photos to the Joseph Civic Center, where the Oregon Arts Commission is meeting tonight.

August 24—The mornings are cool now, and the days bright. This is the day to slice the sweet pickles and pour a boiling sweet and spicy syrup over them. The kitchen smells wonderful. Swiss steak simmers in the dutch oven, smothered in fresh peppers, tomatoes, and onions.

Sweet peas bloom alongside the garden fence. The first giant sunflower has opened its golden face to the sun. Several small lightning-caused forest fires have been contained. Nearly dark by 8 p.m. now, as the days shorten noticeably.

Willie Locke is baling his second cutting of hay.

August 25—My grown children scurry around getting their children ready for school, like I used to do. Son Todd filled his cow elk tag somewhere out in the Zumwalt country.

My own backpack is ready to go. Four of us ranch women will leave early in the morning to hike to the Minam Lodge in the heart of the Eagle Cap wilderness for two days. A full moon rises, lovely beyond description, over the dry eastern hill. The August moon... saying goodbye to summer.

August 26—Arising at 4 a.m., the bright moon still high in the sky. By 5:30 the four of us—Linde, Helen, Jan and I—are heading out of Wallowa County in a beautiful dawn that promises an equally beautiful day.

By 8 a.m., we are on the tail to Red's Horse Ranch via the trail from Moss Springs. All the cares of civilization fall away as we head into this vast wilderness, entering another world. We nibble thimble berries, and pick and save huckleberries to take to Laney, the cook at Minam Lodge. We cross over the Little Minam River, pass Jim White Ridge, and rest and eat lunch on Backbone ridge, a hogs back just above the Horse Ranch.

After descending the steep switchback trail to Red's, we walk another mile downriver to Minam Lodge. Both places are accessible only by horseback or airplane, according to the brochure. But we walked!

I don't advise walking, however. The Minam trails are horse trails in horse country. If one doesn't realize the distances to be traveled in there, just look at a map of the area. It is a long way from anywhere!

Both the Horse Ranch and Minam Lodge are privately owned and located in the middle of the largest wilderness in Oregon. Cal and Betsy Henry of "High Country Outfitters" now run Minam Lodge, where there is a 2,600-foot two-way dirt and sod airstrip located in a natural meadow that borders the Minam River.

Hot, tired and thirsty, we are welcomed with hugs from Laney, cook and housekeeper, whom we've known from Red's in the past. She bids us to sit down o the deck, take off our packs, and drink a refreshing glass of cold tea. I produce from my pack a letter from Laney's husband, Jim, who lives on "the outside." Laney shows us where our camping area is, pointing off down the airstrip meadow toward the river.

The rustic lodge, situated on a hill, overlooks the meadow and is flanked on west and east by steep rim rocks, which are characteristic of the Minam area. There are cabins, but we have chosen to rough it.

New peeled pole corrals and hitching racks spruce up the place, and we learn a young man named Cary and another fellow we knew last year at Red's, are responsible. Mike, plus Cal and Betsy Henry, will soon be packing in a skeleton crew, along with animals for further filming in a wilderness setting, for "The Incredible Journey!"

After walking what seems like yet another mile, we shed our clothes, don bathing suits, and like young school girls, shriek as we plunge into the cold clear waters of the Minam!

After that refreshing swim in the Minam to wash off trail dust and limber our limbs, we walked upriver to Red's Horse Ranch to visit the cook, Margaret Botts. Red's, under new management now, has undergone a facelift, but retains its original rustic charm.

By the time we hiked another mile back to Minam Lodge, Laney had supper ready—and what a supper. Roast beef, mashed potatoes, three kinds of vegetables, homemade bread, and warm-from-the-oven meringue-topped cream pies.

After browsing through some old scrapbooks that Laney brought from Red's, we walked down the long meadow to our Minam River camp. A loud crashing sound broke the stillness and we peered through the darkness, wondering if it was a bear or an elk. After brushing our teeth, we climbed into our sleeping bags, which were spread under the stars. The night was mild and smelled of river and meadow. I awoke later to see the golden moon glimmer through pine boughs, then sail free among the stars.

August 27—After one of Laney's famous breakfasts, which featured the huckleberries we'd picked, baked in a pfannenkuchen (a wonderful combination of eggs, milk and flour, sprinkled with fruit and served hot from the oven), we opted for no lunch, and decided to hike up the Minam River trail to the Splash Dam.

This historic spot, just five miles upriver from Red's, is a long five mountain miles. We glimpsed whitewater rapids flashing through forested glades alongside the trail, and drank in the wonderful autumn air. The day was cool and made walking pleasant.

I led my friends to the remembered meadow where we rested and experienced the far reaches of the upper Minam. The river makes a wide bend through the meadow, bordered by a sandy beach. Farther down, remnants of the old splash dam can still be seen. In early logging days the dam was constructed to store logs, then, at a given time, the water was released to flush the logs downstream 30 miles to the mill.

A natural rock face forms one side of the dam. Huge timbers, dragged there by teams of horses and men, provide the dam on the opposite side. Today, water flows over solid rock colored many shades of earth tones, pooling in carved formations that are beautiful to see. As it has for years, the Minam passes through this rotting monument to man's determination to solve the problem of transporting logs downriver.

After the walk back and another brief visit with Margaret and Johnnie, the wrangler, we were ready for another fabulous supper: pork chops, creamed asparagus, homemade whole wheat bread and rice, topped off by an apple cream roll.

While walking down at dusk to our meadow camp, we were watched by six cow elk. Then the noise again, only this time a splashing in the river. A bear catching a migrating salmon?

Awakened at 4:30 a.m. by a few drops of rain, which quickly ceased. After another tasty breakfast, we shouldered our packs, said goodbye to Laney, and headed up the trail carrying more memories to store away.

August 28—I got caught up and baked an apple pie so Doug and I could leave in our motor home to camp a couple of days along the Imnaha River to hunt grouse and relax with friends. Another column.

Then home to bake two raspberry pies for the Cowboy Poetry Gathering that night. And be ready for the Labor Day steak feed the next day. In between all this I put up apples, made sauerkraut and finished in time to leave for Baker City with Doug to attend an old farm equipment show. Material for yet another column.

September 4—"My life is a poem I might have writ, if I had time to live and utter it!" Don't know who wrote that phrase, but it sure describes my life. Even though I don't really have time to "utter it," I will anyway...as a bucket of transparent apples waits to be turned into apple sauce and pie filling, my green and purple beans beg to be picked, the lawn cries out for water, the floor for sweeping, and this gorgeous fall day beckons.

September is my month; when the wanderlust, vagabond blood stirs; when mornings are crisp, the days wine-bright, and the harvest of vegetables and fruit all ripens at once. As summer fades, a sort of madness grips all of us here in Wallowa County. We must squeeze in as many activities as possible.

We all seem to be caught up in this great frenzy, getting in one last campout, putting food by for the winter, gathering wood, putting on a cowboy poetry gathering, followed the next day by our Labor Day sale and steak feed, which only leads to Mule Days and Alpenfest. Grouse season opens, bow season, huckleberrying, fishing, and just plain camping. The second cuttings of hay are ready, the ranchers and farmers still irrigating and moving cattle from one pasture to another.

As if this weren't enough, Wallowa County is the setting for a movie, being filmed as I write. The Fred farm on Hurricane Creek road has been turned over to the movie company for shooting segments of "The Incredible Journey," which will be released next April. Our little town of Joseph is full of show people, and many of our locals are cast as doubles, or acting as assistant producers, or hired as security.

What has happened to our once quiet valley?

September 10—On my 57th birthday, I bought a mule.

On my 58th birthday, yesterday, I climbed a mountain, namely, the mountain known as Ruby Peak, which rises 8,874 feet in the northern Wallowas. Actually, my friend and hiking companion, Linde, wanted to climb Ruby Peak on her birthday last month, but I couldn't get away that day.

So, yesterday morning, despite a thick layer of clouds and a thunderstorm forecast, we decided to go for it. As luck would have it, it couldn't have been a more perfect day for hiking: cool with no wind or rain. We had the entire area to ourselves, partly because it was Monday, and because this rugged part of the Wallowas is off the beaten track.

Following an old stock drive, we started up the trail around 9 a.m. This recently restored trail, grubbed out by local volunteers, climbs out of the woods that flank the upper reaches of Alder Slope and becomes a high, rocky trail that affords a splendid view of the valley below.

The trail isn't a horse trail. Due to the steepness of the terrain and narrowness of the trail a horse could slip over the edge very easily. It is a trail to be savored slowly, on foot, with time taken to enjoy the views.

Just under Murray Gap we came to the old trail and climbed up through the gap. Below lay the valley, and to the west and south lay the vast area known as the Silver Creek Basin, flanked by the awesome crest of Traverse Ridge. Anyway you cut it, this hike to the summit of Ruby Peak is not for the faint of heart, and requires strength and determination.

I wanted to show Linde this lovely, wild Silver Creek country, so we veered from the more familiar course that I usually follow, and took a route that led us two ridges and several steep draws away from Scott Creek saddle, which we needed to attain to achieve the final ascent.

Along the way, we picked and ate bright red grouse whortleberries, so full of flavor now and loaded with vitamin C. We marveled at the lush greenness of the places where purple asters, cinquefoil and fading fireweed bloomed amid trickling springs, and wild onion grew in boggy areas. We listened to the alpine birds and the yelping of coyote puppies. We followed game trails, mostly, as there is no trail to Ruby Peak. We were in the home of mountain sheep, elk, bear and mule deer. Noisy squirrels, pikas and chipmunks were storing food for winter.

Surrounded by thick forest, jewel-like meadows stair-stepped down toward the Lostine and stopped short of steep talus slopes and boulder strewn slides. Traverse Ridge loomed above and, out of breath, we topped a ridge that brought into view Scotch Creek saddle, still far away. It was already noon. We scrambled down into yet another meadow and ate lunch beside a meandering stream, before beginning the final pull to the saddle, one foot above the other, slowly making our way to the top.

When we reached this point we could see the valley below again, and the views were far-reaching. A gentle breeze stirred, reviving our spirits as we climbed slowly up the jagged backbone of the ridge. As we climbed, the views took our breath away. Far below lay the towns—Lostine, Enterprise, Joseph—and nestled in the perfect moraine lay Wallowa Lake. All around lay the fertile agricultural lands, the very wealth of the area, in September colors, earth tones of harvested grain fields, golden in rays of sunlight, hayed alfalfa, the quiet serenity of ranches and farms. Hopefully, this will never change.

The vast hill land stretched north to timber and Idaho and Washington, and eastward to the breaks of the Imnaha and the Snake. Twin Peaks rose dark and dramatic in the cloudy sky, and we gazed in awe at old Sawtooth, and at the Matterhorn. We could see the old snow clinging to the edges of the north faces of raw mountains and knew one dirty snow patch lay just above LeGore Lake.

Each step brought into view more vari-colored rock ridges, awesome and stark, creating a picture no artists could paint or photographer capture. We finally literally clawed our way to the top. We'd made it—it was 2:30 p.m. Such an exhilarating feeling!

We had such fun reading the names and accounts in the register stored in a tin box under a pile of rocks. We even found notes I'd left on previous excursions, stored and preserved from the harsh winter storms in glass jars.

The best birthday present of all was reading the scrawled accounts left by five of my grandsons who had scaled the peak, and knowing my children, and now their children, have discovered this ability to enjoy simple outdoor wonders and climb mountains. Climbing mountains in their youth will enable them to climb mountains as adults, and better overcome obstacles, obstacles that are as inevitable in life as death.

In lieu of a birthday cake, Linde produced s'mores from her pack, which are usually fixed over a campfire, where you melt chocolate and marshmallows between graham crackers. Without the melting and the marshmallows they were, nevertheless, delicious, and fit the occasion. What a birthday! We felt as free as the golden eagle we spied soaring earlier over Murray Gap.

The air suddenly changed to a familiar autumnal cold when we began our steep, stiff, and sometimes, for me, painful descent, as 58-year-old legs don't bend like they used to. We returned to our homes with the wonderful tiredness brought on by physical exertion. I cooked up fresh corn-on-the-cob, reheated some barbecued ribs, and cooked some summer squash for Doug and me, then soaked in a tub of hot water and crashed.

And now, as I write, a cold rain drizzles down outside, and you can bet the first snow of the season will dust the high places.

September 17—As I type at a picnic table in our front yard, a sprinkler irrigates the wildflower patch, because thirsty bachelor buttons, Icelandic poppies, purple asters and California golden poppies need moisture to continue blooming. What a joy my wildflower patch has been all summer.

Last Christmas, sister Mary Ann gave me a box of seed that was labeled "Moonlight Gardens." According to the label the mix was supposed to bloom in colors that reflect the moonlight. So, late in the spring. I scattered the seed in a bare corner of the wildflower patch. The delicate pink and white blooms are at their peak of beauty now, ready to reflect the harvest moon that has already begun to grow. How I wish Mary Ann could see her moonlight garden this morning.

At last, the raspberries have ceased their incessant ripening and bearing. Recent frosty nights have nipped the green beans. Thank goodness. I was contemplating doing them in with a shovel. Zucchini and crookneck summer squash continue to bear, even though their vines are somewhat blackened by September frosts. The giant sunflowers, their heads so heavy they can't follow the sun, droop their golden faces downward.

The Barred Plymouth Rock pullets sing and cackle loudly after laying each egg. Chester the rooster, showing his age, has lost most of his tail feathers somehow, and walks slightly arthritic. Limbs on the old-fashioned apple tree planted by one of Prairie Creek's first settlers hang heavy with cooking apples, some of which are stored away in the form of applesauce. Out in our shop there is a great clanging and banging as the men ready the big diggers for the potato harvest, which gets under way Monday.

Tomorrow, Mike McFetridge and Ben and I will drive some of our fall calving cows and their calves down off the high moraine range to lower, greener pastures. Things are very dry up there. In fact, if it weren't for the irrigated lands of the farmers and ranchers, things would be dry all over the valley. We could do with a good rain.

As often happens when I begin to type this column, I get the urge to bake a pie. So I go to the garden and pick some of the last gooseberries to combine with the cooking apples. Now, as I continue with my typing, that cinnamon aroma of apples, spice and gooseberries fills my kitchen with the smells of fall. And when my husband returns, he will be happy. He had to drive to La Grande to pick up parts for the potato digger.

Lately it seems we've been camped along widely scattered rivers in Wallowa County. First it was the beautiful Minam, then the upper Imnaha, and last Saturday night we slept near the Grande Ronde River, which flows past the little settlement of Troy.

Our two nights on the upper Imnaha were wonderful. We took the mini-motor home and parked at our old campsite in a stand of ponderosa pines. After feasting on antelope back strap barbecued slowly over oak wood coals, freshly picked corn on the cob roasted in their husks, freshly dug red potatoes and onions fried in an iron skillet, and transparent apple pie, we sat around the campfire, relaxed and listened to the river running.

Next morning, we were up at dawn and headed toward McGraw to hunt grouse. The sun came flaming up over the Seven Devils range in Idaho as we tromped along old roads and game trails in search of some birds. We all got in some shooting and each bagged a grouse. Doug limited out. Linde shot her first grouse and now she's hooked.

We returned to camp and fixed breakfast over the sheepherder stove. Pat and Doug had picked enough huckleberries on the way in to put in the sourdough hotcakes. It was pretty hard to take two days of this kind of life! More friends joined us Saturday night and it almost seemed like the entire county was camped on the upper Imnaha over Labor Day weekend. The roads were dusty, and many campers headed toward Indian Crossing and Coverdale.

Two grandsons were camped not far from us with friends. Rowdy floated by with a friend in an inner tube one hot afternoon, and Chad had been bow hunting. We fried some of the grouse for Sunday breakfast.

Last Saturday evening found us on our way, in the motorhome again, with Linde and Pat to attend a benefit barn dance along the Grande Ronde River to raise money for Doug Mallory, a local rancher who recently suffered a heart attack. The dance was held in the Kieseckers' barn, about five miles upriver from Troy. On our way "out north," as we say, we stopped to eat supper at the Rimrock Inn, a restaurant that is perched above the scenic Joseph Creek Canyon.

We could make out the glimmer of lights in Troy, far below, which lies near the confluence of the Wenaha River and the Grande Ronde. After rattling across the narrow bridge at Troy, we headed upriver to the Kiesecker ranch. It was after 9 p.m. when we arrived, and the dance was well under way.

We parked our motorhome alongside others in a long meadow just across the road from the river. Linde and Pat set up their camp cots outside under the starry sky—and what stars! The big dipper was just beginning to disappear over a huge rimmed ridge. The Milky Way cut a brilliant path across the sky and the night air was fresh with fall.

A large crowd had already assembled, driving from miles around. There were cowboys from neighboring ranches, and folks who live on Lost Prairie, Eden Bench, Bartlett Bench, Grouse Flats, Anatone, Paradise, Flora and Troy, along with people like us from the valley. The Twin River Band played such foot-stompin' music we couldn't sit still for long, and soon we joined in the fun. The band soon added a fiddler, who really made things jump.

We visited with Bob and Terri Morse, who have a cattle outfit out on Lost Prairie. Terri said they had to get up and ride in the morning, so they left before the dance ended, which was well after midnight. We had been in bed only a short while when the music stopped at 2 a.m. We slept until late the next morning. Around 8 a.m., just as the sun crept over the high rim rock ridge to the east, we were already up, talking with Lester Kiesecker, who had come out to see how the happy campers were.

We drove to Troy and had a late breakfast, a real treat for us cooks. I remembered a sign over a Baker City restaurant last week. It read: *Eat Out, The Wife You Save May Be Your Own!* Although both Linde and I love to cook, it is a relief to eat out once in a while.

We ordered a "Shiloh breakfast" and recognized one of the waitresses, who had been at the dance. She was bright-eyed and cheerful even though she had spent the night dancing.

Doug and Pat did some steelhead fishing along the Grande Ronde before we headed up the long, winding road to Flora, then on out to the north highway and home. Round trip, about 100 miles or more.

The sauerkraut was ready to can. The ripest tomatoes we'd picked earlier in the week at Imnaha were, too. So were the pears from the Grande Ronde. So I canned the sauerkraut and fixed a nice supper from the garden, and crashed at 8 p.m.

Yesterday I canned the pears and stewed the tomatoes with peppers, onions and seasonings to put in the freezer for soups and stews. One day at a time. We are so lucky when we have our health, can live in such a beautiful country, and enjoy working as well as playing.

September 24—Yesterday was the first day of autumn. The full harvest moon appeared early last evening in a rose-tinted sky, glowing golden above the frosted and sunburned hills.

All in all, it was quite a day.

Yesterday morning, we began digging the seed potatoes. The first day is always the hardest, until most of the "glitches" are worked out. Our weather continues warm and dry during the daytime, so Doug has been irrigating the potato fields to soften the soil for digging. It was in the 70s yesterday, and feels even warmer today. Although some mornings are frost-less, like this morning, others have gotten pretty cold, like last week when the temperature dropped to a chilly 26 degrees and finished off the vegetable garden.

In the cold moonlight, sister Mary Ann's "Moonglow" flower mix frosted. The lovely pink and white blooms, glowing softly, were stilled at the peak of their beauty. Today they are withered and frost-burned, giving no hint of their former glory. Stubborn poppies and blue bachelor buttons continue to bloom among a fall mix of weeds, and the heavy heads of sunflowers sway on their huge stalks as occasional breezes play among the withered rows of corn.

Huge green and yellow zucchini lay exposed among blackened squash vines, and my own red potatoes are ready to dig and store. The flowers that grow alongside the house, such as geraniums and petunias, have escaped the frost. Knowing their days are numbered, I have potted some of the geraniums to keep indoors through winter.

Am outside typing away on the picnic table again, where I can enjoy the golden afternoon. The three young Northwood maples' leaves have turned to flame. What a sight they are, with the autumn sunlight striking them at different angles. While I write, I can hear the squeaking and whining of our potato equipment as the men and women work to pick rocks and dirt clods out of the potatoes that pass before them on a moving conveyor.

This first digging is our own seed that will be kept to plant next year, and stored in the small cellar near our house. The remainder of the 140 acres of seed will be stored in a large dome cellar near Joseph. Every so often one of our ancient potato trucks loaded with potatoes chugs slowly past, or an emptied one returns to the field for another load. Or son Steve roars up the driveway in his 4-wheeler after a tool in the shop.

Above the noise, I can hear the plop of an apple falling from the tree, and the buzzing of flies, which, like my geraniums, seemingly survived the frost.

After arising early yesterday morning to cook Doug his favorite breakfast (sourdough hot cakes, sausage and eggs), then making his lunch, I typed out "CattleWomen's Corner" for our local newspaper. I spent the remainder of the morning running various errands in town.

I returned home to put a pork roast to bake slowly in the dutch oven, then drove to the potato field where I was to relieve daughter-in-law Angie, who had an appointment in town. I climbed aboard the big harvester and joined Scotty, Julie, Teresa and daughter Jackie, who all have such a good sense of humor they can make throwing dirt clods and rocks into a moving trash eliminator almost fun.

At the end of each row we took turns walking behind the digger to pick up any potatoes left in the dirt. Because one of the loaded potato trucks got stuck and had to be towed out, and a breakdown at the cellar earlier had delayed trucks in the field, we didn't set any records for yesterday. But today things appear to be moving right along, judging from the trucks going by. Since the potato field is some distance away from here, it requires time driving to and fro.

I returned to the ranch to gather eggs, pick corn (still sweet) from the withered corn stalks, make a coleslaw, and serve it with pickled beets, fresh applesauce and sliced tomatoes to accompany the done-to-perfection roast pork. Nothing beats good old-fashioned food for working people.

Prairie Creek farmers are just now finishing up their grain harvest. Large clouds of grain dust can still be seen following in the wake of harvesters as they slowly chew their way across golden fields of sun-ripened grain. Second cuttings add more length to the already long stacks of hay. Security against the Wallowa winters.

Wallowa Lake's Alpenfest is history, and all those tourists who travel to such things have left. The movie people, too, have moved on to Bend to continue filming "The Incredible Journey."

This weekend mule deer buck season opens. Doug and I didn't get in the drawing so we won't be hunting deer this fall. I will be looking forward to a visit from grandchildren instead. Not work, but fun for me.

Windfall apples are being made into applesauce, some of which I give away to grandchildren because they love it so, and grandma can't bear to see apples go to waste—a trait inherited from my grandmother.

Last week, old-hand Mike McFetridge, Ben and I gathered cows and their fall calves off the east moraine, then sorted out 40 pairs and drove them down to greener pastures. The weather was splendid and the air so fresh, Mike and I smiled at each other. Good to be on horseback again. Riding along the back roads of upper Prairie Creek was a pleasure on such a fine day. We watched ranchers working their fields, raking and baling hay. These widely scattered small farms and ranches provide a sight far more pleasing than mile after mile of subdivisions, I mused, cringing at the thought.

Nothing can match the unique charm of these small family-owned and operated places. The love of the land is evident in all they do, year after year, generation after generation. It seems sad knowing that this, too, could change. As it already has in areas similar to ours. Whatever the future may hold for our special home, I will forever hold dear in my heart the way it looks today, and will, with others, fight to protect these last frontiers of the Western family-owned farms and ranches.

October 1—September's golden days are gone, and this first October morning seems not much different than yesterday. Then, shortly before noon, a cool wind ripples through the grasses in the hay field, rattling the withered corn stalks in the garden. And above, in the wide autumn skies, a few clouds appear, whispy "mare's tails", drifting in the wind.

It is so dry, we have been locked into this unusually hot weather pattern. High temperatures, mild and starry moonlit nights, cloud-less daytime skies, and not a hint of morning frost. The threat and danger of forest and range fires is always present, an unspoken fear among those of us who live here.

We are into the second week of digging seed potatoes. Those glitches I mentioned last week continue to plague us. Breakdowns, somehow, are synonymous with all types of farm work. Each year it becomes increasingly difficult to find workers to hire during harvest, and this puts an added strain on our family, for we must pitch in and help on the diggers.

Daughters, daughters-in-law, grandsons, and grandma must fill in whenever needed. The opening morning of mule deer buck season found Doug, daughter-in-law Jo, grandson Shawn, and yours truly working on the potato digger. Shawn who returned during the wee hours of the morning from playing football (Enterprise vs. Vale at Vale), gamely kept up. His dog, Susie, followed alongside or rode in one of the potato trucks up and down the rows.

I had the two youngest grandchildren for several days during this time, which meant having them up early, dressed, and fed breakfast before driving them over to granddaughter Carrie's, who watched them on Saturday while grandma worked on the digger.

The first day they were here, we went fishing in the creek across the hill from our house. The trout were feeding on grasshoppers, which are numerous this fall, so we had a nice rainbow each time our hook touched the water with a squirming grasshopper. The last one James pulled out was a whopping 12 inches. The children and I jumped up and down, yelling and laughing over our good fortune.

We trooped back through the high grasses, James dragging the forked stick of a cottonwood branch which held the fish, and Adele holding a plastic carton containing a tree frog she had captured. For three nights I slept in the old sheepherder's wagon with the two children. Being a grandma is great fun, but I must admit my own bed felt good last night. I do miss the children's friendly chatter this morning, however, and they weren't here to help feed the chickens and the kittens...or bring me flowers that continue to bloom in the garden.

In these five-year-old and three-year-old eyes shine such adoration for their "gramma." I am constantly amazed at this pedestal they place me on. May as well enjoy it while I can. All too soon the world will take them away. Hopefully, some of this little boy and little girl time will hide in their hearts, to resurface after they, too, become grandparents.

Last Sunday morning, the children and Doug and I drove to Imnaha for the dedication of Imnaha's first church. The canyon colors were just beginning to turn, and the sumac is reddening up among the rim rocks.

Perched under one of those rims now sits the brand new church. The new pews were all filled, and chairs placed on both sides were also filled with people who had come from near and far for this momentous occasion; people like 97-year-old A. L. Duckett, who donated the land for the church to be built; local rancher Don Hubbard, who contributed in so many ways to making a dream become reality; and Ken Stein, Paul Kriley, Pastor Richard Smith, and wife Linda; Max Gorsline, who said the plans for the church were too big, but where would all the people have sat, if it had been smaller?

Rose Glaus, driven here from Montana by her son and daughter-in-law, was there with her infant granddaughter, remembering how her husband, Warren, had worked so hard on the church. Many more people, more than could be listed here, have made this church a reality. Doug, who restored, with Max Gorsline's help, the ancient bell that now sits proudly in the bell tower, was asked, along with Max, to ring the bell.

What a lovely sound. On that hot, autumn morn, that last day of September, the bell tolled and was heard up and down the river. After the services and dedication, we were treated to one of those famous church potlucks, after which we photographers took several shots of all those people standing outside the church. It was a mite difficult, with the children running in and out of focus, but we managed to get most of the people in.

We went on up Camp Creek to visit daughter Jackie's family, and let the grandchildren play with their cousins. Son-in-law Bill's father and mother from Roseburg were visiting and we listened to the deer hunting

James Nash, 5, and his sister, Adele, 3, proudly show off the rainbow trout they caught. They're standing in the door of the old sheepherder's wagon.

story of how grandpa Bill shot his buck. James' dad also shot a big muley on opening morning. We noticed quite a few hunting rigs and camps on Imnaha, but due to the drawing neither Doug nor I had a tag this year, so didn't hunt.

Two weeks or so ago, Linde decided to surprise neighbor Betty Van Blaricom on her birthday. Between the two of us we cooked up a real surprise. I spent the morning baking a fancy Reuben loaf, a delicious mixture of sauerkraut, sliced beef and swiss cheese, baked in rye bread dough, and Linde baked a Black Forest cake.

Linde called Marian Birkmaier, way out on Crow Creek, nearly an hour's drive away, and arranged that we would kidnap Betty and, along with other CattleWomen, take her out there for lunch. It all came off without a hitch and Betty was really surprised. Fun!

October 8—We are into the third week of potato harvest. Days continue warm and dry, and mornings now have that October chill, the kind that adds crispness to apples and pains fingers.

This Tuesday morning, the ranch seems comparatively quiet, at least compared to yesterday. After arising before dawn to cook breakfast, I had just finished my outside chores when the day began to take a different twist. Our CattleWomen's president, and neighbor, Linda Childers, was to come over and help me bake 300 sourdough bread sticks for a Chamber of Commerce dinner we CattleWomen are catering Saturday evening at Cloverleaf Hall.

I zipped through some necessary household chores, then set four large bowls of sourdough to rise, placing them at various locations around the kitchen so they would catch the warmth of the sunshine. The phone rang several times, mostly people wanting to work on the potato digger or glean potatoes in the wake of the digger.

One call was from Linda. Her daughter had to be picked up at school and taken to the emergency room of the hospital. She'd be late, she said. The phone rang again. This time it was the proprietor of a local video store in Enterprise, and she was phoning to tell me that the wife of one of our potato truck drivers had been involved in an automobile accident in front of their store. The wife, who was pretty shaken but not hurt, wanted me to find her husband, who was in our potato field.

So...leaving the rising sourdough, I drove to the field, deciding to take a shortcut, which turned out not to be one, that I had been traveling all week. To my dismay I realized I couldn't drive to where they were digging, because the road along the harvested field had just been freshly disced under. Nothing to do but walk a mile over the freshly tilled ground to the end of the field, where I could just barely see the diggers making their slow way up and down the rows.

When I finally arrived, I found that the man I sought was at the end of a row on another digger. After climbing into a parked pickup, I drove to the digger, found and delivered my message to Don.

Borrowing another pickup, we returned to my car via another, much longer, route. Don went to his wife and "meanwhile back at the ranch," I dealt with the overflowing sourdough. Linda called again, saying she had her daughter under control, but had to swing through town again for parts!

"Isn't it fun being a ranch wife?" we laughed. Just as I was kneading the dough and beginning to shape the first bread sticks, someone knocked on the back porch door. Standing there, smiling broadly, were Ernie and his wife, Rose, from Dixon, California, who had driven up to visit daughter Ramona's family. Ernie carried in a huge lug box of tomatoes, plus apples and grapes picked for us in Lodi.

Ernie and Rose are part of a family-owned diversified farm and ranch operation that includes the production of tomatoes, sunflower seeds. beans, sugar, alfalfa hay, and other commodities including milk from a large dairy on the ranch. They are delightful people. Rose, born in Switzerland, said Wallowa County reminded her of home.

She was soon helping me shape bread sticks. We were visiting and having a great time when Linda arrived with her house guest, Ronda, who was an old school chum visiting from Utah. The three women happily shaped bread sticks, which we now called "international bread sticks," while I mixed and kneaded the other three batches of dough.

Suddenly, we wondered where Ernie was. He had quietly left. An hour or so later he reappeared, having found the potato field, jumped aboard one of the diggers, and visited my daughter Jackie and good friend Scotty, whom he'd met two years ago. Without gloves, he'd even helped sort out rocks and dirt clods.

By 12:30 we had 150 bread sticks under control and everyone left. Somewhere in my busy week I will have to bake the other half.

Meanwhile, because we had these wonderful tomatoes, Ernie suggested we invite friends and daughter Ramona's family over that evening for BLT's for an easy supper.

"We will pig out on BLT's," he said. Sounded wonderful. After cooling and freezing the bread sticks, I grabbed a quick bite of lunch between typing out CattleWomen's Corner, then drove to the newspaper office in Enterprise. A stop at the grocery store, then home to bake two raspberry pies for supper, as Rose had said Ernie's favorite pie was raspberry.

Since Linde works on the digger, and son-in-law Charley had to work late, we didn't eat until nearly 7:30. Everyone built their own bacon, lettuce and tomato sandwich and then ate raspberry pie while watching a Baxter Black cowboy poetry video on our TV. Doug, looking incredibly weary and dirty, showed up after everyone left. I fixed him some hot stew, and we both crashed.

Last Sunday, Ben, Doug and I gathered 70 pair of cows and calves off the east moraine and drove them to the home ranch. The cows and their new fall calves were scattered way back up in the timber that flanks the sides of Mt. Howard. It required lots of riding and searching, then driving them into one bunch. After we got them out onto the road, several calves decided to run back or join neighboring cattle in an adjoining pasture. While I held the lead, Ben watched the rear and Doug rounded up the errant calves, no small feat.

I had my hands full with the mama cows in the lead. They knew where they were headed and wanted to get moving. As the day warmed, the little calves got tired and had to be pushed every inch of the way. It was nearly 2 p.m. when we wearily rode up to the bunkhouse and unsaddled our horses. We are still out more cows and calves, and will have to backride for them another time.

High up on the mountain slopes the tamaracks are just now beginning to turn golden. How I'd love to be sitting there in some high meadow near a seeping spring where, perhaps, I could hear a bull elk bugle, or watch the floating cobwebby filigree drift in the hazy autumn air.

October 15—A glowing orange-colored sun rose through a smoky haze this frostless morning. It is the 68th day of no measurable rain. The smoke seems to have drifted in from somewhere, possibly Union County. Our canyons, hills and forests are extremely dry. The irrigated valleys remain green and the winter grain fields, which had to be irrigated to make them sprout, resemble spring, not fall.

Owing to the dryness, the autumn colors are especially lovely. Green-gold willows and cottonwoods by the creeks and ditches; the tamarack, whose rusty gold needles take on a deeper hue each day; in the high country, aspens glitter gold, their falling leaves floating upon the waters of Hurricane Creek. Throughout the dry forest and along the dusty trails, the bushes wear rusts, reds and burnt sienna, which mingle with the whiteness of snowberry.

Early yesterday afternoon, our two potato harvesters clanged their noisy way down the final rows. The cellars are full. The weary crew is glad, and today a few remain for the clean-up.

Friday evening, we will invite all 25 workers and their families to our traditional harvest dinner in the shop. Before concentrating on all that cooking, Doug and I plan to take a little R&R ourselves and head to Cow Creek tomorrow, and maybe get in a little steelhead fishing. Of course I'll take my camera along, as the Imnaha Gorge is one of my favorite subjects.

Last Tuesday, I took Scotty's place on the digger in the afternoon while she attended a class in Enterprise. We gals wore masks or scarves over our noses, and goggles to keep out the dust and dirt. Not a pleasant job. After a while, one of the truck drivers relieved me so I was able to return home to my typewriter and finish last week's column.

During these final days of potato harvest Doug has been battling a bad bout of flu. With the responsibility of harvest behind, he can hopefully recover.

Wednesday morning I assembled my canning supplies, and Ernie and Rose came down to help me tackle those tomatoes. While Ernie peeled onions and garlic, and cleaned bell peppers for me to put in the food processor, Rose diced tomatoes. My kitchen fairly hummed with activity and conversation, and soon we had two batches of salsa ready to can.

For lunch we cleared a space among the salsa and made Reuben sandwiches, using some of my fresh sauerkraut. After Ernie and Rose left, I canned 15 quarts and five pints of salsa, plus five quarts of tomato juice. That evening, leaving Doug to rest, I joined family and company at Linde and Pat's for an enchilada and refried bean supper. Our salsa passed the taste test!

On Thursday I washed four loads of clothes, hung them on the line, then baked another batch of sourdough bread sticks to freeze for Saturday's dinner. Cleaned eggs to sell and was ready by 10:45 to pick up Rose and take her with me to the CattleWomen's meeting.

On the way through Joseph, I picked up a box of plums that John and Ruth Steel had saved for me to make jam. Rose and I had lunch at the Cloud Nine Bakery in Enterprise where our CattleWomen meet. She enjoyed meeting other Wallowa County ranch women.

We had a large turnout of members at this meeting, and it was gratifying to see so many young ranch wives becoming involved. Soon, they will be the ones to carry on after we older ones step back. Our new young and capable president, Linda Childers, presided and we completed plans for catering the Chamber of Commerce dinner Saturday evening.

I was supposed to watch grandchildren on Friday while mom worked on the digger, as there was no school in Imnaha that day, but other arrangements were made. Daughter Ramona got a day off and son-in-law Charley said he'd watch grandson Bart, so we ended up taking Rose and Ernie for a hike up in our mountains. It was only a short hike up Hurricane Creek to Slick Rock Creek and back, but it did give them a taste of our high country.

The skies were deep blue in color, the fall foliage was very colorful and the waters of Hurricane Creek were so clear you could see every rock on the bottom. The trails were very dusty and it is the driest I've ever seen the mountains this time of year. We were surprised to see snow patches left on the northern flanks of Sacajawea. Otherwise, the awesome peaks were bare, painted many colors by the different types of rock formations. The cottonwood and aspen thickets trembled gold as a fall breeze wafted down the canyon. We ate our lunches alongside the creek, near the cutoff to Thorpe Creek basin.

Returned home to make a batch of plum jam. That evening, grandson Bart, Doug and I listened on the radio to the football game. The Enterprise Savages were playing Grant Union (John Day) here, and Bart's brother and cousin played. They are both seniors and the Savages won. Yeah!

Saturday was spent baking the final 100 sourdough bread sticks needed for the chamber dinner that night. Meanwhile, all over the county, CattleWomen were busy preparing more food. Linde had her hands full with a Greek salad, which took most of the day. Then she stopped by to pick up neighbor Betty Van's cake, and drove down here. Together, we picked up Ardis Klages and headed for Cloverleaf Hall. Trudy Allison was already there, busy with the tri-tip beef roasts.

Everything was ready to serve by 7 p.m. All our hard work paid off; the meal was a success. We wearily cleaned up the tables and kitchen, and headed back to our country homes.

Sunday found Doug, Mike McFetridge and me in the saddle again, back-riding for those missing cows and their fall calves. Doug and I rode over a large area, but all we saw were cow tracks. No cows! Doug rode on up a ridge and I returned to the meadow where we'd seen five pair earlier. Just before I reached the meadow, here came Mike, trailing 25 pair off the hill. Old hand Mike had saved the day.

Even though we were still out three more, we went out on the road with what we had. The day warmed up rapidly, as usual, but the cows and calves traveled better this time, and we arrived at the ranch around 4 p.m.

Son Todd was here yesterday to reset the shoes on our horses. And this afternoon we must move the 40 pair we brought off the moraine earlier, to another rented pasture. Ben and I gathered and drove the herd to Hockett's and so I didn't get this column typed.

Now it is 5:30 a.m. on October 16 and I am sitting at the kitchen table typing the final copy so I can get this in the mail before the deadline...and we can go fishing.

October 20—There is a good three inches of snow on the ground this morning. All of a sudden it is winter. A fire crackles in the old Monarch and the Revere-ware tea kettle is steaming. I threw some hay to the two milk cows and their six calves, and treated Alfie to some, too.

Ben and Steve are headed to the hills to haul in the bulls, and Doug is off to the potato cellar to run sonic potatoes that were left over, so the Enterprise FFA Chapter can sell them for a money-making project.

After all that cooking for the harvest party last week, not to mention the scrubbing of heavy pots and pans afterward, I called Marilyn Goebel, a member of our photo club, to ask if she would like to drive to Cow Creek with me and photograph the Imnaha Gorge.

"Sure", she said. After a late start, we arrived at the Cow Creek bridge just before noon. The colors may not be as vibrant as last year, due to the dry conditions, but the gorge is always a photographer's dream. Clouds gave way to sunlight and made for lovely effects against the canyon walls. Coming out the long, winding, narrow dirt road, we witnessed the moon's appearance over those awesome rim rocks. As the last light of day lingered on the highest rims, the moon hung suspended above them.

Knowing the golden-blue days of October were numbered, Linde and I paid a visit to Kathy Hadley, who is herding sheep out in the north end of Wallowa County. We had become acquainted with Kathy as a result of her husband, Jay, working on our potato cellar crew. They both attended the harvest party and, after I expressed an interest in writing about her life, she said to come on out—so we did.

Golden tamarack needles sift down in the wind to land on the dry, frosted grasses that grow in a sparsely forested area near the edge of a long meadow. Ponderosa pines whisper as, far off in the distance, the blue outline of the snow-less Wallowas traces the skyline.

Kathy Hadley, leading her saddle horse and accompanied by two border collie dogs, emerges from the timber behind her band of 1300 sheep. The young woman's sheepherder wagon is parked on a ridge further up the wooded hill. It is late morning and the sheep are wandering, grazing their way slowly down from the timbered bedground to the meadow, heading in the direction of a large pond where they will drink.

Aside from the tinkling of sheep bells and the gentle signing of the wind, there is no other sound. The air is gentle and the sun is warm, but the wind clouds are gathering overhead; the weather is changing.

October's Indian Summer days are dwindling, and soon Kathy and her sheep will return to Ione for the winter.

Kathy has been herding sheep for 17 years, working for outfits in Utah, Wyoming and Idaho before being hired by her present employer, Skye Krebs, whose family-owned operation runs 4,500 sheep. The Krebs family runs five summer hands and three winter hands. Kathy's band includes 900 lambs, 300 yearling ewes, and 20 bucks. They are Targhees which are a relatively new breed: bred, she says, for their herdability. Kathy says Targhees are a Rambouillet and Columbia cross, with some Merino thrown in.

Asked how she became a sheepherder, Kathy said, "When I was first married, my husband, Jay, was an auto mechanic. When spring came, Jay would look longingly out the window, wishing he could be up in the mountains. One day, he quit his job and we took what money we had, purchased enough supplies to last all summer, and lived in a tent in the mountains until fall."

Kathy recalls, "The worst time was when we had to return to town to find a job. We both loved living far out where it was peaceful and quiet. One day, while driving around Idaho, we met up with a sheep herder. We asked him if we could become sheepherders, and he replied, 'Sure, just come up to my camp, bring a case of beer, and I'll show you how to become a sheepherder'."

Kathy and Jay took the fellow up on his offer and, armed with a case of beer, they found the herder in his camp. Kathy said the herder proceeded to drink the beer, and they didn't learn a single thing about herding sheep. Pretty soon the old fellow drove off in his pickup and, thinking he was finally going to do something with the sheep, they walked over to where he had gone, only to find he had dumped beer cans over a hill into a dump pile consisting of hundreds of beer cans.

Some good did come from their visit, however, as the old herder gave them names of several sheep outfits that might hire them. That winter, Jay went back to being a mechanic, but the desire to find a shepherding job still haunted them.

They drove around Utah and Wyoming, until, finally, at Bear Lake, Idaho, they found a herder, a wino, who claimed he herded only one side of his band.

"The outfit was so hard up, they hired us on the spot," said Kathy. She said herding sheep was hard to do, but having two people helped. She claims there isn't any one way to herd sheep, that there are as many ways as there are sheepherders.

"One must be ready to make quick decisions at a given situation," she says. "Any kind of a job is an extension of one's personality," and has to do with the number of decisions to be made. "It's a stylized thing. Each herder has his own style. For instance, an insecure person will herd the sheep tight."

"Sheep," says Kathy, "have natural instincts, and you soon learn how they react to different situations." The looser they graze, she feels, the better. "That way, the grasses won't be overgrazed; but then again," she adds, "One can't lose any sheep. The boss wants them found. There must be a balance, which is achieved by knowing the sheep's habits, as well as the perimeter of their territory."

When it's stormy, she says, sheep will run around a lot more. "Different breeds react differently to similar conditions. Sheep like to go up at night and down in the morning."

Kathy and her saddle horse, an Arabian gelding named "Roger," follow the sheep, watching the lead. She says each band has its leaders and followers, like people, and she has control of the band when she can control the lead.

There are no rigid rules to follow when herding sheep, says Kathy. "Every day is different. The largest factor affecting herders is being alone. When you're alone, you have no input from other people. It takes time to work out problems, but when you are out here, in the quiet, with the sheep, you can sort through things and come to grips with problems easier.

"You become an exaggerated extension of yourself. You notice things more, too. When you do meet someone, you notice all the intricacies of their personality. Someone has come into your space!" When she and Jay visit a big city, it is a culture shock, she says.

Kathy, wearing an often-patched Levi jacket, talks in a soft, soothing voice. There is a look of serenity in her face and sincerity in her words. I ask whether Kathy and Jay have any children.

"The sheep are my children," she says, as she unbuckles her horse's hobbles and rides off toward her sheep, heading for the watering hole. The wind is rising and the dark clouds nearly obscure the distant Wallowas.

And now, as I write here at home, I try to envision Kathy out there in the snowy north country, herding her sheep. Perhaps smoke is curling up from the stove pipe in her sheepherder's wagon. The long drought has broken, and once more it is safe to have a fire.

October 21—In the pre-dawn cold, I heard the geese calling in the silence created by falling snow. At first I thought I was hearing crows until, at daylight, I saw their long, wavering skeins of geese flying southward, dull-dark in the leaden sky.

Now, at mid-morning, the silence is replaced by the bawling of cows and calves as the men brand and work our fall calves, and spray the cows. The early morning snow that sifted so quietly down has melted, but the white snowline lies just above us on upper Prairie Creek. Up there, next to the timber, last week's snow remains, and every day since has added its accumulation.

The mountains are shrouded in clouds. I caught a glimpse of Ruby Peak up there earlier, exposed briefly in the swirling mists; a breathtaking, sunlit, snow-covered fragment glowing in the cold before the clouds once more claimed the mountain.

An apple pie bakes in the oven, its fragrance permeating the kitchen; long johns hang, drying at the back of the wood stove; a pot of vegetable/beef soup simmers and bubbles on the old Monarch. My Barred Plymouth Rock pullets have the run of the garden now, and also the raspberry patch, as they happily scratch for bugs and worms.

October 23—Three inches of snow fell last night. Linde and I drove to Alder Slope and picked apples for making apple cider. We trudged to and fro from the orchard to the Jeep, lugging buckets and boxes laden with four varieties of crisp, sweet fall apples.

We wore gloves to keep our hands warm, as snow still clung to the branches and fell down our necks when we reached from the ladder to pick the big apples growing up high. We laughed when the Jeep was loaded. There were so many apples—we had picked three trees clean.

"Takes a lot of apples to make cider," I said. Linde drove real slow because of the load. Tomorrow, we will make cider at her place.

Doug appeared at the door this evening bearing a cock pheasant he had shot. Supper! I fried the bird in a skillet on the wood cook stove, and made mashed potatoes and gravy.

October 24—Today found Doug, Bill, Linde and me in Pat and Linde's big barn, pressing apple cider. Snow showers swirled over the Wallowas and it was bitterly cold, but Linde's husband, Pat, had set up a sheepherder's stove mounted on legs, so we could warm our hands. As it warmed up, snow began sliding off the barn roof where we were working. *Swoosh!* A blue jay scolded us from a tall pine tree, the bright flash of blue a cheery sight.

We began washing the apples in a tin wash tub, then quickly got a system going where one of us fed apples into the grinder, someone else cranked down on the press, and a third person poured the strained juice into a bowl and began filling empty jugs. We set up the old-fashioned handmade press in the barn, out of the weather, in case it snowed again. When the press was cranked down, the beautiful golden juice flowed out below and ran into the clean bucket. It was both fun and work.

Linde took some of the apple pulp to her hogs, and later deer would come down out of the woods to have themselves a feast. We couldn't wait to taste our product and passed around a quart jar of the cold cider. Contained therein was the very essence of fall. We tried to mix the different varieties so the flavors would blend, but all the jugs were a slightly different color. The sun came out briefly; all 29 gallons glowed golden in the light, and Linde snapped a picture. We finished just as another snow storm came swirling down off the mountain.

It was noon after we finished hosing down the press and washing up, so we retreated to the warmth of Linde's log home and warmed ourselves by the big stone fireplace before eating lunch. After partaking of hot Reuben sandwiches, we feasted on Linde's German plum pastry, fresh from the oven, made with Alder Slope plums, also picked yesterday. A perfect ending to a perfect time.

I returned home just in time to greet two grandchildren who will spend tonight at grandma's house.

October 25—Big, fat flakes of snow fell out of the sky this morning. The children and I looked up and imagined someone up there letting loose hundreds of cotton balls. The snow was nearly gone by noon, the eaves were dripping with the melting.

October 26—Today dawned a nice fall day, wet and without any frost. Doug announced that he and neighbor Pat were going fishing down on the Imnaha, so I packed him a lunch and he was off. It is good to see him feeling well again after being under the weather so long.

October 27—I began a frenzy of house-cleaning; packed all the junk out of the back porch, scrubbed the cement floor, and then had to deal with what to do with all that "stuff." Boy, things sure do accumulate on back porches, especially on our ranch.

In between cleaning, I baked a loaf of sourdough french bread and delivered it, warm, to the people who loaned us the cider press. Then home to make sourdough biscuits for Doug and me to go with our supper soup.

The evenings are long now; I've taken to reading again. Am halfway through *Talking Leaves,* an anthology of contemporary native American short stories, edited and introduced by Craig Lesley. Craig, whom I met at "Fishtrap," is the award-winning author of *Winterkill* and *Riversong.* This collection of short stories echoes the voices of Cherokee, Chippewa, Sioux, Navaho and Modoc. The stories are uniquely their own; each author writes of what he knows best.

October 28—I had spent a busy day today, finishing my column so I could devote the remainder of the week to Sandra. I baked an apple pie and continued with house cleaning. Sandra and Fred arrived in time for supper, which consisted of trout that Doug caught in the Imnaha, fried red potatoes, corn on the cob from our freezer, and sourdough biscuits.

October 29—Crawled out of bed at 5 a.m. to find it snowing outside, as cold Canadian air has begun moving into our area. Good thing our company arrived last night.

After the wood cookstove heated up good and hot, I fried up a big cast iron frypan of fresh mountain oysters, scrambled eggs and warmed the sourdough biscuits. Somehow we couldn't talk Sandra into eating any oysters, but Fred tackled them with gusto. Sandra remembered they were here during branding of the fall calves last year, and was wise to "mountain oysters." The men branded another bunch of fall calves that day, but one of the dogs ate every oyster! Sandra was happy.

Due to snowy and icy road conditions, Sandra and I stayed inside our cozy house and caught up on a year's visiting. The temperature continued downward all that day, so we fed the fire and cooked up a big batch of sweet'n sour spare ribs to go with a kettle of rice for supper.

To bed early, as Doug and I will begin our cow elk hunt in the morning.

October 30—It was a crispy-cold five degrees when I ventured outside at 5:30 a.m. with my tea kettle of hot water to thaw out the chickens' water, and feed hay to the milk cows and their calves. Moonlight sparkled off the snow in that silent, cold dawn.

It felt good to stomp off the dry snow and return to the cozy warmth of the wood cookstove to cook oatmeal, bacon and eggs for breakfast, make lunches, gather up hunting gear, and leave for the hills. Fred rode along with us, but Sandra, on her vacation, decided to sleep in and keep the home fires burning.

Out in the wintry Zumwalt country, the sun looked more like a moon as it rose through a cold layer of ghostly ground fog. Hoarfrost covered every blade of grass and weed. Eventually, the sun burned through the fog, resembling a Halloween pumpkin, its golden light seeping into the frozen hills. Cobwebby fog snagged in the draws, and far off we could see the muted blues of the Seven Devil Mountains in Idaho, as well as the distant Wallowa range. The bitter cold creates its own beauty.

Several hungry coyotes were out hunting, as were golden eagles, hawks and crows. As we drove past our cattle range, it resembled "diamond fields" as the bunch grass glittered in the morning light. Once in a while a wandering breeze would shatter the frozen grass and send crystals floating into the cold air. Stock ponds and creeks were glazed with ice. Not a single elk or wapiti track did we see.

We stopped on a high hill to glass the miles of open country that lay in all directions, drinking hot coffee and chocolate from our thermos, and ate some of Sandra's banana bread.

We met Dick Hammond on his saddle horse, leading a pack horse alongside the Pine Creek road. He hadn't seen any elk either. Dick's wife, Betty, who had been waiting for him in the pickup while he hunted, said she had visited more people this morning than she had in years. As friends drove past, she just stepped out and had a good visit. One thing led to another and pretty soon Dick began recounting previous hunting experiences.

As we drove off, Betty and I agreed we should just plan a potluck out there along the Pine Creek road next year, and that way we could take time to see friends we don't seem to have time to visit in the valley.

After eating our lunches and glassing more of those cold hills, we headed home to Sandra. That night we didn't have any elk stories, but we did enjoy antelope steaks for supper.

October 31—A north wind shifted to the south, the weather warmed to 26 degrees and it began to snow. I carved a jack-o-lantern pumpkin and made rice-crispie squares, but it was such a cold, snowy night, no trick or treaters made it this far out on Tenderfoot Valley Road. We ate roast beef, mashed potatoes and gravy as a candle glowed orange inside the pumpkin on the doorstep, and and the snow fell softly into the night.

November 1—November came to Prairie Creek with a 30-degree reading and seven inches of new snow on the ground. Tree limbs drooped and pole fences were lined with snow. I sloshed through the deep white stuff to feed my animals. While feeding the pullets, I caught our black cat in the act of eating eggs. And I had been putting the blame on the cold weather for the decline in egg production!

I made lunches for Doug and Fred, and they drove out with the crew to haul several truck loads of spring calves in from the hills to wean. Sandra and I ate lunch in town, after which we attended a high school football game, Enterprise vs. Joseph at Joseph. We bundled up in blankets and watched the Savages beat the Eagles on that snowy football field.

Every so often, Chief Joseph Mountain's snowy summit would appear between dark clouds. A weak November sun came out briefly, but by the time the game was over that familiar chill had settled over the valley.

While cattle truck loads of bawling calves arrived, Sandra and I fixed hot tamale pie for supper.

November 2—Clear, cold and five degrees, but we at least could see the mountains again. To warm us up I fixed sausage gravy over hot buttermilk biscuits.

The men ran our weaned calves through the chutes and moved a bunch of fall calvers to the ranch. That evening we all celebrated Sandra and Fred's 40th wedding anniversary in Vali's Alpine Delicatessen at Wallowa Lake.

November 3—About six inches of cold, wet snow is beginning to melt around here this morning, and I can watch the dripping icicles through the windows. Sporadic gusts of wind toss purple clouds across the dark Prairie Creek skies. A curtain of falling snow obscures the mountains. The weaned spring calves have ceased their bawling and settled down to eat hay and grain. Ben and Steve are hauling more calves in from the hills today, so our quiet will be short-lived.

Brightening our kitchen table are some bright orange persimmons that repose in one of Olaf's pottery bowls. The persimmons are a gift from my childhood chum Sandra and her husband, Fred, who arrived Monday night to spend a week with us.

People often mistake Sandra and me for sisters. We were both raised in Placer County, California. We both grew up on small ranches in that sparsely settled, rolling foothill country known as the Mt. Pleasant District; we rode the same school bus, graduated from Lincoln High School, and although Sandra was a grade ahead of me and a year older, we've remained close friends for nearly 50 years.

I was matron of honor at Sandra and Fred's wedding, November 2, 1951, when my first-born daughter, Ramona, was just a month old. Yesterday, Saturday, 40 years to the day later, we had lunch together; Ramona, Sandra and I. How quickly the years slip by.

November 7—Our photo club held its annual dinner meeting this evening, at Vali's Alpine Delicatessen at Wallowa Lake. We enjoyed a delicious steak dinner prepared by Mike and served by his friendly wife, Maggie. The small eatery overflowed with members and spouses.

November 8—Partially clear after the night-time fog crept away, leaving hoarfrost forming in spider web patterns on every weed, stick and blade of grass. Most every morning now we hear the wild geese winging overhead. Our resident geese stay through the winter, while others continue to fly southward. It is refreshing to hear them and step out of a morning to breathe deeply the cold autumn air. Gets the old blood going to meet the day.

Elk hunters have invaded our valley again. Pulling trailers full of horses, mules, and ATVs; driving motor homes or towing camp trailers; they come, mostly to get away, to take to the woods. Many don't care if they shoot an elk or not. They look forward all year to this annual escape. Some set up elaborate tents with sheepherder stoves to keep warm. Lucky for them, our snowy weather changed to fairer skies that were followed by warmer temperatures. The tamarack trees on the slopes of the mountains are at their peak of color now, and the snow-covered tops above make a beautiful backdrop to their hunter camps.

Reports filter in...rumor has it, one camp shot three bulls opening morning! Or "We just saw cows," or "That six-point was just out of rifle range." It is entertaining to listen in on the conversations at local coffee gathering places. Quite often a hunter doesn't return to camp, and then our local Search and Rescue patrol is called out to comb the area in which he was last seen.

November 9—It was such a nice warm, clear day I decided to do some photographing and ended up walking about four miles in my "barn boots," which made for sore heels. I hadn't intended to walk far, but one thing led to another and I just kept stumbling onto interesting subjects.

Returning at noon, I mixed up a batch of Sylvia's bread dough, then tuned into our local radio station and listened to the Enterprise-Umatilla state playoff game. Umatilla won, but it was an exciting game, and the last high school football for my two grandsons, who are now seniors.

Having dug the last of my garden carrots and beets that morning, I made a fresh batch of pickled beets and scrubbed the carrots for supper. We invited Max and Millie and their two grandsons over for supper, for fresh bread, antelope roast, mashed potatoes, gravy and fresh vegetables. I also baked another batch of persimmon cookies for dessert.

November 10—After all that cooking yesterday, Doug took me out to breakfast Sunday morning at "Kohlhepp's Kitchen" in Joseph, which was like old home week because we were joined by friends Bud and Ruby Zollman, whom we had a good visit with over breakfast.

Later I rode to Lostine with Doug to pick up some lumber he'd ordered to repair a loading chute and a bridge on the ranch.

As early darkness crept upon Prairie Creek, I walked outside to shut my chickens in for the night. High up in the old willow trees, two great horned owls called to each other; then, echoing from every fold in the hills…coyote music. Another reason we enjoy living here, where we can share a link with the wilderness that surrounds us.

November 12—It is early afternoon and the nice warm rain that fell all morning has ceased. As a brisk wind blows away the rain curtains, our dark blue and snowy white mountains are revealed to us again.

More bawling down at the corrals as we receive some purchased calves. Due to such nasty weather, the men didn't run the calves through the chutes to vaccinate them this morning, but now that the rain has let up they are going ahead with it.

Thirteen-year old granddaughter Carrie has been staying with us since yesterday. She is a delight to have around. Yesterday afternoon, she and I cooked up a storm. We made lasagna, which we delivered to a neighbor who was at home after having surgery. We made another casserole for our supper and popped it into the oven before we left.

We drove up Sheep Creek Hill and taking a dirt road that wound up a draw to a ranch that lies east of ours. Armed with a loaf of homemade bread, a tossed salad, and a basket of persimmon cookies to go with the hot lasagna, we trooped into Diane's kitchen. She was very grateful for the food. All week long, our local CattleWomen have been taking turns preparing meals for Diane's family.

People helping people is one of the reasons we enjoy living in Wallowa County. Another example was last Wednesday night, "Taco Night" at the Lostine Tavern. *Buy one taco for $1.50, get one free. Bring a pie for the pie auction,* which was a benefit for a little Lostine boy who must undergo treatment for cancer. Doug bid on a pecan pie and ended up paying $40 for it, after which two lemon pies sold for $100 each! More than $53,000 was raised that night for the needy family.

After driving Carrie to school this morning, I went by the vet's to pick up vaccine for working the new calves.

Returning to the ranch on this wet Tuesday, I passed neighbor Bob Perry, afoot, moving his band of sheep. Just Bob, his quick-moving little border Collie, and his sheep, all walking in the rain.

My husband returned from town this morning, a can of pumpkin in one hand and a carton of whipping cream in the other. I took this to be a pretty strong hint to bake a pumpkin pie. So, after the old Monarch's oven registered 400 degrees, I placed two spicy pumpkin pies in there to bake. What is it about a wood stove oven that makes pies taste better?

While on the subject of baking I hope you readers tried out Sylvia Talich's bread recipe, which appeared recently in Agri-Times. It's delicious. I baked two loaves last week and made more today. Now, as I type, that wonderful aroma of bread baking floats through the house, that yeasty smell that warms the heart.

The six calves have been weaned off my two milk cows, and although Startch and her daughter bagged up some, they don't seem to miss their offspring and adopted calves at all. Each morning now, I go out and put hay in their feeder so the new calves growing in their bellies can grow.

November 13—A sudden snow flurry erupts as I walk to the barn lot to hay my cows. Soft wet flakes, driven toward me by the wind, stick on my coveralls like goose down. Through the falling feathers I see my two cows, patiently awaiting their breakfast. The ground, only days before dusty and dry, is now muddy.

Carrie went home last night, as her parents returned safely from Salem. I miss having her around.

November 18—Doug and I will leave in the morning for Portland. As always, we will experience a bit of "culture shock" in the big city. Instead of looking out our window in the morning to see our quiet hills and mountains, we will look down from our room at the Red Lion to see a teeming city.

If we are lucky, it will be clear enough to see Mt. Hood rising above it all, but we will awaken to the sounds of Portland instead of Chester's crowing, the bawling of cows and calves, or Alfie's braying. Country sounds will be replaced by sirens, traffic noises, and people in a hurry to catch the next light rail. We won't be able to smile at familiar faces on the street, but perhaps we can still smile. And maybe some will be returned.

Around 6 a.m. we should be in the Beef Council office, picking up our supplies for the Beef Blitz and taking time to have coffee, juice and sweet rolls with Diane Byrne and her staff, as well as other Oregon CattleWomen and Cattlemen who will be taking part in the school blitz.

Hopefully, by 9 a.m. Doug and I will be in Jan Preedy's classroom at Thomas Junior High School in Hillsboro like last year, presenting our

Beef Education Blitz. This year's theme features Chuck Wagon Cooking, with a "Come an' get it" style!

It should be fun, and draw attention to the new "Cowboys Then and Now" museum, of which our industry is so proud. While the museum tells the story of Oregon's cattle ranching history, Doug and I will bring "the human element" of contemporary cattle ranching to the classroom. We will also demonstrate how to make beef jerky, and talk about sourdough biscuits and beans, which were and still are an important part of the working cowboy's diet. Along with dispelling some of the myths and righting some of the wrongs that come across in the media these days, we will show videos and give each student a chance to ask questions about our lives "east of the Cascades."

That evening, along with other CattleWoman, Cattlemen and leg-islators, we will meet with our "adopted legislator," Bill Dwyer, in the recently opened museum.

Thursday and Friday will be devoted to the annual OCA/OCW con-vention, which will keep us busy attending meetings.

On Sunday we travel to Salem to visit a daughter and a grandson, then return to our ranch, which lies at the opposite end of the state. Looking at my calendar I discover Thanksgiving is only a few days after our return! How does one slow down the time?

A fine snow falls outside this morning, but it is having a hard time sticking to the ground. Yesterday was cloudy, and a warm, misty rain fell into the night. All this moisture is extremely welcome and we refer to this bad weather, as good. Even the newly purchased calves have ceased their bawling now, and settled down to life without mama. Mother cows continue to range the hill pastures, but if it snows up there again, they will be trailed ink. he valley and fed hay all winter.

Last Saturday morning Linde and I drove to Imnaha, which still retains much of its pretty fall color. A gusty wind followed us down along Little Sheep Creek and tall pines thrashed above us as we left frozen Prairie Creek "on top." It was much warmer in the canyons.

As we approached the bridge spanning the Imnaha, just below where Little Sheep Creek joins the river, we noticed these small handmade "Burma Shave" type signs. All in a rhyme, proclaiming the Tomahawk 4-H Club's bake sale being held at the Imnaha store. The last sign merely read "hungry?"

We were abruptly stopped on the bridge itself by an energetic group of 4-H'ers led by one of my own grandchildren, who said we must pay a toll before crossing the bridge! After paying the toll at the toll booth, cleverly constructed of cardboard, we received a cookie in return and proceeded on up the steep hill to the Imnaha store.

Two weathered wooden Indians stood guard at the door as we walked inside to where tables fairly groaned with homemade goodies. There were donuts, cinnamon rolls, blackberry custard pies, pumpkin and apple pies, cookies of every description, and packages of mouthwatering carmel corn.

The 4-H'ers were doing a land office business. Hunters, far from home, were some of their best customers, as were members of the community from up and down the river. They came to sip hot coffee, visit neighbors and buy homemade pastries. 4-H leaders and parents, too, were there supervising the activities.

The brisk wind continued to blow, but did nothing to discourage those youngsters. They blew about in the street, like the leaves falling from the trees, and above them loomed the steep rim rocks. As the leaves provide humus for the earth, so shall the children enrich our lives.

The money raised will be put to good use, purchasing supplies needed for their various projects. Linde and I visited several of our canyon neighbors before heading up the long road to Prairie Creek.

In an old orchard along the road we saw several mule deer feeding on fallen apples shaken down in the wind. And cows. There are always cows ambling along the Imnaha highway this time of year. Their calves having been weaned, they are heading home.

After running some errands in town, Linde and I returned to my kitchen where we peeled and chopped apples to make mincemeat. Earlier, I had simmered some elk from the freezer until tender, then ground the meat in my grinder. To this we added the apples, apple cider, vinegar, raisins, spices and sweet things. The fragrant mixture was then cooked in a large heavy kettle on the old Monarch until the apples were tender and thick. Now I have mincemeat in the freezer and kept some out fresh for Thanksgiving pies.

Remember the black cat that was found eating eggs in the chicken's nests? Well, Doug captured it in a gunny sack and promptly delivered it to granddaughter Carrie on upper Prairie Creek. The next day my egg production shot up dramatically and the problem appears to be solved...until yesterday, when I spied a black cat climbing over the chicken wire pen and making her way into the hen house.

Quickly I ran up there, and caught the cat in the act of sucking eggs! Only it wasn't the same black cat, it was a stray. Now I'm wondering if we wrongly accused one of our raspberry kittys.

Anyone (without chickens) need a black cat?

November 22—Peering out our front window into the wet gray dawn, I watch misty rain meet ice-crusted snow. The constant sound of city traffic is replaced by solitude stored in hills, prairie and mountains. After nearly a week of big city hype, I can relax, collect my thoughts, and reflect on the experience.

A heavy frost lay thick over Prairie Creek last Tuesday morning as Doug and I packed our bags and drove out of the country toward the city. Snow whitened the roadside forests as we sped over the summit of the Blue Mountains. We ate lunch at Fontaines in Hermiston, where Doug attended a meeting of the Blue Mountain Potato board. It was late afternoon by the time we pulled onto the freeway again, heading down the Columbia Gorge in a pouring rainstorm to supper in Cascade Locks.

I caught glimpses through car headlights of autumn color lining the river. Cars hydroplaned by us at frightening speeds and we, too, skimmed over great pools of water in the road. Passing trucks blinded us in spray. Luckily, we exited the rainy speedway at Troutdale without incident and pulled up to a Shiloh Inn to spend the night.

We left Troutdale before dawn Wednesday morning and drove to Oregon Square, where we found the new Beef Council office. Other ranchers, like ourselves, were sipping coffee, munching sweet rolls and visiting before receiving packets containing instructions for our beef school blitz.

I had phoned Nancy Forth earlier in her room at the Red Lion, wanting to know what to do with the items we had for her Country Store. Nancy thanked me for providing "wake-up service." Since we had an hour before leaving for our school, we took the opportunity to view for the first time the new Cowboys Then and Now Museum.

Mick Scott, of the Oregon Beef Council, gave us a tour and activated the talking cowboy mannequin, whose voice and expressions were so real that we were tempted to talk back. An authentic chuckwagon donated by Mike Hanley, a Jordan Valley rancher, stole the show. Parked on real Eastern Oregon dirt and surrounded by sagebrush, it was bordered by a true-to-life mural of Oregon's high desert. A chuckwagon cook wearing a soiled flour sack apron stood by a dutch oven of beans soaking next to a sourdough jug. You could almost smell the steaming coffee and hear the far-off wail of a coyote.

Taking up an entire wall was a time-line depicting in words and photos the history of Oregon's cattle industry. Reading along the time-line I felt a renewed sense of pride in the way we make our living:

The Oregon Territory opened to settlement in the 1830s. To meet the need for cattle, Willamette Valley settlers formed the Willamette Cattle

Company. A veteran trail hand, Ewing Young, was their leader, and in 1837 they went to San Francisco to sell stock and purchase 830 Mexican cattle.

Ewing and eight other men drove the Longhorns northward, arriving 120 days later at Champoeg, near the Willamette River, with 630 head remaining. This was the beginning of commercial cattle raising in Oregon. By 1850 there were 123,093 settlers in Oregon, mostly in the north Willamette Valley. When Oregon asked for statehood in 1859, the senators said only western portions should be admitted; obviously, no one would ever live in Eastern Oregon!

But a few hardy souls did venture into this last frontier, and discovered grass, the primary ingredient in cattle raising. Today, great herds continue to graze the vast ranges that lie east of the Cascades. So, Western Oregon can eat beef and benefit from the hundreds of by-products produced from cattle.

An exact replica of a tack room has been constructed in the museum, where visitors are invited to "come sit a spell" on a bench surrounded by saddles and tack. A sign reads "Please Touch," and young visitors can ride a real saddle mounted on a springy log. We were happy to see the Hamley saddle that once belonged to Jidge Tippett, Doug's dad, displayed there, along with his rawhide riata.

A library opening off the museum provides not only a great resource center but serves as a meeting place as well. A small theater situated at the far end plays continuous videos projected onto a large screen. Through colorful images, "our story" is tastefully told.

After finding our way to Hillsboro and the Thomas Junior High School, we were greeted by Jan Preedy, same as last year, except for a different group of students. Doug and I began by telling the class about our lives and pointed out on an Oregon map where we lived. After answering questions, showing a video and talking about the cowboy museum, we demonstrated making jerky.

We repeated the presentation for four classes and during the last class we encountered a rather rambunctious group. One boy in particular was causing quite a stir. So I asked him what his name was.

"Benny," he replied.

"Benny, who don't you come up front and help with making jerky," I suggested. Doug proceeded to keep Benny so busy he didn't have any more time for troublemaking. After the class, I took his picture, which made him feel even more important.

As in years past, Doug and I felt good about this contact with our city cousins, and hopefully it helps bridge that very large gap that exists in our world today between producer and consumer.

All along the route, maple trees flamed red, orange, yellow and rust as we sped back to the Red Lion. By 5 p.m. Doug and I were attending a reception in the museum for school blitzers and our adopt-a-legislators. We visited with our adopted legislator, Bill Dwyer, whom I met for the first time while sampling chef Wayne Philen's tri-tip roast served with horseradish sauce, buns and relishes. I was most interested to learn from Bill that he has been involved in horse logging in the past.

The museum fairly hummed with conversation as we all shared our experiences in 22 schools that touched 2,000 students in and around Portland. Chiloquin CattleWoman Gerda Hyde walked back to the opening of the trade show with us under a sky full of stars that tried hard to compete with the bright lights of Portland.

November 25—One morning while we were in Portland, during some free time, I wandered across the street from the Red Lion and entered the newly-covered mall at Lloyd Center. The sun was out between showers, and Portland was all rain-washed. It seemed to me that morning that the city was made of sky and cloud, reflections of which glimmered in high rise windows. The mall, enclosed now under a many-windowed roof, glowed with natural light. Meier and Frank glittered with Christmas greenery and tinsel, tempting shoppers with myriad choices of baubles.

I entered the flow of humanity browsing along the mall, only instead of looking into the shops, I gazed upward like a country bumpkin at enormous wreaths that seemingly hung suspended from the sky. White doves flew from the wreathes with ribbons held in their beaks. High above, on a sky walk balcony, people ate at small tables under cloud and sky. Specialty shops beckoned at every door. Caramel corn, See's candy, and my failing: bookstores. Resisting the urge to purchase several, I settled on just one.

Doug and I enjoyed visiting Agri-Times editor Virgil Rupp over lunch in the Trade Show area, after which we all got down to the serious business of attending convention meetings.

After packing our bags Saturday morning we headed in pouring rain south to Salem. We took 99-E and wandered off on a back road that eventually led to a bank of the Willamette River and dead-ended. A sign read *Canby Ferry. $1.00 per vehicle, wait until the signal to drive on the ferry.* And sure enough, across the slowly-moving waters of the Willamette, a ferry made its steady way toward us.

We drove onto the old ferry and were soon transported peacefully to the far bank, then wound around over hill and dale, through green countryside displaying lots of autumn color, until we came to the small town of Aurora, which turned out to be filled with little else than antique shops.

Scurrying out of the rain, we popped into a little shop and sipped specialty coffee and found some interesting items we really didn't need, but thought we did...Like the Golden Guernsey milk bottle I found tucked into a dusty corner, and a cookbook on biscuits and scones.

We arrived in Woodburn and took Aunt Amey to lunch, then continued on to Salem to spend the night visiting daughter Linda and grandson, Jordan.

The next morning we headed east of the Cascades with a broader outlook on life, having sampled life on the western side for awhile. People, we found, are just people, east or west. All of us share the same basic needs, but, like always, we were glad to be home and re-establish the fact that we're pretty lucky to live here.

November 27—I spent the early part of this week meeting photojournalism deadlines before concentrating on Thanksgiving. While we were gone, the sourdough bread I donated to the 4-H radio auction had sold to Jan Bailey for $20.

So, because I had to bake all day anyway today, I baked Jan's loaf of bread. During that day I also baked one mincemeat and two pumpkin pies, a batch of rolls, cooked cranberry sauce and candied yams. It was a good day to spend in my warm, cozy kitchen as the wind blew snow around outside.

We sampled the fresh rolls that evening with clam chowder.

November 28—Thanksgiving Day dawned cloudy, but not as cold, and by mid-morning the clouds lifted to reveal sunlight that streamed through our windows and warmed up the house enough to let the fire die down.

Before morning chores, I mixed up the dressing, using the dried sage from my garden. The savory steam escaping from the giblets, cooking with onion and celery soon filled our house with that traditional smell. When the 20-pound turkey was stuffed and in the oven, I went out to feed Thanksgiving breakfast to my milk cows and chickens.

Granddaughter Carrie helped set the table, which we decorated with the pretty colored maple leaves brought back from the Willamette Valley. There were 13 of us around the kitchen table, which overflowed into the living room. As always, Thanksgiving was a fulfilling time for me, just having family around, sampling crisp skin on golden turkey, mashing potatoes, conversing while stirring gravy...Then finally sitting down to give thanks for it all.

After the feast the children raced around outside and inside, and consumed quantities of punch and pumpkin pie with whipped cream. It always seems to me that during these special occasions, love of family and friends, and food preparation are all linked together. Cooking delicious food is an act of love for those we love. Always has been, always will be.

November 29—In complete juxtaposition to yesterday's weather, a blizzard blew drifting snow across Prairie Creek this morning. Sculpted snow quickly formed drifts under the living room window. The chickens stayed in their hen house, cattle huddled in fence corners, and my mare Cal turned their backs to the storm.

After breakfast, Doug hauled a truck-load of hay to the hills to feed the cows out there, and got stuck, mired down beneath the snow. He walked to the horse pasture, caught a horse and saddled him, and rode to Dorrance Grade where he ran into Mt. Joseph Cattle Company's cowgirl, Sharon Tartar, who gave him a ride to the valley.

With a turkey sandwich and apiece of mincemeat pie under his belt, Doug drove one of our big tractors back out there and pulled the stuck truck out. I followed in another pickup and helped finish feeding hay.

By the time we hauled the horse back and Steve showed up to drive the tractor home, it was close to 8 p.m.

November 30—Our thermometer plunged to a frigid nine degrees, and our cattle began their long trek to the valley.

December 2—Today was Aunt Opal Tippett's funeral. Her obituary in the local paper told how she was born in Iowa on June 25, 1899, she is survived by five children, and she leaves 19 grandchildren and 32 great-grandchildren...But it left out that she had several great-great-grandchildren.

It told how she married Charley Tippett on December 29, 1915, but it didn't say she and Charley lived 50 years way out on Pine Creek, more than 30 miles north of Enterprise. The little house in which Opal and Charley lived and reared their family is still there, and the surrounding country hasn't changed much in all those years.

Alder Creek and Salmon Creek still join Pine Creek at the forks, just below their house. I remember Aunt Opal telling us that the forks was a favorite camping spot for the Nez Perce traveling through the country at that time. Charley and Opal farmed, raised livestock and grew their own food.

Aunt Opal always said life was hard, but good. It was there she bore her children, cooked, washed, and made do without the aid of the modern conveniences enjoyed today by her children and grandchildren. Once, she told about their infrequent trips to town in a horse-drawn wagon to purchase supplies.

"One time," she said, smiling at the recollection, "Charley forgot me, left me in town. He didn't even miss me until he came to the first gate!" Opal's Charley passed away in 1974. This grand little lady, who witnessed myriad changes in her lifetime, was a charter member of the Wallowa County CowBelles, and awarded an honorary lifetime membership in that organization.

Like so many others who are leaving us, Opal Tippett's life completes a chapter in Wallowa County's colorful history. And, at long last, she rests beside her beloved Charley in the Enterprise Cemetery, which overlooks the mountains they both loved.

We invited neighbor Pat to supper this evening, as he was "batching it," while wife Linde was off to Hawaii to help her mother-in-law move.

December 3—An icy breeze wanders over Prairie Creek's frozen snowfields on this clear, sunny morning. Golden dry grasses, sticking up through the snow, shudder in the invisible wind. Irregular dark lines of cattle feed on their daily ration of fragrant meadow hay scattered over their white pastures.

The final 300 head of cows and heifers trailed in from the hills over the weekend. Life will be a little easier for them now; no more rustling between frozen hills in search of grass. Large cattle trucks and trailers arrive at our loading chute this morning to haul our weaned calves to Hermiston, where they will spend the winter in warmer climes.

December 5—I awoke yesterday morning in time to see a thin crescent moon keeping company with the morning star. I was up early to be ready for grandchildren whom I'd been looking forward to seeing all week. The children spent the night and we caught up on reading and playing.

This morning, I drove James into his kindergarten to meet mom, who picked up Adele. As usual, I missed the children when they were gone.

December 6—It rained last night and into this morning, and melted most of our snow. Doug is away, attending the Winter Farm Fair in Hermiston.

The big Handcrafters' Holiday Bazaar opened today at Cloverleaf Hall. Each year this thing grows. Hope McLaughlin was there, sitting back in a corner, making colorful potholders from scraps left over from

Winter comes to Prairie Creek in this view of the Tippett barn.

sewing her lovely quilts. Husband Harold was there, too, selling his well-constructed folding wooden stools, tables and other wooden items.

Other booths offered homemade candy, dough art, paintings, ceramics, Christmas ornaments, and if you were hungry, the Imnaha Grange ladies would feed you homemade soup and pie. The old-time fiddlers were there fiddling away. There was even something for your horse.

Jim Blankenship had a table full of handmade horse-hair reins, bosals, hackamores, and saddle bags. Jim is into braiding rawhide, which is nearly a lost art, and he also makes chaps and other cowboy gear. As in years past, Jim would take his turn being "Santa" again.

For the first time in years, I wasn't involved with taking photos of children sitting on Santa's lap. Local high school photo students took that project on this year.

While I was in town I watched grandson Chad wrestle in a tournament at the Enterprise High School gym.

December 7—Doug and I joined friends for dinner this evening at the home of fellow rancher-neighbors Melvin and Mary Lou Brink. Mary Lou outdid herself in the kitchen, creating Chinese food that I will dream about. During this busy season, it feels good to take time for camaraderie with family and friends.

December 8—Grandson Shawn arrived early to help son Steve do the feeding. Grandma offered hot cocoa and cinnamon rolls to brave the cold, windy morning. After doing my own chores, I put a kettle of beef stew meat on the wood cookstove to simmer. I added onion, garlic, hay leaf and celeriac to the broth; when the meat was tender, I added tomatoes, cabbage, carrots and some small pasta.

Thick slices of home-made whole wheat/rye bread, dunked in that hearty soup, provided lunch and supper. That evening I curled up with the *The Snow Leopard,* and let author Peter Matthiessen transport me to the Himalaya. What an adventure that 250-mile trek was, from Pokara to the Tibetan Plateau. An adventure of the mind as well.

December 9—It was cold and clear in the hour preceding dawn, except for scattered dark clouds smeared across a mauve sky. As daylight seeped into Prairie Creek, dark etchings of mountains appeared and their snowy ramparts soon brightened with amber light as morning came. No matter how hectic my days, my mornings are calm; my favorite time.

Scattered remnants of snow follow fence-lines and frozen watercourses, and trace both sides of our country roads. The permanent snowline remains steadfast just below timberline on upper Prairie Creek. An icy, restless wind sweeps down from the wintry world of nearby snowy peaks. On the high exposed ridges of those peaks, the wind kicks up loose snow that swirls in white banners across the Wallowas. The cold December sun provides light, but no heat.

The men are sorting cows this morning, deciding which to cull and which to keep. In addition to their hay, the fall calvers and their growing calves are now being fed silage. Feathers ruffled and blown about in the wind, my Barred Plymouth Rock pullets search under the bare raspberry canes for dormant bugs.

Since the "cat problem" was solved, as the stray black cat mysteriously disappeared, egg production is back to normal. A small nativity scene, a gift from daughter Ramona, graces our piano top. The Christmas cards and letters are in the mail, and I've finished my gift list. I am creating pomanders, so their old-fashioned spicy fragrance fills my kitchen.

Using oranges, studded with cloves, they are now in a pottery bowl and curing in a mixture of spices. Doug built a frame to accommodate my state flower quilt, which takes up most of the living room. Now, whenever a granddaughter or neighbor comes by we can sit down, hand quilt, and visit. That is, at least until the tree goes up.

Doug was late for supper, so I went for an evening walk along our country road under a salmon-colored sky. Glowing snowfields reflected the sky's pink hues and, because December light fades quickly, it was soon dark.

A calico flash jumped from a roadside haystack and followed me home...purring all the way!

December 10—The two milk cows wait for me each morning, eyeing me silently like two old, comfortable friends. I scratch each one under the throat and they lift their heads and stretch their necks in ecstasy with the rubbing.

Since most of the snow has melted, I've been letting my Barred Rock pullets have the run of the place. It's entertaining to watch them through the kitchen window; they somehow remind me of a group of women...gossiping, fluffing their feathers, stalking off from one an-other in a tiff, or busy huntin' and peckin', engaged in friendly clucking. "Mighty banty" Chester struts among his harem, putting on a show for a seemingly oblivious audience.

Before sun-up I have chored, made the bed, cooked breakfast, done the dishes, and begun quilting the State Flower quilt. Later, I finish my column and bake a four-layer birthday cake to freeze for daughter Jackie's dinner here Friday evening. Split wood for the cookstove and took a walk along the creek, where I chatted with a hawk perched high in an old hare-limbed cottonwood.

Then, home to cook carrots and parsnips to add to lamb ribs which are roasting in the oven. All in all, a great day!

December 11—Sweet buttermilk pancakes and fresh eggs for break-fast. I highly recommend a pancake mix developed by Northwest Country Products Inc., which was founded in 1990 by ten farm families in Umatilla County. It is a product of their own soft white wheat, and contains no preservatives or artificial flavorings.

Predicted snow showers didn't arrive; the day partly cloudy, but not too cold. Made a batch of yeast doughnuts and treated the men who are working in the shop to some while they were still warm.

Doug and I attended a concert tonight in the Enterprise High School gym. Our local sheriffs department was responsible for bringing the program here, the proceeds of which benefit the local substance abuse prevention and education program. It was marvelous entertainment, as singer Patsy Sledd wowed us with her spunky songs and the way she tickled those piano keys.

Marty Davis was there and enthralled his audience, especially 90-years-plus Rota Thornburg. Remember "The Maddox Brothers and Rose"? Well, Rose was there, minus the brothers, most of whom have passed away. Despite having undergone open heart surgery. this top entertainer sang some of those songs of days gone by, which brought back many memories. The band that accompanied them was equally outstanding.

We enjoyed the show, as did a full house of local folks, some of whom had driven many miles to see the performance.

December 12—A restless wind began to blow, accompanied by a spattering of rain, mixed with sleet. By noon a gale forced its way into cyclonic gusts that toppled trees and blew down power lines.

After baking an appetizer for our CattleWomen's Christmas party, I attended a hearing on a proposed subdivision at Wallowa Lake, and made it to the CattleWomen's meeting by noon. Locally, several people have been organizing a food drive to fill Douglas County's diminished food bank, and our CattleWomen donated beef certificates to that drive.

I can't help but wonder what is happening to our world, when a developer wants to build second homes ($200,000) where a select few can live during summer months, while people across our state are going hungry. Thousands of timber-related workers' families have been without work for over a year now, as a result of decisions made concerning forest management practices, and someone proposes a subdivision, made of wood, for people who already have one home! Something is out of balance here.

We who live in Wallowa County are blessed with natural beauty all around us. We are doubly blessed by a natural moraine, the likes of which appears to be unique from any other in the world. And now, for monetary gain, this perfect example of a glacial moraine is being threatened. Hopefully, this will never come to pass. Hopefully, before it is too late, this terrible mistake will not become a blot in the pages of history, as well as on the landscape.

As if in defiance of this proposal, the terrible winds continued on into the night. Our electricity was off from 11:30 til 8:30 p.m. We didn't suffer—we had the old Monarch for cooking and heating. Actually, the soft glow of lamplight and candles was nice for a change.

December 13—Doug left for Hermiston to attend meetings and help round up and load donated food items destined for Douglas County.

This evening, we had a birthday supper here for daughter Jackie. Our house overflowed with family and friends, who ate their way through Chinese food as fast as it was stir-fried. Then the children carried out the Black Forest cake, smothered in whipped cream and filled with cherries. We sang Happy Birthday, and lit the candles. Once again, I was filled with happiness, just to have loved ones around.

December 14—My friend Linde returned from Hawaii and we went for a long hike with another friend today. Breathing that fresh clean air and experiencing the freedom of the hills, after Honolulu's congestion and 80-degree humidity, Linde decided she'd be able to face the world again.

December 17—By the time you read this, Christmas will be over, and a brand new year will soon follow. What will 1992 bring? Things will change, of that we can be sure. Time, and life, roll on, regardless. It is up to each of us to see that both are spent wisely. They are both precious...and fleeting.

Icy patches of snow continue to dot the landscape, and the frozen ground is white with frost this morning. Our Christmas tree is up and decorated, and packages, containing small items for myriad grandchildren, are piled beneath Douglas fir boughs.

December 22—A rainbow-colored halo rings the full December moon as it slowly sinks north of Ruby Peak on this first day of winter. The sun has moved its greatest distance north of the celestial equator, and stands still for a moment before continuing its southward ecliptic.

Stepping out in the cold morning to savor the moon and solstice, which means "sun stands still," in Latin, I wonder just when this pause will occur. Snow, crusted with drops of last night's freezing rain, crunches underfoot as I walk to the barnlot to feed the milk cows. Two silent shapes begin to munch hay, two dark bodies outlined in moonlight.

While tossing several flakes to the horses and mule, I watch ragged dark clouds move slowly across the moon's face, which reappears briefly only to disappear behind the pump house. During these last two clear nights Chief Joseph Mountain has been bathed in moonglow. Cold produces its own beauty.

The cinnamony yeasty aroma of Tannenbaum Brot, the Christmas tree bread, fills my kitchen this morning. This traditional fruit bread will be given away as gifts.

Shawn and Steve have finished the Sunday feeding, and Doug is making some Christmas visits while I attempt to complete this column early enough for the Agri-Times staff to enjoy their holiday.

Christmas cards decorate the entrance to our living room. I love the ones that contain letters. How time changes things. Little children, when last seen, are now sending pictures of their own; friends from far away places write of a life alien to ours. Mostly though, we share the same hopes, joys and disappointments.

When the bread comes fragrant from the oven, I eat a bite of lunch. Then, because it's such a lovely warm day, I set out on a walk. From a large, bare-limbed willow in Rosser's yard, I am greeted by a flock of starlings singing a Sunday serenade to the solstice.

Deciding to hike up Echo Canyon, I follow a coyote track in the snow that leads me across an alfalfa stubble field. I pursue the paw prints to an irrigation ditch that provides winter stock water for our Prairie Creek ranches. Ice has formed over the ditch, but today's warmth has opened the middle channel and dark water flows smoothly between ice crystals. At one particular spot, I watch fascinated as dark water, loosened by the warmth of the sun, moves amoeba-like through the lacy, frozen edges of the ditch.

Then, at mid-day, coyote calls echo from the draw. Perhaps they, too, are signaling the solstice. Continuing to pick my way between frozen hummocks and cold rocks along the ditch bank, I spy a dark, furry movement in some open water. The muskrat splashes under a section of ice, which breaks away from the bank and floats free down the ditch. It is nearly two in the afternoon when I head back to our ranch.

Imagining the sun is "standing still," I look up in surprise to see a "sundog" or some sort of atmospheric reflection on a nearby cloud. The soft colors are similar to this morning's moon halo. While the neighboring clouds remain color-less, this one changes, chameleon-like: violet, rose, indigo, blue, then a glowing white. The phenomena lasts only minutes before this chosen cloud is again no different from the rest. The sun then seems to lose much of its form warmth and at once I am shivering.

Hurrying across the field I climb a fence onto Tenderfoot Valley Road. Alfie comes running to greet me, and a small white weasel pokes his pink-white heap up through a pile of rocks to look directly at me. Refreshed and inspired from my long walk, I return to the typewriter to record and share my experiences.

One of the happiest happenings of the season is when we attend the annual Imnaha school Christmas program. Along with other proud grand parents, we look forward all year to this one. To provide more seating for the popular event, it would be held in the new church under the rimrocks. Granddaughter Mona Lee said this year's theme would be "Christmas From a Distance."

Neighbors Linde and Pat invited us up to supper that evening, after which we'd all go together to Imnaha. Driving up their snowy road, glimpsing their log home, all a-twinkle with colorful lights, was like slipping into a Christmas card. After a delicious meal, we bundle up and drive the 30 miles to Imnaha. Leaving the snow behind as we descend into the canyon country.

It is a mild 40 degrees when we pull up to the church, located above the Imnaha River and overlooking benches and rimrocks that march upriver. The bell tower is aglow with Christmas lights. Across the way we see horses grazing a high, grassy bench in the moonlight.

The parking lot is already full and, inside, little actors and actresses are wired with excitement. After we take a seat, the program begins with the kindergarten children singing (and giggling) a song. The audience is sprinkled with babies, ranging in age from newborn to 4. Baby sounds and the resulting shushing of parents accompany the hour-long program.

Then, it's the first to eighth graders' turn to perform. As proud of all the children as we are of our own grandchildren, we glow with pride as little Hope recites her poem, and brother Luke plays his harmonica, Sarah plays the piano, and Buck and Mona recite their pieces. Every year we notice the children's steady growth and know the Imnaha has put its stamp on them.

A skit follows whereby the entire school takes part in portraying Christmas around the world, "From a Distance." A large world map hangs behind the scene and each child points to his chosen country; then, dressed in ethnic costumes, they act out their particular Christmas traditions.

What really warms hearts is the singing of "The Twelve Days of Christmas," all pantomimed and sung by the first through eighth grade. A little girl at the end of the line, who plays the partridge in a pear tree, stole the show.

Throughout it all we are, as usual, impressed by the children themselves. In a world strewn with so much sorrow and unhappiness, these children show a genuine happiness in their faces, content with their simple lives, far-removed from the outside world. They aren't just performing, they are enjoying. Much of the credit goes to their teacher, Claudia Boswell, and helpers, like Pat Stein, as well as former teacher Char Williams, who in the past has helped shape these young lives. Char was in the audience. She couldn't stay away.

With a great jingling of bells and a *ho, ho, ho,* Santa comes galloping down the aisle, producing from his bulging pack small brown bags full of oranges, apples and candy, one for every child there.

Driving home under the glowing moon, we top out over Sheep Creek Hill and marvel at snowy mountains, the valley laying below. Bright as day, peaceful as a holy night. Winds of change are beginning in our valley. As that change occurs, I will forever remember the way it is tonight.

December 24—Son Steve and his family came over for clam chowder and our traditional tree. It was a very peaceful night, and all the stars in the heavens shone down upon Prairie Creek.

December 25—Christmas day 1991 has been, compared to other years, much calmer, since our grown children elected to spend the day with their own families. After the feeding was done, Doug and I, bearing gifts, made the rounds of these scattered offspring and "pecked" in on each family's Christmas. It was fun, seeing them all together, enjoying their own traditional activities.

Five of our children live here in the country, from Imnaha to Alder Slope. We ended up at son Steve's home on Alder Slope for Christmas dinner, a real treat: barbecued tri-tip roast. After eating too much and playing several games at the kitchen table, we returned to Prairie Creek. Guiding us home was a brilliant orange-colored half moon, which hung suspended over Echo Canyon. Our porch thermometer read 17 degrees. We have so far been spared the bitter sub-zero cold of last December.

December 26—Ruby Peak blushed pink around 7:30 a.m. as I walked in from doing chores. Because the weather has been so mild, I have continued my daily walks along our country road. Returning from this afternoon's jaunt, I stopped to get the mail out of our roadside mailbox and received a late Christmas card from Doug's sister, Barbara, who spends her winters in Hawaii. Somehow I get the feeling she misses Wallowa County at Christmastime.

On the card she penned the following, as she often does, remembering her growing-up years on the big cattle ranch along Joseph Creek: *This time of year I reflect on the arrival of the Christmas trees by mule back when they brought home the cattle from the fall ride to winter on Joseph Creek. Bob and I marked our joint birthdays by the setting up and decorating of that magical tree. The pack mules carried a tree for us, one for the schoolhouse, and many times one for a needy neighbor.*

Birthday gifts were rare, except for the 5-cent candy bars (large in those days) that came from the Rogersburg store, via Clarence Spangler, who worked for us so many years. And how do you share 10 candy bars (a once-a-year gift) with six kids, two parents, and assorted cowboys? No doubt we took the sack and hid out in the haymow, or disappeared behind the barn. Bob's birth on that cold and lonely day, delivered by the postman, will always be of wonder to us all.

Doug's brother Bob was born in Rogersburg, there along the Snake, while his mom, Jesse, waited for a boat that would take her out to civilization. Bob is gone now, but the story of how he came into the world is sure to be kept alive for generations to come.

Daughter Jackie's family returned safely tonight from Roseburg, where they had spent Christmas with Bill's folks. They stopped by on their way home to Imnaha, leaving Buck and Mona here to spend two nights with us.

December 27—I took the children sledding up near the ski run. What a fun time! Sunlight spilled across the snow, casting ever-green shadows. The woods were quiet save for sled runners swooshing past, and the air was clean and cold. It was a day of red cheeks, laughter, and cold noses. Home to shed dripping mittens and snowboots, back up to the old Monarch and sip hot chocolate.

Granddaughter Tamara is home for the holidays, taking a break from her senior year at Cal Poly. Boyfriend Matt Lauchland drove up after Christmas so I cooked a prime rib dinner in their honor, which included baked potatoes, salad, sourdough bread and fresh pies.

All of a sudden there were 20 of us. Our family must seem a bit overwhelming to Matt, but he was a good sport. He is part of a family-owned wine grape operation in Lodi, California.

December 30—Doug and I piled into our van, along with Tammy, Matt, granddaughter Carrie and son-in-law Charley, and drove down to Troy, where we all went steelhead fishing in the Grande Ronde. The river was free of ice, and we left the fog and snow at home. Green grass was already visible under the old dead stuff.

Ice falls, the mute evidence of previous cold snaps, spilled from canyon crevices and formed enormous icicles. Leafless Hackberry harbored several birds, and other than their soft twitterings and the river-songs, the canyon was peaceful.

Matt couldn't get over the abundance of water. California, now in its seventh year of drought, is water-starved. He tells us how every time another well is drilled, the water tables just keep dropping. Although we didn't catch any fish, we did witness one being caught where the waters of the Wenaha mingle with those of the Grande Ronde.

We ate lunch at the small Shiloh restaurant there at Troy; good ol' burgers with seasoned curly fries. We listened to fish stories of other fishermen who came in wearing hip boots. From what we gleaned from various conversations, fishing hadn't been too hot that week.

After fishing one more hole downriver, Doug drove us home by way of Rattlesnake Grade. When we topped out it was snowing lightly, and the fog was gone.

December 31—My world has shrunk to the immediate area beyond our windows this foggy morning. Every so often, a hairy and frosted shape of a mule or horse ambles into that space. The last day of 1991 brings both sadness and gladness; sad because the year is ending much too soon, and glad anticipating that which is to come.

Tonight we will gather on upper Prairie Creek in Linde and Pat's cozy log home to see in the New Year with friends and neighbors.

This morning Linde and I turned out 34 sourdough pretzels in her kitchen. We had a great time rolling out long strips of dough and tying them in a bow knot. Between sips of hot spiced cider, we blew up three packages of colored balloons. Outside, the fog lifted briefly, revealing a robin's egg blue sky hanging over a gleaming Chief Joseph Mountain.

All in all, it has been a wonderful holiday season. Aside from some anxious moments of worrying over several sick grandchildren, it couldn't have been better. As we continue with the 1990s, the ongoing struggle of how to manage what land we have left goes with us. Decisions must be made wisely.

I'd like to leave you with a quote from J. Frank Dobie, *The earth does not think and does not care what people think, but it gives and takes with undeviating justice, and it remembers...*

Index

Doug Tippett appears too frequently to be included in the index.

Photos of Doug appear on page 134.
Photos of Janie appear on pages 134, 212, 237, and 452.

CPSIA information can be obtained
at www.ICGtesting.com
Printed in the USA
BVHW081355261021
619919BV00001B/6